ALSO BY NANCY GIBBS AND MICHAEL DUFFY

The Preacher and the Presidents

THE PRESIDENTS CLUB

INSIDE THE WORLD'S MOST EXCLUSIVE FRATERNITY

NANCY GIBBS

AND

MICHAEL DUFFY

SIMON & SCHUSTER
OCN 741542754
New York   London   Toronto   Sydney   New Delhi

Simon & Schuster
1230 Avenue of the Americas
New York, NY 10020

First Simon & Schuster hardcover edition May 2012

SIMON & SCHUSTER and colophon are registered trademarks
of Simon & Schuster, Inc.

For information about special discounts for bulk purchases,
please contact Simon & Schuster Special Sales at 1-866-506-1949
or business@simonandschuster.com.

The Simon & Schuster Speakers Bureau can bring authors to your
live event. For more information or to book an event contact the
Simon & Schuster Speakers Bureau at 1-866-248-3049 or visit
our website at www.simonspeakers.com.

Designed by Joy O'Meara

Manufactured in the United States of America

10   9   8

Library of Congress Cataloging-in-Publication Data is available.

ISBN 978-1-4391-2770-4
ISBN 978-1-4391-4871-6 (ebook)

CONTENTS

THE
PRESIDENTS
CLUB

INTRODUCTION

So you've come to talk about my predecessors." Bill Clinton greets us in his Harlem office, looking thin, sounding thin, his voice a scrape of welcome at the end of a long day.

It is late, it is dark, pouring rain outside, so beyond the wall of windows the city is a splash of watery lights and street noise. But inside, past the two armed agents, behind the electronic locks, the sanctuary is warm wood and deep carpet, a collector's vault. A painting of Churchill watches from the west wall; a stuffed Kermit the Frog rests on a shelf, while a hunk of an old voting machine, with names attached and levers to pull, sits behind his desk. "This is my presidential library, from Washington through Bush," he says, pointing to bookcases full of memoirs and biographies, and in the course of the séance that follows he summons the ghosts not just of Abraham Lincoln and Teddy Roosevelt but Franklin Pierce and Rutherford B. Hayes.

He dwells on one president he misses—Richard Nixon—and another that he loves: George H. W. Bush. "A month to the day before he died," he says of Nixon, "he wrote me a letter about Russia. And it was so lucid, so well written. . . . I reread it every year. That one and George Bush's wonderful letter to me, you know where you leave your letter to your successor."

That was the letter that said, "You will be our President when you read this note. . . . I am rooting hard for you."

Along the windowsill are dozens of pictures; he looks at the signed photo of Lyndon Johnson, a prize given to him forty years ago when he worked on a campaign in Texas. "Over time," he predicts of LBJ, "history will tend to be kinder to him."

In the meantime, it falls to the presidents to be kind to one another. "There's just a general sympathy," he says, among the men who have sat in the Oval Office. "President Obama and I didn't talk much about politics when we played golf the other day." There are plenty of other people around a president to talk politics; sometimes you need someone who just makes you laugh. Or tells you not to let the bastards get you down. Clinton was exhausted that day, he recalls, but "when my president summons me, then I come and I would play golf in a driving snowstorm."

My president, he calls him, which suggests how far the two men have come since their proxy war in 2008. Such are the journeys this book attempts to trace: the intense, intimate, often hostile but more often generous relationships among the once and future presidents. It makes little difference how much they may have fought on the way to the White House; once they've been in the job, they are bound together by experience, by duty, by ambition, and by scar tissue. They are members of the Presidents Club, scattered across the country but connected by phone and email and sometimes in person, such as when five of them met at the White House after the 2008 election to, as President Carter told us, "educate president-elect Obama in a nice way without preaching to him."

Throughout its history, the club has never numbered more than six. At the moment, there are branches not just in Washington and New York, but in Atlanta, Dallas, and Kennebunkport, Maine, in a saltbox cottage on the grounds of the Bush family compound. You climb the creaky staircase lined with framed photos so treasured they aren't even in the Bush presidential museum. It is here that the elder Bush brought Clinton, the man who had defeated him, to play golf, spend the night, hurdle the waves at breakneck speed. From the moment the two men bonded in 2005, they didn't talk much about politics either, or world affairs or strategy and tactics. It has always been more about fellowship. "You are right," President Bush explains in an email. "We don't talk about it. You don't have to. No matter the politics, you know and understand the weight of the decisions the other guy had to make, and you respect that."

The Presidents Club has its protocols, including deference to the man in the chair and, for the most part, silence about how the members of the world's most exclusive fraternity get along and the services they provide one another. Harry Truman privately offered to serve as Dwight Eisenhower's vice president if Ike decided to run in 1948; Nixon's secret letters to Ronald Reagan in 1980 and 1981 were a virtual blueprint for setting up his White House; Carter promised not to talk to reporters about a mission he undertook for Obama in 2010. "When your ambition is slaked, it becomes more important to see something good happen for your country than to just keep winning arguments," Clinton says. "At some point, you're just glad when the sun comes up in the morning, you get up and you want something good to happen. I don't think it's because we all become saintly."

The Presidents Club, like so much else, was founded by George Washington, thanks to the second-best decision he ever made. The first was agreeing to take the office in the first place; but then he chose to leave it, retiring in 1797 after two terms. Which meant that rather than becoming America's President for Life, he instead became its first former president.

Everything Washington did set a precedent: to accept a salary though he didn't need one, so that future presidents would not all need to be rich; to go by Mr. President rather than Your Excellency, so that future presidents might remain grounded; but most of all to relinquish his power peacefully, even prematurely given his immense stature, at that time a striking act of submission to untested democratic principles.

With that decision Washington established the Presidents Club—initially a club of two, once John Adams took office. Faced with the threat of war with France, Adams named the revered Washington commander of the Army, where he served until he died the next year. Adams was the first to discover that, whatever jealousies lingered in private, a former president could be highly useful.

He would not be the last.

In the two centuries that followed, the club's ranks rose and fell. It grew to six under Abraham Lincoln, though that was partly because none of his living predecessors had managed to win a second term. The club would not be that large again until Clinton's inauguration in 1993, when Nixon, Ford, Carter, Reagan, and Bush all stood ready to assist. Some presidents—Adams, Jefferson, both Roosevelts—had only one president in reserve. Like Washington, Richard Nixon, upon his reelection in 1972, had none: Harry Truman died just after Christmas, Lyndon Johnson a month later. At that dangerous moment in American history, the club disappeared entirely.

So why does this matter?

First, because relationships matter, and the private relationships between public men matter in particular ways. For the former presidents, the club can be a vital, sometimes surprising benefit of post-presidential life. They have relinquished power, but not influence; and so their influence becomes a piece of the sitting president's power. They can do more together than apart, and they all know it; so they join forces as needed, to consult, complain, console, pressure, protect, redeem.

As voters we watch the presidents onstage, judge their performance, cheer their successes, cast them out of office for their failures. This is the duty of democracy. But judgment is not the same as understanding, and while *what* a president does matters most, *why* he does it is the privilege of history. To the extent that we learn about these men by watching the way they engage with their peers—the loyalty, the rivalry, the pity, and the partnerships—the club opens a new window into the Oval Office.

Second, it matters because the presidency matters, and the club serves to protect the office. Once they've all sat in the chair, they become jealous of its powers, convinced that however clumsy the other branches of government can be, the president must be able to serve the people and defend the nation when all else fails. They can support whomever they like during campaigns; but once a new president is elected, the others often act as a kind of security detail. Thus did Johnson once present Eisenhower with a pair of gold cuff links bearing the Presidential Seal. "You are the only one along with Harry Truman who can legitimately wear these," Johnson observed, "but if you look closely, it doesn't say Democrat or Republican on them."

These relationships don't just reveal the nature of the presidency; they reflect the forces that have shaped our politics over the last half century. In the docile 1950s, Eisenhower cemented Franklin Roosevelt's legacy: a Republican in office for eight years who did not rip up the New Deal effectively endorsed it. By 1968, the country was so divided that Lyndon Johnson fought as fiercely with his vice president, Hubert Humphrey, as with the Republican challenger, Richard Nixon. In ways that tell more important tales, the long, complex, and conflicted relations between Reagan and Nixon or, later, between Reagan and Ford, defined the ideological struggles inside the Republican Party for two generations and counting. In the same way, the complicated relationship between Bill Clinton and Barack Obama mirrors the Democrats' generational fight about how best to yank a center-right electorate leftward—or whether it can be done at all.

Finally, it matters because the club has become an instrument of presidential power. It is not in the Constitution, not in any book or bylaw, but neither is it a metaphor nor a figure of speech. It is an alliance the former presidents are conscious of building, and the sitting presidents of using, both to promote themselves and to advance their agendas. There is no fraternity like it anywhere, and not just because of the barriers to entry or the privileges of membership. For all of the club's self-serving habits and instincts, when it is functioning at its best, it can serve the president, help solve his problems, and the nation's, even save lives.

The Modern Club

On January 20, 1953, at the inauguration of Dwight Eisenhower, Truman greeted Herbert Hoover on the platform. "I think we ought to organize a former presidents club," Hoover suggested.

"Fine," Truman replied. "You be the President of the club. And I will be the Secretary."

Up to that moment, the club was more an idea than an institution. Some sitting presidents consulted with their predecessors, but beyond sharing war stories, there were limits to what a former president could do—unless he applied for a new job, like congressman (John Quincy Adams) or Supreme Court justice (William Howard Taft). Calvin Coolidge, shortly before he died in 1933, remarked that "People seem to think the presidential machinery should keep on running, even after the power has been turned off."

But in our postwar age of global celebrity, presidents live longer, and larger, than ever, and even when the power goes off, their influence remains. Truman was a mortal political enemy of Hoover's, but he also knew that only Hoover had the experience and stature to overhaul the executive branch to meet the challenges of the nuclear age. As a result of their partnership, the Hoover Commission, which Congress created, Truman sanctioned, and Hoover chaired, produced the greatest transformation of the presidency in history: a concentration of power that ultimately yielded the CIA, the National Security Council, the Council of Economic Advisors, the General Services Administration, a unified Defense Department, and much more.

Every president who followed would have reason to thank them. Eisenhower, through an act of Congress in 1957, granted the club formal privileges: members received an allowance, office space, mailing rights, a pension. John F. Kennedy, the youngest president in a century, understood the club's political uses, and he looked for any opportunity to summon his three predecessors back to the White House for the photo op; Johnson discovered its personal uses, seeking both counsel and comfort as he staggered into office in the wake of a tragedy.

"I need you more than ever now," Johnson told his old sparring partner Eisenhower on the night of Kennedy's murder, and Ike drove to Washington, came to the Oval Office, and wrote out on a legal pad what he thought Johnson should say to an emergency joint session of Congress. Johnson extended all the former presidents Secret Service protection, helicopters, even a projectionist so that if they were being treated at Walter Reed Medical Center, they could watch movies from the White House library. When Truman called to congratulate him on his landslide victory in 1964, Johnson responded like a brother. "And I just want you to know," he told Truman, "that as long as I'm in that office, you are in it, and there's not a privilege of it, or a power of it, or a purpose of it that you can't share. And your bedroom is up there waiting for you, and your plane is standing by your side." A year later, Ike's private advice on how to handle the Vietnam War had become so crucial that Johnson told him "you're the best chief of staff I've got."

Nixon, the man who eternally longed to belong, actually created a private clubhouse, a brownstone across the street from the White House, purchased discreetly by the government in 1969 for the use of former presidents. It is still in operation. He and his wife, Pat, organized the first club reunion, researching all the living members of the first families and inviting them to the White House: Calvin Coolidge's son, Grover Cleveland's grandchildren, various Roosevelts, and dozens of Adamses.

Nixon had a particular reason throughout his first term to stroke Johnson; their relationship over the years involved camaraderie, conspiracy, and blackmail. This book will argue that the collapse of the Nixon presidency owed a great deal to his need to protect some secrets only the two club members shared.

Nixon in exile had the longest road to redemption of any of them; and so with Reagan's election in 1980 he made sure the incoming president understood how valuable a former president could be: "President Eisenhower said to me when I visited him at Walter Reed Hospital after the election of 1968, 'I am yours to command,'" Nixon told Reagan. "I now say the same to you." George H. W. Bush launched a kind of club newsletter, letters stamped SECRET sent to some of his predecessors, and offered each a secure phone line to the Oval Office. After Clinton took over with five former presidents standing by, he came to see how, in the case of Carter and Nixon, he could use them as an arm of his foreign policy, and in the case of Ford, part of his impeachment legal defense team. Clinton understood that "being a former president is an asset," his advisor John Podesta observed. "But it's the current president's asset to deploy."

This story is told chronologically, but that line sometimes needs to bend, because the club has its own life cycle; each president discovers its value in his own time, uses it in his own way. And it is necessary, too, to travel back to understand how the relationships unfolded. The feud that raged in the 1950s between Eisenhower and Truman only makes sense when you understand how closely they had worked together while Ike was still in uniform. Reagan's encounters with Nixon began not when Reagan was elected in 1980, but in 1947 when a freshman Republican congressman sat down with a then Democratic movie star to talk about communists in Hollywood; their correspondence stretches across half a century. And of course the tale of the Bushes began forty-three years before either reached the Oval Office. Presidents naturally take a fierce interest in who might one day be joining their fraternity—especially because they have little control over it. They act as talent scouts and bouncers, they test the pledges to see who might have the makings of a brother. The club is a peerage; but future presidents play a part in its evolution, and so those stories sometimes need to be told as well.

The Bind That Ties

"There is no experience you can get," John F. Kennedy admitted after two years in office, "that can possibly prepare you adequately for the Presidency." Nor is there any advice, any handbook, since every president enters office determined to turn the page. Kennedy couldn't wait to toss out Ike's military management style for a more supple, activist alternative. "They behaved as though history had begun with them," said advisor Clark Clifford of Kennedy's men. Ford practiced radical normalcy—his wife even discussed her mastectomy—to send the clearest possible signal that the dark age of Nixon was over. Clinton wanted to prove he was not the second coming of Jimmy Carter; George W. Bush was all about not being Clinton; Barack Obama was about not being either one. Each had to learn how much they had to learn, before the club could be of much use—but eventually, they all find themselves reaching out for help. "That connection begins the first time you receive the daily intelligence briefing," argues the first President Bush. "We all understand the magnitude of the job when we decide to run for President. At least we think we do. But it's not possible to fully appreciate the responsibility that comes with being President until you get that first briefing."

One senior advisor to three presidents recalls watching the revelation unfold, as talented, confident men realize what they've gotten themselves into. "When you get in, you discover nothing is what you expect, or believed, or have been told, or have campaigned on," he says. "It's much more complicated. Your first reaction is: *I've been set up.* Second is: *I have to think differently.* Third is: *Maybe they had it right.* And it isn't long before they ask, who am I gonna talk to about *this*?"

The problems a president faces, Eisenhower said, are "soul-racking. . . . The nakedness of the battlefield, when the soldier is all alone in the smoke and the clamor and the terror of war, is comparable to the loneliness—at times—of the presidency, when one man must conscientiously, deliberately, prayerfully scrutinize every argument, every proposal, every prediction, every alternative, every probable outcome of his action, and then—all alone—make his decision."

All alone—because just when a new president needs allies, his circle of trust shrinks. No one, with the possible exception of his family, treats him the same, and no one, with the exception of his predecessors, knows what this is like. "The sycophants will stand in the rain a week to see you and will treat you like a king," House Speaker Sam Rayburn warned Truman when he took office. "They'll come sliding in and tell you you're the greatest man alive—but you know and I know you ain't." Everything a president says, even to his inner circle, is analyzed, interpreted, acted upon; even questions are read as decisions. So he trains himself: no idle comments, no thinking out loud, and grows increasingly guarded; he worries that people only tell him what they think he wants to hear. "The Presidency," Kennedy observed, "is not a very good place to make new friends." He and his brother Bobby used to imagine a book they'd write one day—*The Poison of the Presidency.*

But that poison is not something they can talk about; how can you complain about a burden you fought to bear? Thomas Jefferson called the presidency "a splendid misery." They face only hard choices and high stakes: the easy decisions never make it to the president's desk. When Eisenhower was ridiculed for playing so much golf, Truman, no friend of Ike's at the time, defended him: "I am sure that the problems of the President follow him around the golf course . . . and anywhere else he may go." But they bond in the locker room, since they all got into the game, "dared greatly," did not remain on the sidelines. If there is a club manifesto, it is Teddy Roosevelt's gauntlet, thrown down to all the armchair generals and righteous pundits: "It is not the critic who counts, not the one who points out how the strong man stumbled," he argued. "The credit belongs to the man who is actually in the arena, whose face is marred with sweat and dust and blood; who strives valiantly; who errs and comes short again and again . . . who, if he wins, knows the triumph of high achievement; and who, if he fails, at least fails while daring greatly."

That also accounts for a regular club refrain, when they refuse to criticize their successors on the grounds that presidents act on information—and bear responsibilities—that outsiders can't fathom. "No one," Kennedy told historian David Herbert Donald early in 1962, "has a right to grade a President—not even poor James Buchanan—who has not sat in his chair, examined the mail and information that came across his desk, and learned why he made decisions." Truman and Eisenhower went for a drink together after Kennedy's funeral; they talked about how no one ever really understands why presidents make the decisions they do:

"We know what we did," Truman said.

"We surely do," Eisenhower agreed.

So against all expectation, they all talk to each other: Kennedy had called Eisenhower on the morning he was set to announce the U.S. quarantine of Cuba, which posed a reasonable chance of triggering a nuclear exchange. Only one other man alive really knew what that felt like. "No matter what you find that you have to do," Eisenhower told him, "I will certainly . . . do my best to support it." Two years later, once Johnson took over, he would ask Eisenhower to concoct a cover story for why he needed to be in Washington, so he could come by the White House and give Johnson some much-needed guidance, even spend the weekend. Clinton would call Nixon and describe his schedule—when he got up, when he exercised, how long he worked, in order to hear if that was *normal* for a president. After Nixon died, Clinton said it felt like the loss of his mother: "Just today I had a problem and I said to the person working with me, 'I wish I could pick up the phone and call Richard Nixon and ask him what he thinks we ought to do about this.'"

When they can't talk to each other, they study each other. Every president may enter office promising a new day, a new deal, a new frontier. But they all inherit the successes and the failures of the men who came before. "The things that Jerry Ford decided when he was in office affected me daily," Carter said. "Even the things that Harry Truman decided 30 years before I went into office affected me daily." Nixon could tell you every detail about many of his predecessors—who took sleeping pills, who had hemorrhoids. Obama quizzed Reagan's team about how he managed to stay focused on the horizon and not get pulled down into the weeds—and whether he got discouraged and how he kept the public from seeing it. These are men who have worked at the same desks, slept in the same beds, shaved in the same mirrors, raised their children in the same backyard. When they return to the White House to visit, they check out how the new tenant redecorated. But they all know that in fact the man does not remake the presidency. It's the other way around.

A few weeks after his reelection in 2004, George W. Bush sat in the Oval Office beside a Christmas tree flocked with eagles, with an air of equanimity you might expect from a president who had just won reelection despite an unpopular war, an economy on tiptoes, and a public conflicted about many issues but most of all about him. He was asked whether he thought more or less highly of his predecessors, now that he'd been in the job awhile.

"Of my predecessors? Very interesting," he replied, and then, without hesitation, "More highly of them all."

Why? Because "I've got a much better appreciation of what they've been through."

That included even Clinton, with whom he went on to form the next club alliance. "There is no conversation so sweet as that of former political enemies," Truman observed. It was the scars of war and scandal, says an official who worked for both Clinton and Bush, that enabled such natural adversaries to become friends. Both men "went through impossible circumstances and they both came out with a lot of scar tissue and so they both have to be asking themselves, how do I find peace in my life? I've been through a meat grinder; maybe a friendship with a person who has been through something like this could bring me to a different place as a human being; it detaches me from the old and gets me to a new place. It's just a way of finding peace. But I can't find peace with a lot of people because so few are my equal."

Or as Jimmy Carter puts it, "We always have sorrows."

The Other Secret Service

The club has an operational wing, whose use depends on the needs of the president and the skills of predecessors. Truman sent Hoover to twenty-two countries in fifty-seven days in 1946 trying to prevent a postwar humanitarian crisis. Reagan conspired with Nixon when he traveled to the Soviet Union to weigh Mikhail Gorbachev's true intentions. Bush 41 tapped Ford and Carter to monitor the elections in Panama in 1989. Obama dispatched Clinton to North Korea to win the release of two jailed American journalists.

On such missions the stakes can be high, as are the risks. "They have a power because of their position that's unique," observes President Bush 41's advisor Brent Scowcroft of the former presidents. "But it's dangerous to use them because, not unreasonably, they think that they know much more than we do." Some members proved both immensely useful and infuriatingly mutinous, as Carter did when he undertook a mission to North Korea in 1994 at Clinton's behest. His brief was clear: deliver a message and bring back intelligence about Kim Il Sung's nuclear intentions. Instead he brokered a deal to forestall a crisis—which he announced on CNN. White House officials, gathered around a television in the West Wing, did not try to contain their fury; one cabinet member called Carter "a treasonous prick."

Carter was not unusual in wanting to experience one more time the rush of power, and believing he was uniquely positioned to help. Many leave office with agendas more complex than those they brought in, which play out in the books they write, the foundations they lead, but also the advice they offer. That's the crucible in which the club does both its best work and its worst. A sitting president lends them a halo, a script, an airplane; they can serve the country, or serve themselves. "No one who has been in the Presidency with the capacity and power to affect the course of events can ever be satisfied with not being there," Nixon said years after he stepped down, and so they may insert themselves into events whether the sitting president invites them or not. Nixon promised Ford he'd stay out of sight in 1976—and then went prancing around China in the middle of the New Hampshire primary that year. Carter and Ford presented George Bush with a proposal to raise taxes just a few weeks after he'd been elected on a promise not to. Bush did not appreciate Carter secretly lobbying the U.N. Security Council against the Gulf War. Sometimes a former president is best neither seen nor heard.

This is the club's constant tension: among its crucial services is the repair of ragged reputations. When former presidents, like Nixon or Carter, do this at the sitting president's expense, all hell breaks loose. But members more often conspire than collide. They extol each other at library dedications. They exalt each other in eulogies. They line up together with fat bristle brushes to whitewash the stains on their records. Go to WhiteHouse.gov and read the presidential biographies; they are feather soft and heartily heroic, valentines straight from the Oval Office. Under Bill Clinton, "the U.S. enjoyed more peace and economic well being than at any time in its history." He got into trouble over his "indiscretions with a young White House intern," but "apologized to the nation for his actions and continued to have unprecedented popular approval ratings for his job as president." George W. Bush "cut taxes for every federal income taxpayer . . . modernized Medicare . . . empowered America's armies of compassion . . . built global coalitions to remove violent regimes in Afghanistan and Iraq that threatened America; liberating more than 50 million people from tyranny."

You can view the work of rehabilitation as purely self-interested: they all compete for history's favor. But they may also defend each other, not out of sympathy or affection, but because the club functions as the protective arm of the presidency itself. That role sharpens their advice, mostly ensures their silence, and offers the promise of a gentling redemption they will need someday, too. It is a shadow Secret Service, patrolling the power and privilege of an office that its members think America needs now more than ever. Sometimes burnishing a legacy serves to bolster the institution, so that presidents like Truman who were reviled in office are revered in retrospect, and everyone wins. Club members do not want to see the president look bad, no matter who it is.

But the club's most secret handshakes are less about membership than stewardship. In 1960, after one of the closest elections in history, both Hoover and Eisenhower quietly told Nixon not to contest the results, even as rumors spread of Chicago precincts where machines registered 121 votes from 43 voters. It was not because they wanted to see Kennedy in the White House; it was to protect the presidency from a crisis of legitimacy. "I think we are in enough trouble in the world today," Hoover told Nixon. "Some indications of national unity are not only desirable but essential." When Kennedy and then Johnson came under fire for foreign policy decisions, Eisenhower stared down his fellow Republicans: at a time of crisis, he said, "there is only one thing a good American can do, and that is support the president." Ford pardoned Nixon not to save the man but to restore the office and let the country move on; he lost the next election, but forever defended the choice. It fell to the Kennedys twenty-seven years later to give Ford a Profile in Courage Award, the family of one president symbolically pardoning another for deciding to pardon a third. "We want you to succeed," George W. Bush told Obama after the 2008 election. "All of us who have served in this office understand that the office transcends the individual."

When the political culture is splintered and siloed, the president alone serves all the people. The sight of the presidents meeting in the Oval Office after a tough election, or hitting the road together to do hurricane relief, the sight of them standing side by side, old enemies reconciled, can offer a rare moment of truce when politics is turned off and the common good wins out over personal pride or public ambition. When Bill Clinton and George H. W. Bush began working together raising relief money for disaster victims, they knew their buddy movie ran completely against the bitter grain of the times; that was partly why they delighted in doing it. "Americans like politics," Clinton said. "They like us to air our differences, because they know we have got to have an honest debate to come to a good answer. But then they also think that debate ought to have limits to it." For too long, politicians did not just disagree with opponents: they despised and demonized them, he observed, and the country suffered for it. "It keeps us from solving a lot of problems and doing a lot of things that we could have done otherwise. So I think people see George and me and they say, 'That is the way our country ought to work.' "

So just how crucial is the club in the early twenty-first century? In every age, three factors determine its performance: the needs and choices of the sitting president, the needs and talents of the former presidents, and a climate that welcomes or deplores their partnership. It was no accident that the club's founders had all three factors in their favor. Hoover and Truman showed just how much good they could do, through an alliance that was as productive as it was unexpected. Much about the country, and the world, was broken in 1945: neither the Congress, the parties, the press, nor the public was going to throw up much resistance to two men so resolutely committed to fixing it.

That episode, while formative, was also unusual. Under Eisenhower, the club lost much of its clout; in that case, the president simply didn't feel the need. Later presidents would feel the need but lack the resource; there was not much help Nixon could offer Gerald Ford, other than to remain as quiet as possible. But the club has proven over time that it is a force in itself, able to change the course of history by bringing out the best and the worst in its members.

Back in the beginning, when the club was born, the very idea that it would exert its own power was so outlandish that even the two presidents who started it were wrong about how it would all turn out.

TRUMAN AND HOOVER:

The Return of the Exile

——————— ⚷ ———————

The modern Presidents Club was founded by two men who by all rights should have loathed each other.

There was Harry Truman, the humble haberdasher from Missouri, hurled into office in the spring of 1945, summoning to the White House Herbert Hoover, a failed Republican president who had left town thirteen years earlier as the most hated man in America, his motorcades pelted with rotten fruit. They were political enemies and temperamental opposites. Where Truman was authentic, amiable, if prone to eruptions of temper, Hoover could be cold, humorless, incapable of small talk but ferociously sure of the rightness of his cause. Yet they shared some personal history and, more important, some public goals. Though they saw the world differently—Hoover's faith lay in private initiative, Truman's in the promise of benevolent government—they were men of Middle America, of Iowa and Missouri, the first and second presidents born west of the Mississippi, with a shared suspicion of elite Easterners and a common commitment to Wilsonian idealism. Both men were more loyal to their parties than their parties were to them.

"I'm not big enough. I'm not big enough for this job," Truman said to a Senate friend the day after Franklin Roosevelt died. But he was, not least because he did not let his pride interfere with his needs—and during the crucial postwar years, Truman's needs and Hoover's gifts were perfectly matched. Across a devastated Europe, a hundred million people were at risk of starvation. Truman was determined to help them, Hoover was the man who knew how, and from that simple equation, an alliance was born. Together, Truman and Hoover probably saved more lives than any two players on the stage of the twentieth century.

Hoover served Truman so well that Truman next enlisted him to help sell a suspicious Republican Congress on the notion of an entirely new role for America in the world, promoting European recovery as a counterweight against Soviet influence. And if that was not enough, Hoover then proceeded to lead the top-to-bottom overhaul of the presidency itself, strengthening the office to meet the demands of the modern age. It was the gift the two unlikely partners bequeathed to all the rest who followed.

Truman gave Hoover what any failed president dreams of: a chance to rewind the tape and replay it, reveal the compassion obscured by the caricature, and erase the image of a hapless president by being the one who saved the presidency. It didn't matter that Truman thought Hoover was "to the right of Louis the Fourteenth." He was honest and honorable, and they never talked about politics anyway, since they had something more important in common. "We talked," Truman said, "about what it was like being president."

As for Hoover, as emotionally austere as any president ever, he would one day write to Truman that "Yours has been a friendship which has reached deeper into my life than you know." Truman was so moved by the letter, he framed it so it could remain on his desk until the day he died.

1

"I'm Not Big Enough for This Job"

—HARRY TRUMAN

Harry Truman had fond memories of his first White House meeting with Herbert Hoover.

It was May 1945. He'd been in office less than two months, and a week after the German surrender on May 7, newspapers were already warning of the next disaster: "the most stupendous feeding problem in history," as the *New York Times* described the hideous famine facing 100 million European civilians. Roads out of Germany were a cortege of refugees, many too weak to walk; in Dutch cities people were making soup by cutting the poison centers out of tulip bulbs and boiling them. One in three Belgian children was tubercular; one in four children in Belgrade died before their first birthday.

"I knew what I had to do and I knew just the man I wanted to help me," Truman recalled many years later. Hoover had made his fortune as a mining engineer, but had made his reputation as the man who saved millions from starvation as Woodrow Wilson's food czar during the First World War. So Truman invited the former president to meet with him in the Oval Office.

"Mr. President," Truman said, "there are a lot of hungry people in the world and if there's anybody who knows about hungry people, it's you.

Now there's plenty of food, but it's not in the right places. Now I want you to . . ."

As Truman supposedly told the story to oral historian Merle Miller, it was at this point that Hoover started to lose it.

"He was sitting there, just as close to me as you are, and I saw that great big tears were running down his cheeks." Truman said he was pretty sure he knew what the problem was. "It was the first time in thirteen years," he told Miller, "that anybody had paid any attention to him."

Such a sweet story; such a testimony to a sitting president's magnanimity and a former president's gratitude for a chance to serve once more.

And such a sentimental whitewash of what actually happened.

Being president involves a crash course in mythmaking, and many of these friendships would acquire a glaze of nobility that was often missing in real time. Memory can work that way; by the time Truman was writing his memoirs and talking to Miller, he and Hoover had indeed become unlikely brothers. But back in 1945, relations between the two men were by no means so warm. Much as both men wanted it, their first date nearly didn't happen because they were so suspicious of each other's motives—and both left with their doubts intact. While pleased at being back inside the halls of power, Hoover dismissed the meeting as "wholly political," designed to show that Truman was above partisanship; there was no chance Truman would actually let any Republican participate in his administration.

"Nothing more would come of it," he concluded in his memo of the meeting.

That turned out to be wrong.

The Most Despised President

Truman had no use for posers: he was suspicious of wealth and privilege and the entitled ease of the country club. His happy Missouri childhood took a hard twist after his father lost everything betting on wheat futures; from the age of eighteen, hardly a day went by that Truman wasn't worried about money. His path to the White House moved from the mailroom at the *Kansas City Star* to railroad timekeeper to bank clerk to farmer to soldier to haberdasher to machine politician in Kansas City, where he was distinguished by a refusal to enrich himself at the public trough. When he ran for reelection in 1940, he couldn't afford the stamps to write to old friends asking for money. He knew what it was like to have to sleep in his car; and he was a man for whom there was no place like home.

So how could he ever forge a bond with Hoover, so rich, so remote, a true man of the world who, when he and his wife didn't want to be overheard in the White House, used to speak to each other in Chinese? By 1945 as Truman moved into the White House, Hoover was living in a $32,000-a-year suite in the Waldorf Towers in Manhattan, alongside neighbors like the Duke and Duchess of Windsor, Cole Porter, and the shah of Iran, with cooks at their command who could prepare chicken seventy-one ways. A self-made man, he lived so well that most people forgot that as a child he had learned the meaning of poverty from actual experience.

Truman, however, came to appreciate qualities in Hoover that many people missed. Hoover "wasn't one of those fellows born with a gold spoon in his mouth," Truman observed in one of his memoirs. "His father was a blacksmith in West Branch, Iowa and both of his parents died before he was nine years old, and he and his brother and sister were split up and sent to relatives."

Some combination of independence, ingenuity, and force of will carried Hoover to Stanford to study geology, then into the mining business, eventually taking him all around the world as an engineer. His organizational prowess and urgent Quaker philanthropy drew him into public service under Woodrow Wilson during World War I. Wilson put him in charge of managing food shortages; until that point, it was not uncommon for as much as a third of the population in a war zone to die of hunger. Hoover, Truman said, "had the skill and the humanity to save millions of people threatened with starvation." Streets would be named for him in Belgium. In Finland his name became a verb, meaning "to help." Both parties flirted with him as a candidate in 1920. "He is certainly a wonder," a young Franklin Roosevelt said at the time, "and I wish we could make him president. There certainly couldn't be a better one." A poll of the Harvard faculty preferred him two to one over any other contender.

By the time Hoover actually became president in 1928—he won with 444 electoral votes—he had added to his reputation the rescue of victims of the Great Mississippi Flood of 1927, leaving many people convinced there was not a problem on earth he couldn't solve with his technical and organizational acumen. America, he declared, was "nearer to the final triumph over poverty than ever before in the history of any land. The poorhouse is vanishing from among us." Even eight months later when the markets crashed, he was praised for his handling of the crisis. "No one in his place could have done more," affirmed the *New York Times.* "Very few of his predecessors could have done as much."

Four years later Franklin Roosevelt would carry all but six states; *Time* christened Hoover "President Reject," the lame-duck Congress considered impeachment, and a would-be assassin tried to kill him. Herbert Hoover, "the Great Humanitarian," was accused of callous indifference to the suffering of his own citizens, the man who fed his dog T-bone steaks in the Rose Garden while proud men were reduced to selling fruit on street corners. "We'll hang Herbert Hoover to a sour apple tree!" cried the protesters marching on Washington.

How had it all gone so wrong? There were a great many theories, but for our purposes Truman's is the most relevant. "I think he and his administration were blamed for things that were not their fault," Truman argued, once he too was safely out of office and no longer invoking the "Hoover Depression" during his campaign speeches. Hoover, Truman said, was handicapped by having arrived at the White House too easily. The only political job he had ever held was as commerce secretary; he'd never had to run for Congress, or even for sheriff, and had informed his advisors in 1928 that "I'll not kiss any babies." Without a strong attachment to the grass roots, Truman observed, "he didn't really understand . . . the needs of the American people."

Or at least that was the impression he gave, and Roosevelt did everything he could to promote it. Between election day and Roosevelt's inauguration in March, the nation's banks began to wobble. Hoover tried to enlist his successor to act with him, although in ways that could have undercut Roosevelt's own progressive agenda. Roosevelt rejected the overture: "It was also his ego, I think, that prevented [Roosevelt] from even listening," Truman concluded. "The campaign had been a pretty rough one, and many people were blaming Hoover for the depression as though he'd caused it all by himself, calling cardboard shanties Hoovervilles and empty pockets Hoover flags. . . . Roosevelt decided that he was smarter than Hoover in every way and [that] Hoover just didn't know what he was talking about when he suggested closing the banks. But the bank closings were an absolute necessity."

That refusal on Roosevelt's part helped ensure he would take office in an atmosphere of total desperation—and that Hoover would become as widely hated as any president in history. There were rumors that he'd been arrested trying to flee the country aboard financier Andrew Mellon's yacht, with $200 million in gold. When stock markets rose, comedians asked, "Did Hoover die?" Roosevelt did nothing to divert the blame from his predecessor, and actually worked to deny him credit for his successes. That first spring in office, Interior Secretary Harold Ickes ordered that the immense dam on the California-Nevada border that Hoover had launched as commerce secretary, and that was referred to in multiple appropriations bills as Hoover Dam, be known as Boulder Dam; Hoover was not invited to its dedication in 1935. His tax returns were audited; there were no routine birthday greetings from the Oval Office.

His own party pretended he didn't exist; during the 1940 campaign, Connecticut Republicans asked him not to appear in the state, since his presence was poison. "I shall never understand the long neglect of Herbert Hoover," Truman once observed. "He deserved better treatment at the hands of his own party."

After Pearl Harbor, Hoover spoke out in support of Roosevelt's response and offered to help in any way; given his experience after the First World War, he thought he might be able to serve again. Belgium, Norway, Poland, Holland, and Finland all tried to enlist Hoover's aid; Congress asked his advice. Secretary of State Cordell Hull tried several times to convince Roosevelt to call him. But both Roosevelt and British prime minister Winston Churchill rejected Hoover's initiatives to get food to the occupied countries, on the grounds that this amounted to aiding Hitler by relieving him of his obligation to feed the nations he overran. Hoover was pilloried in some quarters as a pro-German isolationist. "Roosevelt couldn't stand him," Truman told friends, "and he hated Roosevelt." For the Democrats, involving Hoover in a humanitarian mission would have meant rehabilitating the most useful scapegoat the party had ever had. "I'm not Jesus Christ," Roosevelt declared, after financier Bernard Baruch recommended soliciting Hoover's help. "I'm not raising him from the dead."

All Roosevelt would agree to were arm's-length meetings between Hoover and various cabinet officials, who would then report back to the president. *Newsweek* cast doubt on the sincerity of any White House overtures, on the grounds that "few Administrations in American history ever went to greater lengths to smear a predecessor than this one."

At the Democratic convention in 1944, the moment when then Senator Truman's star suddenly rose and he found himself anointed as FDR's running mate, Hoover was still very much the enemy: candidates "invoked Herbert Hoover as the man they prefer to campaign against. We ought to be eternally grateful to Herbert Hoover," one New Dealer remarked, "who has been our meal ticket for twelve years."

But in 1945, when Roosevelt died and Truman suddenly found himself occupying the office Hoover once held, he approached his Republican predecessor very differently. Though a Democrat to his bones, Truman was not wired to see every decision as a political calculation. Neither Truman nor Hoover had Roosevelt's gift for making politics a great show, or his subtle sense of human nature, or the patrician bravado that allowed him to embody the office rather than merely occupy it. Hoover was the only man alive who knew what it was like to sit in the chair in a crisis—and to be eternally compared to the sainted Roosevelt. So Truman was not allergic to the idea of inviting Hoover back to the White House in the spring of 1945, when he found himself facing a food crisis in Europe.

Truman had just as vivid—and selective—a recollection of how that meeting came about as he had of Hoover's demeanor during it. He recalled how that morning he'd read in the paper that Hoover was in Washington, staying at the Shoreham Hotel. So he picked up the phone in the Oval Office and asked the chief operator to connect him to the hotel. She was shocked by the idea of a president placing his own call, but no more so than the man at the other end.

"How are you, Mr. President?" Truman said.

"Who is this?"

"This is Harry Truman," he said. "I heard you were in town, Mr. President, and I called to ask if you would care to come over and see your old home."

At this point, Hoover had not stepped foot in the White House since the day Roosevelt was inaugurated in 1933.

"Well, Hoover was just flabbergasted," Truman recalled.

"Mr. President, I don't know what to say."

Truman told Hoover he'd like to talk to him, and would even come to see him at his hotel.

"I couldn't let you do that, Mr. President. I'll come to see you."

"That's what I figured you'd say," Truman replied. "I've got a limousine on the way to pick you up."

Another very nice tale of a spontaneous meeting of minds; but once again the record tells a different story. Presidential meetings hardly ever happen that easily, especially when the practice had gone out of fashion during the Roosevelt years, and much of the White House staff is opposed to it. It took multiple matchmakers and an elaborate courtship over a period of weeks before Hoover would come anywhere near the Oval Office. He knew he still had enemies in the neighborhood. If Truman had just happened to pick up the phone and summon his predecessor, how was it that the *New York Times* already knew about the meeting in that morning's paper?

The real story was much more complicated. Hoover had been desperate to help as the war wound down. He just had certain conditions, since he knew how easily he could be undermined by Roosevelt's palace guard, and he bore some grudges of his own. He'd been trying all through the spring to make his voice heard. He helped lead a nationwide drive to collect 150 million pounds of donated clothing. He blasted the inefficiency of the United Nations Relief and Rehabilitation Administration (UNRRA), formed the year before; if the agency couldn't manage to get food to starving children, let the War Department take over. "It is now 11:59 on the clock of starvation," he warned again and again. Apart from sheer humanitarian concern, the safety of American troops and the need for order required getting food to an increasingly desperate population.

On April 12, 1945, the day Roosevelt died, Hoover sent Truman a telegram. "All Americans will wish you strength for your gigantic task," he cabled the new president. "You have the right to call for any service in aid of the country."

Including, of course, *his* service. Truman wrote back a perfunctory note of thanks for the good wishes, but with a scrawled handwritten postscript: "I assure you I shall feel free to call upon you. Thanks for the offer."

It was the opening Hoover had been waiting for: he told a friend that "now that there has been a change in Washington, I may be on the move often." His hopes unleashed, he mused that if Truman would just name him secretary of war to replace the aging icon Henry Stimson, he'd be in the perfect position to get the relief where it was needed.

Republican congresswoman Clare Boothe Luce returned from a European tour aghast at the devastation and calling for appointment of some sort of "Super Hoover" to coordinate relief. And she was not alone. By early May, Stimson himself was playing matchmaker. A lifelong Republican who had served as Hoover's secretary of state and as Taft's, Roosevelt's, and Truman's secretary of war, he was a titanic figure in Washington—and the perfect presidential back channel. It's time to call Hoover, he quietly urged Truman; the president, Stimson wrote in his diary, was "cordially acquiescent" to the idea, and made it sound like he was expecting Hoover to drop by any day now.

But no official invitation came. Friends urged Hoover to offer his help again. Over lunch, Bernard Baruch too pushed him to call Truman, "and for the fourth time," Hoover recorded, "I had to explain that I would not go to Washington except at the direct invitation of the President." Friends kept telling him that if he presented himself at the White House he would be warmly received and offered "a big job in Europe." But Hoover was convinced they were playing games, resisting any official initiative in order to avoid offending "the left wingers." If Truman wanted his advice, he could ask for it, the former president concluded. "Because of the pettiness and vindictiveness of the group in Washington . . . my own inclination was to tell them to all go to Hell."

So on May 13, Stimson invited Hoover for Sunday lunch at his Long Island home: it was "very hush hush," Hoover's close friend Edgar Rickard wrote in his diary. Hoover did not hide his pride or bitterness. Democrats had been beating him up for years: if Truman wanted to mend fences he needed to do it properly. But he was softening; Hoover was impressed by the reports of Truman's administrative style, and told Rickard he thought Truman would make a decent president "even though he is a Democrat."

But when Stimson proposed later that week that Hoover come to Washington to see him and some aides to discuss the situation in Europe, Hoover balked. An informal lunch between old friends is one thing; this meeting sounded too official, and Hoover didn't want to be seen as angling to get back inside. Stimson said he was "making a mountain out of a molehill." But Hoover had been hearing reports of people around Truman who wanted to have nothing to do with him: press secretary Steve Early, a Roosevelt loyalist, was reported to have said that "if Hoover wanted anything he would have to come down on his knees to get it."

This would come to be a club puzzle: how do you navigate the advisors who often have an interest in keeping presidents apart? Hoover knew his way around the White House, knew what can happen when a president wants to reach around his aides for advice. The only way he would get a real hearing internally was if Truman himself asked for it.

And so it was that on May 24, Truman personally mailed a letter, handwritten on White House stationery:

My dear Mr. President:

> *If you should be in Washington, I would be most happy to talk over the European food situation with you.*
> *Also it would be a pleasure to me to become acquainted with you.*

> *Most sincerely*
> *Harry S Truman*

That gesture would require Truman to do some blocking and tackling. The Roosevelt loyalists "had lost their leader and they were down in the dumps," Truman observed. They were watching closely, keeping score of Truman's departures from Roosevelt's rules, and rehabilitating Herbert Hoover was a cardinal sin. He waited until the staff meeting the next morning to break the news. As aide Eben Ayers remembered it, "the president said he was going to tell us of something he had done last night on his own—and we might all throw bricks at him."

Hoover wrote back immediately and the meeting was set for May 28; his friend Rickard observed that Hoover was "elated" at the invitation. In an editorial on the morning of the visit, the *New York Times* celebrated the foundation of the modern club: a summit that brings together "the two men who, working in concert, should be able to do more than any two men in America toward relieving the distress of 100,000,000 people. . . . Mr. Hoover's advice has been available but unsought for a long time."

Hoover arrived a little early, taking in the sights and smells of the halls he hadn't seen in so long. He greeted employees who had served while he lived there. And then he greeted Truman in the Oval Office. His account of the meeting was much less moist than Truman's later recollection.

Hoover approached problems like a clock to be dismantled, and so laid out for the president his sense of the food challenge and how to meet it. The next three months until the harvest would be key: it would take a million tons of wheat per month to stave off disaster. He reminded Truman that when Wilson put him in charge of relief after World War I, he had had the authority to cut through red tape, as well as the advantage of having the Big Four powers gathered at the peace talks in Paris to help break down any obstacles he encountered. "During the next ninety days . . . no organization could be formed that could cut through the maze of red tape except the Army." He stressed the strategic imperative as well as the humanitarian one: "Bare subsistence meant hunger," he told Truman, "and hunger meant Communism."

At home, Hoover said, Truman should create an economic equivalent of the War Council to battle bureaucracy, develop policy, and relieve Truman of the burdens on him. And the agriculture secretary needed much more authority over how food was grown and distributed.

They talked about Japan, and how to sue for peace; they discussed the perils of a war with the Soviet Union. Truman asked if Hoover would write him a memo with his ideas.

The meeting lasted nearly an hour, which was noteworthy given that Truman was stingy with his time, cutting the length of cabinet meetings in half and holding most visitors to fifteen minutes. When they finished, Truman recalled, he invited Hoover to stay over at the White House if he wanted; Hoover thanked him, but said he preferred a hotel. "This is the same answer I would have given if I had been in his place," Truman wrote later, but added that he made sure that every courtesy was extended to Hoover whenever he came to Washington.

The reporters who greeted Hoover afterward were eager to hear all about what had happened. There he stood, in front of the cameras again, with the press corps hanging on to what he had to say about his foray back into the heart of the action. It was a moment Hoover had been awaiting for a very long time. But in a gesture establishing the first club protocol, the former president let his successor shape the message. "The President of the United States has the right to make his own announcement concerning anything he may have said to visitors or what visitors have said to him."

Truman did reap a political benefit. The Hoover visit, *Time* pronounced, was "as shrewd as it was generous. In one master stroke, he had won the applause of Republicans and had sharply reminded the nation of the immediate necessity of feeding Europe." Hoover suspected there was more theater than substance to the effort. In his own notes he concluded that Truman "was simply endeavoring to establish a feeling of good will in the country."

Hoover went back to the Waldorf to write the memos he had promised. Still skeptical of the palace guard, he sent them to Truman through his new press secretary, Charlie Ross, with a note: "I am sending it to you as I do not know how many hands these things go through under the present mechanism." Ross made sure Truman got them, and the president in turn passed the memos around his cabinet, asking the State Department to analyze the Japanese peace proposal. He gave the military a stronger hand in the immense relief effort, laying the foundation for what he and Hoover would undertake the following year. Hoover publicly praised the president a week after their visit for doing an "admirable" job.

But it is Truman's takeaway from the meeting that sheds the most light on a president's unusual needs. It would be three days before he got around to writing about the meeting in his diary, and he had nothing much to say about food relief or Japan or anything else, other than that the discussions had been "pleasant and constructive."

What stayed with him was what the two men shared about "the general troubles of U.S. Presidents—two in particular."

Truman had once observed to his mother that Washington featured more divas per square foot than all the opera companies combined. Hoover knew something about that.

"We discussed our prima donnas and wondered what makes 'em. Some of my boys who came in with me are having trouble with their dignity and prerogatives. It's hell when a man gets in close association with the President. Something happens to him." This was even true of Truman's old Senate comrades, who would stop by to chat and drink his bourbon, then go out and tell reporters how they were helping Harry save the world. "That publicity complex is hell and few can escape it here. When a good man comes along who hasn't the bug I try to grab him."

And what else was on the president's mind that night, as the world bore down hard around him? The unique loneliness of being the most public man on the planet. That morning he had walked across the street to St. John's Church and slipped into a back pew. He didn't think more than six people recognized him. "I'm always so lonesome when the family leaves," he wrote in his diary. "I have no one to raise a fuss over my neckties and my haircuts, my shoes and my clothes generally."

In his note of thanks to Hoover, Truman added a postscript: "I appreciated very much your coming to see me. It gave me a lift."

The Committee to Save the World

Two months later, Truman got to see for himself how bad things were in the war zone. During his August 1945 trip to the Potsdam Conference outside Berlin, he drove through flattened cities filled with sick, broken people living at the edge of despair. No war president, observed historian David McCullough, not Lincoln or Wilson or Roosevelt, had ever seen anything like what Truman confronted. Berlin was "an absolute ruin," the president said. The empty look on people's faces was haunting.

In the weeks that followed things got even worse; too many European farmers had been turned into soldiers, too much fertilizer had been diverted to make explosives, and too many farm machine factories had been converted to churn out munitions. By September it was clear that the harvest would be bad, and hunger a growing threat. The Soviets were showing how casually they viewed the provisions of international agreements, as they swallowed one weakened state after another. Meanwhile American workers were restless, the housing shortage critical, Truman's cabinet partially mutinous, and many in Congress were shocked to find that Harry Truman was a liberal, after he sent up a sixteen-thousand-word message laying out his goals for health insurance, housing, education, unemployment, and the minimum wage that left Republicans and Southern Democrats growling.

Hoover and Truman continued to correspond, and the former president watched the fall wrestling matches with interest. "He does not have the abilities of his predecessor in adroit coercion and bribing with political spoils," Hoover observed to a friend. Hoover could sympathize; he'd managed to alienate a Republican Congress during his presidency, to the point that even a friendly columnist declared him "the most left-footed President politically the world ever saw."

And Truman wasn't exactly enjoying himself. At Christmas he went home to Missouri with Bess, but that didn't go very well. Back at the White House a few days later, he wrote her one of those cranky letters he had the good sense to stick in a drawer. "I'm here in the White House, the great white sepulcher of ambitions and reputations," he began. Bess hadn't been very supportive lately, he suggested, and he sounded frustrated. "No one ever needed help and assistance as I do now. If I can get the use of the best brains in the country and a little help from those I have on a pedestal at home, the job will be done."

For at least one of his immediate problems, the "best brain" happened to be lodged in the head of Herbert Hoover. A few days later, on January 4, 1946, new British Labour prime minister Clement Attlee cabled Truman warning that widespread food panic was making the task of reconstruction massively harder. Europe's wheat crop and Asia's rice crop had come in below expectations; much of Holland was underwater from flooding where dams had been destroyed. There were food riots in Hamburg, looting in Sicily; Romanians and Hungarians were reduced to eating acorns. Drought and locusts wrecked crops in Africa and India, and even Canada's wheat production was down 25 percent. Attlee, Truman said, "pleaded for my personal and active interest."

Agriculture Secretary Clinton Anderson, who would be a crucial in-termediary in the coming months, walked into a cabinet meeting and declared that no matter how much wheat American farmers produced, there would not be enough to meet U.S. commitments abroad. He called Hoover, who understood both the scope of the problem and the limits to how Truman could address it: the winter of 1946 was not an easy time to ask Americans to cut back their own consumption in order to free more food for export. With the war over, sacrifice no longer felt like service, but like suffering. People lined up to buy sugar and stockings and wash-ing machines; as wartime price controls frayed, the threat of inflation grew while workers pressed for higher wages.

But Hoover didn't believe in rationing and government control any-way. He was an evangelist for voluntarism: many people still remem-bered his leadership during the First World War, the "Hooverizing," the Wheatless Wednesdays and Meatless Mondays that Hoover had orga-nized as Wilson's food administrator in 1917 to conserve food that could be sent abroad. Convince the president to launch such a voluntary con-servation program, Hoover advised Anderson, which Truman promptly did. On February 6, Truman outlined a nine-point emergency food plan, including cutting U.S. whiskey and other grain alcohol production, lim-iting the use of grain to feed livestock, and extracting more flour from wheat, thus turning bread a little grayer.

Truman's radio address came as a rattling shock. Most Americans knew that the job of feeding the world now fell to them—but most also thought they were doing a pretty good job. Now, without significant cut-backs to free up food to export, Europe faced disaster. A hundred million people were getting by on less than half what the average American ate: "More people face starvation and even actual death for want of food today than in any war year and perhaps more than in all the war years combined," Truman declared.

Hoover immediately pitched in, warning of "the stern job ahead," and urging Americans to heed their president, in a statement issued from his apartment at the Waldorf. But Truman needed more than cheerlead-ing. Hoover was on a fishing trip in Florida in February when Anderson tracked him down. Would Hoover be willing to come immediately to Washington to chair an emergency citizens commission to raise awareness and promote conservation? They'd be willing to send a special plane, land or amphibious, to fetch him.

And there was some flattery: Anderson said that Hoover had given him better advice than anyone else the previous summer, and everything he'd warned about had come true. Lest Hoover worry about a trap, Anderson preemptively assured him that this "was not a politically cooked up arrangement."

Hoover sent back a telegram, suggesting he was ready to help, but not to waste his time. A citizens commission can't do enough, he argued: he had told Truman last May that all control over food should be placed in the agriculture secretary's hands. "I am advised that this was not done," Hoover complained to Anderson. "It should be done now." He then walked Anderson through the next steps, including the need for a global assessment of food needs and surpluses, a national conservation plan, and coordination of the entire food industry. Anderson listened carefully—and Truman acted on the advice.

The next day, February 27, 1946, Truman sent a telegram to a handful of the most influential men and women in the country: Time-Life founder Henry Luce, *Washington Post* publisher Eugene Meyer, pollster George Gallup, the chairman of General Foods, and the presidents of the U.S. Chamber of Commerce and the League of Women Voters.

"I am asking you and a very few other public spirited citizens to meet in the East Wing of the White House at three o'clock, Friday afternoon, March first," Truman wrote, and then added a sweetener: "Ex-President Hoover has accepted my invitation and will be there. I count on your support." Truman didn't care that his mail ran two to one against having anything to do with "that contemptible character." He called this "the most important meeting, I think, we have held in the White House since I have been the President."

Hoover arrived early to meet privately with Truman, before the full committee gathered. They talked about the gap in Anderson's estimates of food supply and demand, with Hoover noting that the numbers were "appallingly far apart, that if the figures were right, the world was faced with a gigantic catastrophe." The best they could hope was to minimize the loss of life. "I have a job for you that nobody else in this country can do," Truman told him. Somehow they needed to find a way to get the food from the people that had it to the ones that needed it—and come up with eleven million extra tons of cereal to close the gap. "You know more about feeding nations and people than anybody in the world," Truman said. Take my plane, he offered, pick a staff, take whatever time you need but go see what we can do.

Recalling the request later, Hoover claimed that "I accepted with reluctance, since I was 71 years old and my time was committed to administer several educational, scientific and charitable institutions at home." But Hoover, while often shy, was seldom modest, and he didn't think anyone else was up to the job. Someone with stature needed to meet with the top people, face-to-face, as well as talk to the local people and press. Who better than a former president, who was already a hero to the hungry?

When the full committee met with Truman, Hoover, and key cabinet members later that day, it called for a 25 percent cut in wheat consumption, and cuts in fat consumption as well, long enough to see Europe through to the next harvest. "The fate of civilization," Hoover declared when the meeting adjourned, "depends on whether the American people are willing to make a sacrifice for the next four months, if they are willing to save the world from chaos." He stressed again the need for a central food czar to unblock bottlenecks and end the feeding of precious grains to livestock rather than starving people. But once again, he respected Truman's presidential prerogatives. Asked by reporters how hard he had pressed his idea of a food administrator on Truman, he demurred. "I make it a practice to never say what I say to a president." And everyone smiled.

Four days after Hoover and Truman met at the White House, Truman was back in his home state with Winston Churchill, who shook the very foundations of the postwar peace with the speech he gave in Fulton, Missouri. He too warned of Europe's condition: "None can compute what has been called 'the unestimated sum of human pain.'" But hunger was not the only threat. "From Stettin in the Baltic to Trieste in the Adriatic an iron curtain has descended across the Continent," Churchill warned, and certainly underlying Hoover's mission was a determination not to let that Soviet sphere grow any larger because of a complete breakdown of order among desperate people.

Feeding them was important. Winning their allegiance even more so. The next day, the *New York Times* ran a pointed editorial tying the two together. "The United States has lost some popularity abroad since VE and VJ days. It is pleasant to think that by a neighborly act now we can recover much of it." Hoover's trip could serve many useful purposes, the paper suggested. "The 'American Way' will have an advantage over other and different 'ways' if it obviously stands for food for the hungry. Mr. Hoover taking up where he left off so long ago is a splendid argument for Americanism."

Herbert Hoover had become Truman's first weapon in the Cold War.

The Fifty-Thousand-Mile Mission

Before leaving, Hoover delivered a national radio address, invoking America's moral duty to rise to the occasion. Half a billion people were at risk, and the available food surpluses would only solve half the problem; creativity and conservation would have to do the rest. If your neighbor were starving, he argued, you would feed them: "Could you not imagine one of these helpless women or children as an invisible guest at your table?"

After a week of consultations, on Sunday, March 17, Hoover and his team took off from LaGuardia Airport aboard an Army C-54 nicknamed the "Faithful Cow," because of the mooing noise it made on takeoff and landing. The trip would cover twenty-two countries in fifty-seven days. What he saw in the weeks that followed haunted him for years. Touring Warsaw, where nine of ten houses had been destroyed, he observed that "the city was a horror of vengeance." He visited slums and soup kitchens and orphanages; "we are weary of dying," one woman told him. When the team went to Rome to enlist the pope's help, one member noted that even the luxury hotel menu was "just sufficient for a robust canary."

It was the ultimate puzzle, collecting the data and then putting the pieces together both to increase the supply of available food and to direct it to where it was needed most. In Norway, Hoover learned that the 200,000 tons of surplus fish could more than double if only there were more salt to preserve it; so he arranged through American officials in Germany to get the needed salt supply.

"He dug out a tremendous amount of stored food and black market supplies that we probably would have missed had we not had his knowledge, background, understanding and acquaintance with the communities themselves," observed Treasury Secretary John Snyder, recalling Hoover's relentless crusade. "Because of his experience and because of his stature, [it] worked out to our great advantage, as we knew the tricks that the citizens and the governments had worked in the past."

Still, Truman was coming to the realization that Hoover was not just a useful stand-in overseas; if played right, he could help Truman even more at home. As Hoover headed to Cairo in mid-April, Truman had lunch with Anderson and Famine Emergency Committee head Chester Davis, and decided he wanted to bring Hoover back home to make speeches and raise awareness. The president sent a cable the next day. "An urgent need has developed in this country to bring forcibly and dramatically to public attention," Truman wrote, "as a spur to the food-for-famine-effort, the facts about conditions in Europe which your visit and inquiries have brought to light."

Hoover pushed back hard. For one thing, people in India, China, and Japan would be very disappointed, at some cost to goodwill, if he postponed his trip. But he proposed something more radical and unprecedented: the first ever club radio broadcast in which a sitting president facing multiple pressures at home enlisted a former president to be his partner and enhance his clout. And so they prepared a joint message delivered from Truman in the White House and then Hoover in Cairo, which would air on all four networks on the night of April 19.

Truman went first: Hoover's reports from the front lines, Truman said, "have driven home again and again the desperate plight of the people over there. . . . Millions will surely die unless we eat less." He asked Americans to go on a European "austerity" diet two days a week. And in a tacit admission that voluntary conservation would not be enough, he added some muscle to the effort. That night Anderson announced a reduction of wheat used by bakers, a huge government purchase of oats for export, and an extra 30-cent bonus above the ceiling for every bushel of wheat delivered before May 25.

It was Hoover's turn next. Where Truman was practical, Hoover was preacherly, searching for language to scrape the conscience. Though he had been sounding the alarms for years, Hoover sensed that this was the first time people were really paying attention. Tens of millions tuned in, by far the largest audience he'd had since leaving the White House. He argued the strategic imperative and for personal duty. "The saving of these human lives is far more than an economic necessity to the recovery of the world," he said. It was "a part of the moral and spiritual reconstruction of the world."

By this time Hoover was acting not only as Truman's ambassador and proxy; he was his intelligence officer abroad and his public relations manager at home. A few days later he warned Truman of "a very active propaganda" campaign in various European countries to blame the United States for any failure in food supplies. He included a cartoon from Britain's *Punch* accusing the United States of greed and selfishness. Truman sent back an eyes-only cable, thanking him for the heads-up, and for all Hoover was doing to see that America got credit for her efforts. "I fully recognize the personal sacrifice and risk which you have taken in taking such a hazardous journey," Truman wrote, "but the excellent results which you have obtained will be of inestimable value to this country."

Selling Sacrifice

When the two presidents met again in person, their fourth encounter in a year, they had more on their minds than hunger. Most of their conversation was about the Soviets; Truman complained about how hard they were to deal with. "I told him," Hoover recorded in his notes, "that there was only one method of treating this present group of Russians and that that was with a truculent spirit." That was the only language they would understand. Hoover even drafted a telegram for Truman to send to Soviet leader Joseph Stalin, urging that the Soviets increase their food aid to Finland, Poland, Czechoslovakia, and Yugoslavia to help ease the crisis.

Then Hoover was back on the radio with a passionate sermon unlike any he had ever managed as president. "Of the Four Horsemen of the Apocalypse, the one named War has gone—at least for a while," he said. "But Famine, Pestilence and Death are still charging over the earth. Hunger is a silent visitor who comes like a shadow. He sits beside every anxious mother three times each day. He brings not alone suffering and sorrow, but fear and terror. He carries disorder and the paralysis of government, and even its downfall. He is more destructive than armies, not only in human life but in morals. All of the values of right living melt before his invasions, and every gain of civilization crumbles."

There was one more chance to turn the corner: but that involved getting Latin America, especially Argentina, to step up its food exports. And that made for some delicate diplomacy, not just with the new president, Juan Perón, but among Truman, Hoover, and the U.S. State Department.

Regarding the idea of sending Hoover to Latin America next, Anderson warned Truman that "the State Department will protest." Professional diplomats tended not to welcome freelancers, even when they are former presidents. To which Truman replied, "we won't give them a chance. I will announce it at once." The United States had worked hard to prevent Perón's ascension; as a result, relations with Argentina were so bitter, Hoover wrote in his diary, that the effort could be a total waste of time. But the stakes—possibly adding a million tons of food—were too high not to try.

So this was Hoover's next mission for Truman, in June of 1946. It was not a happy trip, through eleven countries in twenty-five days. In Venezuela, he fell in a bathtub and broke several ribs. In Argentina he attended a state dinner and was seated 196th out of 219 guests: but "I was resolved . . . to eat even Argentine dirt if I could get the 1.6 million tons."

Perón had been in office all of forty-eight hours when Hoover landed in Buenos Aires. The U.S. embassy had served as a kind of opposition headquarters during the election campaign, in a "total war" against Perón, and the U.S. ambassador stalled in any effort to set up a meeting for Hoover. But the Mexican ambassador pitched in and the pope had already laid the groundwork. Hoover had two meetings with Perón, who was "most cordial." Perón even attributed the size of his victory to the American opposition: it allowed him, he told Hoover, to rally his countrymen to "fight off tyranny of the Colossus of the North." Perón's wife, Eva, Hoover observed, had the brains of Eleanor Roosevelt and the looks of Hedy Lamarr.

Perón complained that even ten months after the war's end, the United States had not lifted its wartime trade restrictions, which were driving up Argentine unemployment. Plus, Argentina's gold reserves were still held frozen in New York's Federal Reserve Bank. Could Hoover do anything about this?

His fight was not with the people of Europe, Perón added, and issued an executive order to release more grain within a matter of weeks. Hoover kept his promise as well: he met with Truman as soon as he got back to Washington and told him about the gold seizure and trade restraints. As Hoover remembered it, Truman said he couldn't believe this was true, picked up the phone, and called the State Department.

"I heard only one side of the conversation," Hoover recalled, "but that was sufficient." The president ordered the trade barriers lifted and the gold released. Hoover asked if he could let Perón know, "as it would relieve the strain between the United States and the Argentine. Mr. Truman agreed, and I sent a cordial telegram to President Perón."

In barely a year Truman and Hoover had gone from total strangers and political foes to trusted teammates at home and abroad, in public and private. Together they broke through the red tape, defied the bureaucrats, wooed the dictators, moved a mountain or two. The first year of Truman's presidency was played for the very highest stakes—and it was Hoover who ensured his victory. By the end of that month, Truman could announce that America had shipped five and a half million tons of grain, thereby keeping the nation's promise and forestalling a humanitarian disaster.

"Every molecule in my body yells at me that it is tired," Hoover told a friend. "I am going away for a rest."

"Yours was a real service for humanity," Truman wrote privately to Hoover as the year came to an end. By now the two had battled enough common enemies to have seeded something like a friendship. "I know that I can count upon your cooperation if developments at any time in the future make it necessary for me to call upon you again."

2

"Our Exclusive Trade Union"

—HERBERT HOOVER

Together Truman and Hoover prevented a humanitarian catastrophe. Now all that remained was preventing another war.

It was already clear that the Soviets and the Americans held very different visions of the future of Europe and the balance of power. At a time when Americans wanted nothing more than to retreat, recover, rebuild, and reject any further involvement in the continent that kept sucking the United States into wretched wars, Truman understood that there was no going back. This was now the American Century, and America would have to lead.

Selling that idea to the American people, however, much less a Republican Congress, would take energy, ingenuity, luck, and the help of the kind of super-lobbyist that only the club can provide.

What Truman set out to do was way too ambitious to do on his own—even if he hadn't run into hard political times. When the war ended, Truman's approval rating topped 80 percent; toward the end of 1946, it sank to 32 percent. He was called stupid, vulgar, late for cabinet meetings because he woke up stiff in his joints from trying to put his foot in his mouth. In the 1946 midterm elections, Democratic candidates asked him not to campaign for them; some ran recordings of old Roosevelt speeches at rallies. His party was crushed anyway, leaving Congress in Republican hands for the first time in sixteen years.

The German Problem

Truman's immediate challenge at the start of 1947 was what to do about Germany, a flashpoint since the war ended. Do we keep it weak, a nice pastoral state that would never pose a threat again? Or was Germany fated to be the economic engine of Europe, in which case the sooner it was back on its feet, the better for everyone? Truman and Hoover agreed on the latter course; now the trick was persuading a tightwad Republican Congress to go along with a massive German aid program.

Truman had his own reasons for needing the emissary to be someone of Hoover's international stature and domestic political clout, rather than some anonymous bureaucrat or diplomat. The president's political motives were transparent even at the time: "President Hopes Investigator's Findings Will Impress Republicans in Congress" read the headline the next day. Truman was looking for $300 million; if Hoover came back affirming that the U.S. approach was sound, the odds were much better that he'd get it. Of course, if Hoover came back from a third overseas mission rejecting Truman's priorities, the president would have even bigger problems. It was a measure of his growing trust in Hoover that he was willing to run the risk.

By now there were elements in the administration that were actively conspiring to undercut the club's clout. Sending Hoover back to Europe as a super-ambassador ruffled feathers in the War Department and raised "serious misgivings among career diplomats," as the New York Times put it. German economic unification was supposed to be high on the agenda for incoming Secretary of State George Marshall, who was soon to attend the Moscow Conference of Foreign Ministers to discuss final peace terms for Germany and Austria. Calling Hoover in, the sources said, was "puzzling to us who know how delicate the problem is at this stage." Germany was suffering a terrible winter, with temperatures in Berlin falling to zero, people dying of cold, and too little food or fuel or basic goods, and Hoover's view was that Germany needed to begin supporting itself. But the State Department believed that making Germany anything other than a ward of the West would require rewriting the rules of Potsdam, which kept German industry so weak that waging future wars would be impossible. "I was not in a particularly conciliatory mood when I responded to the call to Washington to talk with the President," Hoover recalled, but he went anyway. He made sure to meet with Republican leaders on the Hill before heading to the White House; some members later admitted that while they wanted to support Truman's foreign policy, in the honored tradition of politics stopping at the water's edge, they would welcome some political cover. "If the views expressed by Mr. Hoover in his report happened to coincide with those of the President," reported the *Times*, the Republican lawmakers "would then vote their convictions without any liability for following the Administration's program."

When Hoover reached the White House, Truman referred to the critical newspaper leaks "with considerable indignation," as Hoover told it. At one point Hoover actually sat at Truman's desk and wrote out, in pencil, his view of the mission, just so there would be no misunderstanding. He agreed to undertake a "long-range study" of German recovery, with a guarantee of complete freedom, though Truman warned him about "some of my prima donnas in the State Department."

Hoover set off on February 2 for a three-week mission, and this was no junket. Now seventy-two, he worked fifteen-hour days in unheated government buildings, where he sat wrapped in overcoats and blankets. He suffered a series of bad colds, and a rapid descent into Newfoundland in the unpressurized DC-4 ruptured his eardrum and damaged his hearing permanently. Food was once again terribly scarce; among his initiatives was the creation of canteens and soup kitchens across Germany, drawing on surplus Army rations, to give 3.5 million schoolchildren a hot meal at midday.

Upon his return, he reported to Truman of the grinding suffering Germany faced. He spent the next day talking with cabinet officials, including a two-hour meeting with Secretary of State Marshall. He testified before the House Foreign Affairs Committee and had lunch with twenty-five lawmakers.

Back in New York, Hoover wrote up his report on Austria, and arranged to meet with Truman again. Upon reading it, the president sat down to write a note of thanks. "I want to express to you again my very high appreciation for your willingness to undertake these two surveys for the Secretary of War and me," Truman wrote to Hoover. "You have made a very decided contribution to the situation in Germany and Austria and I am sure that it will have a bearing on the conference in Moscow." He had all the more reason to be grateful, since he had just invited key lawmakers to a secret White House meeting to prepare them for news that Britain, its economy on life support, could no longer be responsible for saving Greece and Turkey. That job would fall either to the United States—or the Soviets. What would come to be known as the Truman Doctrine would decide which. No longer could the United States sit back safely on her side of the ocean and let Europe sort out her own affairs.

On Wednesday, March 12, Truman and Hoover met in the morning; Hoover declined the job of overseer of American relief, but stressed again the importance of controls on how aid money would be used. Afterward Truman headed to the Hill—where he proceeded to lay out an entirely new framework for the use of American aid and power. He asked for $400 million in aid to Greece and Turkey, arguing that coercion and intimidation of free people by rising totalitarian regimes undermined world peace. "I believe it must be the policy of the United States to support free people who are resisting attempted subjugation by armed minorities or by outside pressures," he declared.

The stunned lawmakers seemed "somewhat bewildered," reporters observed, as they "saw their country's foreign policy undergo radical change in the space of twenty one minutes." There was evidence of "a congressional storm of great dimensions in the making." Republicans in particular were in no mood to write a Democratic president a blank check to remake the world in America's image.

So in this crusade, the hardheaded Hoover was an essential ally. He testified all through the spring on the importance of American aid—especially if administered with safeguards against misuse and constructed around the premise that it would eventually be paid back.

He arranged to have breakfast with ten Republican lawmakers, but told his friend Rickard he would not accept Truman's offer to stay at Blair House "as [it] will not provide independence he desires; suggests that Blair House may be wired." Hoover was working both sides in what he believed to be the national interest: he didn't trust Truman's bleeding-heart profligacy or the Republicans' reflexive isolationism. As the bill finally took shape, it did incorporate many of Hoover's cost-control suggestions. And so from the foundations he and Truman laid together arose the great edifice of American statesmanship that was the Marshall Plan. Once again, Truman had every reason to be very grateful for his surprising—and therefore especially influential—ally.

Over the course of that year of 1947, Truman offered a series of olive branches to his proud partner. In April he signed a congressional resolution restoring the name of the Hoover Dam: he used four pens, and asked that they all be sent to Hoover.

A month later the unprecedented partnership finally went public, when Hoover appeared at the annual Gridiron Dinner of Washington's power elite for the first time since 1932. Since Truman had a reelection campaign approaching, Hoover said in his remarks that he wanted to avoid "an indelicate implication that I am seeking to recruit him to my exclusive union of ex-presidents." He commiserated about the ordeal of handling an opposition Congress: "Here again I can sympathize with Mr. Truman more than any other living person," he said. He went on to praise Truman for his strength and principle: "Amid the thousand crises which sweep upon us from abroad, he has stood firm with his feet rooted in the American soil. He has brought to the White House new impulses of good will toward men."

When Hoover finished, Truman reached over and wrote a note on his program: "with high esteem and keen appreciation to a great man." In December Truman invited him to a White House reception; the following month he offered him the use of the presidential retreat in Key West. Hoover was especially touched when the Trumans hung a portrait of his wife, Lou, in the White House.

The longer Truman occupied the office, the more aware he was of ways that his predecessor, perhaps uniquely, could help him, and he was not too proud to ask. Hoover found ways to return the favor; it had been during the last year of his administration that Congress had made all government salaries, the president's included, taxable. This made little difference to independently wealthy men like Hoover and Roosevelt, who by 1944 was paying more than half his salary in tax, but made quite a difference to the permanently pinched Truman. The salaries of the White House staff and servants were paid by the government, but not their meals. When it was just the family eating, it was usually leftovers. Truman told friends his typical weekly take-home pay was about $80.

Hoover helped lead the charge to get the president a raise. Truman was lucky, Hoover argued, if he had enough left over each month for cigarette money (Truman didn't smoke). Early in 1949, Congress finally voted to raise his salary by a third, to $100,000, and added $50,000 tax free to his expense account to use as he chose.

A Gift for the Club

It's one thing for Congress to provide the president more money; quite another to grant him more power.

Truman, again, would turn to Hoover to help him get it.

There had been at least a half dozen attempts, starting in 1798, at a comprehensive reorganization of the executive branch, all sorts of commissions and committees that began with high hopes and went largely nowhere.

Most efforts at executive branch reorganization were aimed at keeping the president in a box—but modern presidents were ill served by the tangled mess of agencies beneath them. In his first message to Congress in May 1945, Truman asked for the authority to restructure the executive branch. Hoover backed him up at the time; he wrote to Ohio congressman George Bender (and made sure Truman saw a copy) that "six successive Presidents over 35 years have recommended such reorganization. The overlap, waste and conflict of policies between executive agencies have been a scandal for the whole 35 years." Truman appreciated the boost. "The fight for this measure has been long and futile," Truman wrote to Hoover. "It is heartening to know that you approve the bill in principle." And useful knowledge for the battles to come.

But throughout Truman's first term, Congress managed to foil most of his reorganization efforts. Especially after the Republicans took over in 1946, they were looking mainly for a smaller government, not a more effective one. Hoover's administration had cost $4 billion a year; in the postwar years, Truman's was running more than ten times that. The 604,000 civilian employees were now two million. The government owned a quarter of the continental United States, more than five thousand buildings, a million cars and trucks, paint factories, sawmills, a distillery in the Virgin Islands, and a $20-million-a-year fertilizer operation in Tennessee. A single salmon in the Columbia River swimming upstream to spawn came under the jurisdiction of twelve different federal agencies.

So in July of 1947 Congress created the Commission on Organization of the Executive Branch of the Government, which had more latitude than any past attempt at restructuring. The commission's stated goal was to "promote economy, efficiency, and improved service" in going about the public business; its report was due after November of 1948, neatly ensuring that the proposals could be a blueprint for housecleaning by a new Republican president. Speaker Joe Martin appointed Hoover to the panel, who, characteristically, refused to serve unless he was named chairman.

As the only living ex-president, he was a natural choice: an esteemed elder statesman with close ties to congressional Republicans. Those most intent on rolling back Roosevelt's legacy trusted Hoover to deliver the fatal blow to "the traitors who call themselves liberals," as he had been known to call New Dealers, and introduce sound management practices to the public sphere.

But Truman by this time understood something about Hoover that his Republican backers did not. It was a powerful impulse shared by virtually all former presidents: you protect the office, regardless of who holds it at the moment. "Mr. Hoover was not about to take part in any attack on the Presidency," observed his commission aide Don Price. Hoover had sat in the chair during a national crisis and taken the blame for failing to do enough to relieve it; if he managed to transform the office, he could protect his successors from a similar fate.

Some Democrats thought Truman was naive to sign off on what could only be a plot to roll back his entire progressive agenda. But Truman sensed by now that Hoover was not opposed to the notion of the enhanced, institutionalized presidency, merely with how Roosevelt had chosen to use it. Truman told the commission to send back "the most honest findings you can get and don't worry whom it might or might not please." When the once and future house speaker Sam Rayburn protested, Truman brushed him back. Hoover, he declared, was "the best man that I know of, and he'll do the job for me. . . . You politicians leave him alone and we'll get an organization in the government. Now Sam, that's all—you help!"

Hoover called it his "last public service." The commission had a mandate to examine 2,500 departments and agencies, in hopes of whittling down a $40 billion budget. About half the government's purchasing orders, for instance, were for items that cost less than $10—and the paperwork to process them cost $11.20. Hoover predicted that creating a central purchasing agency to cut red tape could save $250 million a year.

Hoover set up two dozen task forces, which met in private; he hired research staff and recruited hundreds of specialists, including two former cabinet members, thirteen undersecretaries, three former senators and five governors, and ten university presidents. Many had a conservative, pro-business bent, and helped steer the commission in that direction, though the group never split purely on partisan lines. Truman's delegates worked to hold off the assault on New Deal agencies, but they were outnumbered. "Hoover definitely thought he was going to use the Commission as a vehicle to overturn the New Deal in substance," recalled member James Rowe, a lawyer, New Dealer, and advisor to every president from Roosevelt to Johnson. "I think he was a very earnest, very sincere man, and worked like the devil. He was seventy-five at this time. I remember we used to break up Saturday morning and he'd say, 'I'll be back Monday morning with three drafts of various reports.' He'd get on the train; he'd work all Saturday and all Sunday; and on the train coming back he'd have these reports written. They weren't very well written, they had terrible style, but he'd been working on them."

Helping government "do more with less" was the nominal mission, but for conservatives it was actually "do less with less." In a memoir of the commission that he never published, Hoover described Truman's representatives as "sycophantish. . . . They all believed the Republicans would win the campaign and their remarks were seldom complimentary to Mr. Truman. I seemed at times the only member who spoke kindly of him."

There was one area of inquiry Hoover declined to delegate: that would be the treatment of the presidency. "I guess I'll take that one myself," he said. "Who is there who ought to know more about it?"

He reached out to Truman's budget chief, James Webb, for help, and told him he'd be investigating the demands of the presidency personally; this, Webb told Truman, was "a happy development." There were all sorts of ideas being floated, Webb noted, and "the evaluation of such proposals by persons who have not either occupied the Presidential office itself, or worked in extremely intimate relationship with it, is extraordinarily difficult. From my several conversations with Mr. Hoover, I am convinced of his appreciation of the difficulty and delicacy of dealing with the whole problem."

Meanwhile, the Other Campaign . . .

Hoover was not inclined to make things worse for a president who faced long odds going into the 1948 campaign against New York governor Thomas Dewey. He also did not want his precious commission to become a partisan football. He had lunch with Truman's press secretary, Charlie Ross, and told him that he'd turned down an invitation to deliver the keynote address at the Republican convention—which tells you how far his rehabilitation had progressed. He'd take a smaller role, he assured Ross, and avoid any attack on the president. The gesture was not entirely welcome news at the White House. At a staff meeting, according to assistant press secretary Ayers, "[Clark] Clifford and others laughingly expressed regret that he was not going to be the Republicans' keynoter as they felt it would be a help to the Democrats."

Hoover gave his convention speech; "Few Republicans had been so bitterly assailed during the years of Democratic supremacy," *Time* observed, "but Hoover's prepared speech cast aside partisanship to talk of the nation's place in the world." He affirmed the importance of strengthening Western Europe and defending liberty. "If you follow the counsel of those who believe that politics is only a game to be played for personal advantage, you are wasting your time," Truman wrote to him, praising it as "the utterance of a statesman."

So one might have expected that the general election would unfold without the two men drawing blood. Truman professed to believe in gentlemanly campaigning. "If you can't win an election without attacking people who've helped you and who're friends of yours," Truman once said, "it's not worth winning." But that was a belief he suspended as the contest reached a fever pitch.

Maybe the habit was just too entrenched—that the only Republican any living Democrat knew how to run against was Herbert Hoover. Truman cast the race as a battle between the common man with his small-town values, and the Republican "power lobby" looking to cheat him at every turn. In one speech he mentioned Hoover sixteen times; not once was it to praise him. If only Al Smith had beaten Hoover in 1928, Truman declared, "we and the world would have been spared untold misery and suffering." After Dewey's campaign train accidentally backed up into an Illinois crowd and Dewey called the engineer "a lunatic," Truman couldn't resist the analogy: he began referring to Hoover as an engineer who "backed the train all the way into the waiting room and brought us to panic, depression, and despair."

To Truman, this may have been perfectly acceptable political jousting, but "Mr. Hoover was absolutely shocked," recalled James Rowe. "He didn't see how a man who had been so nice to him could say such things about him. But I'd say, 'Mr. Hoover, this is politics, he's got to do that.'"

"Well, I suppose he does," said Hoover. It would have been small comfort, but Truman didn't mean a word of what he was saying, he confessed to John Steelman, his chief of staff: "Hoover didn't have any more to do with the Depression than you or I did."

And all the while Hoover kept his weapons sheathed. It's hard to imagine, through the lens of twenty-first-century political warfare, how a leader of one party could have lethal ammunition to use against the other and choose not to deploy it in the name of some larger good. If the material gathered by his commission had been shared with the Republicans during the presidential campaign, James Reston wrote once it was all over, it would have been "fairly inflammable [*sic*] stuff. Mr. Hoover and his staff, however, were scrupulous in keeping the enormous collection of facts about inefficiency, disorganization, duplication and waste under wraps until after the campaign was over." Hoover appeared to steer by the principle that a successful overhaul of the presidency was more important than any individual campaign for it—even if that meant keeping the Democrats in the White House for four more years.

Mr. Truman's Salesman

Truman went on to win his historic upset victory, with Hoover maintaining his dignified silence. There were rumors that he would resign from the commission; the Democrats won back control of Congress as well, which meant that the liberals on the commission, led by future secretary of state Dean Acheson, could now assert their power. Acheson urged that Truman just walk away from the whole effort.

By this time Hoover had invested fourteen months and countless hours, and produced some two million words to be boiled down to nineteen reports that would surely be picked apart in the press and the Congress. His best hope was that the sheer logic of the commission's proposals would overcome arguments of privilege or partisanship.

Hoover asked Truman's aide Webb to have lunch with him, and vented all his frustrations: they had worked so hard, and he'd been so sure there would be a Republican president in place to carry out their proposals, and now it was all lost.

"I just sort of let him have it," Webb recalled. "I said, 'This is no way for a former President to talk. If your work was good yesterday it will be good tomorrow. If you really believe yourself it's good, I'll get hold of Mr. Truman and see if we can't continue our cooperation.' Well, his face lit up in a smile—he thought he was going to be kicked around like FDR kicked him around."

The two men walked together back to Webb's office, still talking; then Webb placed a call to Truman, who was savoring his victory in Key West. Webb was convinced of how much more Truman stood to gain if he and Hoover joined forces, and laid out his argument in a memo to the president three days after the election.

Republicans had typically been suspicious of a strong presidency, Webb observed. But "based on my relations with Mr. Hoover . . . I believe there is now a possibility of getting the last Republican President to urge you to accept an . . . organization for executive responsibility that the Republican Party has historically denied to Presidents.

"If that can be managed," Webb argued to Truman, "you will undoubtedly be able to achieve—with at least a show of bipartisan agreement—a new level of Presidential leadership . . . unknown in our history."

Hoover seemed to have gotten religion on the question of whether the government was too big, or just too untidy. "Our job is to make every Government activity that now exists work efficiently," he told reporters after the election. "It is not our function to say whether it should exist or not." As though on cue—which, actually, it was—Truman came out the next day and publicly renewed his support for Hoover's investigation. The executive branch "imposes handicaps on effective and economic administration and must be brought up to date," Truman affirmed to Hoover. "The task, as you and I have seen from our experience, is to crystallize this general belief into concrete and wise proposals for action."

A couple of weeks later both presidents privately promised to join forces. Truman all but offered a secret club handshake: "As soon as I can dig out from the letters of congratulations and things of that sort," Truman wrote, "I'd like very much to have a conversation with you on the whole subject. I believe we can really accomplish some good results, as you and I are fully acquainted with what is necessary to make the Government run more efficiently."

Hoover, however, remained suspicious of Truman's delegates on the commission. "They went along until November election and then began giving trouble," Rickard recorded in his diary after visiting with Hoover, "as undoubtedly any real, vicious New Dealer does not want the misrule of the last 15 years exposed." Hoover came to suspect that the New Dealers were now working against Truman's own interests in muscular reorganization. He continued to pour everything into the commission's work, even as he doubted that any good would now come of it with the Democrats back fully in charge.

In the months that followed, the first commission reports were released to the public. Hoover faced a delicate political calculation, which wasn't exactly his strong suit. He had to decide whether to ask for what he wanted, or for what he thought he could get. Should he water down his findings to appease Democrats, or let the chips fall?

Truman and Hoover met on January 7, 1949, to get down into the weeds; how many agencies to eliminate or streamline, how to get cabinet members to support the commission's recommendations. You now had two presidents from different parties conspiring together to supercharge the powers of the office they had both held.

A week later Hoover went before Congress urging them to give Truman the power to restructure the executive without first asking the law-makers' permission, and without exempting certain agencies. The first report was submitted on February 7. The "critical state of world affairs," it stated, required that the president have the ability to act decisively, and be held accountable to the people and to Congress. Hoover offered twenty-seven specific recommendations, including that some sixty-five departments and agencies that reported directly to the president be cut down by two thirds. Congress would still have the right to reject any reorganization within sixty days by a majority vote.

In the past, protecting its patronage powers and influence, Congress had always resisted granting the president such blanket authority. When Roosevelt sought more modest reforms, he was charged with dream-ing of an "Executive dictatorship." But there had never been a study that approached in scale or comprehensiveness what Hoover had pro-duced, nor had the need and timing been so suited to reform. Finally, columnist Arthur Krock wrote, "none has gone to the Capitol with such powerful . . . sponsorship as that jointly assumed by a President fresh from a great election triumph and a former president who is ac-knowledged to be the greatest living authority on the functioning of the American government." In other words, never before had a president and former president joined forces to defend the Oval Office agenda against the parochial interests of the rest of Washington. This was, in fact, the first true test of the club's potential.

On February 7, 1949, the day Hoover submitted his first report, the House approved a reorganization bill. The *Times* called it "one of the most remarkable votes taken in that branch of Congress in years. Here was a measure which challenged inertia, defied tradition and gave the president power to undo . . . some of the favorite handiwork of Con-gress itself. Yet it was approved by the almost unprecedented margin of 356 to 9."

In the weeks that followed, the commission submitted further re-ports on restructuring the State Department, unifying the national se-curity and defense apparatus, bringing logic to agriculture programs, and centralizing purchasing authority to reduce excess inventories and waste. Based on the commission's recommendations, Truman sent one reorganization plan after another to the Hill for approval, and Hoover continued to lobby as the two corresponded throughout the summer.

Testifying before the Senate in July, Hoover brushed back challenges to the president's plans: "Senator, don't try to create any difference between the President and myself," Hoover chided Louisiana's Democratic senator Russell Long, "because the President has been most cooperative in this whole work."

Rebirth of a President

Given the scope of the recommendations, it would take years before they were fully enacted; but eventually fully 70 percent of the Hoover Commission's proposals went into effect, providing the president with enhanced powers, reduced legislative interference, and a streamlined chain of command—as well as savings conservatively estimated in the billions. As late as 1961, notes historian Richard Norton Smith, Kennedy's Defense chief, Robert McNamara, thanked Hoover for helping save billions in the Pentagon budget.

And so it went: an unlikely partnership had produced a new kind of presidency. It was an arrangement that favored them both; by 1951, Truman and Hoover ranked three and five on Gallup's list of Most Admired Men. Together, the two presidents had pushed through the greatest transformation of the presidency in history. A commission created to kill the New Deal instead helped save it, by making the structures it created more effective. In fact, on his last night in office in 1953, Truman was said to have observed proudly that he had reinvented the White House office in such a manner that no future president could make a mistake.

Truman left office convinced that former presidents still had much to give after their terms had ended. "A man who has the experience of a President, or a Vice President, or a Speaker of the House, gets a chance to become much more familiar with our government than anyone else," he wrote years later. "These are the men to whom we must look for help and counsel. That is why we must not shelve or thrust into obscurity men with such unique experience. And least of all, our former Presidents."

Of course when Truman wrote this, he too was a former president, who had by then watched a former friend and ally take over the office and show little inclination to heed his advice. Upon Dwight Eisenhower's election in 1952, the club finally had two retired members, and this time they were actually friends. It was a friendship that deepened over the next decade, enlivened in part by their surprising mutual antagonism toward the general who had taken over the job. Truman, observed his budget director, Frank Pace, "really gave Mr. Hoover all of the honors and attentions due a former President . . . I know that Mr. Hoover was most appreciative of it. Although they were quite different kinds of men, I know how deeply Mr. Truman's treatment affected him."

From Partners to Friends

Out of office, their political battles behind them, Hoover and Truman continued to correspond; they visited together in New York, Independence, and Key Largo, and consulted on official club business as needed. Since they were frequently enlisted to lend their names and prestige to various causes, Hoover proposed protocols, lest they get drawn into unworthy enterprises: "I think we need an agreement," he wrote to Truman, "that we will not allow promoters of causes to trap us into joint actions for their schemes without our having prior consultations."

Truman invited Herbert Hoover to his presidential library dedication in July of 1957. Shaping one's legacy is the mission they all share—even when they find themselves doing it at one another's expense. Among the modern presidents, the workshop where legacies are polished and framed is their libraries, and so the first presidents to build them took an enormous interest in one another's efforts.

Hoover, rearranging his travel plans, promised to be on hand "except for acts of God or evil persons," since "one of the important jobs of our exclusive trade union is preserving libraries."

"Yours was one of the nicest letters I have received," Truman wrote back, "and, as we say in Missouri, I am all swelled up about it."

"I feel that I am one of his closest friends," Truman said when it was his turn to help dedicate Hoover's library in 1962, "and he is one of my closest friends." The two men exchanged the books they were writing; upon receiving a copy of Truman's latest, Hoover wrote back the most heartfelt and intimate of all the letters they exchanged. The book, he said, "goes into the file of most treasured documents." And he proceeded to unspool a tribute to his Democratic friend that belied both his political instincts and his deep Quaker reserve:

> *This is an occasion when I should like to add something more, because yours has been a friendship which has reached deeper into my life than you know.*
>
> *I gave up a successful profession in 1914 to enter public service. I served through the First World War and after for a total of about 18 years.*
>
> *When the attack on Pearl Harbor came, I at once supported the President and offered to serve in any useful capacity. Because of my varied experiences during the First World War, I thought my services might again be useful, however there was no response. My activities in the Second World War were limited to frequent requests from Congressional committees.*
>
> *When you came to the White House within a month you opened the door to me to the only profession I knew, public service, and you undid some disgraceful action that had been taken in the prior years.*
>
> *For all of this and your friendship, I am deeply grateful.*

If Hoover and Truman could forge such a bond, there was no telling what two presidents who actually had something in common might do together.

EISENHOWER AND TRUMAN:

Careful Courtship, Bitter Breakup

Some presidents—a Lincoln, an FDR—achieve Olympian status in office, though neither of those lived to leverage it later. But alone among twentieth-century figures—or really any figure other than Washington—Dwight Eisenhower was bigger than the office before he even held it. In his role as Supreme Allied Commander during the war, he had faced burdens and pressures comparable to those of a head of state—heavier, in fact, than many presidents ever face. And so when it came to solace or guidance from his presidential predecessors, his needs were minimal. As for polishing his legacy, he was the rare president who both entered and left office more popular than any man alive.

That made him a particularly powerful member of the club he never really set out to join.

Eisenhower and Truman met in 1945 at the hinge of history, just weeks after Truman had taken office and Eisenhower had defeated the Nazis. Together they built the scaffolding of the American Century, reviving Europe, reforming the armed forces, establishing NATO, and building a national security structure to meet the challenge of the Cold War. Eisenhower called their friendship "priceless"—until it all fell apart in the hot campaign of 1952, the moment the general hung up his uniform, turned into a politician, and came quickly to find that among his fiercest enemies was his old friend Harry Truman. The fight was never really about policy, or even politics; the hostility was deeply and devoutly personal, the conviction on Truman's part that Eisenhower, though a great soldier, was a moral coward for failing to confront the worst elements in his party. Ike would grow just as contemptuous of Truman—a contempt, however, mixed with some measure of guilt that on at least one scarring occasion, Truman was right.

By inauguration day 1953, they were barely speaking. For a decade they alternated between ignoring and insulting each other. It would have to wait until they were both out of office and found themselves suddenly riding side by side—in the funeral procession for the man who replaced them—for the club to make peace.

3

"The News Hounds Are Trying to Drive a Wedge Between Us"

—HARRY TRUMAN

U seful as a former president like Hoover could be to a rookie chief executive, a future president's star power proved just as valuable.

In 1945, one month after Truman turned to Hoover for help, he made the acquaintance of the hero of Western civilization, General Dwight David Eisenhower, who was every bit as revered as Hoover had been reviled. In those two men, Truman found the allies who would help him shape the postwar world.

Like millions of his countrymen, when Eisenhower heard the news of Harry Truman's sudden vault into the presidency upon Roosevelt's death in April 1945, he admitted that he "went to bed depressed and sad."

It was nothing personal—he had never met the vice president, and Eisenhower had not been one of Roosevelt's pets. But to him and the other generals, "this seemed to us . . . to be a most critical time to be forced to change national leaders." He knew better than most people the weight that was about to fall on Truman's shoulders, the new threats rising even as a great enemy was finally routed. Just a few weeks later Eisenhower was accepting the German surrender in a small red-brick schoolhouse in northeastern France, the signal, Winston Churchill said, "for the greatest outburst of joy in the history of mankind." And on June 18, 1945, Truman gave thousands of government employees the afternoon off so they could burst out themselves, and greet the supreme commander of what was being called the greatest victory in the history of warfare.

A million people jammed the hot, flag-wrapped streets of Washington, hung from windows, perched in trees to watch the parade and celebrate at last. Eisenhower arrived in a four-engine Skymaster at Washington's National Airport, where Mamie waited for the husband she had seen only once in the last three years. He ran down the steps, caught her in his arms, and kissed her. Twenty bands played; dozens of fighter planes and bombers flew overhead in escort as the parade made its way through the capital. A "rush and storm of joy" swept the city, the *New York Times* marveled. "Stand up, so they can see you!" urged General George Marshall. So he stood in his jeep as it moved down Pennsylvania Avenue, his arms raised, delighted, embarrassed, his grin almost wider than his face.

"Isn't he handsome?" said the voice in the crowd.

"He waved at me."

"He's marvelous."

Ike arrived at the Capitol to address a joint session of Congress, the cabinet, ambassadors, and the justices of the Supreme Court, as though he were delivering his first State of the Union, only to an audience far more worshipful than any president of either party had ever faced. Yet every wave and bow, he insisted again and again, he made only as a representative of the three million soldiers he commanded. "They who earned your commendation should properly be here to receive it," he said, but, "I am nevertheless proud and honored to be your agent in conveying it to them." And the chamber erupted in a great rolling cheer.

"The U.S. liked what it saw," *Time* swooned, "a kindly, common-sense man; a warrior who remembered that he was a citizen; a son of the Middle-West, unhardened by war, unspoiled by fame."

That afternoon the towering hero of the age would meet for the first time the "little haberdasher." That was not an easy day for the rookie president. "I have to decide Japanese strategy," Truman wrote in his diary the night before. "That is my hardest decision to date." He met with his War Cabinet to discuss the costs of mounting an invasion of the Japanese home islands—and the chance that more than a quarter million U.S. soldiers and many more Japanese civilians would die. Unless fate intervened. "We are approaching an experiment with the atom explosion," Truman recorded. "I was informed that event would take place within a possible 30 days."

At least the other war was over, and Truman, almost a bystander on a day of adulation, got to thank Eisenhower personally. In a ceremony on the White House lawn, Truman added a second oak leaf cluster to the general's Distinguished Service Medal, praising "his modesty, his impartiality and sound judgment . . . and his great abilities as a soldier and a diplomat." But his private message was more revealing. Truman, whose bad eyesight had prevented his attending West Point, who had had to memorize the eye chart in order to enlist in the Missouri National Guard, who at age thirty-three left his farm and family to command a field artillery battery in France during World War I and saw some of the most intense fighting of the war, pulled the great general aside: I'd rather have the medal, he whispered to Eisenhower, than the presidency.

Truman invited Eisenhower to a stag dinner at the White House that night, "as simple and homey as a community supper in Missouri," said Eisenhower's aide Harry Butcher. At Ike's table were Secretary of War Stimson, House Speaker Sam Rayburn, Chief Justice Harlan Stone, Marshall, and Truman himself. "It had been General Ike's first opportunity to visit with the new president, although he had seen him briefly that afternoon," Butcher said. "What he saw and heard, he liked."

Truman felt the same way. "He is a nice fellow and a good man," Truman wrote home to Bess, calling the dinner "a grand success."

"He's doing a whale of a job," he went on, and already the political implications were apparent. "They are running him for president, which is ok with me. I'd turn it over to him now if I could."

And so for the first of many times, Truman imagined stepping aside for a man who people were already calling "Our Next President." Eisenhower didn't think this even merited a response. "There's no use denying that I'll fly to the moon because I couldn't if I wanted to," he said. "The same goes for politics."

Had that resolve remained untested, the story of Truman and Eisenhower's jagged relationship might have a very different ending.

Brothers in Arms

Where Hoover and Truman could hardly have been more different, Truman and Eisenhower had much in common. Raised 150 miles apart in solid families, both nearly died from illness as children, and both watched their fathers lose everything in a business calamity. Truman and Eisenhower's brother Arthur had even been roommates in a boardinghouse in Kansas City in 1905. Both married women of higher social standing, and launched themselves in careers (or in Truman's case, multiple careers) with no particular flavor of destiny about them. They were avid readers of history, though Truman's preferred relaxation would be at the piano, Eisenhower's at an easel. Both were late bloomers, who owed their ultimate glory to Franklin Roosevelt but were never in his inner circle and bridled at his deviousness. Both were patriots, ever and instinctively putting their country before their comfort and convenience; and both were ardent internationalists whose roots in, and love for, the American heartland did not prevent them from embracing a new role for the young superpower in a suddenly more dangerous nuclear age.

When they met, however, both were public men, and the stature gap between them was vast. While Truman's popularity was high in 1945, he was never revered the way Ike was, and quickly came to be derided by critics as mediocre, insignificant. He was one of history's "wild accidents," wrote liberal columnist Max Lerner, "whose basic weakness lies in his failure to understand imaginatively the nature and greatness of the office he holds." He was surrounded by "moochers" and "big bellied, good-natured guys who knew a lot of dirty jokes," charged the ecumenically lethal columnist I. F. Stone. Far from feeling like the seat of a great democracy, Truman's White House, columnist Joseph Alsop observed, was like "the lounge of the Lions Club of Independence, Missouri," rank with the odor of "ten cent cigars."

Eisenhower, on the other hand, had by this time earned the adulation not just of privates and sergeants but kings and queens and heads of state, all of whom jostled to shower honors on him: the French Legion of Honour, Grand Croix, the British Order of Merit (never before bestowed on a foreigner), the Greek Royal Order of the Savior, the Danish

Order of the Elephant, even the Soviets' diamond- and ruby-studded Order of Victory.

As Eisenhower would later tell the story, Truman first offered to serve as his political patron that same summer of 1945, when they met again during Truman's trip to Potsdam. They were driving with General Omar Bradley, discussing what the war's leaders would do with themselves in peacetime. Ike affirmed that he had no ambition beyond retiring to a quiet home—at which point Truman declared, "General, there is nothing that you may want that I won't try to help you get. That definitely and specifically includes the presidency in 1948."

"I doubt that any soldier of our country was ever so suddenly struck in his emotional vitals by a President with such an apparently sincere and certainly astounding proposition as this," Eisenhower recalled. So he laughed it off.

"Mr. President, I don't know who will be your opponent for the presidency," he said, "but it will not be I." If Truman, a faithful Democrat, was listening closely, that mention of "your opponent" should have clarified at the very least which party Ike identified with—an allegiance he would not profess publicly for another seven years.

The men parted in Germany with a renewed sense of mutual admiration, though Eisenhower's respect was as much for the office as the man who held it, and he was not above a certain amount of ingratiation. Eisenhower called Truman "sincere, earnest, and a most pleasant person with whom to deal." Once back in Washington, Truman was surprised to find a gift awaiting him: the immense globe he had admired at Eisenhower's headquarters, with the engraving: "Presented to President Harry S Truman by General of the Army Dwight D. Eisenhower, who personally used this globe throughout the campaign of 1942–1945."

Years later, when things had turned bad and the notion of Eisenhower in the Oval Office was anathema to Truman, he'd repeatedly deny making any offer of political support. "I told him how grateful the American people were for the job he'd done, and we talked about the fact that a lot of wartime heroes get into politics," Truman reported. "And he said that under no circumstances was he going to get into politics at any time. And that's all there was to it." But Bradley confirmed Ike's account, as did Truman himself to reporters covering him at the time.

And it would not be the last time Truman would try to tempt the charismatic general into a new line of work—provided, of course, that Eisenhower would reveal himself to be a good Democrat under all that brass. Partly this reflected Truman's modesty; he developed a deeper respect for the general as they tackled together some of the toughest challenges of the postwar era: the reconstruction of Europe, the resettlement of the Jews, the trial of war criminals, the ambitions of the Soviets. When George Marshall stepped down as army chief of staff in 1946, Truman tapped Eisenhower to take his place: "I told him I'd much rather retire," Eisenhower recalled, "but he said he had special need of me at the moment."

Retooling a war machine for peacetime was no small assignment, at a time when wives were sending baby shoes tagged "bring daddy back" to congressional offices and riots were erupting overseas among soldiers demanding a boat home. Eisenhower appreciated Truman's commitment to returning veterans, his push for housing, health care, for the GI Bill; at one point veterans services consumed 20 percent of the federal budget. The reorganization of the armed forces was a priority for both men: while the Army favored unification, the Navy and allies in Congress were largely opposed. Truman stood little chance of getting a new structure past various congressional fiefdoms without Eisenhower as his offensive lineman. But it was a mission that required compromises and retreats and frustrations, a far less gratifying one than leading a wartime crusade. One day late in 1946, Eisenhower sent Truman a bottle of scotch: "I think I'll inhale it rather than pass it out to these 'thugs' who hang around here and drink my whiskey," Truman wrote in thanks. "Maybe you and I could think up an occasion when we could share it."

The two worked well together, though their dealings were largely formal. The following year, when the trustees of Columbia University offered Eisenhower their presidency, he accepted it with Truman's blessing. "What a job he can do there," Truman wrote in his diary in July of 1947, after a long talk with the general. Among other things, Truman recalled, the two had discussed the political ambitions of another general: Truman's brilliant, cantankerous Supreme Commander in Asia, Douglas MacArthur. They mused that MacArthur planned to make a triumphal return to the United States just in time for the 1948 Republican convention.

"I told Ike that if he did that that he [Ike] should announce for the nomination for President on the Democratic ticket and that I'd be glad to be in second place, or Vice President," Truman wrote. "Ike & I could be elected and my family & myself would be happy outside this great white jail, known as the White House."

The conversation ended with an understanding: Ike won't quote me, Truman vowed, "and I won't quote him." Eisenhower, in his own diary, called the talk "astounding. . . . I wonder whether five years from now HT will (or will want to) remember his amazing suggestion!!"

You have to wonder if Truman foresaw the potential of political ambitions to pull the friends apart. On January 1, 1948, Eisenhower called Truman to wish him happy new year. He noted in his diary how Truman had said to him, "Ike, no matter what you do or whatever your plans, let us both resolve that nothing shall ever mar our personal friendship."

The Roosevelt Rebellion

Truman was one of the very few people who took the general at his word when he said he wasn't interested. "All journalists know that political life can be rugged," Eisenhower observed, "yet each assumes, automatically, that every man who has the chance wants to get into political life and that anyone who denies such ambition is a liar." But it wasn't just the journalists. A majority of people, according to one 1947 poll, didn't even know which party he belonged to—and didn't seem to care. Beginning that fall and into the election year of 1948, polls showed that while Truman would narrowly defeat the likely Republican nominee, whether New York governor Thomas Dewey or Ohio senator Robert Taft, Eisenhower would crush them all. "Draft Eisenhower" groups vowed to enter his name in the New Hampshire and Pennsylvania primaries whether he liked it or not.

"The tossing about of my name in the political whirlwind is becoming embarrassing," he wrote in his diary in January of 1948. But acting coy was just assumed to be part of the game, and reporters insisted the general was enjoying the circus. Laying a wreath on Ben Franklin's grave, he was stopped by a man wearing a "Draft Eisenhower" button in his lapel. "Take that thing off and throw it away," Eisenhower said. But, one reporter remarked, "he wore his widest grin as he said it." A week later he had officially and emphatically bowed out of the race he had never actually entered, in a letter to a New Hampshire publisher who had been stirring the draft movement. Among his reasons: a reluctance to campaign against his commander in chief, who, he knew, would put up a tough fight; a general distaste for partisan politics; and a conviction that "generals in politics were bad for the nation and bad for the Army." He affirmed that politics was a noble profession, then added, in what he'd later call "a model case of a cracked crystal ball: 'My decision to remove myself completely from the political scene is definite and positive.'"

That same day, he resigned as Army chief, and prepared to take up his life as a college president. In a warm letter to Truman, Eisenhower observed that "your encouragement, understanding and above all, your friendship, have always been priceless to me."

This might have been the end of Eisenhower's political career. The Republicans were so convinced they were finally going to win the White House back from the increasingly unpopular Truman that party leaders didn't actually want to deal with an immensely popular war hero whose views they didn't know and whose actions they couldn't control. They were quite happy with Dewey as their standard-bearer. It was the Democrats who sparked the first political battle between Truman and Eisenhower—as it happened, against the wishes of both men.

As the Democrats approached their 1948 party convention, many were concluding that, in the words of one New York delegate, "Our dear President Truman, of whom we are all so fond, cannot possibly be re-elected." Party bosses and big-city mayors and sitting senators called on him to retire. True-believing liberals were breathing fire: "You have the choice of retiring voluntarily and with dignity," Roosevelt's faithful advisor Harold Ickes wrote to Truman, "or of being driven out of office by a disillusioned and indignant citizenry." Editorial writers were less delicate. He is "an incompetent," declared the conservative *Chicago Tribune*, "the most complete fumbler and blunderer this nation has seen in high office in a long time," said the *Los Angeles Times*.

And now the surviving Roosevelts arose in mutinous assault. "No President in memory, not even Herbert Hoover in his darkest days," wrote historian David McCullough, "had been treated with such open contempt by his own party." Ten days before the convention opened,

Roosevelt's sons Franklin and James and wife, Eleanor, spurred the newly formed Americans for Democratic Action to launch a Dump Truman movement, and recruit—of all people—Eisenhower to lead their crusade.

Thus did the family of a former president turn their fire on his handpicked successor. They sent telegrams to every Democratic delegate, dangling Ike's name as the alternative to Truman and hoping to win enough delegates to block him on the first ballot. Never mind that Eisenhower had no interest in being a stalking horse—or a Democrat. "Here was President Truman who had met every liberal test that existed in that period," recalled presidential advisor Clark Clifford, "and here was supposedly the professional liberal organization who demonstrated their true colors. They weren't interested in a liberal candidate; they were interested in the candidate who they thought could win."

So once again, Eisenhower was forced to step up and flatly declare that "I will not at this time identify myself with any political party and could not accept nomination for any public office or participate in partisan political contests." As for Truman, he had come to like the job, and he loved a good fight, with Southern Democrats who didn't like his stand on civil rights, with New Dealers who felt he'd abandoned them, with the city bosses who worried he'd lose so badly they'd be tossed out as well.

"When the President in the White House decides he wants to be renominated," Truman said later, "nobody can keep him from it."

Once Truman went on to win the upset victory of a lifetime, Eisenhower, though he had not voted for him, sent warm congratulations. In all our political history, he wrote, no one ever managed a greater accomplishment "that can be traced so clearly to the stark courage and fighting heart of a single man." Eisenhower reaffirmed his loyalty and offered his services at any time.

He had reason to be especially grateful: thanks to Truman's personal intervention, the IRS judged Eisenhower to be a nonprofessional writer and so taxed his income from his war memoir *Crusade in Europe* at the 25 percent capital gains rate rather than the 75 percent income tax rate, which among other things meant that Mamie Eisenhower got her first mink coat. Eisenhower sent Truman a signed copy, the first volume he gave anyone outside the family.

War Again

It didn't take long for Eisenhower to get restless at Columbia. "You can call on me at any time for anything," he wrote to Defense Secretary James Forrestal after six months, and he was ready in February 1949 when Truman asked him to serve as a military advisor. Truman recruited Ike for a new kind of war: a bureaucratic one. He needed someone with Eisenhower's stature—and skill at mediating between interests and egos—to soothe the vengeful admirals, corral the generals, persuade the various services and their congressional allies to bring the U.S. defense establishment under a more unified command structure when they were still fighting over the color of their uniforms. After a long session with Truman, "the one disturbing thing," Ike reflected, "is the president and Mr. F. [Forrestal] apparently assume that I have some miraculous power to make some of these warring elements lie down in peace together."

Truman needed his cantankerous generals to settle down because he would soon need them for some real fighting. On September 23, 1949, the White House revealed that it had evidence that the Soviets had exploded their own atom bomb. A week later, China fell to Mao Zedong's communist revolutionaries. In the months that followed Albert Einstein warned that "general annihilation beckons," Los Alamos scientist Klaus Fuchs confessed to espionage, and an obscure, dissolute Wisconsin senator named Joe McCarthy declared that he had a list of two hundred communists at the State Department.

And then, the real test: on June 25, 1950, the North Korean army crashed across the 38th parallel into South Korea, turning the Cold War hot and wrecking Truman's hopes for a lasting peace. "My father made it clear from the moment he heard the news," recalled Truman's daughter, Margaret, "that he feared this was the opening of WWIII."

An aggressive response to this communist-backed challenge could ignite a wider war in Asia; but a failure to act would signal America's lack of will to fight. As North Korea's Soviet-made tanks swept into Seoul, many feared this aggression was being directed by the Kremlin to draw America's strength and attention away from Western Europe and leave it vulnerable to Soviet conquest. A mere twelve Western divisions were up against 175 Soviet divisions stationed in Eastern Europe. One Western staff officer, asked what the Russians would need to conquer the West, replied: "shoes."

Eisenhower stood right by Truman's side; he immediately supported Truman's decision to rally the United Nations to South Korea's defense and commit American soldiers to war, denouncing the "outrageous invasion" and calling Truman's response "inescapable." The next day he and Marshall had lunch with Truman at the White House, both saying strength and speed were essential. "We encountered good intentions," Eisenhower recorded, "but I'm not so sure we met full comprehension."

The months that followed would be among the most punishing of Truman's presidency. By the beginning of October, thanks to MacArthur's daring raid at Inchon, American and South Korean forces had retaken the country back to the 38th parallel; but the decision to try to destroy the North Korean army and reunify the country by force brought 260,000 Chinese troops pouring into the fight. Truman flew fifteen thousand miles to meet with MacArthur at Wake Island; the general would only give him a two-hour briefing, and was too busy to have lunch. Eisenhower's private doubts about Truman's military capacity grew. Poor Harry, he concluded, is "a fine man who, in the middle of a stormy lake, knows nothing of swimming. Yet a lot of drowning people are forced to look to him as a lifeguard. If his wisdom could only equal his good intent."

Now all of MacArthur's promises of having the boys "home by Christmas" were gone. The general wanted a naval blockade of China, permission to bomb Manchuria and mainland cities, an all-out counterattack, including the use of nuclear weapons. Joe McCarthy called on Secretary of State Dean Acheson and Marshall to resign, and for Truman to be impeached. Truman meanwhile shared the fear of his Joint Chiefs of Staff chairman, General Omar Bradley, who warned Congress that expanding the Korean War would involve America in "the wrong war, at the wrong place, at the wrong time, and with the wrong enemy."

Supreme Allied Commander, Redux

The day after the Chinese entered the war, Truman tracked down Eisenhower, who was on a train in Ohio, and asked him to come see him. The president now needed more than Eisenhower's friendship and advice; he needed him back in uniform, eventually overseas to lead the West once more but first at home to persuade a reluctant Congress and public to embrace the kind of entangling alliances that America had so long resisted.

The Western powers had signed the North Atlantic Treaty Organization pact more than a year earlier, to provide for the common defense against the Soviet threat: but it was more an idea than an army, until Korea brought home the need to take collective security seriously and put in place a real force under a unified command. The member countries were now committed to mutual defense—and Eisenhower, Truman said, was the unanimous choice to serve as NATO's Supreme Allied Commander. Eisenhower was more than ready to be back at the center of history: "I consider this to be the most important military job in the world," he told his son John. When a friend suggested that maybe Truman was taking advantage of him, Ike retorted that "I rather look on this effort as about the last remaining chance for the survival of Western civilization."

Truman knew Eisenhower was the only person who stood even a chance of getting twelve countries to work together; to persuade them to reinvest in their military strength rather than count on hiding beneath America's nuclear umbrella; and to solve the hard practical and political question of rearming Germany. Truman also knew he would need every watt of Eisenhower's star power to sell the idea that this level of commitment abroad was essential to national security.

"You know, that little guy is truly amazing," Acheson told a State Department colleague after discussing the appointment with Truman. "I think he was conscious of the fact, that maybe by making this decision, he was creating a future President of the United States, who might be a Republican." But, Acheson said, "He didn't bat an eye. He said, 'If that's what we need, that's what we need.'"

Only from this distance can we savor the moment when a sitting president deployed a future one to battle a former one. For into the fray stormed Hoover, seventy-six, who had emerged from his long exile to take his place as the elder statesman of the Republican Party. Just because Hoover and Truman were partners in reinventing government did not mean they agreed on everything—especially America's foreign policy posture. They had worked successfully on humanitarian relief in Europe. But Hoover always worried that Europe wanted a free ride back to recovery under America's protective wing. In a national radio address on December 20, 1950, Hoover offered the conservative counterargument to Truman's expansive policy. Rather than sending troops and treasure overseas, he argued, America should rely on its air and naval power to create "a Gibraltar of Western Civilization" at home. Not a dime or a soldier should be sent to Europe until its nations had shown a willingness to defend themselves.

And so the gauntlet was thrown down, with Truman and Eisenhower and the internationalists on one side, against Hoover, Taft, and the isolationists on the other.

Eisenhower had always respected Hoover, and the two spent some time over the summer at the elite enclave of Bohemian Grove—where, among other things, Hoover introduced Eisenhower to a rising star named Richard Nixon. But Eisenhower was appalled by Hoover's vision. Though he was a man "I've admired extravagantly . . . I am forced to believe he's getting senile." But he too was concerned about America making a commitment to defend countries that hadn't the stomach to fight for themselves. He told Truman the first task was to assess Europe's appetite: at the beginning of January 1951 he clasped hands with Truman, Acheson, and Marshall at National Airport, kissed Mamie goodbye, and set off at Truman's behest on a thirteen-thousand-mile trip to visit twelve capitals in eighteen days. "He would have to persuade a warweary, unconfident Western Europe that it must make sacrifices and get ready to fight again," declared *Time*. "He would have to do it while his own country's councils were divided about his task."

The "Yanks Go Home" posters that greeted him were not auspicious, and the trip was a hard one. He landed in Oslo in a blinding snowstorm, and had a smallpox scare in London that required a vaccination that left his arm sore and swollen for days. As the general moved across the continent, Truman was under siege at home. He once more found himself derided as the Missouri machine pol without so much as a college degree, overwhelmed by forces well beyond his skills. Korea was a catastrophe: the Chinese had pushed MacArthur's forces back, and the commander was still pressing for an all-out assault. Meanwhile congressional Republicans charged that Truman did not have the constitutional power to send troops to Europe in peacetime.

In his State of the Union address, Truman clung to Eisenhower like a life preserver. Calling him "one of our greatest military commanders," Truman insisted his mission was "vital to our security. We should all stand behind him, and give him every bit of help we can."

When Eisenhower returned, he holed up for four days in a cliffside room at the Thayer Hotel at West Point, getting his thoughts on paper. "Few speeches have ever given me so much trouble," he later admitted, since he needed to capture both Europe's total weakness and vulnerability, and its spiritual readiness to rebuild. He knew the weight his assessment would carry.

And he also knew that one private meeting he planned as he returned to Washington could be most important of all.

He flew into Washington in an ice storm, to be greeted by a shivering committee of generals, cabinet officials, ambassadors, and President Truman, who wrung his hand and led him to his limousine, shooing off photographers with the warning that "We can't give this fellow pneumonia." They had lunch privately at the White House, so Truman could hear the message Eisenhower would deliver to the 82nd Congress and then in a national television appearance. It came down to this: the United States couldn't afford to let the rest of the world fall to the communists. The defense of the West was both necessary and feasible if only the United States found its will.

"Each of us must do his part," Eisenhower declared in his national address. "We cannot delay while we suspiciously scrutinize the sacrifices made by our neighbors, and through a weaseling logic seek some way to avoid our own duties." He was urgent, unwavering, unfailingly optimistic that while the challenge was great, America's ability to meet it was greater still. "If we Americans seize the lead," he promised, "we will preserve and be worthy of our own past."

With that performance, *Life* magazine declared that he had "once again shown himself to be a foremost symbol of all that is right and good and strong in American policy and purpose." And in the process, said *Time*, "he had done for the President what Harry Truman could not do for himself. Ike appeared to have routed the calamity-howlers and the super-cautious—the Hoovers, the Kennedys . . . the Tafts. By the end of the week, congressional opposition to the Administration's main military plans had all but collapsed. Congress and the people were behind the second Eisenhower crusade."

But when one looks back at the Great Debate, as it came to be known, one fateful encounter stands out—one that very few people knew about at the time. Even as he took on his NATO assignment, the political pressures on Eisenhower were just as strong as ever; he would have happily shut the speculation down once and for all had he not feared that the hard-line isolationist wing of the Republican Party would prevail in his absence.

So with an eye toward killing two birds at once, he arranged a secret meeting with Ohio senator Robert Taft, himself the son of a president and a leading contender for the 1952 Republican nomination. All Eisenhower wanted from Taft was an assurance that he would help make the collective security of Europe the center of a bipartisan U.S. policy. If Taft agreed, Ike would devote himself to carrying it out, and take himself out of the running for 1952 once and for all. He wrote out a statement in pencil, folded it up, and tucked it in his pocket: "Having been called back to military duty, I want to announce that my name may not be used by anyone as a candidate for President—and if they do I will repudiate such efforts."

Then he drove over to the Pentagon for the private meeting with Taft. The general and the senator talked for a long time. "I think he may have been suspicious of my motives," Eisenhower concluded, which would have been natural, since the groundswell beneath an Eisenhower candidacy was clearly visible to even the most cross-eyed political landscaper.

"I used all the persuasion I could, but Senator Taft refused to commit himself," Eisenhower recalled. Eisenhower didn't even try to extract a promise for a certain number of troops; just general support for collective security as Europe's best defense, and America's vital role in that alliance. But even that was too much for Taft, who feared it would just provoke the Soviets further and drag the United States back into Europe's ancient battles. After Taft left, the general called his aides back into the room and tore up his statement in front of them.

"I finally concluded that it might be more effective to keep some aura of mystery around my future plans."

The Shadow Campaign

About six months later, on a hot August day in the summer of 1951, when the news was slow, *New York Times* reporter William Laurence decided to ask Truman about that offer he'd made to Eisenhower back in 1948. He'd said he would support Eisenhower if he ever ran for president. Does that promise apply to 1952—when, it should be noted, Truman was still eligible to run again as well?

"It certainly does," Truman said. "I am just as fond of General Eisenhower as I can be. I think he is one of the great men produced by World War II, and I think I have shown that, by giving him the most important job that is available for his ability."

"Good Lord," breathed Laurence, as he slid back to his chair and scribbled in his notebook. The headline practically wrote itself: TRUMAN BACKS IKE FOR PRESIDENT. Then an NBC reporter asked the follow-up: "Does that mean that if Ike wants to be President, you will help him get it?"

Well now, Truman replied, that's not what he was saying at all. "I don't think he is a candidate for president on the Democratic ticket," he said, "and I couldn't very well help him to be a candidate on the Republican ticket, because I don't think that would do him any good." This was an understatement. That summer of 1951, amid a continuing stalemate in Korea, charges of influence peddling, and rising attacks from McCarthy and his henchmen, Truman's popularity had hit a record low of 24 percent.

Ambassador Averell Harriman, passing through Paris, visited with Eisenhower at NATO headquarters and suggested that Truman wanted to meet with him in Washington. Eisenhower got the impression that this was to be a secret meeting, which seemed ill-advised to him; it was bound to leak, and Congress was caught up debating a military aid bill, which he did not want to get sucked into.

He cabled George Marshall with a top secret message for the president, suggesting a later date. Truman wrote back, by hand, to reassure him: "I had never expected to have a secret meeting with you," he assured the general. He'd just heard reports that Eisenhower was "not getting the proper support and cooperation from other departments," and wanted to help make his job easier. He also didn't want Eisenhower to be "harassed by these nutty congressional committees. One man is enough for them to pick to pieces—and I'm accustomed to it."

So it would be some months before the two men met again, by which time the speculation about an Eisenhower candidacy was in full flame. "There are many things I want to talk with you about," Truman wrote to Eisenhower in late September 1951. "I am sure you and I understand each other. You are doing a grand job."

When he flew home from Europe the following week to confer with Truman about NATO, Ike said the talks were to be "strictly military." But there was only one topic on everyone's mind. Would Truman offer to step aside if Ike agreed to run, and if so, who would take over NATO, and by the way, does anyone know yet if he's even a Democrat? *Collier's* magazine went so far as to offer him $40,000 just to reveal what party he belonged to. Taft had just officially declared his candidacy and had deep party support. But polls showed Eisenhower leading both Truman and Taft by better than two to one.

On November 5, Truman and Eisenhower had lunch at Blair House, where the Trumans lived while the White House was being renovated. Truman showed Eisenhower pictures of the renovations, as though demonstrating what a nice place it would be to call home. Once again Truman offered his full support; the president could deliver him the Democratic nomination with a bow on it, if Ike would just declare himself a candidate.

Truman's offer, revealed *New York Times* bureau chief Arthur Krock, was the culmination of a long campaign by Democrats to reel the general into their camp. Party emissaries had flown to Paris some weeks earlier to inform him that he had just to say the word and the nomination was his, with Truman's support.

Ike's reply? He had been a Republican all his life, if a nonvoting one. "You can't join a party just to run for office. What reason have you to think I've ever been a Democrat?" He also thought twenty years of Democratic rule was enough; someone had to save the two-party system. Plus his disagreements with Truman's progressive Fair Deal policies were long and deep. "It never occurred to the President that I might be a Republican," the general reflected later. "He believed in Democrats so much that he assumed that anyone who had any sense would become a Democrat."

Both Eisenhower and Truman denied that they had talked politics; when asked about Krock's story, Truman said "no comment." For all the public denials, in private Truman wanted Eisenhower to know there were no hard feelings. He still had made no announcement about whether he'd be running again, though he had privately decided more than a year earlier that he would not. "There is a lure in power," he observed in a note he had written and stuck in a drawer. "It can get into a man's blood just as gambling and lust for money have been known to do."

In mid-December he wrote to the general. "The columnists, the slick magazines and all the political people who like to speculate are saying many things about what is to happen in 1952. As I told you in 1948 and at our luncheon in 1951, do what you think best for the country."

But then he said something extraordinary. For all their domestic policy differences, both men were fully committed to America's role in leading a Western alliance. So long as the next president shared that vision, they would each be quite content to retire to a quiet life. For Truman, "my own position is in the balance. If I do what I want to do I'll go back to Missouri and *maybe* run for the Senate." But if Eisenhower declined to run, he went on, it would be Truman's mission to keep the isolationists out of the White House. If that meant breaking his private vow not to run again, so be it. "I wish you would let me know what you intend to do. It will be between us and no one else.

"I have the utmost confidence in your judgment and your patriotism."

Eisenhower wrote back to Truman. "I'd like to live a semi-retired life with my family," he said. "I do not feel that I have any duty to seek a political nomination." But by now he was discerning a difference between seeking the nomination and responding if called. So five days later, his most ardent backer, Senator Henry Cabot Lodge, forced the issue by entering Eisenhower in the New Hampshire primary, and preemptively revealing that Eisenhower was indeed a Republican. Though annoyed at being cornered, Ike finally affirmed that if the Republicans offered him their nomination, he would accept it.

Now that his affiliation was finally cleared up, reporters were desperate to get Truman to dish about Eisenhower. But he wouldn't play. At a January 10 press conference, he declared once more that he thought Eisenhower was "a grand man. I have the utmost confidence in him, and

I gave him one of the most important jobs that this Government has to offer." As far as his NATO assignment went, the timing was now in Eisenhower's hands—though Truman was not subtle about the choice he hoped he'd make. "If he wants to get out and have all the mud and rotten eggs and rotten tomatoes thrown at him, that is his business, and I won't stand in his way."

And then they came to the crux of the matter, since Truman's intentions were still a mystery. "Mr. President," one reporter asked, "how could you run against a fellow you liked so well?"

"Easily," Truman replied. "I have done it before."

That led Truman to write to Eisenhower once again, in a remarkable exchange of letters between two men dancing around each other and the most powerful office in the world. Truman enclosed a full transcript of the news conference, just so there would be no misunderstanding about what had been said. "As usual," Truman wrote to Ike, "the news hounds are trying to drive a wedge between us. As far as I am concerned, that will never happen."

Eisenhower wrote back from Paris, wondering why people seemed so keen on producing "irritation or mutual resentment between us. I suppose the hope is for an impulsive and possibly critical statement from one of us with respect to the other, thus making news. I deeply appreciate your determination to avoid any such thing—a purpose which does and will govern my own conduct."

To which Truman replied, "You can rest assured that no matter what the professional liars and the pathological columnists may have to say, you and I understand each other."

In March Eisenhower won the New Hampshire primary in a walk, without shaking a single voter's hand; he declared himself "astonished" and "deeply moved." A few weeks later Truman finally announced what he'd known for two years: that he would not be running again in 1952, even though he was constitutionally eligible, having served only part of Roosevelt's term. This meant that Eisenhower would not be in the position of challenging his commander in chief, and freed him to announce that he would step down as Allied commander and return to the United States in June to take up his campaign. "I clearly miscalculated," he wrote to Truman, when he assumed anyone would believe his statements about aspiring to no political office. He needed to step down, he wrote, "so that any political activity centering about me cannot possibly affect the military service."

Truman remained respectful and supportive. Asked at a May news conference whether Eisenhower's health was strong enough for the White House, Truman declared that "he's in perfect health. He's as fine a man as ever walked." In June of 1952 when Eisenhower returned once and for all to launch his campaign, Truman was asked if he still thought Ike was a nice guy.

"Yes, of course I do. I am very fond of General Eisenhower, and he is entitled to his political views. It's all right with me. This is a free country. But I still like him as well as I ever did."

But once he met Ike the politician, all that would change.

4

"The Man Is a Congenital Liar"

—DWIGHT EISENHOWER

When Eisenhower finally returned to the United States in June of 1952 to throw himself into the presidential race, he reported first to his commander in chief. Rather than meeting in the Oval Office, Truman took the general upstairs to the study. Already the incoming fire seemed fierce: Taft's people were spreading stories about Mamie's drinking, about Ike's relationship with his aide, Kay Summersby, about Eisenhower being secretly Jewish. Eisenhower was furious; Truman basically told him to brace himself. "If that's all it is, Ike," he said, "then you can just figure you're lucky." He urged that Eisenhower "go right down to the office of the Republican National Committee and ask them to equip you with an elephant hide about an inch thick. You're going to need it."

Both men reaffirmed that nothing in the coming campaign could damage their friendship. Ike gave Truman one final NATO briefing, and the next day Truman presented the general with his fourth oak leaf cluster in the Rose Garden. When, in his acceptance speech at the Republican convention, Eisenhower declared that his goal was to "sweep from office an administration which has fastened on every one of us the wastefulness, the arrogance and corruption of high places . . . the bitter fruit of a party too long in power," Truman didn't take it personally; he had been in politics a long time, and he knew the rules of the game.

But even he did not expect that Eisenhower would so quickly find a way to annoy him—a way matched only, as it happens, by the Democratic nominee, Illinois governor Adlai Stevenson.

Stevenson and Eisenhower shared a similar problem: creating a hygienic distance between themselves and an unpopular and scandal-plagued administration whose policies—domestic for Stevenson, foreign for Eisenhower—they basically supported. It was one thing for Eisenhower to try to shine as a beacon of courage and conviction, floating high above the fray, a hero leading his next "Great Crusade." He was revered by people who were tired of ugly politics and looking for a nice, commanding figure to help America settle into a prosperous middle age.

But it was quite another to try to wrap that aura around the fretful, fractious, increasingly desperate Republican Party. Eisenhower had never been a party man and was as hostile to what he called the "disciples of hate" in the party as he was to the opposition. He believed the president, like a military commander, should be above politics. He still had not decided how to handle powerful bottom-feeders like McCarthy and Indiana's William Jenner; he'd been warned by his advisors about denouncing them, but was appalled by the idea of embracing them. His party, now twenty years in the wilderness, included many for whom purity mattered more than victory. That would never be Eisenhower's way, and there were plenty of Republicans who were skeptical about his devotion to their principles.

So his first task upon winning the nomination was to unite his party behind him. Eisenhower holed up in an eighth-floor suite at the Brown Palace Hotel in Denver, getting a crash course in obscure corners of domestic policy, brokering peace with the Taft wing of the party, and conceding to one friend the possibility that "some day I shall conclude that I made a mistake in allowing myself to be drawn into the political whirlpool." In his military world his judgments were solid, born of instinct and long experience; in this new political arena he had to weigh the conflicting advice of myriad advisors and well-meaning but inexperienced friends, many of whom were now looking to him to lead them to political war. "The whole atmosphere is so different from that to which soldiers of long service become accustomed," he wrote plaintively to George Marshall, "that I sometimes find it difficult indeed to adjust myself."

The first "adjustment" occurred in mid-August, when news came that Stevenson had been invited to the White House for an intelligence briefing by national security officials. Between Korea and the unfolding tensions in Europe with the Soviets, the need for continuity was greater than ever. Truman, a man who landed in the Oval Office with no preparation whatever, was determined that whoever succeeded him be fully up to speed. It was an unprecedented gesture born of a patriotic instinct, but it also ignited a political firefight.

Stevenson did attend the intelligence briefing, followed by lunch with the entire cabinet and a tour of the restored White House. Then he and the president talked campaign strategy in the Cabinet Room. While Truman was eager to help any way he could, Stevenson was noncommittal. The whole Republican message was that it was "Time for a Change," and vice presidential nominee Richard Nixon was hammering Stevenson as the apostle of "Trumanism." Stevenson couldn't afford to be seen as just a new name on a tired empire. Party officials speculated that he'd ask Truman to limit his campaign appearances to a few big cities.

Eisenhower meanwhile was under growing pressure to sharpen his rhetoric, especially from party regulars who weren't quite convinced he was on the team. Some Taft loyalists publicly suggested that Republicans forget about the presidency and just concentrate on electing a Republican majority to Congress, rather than wasting energy just to turn the White House over to a "crypto Democrat" like Ike. They had no patience with the high-minded rhetoric of his Great Crusade, which *New York Times* reporter James Reston described as appealing "not to the mind but to the heart. . . . His language was filled with the noble words of the old revivalists: frugality, austerity, honesty, economy, simplicity, integrity." One late-August front-page editorial in the *New York World Telegram and Sun* said plaintively: "We still cling to the hope that when he does start campaigning, he will come out swinging." But at the moment, "Ike is running like a dry creek."

The Stevenson briefing offered a perfect opportunity for Eisenhower to put some righteous distance between himself and the White House. Privately he told CIA director Walter Bedell Smith—Ike's chief of staff during the war—that his campaign headquarters was in "a steaming stew" over the Stevenson meeting, though he added that "I am amazed to find out how important these things are considered in the political world." In public, Eisenhower called the meeting an "unusual spectacle" that raised "disturbing questions" about whether Truman was using government resources to influence the campaign. The American people, he said—in what the *New York Times* called "the bluntest statement of campaign issues" since his nomination—wanted a genuine change from the "corruption . . . reckless spending . . . mismanagement in foreign affairs" of the Truman presidency.

The next day Truman sent Eisenhower a cable, offering the exact same invitation; a briefing, a lunch with the cabinet, and a chance to meet with anyone on the White House staff he chose. "I've made arrangements with the Central Intelligence Agency to furnish you once a week with the world situation as I also have for Governor Stevenson."

For the first time in his life, Eisenhower rejected a White House invitation. In a telegram to the White House, which his campaign immediately made public, Eisenhower noted that since there was no "grave emergency" that would compel his attending, it was his duty as the Republican nominee to remain free to criticize the administration's policies and those of its handpicked successor. Any communications between him and Truman "should be only those which are known to all the American people. Consequently I think it would be unwise and result in confusion in the public mind if I were to attend" the briefings.

Of course there was never any suggestion that by attending an intelligence briefing Eisenhower relinquished the right to criticize any policy he wanted to. The telegram was a little piece of theater, written for an audience well beyond the White House, and it had its desired effect: conservatives, noted Ike's campaign manager, Herbert Brownell, "were greatly reassured."

Truman, however, was livid. He did not play games with the country's security. At his press conference, Truman slapped down the charge that he'd only planned to brief Stevenson until Ike protested. He had discussed briefing both candidates the week before, he said, and left it to General Omar Bradley, now chairman of the Joint Chiefs, to communicate with Eisenhower. Bradley said he would have issued the invitation more quickly had he known its timing would become a political issue. "Most of this information is not for general distribution," Truman told reporters, "and it cannot be used publicly because it is top secret."

Truman then sent Eisenhower a private letter, which suggested that the general had allowed himself to be hijacked by political opportunists.

"I am sorry if I caused you embarrassment," he began. His only goal was a stable and consistent foreign policy: "Partisan politics should stop at the boundaries of the United States. I am extremely sorry that you have allowed a bunch of screwballs to come between us.

"You have made a bad mistake, and I'm hoping it won't injure this great Republic. . . .

"May God guide you and give you light.

"From a man who has always been your friend and who always wanted to be!

"Sincerely, HST."

Now Eisenhower was angry too, though his response to Truman was gracious and, as ever, measured. Truman's letter, he told the CIA's Smith, "breathed injured innocence, and warned me solemnly of the great error I was making in allowing 'screwballs' to come between us and twist my thinking."

It might have been some consolation had Eisenhower known that Truman was every bit as fed up with Stevenson, who was now treating Truman like a crazy uncle best hidden from polite company. Stevenson named his own party chairman, set up headquarters in Springfield, and, in answer to a reporter's question, insisted that he'd be able to "clean up the mess in Washington," which was taken as Stevenson's confirmation that Washington was, indeed, a mess.

Publicly, Truman said he couldn't comment because he knew of no such mess. Privately, he vented in more unsent letters: "I have come to the conclusion that you are embarrassed by having the president of the United States in your corner in this campaign," he wrote to Stevenson. "I'm telling you to take your crackpots, your high socialites with their noses in the air, run your campaign and win if you can."

Enter McCarthy, Stage Right

It took various misunderstandings to raise tensions in both the Truman and Eisenhower camps; but it fell to the Great Divider, Joe McCarthy, to set the two men at war. It was all the more ironic that their feud should have revolved around McCarthy, a hatemonger they both reviled, and George Marshall, a statesman both men revered.

Eisenhower owed his mentor everything; Marshall had recommended him to lead the Allied war effort while Marshall stayed back in Washington. Churchill referred to Marshall as "the true architect of victory"; Truman called him "the greatest living American." It was Eisenhower whom Truman dispatched to Shanghai in May of 1946 to ask Marshall to serve as secretary of state.

But to Joe McCarthy, delivering one of the more vile speeches ever made on the Senate floor, in June of 1951, Marshall was a traitor who had weakened the country by failing to prevent China from falling to the communists. McCarthy accused him of "a conspiracy so immense, an infamy so black as to dwarf any previous such venture in the history of man." How else to explain continued communist successes, if they did not have accomplices in the highest branches of the American government?

Of course, Eisenhower had been a military advisor while Marshall was busy "losing" China; he had not raced the Russians to Berlin in 1945; he had been a strong supporter of the Truman Doctrine, the Marshall Plan, NATO. He was, in other words, a star player in the foreign policies that the isolationists in his party deplored, and that would require some explaining.

During the primaries, McCarthy had supported Taft, so Ike didn't owe him anything; Eisenhower announced in August that he'd never campaign for him. He denounced any "un-American methods" of fighting communism—though without mentioning McCarthy by name. As for Marshall, Eisenhower declared at a Denver news conference that "there was nothing of disloyalty in General Marshall's soul . . . if he was not a perfect example of patriotism," Ike went on, "I never saw one."

But soon Eisenhower's arguments grew more nuanced, finding a distinction between "an endorsement" and "a blanket endorsement." If Republican primary voters chose to nominate people like McCarthy and Jenner, then it would be presumptuous of Eisenhower to reject their judgment. He could support them as Republicans, even as he rejected their tactics. Or so he thought.

Indiana's William Jenner, who had voted against NATO and liked to call Marshall "a living lie" and "a front man for traitors," introduced Eisenhower at a rally in Indianapolis on September 9; the crowd roared as Eisenhower promised to cast out "the incompetent, the unfit, the cronies and the chiselers." He made no mention of Jenner, who took every chance to slap his shoulder and squeeze into the picture, finally grabbing Eisenhower's arm and raising it triumphantly overhead. "Charlie, get me out of here," Ike barked to Indiana congressman Charles Halleck. "I felt dirty from the touch of the man," he told his speechwriter Emmet Hughes. Truman was shocked by the sight. "When Eisenhower threw his arms around Jenner, he lost Truman," said international news service correspondent Robert Nixon. "That was the end of the line."

That same night, McCarthy won the Wisconsin Republican Senate primary by better than two to one. Eisenhower still had no desire to campaign in his state; but party officials argued that Wisconsin's moderate Republican governor, Walter Kohler, faced a tough reelection challenge; control of the Senate was also hanging in the balance. Truman had won Wisconsin in 1948; the Republicans needed to get the state back.

Eisenhower still didn't want to go, and some moderate advisors, especially Thomas Dewey, agreed. In his memoirs, Ike blamed a staff "blunder" for scheduling a trip. But forced into a visit, he thought he could make a point as well: he told speechwriter Hughes that he wanted to include in his big Milwaukee speech a defense of Marshall, right in McCarthy's home state. That would have gone a long way to bolster Marshall and bury McCarthy.

No one knows who tipped off McCarthy; or maybe he just had a good enough read on Eisenhower to worry about what he might say. In any event, on October 2, as Eisenhower's campaign train rolled through Illinois on its way to Wisconsin, McCarthy flew into Peoria unannounced and paid a visit to Eisenhower's hotel.

The two men talked privately for a long time.

Afterward McCarthy told reporters they had had "a very, very pleasant conversation." While he and Eisenhower didn't agree on everything, he said, he left the meeting with "the same feeling as when I went in, and that is that he's a great American who'll make a great president, an outstanding president."

One of Ike's speechwriters, Kevin McCann, who was sitting outside the suite, told a different story. Eisenhower let McCarthy know exactly what he thought of McCarthy's thuggish tactics and his attacks on Marshall. The fight had been so fierce it turned the air blue. "I never heard the General so cold-bloodedly skin a man."

En route from Peoria to Wisconsin, however, Eisenhower's determination to defend Marshall publicly in McCarthy territory got derailed. His campaign manager, Sherman Adams, had a draft of the speech, including the section praising Marshall. Governor Kohler and Republican national chairman Arthur Summerfield warned Ike that defending Marshall would be read as such an intentional attack on McCarthy that it could cost the party the state. As his advisor William Ewald recalled their argument, they told Eisenhower that "You cannot go into Milwaukee, Wisconsin, get up on the stage in the largest public auditorium in this city, have Joe McCarthy sitting there, running for the Senate—you're running for the presidency on the Republican ticket—and punch him in the nose."

Eisenhower's team hashed it out; should he or shouldn't he come to Marshall's defense? Some advisors were adamant that the speech had to be delivered as written. Adams, however, agreed that the Marshall section seemed gratuitous and out of place. At one point Eisenhower returned from a forward car of the train, where he'd gone to talk with Adams further, looking "purple with anger." But in the end he agreed to cut the passage. Eisenhower later told people he agreed to take it out only after he'd been warned that attacking McCarthy in Wisconsin could incite a riot at his rally. In his memoirs, he offers the reasoning that having just recently defended Marshall, doing so again "could be interpreted as a 'chip on the shoulder' attitude. By thus arousing new public clamor, I could be inadvertently embarrassing General Marshall."

As the train pulled in to Green Bay, McCarthy scampered onto the train platform to greet crowds that cheered him louder than they cheered for Eisenhower. He got to introduce the general in his hometown of Appleton, after campaign aides said he wouldn't. All day aides who did not know that the speech had been changed were telling reporters, just wait, just wait, you'll hear what Ike really thinks of McCarthy tonight.

In his big Milwaukee speech, with McCarthy sitting behind him on the stage, Eisenhower did warn against "violent vigilantism," but he hardly sounded hostile: "The purposes that [McCarthy] and I have of ridding the Government of the incompetents, the dishonest and, above all, the subversive and disloyal are one and the same," he declared. "The differences apply to method." Truman's indifference to communist infiltration, he added, had resulted in "a calamity of immeasurable consequences."

Gone from his remarks was this line from the original he had prepared: "I have been privileged for 35 years to know General Marshall personally. I know him, as a man and as a soldier, to be dedicated with singular selflessness and the profoundest patriotism to the service of America. And this episode is a sobering lesson in the way freedom must not defend itself." Then the photographers finally got their picture: "Standing so far from Joe that they looked like two men reaching toward each other across a trout stream," *Time* wrote, "Ike grabbed the Wisconsin Senator's hand, pumped it once and abruptly let it go."

What Eisenhower did not know was that the *New York Times* had a copy of the complete original text. And so the headline from the trip was that McCarthy had bullied Eisenhower into silence; that the hero who stood up to Hitler had been cowed somehow by the domestic fearmongers. The *Times*'s publisher, Arthur Sulzberger, sent Adams a telegram: "Do I need to tell you that I am sick at heart?" Eisenhower flatly denied that he had caved; he had defended Marshall before, his aides argued, so there was no point in doing so again. "It was a mistake," Ewald recalled, "a grievous mistake that I feel certain pained Dwight D. Eisenhower to his last day."

Marshall himself didn't say anything, though his wife later described how the retired statesman would sit in front of the radio night after night, waiting to hear Eisenhower defend his honor.

His failure to do so sent Truman over the edge. "When anybody criticized Marshall to Truman it was like criticizing his own father, and he took that very strongly, personally," explained his aide Matt Connelly. Truman had been restrained after the Jenner endorsement, offering only a "no comment." But Truman later charged that the "ugliest and dumbest thing" Ike did was to duck the McCarthy fight, "even when good, decent people around him were being hurt by that awful and horrible man."

Many years later a question would arise over whether there was even more to the Truman-Eisenhower-Marshall relationship than anyone knew. In his controversial oral history *Plain Speaking*—published in 1973, after Truman died—Merle Miller claimed that in June of 1945, with the war finally over, Eisenhower had written to Marshall saying he wanted to come home and divorce Mamie so he could marry his wartime driver, Kay Summersby. Marshall wrote back that if Ike attempted such a thing, "he'd see to it that the rest of his life was a living hell," Miller reports Truman as saying. "General Marshall didn't very often lose his temper, but when he did, it was a corker." One of the last things Truman said he did as president, Miller wrote, despite his intense dislike of Eisenhower at that point, was to take the letters from the Pentagon files and destroy them.

Though some of *Plain Speaking* was based on taped interviews with Truman, Miller had no recording of the conversation concerning the sensational letters—and Truman was no longer alive to confirm it. The only corroboration came from Truman's garrulous aide Major General Harry Vaughan, who claimed that there had indeed been a damaging exchange between Eisenhower and Marshall regarding divorce, which Eisenhower's enemies got wind of and wanted to use against him in the 1952 campaign. Vaughan also alleged that Truman interceded, retrieving the letters and sending them to Marshall to destroy.

The surviving evidence tells a different story. Ike did write to Marshall in June of 1945; but it was to ask that Mamie be allowed to join him in Germany for what promised to be a long occupation. It was an unusually intimate letter: "I will admit that the last six weeks have been my hardest of the war," he confided. "My trouble is that I just plain miss my family." Mamie had fallen ill; she weighed barely a hundred pounds. The war had been a great strain on her, he wrote Marshall, and "I would feel far more comfortable about her if she could be with me."

As a matter of protocol, the request was unnecessary; MacArthur, serving in Asia, had simply sent for his wife to join him. But even though they were now of the same rank, Eisenhower respectfully asked Marshall for permission, and Marshall took the letter to Truman for his advice. Truman told him no, it would not be fair to other soldiers who were separated from their families. Eisenhower's response? He apologized to Marshall for even asking.

On the Warpath

Eisenhower's very public failure to defend Marshall, for whatever reason, turned the 1952 campaign into what the *New York Times* called "a bitter Eisenhower-Truman affair," to the point of overshadowing Adlai Stevenson completely. Truman went on the warpath, with a carefully prepared speech in Colorado Springs. Eisenhower, Truman charged, was a coward. Rather than condemn the "moral scoundrels" and "pygmies" like McCarthy and Jenner who "tried to stab an honored chief, friend and benefactor in the back," Ike had embraced them and "humbly thanked [McCarthy] for riding on his campaign train. And why? Because he thinks these two unprincipled men will bring him votes in November." Any man who would bow to such political pressures, Truman charged, was unfit to be entrusted with the presidency or the nation's atomic arsenal. "I skinned old Ike from the top of his bald head to his backside," Truman later told a *Washington Post* reporter.

And that was just the beginning. Truman climbed aboard his armor-plated presidential railroad car, the *Ferdinand Magellan*, for his first whistle-stop tour of the campaign, through twenty-four states. In a lovely bit of political jujitsu, he attacked Eisenhower by embracing him, reminding voters that he was "the man I chose to be a chief lieutenant in some of the greatest and gravest undertakings of my Administration." But now Ike was attacking the very policies he'd helped shape, Truman charged. In just one October day of stops across New York state, Truman called Eisenhower a liar, a fool, a hypocrite, so ignorant of government after a life in the military that he was at the mercy of the party bosses, "a babe in the woods of Senator Taft . . . a military man who doesn't know anything about civilian problems, in the hands of the reactionaries who speak and work for the banker, the power lobby, the real estate lobby, and all the other special privilege boys."

"I knew him. I trusted him," Truman confessed to his party faithful in the heat of the campaign. "I thought he might make a good president. But that was a mistake. In this campaign he has betrayed almost everything I thought he stood for."

Like a brass band building to the coda, Truman ran higher and hotter, and always, it came back to Marshall and McCarthy: "This much is clear to me. A man who betrays his friends in such a fashion is not to be trusted with the great Office of President of the United States."

Eisenhower wasn't exactly wearing kid gloves when he referred to Truman as an "expert in political demagoguery." But for all the charges of political naivete, Eisenhower was as shrewd as he could be about reading public opinion and private motives, and understood that his political "inexperience" actually gave him an advantage. His language and demeanor were designed to set him apart from the bar fights of recent political life. While the hard-liners in his party wanted him to take Truman down at every chance, he knew he needed the votes of independents who were already alarmed by his handling of McCarthy.

And he may have understood what reporters covering the race discovered: that Truman, blinded by his own disillusionment, underestimated people's personal devotion to Eisenhower, the sheer power of his presence. "It is not uncommon for people to risk injury from rotten branches and high tension wires," wrote *New Yorker* columnist Richard Rovere in September, as spectators climbed the trees along a parade route to get a better view. "Three times during the tour of Minneapolis and St. Paul, the crowds broke through the police cordons, forcing the motorcade to stop." Especially at his whistle-stops, Truman would be all but drowned out by crowds shouting "We like Ike! We like Ike!" When Truman started accusing Eisenhower of "moral blindness" and anti-Semitism and anti-Catholicism, it backfired. "Many Believe He Is Harming Stevenson's Chances" read the *New York Times* headline.

Having found in Herbert Hoover how vitally useful a former president could be to a new one, Truman seemed unaware that he was precluding such a role for himself. There was little chance that even a remnant of his friendship with Eisenhower could survive the campaign brawl. Eisenhower was a supremely confident leader, and might never have felt inclined to turn to Truman in any case; but the wounds of the 1952 race ruled out even the most minimal club camaraderie. Eisenhower, his onetime friend Averell Harriman later told his grandson David Eisenhower, "just didn't understand politics. He had no idea of the difference between opposing a man politically and personally." Eisenhower came away from the campaign doubting Truman's honor and leadership and respectability.

In the end, there is probably nothing Truman could have done that would have changed the outcome either way. Eisenhower won thirty-nine of forty-eight states, including Stevenson's and Truman's home states, with a six-million-vote edge—the most votes ever received by a candidate to that point—while carrying the House and Senate. Stevenson conceded at 1:30 A.M.; after a brief speech, Eisenhower went back to his hotel suite and collapsed on a bed. But there was one last task before sleep.

It was Clare Boothe Luce, the former lawmaker Ike would name ambassador to Italy, who came to him. "I know how tired you are," she said. "But there is one more thing you *have* to do." Obediently, he went to the phone and called Herbert Hoover, the last Republican to win the White House, twenty-four years before.

The mere mention of Truman's name to Ike after the 1952 campaign "would forever bring a tightening of the jaw and a reddening of the face," observed Ewald. Eisenhower's wrestling coach at West Point had taught him to always come back off the canvas with a grin on your face—but "Eisenhower's insouciance was an exercise in iron self-discipline," Ewald said. "Underneath, the venom worked; and it shaped the course of history."

The Very Ugly Handoff

"Congratulations on your overwhelming victory," Truman cabled to Eisenhower. "The 1954 budget must be presented to Congress before January 15th. . . . You should have a representative meet with the Director of the Budget immediately." Truman already had a clear vision for handling the first turnover of power between parties in two decades. It just didn't happen to be one that Eisenhower shared.

Eisenhower and Mamie, with their daughter-in-law and three grandchildren, had just settled in to Bobby Jones's cottage at the edge of the Augusta National golf course when another telegram arrived, inviting him to the White House. Truman, who had had no chance to prepare for his ascension at Roosevelt's death, was determined that his successor have a better foundation to build on. So he also urged Eisenhower to send in his top advisors to meet their counterparts at key agencies, and instructed people at every level to offer any cooperation they could.

Right away, Eisenhower's aides made it clear that until inauguration, Eisenhower would possess "no authority of any kind." As for Truman's outreach, they believed it warranted only the most limited response. "Ike and his advisors are afraid of some kind of trick," Truman wrote in his diary on November 15. He understood that outgoing presidents were perfectly capable of setting booby traps for their successors: "I could have clotted things up so he wouldn't get straightened out for a year," he told one reporter on the eve of the inauguration. But that was not his intent. "I am very much afraid that Ike's advisors have convinced him that he is dealing with a man who wants to embarrass him," he wrote. "That is not true. All I want is to make an orderly turnover. It has never been done."

That wasn't precisely true, but it was close. When Eisenhower came to the White House just before two on the afternoon of November 18, it was only the fourth meeting of its kind in U.S. history, and like the first, between Jefferson and Adams, produced only acrimony. The second and third such meetings were between Hoover and Roosevelt, and those were positively toxic. For Truman and Ike this would be the first face-to-face meeting since Eisenhower's return in June. Following the Roosevelt script, Eisenhower insisted the meeting would be "wholly informal and personal," with no joint action whatever.

It was Eisenhower's first time back in the capital since the election; half a million people turned out to see him as his motorcade moved from the airport to the White House; Truman had even given government workers time off to see his successor.

"Good morning, folks," Eisenhower said cheerily to the newsmen and White House staffers who packed the lobby. He and Truman met privately at first in the Oval Office. Truman concluded right away that Ike "had a chip on his shoulder." Truman offered to leave various pictures of Latin American liberators given to the office. "I was informed, very curtly, that I'd do well to take them with me—that the governments of those countries would, no doubt, give the new President the same pictures." Truman returned the magnificent globe Eisenhower had given him back in the summer of 1945. "He accepted that—not very graciously." (Eisenhower actually tried to correct that awkward moment about two weeks after he took office. "I have just noticed the inscribed plate you had attached to the globe in this office," he wrote to Truman, "and I remember that I failed to thank you for your courtesy in returning it to me. It was a friendly gesture that I much appreciate.")

They talked about the fighting in Korea, and agreed on the need for continuity on foreign policy. But Truman also tried to prepare Eisenhower for what lay ahead—give him a window into the office and the keys to success in it. He needed to find a skilled diplomat as his appointments secretary, Truman advised, who was "able to say 'No' nine tenths of the time and make no one angry." He'd need a shrewd press secretary able to keep reporters in line. Then they went to the Cabinet Room, where the secretaries of state, defense, and treasury briefed him and answered questions.

Truman came away from the meeting convinced that Eisenhower had had a rude awakening to the ordeal ahead; that he was "awestruck by the long array of problems and decisions the President has to face. If that is so, I can also understand his frozen grimness through our meeting."

Ike reported no such reaction: the meeting, he said, "added little to my knowledge, nor did it affect my planning."

Watching the tension between the two men, Acheson was puzzled. Eisenhower's easy charm was nowhere in evidence. "He seemed embarrassed and reluctant to be with us—wary, withdrawn, and taciturn to the point of surliness," Acheson observed. "Sunk back in a chair facing the President across the Cabinet table, he chewed the earpiece of his spectacles and occasionally asked for a memorandum on a matter that caught his attention."

Before Ike left, Truman handed him three loose-leaf volumes summarizing U.S. security policies and top secret plans in case of an all-out communist attack on Korea, Yugoslavia, or Iran. Talking with his staff, he imagined what awaited his successor. "He'll sit here and he'll say, 'Do this, do that,' and nothing will happen. Poor Ike. It won't be a bit like the Army. He'll find it very frustrating."

He savored the prospect of Eisenhower's steep learning curve once the burdens of the office fell on his shoulders. "This fellow," he told reporters as inauguration day approached, "don't know any more about politics than a pig knows about Sunday."

The closer inauguration day drew, the happier Truman became. "Why you'd have thought the President won the election, the way he acts," a

White House valet told the *Washington Post*. He seemed unbothered by the shadow of so bitter a campaign, the prospect of moving out, the complete uncertainty about the future. Even his critics, like columnist Walter Lippmann, would say that "in the manner of his going, Mr. Truman has been every inch the President, conscious of the great office and worthy of it." But one critic—the one who was about to take his place—refused to see this.

No Top Hats

Inauguration day is democracy's secular feast day, a celebration of pride and patriotism and the peace that follows partisan warfare. But there is also a long history of gale winds on those mornings, often inside the White House itself. And so it was in 1953, which may rank as the most rancorous inauguration day of the twentieth century. Ike had warned an aide that "I'll never ride down Pennsylvania Avenue with him. I'll meet him at the Capitol steps."

That's very nearly what happened.

The first fight was sartorial; custom demanded that the president-elect wear a top hat and cutaway coat. "It's this sort of thing where everybody goes over to a tailor and for the day hires an outfit with an ascot tie," correspondent Robert Nixon recalled. But Eisenhower rejected the top hat in favor of a homburg—without conferring with his predecessor. Truman acceded graciously—"I don't want to get into any hat controversy," he told the *Washington Post*, but he later wrote that he felt the occasion of an inauguration warranted more formal attire. (For the record: Ike wore a morning coat for Kennedy's inauguration eight years later.)

Eisenhower was aiming for a "simple and dignified" celebration, but it was just the nature of the times, so much pent-up celebratory fervor and hunger for a change, that it turned out to be one of the biggest, costliest, longest extravaganzas the capital had seen in years. It was a beautiful sunny day; three quarters of a million people lined Pennsylvania Avenue, some peering over the crowds through cardboard periscopes.

By custom the incoming president comes to the White House to pick up his predecessor and ride together to the Capitol. But Eisenhower sent word that he wanted Truman to come pick him up at the Statler Hotel. "Well, I wouldn't do it of course," Truman recalled. Bess Truman had prepared a small luncheon for the Eisenhowers. "We were disappointed when the invitation was refused and the custom ignored." Eisenhower pulled up just in time to head to the Capitol—and even then, he refused to get out of the limousine. Ike could be an unforgiving enemy—but this was especially graceless in victory. Only when the Trumans emerged did Eisenhower get out of the car. "It was a shocking moment," said CBS newsman Eric Sevareid. "Truman was gracious and he had just been snubbed. He showed his superiority by what he did."

So it was a frosty ride to the ceremony. "It's interesting that a single thing, that great smile of Eisenhower's, gave him the worldwide and life-long reputation of being a sunny and amiable man," Truman reflected, "when those of us who knew him well were all too well aware that he was essentially a surly, angry and disagreeable man."

When they reached the Capitol, they went to the sergeant at arms office to await their summons to the platform. It was at this point that Eisenhower turned to Truman and asked: "I wonder who is responsible for my son John being ordered to Washington from Korea? I wonder who is trying to embarrass me?"

"The President of the United States ordered your son to attend your inauguration," Truman replied. "The President thought it was right and proper for your son to witness the swearing-in of his father to the presidency. If you think somebody was trying to embarrass you by this order, then the President assumes full responsibility."

If you were to judge only by the letter Eisenhower wrote three days later, he was actually grateful for Truman's thoughtful gesture in bringing John home for the occasion. He thanked Truman for "the very many courtesies you extended me," all his efforts to smooth the transition, and also, "on the personal side, I especially want to thank you for your thoughtfulness in ordering my son home from Korea for the inauguration; and even more so for not allowing either him or me to know that you had done so." Truman wrote back by hand: "It was a pleasure to help all I could in the orderly transfer from my administration to yours. I would never have mentioned the incident of your son, had you not asked me about it."

Maybe the letters were perfunctory gestures of statesmen; maybe there was a momentary truce that simply couldn't last. For whatever reason, the incident became another flashpoint between the two men. "Eisenhower didn't like it," Robert Nixon said. "He felt that Truman was interfering in his private life and the life of his family. Even more than that, Truman was calling his son back from an atmosphere of combat. He felt his son should be there fighting. . . . Under no circumstances did he want his son to be called back to Washington just to see his father inaugurated President.

"Truman, of course, was flabbergasted," Nixon went on. "Here, out of the kindness of his heart, and a genuine feeling for family, he had made what he thought was a nice gesture. For whatever were the reasons, this turned out to be another breach between these two men. One trying to be nice, thoughtful and kind, and the other resenting it."

It was all so bitter that Truman wondered whether he and Bess would be left to walk to the train station when the ceremonies were over. But the White House provided a ride, and the crowd waiting at Union Station to send him off was so big he had trouble getting to his train. "Make way for the President," boomed the public address system. People cheered and sang "Auld Lang Syne." "In all my political career I have never had anything like this," Truman said. "I'll never forget it if I live to be a hundred, and that's just what I expect to do."

He was a man with great hopes but few plans and less money. He had already turned down various lucrative offers, since he didn't want to cheapen the presidency by selling his name. But he had a model to steer by.

"I think Herbert Hoover has handled himself perfectly," he declared.

Truman in Exile

The first time the Trumans returned to Washington, in June of 1953, reporters asked if he'd visit Eisenhower. No, said Truman lightly, "He's too busy to see every Tom, Dick and Harry that comes to town." When asked at a county fair why he'd been so mild in his post-presidential statements, he smiled and observed, "If we point out the Republicans' errors, they might mend their ways, and we would not have the chance to take them to task."

Besides, he was enjoying himself. Truman's retirement offered him the chance to rest, to travel, to reflect on his journey; he visited Churchill in London, received an honorary degree from Oxford, had an audience with Pope Pius XII, played Mozart's piano in Salzburg.

But over time, the silence from the White House became conspicuous. Eisenhower never called to ask advice or offer a visit; he seemed intent, in fact, on erasing all signs of Truman ever having served there. Truman's portrait was removed from public rooms, along with his piano, and a favorite chandelier; the bowling alleys built by friends of Truman's from Missouri were taken out. This fight, Fletcher Knebel wrote in *Look* magazine, "is no ordinary case of ruffled feelings in the wake of a heated political contest, but one of the real hell-for-leather grudges of our era."

Relations were so tense in the fall of 1953 that a furor erupted simply over whether Eisenhower ignored a phone call from Truman when the president was visiting Kansas City. Ike was staying at the Muehlebach Hotel, where Truman regularly had lunch with friends. According to Truman, he called the hotel to pay his respects to the president: "I was very curtly told that the President's time was all taken up and that there was no opportunity for that to happen."

Some Eisenhower aides suggested that Truman never called; others blamed a hotel operator, who allegedly said that when Truman identified himself, he replied, "And I'm Julius Caesar." Ike's friend George Allen recalled Eisenhower ordering the Secret Service to look into what had happened. Years later during the 1960 campaign, the issue was still tender. "Oh, that was wrong," Richard Nixon told Edward Folliard. "The President should have called up Mr. Truman and told him he was sorry, and that would have ended the whole thing." As for Eisenhower himself, years later when he was working on his memoirs, he was still convinced Truman had invented the whole incident. "The man is a congenital liar," he told his aide William Ewald.

But it was not just the call; within two months a far more serious assault was under way, by Eisenhower's attorney general, Herbert Brownell. He opened an investigation into whether Truman had knowingly promoted a Soviet spy named Harry Dexter White to become executive director of the International Monetary Fund. "The effort of Herbert Brownell to picture Mr. Truman as a traitor," argued Truman's aide Clayton Fritchey, is "one of the ugliest chapters in our history." Eisenhower had to have given his consent, Fritchey charged, because "having told the country that Washington was teeming with Communists and security risks, they had to find some."

Things got so out of hand that Truman was subpoenaed to appear before the House Un-American Activities Committee; he refused, on the grounds that the charge was pure political payback, and an appearance abridged the doctrine of separation of powers. He spoke on television instead, defending himself in a national address against what he called "shameful demagoguery" in the service of "cheap political trickery."

That showdown is worth noting for the tone it set and the precedents it left. The power of the president had increased immensely during the 1930s and 1940s; so the power of former presidents increased as well. Truman was the first to claim executive privilege for the ex-president; constitutional experts debated his premise, but the public was on his side. He never appeared, and the investigation was dropped. Decades later, Richard Nixon would have Truman to thank for the foundation he laid.

So it went, throughout Eisenhower's presidency. When Truman, living on a tiny military pension, published the first volume of his memoirs in 1955, Eisenhower declined to return the favor Truman had granted him as amateur author; Truman had to pay two thirds of the royalties in income taxes. Upon Ike's overwhelming reelection in 1956, Truman wrote another letter he never sent, which signed off with "Best of luck and may the honest Democrats and Liberal Republicans save you from disaster." In his private writings, he made his feelings plain: "I'm not one of Eisenhower's admirers. I'm sure he has some, perhaps many, though for the life of me I can't tell you why." Soldiers just aren't suited to be president, he said; too hierarchical, too divorced from civilian reality.

But his greatest objection appears to have been born of rejection. Presidents, he argued, need to build on the successes of their predecessors, "and not try to abandon them simply because the previous president ... belonged to a different political party." And then he laid out the essential challenge of club membership, where the public and private demands collide.

"Most Presidents don't seem to want to talk to former presidents," Truman admitted. "And from my own experience, I know that's pretty natural behavior. A new president wants to be president on his own hook and not have a former president around trying to give him advice. It's customary for the president, after he's elected, to want to run things himself. . . . But the really terrible thing is when a president sets out to actively discredit the policies of the former president, and that's what happened when I was succeeded by Dwight Eisenhower."

Eisenhower could be petty to the point of hostility—as when the White House asked Herbert Hoover not to attend Truman's library dedication in 1957. Roosevelt's press secretary and later radio advisor Leonard Reinsch was assigned to herd the dignitaries at the dedication ceremony and told Hoover how gracious he was to be there. "I wouldn't miss it," Hoover told him, having ignored the administration's request. Eisenhower sent Truman a "congratulatory" letter, to be read by the General Services administrator, that was so chilly "you could almost see the icicles on it on a hot July day," said Reinsch.

"President Eisenhower still harbors a fierce personal distaste for his once generous patron," concluded the *Chicago Daily News*. "Only if he had sent the GSA employee who is up for night watchman at the library could Mr. Eisenhower have expressed his cold detachment more pointedly."

Meanwhile Truman would continue to hammer at Ike and his domestic policies all through the campaigns of the 1950s—but he also took opportunities to come to the president's defense on some matters of club principle. In 1958, with the economy in recession, Eisenhower was attacked for using a government plane to take Mamie to an Elizabeth Arden resort in Arizona. Truman, who had once been criticized for using the plane to visit his dying mother, defended the flight: "Whatever the President sees fit to do for the welfare of his family, he should be allowed to do without a lot of people jumping on him," he said. "I don't believe in attacking a man through his family."

Even more important, Truman consistently spoke out in support of the president's foreign policies, whether sending Marines to Lebanon or vowing to defend the islands of Quemoy and Matsu in the Taiwan Strait. He said he hoped that "those who are trying to destroy the free world will clearly understand that we will unanimously support . . . the President of the United States." In this posture, Truman was at odds with his own former secretary of state: "Please don't be hooked on one of those my country right or wrong gambits," Dean Acheson wrote to Truman, for "in this way Foster [John Foster Dulles, Ike's secretary of state]

can always drive us like steers to the slaughter pens." On another occasion Acheson questioned Truman's assertion that "we must . . . accept
the President's assessment of what the situation is [because] only the
President is in possession of all the facts." But at that moment Truman
was expressing kinship with a man who knew what it was like to bear the
burden, to live with the full knowledge of the dangers the country faced.
Let the armchair critics with their blinkered view have at it; presidents
know that there are some things only presidents know, and so Truman,
for all his issues with Eisenhower, would still grant him the benefit of
the doubt.

After that there were signs of thaw in Eisenhower as well; he invited
Truman to a Memorial Day lunch at the White House in 1958, and to a
NATO anniversary celebration the following year, neither of which Truman could attend due to scheduling conflicts. Their reunion would have
to wait, for a moment that suited both irony and history.

Funerals for Their Friends

In October of 1959 the two presidents were reunited for the first time in
six years at a chapel near Arlington Cemetery. The funeral was for, of all
people, George Marshall. Truman was already seated in the pew when
Eisenhower arrived and sat beside him.

"How do you do, Mr. President," Eisenhower said, offering his hand.

"How are you, Mr. President," Truman replied. When the service was
over, the men stood side by side as the casket was removed; Eisenhower
saluted his former commander in chief—and Truman returned the salute. Then they left through separate doors.

A year later, Eisenhower would be getting ready to turn over the
keys to the Oval Office and reenter civilian life. More than most of his
predecessors, that adjustment was complicated. It had been decades since
he had stepped foot in a clothing store or a barbershop; as Stephen Ambrose recounts in his biography, Ike had never paid a turnpike toll, and
he couldn't remember how to type, adjust a television picture, or make
orange juice. He even had to be shown how to place a phone call. And he
had some bridges to rebuild.

By 1961, with John F. Kennedy in the White House, Truman had been restored to his place as revered elder statesman. That November he paid the young president a visit, and took the opportunity to blast Eisenhower's "wrong and unwise policies," in a speech at the National Press Club. Asked about the possibility of forming "a troika of former presidents," Truman smiled and revealed that he and Hoover had already started the Presidents Club. "He's the president and I'm the secretary. The other fellow [Eisenhower] hasn't been taken in yet."

Eight days after Truman's White House visit, historian Steve Neal recounts, "Ike applied for membership." He was designing his library in Abilene, and wanted to see how Truman had organized his. He was already planning a trip to Kansas City to help rededicate a war memorial, so a stop in Independence was discreetly orchestrated.

Truman insisted that Eisenhower call on him in his private office at the library. "I want to have some time with him," Truman had instructed.

"Come in, come in," he welcomed Eisenhower. The two presidents talked in private for about a quarter hour before beginning their tour. Should he sign the guestbook? Eisenhower asked.

"Definitely," Truman teased. "Then if anything is missing, we'll know who to blame."

They explored the replica of the Oval Office, re-created down to the gadgets on the desk. Ike would eventually send back the globe that the men had now passed back and forth three times. Eisenhower noticed that his portrait was in the place of honor, to the right of the entrance; Truman's was on the left. "You know that fellow," Truman said, smiling. He noted that it had been given to the library by Eisenhower's friend Kansas senator Harry Darby.

"But you got it on the preferred side," Eisenhower observed.

"Yes sir, General," Truman replied, "and I had it put there."

Truman also pointed out the signed copy of *Crusade in Europe*; Eisenhower read his flattering inscription, Truman's aide Rufus Burrus said, and turned red. Eisenhower told him after the tour that he wished he had visited sooner: "He said he would have made some changes in his own Library, because he liked the arrangement better here."

"It was obvious to all observers," the *New York Times* proclaimed, "that Mr. Eisenhower had been admitted to the 'Former Presidents' Club.'"

About a week later one of the giants of their generation, House Speaker Sam Rayburn, died at the age of seventy-nine. His Texas funeral would bring together Presidents Kennedy, Eisenhower, and Truman, and Vice President Johnson in the pew at the First Baptist Church in Bonham, Texas. "You know, having met as we did at the Library before that," Truman recalled, "it made it less awkward to meet at the funeral service. I'm glad we had the chance to do that." Eisenhower flew the last leg of the trip in a helicopter with President Kennedy. He and Truman chatted at the graveside.

They met again at Eleanor Roosevelt's funeral at Hyde Park a year later. But it was their encounter in November of 1963, after the assassination of John F. Kennedy, that made all that had come between them seem suddenly rather small.

KENNEDY AND HIS CLUB:

The Hazing

——————— ⚷ ———————

If Eisenhower, given his stature and circumstances, had little need to call the club into action, John F. Kennedy was a different story. Maybe it was the lingering concern about his narrow victory, or relative youth, or the fact that his ability to get anything done depended on a measure of bipartisan support. But it may also have been that Kennedy knew that a predecessor, if not handled correctly, could do a president more harm than good.

He didn't need to worry about Truman, the faithful fellow Democrat, or Hoover, an old friend of his father's. It was Eisenhower who mattered, his popularity still vast, his authority unassailable, and his contempt for Kennedy palpable. "I think he always felt that Eisenhower was unhappy with him," Bobby Kennedy said soon after his brother's death. "And so . . . he always went out of his way to make sure that Eisenhower was brought in on all matters and that Eisenhower couldn't hurt the Administration by going off and attacking . . . not that Eisenhower ever gave him any advice that was very helpful."

The record suggests otherwise. Presidents typically land in office thinking they know better than their predecessors; having just spent an entire campaign convincing voters this is the case, they naturally come to believe it themselves. But then something like a chain reaction occurs: they win the office, then the office strikes back, challenging a president, chastening him, confronting him with all he doesn't know. Kennedy's humbling came within months, with the disastrous Bay of Pigs invasion—a result of, among other things, his determination to blow up the decision-making machinery that Hoover and Truman built and that had served Eisenhower well. Whatever his appetite for instruction at that moment, Kennedy knew the world needed to see the two presidents together, an insight that yielded the iconic, page-one photo of the old president and the new one walking the paths of Camp David together, deep in conversation.

Thus did the club become the woodshed for a talented president who still had a lot to learn.

5

"He Had No Idea of the Complexity of the Job"

— DWIGHT EISENHOWER

P resident John F. Kennedy had a slip of paper he liked to carry around in his pocket: 118,574, it read, reminding him of the sliver of votes that he had to stretch into a mandate to do the job he had fought so hard to get.

That alone set him apart from the club's members, to say nothing of the vast differences in age, experience, and temperament. Hoover hadn't liked being president; Truman and Eisenhower hadn't expected to be. Kennedy was eager, impatient, unwilling to wait his turn. Though he ascended at a moment of existential threat, it was not a burden he shrank from. "Sure it's a big job," he told a *Time* reporter, sitting in his Georgetown living room just before his inauguration in January 1961. "But I don't know anybody who can do it any better than I can.... It isn't going to be so bad. You've got time to think—and besides, the pay is pretty good." But from his very first days, his toughness was tested by both his enemies and his advisors, including the seasoned soldiers of the Joint Chiefs of Staff, which he did not have the advantage of ever having chaired.

This is one reason why, of the club's members, he would court most faithfully the one he liked least: that would be Eisenhower.

It is testimony to Kennedy's lowly place in the Senate hierarchy that he and Eisenhower never met when Ike was in the White House. They had, however, crossed paths a decade before, in 1945 when Kennedy was a twenty-eight-year-old war hero traveling with Navy Secretary James Forrestal to Potsdam. When Forrestal's plane landed in Frankfurt, one journalist recalled, "the plane doors opened, and out came Forrestal. Then, to my amazement, Jack Kennedy. Ike was meeting Forrestal. So Jack met Ike."

Kennedy's icon was Roosevelt, the model he leaned on and learned from across a generation. He was endlessly curious about FDR, recalled his advisor Arthur Schlesinger, even adopted some of his mannerisms. Both men were urbane, patrician, easy with power, strengthened by the suffering of afflictions they worked hard to conceal. Roosevelt's handicap was more obvious—but Kennedy received last rites at least four times in his adult life, and "in a lifetime of medical torment," biographer Richard Reeves observes, "Kennedy was more promiscuous with physicians and drugs than he was with women."

Like his hero, Kennedy wanted America to see herself anew, though his challenge was very different from Roosevelt's in the midst of a crushing Depression. Climbing to power during the placid 1950s, Kennedy didn't look to raise hopes; he wanted to raise questions, make people restless and adventurous. He rejected less Eisenhower's policies than his pieties; he saw the Eisenhower years as soul-crushing, humorless, anti-intellectual. "In some influential quarters," Schlesinger charged of the Eisenhower years, "it was almost deemed treasonous to raise doubts about the perfection of the American way of life."

The antagonism was political as well as cultural and generational: JFK thought Eisenhower didn't grasp the full power of the presidency. Ike's landslide victories and long coattails had granted him immense power, which Kennedy felt he squandered. Kennedy had his micro margin and a Democratic majority in name only, since lawmakers owed him nothing and conservative Southern Democrats who rejected most of his priorities controlled much of the legislative machinery. "The word 'politics.' I have no great liking for that," Ike once said. This was mystifying to Kennedy. "I do have a great liking for the word 'politics,'" he said. "It's the way a President gets things done."

Finally, there was something personal; whatever reverence Ike deserved as a general, Kennedy did not extend to the man himself; he called him "that old asshole."

"I could understand it if he played golf all the time with old Army friends," he told Schlesinger as the campaign was just getting under way. "But no man is less loyal to his old friends than Eisenhower. He is a terribly cold man. All his golfing pals are rich men he has met since 1945."

No one knew that better than Ike's political "partner," and Kennedy's 1960 opponent, Richard Nixon. It is one of those forgotten plot twists that Kennedy and Nixon had been friends early on—closer, you could argue, than Nixon would be with Eisenhower during his formative political years. Nixon and Kennedy entered Congress together in the Class of 1946, two young Navy officers returned from war as passionate anticommunists and pragmatic reformers, with offices across the hall from each other. Kennedy was the golden boy from Harvard whose father's money lubricated his path to Congress; Nixon had won a scholarship to Harvard but couldn't take it, since he couldn't afford the travel cost to get there. But very quickly, it was Nixon who was the star, vaulting to national fame by taking down the great patrician traitor Alger Hiss. Jack appeared at his door one day in the summer of 1950 with $1,000 from his father, for Nixon's Senate race. When Kennedy applied for membership at the Burning Tree Club, Nixon wrote the sponsoring letter. They even shared a sleeper compartment, traveling back to Washington by train one night after a debate in Pennsylvania; they drew straws for who got the lower berth. Nixon was invited to Kennedy's wedding in 1953; the only reason he missed it was to accept a rare invitation to play golf with Eisenhower. The following year, Kennedy lay near death, after surgery to insert a metal plate in his spine; he got an infection and fell into a coma. Nixon wept: "Oh God, don't let him die." He told Jackie that if there was a tie vote in the Senate in Kennedy's absence, he would not exercise his right as vice president to cast the deciding vote.

Ike had tapped Nixon as running mate in 1952 and yet throughout the next eight years in the White House never once invited his vice president up to the residence or to his farm in Gettysburg. It was a relationship of king and courtier; Nixon was unfailingly respectful and loyal to Eisenhower, even when he was given the ugly jobs of firing cabinet members Ike didn't want to confront, or being sent out as the political hit man so Ike could remain above the fray.

Nixon *was* the fray; his essential nature—so resentful, so suspicious, with a drive unique to a man who lost two brothers, one of whom had been the family golden boy. After brother Harold's death, Richard "sank into a deep, impenetrable silence," his mother, Hannah, recalled. "From that time on it seemed like he was trying to be three sons in one." Nixon's father, a bully and blusterer, who at various times worked as streetcar motorman, farmhand, butcher, housepainter, sheep rancher, and telephone pole climber, claimed as his greatest achievement that he once shook hands with President William McKinley.

Imagine what it would mean if his son could win that prize?

Into Battle: The 1960 Election

Since in 1960 Eisenhower remained the most popular man in the country, both Nixon and Kennedy knew better than to cross him, even as they tried to satisfy voters hungry for change. The substantive differences between Eisenhower, Kennedy, and Nixon were marginal at best; Schlesinger even dashed off a quick 1960 book, *Kennedy or Nixon: Does It Make Any Difference?*

Instead the campaign was about other things; age and energy and a vision for a new decade. Kennedy would "get the country moving again." He would jostle the economy out of stagnation, rebuild the muscles of a country gone flabby under its war hero president, restore its prestige—all promises precisely engineered to drive Eisenhower crazy.

Eisenhower was proud of his success in keeping the country safe and sound: safe from attack, without going bankrupt in the process. He had killed weapons systems, pursued a test ban treaty that both the Democrats and the military opposed, ignored Soviet premier Nikita Khrushchev's boasts about "cranking out missiles like sausages" because he knew that it was more talk than action. The two leaders were silent partners, resisting calls in both countries to hurl billions more into missile systems and civil defense networks. "I don't believe we should pay one cent for defense more than we have to," Eisenhower declared at a press conference early in 1960. Pressed by reporters about "adequacy of defense" Ike replied, in essence, Trust me. "I've spent my life in this," he said, "and I know more about it than almost anybody." Now here was this junior senator, egged on by allies in Congress, accusing him of placing fiscal security ahead of national security, and warning of a "failure of nerve" that allowed the opening up of a "missile gap."

Ike was so annoyed at Kennedy's portrait of him as a caretaker president that he went to battle more to defend his own image than to enhance Nixon's. Eisenhower had never felt much warmth toward his vice president, a man he barely knew when he hoisted him onto the ticket in 1952, and he had a list of Republicans to whom he'd have rather handed the keys, like his treasury secretary, Robert Anderson. He refused to endorse Nixon before the Republican convention. Once Nixon's nomination was assured, his praise was so thin you could see through it: "I am not dissatisfied with the individual that looks like he will get it." He managed to deliver his prime-time speech at the convention in which he celebrated the achievements of the past eight years, the "unprecedented prosperity" and "the strongest security system in the world," without once mentioning Nixon's name—only his prayer that "the next President of the United States will be a Republican." He would come to regret his failure as president to do more to shape the Republican Party, build a new generation of leaders in his image. Instead there he was, delivering lethal injections into the campaign, like his remark, when asked for an example of Nixon's role in a key decision, "If you give me a week, I might think of one."

If it was any consolation, at least Kennedy was having the same problem with his party elders. During the Democrats' nominating process Truman was no more help to Kennedy than Eisenhower was to Nixon—in fact Truman did everything he could to block him. He disliked Kennedy's faith, his father, and his fortune. Given the fact that he had experienced a party mutiny himself in 1948, when the surviving Roosevelts tried to topple him, Truman's efforts to derail Kennedy spoke both to the depth of his hostility—and his reflex, shared by many former presidents, to flex his clout as kingmaker. After the hard-fought primary season against Hubert Humphrey, and a mere three days before the Democratic convention opened, Truman held a nationally televised press conference in which he attacked the convention as "a prearranged . . . mockery . . . controlled . . . by one candidate."

"Senator," Truman intoned, "are you certain that you are quite ready for the country, or that the country is ready for you in the role of President?" Such dangerous times called for "a man with the greatest possible maturity and experience . . . may I urge you to be patient?"

Patience was nowhere in Kennedy's repertoire, nor deference to the Old Frontier. Kennedy called a news conference of his own at New York's Roosevelt Hotel, and retorted that "Mr. Truman regards an open convention as one which studies all the candidates, reviews their records and then takes his advice." He demolished the experience argument so effectively that he should have thanked Truman for raising it: if fourteen years in elective office were not sufficient preparation, Kennedy declared, then that would have ruled out the candidacies of every Democratic president of the century—including Wilson, Roosevelt, and Truman himself.

But Truman was not the only one out to stop the Kennedy juggernaut. Lyndon Johnson, the towering majority leader of the Senate with whom Eisenhower had cut many a successful legislative deal, was just as intent on derailing Kennedy, though in his case it was to clear the way for himself. The Democrats' convention was due to open in Los Angeles on July 11; Lyndon Johnson finally declared his candidacy on July 5, and on the night before he flew to the West Coast he stopped by the White House to have a long talk with his Republican friend.

Kennedy, Johnson complained to Eisenhower, was a mediocrity, "a nobody who had a rich father," and insisted, "Ike, for the good of the country, you cannot let that man become elected President. Now, he might get the nomination out there, he probably will, but he's a dangerous man."

Of course, it would only be a few nights later that Eisenhower got a big surprise when he turned on his TV. As he told interviewer Earl Mazo, "there was that son of a bitch becoming a vice presidential candidate with this 'dangerous man.'"

All the candidates and their prospective patrons continued this rugby match through the summer: having secured the nomination and roped Johnson tightly to his side as his running mate, Kennedy set out to appease his elders. He went to Hyde Park to woo Eleanor Roosevelt, with whom he had had a long and prickly relationship. In early August he flew to Missouri to pay homage to Truman. He was a hard case: "I never liked Kennedy," Truman told one Senate friend. "I hate his father." But

Truman would embrace the enemy of his enemy. "That no good son-of-a-bitch Dick Nixon called me a communist and I'll do anything to beat him."

And likewise on the Republican side, what finally got Eisenhower into the ring was less his commitment to Nixon and his running mate Henry Cabot Lodge than his contempt for Kennedy. By October he told one Oval Office visitor, as he jabbed a finger toward his desk chair, "Listen, dammit, I'm going to do everything possible to keep that Jack Kennedy from sitting in this chair." He referred to Kennedy as "Little Boy Blue," or "that young whippersnapper," a celebrity and dilettante buying the office with his father's money. And he started flashing a Nixon-Lodge badge as big as a butter plate.

Ike hated the substance of Kennedy's campaign, even though—or maybe because—it relied every bit as much on personal charisma and celebrity as Eisenhower's had. Kennedy warned of America's growing weakness, economic decline, failing prestige in the world. "To a country that has marched down the middle of the road behind Dwight Eisenhower to the highest level of shared prosperity of any nation in history," *Time* observed, "he campaigns with Depression fervor for welfare-state reform ('I am not satisfied that 17 million Americans go to bed hungry every night. . . .'). Kennedy's panacea for these problems is simple: himself. Elect me, he says, and I will start the U.S. moving forward again."

Ike had remained largely offstage through much of the campaign. But he charged in during the final days, the cavalry appearing at the crucial moment, firing back at Kennedy's "amazing irresponsibility" and "unwarranted disparagement of our moral, military and economic power" in a nationally televised speech, his most forceful in years. "Where did this young genius acquire the knowledge, experience and wisdom," he charged, "through which he will make such vast improvements over the work of the Joint Chiefs of Staff and the dedicated civilian and service men who have given their lives to this work?"

That Ike had appeared at Nixon's side at the end made his presence all the more powerful. "If Nixon had brought Eisenhower into the campaign earlier," Kennedy's friend Ken O'Donnell observed, "Kennedy would have charged him with hiding behind Ike's favorable image and being unable to stand on his own record and merits."

As withering as Ike's broadsides were, Kennedy knew he could not attack directly such a popular president. He had to move carefully, remain statesmanlike. "With every word he utters, I can feel the votes leaving me," he told his friend Red Fay as he soaked in a bathtub at the Palace Hotel in San Francisco. "It's like standing on a mound of sand with the tide running out. If the election were held tomorrow, I'd win easily, but six days from now, it's up for grabs."

But even as Ike drew immense crowds in the final days, it was clear his halo was not transferable—at least not to Nixon. WE LIKE IKE; NIX ON NIXON read the signs. Or WE LIKE IKE; WE BACK JACK. Ike's popularity averaged an astonishing 61 percent throughout his last year in office; Truman's in 1952 had been 32 percent. "Kennedy saw no reason to take him on except by indirection," said his advisor Ted Sorensen, and showing respect for the club enhanced his own claim to be worthy of joining it. When he mentioned Ike at a speech at Dartmouth and the audience hissed, Kennedy issued a rebuke: "You mustn't hiss the President of the United States." When Democrats at a meeting in Tucson condemned Mamie's trip to the "beauty ranch" Kennedy defended her: "I wouldn't criticize anything she does—she is a very fine woman."

Nixon went him one better: demonstrating his precocious sense of the club's power, he proposed on the eve of the election that if he won, he would send all three former presidents to the Soviet bloc nations on a goodwill tour, and invite communist leaders to the United States. He claimed to have discussed the idea with Eisenhower, and that it was the president who had proposed including Hoover and Truman as well. "We have our differences at home," he declared, "but abroad . . . Mr. Truman is honored because of the Marshall Plan, which I supported and which resulted in the rebuilding of Europe." Never mind that the first Ike heard of the joint mission was when Nixon announced the idea. According to Eisenhower's faithful secretary Ann Whitman, the president was "astonished" at the proposal, and "did not like the idea of 'auctioning off the presidency' in this manner." He was so angry at Nixon's speech he considered having his press secretary issue a denial before he cooled down.

But in the end even that club gambit was not enough, and Nixon fell just barely, microscopically short of the prize. "Ike's blunder in dismissing Nixon's claims of executive leadership," argues historian Robert Dallek, recalling Ike's remark about not remembering any decision Nixon had participated in, "and his failure, because of health concerns, to take a larger role in the vice president's campaign may also have been decisive factors in holding down Nixon's late surge."

Two years later, Eisenhower would publicly admit that "one of the biggest mistakes of my political career was not working harder for Dick Nixon in 1960." But the mistake was not his alone. Nixon told the story of how Mamie Eisenhower had privately implored him not to exhaust her ailing husband on the campaign trail, and Nixon had agreed, in a gesture of loyalty and sacrifice. But years later, his daughter Julie Nixon disputed the account. "Mamie says that story isn't true about her asking my father in the 1960 campaign not to call on Ike so much because of his health," Nixon's aide William Safire recalls Julie telling him. "My father had said to Ike, 'It's got to be my own campaign.'" That bit of personal pride would help delay the Nixon presidency by eight years.

The Club Brokers a Cease-Fire

The votes had barely been counted before Nixon's supporters charged that the election had been stolen; they told him about Texas counties where there were 4,895 voters on the rolls but 6,138 voted; of precincts in Chicago where after 43 people had voted, the machine had counted 121. Kennedy had won Illinois by 8,800 votes—and the ballots were quickly destroyed. Many close friends as well as party officials urged Nixon to press for an investigation; his daughters would donate their Christmas money to the recount effort.

Kennedy knew that the way the election played out posed a real threat to his legitimacy. His first mission was to establish, clearly and firmly, his rightful claim to an office he had won so narrowly and ruthlessly. He needed to send the message that the good of the country was bigger than party, beyond partisanship—a message that would only have meaning if Nixon affirmed it. Nixon wasn't saying anything yet. He hadn't demanded a recount, but hadn't explicitly rejected the idea either. Privately, Nixon was inclined not to contest the vote; it would have caused chaos, delayed the handover for months, risked a constitutional crisis, and set a disastrous example for emerging democracies around the world.

But Kennedy didn't know that. The stakes could not have been higher, and it is for precisely such missions as this that the club exists.

Kennedy enlisted it not on his own behalf, since he had as yet so little standing with its members, but on behalf of the office they all had held.

The initial overture would come from a pair of cross-party allies: President Herbert Hoover and Ambassador Joseph Kennedy. Joe Kennedy had been a mainstay of the first Hoover Commission, and through the decade the two old Fortress America warriors had remained friends.

In the days immediately following the vote, an exhausted Jack Kennedy was resting at his father's sprawling white stucco mansion in Palm Beach, Florida, so wiped out by the long ordeal that his hands shook at his press conference. Nixon and his family had flown down to Miami, crushed, exhausted, "more unresponsive than at any time I had known him," recalled his aide Herb Klein. "He was completely depressed and had finally realized, four days later, that he'd lost the election."

But the fact that both men were in Florida provided the opportunity for a conspicuous parley. Joe Kennedy called Hoover at the Waldorf; wouldn't it be a good idea for them to meet, be photographed together, to show the country that all was well and let bygones be bygones? Joe said he would arrange for Kennedy, as the victor, to fly to Miami and call on Nixon, provided Hoover could convince Nixon to see him.

Which is how it came to pass that on Saturday night, Dick and Pat were having dinner with friends at the Jamaica Inn in Key Biscayne, when word came from their hotel that President Hoover was trying to reach Nixon. "I knew he would not be calling unless it was a matter of vital importance," Nixon recalled, so he went to take the call.

"Hello, Chief," Nixon said.

Hoover did not waste any time.

"The Ambassador [Joe Kennedy] has just called me and suggested that it would be a good idea for you and the President-elect to get together for a visit," Hoover said. If Nixon agreed, Kennedy would call him to arrange the logistics.

Nixon asked Hoover what he thought he should do. As Nixon recalled it, Hoover replied that "I think we are in enough trouble in the world today; some indications of national unity are not only desirable but essential." As Hoover remembered it, Nixon resisted being party to what he called "a cheap publicity stunt," but Hoover threw that right back at him. Newly elected presidents, he informed Nixon, don't need any help getting publicity. "This is a generous gesture on his part, and you ought to meet it."

So Nixon agreed, and told Hoover to give Ambassador Kennedy the green light. Back at the table, he actually seemed elated at the call: "It was the difference between night and day," Klein recalled. They agreed that he should check in with Eisenhower first, so Nixon placed a call to the White House operator and asked if she could patch him through to Augusta, Georgia, where Eisenhower was on vacation. "He knew that it was my practice never to call him outside office hours unless the matter was of great importance," Nixon said. When the operator got Eisenhower on the line, Nixon told him about Hoover's proposal and asked what he thought. Eisenhower was just as blunt.

"You would look like a sorehead if you didn't," he said. But Nixon was under no obligation, Eisenhower assured him, of agreeing to play a role in the administration. Already there were rumors that given the tight outcome Kennedy would be inviting key Republicans into his government, with Nixon's name floated among them.

They talked for a few minutes before another call came in to interrupt dinner; this time, the maître d' said, it was Kennedy himself.

"I would like to fly down from Palm Beach to have a chat with you—if it won't interfere with your vacation," Kennedy said, and Nixon agreed, even offered to make the trip himself, adding, what were, for Kennedy, the magic words: "After all, that's the proper thing to do in view of last Tuesday's results." No recriminations: no demand for a deal or a recount. Kennedy brushed away the offer: after all, he now had a helicopter at his disposal. They agreed to meet at the Key Biscayne hotel on Monday.

"As I hung up and walked slowly back to our table," Nixon recalled, "it dawned on me that I had just participated in a probably unprecedented series of conversations. In the space of less than ten minutes, I had talked to a former President of the United States, the present president and the President-elect!"

And they, in turn, had all talked not just to the current vice president, but a future president.

When Kennedy was asked why he was making the trip—Eisenhower would never have called on Stevenson after the last two elections—Kennedy replied that "There are some things Democrats must do which

Republicans don't have to do." Or at least Democrats who have just *barely* won.

What are you going to talk to him about, his friend Ken O'Donnell asked.

"I haven't the slightest idea," Kennedy replied. "Maybe I'll ask him how he won Ohio."

It was really all about the visuals. And as it happened, a kind of ritual humiliation. Kennedy was late; Nixon had to stand waiting, surrounded by the army of reporters and photographers and tourists awaiting the president-elect, who arrived with his escort of local police and Secret Service followed by Kennedy's convertible. Kennedy sat in the backseat, Nixon recalled, "looking almost lonely." The two men proceeded to the seclusion of Nixon's Villa 69, following Navy protocol, the now higher-ranking Kennedy on the right. Pat and the girls were down at the beach, so the men sat and talked on the screened porch alone for a little over an hour.

Spokesman Pierre Salinger told reporters the purpose of the meeting was to "resume the cordial relations with Vice President Nixon that existed between them during the 14 years they served in Congress," and refused to rule out a role for Nixon in the new administration.

Now that it was all over, they talked shop; Nixon ran through the names of some career people at the CIA and State Department. They were loyal, the men agreed, but lacking perhaps in initiative and imagination. They discussed roles Republicans might play; would Nixon consider a temporary assignment overseas? Nixon graciously declined, to what he presumed was Kennedy's relief.

He did have some advice for the new president, the advice White House veterans *all* give: make use of Camp David. You will need it. I may criticize your policies, he said, but "of one thing I can assure you: I shall never join in any criticism of you, expressed or implied, for taking time off for relaxation. There is nothing more important than that a president be physically, mentally and emotionally in the best possible shape to confront the immensely difficult decisions he has to make."

Kennedy could listen politely and commit to nothing; he already had what he needed, as was plain when he spoke with reporters afterward about "the very cordial meeting." As a final indignity for the defeated warrior, Vice President Nixon had to preside over the roll call of the

Electoral College. "This is the first time in 100 years that a candidate for the presidency announced the result of an election in which he was defeated," he told the assembled members of Congress. "I do not think we could have a more striking and eloquent example of the stability of our constitutional system." He got a standing ovation.

Nixon's handling of the whole matter was widely praised—especially by Kennedy supporters. "Eisenhower and Nixon, merely by meeting with Kennedy, were patriotically recognizing the certainty of his election, and thus helping to put an end to the bitter charges of fraud, the demands for recounts and the threats of Southern independent electors," declared Sorensen. "In few other nations could so narrow a result have been so smoothly accepted." Cardinal Cushing in Boston nominated Nixon "Good Will Man of the Year." Editorials across the country lauded the Key Biscayne Summit. "Politics may turn into warfare every four years," wrote the *New York Times*, "but doesn't require that everyone stay angry. . . . The two men talking cordially for more than an hour and walking quietly away together across the green Florida golf course—all this was in our best tradition. It was political and human too."

Erasing Ike

No one is ever prepared to be president, because no job can compare to it. But at least Kennedy knew this. "If I am elected," he had told Washington wise man Clark Clifford, "I don't want to wake up on the morning of November 9 and have to ask myself, 'What in the world do I do now?'"

Kennedy asked Clifford and presidential scholar Richard Neustadt to guide him through the seventy-three days between election and inauguration. Transitions can be a series of sand traps, warned Neustadt, whose new book, *Presidential Power,* was already changing the way aspirants viewed the levers and limits of the role. The Constitution provides no machinery, no means or money or method for transferring power; in 1960 this meant 2,380,475 federal employees, a $77 billion budget, and a freshly frozen Cold War. "Everywhere there is a sense of a page turning, a new chapter in the country's history," Neustadt observed. "And with it, irresistibly, there comes the sense, 'they' couldn't, wouldn't, didn't, but 'we' will. We just have done the hardest thing there is to do in politics. Governing has got to be a pleasure by comparison."

That's a mistake many presidents make.

Clifford, having been around the White House since the Truman years, was aware of the risks—of ego as well as ignorance—that came with a new team. He set up a series of meetings between Kennedy's new appointees—who were an average of ten years younger—and their Eisenhower administration counterparts. From the start, he was disturbed by the new men's demeanor in the meetings. "They behaved as though history had begun with them. They regarded both Eisenhower and Truman (and their own Vice-President) with something bordering on contempt," he concluded. "Their new leader, the first President born in the twentieth century, was going to be *different*." With the exception of historian Arthur Schlesinger, Sorensen, and Kennedy himself, the new elite did not appear to show much interest in history, Clifford observed. "I regarded this as a form of arrogance."

Kennedy may not have shared that attitude about history, but he was every bit as eager to make a clean break. The conservatism of Ike's policies, he believed, reflected the conservatism of his process; a rigid military hierarchy that crushed innovation and sapped energy in the procedural sludge. Kennedy wanted the system to be more supple than Ike's, shaped by his strengths, matched to his metabolism, reflecting his faith in personalities over protocols. Ike had learned management in the military; Kennedy, as the child of a big family. "I never heard him talk with real interest on any topic except personalities and politics," National Security Advisor McGeorge Bundy said. One reporter described the two presidents' views of teamwork in terms of football and basketball. "The Eisenhower football method relied on regular huddles and rigid assignments. In the Kennedy Administration all team members were constantly on the move."

Kennedy vowed to be an activist president: no elaborate cabinet hierarchy to clog up the flow of information and leave him with little to do other than approve decisions already made elsewhere. Kennedy reached past Eisenhower to his hero, FDR, who had shared his lack of interest in administrative structures. "He paid little attention to organization charts and chains of command," Sorensen said of Kennedy, "which diluted and distributed his authority." The new president wanted fewer cabinet meetings; he couldn't sit still for long stretches without getting restless, couldn't bear repetition and circuitous argument. "The informality was amazing," said Fred Dutton, who had worked on the campaign and would become a special assistant. He was instructed to study Eisenhower's system—and demolish it. "They'd even have rehearsals for Cabinet meetings," he learned when he met his Republican counterparts. "Kennedy would never have tolerated that."

Ike had assembled credentialed strangers to run the government; Kennedy wanted a band of brothers to blow up the whole contraption. In its place he envisioned the spokes of a wheel, and he would be the hub. On the Monday before Thanksgiving, Clifford informed reporters that Kennedy's executive team would be much smaller than Eisenhower's, without the military system answering to a powerful chief of staff. There would be no such figure in Kennedy's White House, Clifford said, since the president did not want anyone "between him and his staff."

It all sounded just wonderful, but it was a theory that had never been tested in practice. Kennedy had no executive experience, unless you count commanding his PT boat during the war. As a House and then Senate backbencher, it was fine to function as a political freelancer, accountable to no one but the voters. He would later confess that "it was a tremendous change to go from being a Senator to being President. In the first months it is very difficult."

Ike's people tried to warn them: when Bryce Harlow, who managed Ike's congressional affairs, heard that Kennedy planned to handle relations with the Hill himself, he called special assistant Larry O'Brien in and "scared the hell out of him." I like a good political fight as much as anyone, he said, but we shouldn't be fighting over mechanics. Even in the waning days of Ike's presidency, he was fielding 125 calls a day from the Hill, not counting visits; the appointments secretary next door handled four hundred calls. From 12:01 on January 20, he said, "you won't be able to hang it up without it ringing, no matter how many lines you put on it. Now, if you think you can handle all that stuff by yourself. . . . I'm just telling you, you're going to destroy yourself and destroy your president. The President told us to be good to you guys in transition. I'm just telling you that's absolutely mad, stark raving mad."

O'Brien took the advice.

Only years later did historians dislodge from the popular imagination—and their own—the image of a detached Eisenhower delegating to his commanders in the field. Eisenhower had run the Army; he knew all the ways decision making can go off the rails, and insisted on collective debate precisely to prevent senior officials from freelancing, or putting their departmental interests first. For all the formal machinery, Eisenhower was very literally the commander in chief, making the key decisions himself and monitoring closely how they were carried out. Even years after D-Day, when critics needled him for not being on the front lines with the invading forces, he retorted, "I planned it and took responsibility for it. Did you want me to unload a truck?"

"He was a far more complex and devious man than most people realized, and in the best sense of those words," Nixon would observe. "Not shackled to a one-track mind, he always applied two, three or four lines of reasoning to a single problem. . . . His thoughts far outraced his speech and this gave rise to his frequent 'scrambled syntax.'"

In time, Kennedy would come to see that maybe he had something to learn from the old general. But not for a while yet.

The December Meeting

Kennedy got to test a few of his own theories about Ike when the two men met on December 6, the first date in what would be a careful courtship. Eisenhower had instructed his people to cooperate in every way possible; both he and Kennedy were intent on avoiding a repeat of the Truman-Eisenhower bar fight of 1952. Thanking Eisenhower for his invitation, Kennedy wired that "the whole country is hopeful that your long experience in the service of your country can be drawn upon further in the years to come."

A few nights before the meeting, Kennedy was still in Palm Beach, having dinner in the big kitchen with friends. Someone asked if he was nervous about the approaching meeting.

Kennedy laughed. "Good morning, Mr. Ke-e-nnedy," he said, mimicking Eisenhower, who was known to mispronounce Kennedy's name. Then with a bow, he swept off his hat: "Good morning, Mr. Eeee-senhower."

At the White House meanwhile, a dozen painters were putting a fresh coat on the mansion. Eisenhower hosted a farewell luncheon; he glimpsed the inaugural reviewing stands going up across Pennsylvania Avenue.

"I feel," he told friends, "like the fellow in jail who is watching his scaffold being built."

Kennedy was famous for running an hour or two late during the campaign. But on that Monday morning he left his Georgetown home so promptly he had to be driven a roundabout route to avoid arriving at the White House too soon. The cream-colored Lincoln pulled up to the North Portico at 8:58, as the Marine Band struck up "Stars and Stripes Forever" and an all-service honor guard stood at attention. Such are the trappings of the office you are about to inhabit, Ike seemed to be saying, and Kennedy jumped out before the car had stopped, his hat in his hand as he stepped lightly up the stairs where Eisenhower stood.

"Good morning Mr. President."

"Senator."

"It's good to be here," Kennedy said, in a historic understatement. And Ike ushered him into the White House.

They seemed, the *New York Times* suggested hopefully, "genuinely pleased to see each other."

The two men talked for more than an hour in the Oval Office. Kennedy admired the president's immaculate desk; his own was typically buried under a drift of books and papers. They discussed the major problems Kennedy would face—disarmament, NATO burden sharing, Laos, Berlin, Cuba. Kennedy had already been briefed by CIA chief Allen Dulles; but there was much more to learn about the parts of the world most likely to torment him in office.

Kennedy pressed Eisenhower for details about how he managed the National Security apparatus. Ike stressed that the NSC "had become the most important weekly meeting of the government"; it had met 366 times during his presidency, and he had presided at 329 of them. But Eisenhower had a growing sense of Kennedy's determination to tear the whole thing apart. They discussed Pentagon reform: a month before the election, Kennedy had received a report from a study group chaired by Senator Stuart Symington. It proposed drastically centralizing power under the secretary of defense, consolidating combat forces under four unified commands, and eliminating the Joint Chiefs of Staff. Eisenhower knew something of the proposal—"and while I consider it so useless as to be ridiculous," he wrote in his memo of the meeting, "I was careful to say nothing about the report as such."

Where to begin to teach this restless young man what lay ahead? The president ran through the various roles of the White House staff, the relations of the president and the cabinet, all the areas Kennedy was clearly intent on changing in order to speed up and stir up and centralize decision making. "No easy matters will ever come to you as President," Eisenhower warned him. "If they are easy, they will be settled at a lower level." So he urged Kennedy to avoid any reorganization until he had learned for himself the nature of the job. "I pray that he understands it," he wrote that night. "Certainly his attitude was that of a serious, earnest seeker for information."

Conscious of how thoroughly Roosevelt had exiled Hoover, and how Ike had banished Truman from any further service, Kennedy conspicuously propped the back door open. He asked whether Eisenhower would be prepared to serve again in some capacity. "Of course," Eisenhower replied, though given his age and experience, he preferred that it be consultation on something he knew about rather than "errands which might necessitate frequent and lengthy travel."

Eventually they moved into the Cabinet Room to meet with the secretaries of state, defense, and treasury. Eisenhower opened the meeting noting that "it was evident we couldn't turn over the government in the matter of two or three hours, and that he had invited Senator Kennedy to come back and see him and any of his people at any time." According to notes by Eisenhower's chief of staff, General Wilton Persons, the principals discussed Berlin ("This is acute and dangerous," Ike warned), Laos ("the strategic gateway to Southeastern Asia"), Algeria, Morocco, Sudan, India, nuclear proliferation, and Pentagon reform.

In case Kennedy wasn't getting the message, Persons recorded, "the President further pointed out that the great problem is keeping a big war from starting."

Eisenhower was pleased by the invitation to remain involved, as Kennedy had plainly intended. And he was, against all expectations, impressed. Persons later told Clifford that Ike had been "overwhelmed" by Kennedy. "What impressed the President most," Persons said, "was your man's understanding of world problems, the depth of his questions, his grasp of the issues and the keenness of his mind." Ike called him one of the "ablest, brightest minds I've ever come across," and confessed to perhaps having misjudged him.

But he also glimpsed the blind spots. "I think he was pretty quick, but my impression was this," Eisenhower told an interviewer years later, reflecting on that first encounter. "At that time, he looked on the presidency as not only a personal thing, but as an institution that one man could handle with an assistant here and another there. He had no idea of the complexity of the job at that time."

For the moment, Kennedy was glad to hear the charm offensive had worked. But "he still felt that Eisenhower was a 'non-President,'" Clifford recorded, "with only limited understanding of the powers available to him." When he recruited the Ford Motor Company's boy genius Robert McNamara to run the Pentagon after reading a profile of him, McNamara demurred, saying he didn't know anything about government. "We can learn our jobs together," Kennedy told him. After McNamara discussed the job with outgoing defense secretary Thomas Gates, he told Kennedy he was convinced he could handle the job. Kennedy smiled: "I talked over the presidency with Eisenhower," he said, "and after hearing what it's all about, I'm convinced I can handle it."

Eisenhower did have one favor he wanted from the incoming president: that Kennedy expedite Eisenhower's petition to be restored to his five-star rank. Kennedy asked Colonel Ted Clifton, acting as intermediary, about the "eccentric request." Clifton explained that as "Mr. President," Eisenhower would be in the company of Hoover, Truman, and Kennedy; five-star generals were an even rarer breed. Besides, he had worked his whole life to become a general, quite unlike his glide path to the presidency. "And if he is a five star general," Clifton told Kennedy, "he needs no favors from you or the White House."

Turning Over the Keys

Kennedy's final meeting with Eisenhower came on the day before he'd take office at last: January 19, 1961. Kennedy wanted to get together "because it would serve a specific purpose in reassuring the public as to the harmony of the transition. Therefore strengthening our hands."

They spent forty-five minutes together privately in the Oval Office: Kennedy thought Eisenhower looked "very fit, pink cheeked and unharassed."

Then it was time for the general to show the lieutenant what it really meant to be president.

This session was about life and death and power. It was almost taken for granted that a nuclear attack would come sooner or later. Eisenhower talked about the "immediate, split-second decisions" that fell only to the commander in chief. He introduced the nondescript man with the black briefcase containing the nuclear codes who would shadow the president every day he was in office. As president, Kennedy would carry a laminated card at all times, which would allow him to pick from thirty pages of lethal options, activate missile silos, surface the submarines. Ike explained it all with a cool confidence that Kennedy found almost chilling.

And then, one final show. Eisenhower picked up the phone and smiled. "Watch this."

"Opal Drill Three," he said crisply into the phone. Within about three minutes, a Marine helicopter had swooped in and was hovering outside on the White House lawn. Kennedy loved it.

Together they went over to the Cabinet Room, where the incoming and outgoing cabinet secretaries were gathered. "I've shown my friend here how to get out in a hurry," Eisenhower told them with a laugh.

Eisenhower presided; each cabinet officer ran through the problems and responsibilities that would soon fall to the new team. The bulk of the meeting was focused on Laos, and the prospect of dominoes toppling under Sino-Soviet pressure: "It is like playing poker with tough stakes," Ike said. "There is no easy solution."

And then there was Cuba. Kennedy already knew that the CIA was training Cuban exiles in Guatemala in preparation for an invasion. Had he not been briefed by the CIA, he could have read about it in the *New York Times*: "US Helps Train an Anti-Castro Force at Secret Guatemalan Base," declared the headline nine days before—thereby ensuring that the "secret" part, at least, was no longer operative. Eisenhower explained that no specific invasion plan had been set, and stressed the importance of finding a legitimate Cuban leader to set up a government in exile and provide an alternative to Castro. "In the long run," Eisenhower said, "the

United States cannot allow the Castro government to continue to exist in Cuba."

"The tone of the old soldier—on his last day of public service, half a century after entering the United States Military Academy—had a powerful effect on Kennedy," Clifford wrote in his memoirs. Kennedy's men didn't know enough about the situation in Southeast Asia to challenge Ike's assessment. "In retrospect, I believe that President Eisenhower, while sincere, did a disservice to the incoming administration," Clifford said. Having himself resisted getting drawn into a land war in Asia, Eisenhower now took a much harder line—"sensing in the men of the New Frontier," Ewald suggested, "inexperience . . . and a tendency to tilt soft." It "cast a shadow over the early decisions of the next administration," Clifford argued. "Its consequences, moreover, affected Vietnam and even Cuba." Given the colossal failures in presidential decision making in the months ahead, Kennedy loyalists would never miss a chance to lay the blame at least in part at Eisenhower's feet.

When it was over, Kennedy thanked Eisenhower for giving them everything they asked for and offering ideas they hadn't thought to ask about.

"You are welcome—more than welcome," Eisenhower replied. "This is a question of the Government of the United States. It is not a partisan question."

As the meeting broke up, Eisenhower took Kennedy aside, to make one last point. Whatever you may have said in the campaign about a supposed "missile gap" between the United States and the USSR, Eisenhower said, the Soviets were nowhere near as powerful as they pretended. "You have an invulnerable asset in Polaris," he said, referring to America's submarine-launched missiles. "It is invulnerable."

Kennedy came away from this last meeting grateful, and sober, and determined never to cross his popular predecessor if he could possibly help it.

The Torch Has Been Passed . . .

Finally, it was time to celebrate. The entire city had primped and prepped for the big day ahead. The National Park Service sprayed the grass around the Lincoln Memorial with fresh green dye, simulating spring. Trees along the inaugural route were coated in Roost-No-More to repel the starlings. Secret Service agents sealed the manhole covers to foil bombers; there were snipers on the rooftops, five thousand men on security detail. But even they could not protect against the weather.

That afternoon after his White House meeting, Kennedy attended a governors reception, then visited with Truman; the traffic snarled into knots as the first snowflakes fell. By that night at least ten thousand cars were stalled and abandoned. Planes couldn't land; President Hoover, flying up from Florida, had to turn back and never made it to the inauguration. It took Pat Nixon more than two hours to get to her husband's farewell party at the Senate. At the White House, dozens of members of Eisenhower's staff were snowbound for the night, as three thousand men and seven hundred plows worked around the clock clearing the streets.

It was still cold in the morning, but clear. And the atmosphere at the White House was altogether warmer than eight years before. Jack and Jackie had coffee with the Eisenhowers, the Johnsons, and the Nixons, in one of those rare club initiation ceremonies that included future presidents as well as present and outgoing ones. There would be no homburgs this time; Eisenhower and Kennedy emerged in their top hats and rode together in the black, bubble-topped limousine to the Capitol, where they waited for their call to the platform.

It was somehow fitting that their final conversation before the handover of power was about a book Kennedy was reading in which Eisenhower was a character: *The Longest Day*, Cornelius Ryan's book about D-Day. "He was fascinated that Eisenhower had never read the book," Bobby Kennedy recalled.

As Richard Cardinal Cushing rose to give the invocation, little wisps of smoke began to rise from the podium from a short circuit. "If that smoke indicates a bomb and if the bomb explodes while I'm praying," Cushing recalled thinking, "I'm going to land over on the Washington Monument." At that point Eisenhower leaned over and whispered to Kennedy: "You must have a hot speech."

Kennedy was struck again by the sheer force Eisenhower radiated. "The vitality of the man!" Kennedy marveled that night. "It stood out so strongly there at the Inauguration. There was [Secretary of State] Chris Herter, looking old and ashen. There was Allen Dulles, gray and tired.

There was Bob Anderson, with his collar seeming two sizes too large on a shrunken neck. And there was the oldest of them all, Ike—as healthy and ruddy and as vital as ever."

When it was all over, Ike and Mamie slipped out quietly. They realized, Ike wrote later, that "We were free—as only private citizens in a democratic nation can be free." He planned to write, lecture, guide his party into the future. "Believe me," he promised friends, "I'm going to be heard from."

Late that afternoon he and Mamie rode in their Chrysler Imperial back to their Gettysburg farm. Now there was no motorcade, no motorcycles or sirens or lights, just a Secret Service car in front and behind. But people turned out, with WELCOME HOME signs. When they arrived at the farm, the agents honked their horns, did a U-turn, and headed back to Washington.

That night Nixon asked his official driver to take him around the city one last time. He went to the Capitol, through the Rotunda, down a long corridor, and out onto the now empty balcony looking over the west grounds of the Capitol. The Mall was snow-white, the monuments gleaming. "I stood there looking at the scene for at least five minutes," he recalled. But "as I turned to go inside, suddenly stopped short, struck by the thought that this was not the end—that someday I would be back here." And then he hurried back to his car.

Kennedy began tending the club from the very first day. The first letter he dictated was to Eisenhower, thanking him again for all his help. "I am sure that your generous assistance has made this one of the most effective transitions in the history of our Republic."

His first visitor at the White House was Harry Truman, finally restored to an honored place as elder statesman. After dinner, the men strolled around the mansion that the Trumans had helped preserve as a national treasure—and where he had not stepped foot in eight years. At the entrance to the East Wing, they paused in front of the gold-lettered dedication on the wall commemorating the Truman restoration of the mansion. As the story goes, Kennedy remarked dryly to Truman: "The S.O.B. [Eisenhower] had a painting over it."

6

"The Worse I Do, the More Popular I Get"

—JOHN F. KENNEDY

It took less than seventy-two hours from the start of the U.S. invasion of Cuba in April of 1961 for it to become apparent that everything that could go wrong did.

The original plan called for two waves of air strikes in support of the invading Cuban exiles that the United States had been training in Guatemala; one strike would come two days in advance to take out Cuba's air force; at the last minute President Kennedy cut the size of that strike in half, to keep the noise level down. "I believe the president did not realize that the air strike was an integral part of the operational plan he had approved," CIA operations chief Richard Bissell later wrote in his memoirs, and indeed much of Cuban dictator Fidel Castro's airpower survived the initial bombardment. The second planned strike, to support the actual invasion at the Bay of Pigs, was canceled altogether. Again the CIA went along, assuming Kennedy would reverse course and send in U.S. forces "when the chips were down."

The plan also assumed that the invaders could slip into the mountains to take up guerrilla operations; but that proved impossible, which seemed to come as a surprise not only to the president but to many of the other principals involved in approving the mission. "The Cuban armed forces are stronger, the popular response is weaker, and our tactical position is feebler than we had hoped," National Security Advisor McGeorge Bundy wrote in a grim memo to Kennedy. Analysts studying the surveillance films had mistaken the sharp coral reefs of the Bay of Pigs for seaweed—so the landing crafts ran aground that first morning and were raked by Castro's antique jet fighters. Ten days' worth of ammunition, food, and communications equipment was lost when a single freighter was sunk. Castro, well aware of what was coming, had rounded up anyone who might have remotely considered supporting the invaders. So there was no popular support, no sudden eruption of civil war, no relief for the U.S.-trained exiles pinned down on the beach, and no escape to the mountains beyond.

In short, a fiasco.

On the night after the invasion, Kennedy attended a reception honoring members of Congress, then slipped away after midnight, still in formal dress, to meet in the Cabinet Room with leaders from the CIA, Pentagon, NSC, and top aides. "There were all these people in white ties and medals," Walt Rostow, the NSC deputy, recalled. "It was a marvelous demonstration of the limitations of power, the greatest power in the world, and this little operation fails."

That failure would darken Kennedy's first hundred days, enrage U.S. allies abroad, and shake his confidence in the vast military and intelligence machine over which he now presided. When the president's men were pressed in the months and years that followed to explain the disastrous Bay of Pigs invasion, most of them invoked a basic club reality: that presidents inherit the foreign policy of their predecessors. They inherit their wars and their treaties and in this case their covert operations. "It wasn't Kennedy's plan; it was Eisenhower's," insisted undersecretary of state George Ball. "He was very in awe of Eisenhower and, I think, he felt he had no option but to go through with it." It was executed by men Ike had appointed, Kennedy's allies argued; there was no way that a young new president could have rejected the great general's plan to rid the hemisphere of a communist menace without being crucified as a coward.

But while blame is easy, actual responsibility is not quite so simple. Eisenhower would never have approved the absurd, jerry-built invasion plan in its final form, countered others who had served both presidents. Kennedy may have thought he was following Ike's lead, not to mention his CIA director, Allen Dulles; but he had also rejected the checks and balances that Ike had relied on to protect him from such debacles.

The Making of a Disaster

"No man entering upon this office," Kennedy declared in his January 30 State of the Union address, "could fail to be staggered upon learning— even in this brief 10 day period—the harsh enormity of the trials through which we must pass in the next four years. Each day the crises multiply. Each day their solution grows more difficult."

Though you wouldn't know it to hear him talk, "John F. Kennedy had discovered no skeletons in the Eisenhower closet, no cataclysmic secret-intelligence reports," *Time* observed in a story called "Man Meets Presidency." "But he had discovered that even a well-informed, alert Senator and President-elect has no conception of the responsibilities of the U.S. presidency."

Eisenhower's attempt to introduce him to those responsibilities when they met after the election included an update on plans regarding Cuba. Eisenhower's approach to the Castro challenge was political as well as military. At a meeting in March 1960, Eisenhower had instructed the CIA to assemble a plausible Cuban government in exile, step up internal propaganda and intelligence gathering while training a paramilitary force of Cuban exiles in Guatemala—but only training. "I will reserve to myself whether they will actually be committed or not," he said at the time. He wanted flexibility—and secrecy. "Everyone must be prepared to swear that he has not heard of it," Ike said.

Eisenhower's aide Andrew Goodpaster remembers warning him of the risk he was taking just by letting the training commence.

"I said to him 'there is always the danger that this will develop a momentum of its own,' " Goodpaster said. "He kind of snapped back at me, 'Not so long as I'm here.'

"And I said 'Yes sir. That's just the problem.' "

Shortly after the election, Dulles and his operations chief, Richard Bissell, flew down to Palm Beach to brief Kennedy. Already the momentum Goodpaster warned of was building: the original underground operation was turning into a full-fledged amphibious invasion, which would require a far larger force—and therefore a larger U.S. role—to stand any chance of success. According to the CIA's own secret history of the Bay of Pigs operation, the invasion task force had already concluded that it could not succeed without open participation by U.S. forces. "Our original concept is now seen to be unachievable in the face of the controls Castro has instituted." But they didn't mention that to Kennedy.

When Ike and Kennedy met in December and January, Eisenhower still endorsed the goal of removing Castro, without appreciating how the mission was evolving. George Ball recalled that in their final session, Eisenhower told Kennedy that "I am trusting you, as a head of state, to carry this through." The problem is, by that point the outgoing president was no longer in control of the scheme he was handing over to his successor.

Eight days after he took office, on January 28, 1961, Kennedy got his first full Cuba briefing as president; he heard, among other things, that nothing currently on the drawing boards was sufficient to oust Castro from office. He told the CIA to continue with sabotage and propaganda efforts, while working with the Pentagon to develop a viable invasion plan.

By February it was clear that the State Department was worried about the political risks of a plot that was fast becoming an open secret. But despite questions about the CIA's ability to mount a major military operation, the atmosphere at most meetings was one of "assumed consensus. The CIA representatives dominated the discussion," Schlesinger said. "The Joint Chiefs seemed to be going contentedly along."

At a briefing on March 11, Kennedy's own doubts deepened. He did not want his first major foreign policy act to involve being caught invading a sovereign country in violation of all the international principles the United States charged the Soviets with flouting. The plans laid out by Dulles and Bissell were "too spectacular," Kennedy warned. "It sounds like D-Day. You have to reduce the noise level of this thing." The planners agreed, just to keep the operation alive—even though success depended on the invasion triggering an uprising, so it needed to be as noisy as possible. Every action taken to try to reduce the political risk had the effect of increasing the military risk—and therefore the likelihood of failure.

So why did Kennedy let the planning move forward through the winter? In their recollections, his advisors suggest that the ghost of Eisenhower haunted the halls. "He's in office ten days; is he going to call this thing off just because he thinks it isn't going to work?" asked Ambassador Angier Biddle Duke, Kennedy's chief of protocol. "He didn't trust his own judgment at that time. He respected the Supreme Allied Commander, the twice-elected president of the United States, and this venerable figure, Allen Dulles."

Kennedy, who knew something about managing strong father figures, may have shown little respect for Eisenhower in the political arena; but the military was another matter. "Allen Dulles didn't say it—but he didn't have to," Schlesinger recalled, "that in the United States, the notion that a fellow who had been a lieutenant JG in the Second World War would overrule a plan agreed to by the commander of the greatest amphibious invasion in history would not have gone down. He was really trapped by what he inherited."

It was not just the plan, but the people they inherited, Bobby Kennedy claimed in 1964, that had lulled Kennedy into false confidence. "He came into government as the successor to President Eisenhower, who was a great general, a great military figure. . . . He retained the same people in all these key positions whom President Eisenhower had. Allen Dulles was there, [Joint Chiefs chairman] Lemnitzer was there, the same Joint Chiefs of Staff. He didn't attempt to move any of these people out. . . . It was on their recommendations and suggestions and their intelligence information—what they found the situation to be on *their* homework— that he based his decision."

Such excuses simply ignored the fact that Eisenhower had far more experience managing spies and generals, a more careful decision-making structure, and a deep skepticism about posturing politicians. Kennedy had campaigned on the promise that he would be even tougher than Eisenhower and Nixon when it came to the communists and Castro. "Are you really going to tell this group of fine young men," Dulles challenged him, "who are ready to die for their country that they get no sympathy and support from you?" Not to mention that if they were disbanded, they would spread the word that Kennedy had betrayed their mission to depose a dictator who was subverting the hemisphere.

The Floating Crap Game

As planning progressed through March into April, the doubts and debate unrolled: Dulles was not beyond invoking Eisenhower directly. "Mr. President, I know you're doubtful about this," he said during one briefing. "But I stood at this very desk and said to President Eisenhower about a similar operation in Guatemala [when the CIA helped overthrow the Arbenz government in 1954], 'I believe it will work.' And I say to you now, Mr. President, that the prospects for this plan are even better than our prospects were in Guatemala."

Bissell sensed that Kennedy had visions of headlines declaring how he had "lost" Cuba within a few weeks of taking office by throwing away an established plan. Bissell was in a strong position to ease that fear, since he was no ordinary spy. He had a Ph.D. in economics from Yale, had taught at Yale and MIT, even taught Bundy. He was smooth, smart, calm, compelling, a thinking man's spymaster, who many thought was the inevitable choice to succeed Dulles. So together they worked to reassure the president; they came back on March 16 with new alternatives, including moving the invasion from the city of Trinidad to a more remote landing spot called Bahía de Cochinos, or Bay of Pigs. At the end of March, Kennedy stressed again that there would be no overt U.S. military support under any circumstances—and was assured the landing could still succeed and trigger a popular uprising.

What Kennedy did not know was that their confidence in its success depended on how they thought he would react to its failure. They counted on Kennedy to unleash the full might of the U.S. armed forces once the initial incursion met the inevitable resistance. It was either that, or face a humiliation they assumed no new president would accept. They did not mention that two of the top planners wanted to resign, convinced the scaled-back plan could no longer work.

By this point some in the CIA were referring to the White House as "the floating crap game." Kennedy had held only two cabinet meetings, and convened the full National Security Council only twice; he preferred ad hoc task forces that he could form and dissolve at will. "Kennedy really didn't get himself involved in what might be called housekeeping functions; he didn't care about them," Fred Dutton recalled. Something about large meetings just bothered him, Dutton concluded, an invitation for people to act pretentious.

He would pick up the phone and call professors, reporters, lowly desk officers at the State Department; it took a while for bureaucrats to realize that the voice on the phone claiming to be the president was not a crank caller. And Kennedy had a special faith in those on the front lines. "If someone comes in to tell me this or that about the minimum wage bill, I have no hesitation in overruling them," he told Schlesinger later. "But you always assume that the military and intelligence people have some secret skill not available to ordinary mortals."

Senate Foreign Relations Committee chair J. William Fulbright, who opposed the Cuba plan, also frowned on the random quality of the meetings and decision-making process; no hierarchy, no obvious chain of command or responsibility. Kennedy's "spokes of the wheel" management philosophy meant that "there was no locked door to the Oval Office," Salinger said. "There were twelve of us who had access to that office at any time of the day." In the first week of April, with D-Day less than two weeks away, National Security Advisor McGeorge Bundy, the former dean of faculty at Harvard, was sufficiently worried about the process to send Kennedy a memo. "More than once the ball has been dropped," he warned, "because no one person felt a continuing clear responsibility."

The Cuba operation was code-named Bumpy Road. And that about said it all. "I know everybody is grabbing their nuts on this," Kennedy told Sorensen just before the invasion. And it would not be long before their worst fears were realized.

Damage Control

Even as it became clear the invasion was a disaster, its promoters scrambled to avoid the worst. When the principals met in the Oval Office late into the night on April 18, after two days of combat, Bissell was still insisting that the mission could be salvaged if Kennedy sent Navy fighters to provide air support.

"Let me take two jets and shoot down the enemy aircraft," demanded the chief of naval operations, Admiral Arleigh Burke.

"I don't want the United States to get involved in this," Kennedy insisted.

"Hell, Mr. President," Burke shot back, "we are involved."

The meeting was still going on at 4 A.M. At one point Kennedy broke away practically in mid-sentence, went out into the Rose Garden, and walked alone in the cool spring night air for about forty-five minutes. The others just watched him out the windows. "He seemed to me a depressed and lonely man," Sorensen said.

Jackie Kennedy would recall the sheer weight of that failure on her eager, optimistic husband. "He came back to the White House to his bedroom and he started to cry, just with me," she told Schlesinger three years later. "Just put his head in his hands and sort of wept. It was so sad, because all his first 100 days and all his dreams, and then this awful thing to happen. And he cared so much."

In the end Kennedy agreed to one round of air cover for a morning bombing run—which set up one last debacle. The CIA dispatched B-26 bombers from Nicaragua; the Navy sent the fighters from the carrier *Essex*. Since they came from different time zones, they arrived over their target an hour apart. Two of the bombers were shot down, killing four pilots from the Alabama Air National Guard. More than a thousand of the exiles, who had fought valiantly, had no choice but to surrender. The last message from José "Pepe" San Román, the brigade commander, would be "How can you people do this to us?"

"The President," Sorensen observed, "having approved the plan with assurances that it would be both clandestine and successful, thus found in fact that it was too large to be clandestine and too small to be successful."

The full cabinet met the next day: it was, observed Ambassador at Large Chester Bowles, "about as grim as any meeting I can remember in all my experience in government, which is saying a good deal. The President was really quite shattered, and understandably so." Bowles had been among the liberal opponents of the whole enterprise. Now that it had gone bad, Bowles recounted, "reactions around the table were almost savage, as everyone appeared to be jumping on everyone else." As he saw it, Kennedy's confidence had been fed by a life of near misses and lucky escapes. "Here for the first time he faced a situation where his judgment had been mistaken, in spite of the fact that week after week of conferences had taken place before he gave the green light."

But Fred Dutton saw something different at that meeting. He remembered Kennedy talking through what had happened, brutally, painfully, but taking full responsibility for it. "Even with the Cabinet there at a moment like that, he didn't ask them to rally round," Dutton argued. "He didn't say that they were to avoid criticism; he didn't give them a public line they were to take." And the same held true when he faced reporters that Friday. "There's an old saying, that victory has a hundred fathers and defeat is an orphan," he said. "I am the responsible officer of the government and that is quite obvious."

But privately, his aides said, he was asking the same question again and again. "All my life I've known better than to depend on the experts," he told Sorensen. "How could I have been so stupid, to let them go ahead?" The problem was not just that he didn't know them, know their strengths and weaknesses; it was that they didn't know him either. "They couldn't believe that a new president like me wouldn't panic and try to save his own face," Kennedy said, realizing at last that the whole plan depended on him sending troops to salvage the mission. "Well, they had me figured all wrong."

The response around the world was blistering; the denunciation every bit as great as if he had openly invaded. Khrushchev called the effort "a crime which has revolted the entire world." America appeared aggressive and weak at the same time. "You succeeded in Guatemala, and that left a scar," a Latin American diplomat told a U.S. diplomat at the U.N. "You failed in Cuba, and that will leave a double scar." Truman's secretary of state Dean Acheson was in Europe at the time—"and this really shattered the Europeans. It was such a completely unthought out, irresponsible thing to do," he said. "They had tremendously high expectations of the new administration, and when this thing happened they just fell miles down with a crash."

Columnist Walter Lippmann, making his television debut, complained that all Kennedy had accomplished in his first months in office was to be a pale shadow of his predecessor. The administration, he argued, was "like the Eisenhower Administration thirty years younger." In the Kennedy White House there was no crueler taunt.

So he began the damage control, and here Kennedy wanted help from people he could hardly have imagined calling just four months earlier.

He reached out to Nixon, whose daughter Tricia, when she saw the message from the White House, said, "I knew it! It wouldn't be long before he would get into trouble and have to call on you for help." Nixon called back, and Kennedy asked that he come to the White House. They met in the Oval Office: "The atmosphere was tense," Nixon said. He recalled Kennedy pacing angrily, cursing the CIA, the Joint Chiefs, the White House staff: "I was assured by every son of a bitch I checked with—all the military experts and the CIA—that the plan would succeed."

The two talked for nearly an hour. "It really is true that foreign affairs is the only important issue for a president to handle isn't it?" Kennedy admitted. "I mean, who gives a shit if the minimum wage is $1.15 or $1.25, in comparison to something like this?" As Nixon left, he recalled, "I felt empathy for a man who had to face up to a bitter tragedy that was not entirely his fault but was nonetheless his inescapable responsibility."

Kennedy knew Herbert Hoover would not be a problem either. He paid a call on the former president at the Waldorf. "You know I'm a Quaker and I loathe war, but, by heavens," Hoover told Kennedy, "if I were President of the United States I would order the necessary forces into the Bay of Pigs and I would decimate that Cuban army while they're there. . . . I'd end the thing forthright [*sic*]."

But the only meeting that mattered was the one with Eisenhower, who was maybe the only man on the planet with the power to help Kennedy put the disaster behind him. The two hadn't been in touch much: Eisenhower had cabled a thanks in March for Kennedy's proposal that Congress restore his Army rank. But relations were formal and distant, until the moment came when Kennedy needed a serious second opinion.

To this point, Kennedy had never stepped foot on the grounds of Camp David, the presidential retreat established by FDR and renamed for Eisenhower's grandson. The next day, Kennedy climbed into a helicopter to make his maiden trip to the Catoctin, Maryland, mountains— where he would commune with Eisenhower, who came in from nearby Gettysburg and would show him around the place.

"You go down there and tell that little boy to be careful," one woman wired Ike from Iowa. "In fact, you'd better go and take over yourself."

Because this was no time for rookies. "Is there a possibility that if you had been president, the Bay of Pigs would have happened?" his son John asked. Eisenhower reminded him of D-Day.

"I don't run no bad invasions."

To the Woodshed

Kennedy may not have cared what Ike had to say. But he knew he at least had to appear to. If nothing else, the image of the two of them consulting would go a long way to reassuring people that the young president was getting the advice he needed.

Dulles had briefed Eisenhower the day before, so the former president had at least an outline of what had gone wrong.

When Ike arrived at Camp David, Kennedy came to the helipad to meet him, and they immediately set to reviewing the facts. Kennedy struck the older man as candid, and chastened. "He seemed to be very frank but also very subdued and more than a little bit bewildered," Eisenhower said later. "I quizzed him rather closely. He seemed himself at that moment." The two men had quite a different, more raw and private, encounter than they had had during their formal transition meetings only months before.

They had a fried chicken lunch in Aspen Cabin, then sat in the picture window, looking out over the two-hole putting green.

"No one knows how tough this job is until he has been in it a few months," Kennedy admitted.

"Mr. President," Eisenhower replied, "if you will forgive me, I think I mentioned that to you three months ago."

"I certainly have learned a lot since."

Kennedy ran through the whole story, the pressures he had faced, the promises he'd been made, the serial failures of intelligence, timing, transport, tactics. The general listened, and then called him on the carpet.

"The point of pride between the two men," argues Ike's grandson David Eisenhower in his memoir, *Going Home to Glory: A Memoir of Life with Dwight D. Eisenhower, 1961–1969*, "had to do with their differing views about the NSC and Eisenhower's elaborate staff system, which Schlesinger later said Bundy was 'slaughtering' with such glee. To Ike,

Kennedy's most irritating campaign promise had been to restore Roosevelt's improvisational methods of organization."

So Eisenhower pressed Kennedy on how the decision had been made, who had weighed in and how. Eisenhower's military life taught him that talent was a necessary but not sufficient condition for success. The only way to guarantee smart decisions, Ike believed, was to bring all the responsible parties together and have them fight it out. "I do not believe in bringing them in one at a time and therefore being more impressed by the most recent one you hear," he said later. "You must get courageous men, men of strong views and let them debate and argue with each other."

So he pressed the case: "Mr. President, before you approved this plan, did you have everybody in front of you debating the thing so you got the pros and cons yourself and then made the decision, or did you see these people one at a time?"

"Well, I did have a meeting," Kennedy said. But it was never the whole Security Council. "I just approved a plan that had been recommended by the CIA and by the Joint Chiefs of Staff. I just took their advice."

But did you change the plan after the Joint Chiefs had signed off? Having commanded the chiefs himself, he understood that when the generals are talking to the president, their verbal support for a plan carried little weight; a commitment has to be in writing. Kennedy admitted to scaling back the air cover. Ike pressed him on this: why did he change plans after the troops were already at sea?

The challenge, Kennedy reminded him, was to try to hide America's hand in the whole operation. "We thought that if it was learned that we were really doing this and not those rebels themselves, the Soviets would be very apt to cause trouble in Berlin."

That was exactly wrong, Eisenhower shot back. The men in the Kremlin admire strength, and understand coldly calculated self-interest. "If they see us show any weakness, that is when they press us the hardest. The second they see us show strength and do something on our own, that is when they are very cagey." The failure of the Bay of Pigs, Eisenhower predicted, will just embolden Khrushchev to do something that he would not otherwise do.

On that point, Eisenhower would soon be proven right.

As for concealing the U.S. role, Eisenhower was derisive. "Mr. President, how could you expect the world to believe that we had nothing to do with it? Where did these people get the ships to go from Central America to Cuba? Where did they get the weapons? Where did they get all the communications and all the other things they would need? How could you possibly have kept from the world any knowledge that the US had been involved?"

And then he suggested, as he had during their pre-inauguration meetings, that success mattered more than secrecy—which was just what the CIA had assumed Kennedy would think. "I believe there is only one thing to do when you get into this kind of thing," Eisenhower said. "It must be a success." Or, of course, don't get in at all.

"Well," Kennedy replied, "I assure you that hereafter, if we get into anything like this, it is going to be a success."

Eisenhower said he would support anything that prevented the communists from strengthening their position in the Western Hemisphere. But the American people will not support a direct invasion, he warned, unless faced with extreme provocation. At no point, Eisenhower was relieved to find, did Kennedy suggest that the problem was an inherited plan gone wrong.

The two men walked the paths of the 125-acre compound and talked into the spring afternoon. It was surrounded by an electrified fence, guarded by Marines, the cameras corralled at a safe distance—all designed to give them the privacy they needed.

The encounter ended with the all-important photo op, the show of presidential solidarity that would signal the world that even a humbled America remained united in its resolve. "Eisenhower Urges Nation to Back Kennedy on Cuba" ran the front-page headline in the *New York Times*, next to the picture of them walking the paths, heads down, Ike's hands and hat clasped behind his back. "I asked President Eisenhower here to bring him up to date on recent events and get the benefit of his thoughts and experience," Kennedy said. Eisenhower dutifully declared, "I am all in favor of the United States supporting the man who has to carry the responsibility for our foreign affairs."

When it was over, Eisenhower was eager to show his pupil the grounds; he knew his way around, knew some of the personnel. The compound included a bowling alley and movie theater, an unheated pool, a skeet range, and the one- and two-room cabins Roosevelt had had built and equipped with his favorite chiming Navy clocks. He walked him down to a small cottage called Dogwood. "I want you to see what these are like," he said. Then Kennedy drove Eisenhower back to the helipad, and suggested they play golf together soon.

Eisenhower had renamed Roosevelt's Shangri-La as Camp David, and it was of course Kennedy's prerogative to change the name again. Three days after the visit, the White House announced that contrary to any speculation, the official presidential retreat would continue to be known as Camp David.

The Loyal Opposition

Eisenhower proved to be a faithful ally in the days that followed. When New York's Republican congressman Bill Miller charged that Kennedy had crippled the invasion by calling off Eisenhower's air cover plan, Ike spoke up to deny that there had ever been such a specific plan.

A week after the Camp David meeting, the Republican congressional leadership made a pilgrimage to Gettysburg to meet with Eisenhower, hoping to hear a ringing denunciation of his callow successor. Instead he warned them sternly against "witch-hunting."

"Don't go back and rake over the ashes," he insisted, "but see what we can do better in the future."

But privately Eisenhower bristled at the persistent story line quietly pushed by some Kennedy loyalists that Eisenhower was somehow complicit, perhaps even to blame. He was under growing pressure to take Kennedy on; the mystique had cracked—and the Republicans were without a strong voice of loyal opposition. "In the wake of the Cuba news," David Eisenhower recalled, "Eisenhower gave serious thought to the idea of forming something like a 'shadow government' built on maintaining close links to his former cabinet and GOP elective officials." He invited some old friends and counselors to a lunch in Gettysburg, including former commerce secretary Sinclair Weeks, Senator Thruston Morton, former budget director Maurice Stans, Attorney General William Rogers, U.N. Ambassador James Wadsworth, NSC Secretary Gordon Gray, and Agriculture Secretary Ezra Taft Benson.

The lunch guests argued that Kennedy's honeymoon was over; that the administration was doing everything it could to undermine Eisenhower's record and reputation; that the Republicans needed a strong presence on the stage to challenge Kennedy's media dominance. On the Bay of Pigs, Kennedy only reached out to Republicans after the fact, "in an effort to diffuse responsibility," Eisenhower observed. "I will not be held to blame for Cuba having been consulted after the fact."

"People still have faith in you," said Benson, a member of the newly formed archconservative John Birch Society. "Take the gloves off. Opposing Kennedy is not the same thing as disloyalty to the United States." But Eisenhower had always had strong views about not getting into specific personalities; and by this time he had fully internalized the protocols of the club.

"As emeritus," he told them, "I must be silent."

Gordon Gray warned about yelling "failure" after one hundred days, and the group agreed that Eisenhower would remain above the fray.

In the weeks that followed Eisenhower would hear after-action reports from friends back in Washington and around the country. He included in one diary entry a sketch of the invasion zone that he had been given by a former Latin American ambassador who had served as an advisor to the planning. It laid out how at one point the necessary air cover was over the target area but called back on orders from the White House, abandoning the invaders to their fate on the beaches.

He continued to be supportive in public, but his private contempt was sharp. "It is a very dreary account of mismanagement, indecision, and timidity at the wrong time," Eisenhower wrote in his diary. Were it to become public, as he suspected it would, there would be a huge furor. "If true, this story could be called a 'Profile in Timidity and Indecision.'"

Lessons Learned

That wasn't far from the conclusion reached by the CIA's inspector general, Lyman Kirkpatrick, when he conducted a postmortem. His report, one of the most secret documents of the Cold War, accused Bissell and his aides of "playing [the invasion] by ear" by setting up an "anarchic and disorganized" command structure. The operation was doomed by "bad planning," "poor" staffing, bad intelligence, and "a failure to advise the President that success had become dubious."

NSC Advisor Bundy offered to resign, but Kennedy refused. Bundy wrote a long memo, laying out the flaws in Kennedy's manner and methods and comparing them unfavorably to Truman's and Eisenhower's. "We can't get you to sit still," Bundy charged. "Calling three meetings in five days is foolish—and putting them off for six weeks at a time is just as bad." Half the reports Kennedy had asked for were never reviewed because by the time he was available to read them, he had moved on.

Bundy invoked his predecessors, with the clear suggestion that maybe Kennedy could learn something from the old guys. "Truman and Eisenhower did their daily dozens in foreign affairs the first thing in the morning," he noted, "and a couple of weeks ago you asked me to begin to meet with you on this basis. I have succeeded in catching you on three mornings, for a total of about eight minutes, and I conclude that this is not really how you like to begin the day."

The Bay of Pigs changed Kennedy's approach to executive management. He stopped believing that the judgment of professionals was infallible, and he rebuilt part of the Eisenhower system, even reviving some of the committees he had been so intent on stamping out. In 1956 Eisenhower had established the President's Board of Consultants on Foreign Intelligence Activities—with Joe Kennedy as one of the original members. Kennedy originally planned to abolish it, along with the rest of the bureaucratic clutter that interfered with vigorous foreign policy. After the Bay of Pigs he "reactivated it," with a new title, the President's Foreign Intelligence Advisory Board (PFIAB) and named as chairman the man Eisenhower had chosen as his science advisor: MIT president James Killian Jr. And he fired Dulles.

Kennedy found a way to show his gratitude at the end of so tumultuous a year, to the man who had warned him, and then supported him when it counted. He sent his new CIA director, John McCone, an old friend of Ike's, out to Palm Desert, California, to brief the general; McCone arrived a few days after Christmas, bearing a box of golf balls with the Presidential Seal and a handwritten note from Kennedy.

"Dear General," Kennedy wrote, this time using the title Ike preferred,

"I have received these golf balls for Christmas, but regrettably because of my back, I cannot use them for many months. You are the only other golfer I know entitled to them—and I send them with my best wishes."

Eisenhower refused to criticize Kennedy's handling of the disaster; but he had come to realize how much less power an ex-president has than a sitting one to shape the narrative of events. He was sufficiently concerned about how his role would be remembered that just this one time, as historian Stephen Ambrose explained, he set out to have the official record emended to reflect his memory of what had happened.

It all went back to the key meeting of March 1960, when he had first approved the CIA training mission. Two months after the invasion, Ike reached out to his inner circle and asked them for their recollections of that meeting; his aide Gordon Gray replied that he actually had notes of the conversation, stored with Eisenhower's other classified presidential papers at Fort Ritchie in Maryland. Ike sent his son John to retrieve them, and then sat with Gray in Gettysburg going over the record. The account did confirm the importance Ike had placed on there being a plausible government in exile in place before any move was made on Castro. But it was when they came across the word "planning" that Eisenhower recoiled.

"This is wrong," he insisted. "We did no military planning." All he had approved was the training of the Cuban exiles, not a blueprint for their deployment. "With your permission," he told Gray, "I'm going to have this page rewritten to reflect the facts." Gray agreed; more than a decade later, he wrote to the assistant director of the Eisenhower library explaining how the original version of the memo had been misleading, and how they had altered it.

For Kennedy, the Bay of Pigs was the low point, but hardly the only challenge of that first year. He struggled to hold back Soviet influence in Laos, Angola, and the Congo after its president was assassinated. The test ban talks in Geneva collapsed in March of 1961; the Soviets won the race to put a man in space in April; the government of South Korea was overthrown in May. In June, Khrushchev bullied and battered Kennedy at their summit in Vienna. That summer the Soviets resumed nuclear testing after a three-year moratorium. At one point Kennedy opened a National Security Council meeting asking, "Did we inherit these problems, or are these our own?"

"Oh, well," he remarked at another meeting, "just think of what we'll pass on to the poor fellow who comes after me."

On the other hand, the serial challenges—even the disasters—didn't seem to hurt him with the public. Just two weeks after the Bay of Pigs, at the end of April, Gallup pegged his approval at 83 percent.

"Jesus, it's just like Eisenhower," Kennedy said. "The worse I do, the more popular I get."

Fears and Threats

Kennedy's great fear, said his press secretary, Pierre Salinger, was "that he might have to be the President to start a nuclear war."

In the summer of 1961, he returned from his first summit meeting with Khrushchev in Vienna feeling he had never encountered a leader so immune to reason, or so apparently indifferent to the prospect of Armageddon. "He treated me like a little boy," Kennedy complained to Bobby. After the Bay of Pigs, he concluded, Khrushchev assumed he was weak and inexperienced, just as Eisenhower had warned. It was a dangerous impression for him to carry. Asked by a *New York Times* reporter how their meeting had gone, the president was blunt.

"Worst thing in my life," Kennedy called it. "He savaged me."

When he got back to Washington Kennedy began asking his experts: just how many Americans would die in a nuclear exchange? The answer came back: around seventy million. Eisenhower's doctrine of massive retaliation relied on long-range missiles and Polaris missile submarines to respond to provocation with an all-out, almost indiscriminate attack on the Soviet Union, China, and Eastern Europe. In the "Single Integrated Operational Plan" or SIOP, there was no room for maneuver or margin for error, military historian Fred Kaplan notes; in a crisis, the president's choice would be "suicide or surrender."

The plan operated virtually on autopilot—as though there really were a single button to be pushed to signal the end of the world. Once the president gave his assent, the military would take it from there—and there was no going back. When Kennedy first got a briefing on nuclear policy by the chairman of the Joint Chiefs, General Lyman Lemnitzer, Reeves writes, "Kennedy was gripping the arms of his chair so tightly that his knuckles showed white. He left the room with his secretary of state, muttering: 'And we call ourselves the human race.' "

As that first summer unfolded, Kennedy struck people close to him as moody, withdrawn; he sat up late into the night, talking about war. How do we drain some of the drama from the Cold War, make policy more businesslike, less theological? The United States had too little "usable power," as McNamara put it. A time of growing threats was not a time for limited options—especially after Khrushchev began rumbling about absorbing Berlin into East Germany. Khrushchev needed to halt the flow of refugees from east to west: it was a humiliating spectacle, at a time when he was trying to market this vision of a workers' paradise to the Third World.

But Kennedy and the Western powers could not permit him to swallow a free city. The president called Berlin "the great testing place of Western courage and will" and declared that "an attack upon that city would be regarded as an attack upon us all." Tensions rose: tanks rumbled into position.

Then on August 13, 1961, just before dawn, East German soldiers began building the wall in Berlin that would come to divide the city and define the age. That was bad news for East Germans with Western dreams, of whom more than three million—20 percent of the population—had already slipped across the border to the West. But by the perverse moral math of the Cold War, it was good news for President Kennedy.

"This is his way out of his predicament," Kennedy said of Khrushchev to his aide Ken O'Donnell. "It's not a very nice solution, but a wall is a hell of a lot better than a war."

By October, Kennedy had increased production of nuclear submarines by 50 percent and troop airlift capacity by 75 percent. He doubled the arsenal of Minuteman missiles, increased the production of M-14 rifles from 9,000 to 44,000 a month. After the Soviets resumed nuclear testing, a discouraged Kennedy felt no choice but to do the same. When he checked in with the club, Truman was particularly sympathetic. He understood how hard the decision had been. As for Ike, he declared, "Well, I thought you should have done this a long time ago."

Cuba, Again

Khrushchev was well aware of his strategic disadvantage; the United States had far more nuclear weapons and a more nimble force to deliver them. China was gaining ground in the battle for the soul of the non-aligned world. And his standing at home was increasingly shaky as his economy stalled. Those were just some of the motives behind his gamble, in the summer of 1962, to place medium-range missiles in Cuba. "Every idiot can start a war," Khrushchev told his followers, "but it is impossible to win this war. . . . Therefore the missiles have one purpose—to scare them, to restrain them . . . to give them back some of their own medicine."

Though the missile installations were secret, the increase in Soviet military activity was clear and unprecedented. And since the United States was heading into the 1962 midterm elections, it was a perfect chance for Republicans to make Cuba the metaphor for Kennedy's presidency in general. Conservative senators like Kenneth Keating attacked Kennedy as our "do nothing president" in the face of what he insisted was the buildup of offensive weapons in Cuba. An old club rivalry resurfaced at this point, when none other than Harry Truman fired back at critics, saying, "The reason we're in trouble in Cuba is that Ike didn't have the guts to enforce the Monroe Doctrine." Kennedy meanwhile said that he hoped that "in this nuclear age," the American people would "keep both their nerve and their head."

He might as well have been talking to himself.

To the extent that Ike was feeling restless, marginalized, and indirectly rejected after Nixon's 1960 defeat, the 1962 congressional elections offered him another shot at vindication. "He missed political life," Bobby Kennedy speculated of Eisenhower. "He missed the adulation. So he kept wanting to get back in. He said that—in 1962—he was much more interested in politics and the campaign than he had been even when he was President."

This was especially true after Kennedy went to campaign in Harrisburg, Pennsylvania, practically Eisenhower's backyard, in late September, and offered the country a choice: America could "step up the progress that we have already made, or return to drift and deadlock." He reminded the audience of conditions when he took office: "The Nation's engine was idling. . . . Nearly 5½ million Americans were out of work, the largest number since World War II. . . . Around the world the picture was dreary."

Hearing the broadside, Eisenhower was livid; *Newsweek* described him as "fighting mad." The club has its rules, which generally bar former presidents from attacking sitting ones on matters of foreign policy; but there are limits to a man's patience. He contacted a mutual friend with a warning for Kennedy: "One more attack like the one in Harrisburg and my position of bi-partisan support in foreign policy will draw to a permanent end."

On October 15, he stood before six thousand pumped-up Boston Republicans and denounced Kennedy's "dreary foreign record of the past 21 months."

"It is too sad to talk about," Ike declared, and he began hitting back; during his presidency, he said sharply, "we lost no inch of ground to tyranny. We witnessed no abdication of responsibility. . . . No walls were built. No threatening foreign bases were established."

The back-and-forth was enough to inspire the *New York Times* to spank both presidents in an editorial. Ike's attack was "no doubt prompted at least in part by President Kennedy's recent invidious remarks about the Eisenhower record in foreign affairs," the paper conceded. "But partisan discussions of foreign policy in sweeping vague terms perform no public service."

By then, however, Kennedy had other things to worry about. The morning after Ike's speech, on October 16, Bundy knocked on his bedroom door at about 8:45 with a batch of U2 surveillance photographs under his arm.

"Mr. President," he said, "there is now hard photographic evidence . . . that the Russians have offensive missiles in Cuba."

Kennedy called Bobby.

"We have some big trouble. I want you over here."

The group that met that morning would come to be known as the ExComm; it would form the core of Kennedy's decision-making apparatus this time around.

The Cuban Missile Crisis was the ultimate test of presidential game theory. Kennedy and his advisors faced an almost impossible puzzle. Do they launch an air strike to take out the missiles—knowing it almost certainly would not get them all? Or a broader air strike, possibly followed by a full-scale invasion? Do they start with diplomacy, thereby losing the element of surprise? Or a naval blockade/quarantine, with the option to escalate if it failed? The hard-liners were pushing for an all-out assault, the diplomats for diplomacy.

Until they reached agreement, secrecy was essential. Through the week, Kennedy kept up his campaign travel schedule; one night nine members, after meeting at the State Department, crammed into a single car lest a caravan of limousines tip off reporters. Bobby Kennedy rode to the White House on deputy undersecretary Alexis Johnson's lap. The White House mess stayed open day and night; arrangements were made for staff to sleep in the sub-basement bomb shelter.

In explaining to the world his decision to impose a naval quarantine on Cuba, Kennedy needed the club's role to be public and private at the same time. He wanted the full force of his predecessors behind him; on Monday morning, October 22, as he prepared to address the nation that evening, he called Hoover, Truman, and Eisenhower. "Facing the possibility of an imminent nuclear war, the pressure on Kennedy was unimaginable," historian Robert Dallek argues. "It was one reason for his calls to the three ex-presidents. He thought they were the only ones who could imagine his burden."

Eisenhower was especially helpful. He flew up to Washington over the weekend at the invitation of his old friend and now CIA director John McCone, who briefed him on what was happening. "He initially suspected Kennedy of timing the crisis to help Democratic candidates at the eleventh hour," recalls David Eisenhower, which would remain a persistent belief among some Republicans for years. But McCone, who had been essentially acting as Kennedy's liaison with Eisenhower, may have helped adjust his view.

"He pacified Eisenhower," Bobby Kennedy remarked in 1964. "He was the one influence with Eisenhower which was giving him another side and moderating what Eisenhower was hearing all the time."

McCone knew that Eisenhower was constantly hearing from people with axes to grind. "He'd just be filled with poison by all these people who would tell him things and make things up," Bobby said, so McCone would try to correct the record. McCone told Kennedy that Eisenhower really wanted to do the right thing, "so he [McCone] could work with him or at least reason with him a little bit."

On Sunday morning Ike went on TV and performed in full protective club uniform. He contradicted both his speech of the week before and the pronouncement of the Republican chairman that Cuba was the top issue of the campaign. "Eisenhower Bars Any Crisis Abroad as Election Issue" ran the headline in the *New York Times*. "He Calls Current Foreign Policy an Improper Topic for Partisan Attack."

While Republicans can argue over history and long-range trends, he said, those who attacked President Kennedy's handling of international crises weakened and divided the nation. "Any pronouncement he may make respecting an impending crisis is almost sacrosanct as far as I am concerned," Eisenhower declared.

When Kennedy called the next morning, Eisenhower saluted. "No matter what you're trying to do," he promised, "I will certainly . . . do my best to support it." He warned of the likely outcry at the U.N. and in Latin America at unilateral U.S. action. "I think you're really making the only move you can," Eisenhower said.

"It's tough," Kennedy replied. "We may get into the invasion business before many days are out."

From a military standpoint, that was the clean-cut thing to do, Eisenhower observed. "But having to be concerned about world opinion—"

"And Berlin," Kennedy interrupted. He was afraid that any aggression against Cuba would provoke a retaliatory move on Berlin. But here Eisenhower pushed back. He had heard all the arguments before.

"Personally, I just don't quite go along, you know, with that thinking, Mr. President," he argued. "The damn Soviets will do whatever they want, what they figure is good for them. And I don't believe they relate one situation to another." He could be all wrong, he added, but he didn't think the two flashpoints were connected.

Then Kennedy cut to the chase. Until now the call sounded formal, dutiful; but Eisenhower's confidence seemed to invite Kennedy's candor. Because the whole calculation really came down to this: he was about to make a move from which there might be no return. There was only one other man on the planet who knew what that felt like.

"What about if . . . Khrushchev announces . . . that if we attack Cuba, it's going to be nuclear war? What's your judgment as to the chances they'll fire these things off if we invade Cuba?"

"Oh, I don't believe they will," Eisenhower replied.

"You don't think they will?" Kennedy pressed. "In other words you would take that risk if the situation seemed desirable?"

What else can you do? Ike replied. They've planted these missiles in our backyard, and we won't feel safe until they are gone. "Something may make these people shoot em off," he admitted. "I just don't believe this will."

And they shared an uneasy, world-weary laugh. Stay alert, Ike advised.

"Well, we'll hang on tight," Kennedy said.

That night Kennedy went on television to address the largest audience ever for a presidential speech. Looking tired and grim, he condemned the Soviets for lying about their offensive intentions, laid out the challenge, and announced his decision to impose a quarantine. "We no longer live in a world where only the actual firing of weapons represents a sufficient challenge to a nation's security to constitute maximum peril," he noted. "This sudden, clandestine decision to station strategic weapons for the first time outside of Soviet soil is a deliberately provocative and unjustified change in the status quo which cannot be accepted by this country, if our courage and our commitments are ever to be trusted again by either friend or foe."

There was a run on rifle sales in Tampa, and hand-to-hand combat broke out in a Los Angeles grocery store over the last can of pork and beans. Senate majority leader Mike Mansfield called his wife and told her to meet him at the airport. They were flying home to Montana. "YOUR ACTION DESPERATE. THREAT TO HUMAN SURVIVAL," philosopher Bertrand Russell cabled Kennedy. Undersecretary of state George Ball slept on the couch in his office at the State Department the night of the announcement. When the secretary of state awoke him the next morning, it was with this greeting: "We have won a considerable victory. You and I are still alive." Meanwhile Kennedy and his advisors met to discuss how to manage a naval quarantine, to buy time while building support in Congress and the public. McCone offered to call Eisenhower again to get permission to invoke his name when talking to lawmakers and to get "his view of this thing, as a soldier." On Wednesday morning a Gallup poll reported that a majority of Americans believed that an attack on Cuba would trigger World War III. As Bobby Kennedy described his brother in meetings, "His eyes were tense, almost gray, and we just stared at each other across the table. Was the world on the brink of a holocaust, and had we done something wrong? . . . I felt we were on the edge of a precipice and it was as if there were no way off."

Kennedy and his entire cabinet had suspended further campaigning on behalf of Democratic lawmakers; to their annoyance, Eisenhower kept right on helping Republicans, but the next day he did call on all Americans to assist Kennedy in this crisis. "So far as Cuba and Soviet Russia are concerned, in the weeks ahead we cannot be partisans."

By the end of the week, Kennedy would be on the phone with the club one more time, to tell them, essentially, the crisis was passing. Khrushchev would withdraw his missiles and technicians in return for a U.S. promise not to attack the island—and a private understanding that the United States would withdraw its missiles from Turkey. "Now we have to wait to see how it unfolds," Kennedy told Eisenhower, who had expressed concerns that the Soviets could never be trusted to keep their word. His call to Truman was half as long and purely congratulatory on Truman's part: the first words out of his mouth were "I'm just pleased to death the way this thing came out."

So why did this story have the happy ending, after the first challenge in Cuba had ended so badly?

Certainly the U.S. arms buildup had something to do with it; Khrushchev knew he was outgunned once the United States signaled its determination to get the missiles out one way or another. But the military portion was just one piece of a much bigger political puzzle, and here, some historians argue, Kennedy was served both by the lessons he had learned from Eisenhower, and the ways in which he remained different.

On the one hand, Eisenhower's more hierarchical style, argues Michael Beschloss, might not have left him with the flexibility needed to steer the crisis to its peaceful end. "If Eisenhower had been running those meetings, with his Olympian approach, they might not have been nearly so effective. Here, Kennedy's talent for crisis management may have saved the world," Beschloss wrote.

On the other hand, Kennedy handled the two Cuba crises very differently, and had incorporated some of Ike's guidance after the first to steer him through the second. It helped that as of the beginning of October, he had in Maxwell Taylor a chairman of the Joint Chiefs he trusted. Kennedy did not sit in on every meeting of the ExComm; people talk differently—and more freely—when the president is not in the room. As Schlesinger described it, "Every alternative was laid on the table for examination, from living with the missiles to taking them out by surprise attack. . . . In effect the members walked around the problem, inspecting it first from this angle, then from that."

A couple of weeks later, when Westinghouse president William Knox was traveling in Moscow, Khrushchev summoned him for an audience, clearly eager to tell his own story. He would hate to believe, he said, that Kennedy acted as he did because of impending elections. But he noted that while he had had his issues with Ike, he was sure that the former president would have handled things in a more mature manner. Part of the problem in U.S.-Soviet relations, Khrushchev said, arose from the fact that his eldest son was older than Kennedy.

When it was over, Reeves notes, when Khrushchev had backed down, the ships reversed course, the missiles been removed, Kennedy called Tiffany's and ordered thirty calendars made of Lucite, showing the month of October with the thirteen fateful days engraved more deeply and his initials and the various ExComm members in the corners. Tiffany president Walter Hoving proposed that sterling silver would be more appropriate, and offered to pick up the cost.

The Weight of History

Kennedy had many favorite poems. One he recited on the day he learned of the missiles went like this:

> *Bullfight critics row on row*
> *Crowd the enormous plaza de toros*
> *But only one is there who knows*
> *And he is the one who fights the bull.*

By that time, he knew in a way only presidents can how different their role was than that of anyone else in the orbit of the White House. "There is such a difference between those who advise or speak or legislate," he told *Time*, "and . . . the man who must . . . finally make the judgment. . . . Advisors are frequently divided. If you take the wrong course, and on occasion I have, the President bears the burden of the responsibility quite rightly. The advisors may move on—to new advice."

Early in 1962, Arthur Schlesinger's father, also an eminent historian, conducted a poll of scholars to rate presidential performance. He asked Kennedy for his vote; he qualified not just by holding the office but by having analyzed it himself, as a student of leadership and a Pulitzer Prize–winning author.

Kennedy started to fill out the ballot; but then he stopped. He had come, Schlesinger the younger concluded, to "feel the mystique of the Presidency strongly enough to doubt whether the quality of the presidential experience could be understood by those who had not shared it."

So Kennedy wrote back to Schlesinger Sr. "A year ago, I would have responded with confidence," he explained. "But now I am not so sure. After being in the office for a year I feel that a good deal more study is required to make my judgment sufficiently informed." It was easy enough to pick the obvious ones, Washington, Lincoln, FDR. But "I would like to subject those not so well known to a long scrutiny after I have left this office."

He was more blunt with the son than the father: "How the hell can you tell?" Kennedy asked Arthur Jr. There was no way to know how Lincoln would have handled Reconstruction; voters often don't know when presidents are getting credit for doing things they had no choice about, or how much difference their individual effort made. "Only the president himself can know what his real pressures and his real alternatives are. If you don't know that, how can you judge performance?"

Still a partisan warrior, he was pleased, of course, to see when the results were published that Truman had ranked in the "near great" class while Eisenhower drifted down near the bottom of average. He joked to Schlesinger that it was those ratings that drove Ike to dive headlong into his redemptive mission to help Republicans in the midterm elections. "It is all your father's poll," Kennedy asserted. "Eisenhower has been going along for years, basking in the glow of applause he has always had. Then he saw the poll and realized how he stood before the cold eye of history—way below Truman; even below Hoover. Now he's mad to save his reputation."

There was some truth to that; Ike could have ignored the poll as partisan theater. But he took it to heart. "The old man," said Ike's son John, "was wounded by the thing."

The exercise was a reminder that the club had its uses: Salinger especially looked for chances to get the three former presidents together. They all declined the invitation to attend Churchill's citizenship ceremony. Truman and Hoover were invited to serve as honorary co-advisors to the American Food for Peace program; they consulted with each other and agreed to say no. Truman sent a copy of his refusal letter to Hoover, who said he was grateful: "Apparently we have avoided this one."

Kennedy rallied them in support of broadening the president's trade authority, supporting the test ban treaty signed in the summer of 1963, and of course on Cuba, which, given the shared anticommunist convictions of all three, was almost the easiest. With Eisenhower especially, Kennedy made sure he felt consulted, sending McCone out to Gettysburg to brief him regularly.

As for Truman, Kennedy never missed a chance to congratulate him for the honors he racked up in retirement. Both men had May birthdays; in May of 1963, Kennedy wrote to Truman that he was his model for aging well. "It is my hope that forty six years will rest as lightly on me as seventy nine do on you."

Kennedy never had the chance to find out.

7

"How About Coming in for a Drink?"

— HARRY TRUMAN

Until Kennedy's assassination in November of 1963, no American president had been murdered since McKinley in 1901; the sudden death of one so young was like a national heart attack. But for the former presidents it was an especially sharp reminder of the role they had played and the risks it carried. The club was never so close as in death, whether of a member, a friend, or a first lady. But in the modern era, only Kennedy died while still in office, and it brought the others back into service in an instant, to comfort one another, serve the country, and raise Lyndon Johnson suddenly into their ranks.

All three living former presidents had faced assassination threats, which in Truman's case included a failed attempt in November of 1950. "Dad was terribly shaken by it," Margaret Truman said of Kennedy's death. "For the first time in his life, he was unable to face reporters." Herbert Hoover was so upset that his son Allan decided to spend the night at the Waldorf with him. Lyndon Johnson tried to reach him, and the next morning Hoover wrote to the new president, "I am ready to serve our government in any capacity, from office boy up."

Nixon had just flown home to New York from Dallas, where he had attended a Pepsi board meeting; he heard the news in the cab coming from the airport. That afternoon he talked to FBI director J. Edgar

Hoover, who would tell him that *he,* Nixon, was the original target: Lee Harvey Oswald's wife had told Hoover, Nixon wrote in his memoirs, that "Oswald had been planning to kill me when I visited Dallas and that only with great difficulty had she managed to keep him in the house to prevent him from doing so."

Eisenhower heard the news from a policeman in New York; it brought to mind his decision to get a concealed weapons permit, back when he was president of Columbia and would walk across Central Park with a derringer in his pocket. In *The Death of a President,* William Manchester wrote how as a young officer in Haiti, Ike used to wander through the national palace, see the busts of chiefs of state, and realized, by their dates, that two out of three of them had been killed in office. That's how backward nations worked, he thought, but his country wasn't like that. "Now he wasn't so sure," Manchester wrote, "and he felt heartsore."

The funeral brought the world to Washington. The line to view the casket stretched eight abreast for thirty-two blocks from the Capitol. A million people lined the street on the cold, sunny morning of November 25. The city was in lockdown; Truman and his daughter, Margaret, were staying at Blair House; Eisenhower was with Mamie at the Statler. Ike heard that the Trumans were stranded without a limousine.

"I don't know who was responsible," recalled reporter Edward Folliard, "but he was either a blunderer or a genius at protocol." Soon the phone was ringing at Blair House, as Eisenhower declared, "Hell, I'll have my car. He can ride with me."

The drums sounded like thunder. Ike and Truman were not up to the walk to St. Matthew's Cathedral for the funeral mass, but all the presidents were present in spirit if not in fact; the caisson that carried Kennedy's coffin was the one used for Roosevelt eighteen years before, followed by Black Jack, the riderless horse, skittish, tugging at the arm of the Army private leading him. The family walked behind, then President Johnson. In the river of people behind marched French president Charles de Gaulle, Queen Frederika of Greece, King Baudouin of Belgium, Emperor Haile Selassie of Ethiopia, 213 world leaders in all, and the justices of the Supreme Court, the cabinet secretaries, then personal friends, then mourning strangers.

At the requiem mass, Eisenhower and Truman joined the Kennedys, the Johnsons, the Nixons, Billy Graham, Henry Ford II, and Martin

Luther King Jr., who came late and left alone. Among the Bible passages was one from Kennedy's speech the night before he died: "Your old men shall dream dreams, your young men shall see visions." The cardinal wept; the son saluted; the band played on, so sadly, hailing the chief.

As Bobby Kennedy helped Jackie into her limousine, Eisenhower and Truman both came over and spoke to her through the window. Then they rode together to Arlington Cemetery for the burial, past the Lincoln Memorial, another leader martyred, and over the Potomac to the gravesite. They talked about the assassination, whether Oswald had acted alone, or was it some kind of cabal. And they talked about the old days.

Mamie had a bad foot, and the scene at Arlington was a free-for-all; so both presidents ended up, as Ike said, "out in left field." It was approaching twilight by the time the burial was over; on the way back into the city, Truman asked Ike and Mamie about their plans. They said they were driving straight back to their farm in Gettysburg. It had been a long, hard day, and no one had had lunch. Margaret suggested that they come back to Blair House to fortify themselves before the trip. When Truman got out of the limousine, he turned around, and said, "Ike, how about coming in for a drink?" Eisenhower looked at Mamie, who seemed to agree.

And that was it. For eight years Truman had not stepped foot in the Eisenhower White House. For a decade their relations had evolved from actively hostile to carefully formal. But formality cannot withstand the brute, reckless intrusions of mortality, and so it was that in the late afternoon, the two men, along with Mamie and Margaret and a few close aides, sat in the living room at Blair House, eating sandwiches, drinking coffee.

"There were only a couple of us there," recalled Truman's former naval aide Admiral Robert L. Dennison. "I don't know where the magic came from, maybe President Truman inviting him to come in or maybe because of Eisenhower's thoughtfulness in calling up in the first place, but at any rate they sat down by themselves on a couch and started talking and reminiscing."

Including, of course, about their own deaths. The spectacle of the funeral had left its mark on the modest men. "I think I'll probably be buried in Abilene," Ike said. "I don't know whether I'll have a Washington funeral or not, and I'm really not concerned about that." Truman had already planned to be buried in the courtyard of his presidential library in Independence.

As the two sat talking, a Secret Service agent entered to tell them that an Army officer had arrived with a message for them. Admiral Dennison went out to investigate, and found a very sheepish-looking colonel at the door.

"What's your problem?" Dennison asked.

"Well, Mrs. Kennedy sent me over here," he replied. "She's upset and embarrassed because she forgot to invite these two gentlemen to come over to the White House." Many of the foreign dignitaries had convened at the White House for a reception following the burial.

It was Eisenhower who spoke first.

"Well, please tell Mrs. Kennedy that I understand completely," he said. "It was very kind of her to think of us, but we must get back to Gettysburg, so please present our apology." Truman spoke up next, that he too appreciated the gesture and was not at all offended. "I understand why we weren't thought of in the first place. She has so much on her mind. But I, too, am tired and I've got to rest and I'm sure she'll understand."

The relieved colonel departed, and the two presidents went back to talking, poured another drink as the twilight settled. Margaret was dispatched to deal with the tribe of reporters who had gathered outside, sensing a story and demanding to talk to the two presidents. Neither was at all inclined to oblige.

"I thought it would never end," Dennison said, "but it was really heartwarming because they completely buried the hatchet and you'd think there had never been any differences between them and they were right back where they came in when Eisenhower came back from Europe."

When it truly was time for the Eisenhowers to get on the road, Truman, to the horror of the Secret Service, went out to the curb and started talking again while the car waited to take the Eisenhowers away. Margaret kissed Eisenhower. Mamie kissed Truman on both cheeks. And she thanked him for bringing her son home for her husband's inauguration a decade before.

As for the two presidents, "It was a long, lingering, silent handshake," wrote reporter Warren Rogers, "with both men looking into each other's eyes."

Their friendship never fully revived in the years that remained to them; but the hostility dimmed. They met next two and a half years later, on the twenty-second anniversary of D-Day at a Kansas City luncheon sponsored by an organization called U.N. We Believe. They bantered warmly. "I liked what I saw," said Truman's close friend Tom Gavin. "I thought it was great. President Truman does too."

Margaret's husband, Clifton Daniel, sensed what had let the men move on after the funeral meeting. "They had been very closely associated, and on that day they shared something very much in common; they shared with Jack Kennedy the fact that all of them had been President, and this engenders a greatness of spirit in people sometimes they don't otherwise have."

JOHNSON AND EISENHOWER:

Blood Brothers

———— ⚷ ————

Because of who he was, because of what he confronted, but also because of how Lyndon Johnson came suddenly to be president, his relationship with the club was the most intense of any modern president. Truman had recruited Hoover largely because he needed his expertise, though the stagecraft of bipartisan outreach didn't hurt. Kennedy had managed Eisenhower because he knew Ike's opposition could do him real harm. But Johnson was a very different man, and his reliance on the former presidents was at once highly political and deeply personal. If for no other reason than to signal America's stability, he called both Truman and Eisenhower within hours of his swearing in following Kennedy's assassination, and they were at his side at the White House the next day.

He was fully conscious of the power of his predecessors and protective of their privileges. He studied them, fed and tended them, sent flowers, cuff links, statues, put Air Force jets and helicopters at their disposal, had his aides research every single contact he had ever had with any one of them, going back to his earliest Senate days.

Foreign policy is the realm where presidents exercise the greatest power, and where the club can tie its members in knots. However much presidents may disagree with their predecessors on the value of an ally or the danger of an enemy, they are acutely conscious of being the custodians of American credibility, and of the sacrifice of those who have already died for a cause. So just as Kennedy inherited, and mismanaged, Eisenhower's Cuba policy, Johnson inherited Kennedy's Vietnam commitment as well as his team and doubled down on JFK's dubious bet. Pulling back from Vietnam, assistant secretary of state George Ball observed, "would look as though he were repudiating the policy of Kennedy," which was not an option.

But what to do with this "biggest damn mess," as he was calling the war by 1965? As he cartwheeled into the commitment that would ultimately sink his presidency and torment the nation for decades, he reached out to Eisenhower and practically rode on his star-spangled shoulders; at one crucial meeting it was hard to tell which president was the actual commander in chief. Somehow Eisenhower, the warrior who had assiduously avoided military adventures throughout his eight years in office, became more bellicose when the decisions were no longer officially his to make. As with Kennedy but especially now with Johnson, Ike was literally the armchair general. "There are only two other men in this nation that fully understand the problems that come to this desk. You are one of them," Johnson told Eisenhower in the spring of 1966, as the voices of dissent grew louder. "I cannot tell you adequately my gratitude for your wisdom and counsel. And, for the fact that no one has found it possible to divide you and me."

8

"The Country Is Far More
Important Than Any of Us"

—DWIGHT EISENHOWER

President Kennedy was declared dead at 1 P.M. on November 22, 1963; ninety-eight minutes later in the sweltering cabin of Air Force One, surrounded by White House aides in tears and a new widow in a bloodstained suit, Lyndon Johnson took the oath of office for the job he could not have won on his own.

Most men join the club after dreaming of it for decades, campaigning for it for years, and preparing for it for months between victory and inauguration. Johnson realized he was now the president when he walked into the airplane cabin and aides who were like family suddenly jumped to their feet. "It was at that moment I realized nothing would be the same again," he recalled. "A wall—high, forbidding, historic—separated us now, a wall that derives from the Office of the Presidency of the United States. No one but my family would ever penetrate it, as long as I held the office. . . . It was a frightening, disturbing prospect."

To one degree or another every president is haunted by those who went before, but few so literally as Johnson. No president had ever witnessed the slaying of his predecessor or endured such a brutal transfer of power. "I always felt sorry for Harry Truman and the way he got the presidency," Johnson told an aide two days later, "but at least his man wasn't murdered."

Here was a man who had hated being vice president, the job Truman had described as being "as useful as a cow's fifth teat." It had been like a political death for Johnson, to be reduced to presiding as a figurehead over the Senate he once controlled as majority leader, and acting as a daily reminder of the president's mortality. "I detested every minute of it," he told his aide and later biographer Doris Kearns Goodwin. "Every time I came into John Kennedy's presence, I felt like a goddamn raven hovering over his shoulder."

But now Kennedy was gone, and Johnson took custody of a nation in anguish. The country was ripped open, heartsick, shamed; the world wondered about American intentions and resolve. Mythology smothered memory as Kennedy was instantly beatified: Cities around the world began renaming streets, bridges, buildings in his honor. Churches in London held so many memorial services the U.S. embassy nearly ran out of flags to lend. More than a quarter million people gathered to pray in front of West Berlin's City Hall.

Who could hope to compete with that?

"I took the oath, I became president," Johnson told Goodwin. "But for millions of Americans I was still illegitimate . . . a pretender to the throne, an illegal usurper." His home state of Texas was even the scene of the crime. "And then there were the bigots and the dividers and the Eastern intellectuals, who were waiting to knock me down before I could even begin to stand up. The whole thing was almost unbearable."

In the Cold War age, the world was on a hair trigger; no one knew if the Russians were responsible, or the Cubans, and the idea that America was rattled, rudderless, vulnerable, was not just disturbing, it was dangerous. And so from his very first hours in office, Johnson moved shrewdly and systematically to signal that he was in control. Hours after his swearing in, Air Force One landed at Andrews Air Force Base. Bobby Kennedy was there to meet Jackie and the body; leaders of Congress from both parties greeted Johnson, some of them, like Hubert Humphrey, the majority whip, sobbing openly. Johnson talked with Defense Secretary Robert McNamara as they flew together by helicopter past the floodlit Washington Monument to the White House, where they landed a few dozen yards from Caroline and John Kennedy's swing set. The secretaries had already cleared the Oval Office of Kennedy's things, the family pictures, the coconut shell on which he had carved a message after his

PT boat sank; eventually Johnson removed the crimson rug and replaced it with one with the Presidential Seal because the old one reminded him of the murder.

That night Johnson decided he'd rather work in his own refuge at the Old Executive Office Building; he wasn't ready for the Oval just yet. He started making calls, to J. Edgar Hoover at the FBI, Senator William Fulbright; he called Truman, his old poker buddy, at 7:05.

But it was Eisenhower he really wanted, and he placed that call five minutes later.

"Mr. President, this is Lyndon Johnson. This has been a shocking day."

"My heart goes out to you," Eisenhower replied.

"I have needed you for a long time," Johnson told him, "but I need you more than ever now."

"Any time you need me, Mr. President," Ike said, "I'll be there." In fact Ike had already sent a message of support through National Security Advisor McGeorge Bundy.

"I am going to rely on your good, sound judgment and will be calling on you," Johnson said, "but I wanted you to know how touched I was by your message. It was typical of you and you know how much I have admired you through the years."

"The country," Ike replied, "is far more important than any of us." He was coming to Washington in the morning for the memorials, he said, and Johnson seized the opportunity. "Why don't you give me a call right after the service is over," he said. Johnson ordered a Secret Service detail to take up position at Eisenhower's farm.

Texans Stick Together

You could practically hear the echo of 1945, of Truman suddenly assuming the presidency and reaching back to Herbert Hoover for both public continuity and private counsel. Only it was much easier in Johnson's case, since he and Eisenhower had a long history. "Us three Texans got to stand together," Johnson and House Speaker Sam Rayburn used to tease Ike, who had been born in Denison, seventy-five miles north of Dallas. Given Ike's impregnable popularity, Johnson and Rayburn had figured out early on that they had much more to gain from wooing the Republican president than fighting him. There was no need to oppose Eisenhower on foreign policy, since his own party's isolationists had already been taking care of that. On domestic matters they were clear with him about what could pass and what couldn't, amending his proposals just enough that both sides could claim credit. This helped explain how a Republican president with no legislative background got 83 percent of his program through a Democratic Congress—and how the Democrats won back the Senate in 1956, making Johnson the youngest majority leader ever.

"They didn't want to work with Ike; they wanted to kill him, politically I'm talking about," explained Eisenhower's aide Bryce Harlow, of Johnson and Rayburn. "They would have happily and joyously, but they couldn't." The White House knew that a certain amount of Johnson's bipartisan outreach was a ploy, but it worked to both sides' advantage. "Ike," Harlow said, "was never regarded as a Republican by the American people anyway."

Plus, the men just got along well. It's not that Eisenhower especially admired or trusted Johnson: he could see the neediness, the opportunism, the genius for manipulation. But they were the two most powerful men in the country, and if they wanted to get things done, they needed to find common ground. They were arguably a more synchronized team than Ike and his vice president, Richard Nixon.

Johnson had already done the club a great service even before he joined it. In 1957 he made an impassioned plea before the Senate for providing financial support for former presidents, in recognition that even after retirement the American people "still look to an ex-president for advice, for counsel, and for inspiration in their moments of trial." Truman needed some financial help, he told Rayburn, just "to keep ahead of the hounds." Republicans dragged their feet: what's to prevent a former president from using this public money for partisan purposes? they argued. But Johnson led the charge. You sense that by that time he had soaked in the spirit of the presidency, thought about the role, imagined himself in it, even if he feared he could never win it on his own. "No one who fills these functions can ever again be a 'private' citizen," he argued when pushing for the stipend. He cited Hoover's service to Truman as a heartwarming example of how presidents rise above partisanship in their post–White House years: "Personally, I wish we could find ways and means of making greater use of the services of former Presidents. They have a type of experience and knowledge that can be gained by no other men." He proposed a $25,000-a-year allowance, office space, franking privileges, a pension for his widow, and office staff. "For the moment we can content ourselves with taking this one step—a step which . . . recognizes the true nature of the greatest office in our land." It was as though he were honorary club treasurer, and he wanted the American people to pay dues.

So Johnson helped assure that Ike would have a comfortable post-presidency, and Ike often floated the notion that Johnson take his place in the Oval Office. He would warn Johnson against any legislative efforts that might circumscribe or damage the powers of the president, on the grounds that "It's easily possible that you may be sitting in this chair sometime yourself."

"No, Mr. President," said the man from the Texas Hill Country, "that's one chair I'll never sit in."

As the 1960 campaign approached, Eisenhower used to tell aides he thought Johnson was the strongest candidate the Democrats had. When the men would visit during the evening at the White House, Eisenhower would press him: "Why don't you run, Lyndon? You're the ablest guy in the party."

And Johnson would always respond the same way: "Oh, no," he'd tell Ike.

"Maybe it was just a conversational ploy," Harlow says of Eisenhower's kingmaking. "But Ike wasn't that devious, really. . . . I think it probably was rather genuine."

Ike's tantalizing vision became real only in the wake of national trauma. Eisenhower drove down from Gettysburg and arrived at the White House to view Kennedy's body at 11:15 on November 23, 1963, as boxes of the slain president's papers were being moved out.

Johnson's aide Horace Busby recalled the reversal of roles. "Every impulse of the man was to cooperate," he said of Eisenhower, whom he described as being "modest, undemanding, attempting to be unobtrusive." After the viewing, Ike met with Johnson and the two men had lunch. They talked about NATO, civil rights, managing the prickly French president, Charles de Gaulle, shaping the budget, which was due in a matter of weeks.

Eisenhower told Johnson to "be his own man." He mentioned that there was "uneasiness, if not fear," around the country at the tactics used by Bobby Kennedy's Justice Department, including charges that the IRS was being deployed against the Kennedys' adversaries in business, the universities, and foundations. Let a decent interval pass, Eisenhower advised, but then clean house and appoint your own team.

"It is better to be a good president for a year," he told Johnson, "than to hold the job for six years."

By the time they had finished, Johnson asked him for a memo, with specific advice for the days ahead. Eisenhower went into Johnson's outer office, picked up a legal pad, and began writing out ideas. He asked if a secretary he'd known, Alice Boyce, was still working at the White House; he trusted her, and so she was called in to take dictation. He asked that she burn her notes and make only two copies, one for Johnson and one for himself.

He recommended people for Johnson to reach out to, like Ike's treasury secretary, Robert Anderson, and Andrew Goodpaster, who was then working as an assistant to the chairman of the Joint Chiefs. They could help restore the "organizational machinery" of the executive branch.

Next, Eisenhower told him to call a joint session of Congress, and practically dictated the outline for what Johnson should say. "Point out first that you have come to this office unexpectedly and you accept the decision of the Almighty," he suggested, then assure everyone that "no revolution in purpose or policy is intended or will occur." Instead it would be Johnson's mission to carry out "the noble objectives so often and so eloquently stated by your great predecessor." And he should vow to work closely with Congress, business, and labor to do it.

That was remarkable advice: a Republican former president urging an uncertain Democrat to continue and build on the policies of a Democratic icon. Eisenhower knew what the country needed at that moment; it was not a time for partisan positioning. He did, however, take the opportunity to press the case for a sound fiscal policy.

"I had to convince everyone everywhere that the country would go forward," Johnson recalled. "Any hesitation or wavering, any false step, any sign of self-doubt, could have been disastrous." Besides Eisenhower, Truman came to the White House as well that day, so Johnson could ensure that he was photographed with both presidents. Pictures too of him with Secretary of State Dean Rusk, McNamara, and Bundy were all released to the networks in time for the evening news, to show the world that the machinery of government was firmly in his hands.

Johnson rocketed to a 79 percent approval rating, as he stood before Congress five days after Kennedy's death and followed Eisenhower's guidance to underline continuity—from the tax bill Kennedy had championed to the one on civil rights. "No memorial oration or eulogy could more eloquently honor President Kennedy's memory than the earliest possible passage of the Civil Rights Bill for which he fought so long," he said. Eisenhower's advice even made an appearance: "I pledge that the expenditures of your government will be administered with the utmost thrift and frugality," he said. Most fatefully, in the spirit of living up to Kennedy's legacy, he also vowed: "We will keep our commitments from South Vietnam to West Berlin."

On Christmas Day, one month into his presidency, an exhausted Johnson called Eisenhower from the ranch. I not only followed your advice in my speech, he told Eisenhower, but I sent you a leather-bound copy with your initials on it. Then Lady Bird got on the phone, and told Ike how fondly she remembered the days when he and her husband worked together, "and I sure hope we can have more of that in times to come."

Friends in Need

"Of all men in public life, Lyndon Johnson is one of the most friendless," author Teddy White once observed. "Those who come in contact with him are accepted as cronies, or partners, or supplicants, or men he can use—as servants. But of real friends, he has few, for, above all else, he lacks the capacity for arousing warmth. Of all the things to which Kennedy was born and which Johnson lacked—wealth, background, elegance—Johnson probably envied Kennedy most his capacity for arousing love and friendship."

Indeed Johnson tended to build alliances rather than friendships: "I was always very lonely," he told Doris Kearns Goodwin, a condition made worse by his sudden ascension to an office where power acts as a force field, attracting attention but precluding intimacy. The temptation is virtually irresistible for advisors and acquaintances alike to place themselves at the center of action and brag about their access. "One of the burdens of the president's is if he talks to anybody, the news is spread as fast by that individual as he can," observed Ike's treasury secretary, Robert Anderson, whom Johnson did indeed call the day after Kennedy's murder. "And from my own associations with every president I've known well, he's a human being and he needs somebody to talk to . . . somebody who won't talk about them even to the point of saying, 'I talked to the President.'"

Johnson's isolation was also fed by his sense of deficiency, which turned every encounter into a test of manhood, often literally. Johnson was famous for interrupting meetings at the White House with the suggestion that he and his guests—whether publishers, preachers, business leaders—go skinny-dipping in the White House pool. He took meetings in the bathroom. Guests at his Texas ranch were handed rifles and dared to go bring down a deer or antelope, or subjected to a bloodcurdling ride in his convertible. "I want people around me who would kiss my ass on a hot summer's day and say it smells like roses," he would say.

But relations with Eisenhower were different and always had been. Eisenhower was a hero, a man of action, not words, who like Johnson had received his share of condescension from the Eastern establishment. Being treated as an equal by one so formidable as Eisenhower was like a full body massage for the ego. "I never saw Lyndon Johnson talk to President Eisenhower like he would talk to me, leaning over and pointing at me and things like that," Ike's press secretary, James Hagerty, said. "They talked just like friends, only all they're doing is talking about problems that affect the lives of the whole world. Outside of that it was like friends talking."

When Johnson found himself suddenly in the eye of the storm, Eisenhower stood ready to help—but like Hoover with Truman so many years earlier, he waited to be asked. "He wanted the initiative to be taken by President Johnson," Anderson explained, "because, as a former president, he did not feel that he wanted to be in the position . . . of saying to the then-President . . . that 'This is the way I handled it,' or, 'This is what I would have done.'" While Ike's brother Milton believed Eisenhower's affection for Johnson was genuine, Johnson always played the role of sup-

plicant in their calls and letters, promising not to be a "nuisance," laud-
ing Ike as the great soldier and statesman. Eisenhower's responses were
cordial and respectful, but seldom intimate. They were always straight.

"You had to know this man, Eisenhower," Hagerty explained, when
asked whether Johnson really valued his counsel. "There was nothing
sham about him, and there was no double talking. If you asked him a
question you got an answer, if he was going to give you one."

Eisenhower may have enjoyed giving counsel to Johnson in part
because relations with his own party had cooled. As the 1964 campaign approached and Barry Goldwater's conservative revolution gathered strength, Eisenhower looked everywhere for a more moderate
alternative—including his brother Milton, and Herbert Hoover Jr., who
had served in Ike's State Department. But the newly radicalized Republican Party seemed intent on erasing the memory of its most popular
member, to the point that conservative forces at the Republican convention rejected a preamble to the platform praising the record of the
Eisenhower administration.

So it was easy for Johnson, on his way to winning a historic landslide
victory in 1964, to forgive Ike for being a Republican, since his heart
didn't seem in it anyway. He went to great lengths to extend Eisenhower
every possible perk and privilege: helicopters to ferry him to the farm, the
use of Camp David and the presidential suite at Walter Reed. He sent
gifts of blazer buttons with the Presidential Seal, a tie clip, a watch with
a stopwatch, and a constant supply of flower arrangements for Eisenhower's many hospital visits. He moved Eisenhower's portrait to a more
prominent position, so that it would be visible in the background of pictures of Johnson greeting various White House guests.

Most striking, he asked White House researchers to compile records
of every contact he'd ever had with both Truman and Eisenhower, before, during, and after their presidencies: every lunch, every phone call,
every bill signing and state dinner and off-the-record strategy session.
It was as though he could prove, to himself and others, that these were
relationships that were meaningful and real. There was the time Ike and
Johnson flew together to assess the drought in Texas in 1953, the off-
the-record meetings they had held throughout 1959 and 1960. Johnson
was, in this sense, the club's first true recording secretary, the man most

conscious of its potential power. When Johnson gave him cuff links, Ike wrote to thank him, noting, "I think that one day they will find their place in a museum at Abilene together with a notation that they were a gift from you."

Johnson liked that. He attached a memo for his aides: "That's a line we ought to use when people give us things."

Truman too was the object of much tender loving care. He had the invitations, the gifts, including a statuette of Johnson, which Truman promised to keep right on his desk. When Truman called to congratulate him after his 1964 victory—"I feel just as happy about it as you do," Truman said—Johnson took the opportunity to pay homage: "You feel happier because you have always been more for your party and your other folks than you have been for yourself." But then he went further, maybe the most explicit statement ever of the club's unique bond: "And I just want you to know that as long as I'm in that office, you are in it, and there's not a privilege of it, or a power of it, or a purpose of it that you can't share. And your bedroom is up there waiting for you, and your plane is standing by your side."

Those were not just empty words. The following year, at the last minute, Johnson instructed that the big signing ceremony for his landmark Medicare Act take place not in Washington as planned, but in Independence, Missouri, so that Truman could be in attendance and receive the very first Medicare card, two decades after he had tried to create a national health insurance plan. It was, Truman told Johnson, "the highlight of my post–White House days." When aides protested, Johnson brushed them off.

"Don't you understand?" Johnson said, demonstrating once again his acute understanding of the club's therapeutic purpose. "I'm doing this for Harry Truman. He's old and he's tired and he's been left all alone down there. I want him to know that his country has not forgotten him.

"I wonder if anyone will do the same for me."

9

"I Need Your Counsel, and I Love You"

—LYNDON JOHNSON

When Johnson took over the presidency, Vietnam was "a cloud no bigger than a man's fist on the horizon," advisor Jack Valenti recalled. "We hardly discussed it because it was not worth discussing."

At least not until Vietnam started falling apart. Then Johnson needed to come up with a strategy. For years Eisenhower and then Kennedy had provided economic and political support for the South Vietnamese government in its fight against the Vietcong, the communist guerrillas supported by North Vietnam. But after a military coup in Saigon and the November 1963 assassination of the corrupt President Ngo Dinh Diem, that arm's-length support was no longer enough to avoid a collapse in South Vietnam. So the challenge was, just how important was it to Johnson to prevent one from happening?

Whatever he did, Johnson wanted his predecessors by his side; he wanted to continue Kennedy's policies, if only he could figure out what they would have been, and have Truman's and Ike's blessings for whatever road he chose. "I'm a trustee," he told Bundy a few months after taking office. At least until he won an election on his own.

Attorney General Bobby Kennedy was the keeper of the flame, and Johnson, obsessed with his once and future adversary, imagined the accusations if Johnson wobbled on Vietnam: "That I had let a democracy fall into the hands of the Communists. That I was a coward. An unmanly man. A man without a spine. Oh, I could see it coming all right," Goodwin recalled him saying years later. "Every night when I fell asleep I would see myself tied to the ground in the middle of a long, open space. In the distance, I could hear the voices of thousands of people. They were all shouting at me and running toward me: 'Coward! Traitor! Weakling! . . .' They began throwing stones." And then he would wake up.

Just as JFK had feared Ike's condemnation over Cuba, Johnson feared the reproof of JFK—or at least his brother—in Southeast Asia. But for much of 1964, a campaign year, his strategy was largely one of postponement: sound more moderate than Barry Goldwater but more stalwart than the French. He opened a press conference in June of 1964 by reading a letter Eisenhower had written to Diem in 1954, offering to help Saigon build "a strong, viable state," and resist communist pressures following the collapse of the French colonial empire. That afternoon, however, Robert Anderson suggested that Johnson consult Eisenhower; he'd just had lunch with the former president, and among the Republicans "you do not have a greater admirer," Anderson assured him. "Why don't you ask him to come down and talk to you about this thing in Southeast Asia?" But the campaign of 1964 was in full swing, and Johnson was not eager to confer with someone who could potentially leak to the opposition. All in all, the less said the better.

"I don't think it's worth fightin' for," he told Bundy, "and I don't think we can get out. And it's just the biggest damn mess." Still, the contingency planning for an actual ground war was already under way.

No sooner had Johnson secured his blowout victory that fall than he was forced to make a decision. "I'm perfectly willing and anxious to admit," he said, prophetically, to the House Republican leader, Gerald Ford, "just like I know you would be if you wound up here in the morning by fate, like I did! . . . that I don't know all the answers." This was not yet America's war; fewer than five hundred U.S. soldiers had died, and whatever commitment America had to the dysfunctional government in Saigon, it was diluted by the fact that since Diem's assassination that government was now changing every few months in a series of coups. South Vietnam was not even a real country, but more a jury-rigged improvisation created after the French defeat in 1954 to block the rise of the popular revolutionary leader Ho Chi Minh. There was no way to measure how much popular support the communist guerrillas commanded. A special National Intelligence Estimate predicted that the South Vietnamese army would *never* be an effective military force. Stalwart establishment columnists like Lippmann argued that it was "a grievous mistake to have involved ourselves so much in a part of the world where it is impossible for a non-Asian country to win a war against Asians."

"I knew from the start that I was bound to be crucified either way I moved," he told Goodwin. "If I left the woman I really loved—the Great Society—in order to get involved with that bitch of a war on the other side of the world, then I would lose everything at home. All my programs. All my hopes to feed the hungry and shelter the homeless. . . . But if I . . . let the Communists take over South Vietnam, then I would be seen as a coward and my nation would be seen as an appeaser." That would yield "a mean and destructive debate, that would shatter my presidency, kill my administration and damage our democracy."

Indeed conservative columnists like Joe Alsop were invoking Kennedy facing down the Soviets over Cuba and saying that if Johnson walked away from this fight it would be "his defeat, as well as a defeat for the American people." And all he heard from his military advisors, Johnson complained, was "bomb, bomb, bomb," which he was not convinced would do any good at all. He'd always been wary of military men, he said, because of their thirst for glory: "It's hard to be a hero without a war. Heroes need battles and bombs and bullets in order to be heroic. That's why I am suspicious of the military."

What he needed, in other words, was a military man he could trust—one who had already won all the glory he needed, who understood the weapons of war but also a president's reluctance to wield them. He called Eisenhower before Christmas to check in: "I'm not going to drag you in to get any chestnuts out of the fire unless I really get my tail in a crack internationally," he assured him. "And when I do, I'm going to come running."

That would not take very long. The end of January brought yet another coup in Saigon; the army was a mess, the Vietcong growing stronger. Bundy and McNamara warned Johnson that America's current, passive posture "can only lead to disastrous defeat. . . . The time has come for harder choices." After an assault on February 7 at Pleiku killed eight U.S. servicemen, Johnson's military advisors argued for a major offensive, not just tit-for-tat strikes. Bundy, after a quick trip to assess the situation on the ground, argued that the Vietnamese did not believe the United States—meaning, of course, the president—had "the will and force and patience and determination to take the necessary action and stay the course." He urged a full bombing campaign—"Measured against the costs of defeat in Vietnam, this program seems cheap."

But Johnson understood very well the stakes he was facing as he pondered moving beyond military assistance to bombs and boots on the ground. The problem was not political: an overwhelming majority of Americans—83 percent—favored an expanded bombing campaign, and 79 percent supported a policy of preventing the communists from taking over Southeast Asia. The problem was more personal. "I'm not temperamentally equipped to be Commander-in-Chief," Lady Bird overheard her husband tell Vice President Hubert Humphrey as the internal debate raged. "I'm too sentimental to give the orders."

What Johnson really wanted was someone to hold his hand. He didn't want to rally the country to a great cause, or do anything that might distract Congress from the other missions he had set for it. In fact he didn't even want anyone to know how desperate he was to talk to Eisenhower.

"General, I want to visit with you in the next day or so on our problems out in Southeast Asia," he told Ike when he called the night of February 15, "and I just wondered what your schedule was . . ."

Eisenhower, ever the good soldier, replied he could make whatever arrangements were needed.

"I don't want to put it up like we're in deep trouble, because I don't think it's reached that point," Johnson assured him, but then offered to send a jet to pick him up, provided it could be done discreetly: "I'm a little concerned about leaving the appearance that we've got an emergency or something."

"I see," Eisenhower said. "Well, I think I could manufacture something." They debated whether they could pretend he was on his way to see his publisher and just happened to be in town for a visit.

"Why don't you . . . come on down here and spend a day with me at the White House and let me say, for the public, that I understood you were going to be in New York and I wanted to advise with you on general problems . . . so it doesn't look too dramatic, that we've got a real emergency," Johnson proposed. "It's not that deep. But it's deep enough that I want to talk to you. I think that probably you could be more comforting to me now than anybody I know. . . . Why don't you come stay all night with me? I'll put you in Lincoln's bed."

At this Eisenhower chuckled. "Lincoln's bed?" he asked, Lincoln, another great war president, whom Ike revered.

"I wish you would stay at the White House," Johnson pressed. "I need you a little bit. I need a little Billy Graham these days. I need somebody. . . . You come prepared to stay with me for a day or two. Don't be in a hurry, because I need you."

And Eisenhower wasn't the only one.

A half hour after calling Ike, Johnson called Truman.

"How are you?" Truman asked.

"Oh, I'm having hell," Johnson replied, and explained he was in search of advice and inspiration from the man who, in Korea, pioneered the discomfiting concept of a limited war in a nuclear age. "I've been reading history and saw how much hell you had, and you handled it pretty good, and I just thought maybe I could learn something from you."

He was just trying to do the right thing, Johnson insisted, the vision of dead soldiers, past and future, clearly haunting him. "I think when they go in and kill your boys, you've got to hit back. . . ."

"You bet you have!" the feisty Truman said, affirming once again how much easier it can be to take a hard line when the responsibility is no longer yours. "You just bust them in the nose every time you get a chance. And they understand that language better than any other kind."

Johnson issued another invitation—bring "Miss Bess. . . . I'll just send a plane for you and pick you up and you can all spend the weekend at the White House. . . . You don't have to make any presentation. Don't have to raise any hell. We'll just go in there and we'll have a drink or two together and then we'll go to church."

Truman admitted that he hadn't been feeling well lately, and in the end his health was too frail to manage the trip.

"I don't want to tax you," Johnson said, "but I always want you to know I need your counsel, and I love you."

Ever faithful, Truman released a statement supporting Johnson's

Vietnam policy. Ike meanwhile made his way to Washington; the White House told reporters that he was coming to Walter Reed for his annual checkup, and had time to swing by the White House to see his old friend.

And to guide him through the most fateful decisions of his presidency.

The Club War Council

The key players assembled in the Cabinet Room at ten on February 17: Johnson and Eisenhower, McNamara and Bundy, Army Chief of Staff General Earle Wheeler, and Andrew Goodpaster, who kept the notes and would become Johnson's personal emissary to Eisenhower for the next three years. Everything was on the table: Vietnam's history, the role of the French, the Soviets, and the Chinese, the odds of success, the risks of escalation, the case for using nuclear weapons if it came to that.

At this crucial meeting, Ike acted as if he were still the commander in chief—and Johnson let him. Eisenhower began his opening remarks before Johnson was even in the room, and went on for forty-five minutes; it felt like a freshman seminar in the proper use of power. He did not believe in sending small packets of troops to fight "peripheral" wars, or in giving commanders a task and then placing them in handcuffs. He stressed both soft power and hard, the use of "information and inspiration," to buck up an ally and psych out the enemy, and the use of any necessary force if all else fails. Again and again he tried to focus Johnson's intention on something other than choosing the bombing targets. He quoted Napoleon on the importance of morale, and the need to boost Saigon's while breaking Hanoi's.

While he came down hard in favor of air strikes—it was time, Ike advised, to mount "a campaign of pressure"—they weren't going to stop the infiltration from North to South: the goal was to convince the North Vietnamese of the costs of supporting the Vietcong. The Tonkin Gulf Resolution, passed by Congress the previous summer to permit "all necessary action to protect our Armed Forces" without a formal declaration of war, gives you all the authority you need, he assured the president, and "he thought such strikes could be well justified before the world," Goodpaster reported in his notes of the meeting.

The other reason to strike hard now, Ike argued, was to bring peace more quickly. Here he invoked Lincoln, who he said wrote the Emancipation Proclamation and then waited until after a major military victory to issue it, as he was determined that it come from a position of strength. In Vietnam, Eisenhower warned, "negotiation from weakness is likely to lead only into deceit and vulnerability, which could be disastrous to us." The greatest danger was if the Chinese were to conclude that the United States was limiting its reach. "That would be the beginning of the end," Eisenhower argued, "since they would know all they had to do was go further than we do."

Eisenhower reminded the men that they were playing chess, not checkers. Nuclear weapons had political, psychological, and military uses: if the enemy thinks he can wait you out, he gains the upper hand. He recalled how, after years of stalled negotiations in Korea, he had let it be known, through "secret" channels like India's neutralist prime minister Jawaharlal Nehru, who he knew would leak, that unless an armistice was signed soon, he would no longer put limits on what borders could be crossed or what weapons used, including nuclear. Ike said he warned North Korea that "We make a hell of a lot of weapons. We spent a lot of money on them. What the hell do we make them for if we don't ever use them, if we have to." Ike explained that he never intended to do anything except let that view get back to the North Koreans. But it ensured that the North Koreans would want to negotiate with *him*. (That may have been how he chose to remember it; but in his National Security Council meetings then and later in his presidency, Eisenhower seriously weighed using nuclear weapons in Korea in the event of a Chinese invasion, and worked hard to convince U.S. allies of the legitimacy of their use.)

McNamara pressed him about using tactical nuclear weapons in Vietnam. If the Chinese were to intervene now, Eisenhower said, Johnson should hit them from the air, using whatever force was necessary, including nuclear weapons. He doubted that would happen. But the United States has now put its prestige into keeping Southeast Asia free; if that takes "six to eight divisions . . . so be it."

So the man who had resisted intervening militarily in Vietnam in 1954 for fear the jungle would swallow whole divisions was now pressing for a much more aggressive posture. "As he had with President Kennedy in 1961," Clark Clifford argued in his memoirs, "Eisenhower advocated a variety of strong actions which he had never taken when he was president." Maybe this was just the pattern of former presidents; maybe it reflected how much the circumstances had changed on the ground. But Eisenhower's advice was consistent, from his days as a general, to his years in the White House, to his role as veteran counselor: don't fight unless you are in it to win. Don't waste time and lives with half measures. That had to be a hard message for Johnson to hear, for a man "too sentimental" for the hard decisions, and too uncertain of his ability to sell them. On questions like this, he was less sure-footed, and so more dependent on the "wise men," whether Eisenhower, or Acheson, or Clifford, to give him cover, prevent him from looking timid or incompetent.

Johnson got the other thing he needed most at that moment: a picture, on the front page of the *New York Times*, of him and Eisenhower deep in conversation. "Surprise Visitor," read the caption. No halo shined brighter than Eisenhower's; if the Republicans' greatest hero was supporting Johnson, then the president must be doing the right thing.

The Trap

In February of 1965, Johnson quietly approved Operation Rolling Thunder, a sustained bombing campaign named from a verse of his friend Billy Graham's signature revival anthem, "How Great Thou Art." Before it was all over the United States would drop more bombs on Vietnam than were used by all parties in all theaters of World War II. The ground troops would soon follow; first two Marine battalions—about 1,500 men—to protect the air bases at Danang, then by the end of April fifty thousand troops, to support the Marines. "The time has come to call a spade a bloody shovel," wrote James Reston in the *New York Times*. "This country is in an undeclared and unexplained war in Vietnam." And yet all the while Johnson insisted that nothing fundamental had changed—the reflex, as *Time* White House correspondent Hugh Sidey put it, of a president for whom "the shortest distance between two points was a tunnel."

"I continue to draw strength from our conversations," Johnson wrote to Ike in March, and added that members of Congress—from both parties—were reassured that they were consulting. "The Republican leaders, especially in Congress, are standing up magnificently," Johnson said. Goodpaster's briefings gave Ike the ammunition he needed to help keep nervous Republicans from wandering too far off the reservation. It was the Democrats who were giving Johnson problems. And when liberal Republicans like Jacob Javits urged Johnson to open peace negotiations, Ike shared Johnson's annoyance: "When I hear talk about negotiations," Eisenhower told Johnson, "I wonder why people don't recognize that there must be someone to negotiate with, and there must be someone willing to negotiate."

After a landmark April speech at Johns Hopkins University offering to open unconditional peace talks and provide $1 billion in development aid, Johnson felt the winds shift in his favor. The *Dallas Morning News* ran a cartoon showing LBJ in a fighter jet with a bomb in one hand and a billion dollars in the other. Lawmakers called it a masterpiece. Nearly two thirds of voters in the spring of 1965 thought Johnson was doing a good job on the war, even as the number of ground forces rose to 82,000.

But now Johnson faced his next crucial choice. In May, Clifford warned Johnson that getting in any deeper risked getting trapped in "a quagmire." The South Vietnamese military was disintegrating, the government about to collapse yet again. General William Westmoreland, commander of U.S. forces in Vietnam, sent McNamara a request for 150,000 more troops if he was to "take the war to the enemy."

"We're in a hell of a mess," McNamara told colleagues.

Like Kennedy, Johnson was sensitive to military opinion, Bundy would later explain, and had a hard time giving generals orders—unlike Ike, who "had more stars than they did, and Mr. Truman, because he just didn't give a damn. . . . I've exaggerated in both cases, but still on balance, Truman and Eisenhower, and indeed FDR, had more self-confidence in dealing with their senior military advisers than either Kennedy or Johnson did."

Johnson wanted to know what Ike thought. "I don't see that he's overeager," he told McNamara on June 10, speaking of Eisenhower. Goodpaster, who would practically be commuting from Washington to Gettysburg every couple of weeks, briefed Eisenhower on Westmoreland's request, and Johnson asked the former president to come to Washington to weigh in. So on June 30, Eisenhower had lunch with Johnson and McNamara in the White House family quarters. "He's been mighty helpful," Lady Bird recorded in her diary, talking about Eisenhower. "I know the grist for their mill. It could only be serious and bad."

Lady Bird told historian Robert Dallek that the worst thing for her husband was not knowing whether the war was right. "It was just a hell of a thorn stuck in his throat," she said. He "did not have that reassuring strong feeling that this is right, that he had when he was in the crunch of civil rights or poverty or education. . . . True, you can 'bear any burden, pay any price' if you're sure you're doing right. But if you do not know you're doing right . . . ," and she trailed off.

She wasn't the only one to worry. Johnson's growing depression was apparent to his close aides. He was having trouble sleeping. "I'm beginning to feel like a martyr," he told Canadian prime minister Lester Pearson, who came to see him at Camp David, "misunderstood, misjudged by friends at home and abroad." Press secretary Bill Moyers saw a "tormented man," full of self-pity and increasing paranoia; this reflected, Moyers said, "the realization about which he was clearer than anyone—that [Vietnam] was a road from which there was no turning back." Which meant, in effect if not fact, the end of his presidency. Johnson told Moyers he felt he was in "a Louisiana swamp . . . that's pulling me down."

"When he said it," Moyers remembered, "he was lying in bed with the covers almost above his head." And this was only 1965.

McNamara laid out three options for Johnson, which basically came down to withdrawal, muddling through with about 75,000 troops, or a major escalation. He told Johnson that the Joint Chiefs were all in agreement: give Westmoreland what he wants.

On July 2 as the decision loomed, Johnson pressed McNamara for assurances, if I go all in, give you the 200,000 troops you're asking for, what guarantees do I have? "Can the Vietcong come in and tear us up and continue this thing indefinitely and never really bring it to an end?" He called Eisenhower that night just after eleven, wanting certainty, clarity.

"You have to go all out," Ike told him. "This is a war, and as long as they are putting men down there, my advice is 'do what you have to do!' " The only chance of any kind of negotiation would come if Johnson resolved that "hell, we're going to end this and win this thing. . . . We don't intend to fail."

"You think that we can really beat the Vietcong out there?" Johnson asked. He knew the domestic terrain so well, knew the ways of Congress and exactly what his Republican rivals needed to be willing to do a deal. He was the virtuoso of means and ends and practical compromise. But he had no such feel for this enemy, or whether his goals were even achievable. "This is the hardest thing," Ike agreed, since they didn't even know how many guerrillas they were facing, how many imported troops, how many rebels. But once again he made the stakes plain: "We're not going to be run out of a free country that we helped to establish."

Of course Ike might as well have said, "a country that *I* helped establish." He had a personal stake in South Vietnam's independence, even if it was one he had resisted defending militarily when he was in the White House. Following the French defeat in 1954, when Vietnam was divided temporarily by the Geneva Accords, reunion through free elections was planned within a couple of years. But since it was clear that an election would yield a communist government under Ho Chi Minh, the Eisenhower administration blocked reunification and proceeded to build up South Vietnam economically and militarily as a bulwark against the "falling dominoes" of communist aggression. South Vietnam would not have existed as a country if Eisenhower had not effectively created it.

When they finished, Johnson told Eisenhower, "You're the best chief of staff I've got. . . . I've got to rely on you on this one."

In the end Johnson decided that withdrawal would be a disaster and the status quo meant a slow defeat. He would send the troops—200,000 by October—but he wouldn't tell Congress or the public any more than was absolutely necessary. He didn't want to admit what it would cost, as he drove one domestic program after another through Congress: aid to education, housing, Medicare, the Voting Rights Act, community development. He didn't want to admit to a need to raise taxes, or call up 235,000 reservists, or in any way prepare the country for a long and costly war.

And as long as he had Eisenhower's blessing, maybe he wouldn't need to—if all he was doing was continuing Eisenhower's and Kennedy's policy and honoring their commitments. Every chance he got, Johnson invoked like a talisman the "solemn pledges" of those who had preceded him "to help defend this small and valiant nation." Johnson was now carrying around in his pocket a copy of that 1954 letter from Ike to Diem that he regularly cited as the source of America's sacred commitment to defend South Vietnam. He talked about the "great stakes" involved in resisting communist expansion, and framed the escalation as a matter of the nation's honor. Our commitment, he said, dates back eleven years, through the Kennedy and Eisenhower administrations: "We just cannot now dishonor our word . . . or leave those who believed us and who trusted us to the terror and repression and murder that would follow."

Thus he set his own trap, by suggesting there was a virtual treaty, solemn promises that he could not walk away from, even if they had not been his. He put not just Vietnam's future but U.S. credibility on the line. And, of course, his own. As long as he avoided the full national debate, it would never be America's war; it would be Lyndon Johnson's war.

This left Ike in an awkward position, since he had never sworn to defend South Vietnam at all costs. Speaking with reporters on August 17, Eisenhower affirmed that "the communists must be stopped in Vietnam . . . [for] it would be harder and tougher to try it somewhere else." But he gently rejected the notion that Johnson's actions were basically a consequence of his policies. He had never made a unilateral military commitment to defend Vietnam, he insisted; he had only promised Diem "economic and foreign aid." He had refused to provide fighter planes to the French forces for fear of becoming directly involved militarily. The "state" of South Vietnam was an artificial creation; how far would he have gone to defend it?

No one would ever know. Eisenhower could say that circumstances had changed, that there was a reason for Johnson to send in the troops that he never had. In any event, voters were reminded that Ike had steered clear of a land war in Asia. "Military Pledge to Saigon Is Denied by Eisenhower" ran the headline in the *New York Times*.

And now the editorial writers weighed in about what they hinted was a bait and switch by the White House, using Eisenhower as cover for their covert escalation of the war. "Not only was Congressional debate avoided," chided a *New York Times* editorial two days later, "but there were repeated denials that such a decision [to send combat troops] had been made. Indeed the whole effort was to make it appear that nothing has changed in American policy since 1954."

This sent the White House into full damage control mode. He may have been furious at Ike, but he needed him as much as ever. Johnson called Eisenhower right away: "They want to get us in a fight, and they're not gonna do it, as far as I'm here," he said of the press corps.

Eisenhower, Truman, and Hoover, three architects of the postwar world, were honored at Princeton's bicentennial in June of 1947; though Hoover and Ike were the two Republicans, Hoover and Truman became the closer friends. (*Courtesy of Harry S. Truman Library*)

Truman got to visit with Hoover at the dedication of the Hoover library in August of 1962. "I feel that I am one of his closest friends," Truman said, "and he is one of my closest friends." (*Harry S. Truman Library*)

Truman first met Ike when he presented him with the Distinguished Service medal in June of 1945; they had dinner that night. "He is a nice fellow and a good man," Truman told his wife, Bess. (*National Park Service, Abbie Rowe, Courtesy of Harry S. Truman Library*)

Eisenhower wanted to keep his distance from the Red-baiting senator Joe McCarthy, but when they campaigned together in October of 1952, it led to open war with his old friend Truman. (*Dwight D. Eisenhower Presidential Library & Museum*)

Eisenhower welcomed President-elect Kennedy to the White House in December of 1960. The exalted general's shadow would remain long after he left office. (*Abbie Rowe/White House, John F. Kennedy Presidential Library and Museum, Boston*)

In search of advice—
and a reassuring
picture—Kennedy
invited Ike to Camp
David after the
disastrous Bay of Pigs
invasion in April of
1961. (*Robert Knudsen/
White House, John F.
Kennedy Presidential
Library and Museum,
Boston*)

Once Kennedy took
office, Truman was once
more a welcome visitor
to the White House,
pictured here in May of
1961. (*Robert Knudsen/
White House, John F.
Kennedy Presidential
Library, Boston*)

Johnson called Eisenhower the night Kennedy was shot in November of 1963; the general would become a regular advisor. "You're the best chief of staff I've got," Johnson said in 1965. (*LBJ Library photo by Yoichi Okamoto*)

Nixon and Reagan had a complex, forty-year history of cooperation and competition. At California's Bohemian Grove enclave in 1967, Nixon asked Reagan if he was running for president in 1968. Reagan's reply was noncommittal. (*Lawrence Berkeley National Lab*)

LEFT: By the end of the 1968 campaign, Johnson would privately accuse Nixon of committing treason; but once Nixon won, Johnson welcomed him to the White House and worked to ensure a smooth transition. (*LBJ Library photo by Frank Wolfe*)

BELOW: Nixon and Ford met, socialized, and even carpooled together as young congressmen in 1949 and 1950. Against his instinct, Nixon tapped Ford as his vice president in 1973; Ford pardoned Nixon in 1974. (*Courtesy Gerald R. Ford Library*)

Reagan and Nixon, pictured here with HEW Secretary Elliot Richardson in 1971, were rivals for the 1968 GOP nomination. As president, Reagan welcomed Nixon's help and advice—until Nixon found his arms-control policies naïve. (*Associated Press*)

Ford and Carter were bitter foes from the end of their race in 1976 until their flight home from Cairo in 1981. They would team up two dozen times on joint projects at home and abroad. Carter delivered Ford's eulogy in 2007. (*Associated Press*)

Reagan gave Ford serious consideration before picking George Bush as his vice president in 1980. Reagan turned to Nixon for advice about how to help Bush win the presidency in 1988. (*Courtesy Ronald Reagan Library*)

Eisenhower was reassuring. "After all, you know, no one in the international field can be popular everywhere," he said. "There's always a lot of people going [who] know all the answers. And I had my share of it, I assure you."

Bundy wrote a memo to Goodpaster, and made the stakes clear: "Next to the operations in Vietnam themselves, there is nothing more important than the work that President Johnson and President Eisenhower have done over the last 20 months to maintain their close mutual understanding," he advised. He handed over a packet of materials for Goodpaster to deliver to Eisenhower, including copies of Eisenhower's letters to Churchill and Diem from 1954, and a speech Ike made to Congress about the founding of SEATO, the Southeast Asia Treaty Organization. The Churchill letter asserted that the expansion of communism into Southeast Asia "would be a grave threat to the whole free community."

"The President asks that you make these documents available to general Eisenhower," Bundy told Goodpaster, "not because President Johnson has any interest whatever in making a paper record, but simply because he believes that they show clearly the basic line of policy set forth over the last 10 years by all three presidents. . . . He takes enormous encouragement from his belief that General Eisenhower and he see eye to eye on these fundamental principles."

That was the veiled threat: but then there was the sweetener, a letter from Johnson affirming Eisenhower's vital importance to the country and the cause. "No one knows better than you the accumulated demands of the Presidency," Johnson affirmed. "No one gives more attention than you to the best interests of our country," he added, and praised him for "the massive weight of your prestige and wisdom."

He was confident, Johnson said, of the eternal esteem in which Ike would be held: "Patriot, soldier, President, and now as wise counselor to the nation."

"General Eisenhower was most pleased with the letter," Goodpaster wrote, after he met with the general the next day, "and referred to it several times." Eisenhower assured Goodpaster that there was no problem over the issue of continuity and responsibility for Vietnam; the goal has stayed the same, only the means have changed over eleven years. That was fine—but it was the means that mattered most, as Johnson contemplated sending tens of thousands more men into the theater of war.

That day, August 19, 1965, Ike was also meeting with various Republican leaders—including both Richard Nixon and Gerald Ford. In a press conference, Eisenhower insisted that any rumors that he was parting ways with Johnson over Vietnam were "rot." Johnson's current course was the best under the circumstances, he said, which were much changed since 1954. And at a time of crisis, he added, "there is only one thing a good American can do, and that is support the president." The White House meanwhile said that there was no division between the two presidents and that it "doesn't consider any effort by anyone else to use General Eisenhower to promote such divisions as serving the national interest."

Not every Republican agreed, however, and Ford charged that the White House owed Eisenhower an apology for the White House's "irresponsible insinuation" that he was being " 'used' by someone as a puppet for political purposes." He promised that the Republicans in Congress would be releasing a detailed report on the history of the American commitment to Vietnam.

So the White House beat them to it. Before Ford could release his mimeographed "white paper," produced in such haste that the pages were misnumbered, the White House unfurled a slick, green-covered twenty-seven-page booklet called "Why Vietnam?" Ike declined to endorse the Republican paper on the war's history. Johnson called him "a tower of strength."

Despite—or perhaps because of—Goodpaster's regular briefings, Eisenhower's concerns were growing. He sensed Johnson's hesitation, the lack of a firm commitment to the mission, a reluctance to explain or defend it, and a desire to protect his domestic program at all costs. David Eisenhower argues that at some level Eisenhower realized that he *was* being used. Often when he was in town to see Johnson, he would stop by the office of his old assistant Bryce Harlow to preview the meeting, and they would ride over to the White House together. "All the way over," Harlow told David, "the General would bitch and moan and groan about 'Johnson is using me.'" Sometimes Harlow suspected he'd turn around and head back to Gettysburg. "But at the Diplomatic Reception Room, he would see the President and a change would come over him. Suddenly he was all smiles and the picture of affability." The talks with Johnson would be very warm, and "underneath it all," Harlow said, "the General loved it—at least initially."

His former speechwriter William Ewald recalled how Johnson summoned Ike to Washington for a secret meeting in a helicopter at a Washington airport. He was flying back making notes of the conversation, when an aide turned on the radio to get the sports scores; they heard a news flash that "The President has just met with General Eisenhower."

"That sonovabitch!" Ike growled. "He said the meeting would be secret." And he tore up the pages he was writing.

Eisenhower would suffer another heart attack in November of 1965; it meant yet another step back from the political scene. But when the year came to an end, Lyndon Johnson had an approval rating of 64 percent and was the most admired man in the world in a Gallup poll. Eisenhower was second.

A Nation Divided

By 1966, as Vietnam ground to a stalemate; the hawks wanted an all-out offensive and the protesters an immediate stand-down. The chairman of the Federal Reserve, along with several hundred businessmen, took out an antiwar letter to Johnson in the *Wall Street Journal*. A Boston College student set himself on fire outside McNamara's window. Martin Luther King had come out against the war, along with Dr. Benjamin Spock, the patron saint of parenting, who had actually made a campaign commercial for Johnson in 1964. So too did pastors and housewives and people who had never protested a policy in their lives. A young Texas congressman named George H. W. Bush wrote to constituents that "I frankly am lukewarm on sending more American boys to Viet Nam." Johnson wasn't just looking for "spiritual and historical" support, observes David Eisenhower; he was looking for cover fighting an unpopular war, and "sought the sanction of a member of the Presidential fraternity for his historic efforts to carry out a policy against the grain of public opinion."

By the middle of 1967, seventy thousand Americans had been killed or wounded. "There's nothing more brutalizing," Jack Valenti observed, "than to order men into battle and then pick up the phone from the Pentagon and find out how many were lost that day. I once asked Johnson 'how do you stand it?' And he said it was like drinking carbolic acid every morning." When he couldn't sleep, he'd wander the White House with a

flashlight, visiting the portrait of Woodrow Wilson, who had been para-
lyzed by a stroke while in office, or he would go to the Situation Room
at 3 A.M. because there would always be people there with the latest news
and body counts. "He could not rid himself of the suspicion," Goodwin
observed, "that a mean God had set out to torture him in the cruelest
manner possible."

Eisenhower worried about Johnson's inner resources. "A war or combat situation is upsetting and that can . . . throw off judgment," he observed to Nixon, who came to visit at the farm in the fall of 1967, as he
was laying his plans to challenge Johnson for the presidency. Ike feared
that the president "lacked the inner pressure gauge that told him when
to relax. He had no hobbies or interests outside of politics." Johnson
increasingly took comfort in the company of men with long memories, those who had been in the arena. He savored a visit with Truman
in Missouri; he called him "one of the few comforts I had all during
the war."

"You know the great thing about Truman," he told Goodwin, "is
that once he makes up his mind about something—anything, including
the A bomb—he never looks back and asks 'should I have done it? Oh!
Should I have done it?' No, he just knows he made up his mind as best
he could and that's that. There's no going back. I wish I had some of that
quality."

One day when he visited Ike at Walter Reed following gall bladder
surgery, he ran into Eisenhower's pastor, Dr. Edward Elson, who asked
about Ike's spirits. Johnson's reply suggested he himself was just as much
in need of care: "Dr. Elson," Johnson said, "when I need comfort, this is
where I come and this is the man I come to see."

But over time even Eisenhower grew impatient with Johnson's du-
plicity. Where was the honest appraisal of goals and costs? The very notion of a "painless war" of the kind Johnson seemed determined to wage
was offensive to Ike. "The American people," Ike complained, "are being
promised guns and a lot more butter—guns almost smothered in butter.
I don't believe it's possible." Johnson's popularity sank to the lowest level
since Truman's 23 percent in 1951. He was compared to Caesar, Ca-
ligula, and Mussolini. "Lee Harvey Oswald, Where Are You Now?" read
the protesters' signs. Bobby Kennedy called for an unconditional bombing halt. In the spring of 1967 fully two thirds of the country said they

had lost faith in Johnson's leadership. Half the country didn't know what the war was about. That fall at a Selective Service office in Baltimore, a Catholic priest poured two pints of blood over sixteen file drawers of records; a show at Manhattan's New School displayed Johnson flanked by Miss Napalm and other symbols of death. And then there was the March on the Pentagon, which reduced Johnson to urging companies to withhold buses to reduce the turnout.

The White House watched in growing frustration, especially as Hanoi hailed the "valuable support" and "great encouragement" of the antiwar activists. Generals began talking openly of winning the war "over there," and losing it at home. Advisor James Rowe warned that elite opinion was fast turning against the war, and might "eventually convert the people, especially if unopposed." And a presidential campaign was looming.

This was torment of a purely political kind: Johnson, who so wanted to be loved, so wanted to be a great president, concluded that the main obstacle to winning this cursed war was the opposition of a public that no longer trusted him to do it.

While Richard Nixon would build his 1968 campaign around his appeal to the Silent Majority, it was Johnson who first sought to rally the ambivalent middle to his cause—and use the club members to do it. If he couldn't sell this war, maybe they could. The task of taking on the protesters fell to Johnson's canny special advisor John Roche, a former political science professor from Brandeis. Roche was a classic Cold War liberal; he had served as chairman of the Americans for Democratic Action, advised Kennedy back when he was a senator, wrote speeches for Humphrey, and joined the Johnson White House as a resident intellectual. "I will argue to my dying day," he said of Vietnam, "that this was the most idealistic war we have ever fought."

"In politics," Roche liked to say, "a straight line is the shortest distance to disaster." So he came up with a circuitous one to make the case. When Johnson was desperate for allies against all the whining intellectuals and rambunctious protesters, Roche hatched a plan in the spring of 1967 for a high-profile committee of wise men; he promised, in an eyes only memo, that he would "leave no tracks." He even promised squads of letter writers in support of the committee's efforts. Former Illinois senator Paul Douglas was the perfect face, a strong anticommunist who was in favor of civil and labor rights. James Rowe, who also pitched in, thought

Johnson would appreciate having at least two Harvard professors on the list. Johnson agreed with the plan—but "don't get surfaced," he warned.

And so at the end of October, at the National Press Club, Douglas announced the creation of the nonpartisan Citizens Committee for Peace with Freedom in Viet Nam. The honorary cochairs? Harry Truman and Dwight Eisenhower.

The group was presented as a counterweight to the radical Left and Right: "Voices of dissent have received attention far out of proportion to their actual numbers," the committee said in its mission statement. "Our objective is to make sure that the majority voice of America is heard— loud and clear—so that Peking and Hanoi will not mistake the strident voices of some dissenters for American discouragement and a weakening of will." The committee reeked of sage credibility; businessmen, professors, Nobel laureates: there were former secretaries of state Dean Acheson and James Byrnes; former Harvard president James Conant; former governor Pat Brown of California; AFL-CIO president George Meany; author Ralph Ellison; and Omar Bradley, the only other living five-star general.

The world was watching to see whether America's will was disintegrating: "If the silent center in the U.S. can find an effective voice, through the new Citizens Committee or any other channel," *Time* argued, "American foreign policy will carry considerably greater authority with friends and foes alike."

Again and again, former senator Douglas would faithfully affirm the committee's independence: "Despite your implication, we are not a front for the Administration," he said at a news conference some months later, when the committee issued a statement warning that one-sided concessions to Hanoi were the road to surrender. It was too late for any committee of heavyweights to soothe the growing anxieties of Middle America about the war.

Eisenhower would continue to express support for Johnson's efforts, and urged him to get tough right to the end. "Once I complained to him about the trouble Fulbright and his friends were making for me," Johnson recalled. "He told me 'Why, I'd just go ahead and smack them, just pay no attention to these overeducated Senators, that's all there is to it.'" In an interview at Christmastime Ike declared that any Democrat or Republican running for president on a platform of pulling out of Vietnam "will have me to contend with." He warned, "That's one of the few things that would start me off in a series of stump speeches across the nation." *New York Times* columnist Tom Wicker noted "the remarkable bellicosity" of his remarks, and marveled at the distance from the candidate in 1952 who had asked of the Korean conflict "Where do we go from here? When comes the end? Is there an end?"

In any event, Eisenhower's campaigning days were over—and so, in a sense, was Johnson's presidency. By early 1968 he was practically a prisoner of the White House. The Tet Offensive began at the end of January, eighty thousand communist troops hitting more than a hundred cities and towns in the South. By the time it was over, the losses for the North were devastating; but gone too was all credibility, all the Light at the End of the Tunnel promises coming out of the White House and Pentagon. McNamara resigned; Westmoreland asked for still more troops. Once again, as they had against Harry Truman in 1948, the liberals of Americans for Democratic Action plotted mutiny. CBS news anchor Walter Cronkite declared publicly that the war was unwinnable; "I've lost Mr. Middle America," Johnson declared. Peace candidate Eugene McCarthy won 42.4 percent of the vote in the New Hampshire primary—though only later did a close analysis show that 60 percent of his vote came from people who felt Johnson was not *escalating* fast enough. They were just sick of the stalemate, and the lies, and the unending train of bodies coming home.

Johnson announced a unilateral bombing halt on March 31, 1968, named Averell Harriman his personal envoy who would "go anywhere, any time" to make peace, and then the shocker: with "the world's hopes in the balance," he said, he needed to devote every hour, every breath to the "awesome duties of the presidency"—and so he "would not be seeking and would not accept another term."

Thus ended, for all intents and purposes, the extraordinary presidency of Lyndon Johnson. But in the next seven months he'd have occasion to reconsider his decision—especially once he found himself in the middle of the most devious, and dangerous, club collision of the modern age.

NIXON AND REAGAN:

The California Boys

―――――――――― ⚷ ――――――――――

Richard Nixon and Ronald Reagan defined Republican politics in America from 1966 until Nixon's death in 1994. Raised by religious mothers and luckless fathers, they both had roots in Southern California's conservative crucible. But like other men born under the same star, they functioned as much like rivals as allies over the course of their nearly fifty-year relationship.

And as both began to crowd the national stage, it became clear that their politics were nearly as different as their personalities. Where Nixon was a bloodless realist, Reagan was an ardent optimist. Where Nixon was suspicious and calculating, Reagan was trusting and often naive. Nixon was never as personally popular as many of the initiatives he launched at home or overseas. By contrast, Reagan's policies were never as popular as the sunny persona he created through his speeches and stagecraft. Even after they left the presidency, one of them fourteen years after the other, they took separate paths. One man lingered in the public eye for two decades, fighting for redemption. The other disappeared, almost overnight. Their correspondence lasted thirty-five years. Their letters are always friendly, respectful, and proper. But they only begin to tell the story.

―――――――――― ⚷ ――――――――――

10

"You'll Have My Promise—I'll Speak No Evil"

—RONALD REAGAN

Richard Nixon could not get through.

On the June night in 1966 that former actor Ronald Reagan had defeated all comers in California's Republican gubernatorial primary, Richard Nixon, still stinking of the defeats of 1960 and 1962, could not raise the party's new phenom on the telephone.

Reagan had trounced—flattened is a better description—George Christopher, the moderate Republican mayor of San Francisco, winning all but three of the state's fifty-eight counties (and he very nearly won two of those). Nixon, the last Republican to win the gubernatorial nomination, was unable to get a congratulatory phone call through. The telephone lines from New York to Los Angeles were all jammed, as sometimes happened in those days. Western Union was in the midst of a strike. And so Nixon was forced to reach out to the Republicans' hottest property in the worst possible way: through the U.S. mail.

"Your primary race was conducted with great ability, dignity and effectiveness," Nixon wrote Reagan, apologizing for resorting to the Postal Service. "Your refusal to be baited into attacking your primary opponent tremendously enhances your chances in November." Trading desperately on their shared Midwestern heritage—Reagan was born in Illinois; Nixon's parents were from Ohio and Indiana—he added, "I am sure you know the assault on you will reach massive proportions in the press and on TV as [Pat] Brown and his cohort realize they are going to be thrown off the gravy train after eight pretty lush years. There is an old Midwestern expression (my roots are also in the Midwest) which I would urge you to bear in mind as the going gets tougher. 'Just sit tight in the buggy.'"

By the middle of 1966, Nixon had been courting and advising Ronald Reagan for nearly twenty years. But now Reagan's path began to diverge from Nixon's; and though both men took pains to disguise the fact, Nixon and Reagan were no longer allies.

Instead, they were heading for a brawl.

"The Movie Star?"

The two men met in the summer of 1947, when a thirty-four-year-old freshman congressman sat down for a private conversation with a thirty-six-year-old actor in California. Nixon had heard from his political patrons that Reagan, the new president of the Screen Actors Guild, was concerned about communist infiltration of his trade union. To a junior member on the House Labor Committee, which was then investigating communist influence in American power centers, this was a tip worth checking out. And so Nixon paid Reagan a visit while he was back in his home state that spring.

They had more in common than they might have imagined: both were Depression kids who spent happy times in the spotlight at small-town colleges (both men played football and pursued drama), and both by 1947 had young, growing families. But they were otherwise a study in contrasts. Nixon, a Navy vet who'd won a seat in Congress from Orange County the November before, was making a name for himself as a sharpie who was going places. Reagan was in the early days of shooting a dreadful movie with Shirley Temple entitled *That Hagen Girl*, but was spending a growing portion of his time on union politics as his film career began to turn down. Certainly, Dick and Ron were political opposites: Nixon a conservative Republican on the rise; Reagan an outspoken FDR Democrat in a town where politics didn't matter. Where Nixon was reserved to the point of awkwardness, Reagan was relaxed and charming, having cavorted with starlets and sported with other leading men for more than a decade. Reagan's first job out of college was as a football play-by-play man at a radio station in Davenport, Iowa; after law school, Nixon sought a job with the FBI.

Reagan looked like an ideal witness for Nixon's committee. "I was particularly impressed by his attitude and I believe that he can be extremely helpful in the committee's investigation," Nixon reported to Herman Perry, the Whittier banker who had first urged him to run for Congress. "Reagan would make a particularly good witness in view of the fact that he is classified as a liberal and as such could not be accused of simply being a red baiting reactionary."

Reagan did testify in Washington that fall; and Nixon was present for the hearing, though he asked no questions and the actor's remarks were largely inconsequential. And so the Nixon-Reagan partnership went dormant.

The two men had little contact until 1959. In the interim, Reagan had divorced, remarried, moved away from the movie business, and begun traveling the nation for General Electric, giving speeches to its employees—his liberal antifascist philosophy slowly morphing into a conservative antigovernment outlook. Nixon, meanwhile, had defeated a former Hollywood actress (and friend of Reagan's) turned congresswoman named Helen Gahagan Douglas for the U.S. Senate after Nixon labeled her "pink down to her underwear"; and then was lifted to the vice presidency under Dwight Eisenhower at the unlikely age of forty.

In 1959, as Nixon prepared to mount his own bid for the White House, Reagan again crossed his path. This time, he appeared in the form of a speech, called "Business, Ballots and Bureaus," sent to Nixon by an ally in New York City. The speech, which was Reagan's standard stump, was an appealing mash-up of conservative principles, anecdotes about government waste, and stories from American history. It is hard to imagine that Nixon found it remarkable, but being on the verge of a nationwide campaign and knowing Reagan spoke to hundreds, if not thousands, of people each month in his role as GE's spokesman, Nixon saw the chance to reconnect with the man he had met twelve years earlier. "I thought you did an excellent job of analyzing our present tax situation," Nixon wrote. "In recent months, I have been greatly encouraged by the apparent trend on the part of the American people to question the tax and tax, spend and spend . . . elect and elect philosophy. . . . I hope that you will have many opportunities to repeat your wise words." In a brief postscript, Nixon mentioned that he recalled how the two men had met in 1947.

Reagan wrote back a week later in his clean, even cursive to thank Nixon for his note. He seemed to be ready to enlist in Nixon's army. "You were very kind to write me about my talk," Reagan replied, "and I feel honored that you took the time to read it." After explaining that he had been crisscrossing the country and giving speeches that he wrote himself, Reagan noted his surprise at the reaction: "Audiences are actually militant in their expression that something must be done. . . . I am convinced there is a ground swell of economic conservatism building up which could reverse the entire tide of present day 'statism.' As a matter of fact, we seem to be in one of those rare moments when the American people with that wisdom which is the strength of Democracy are ready to say 'enough.' "

Nixon answered Reagan quickly, enclosing a report from the Cabinet Committee on Price Stability for his correspondent's reading pleasure and adding one prophetic observation: "You have the ability of putting complicated technical ideas into words everyone can understand. Those of us who have spent a number of years in Washington too often lack the ability to express ourselves in this way."

This sort of compliment was worth shopping around. On July 8, an item appeared in Hedda Hopper's widely read Hollywood gossip column noting that Reagan "had a note from Vice President Nixon congratulating him on [a] speech Ronnie delivered at [the] New York Waldorf," which Nixon said had shown a "grasp of complex tax issues." Not standard Hedda Hopper fare perhaps, but the item (almost certainly leaked by Reagan or his friends) did its work. Nixon was helping to launch Reagan's political career whether he intended it or not.

Soon, the courtship was working in both directions. Reagan wrote to Nixon in September to congratulate the vice president for taking an uncompromising line with communist dictators. Nixon replied overnight, and sent along copies of some of his other recent speeches. In hopes of meeting Nixon in person, Reagan wrote again in December to let the vice president know he'd be anchoring ABC's coverage of the Rose Bowl Parade on New Year's Day 1960, in which the Nixons would be featured as grand marshals. Perhaps the two could get together afterward, Reagan suggested. But Nixon begged off.

Reagan's wooing of Nixon paralleled his own trial separation from the Democratic Party. Reagan had been nudged to the right by his experience as president of the Screen Actors Guild, his friends, and his father-in-law, Chicago physician Loyal Davis, who had retired to Phoenix and become close to Barry Goldwater. After watching the Democrats nominate John F. Kennedy at their convention in July 1960, Reagan decided to coach Nixon in the finer points of political theater, dashing off a letter urging the Republican nominee to dispense with "the traditional demonstrations which follow each nomination. True, they once had their place when their only purpose was to influence the delegates in the convention hall. Now, however, TV has opened a window onto convention deliberations and the 'demonstration' is revealed as a synthetic time waster which only serves to belittle us in what should be one of our finer moments."

After a few disparaging sentences about Kennedy's boyish appearance, Reagan told Nixon he could pick up millions of votes if he paid more attention to people who don't vote. This note was a harbinger of Nixon-Reagan battles to come. "I don't pose as an infallible pundit, but I have a strong feeling that the twenty million non votes in this country just might be conservatives who have cynically concluded the two parties offer no choice between them where fiscal stability is concerned." Nixon sent Reagan a brief note of thanks in reply.

By now, Reagan felt comfortable enough to advise Nixon on personnel matters, even the most important ones. Nixon was still in the hunt for a running mate at the convention in Chicago that summer when a telegram arrived at the Blackstone Hotel. It read: RESPECTFULLY URGE CONSIDERATION GOLDWATER FOR VICE PRESIDENT. CANNOT SUPPORT TICKET IF IT INCLUDES ROCKEFELLER.

It was signed MR AND MRS RONALD REAGAN.

A scribbled note from a Nixon aide asked the question: "The movie star?" A second scribbled note provided the answer: "Yes."

It would not be the last time anyone in the Nixon camp mistook Reagan for just an actor.

Over the summer, Nixon's aides plotted how best to bring Reagan into the fold. Adela Rogers St. Johns, the famed journalist who grew up with Nixon in Whittier and then went on to an illustrious career with the Hearst newspapers, told Nixon aide Stan McCaffrey that a number of Hollywood types could be lured to the Nixon tent, including Walt Disney, James Cagney—and Reagan if "the right man might get him to come along." Reagan even offered to change parties and publicly endorse Nixon against John F. Kennedy. No, said Nixon, endorse me as a Democrat. It will mean more.

And so, in October 1960, Reagan became the vice chairman of the Southern California Democrats for Nixon. This celebrity conversion, just a few weeks before the election, was cause for announcement. "As a lifelong Democrat, today I feel no Democrat can ignore that the party has been taken over by a faction which seeks to pattern the Democratic Party and its politics after those of the Labor-Socialist government of England," Reagan said in a statement. "This is no longer the Democratic Party I joined as a young man." Reagan's very public pivot prompted a visit from Joe Kennedy himself. "He tried to persuade me to change my mind and support his son," Reagan recalled, "but I turned him down."

Nixon lost narrowly to JFK, and two more years would pass until Reagan finally joined the Republican Party. In the interim, Reagan helped Nixon navigate the increasingly hazardous back alleys of California's Republican politics. It happened this way: after losing the White House, Nixon spent a year living in New York before returning in 1962 to run for California governor. This turned out to be a truly bad idea that even Nixon's wife, Pat, had opposed. While Nixon had his doubts as well, he also had nothing better to do as he plotted his comeback. But Nixon had no sooner moved his family back home after a decade away when he came under attack from—of all places—the Republican Right. A new generation of archconservatives was gaining influence in California since he had last run for a statewide office, some twelve years before. These Republicans didn't trust Nixon, they didn't respect his eight years in Washington at the side of an internationalist like Eisenhower, and they certainly didn't appreciate the carpetbagger image Nixon had brought with him from New York. And so Nixon turned to Reagan, among others, for advice about how to handle the right-wingers; in turn, Reagan worked behind the scenes to convince many of those who found Nixon too liberal to take another chance on him.

But Reagan's own credentials as a go-between were suspect, chiefly because he was still a Democrat. Reagan finally fixed that while speaking on Nixon's behalf at a 1962 Republican fund-raiser near his home in Pacific Palisades. Midway through the speech a woman in the audience stood up and asked Reagan, "Have you registered as a Republican yet?"

"No I haven't," Reagan replied, "but I intend to."

The woman promptly marched forward to Reagan, introduced herself as a local registration official, and placed the proper form in front of him. As the audience cheered, Reagan recalled, "I signed it and became a Republican, then said to the audience, 'Now where was I?'"

It wasn't enough to save Nixon. He lost to Pat Brown by almost 300,000 votes in 1962 and vowed at an impromptu Beverly Hilton press conference the next morning to disappear from politics forever. "You won't have Nixon to kick around anymore, because, gentlemen, this is my last press conference."

The pundits banged out their Nixon eulogies and buried him. "Barring a miracle," *Time* predicted, "his political career ended last week. He was only 49."

But if Nixon had been sidelined, Reagan had been set free. In March 1962, GE cut him loose as the host of the *General Electric Theater* on Sunday nights, setting the stage for his second career. It has become an iconic piece of Republican lore that the CBS network couldn't cope with a program that had an outspoken conservative as a front man. In fact, politics had little or nothing to do with Reagan getting fired; money did. CBS canceled the show because it was losing market share to a western that appeared at the same time on NBC called *Bonanza*.

And so he turned his attention to his second career. He was about to become a full-time politician.

A Little Help from Gettysburg

When the city fathers of Phoenix invited Nixon to Arizona in March 1965 for a testimonial dinner honoring Barry Goldwater, they asked Reagan to introduce him. The choice made perfect sense: the undisputed winner of the 1964 election, other than Lyndon Johnson himself, had been Reagan, whose eleventh-hour, nationally televised "A Time for Choosing" speech on Goldwater's behalf had electrified conservatives and turned Reagan into an overnight sensation.

A few days later, Nixon sent Reagan a note of thanks for his Arizona remarks and included some advice as Reagan launched his own race to be California's next governor. "Resist the temptation of 'striking back' at any of the other potential candidates," he advised. "I do not know what your political plans eventually will turn out to be," Nixon added, which was more wishful thinking than fact. "However, as I told you, I am sure that no one can beat Brown if the Republican primary is a bitter bloodletting battle."

Reagan wrote Nixon back a week later. "I assure you there will be no first blows, or even second, struck by me. Just between us, I wish the other boys would get the idea. But you'll have my promise—I'll speak no evil and I'll act like I hear no evil, but that will test my acting ability."

Nixon would not be part of Reagan's first political campaign. Reagan made sure of that when he told the *Los Angeles Times* in January 1966 that he did not want Nixon at his side. The reasons for this straight-arm were many: the once reliably moderate politics of California—and of Southern California in particular—were turning to the right. The millions of Midwesterners who had poured into the coastal paradise during the 1930s and 1940s for its plentiful jobs, low cost of living, and good schools were waking up to a new purgatory of high taxes, urban riots, campus dissent, and an increasingly unfamiliar social code.

The summer of 1965 had changed everything. Patriotic employees of such San Fernando Valley defense companies as Canoga Electronics, Rocketdyne, Bendix, and Northrop spent the first week of June 1965 proudly glued to their television sets as astronaut Ed White took the nation's first ever space walk outside a *Gemini IV* capsule that they all had helped build. Two months later, in August, they tuned in again, this time to watch the black neighborhood of Watts, just an hour away, explode in flames and then devolve into looting and rioting until fifteen thousand troops from the 40th Armored Division moved in and cordoned off the entire area. Watts was as terrifying to white Angelenos as *Gemini IV* had been thrilling. "Hell in the City of Angels," the TV commentators declared. A war at home. How could a nation capable of such great achievement in space engender—and then permit—such civil disorder on earth?

Reagan charged straight at that question, promising a new "moral crusade in government" if elected. He capitalized on the hopes and fears both because he was part of the great Midwestern migratory tide himself and because he believed that the government at all levels was becoming too big, too expensive, and too liberal. He drew heavily from Goldwater's well of cultural issues but he did it with a smile. He barnstormed the state calling for lower taxes, a stronger military response in Vietnam, and a crackdown on everything from crime to drugs to welfare queens to communist infiltration at home to sexual orgies on campuses. "He believed basically what Barry believed," campaign advisor Stu Spencer recalled. "He said a lot of things that Barry said, but he said them in a soft way, in a more forgiving way."

And people liked what they heard. Reagan captured 1.4 million votes in his race against George Christopher—a stunning number in a primary. Elite opinion makers on the East Coast were rendered nearly speechless: California Republicans "against all counsels of common sense and prudence," said a *New York Times* editorial, "insisted upon nominating actor Ronald Reagan for governor." Certainly, Nixon needed no coaching on what it would mean if Reagan actually won the governor's race in November 1966 against Pat Brown. The smooth and handsome actor-turned-pol would immediately become a contender for the Republican nomination for president in 1968—the job Nixon himself was seeking.

A week or so after his big primary victory, Reagan flew east to consolidate his victory. He stopped first in Gettysburg, Pennsylvania, for a carefully choreographed two-hour session with Eisenhower, who had been watching Reagan for months. "For quite a while I have been reading all I can find about Mr. Reagan," he wrote to California industrialist Jim Murphy in September 1965. "Mostly I see him in TV scenes that are purely entertainment but he does seem to have a very pleasant and appealing personality. The only thing I know about his politics was that he earnestly supported the Republican ticket in 1964." After that, in one of the club's little-known alliances, Eisenhower began sending Reagan advice and ideas directly and through intermediaries. He suggested ways Reagan could lay out a program, shorten his stump speech, and punch up his key phrases. Ike's advice might have seemed basic, but then neither man had chosen politics as a first profession and they shared the surely strange experience of coming to the game relatively late in life (Reagan at fifty-five, Ike at sixty).

For the summit between the party's glorious past and its glamorous future, all three networks sent camera crews to Gettysburg; a dozen other reporters made the hour-long trip from Washington to cover Reagan's arrival at the tiny college where Ike had his office. If Eisenhower favored Nixon, his old vice president, for the 1968 nomination, it was hard to tell that day. "You can bet" Reagan would be a candidate for the White House in 1968 if he beat Brown, Eisenhower said. "It is true that in 1962 I argued that a number of the younger men in the party should make their views known. Our party deserves to have a voice and not sit around and let the nomination go by default."

Then Reagan moved on to Washington, where he was set to do a star turn at the National Press Club. This event was neither beyond Nixon's notice—nor beyond his desire to manipulate. Nixon pulled some levers behind the scenes and got California's senior senator, George Murphy (also a former actor), to coach Reagan about how to handle inevitable questions from reporters about his future plans. Nixon was hoping Reagan would at the very least sidestep any probing about his ambitions in 1968. The tag team was either successful—or Reagan needed no coaching in the first place. For when the questions did come that day, Reagan played the ingenue: "Gosh, it's taken me all my life to get up the nerve to do what I'm doing. That's as far as my dreams go."

In late June it was Nixon's turn to tour. He flew to California, campaigning not for Reagan but instead for his longtime advisor Robert Finch, who was running for lieutenant governor on the same ticket. Reagan and Nixon met privately for dinner, and afterward Nixon told reporters that he was impressed by the way Reagan had repositioned himself as more of a "centrist." Of course, by delivering this line he was merely drawing attention to the fact that Reagan had done no such thing.

When Nixon ran for governor in 1962, he had repudiated the John Birch Society and its members for their extreme views—and lost ground with some conservative voters as a result. By contrast, four years later, Reagan and campaign advisor Spencer had spent a lot of time thinking about how to manage the Far Right challenge and had decided to neither repudiate nor endorse the society. Instead Reagan countered questions about his connections to the group with the following answer: "Any member of the society who supports me will be buying my philosophy, I won't be buying theirs."

It was an artful straddle. But by July, as the general election against Pat Brown approached, the extremist charge had become nettlesome enough for Reagan that Freeman Gosden, half of the *Amos 'n' Andy* team of radio fame and a longtime California Republican, sought help from Eisenhower, his Palm Springs golfing partner. Gosden sent Ike a confidential and somewhat cryptic letter in early July 1966, reporting that Reagan needed a hand getting free of the charge of anti-Semitism, simply because so many Birch Society members were supporting him. "I don't think [Reagan] can come out and say he is not [anti-Semitic] unless there is a question and answer situation," Gosden wrote. "You might have some thoughts on this."

Eisenhower wrote back the same day, proposing a detailed script for a willing reporter and Reagan to follow. This is how Eisenhower imagined the conversation could go:

"Mr. Reagan, I hear that you have disavowed any connection with the John Birch Society, but at the same time I've had reports that you are anti-Semitic. Do you have anything to say on this point."

Ike continued: "His answer could be as emphatic—and as short—as possible. *'I've heard of this malicious accusation. It is not true. Anyone who repeats this rumor is guilty of a deliberate falsehood.'*"

Ike noted: "Then, at another point in the conference, he might say something like this: *'In this campaign, I've been presenting to the public some of the things I want to do for California, meaning for all the people of our state. I do not exclude citizens from my concern and I make no distinctions among them on such invalid bases as color or creed.'*"

And then Ike closed: "Something conveying this meaning might well be slipped in to every public talk—such as, *'There are not minority groups so far as I'm concerned. We are all Americans.'*"

By midsummer, Eisenhower was telling his friends that Reagan was not anti-Semitic—whatever they may have heard. "To scotch such a rumor," he wrote to one New York socialite in July, "is difficult because a candidate cannot, unless specifically questioned, speak out to proclaim 'I am not a thief; I'm not a liar; I'm not anti-Semitic; I'm not an assassin; I'm not a perjurer.' I hope that Reagan will be questioned on the matter—and if he is, I know his answer. He is a decent American and I do hope he is elected."

The issue reached a climax in early August when a young state controller named Alan Cranston chased Reagan down at the Sacramento airport in an effort to personally hand him a twenty-eight-page report alleging anti-Semitism in his campaign because of his connections to the Birch Society. A Reagan aide intercepted Cranston and his document as Reagan was boarding a plane to Los Angeles. Reagan never got to rehearse Ike's lines, but he didn't need to. Instead, Reagan waved Cranston off with a trademark cock of his head. "You've made your grandstand play," he said. "It's no secret I deplore racism of any kind."

But if the Brown forces weren't above raising the Birch Society as an issue in Reagan's campaign, neither was Nixon. That fall, Nixon flew to California once more to campaign for Republican lieutenant governor candidate Robert Finch. Pat Buchanan, then a thirty-year-old aide traveling with Nixon, recalls seeing a former Republican congressman and state party stalwart named Patrick Hillings talking to reporters after one campaign stop. When Buchanan wandered over to listen in, he heard Hillings telling local reporters that Reagan needed to fully repudiate the Birch Society.

Such a suggestion, Buchanan knew, only served to make the apparent connection between Reagan and the Birch Society even stronger. Stunned by this unhelpful remark, Buchanan pulled Hillings aside afterward and asked, "What the hell are you doing?"

Replied Hillings: "The old man told me to do it."

Nixon, who had campaigned strategically for Republican congressional candidates all across the country, watched the 1966 results come in with about forty supporters at a suite at the Drake Hotel in New York. It turned into a huge Republican night, with big gains in the Midwest and West. The party gained forty-seven seats in Congress—including a young congressman from Houston named Bush—and elected a new generation of governors. Nixon roamed the suite all night long, noting, "It's a sweep, it's a sweep."

But it was as much the moment of the Reagan arrival as of Nixon's revival. In California, the former actor who was easy to underestimate won in a stunning landslide, earning 3.7 million votes to Brown's 2.7 million—capturing a million more votes than Nixon had earned four years earlier. The comparison with 1962 was haunting: where Nixon had won just twenty of California's fifty-eight counties, Reagan captured all but three just four years later. Nixon didn't have to worry about getting through to Los Angeles on this night; this time, Reagan phoned Nixon, who took the call alone in one of the bedrooms at the Drake suite.

When he emerged, he said to aides, "He's all right, Ron is—it's a sweep in California, too." Then the whole Nixon party went out for spaghetti.

Within days, Reagan was being mentioned in the *New York Times* as the conservative favorite for the 1968 nomination. Two weeks later, Reagan quietly launched his own campaign to win the White House.

Shadowboxing

What unfolded over the next two years between Nixon and Reagan was the closest they ever came to direct competition, but that didn't make it any less of a fight. It began within days of Reagan's victory.

November 28, 1966

Dear Ronnie:

Warren Weaver's story in the New York Sunday Times magazine section even went so far as to concede your skill in fielding questions. This concession of the Times is a major breakthrough! Pat joins me in sending our very best wishes to Nancy and you for Christmas and the New Year.

Sincerely
Dick

Immediately after the 1966 election, the 1968 Republican primary began. Reagan and Nixon both allowed other Republicans to step out in front: George Romney of Michigan, Nelson Rockefeller of New York, and, though he was a Democrat on paper, George Wallace of Alabama, who was becoming a hero to many of the nation's conservatives.

Despite Nixon's triumph as a surrogate and statesman in 1966, some on Reagan's team regarded him as a loser, a washed-up has-been; the party would never nominate someone with so many scars a second time.

And so Team Reagan quietly launched its own campaign.

According to Lou Cannon's definitive account in *Governor Reagan*, Reagan met at his Pacific Palisades home with a handful of top advisors to discuss a possible presidential bid only nine days after his election as governor. Reagan aides were given assignments to fan out around the country and measure interest among key party players. Not everyone who was contacted was intrigued. But Tom Reed, Reagan's political advisor, met a few days later with F. Clifton White, a key architect of Goldwater's 1964 nomination, at the Apawamis Club in Rye, New York. White urged Reed to make no moves until Reagan had put some points on the board as governor. Reed personally briefed Reagan on the conversation a few days later in San Francisco.

Reagan's first campaign for president was a strange and muddled affair. In a conversation with syndicated columnist Robert Novak, White described the Reagan bid, in fact, as a clandestine operation: Reagan could not run for president so soon after his gubernatorial election; instead, "a few emissaries under cover would try prying delegates from Nixon even though Reagan was not a candidate." Reagan was at times no more than ambivalent about a White House run; some of his aides were more enthusiastic than he was. Stuart Spencer recalled that even as the furtive campaign was unfolding, he kept a back channel going with Nixon's camp to make sure relations did not turn irrevocably sour.

The secret candidate himself was almost fatalistic about his prospects, taking an active role at some stages while turning passive at others. He had a habit of repeating a phrase to his aides that seemed to take the guesswork out of the gamble: "The office seeks the man," he would say, "the office seeks the man." What exactly did this mean? It translated best into a conviction that if the times demanded it, voters would somehow rise up and call you to service. What you did about it in the meantime, under this unusual theory, mattered only to a point. It was surely a comfort to Reagan, who believed deeply that God had a plan for him, that there was only so much he could do to alter it. But it is also clear that over the next two years, Reagan took a variety of steps to prolong his role in the unfolding 1968 Republican nomination drama even when many people both inside and outside his circle were urging him to quit.

Meanwhile, there is no doubt that Nixon came to view Reagan as an obstacle to the prize. Nixon had seen Reagan roll up massive majorities in California over Brown; he knew how smooth and appealing the former film star was on camera and he knew that the rising urban unrest and unhappiness with the Vietnam War was making the Republican Party a more Western, suburban, and conservative coalition than it had been in 1960. Unlike Rockefeller or Romney, Reagan could appeal to Southern and Western conservatives who were playing a growing role in a party long dominated by its more moderate Midwestern and Eastern factions. "Ronald Reagan . . . set the hearts of many Southern Republicans aflutter," Nixon wrote later. "He spoke their conservative language particularly and with great passion. Until I had the nomination, therefore, I had to pay careful attention to the dangers of a sudden resurgence on the right. Equally dangerous would be a serious intraparty split that would deliver the Reaganites to Wallace's camp."

In a private January 1967 strategy session with his advisors at the Waldorf-Astoria in Manhattan, Nixon sized up his rivals, giving Romney even money to win, himself two-to-one odds, and pegging Reagan's chances one in four. But Reagan was enough of a concern that Nixon discussed with his aides—and then abandoned—the idea of promising Reagan the 1972 nomination in exchange for staying out of the 1968 race.

Over the course of 1967 and 1968, Nixon and Reagan squared off in an increasingly public fight for the nomination while, in private, each went to unusual lengths to pretend that the whole thing was a series of perfectly logical misunderstandings.

Each man played his supposedly innocent role all the way to the convention in Miami Beach.

February 24, 1967

Dear Ron:

Through my private intelligence, I have learned that you will be the speaker at the Gridiron dinner on March 1. The purpose of this note is to wish you well and tell you how sorry I am that I will be in Europe on that date on the first leg of my around-the-world tour.

The Gridiron speech, as you know, is quite a test for the average political figure. My guess is, however, that this white tie audience will present no significant problem for you. After the battle of Berkeley, everything else should seem easy!

Pat joins me in sending our best wishes to Nancy and you.

Sincerely,
Dick

Here, in just a few lines, can be found all of Nixon's complex feelings about Reagan and his rise. Seldom has a politician been less qualified to give a rival advice on charming a crowd than was Nixon with Reagan. The wording is friendly and generous enough but the tone makes clear that Nixon still thought of Reagan as a lucky novice who should be somewhat grateful for the advice and compliments of a seasoned vet. Nixon seemed to believe he could keep Reagan in a box, making a point of strutting about his upcoming overseas swing and his own mysterious network of spies. Left unstated but just as likely, Nixon may have been envious that it was Reagan who was tapped by the capital's political press corps to be its toastmaster at Washington's toniest white-tie dinner that spring. "Nixon did not have a high regard for most people and Reagan was no exception there," recalled John Sears, who worked for Nixon in 1968 and later for Reagan. "Nixon disliked people who he thought were just fluff, who he thought were nothing special underneath a good package. That was part of his idea about the Kennedys and, in Nixon's mind, Reagan fit that too."

As 1967 unfolded, Reagan's political ambition became a very public story. In late April 1967, Los Angeles mayor Sam Yorty, who had backed Reagan in 1966, said that the governor was "running for President too soon." In early May, some fifteen million Americans watched as Reagan appeared on a nationally televised CBS broadcast in which he and Bobby Kennedy debated via satellite two dozen students in London about world affairs, chiefly Vietnam. The foreign students were officious, well prepared, and hostile, but Reagan handled them with a cool detachment that Kennedy visibly lacked. Afterward, critics agreed that Reagan, a relative newcomer to politics, easily outperformed the more accomplished senator from New York. Reagan left Kennedy "blinking," said *Newsweek*. Afterward, Kennedy asked, "Who the fuck got me into this?"

It was a boffo performance that did not go unnoticed in Nixon's camp, which was just then setting up its headquarters a block from the White House, at 1726 Pennsylvania Avenue.

May 31, 1967

Dear Ronnie,

I was still in Latin America when the program was carried but from all sides I have heard nothing but the highest praise for your handling of the joint television appearance with Bobby Kennedy.

When Newsweek gives you rave notices, it must have been tops!

I am planning to come to the Bohemian Grove for the weekend of July 22 and 23. In the event that you are in Sacramento at that time, I would very much enjoy the opportunity to visit with you. I think you might find some of the information I have gathered on my world, fact-finding journey of considerable interest.

With best personal regards, sincerely,
Dick

Reagan agreed to meet, but stuck to his campaign schedule anyway, focusing on the very Republicans who had never held Nixon in high regard. In mid-June, Reagan stole the show at the Young Republican Convention in Omaha, where his speech was interrupted twenty times and climaxed with a five-minute demonstration in the city's sports arena that was punctuated with chants, "We want Reagan! We want Reagan." In late June, Reagan easily won the buzz-war at the summer meeting of the National Governors Association, held at Wyoming's Jackson Lake. He even met privately with eleven Western Republican governors, sweeping into the session, one observer said, like a white knight on a charger, trying to capture the party's right flank. "Reagan's rapidly replacing Dick Nixon in one wing of the party," New Mexico governor David Cargo told reporters that weekend. Still coy, Reagan refused to say he was a candidate—or rule out a draft if it came to that. "If the Republican party comes beating at my door, I wouldn't say 'Get lost, fellows.' But that isn't going to happen."

One account of the Teton meetings sent Reagan—and surely Nixon too—around the bend. "Reagan's ascendancy poses the threat of a conservative split," *Time* reported. "Reagan, in fact, said of Nixon to one Republican governor, 'This guy's a loser. Any guy who can lose to Pat Brown can't win the presidency.'"

There it was: the whole rationale for Reagan's supposedly secret candidacy suddenly out in the open. And if *Time* was right, Reagan himself had put it there. And so a few days after the issue appeared, Reagan fired off an angry letter to *Time*'s editors to cover his tracks. "TIME owes it to its readers to name the anonymous Governor whom I allegedly told that 'Dick Nixon is a loser.' It will be especially interesting, since I have never said it or thought it. I am sorry that at a time when Republican leaders are working hard for party unity, TIME would stoop to quoting nameless sources in an effort to destroy that unity."

Reagan then wrote Nixon a sort of half apology and included a copy of his letter to *Time*'s editors.

July 12, 1967

Dear Dick,

I thought you might be interested in seeing the attached letter.

Best regards,
Ron

Nixon wrote back six days later:

July 18, 1967

Dear Ron,

> *Your letter to TIME was right on target. It probably helps to let them know their errors will not go unchallenged.*

> *Best regards,*
> *Dick*

Time, for its part, dismissed Reagan's request for a clarification. "Time's source is not at all 'nameless,'" the editors replied, "but we are bound to honor his request that he not be identified—a request with which Governor Reagan, as a political figure, can surely sympathize."

Five days later, the long-awaited Nixon-Reagan meeting unfolded in the one place where their conversations would go unrecorded, but not unnoticed: at the all-male power broker confab known as the Bohemian Grove sixty-five miles north of San Francisco. There, amid the towering redwoods spread out over 2,700 acres, the nation's moguls, financiers, politicians, and cabinet officers had been gathering for decades to talk business and politics and put on musical skits. It was something of a clubhouse. In 1967, Nixon was set to be the Grove's keynote speaker in the sprawling natural amphitheater and he planned to dedicate his speech to Herbert Hoover, who had introduced Nixon to Ike at the Grove in 1950.

Sometime during the weekend, Nixon cornered Reagan to pin him down about his plans for 1968. Sitting together with California senator George Murphy on a bench in the "Lost Angels" neighborhood of the Grove, Nixon officially informed Reagan of what was already obvious: that he planned to seek the presidency in 1968. Echoing many of their previous conversations, Nixon promised to run not against any fellow Republicans but instead against LBJ.

And what were Reagan's plans, exactly? According to Nixon, Reagan said he was "surprised, flattered and somewhat concerned about all the presidential speculation surrounding him." Reagan told Nixon that he "did not want to be a favorite son" but he would permit his name to be placed in nomination in order to keep California's large slate of delegates unified. In what would turn out to be a promise he could not keep, Reagan also told Nixon he would not be a candidate in the primaries. Reagan historian James Mann has pointed out that each man was able in this conversation to "advance his own political interests while cloaking them in the guise of what was best for the party."

Yet their truce barely made it through the night. The next day, a Nixon aide was quoted in a syndicated column that suggested how Nixon really felt about Reagan's campaign. The column, a particularly arcane Evans and Novak workup of New York state Republican machinations, suggested that "the rise of Gov. Ronald Reagan" had led the Nixon camp to take some steps to isolate Reagan as the candidate of the fringe ultraconservatives. "Let Ronnie have the kooks," the Nixon aide remarked.

Now it was Nixon's turn to apologize. On August 4, he sent Reagan a long, two-page, single-spaced letter of explanation.

August 4, 1967

Dear Ron,

When I returned from the Coast last week, I came across this recent column by Evans and Novak and I wanted to send it along as a sample of what can be expected from those who are trying to create divisions between us. It is ironic that the same small Eastern coterie that divided the party in 1964 is now trying to divide those who sought to unite it in 1964 by supporting the ticket.

As you are aware from the experience with Time Magazine that you related to me at Lost Angels, it is extremely difficult to stop this kind of activity.

. . . Writing a letter asking the columnists to straighten out the facts is going to accomplish nothing. And, as you found in trying to get TIME to retract the erroneous quote it had attributed to you, a letter to the editor often results in re-publication of the original inaccuracy or falsehood. . . .

Sincerely,
Dick

Reagan replied twelve days later and let Nixon off the hook just as Nixon had done for him in July.

August 16, 1967

Dear Dick,

> *Thanks for sending me the column. I'm quite sure the pace of this sort of thing will step up in the days ahead. I think it is very important that all of us on our side keep reminding ourselves and each other that we shouldn't believe any quotes unless we hear them first hand. I'm always reminded of the Hollywood days and how the people in our business would read the gossip columns and your first reaction was always how dishonest they were about yourself, but two paragraphs later you're believing every word when they talk about someone else.*

> *Sincerely,*
> *Ron*

Then Reagan went back to campaigning.

In October, he raised $350,000 at a dinner in Columbia, South Carolina, the biggest fund-raising banquet in the state's history. The next night, in Wisconsin, thousands jammed Milwaukee's cavernous Municipal Arena (some paying $100 a plate; others $5 just to sit unfed in the balcony) to hear Reagan give his trademark speech. "We have some hippies in California," Reagan told the crowd. "For those of you who don't know what a hippie is, he's a fellow who has hair like Tarzan, who walks like Jane and who smells like Cheetah."

Reagan campaigned in Oregon in November and then went to Connecticut in December, where he wooed Yalies with talk of a volunteer military and insisted that "anyone would have to be out of his skull to want to be President."

But with the publicity Reagan was getting, he'd have been out of his mind to stop. In mid-October *Time* splashed both Reagan and Rockefeller on its cover, suggesting that only by harnessing its two undeclared candidates could Republicans defeat LBJ and Hubert Humphrey. The cover story bent over backward to ignore Nixon's existence or any role he might play in 1968, except for a remark or two leveled obliquely at Reagan. "In a world series game," Nixon was permitted to say, "they often call on the seasoned hitter whose recent batting average isn't so good, but who is reliable in a pinch. The next president must have that same judgment, coolness and poise. It can't be his first world series."

The Western Star

When it finally got under way in 1968, Reagan's public campaign was a little odd. Inexperience, just as Nixon had alleged, was its hallmark. Reagan sat out the early states and did not campaign much where he was on the ballot, while Nixon rolled up delegates. When Rockefeller pulled out of the race in March, Nixon phoned aide Bill Safire and said, "The only one who can stop us is Reagan." A week later, Nixon wrote Reagan a veiled cease-and-desist order under cover of a thank-you note.

April 4, 1968

Dear Ron,

Now that the results of the New Hampshire and Wisconsin primaries are in, I just want you to know how much I have appreciated your using your influence to discourage some of your very enthusiastic supporters who understandably wanted to launch a major campaign on your behalf in those states.

I understand completely the very difficult position you are in due to the necessity of your maintaining your Favorite Son position in California. Whatever happens in the balance of the primaries, you can be sure we shall all be working together for victory in November.

With best personal regards,

Sincerely,
Dick

Reagan fired a note right back, which pretended not to hear what Nixon was asking.

April 10, 1968

Dear Dick,

    Congratulations on your excellent showing in New Hampshire and Wisconsin. It's truly good of you to take the time to write and I greatly appreciate hearing from you.
    I'm especially happy to know you understand the touchy position I'm in at this time maintaining a neutral stand while running as California's Favorite Son.
    My wish, like yours, is to have a united Republican Party behind our candidate in November.

Sincerely,
Ron

And then Reagan went to work to become that candidate.

He did a speaking swing in April in Idaho and Colorado, and then captured 22 percent of the vote in Nebraska after spending only $13,500 there. Reagan, Nixon told reporters, had done "very well." Reagan reset his sights on the Oregon primary in late May and there he made his biggest charge, running twenty-second and sixty-second television and radio ads comparing Nixon's poor 1962 showing against Pat Brown to his own triumph over Brown four years later. His aides distributed 750,000 flyers in Oregon newspapers and tried to win CBS's permission to rebroadcast his triumphant debate with Bobby Kennedy. (CBS declined.) But again Nixon trounced him, this time by a three-to-one margin. Less than a week later, running unopposed, Reagan won the California primary. But his win went unnoticed because Kennedy was assassinated late that night in a Los Angeles hotel.

So did the fact that Reagan came out at the end of the 1968 primaries with more popular votes than Nixon.

But delegates, not voters, matter in nomination contests. Even though the primaries were over and Nixon had the nomination virtually sewn up, Reagan kept on fighting. He next launched a swing through a handful of Southern and border states, which, under the cover of party fund-raising, was a last-ditch hunt for stray and undecided delegates. Reagan flew from Sacramento to Amarillo to Little Rock to Charlottesville, and then on to Baltimore, Cincinnati, and Kentucky, and finally to Birmingham. This barnstorming tour was doomed to fail, but it gave Reagan his first real taste of nonstop presidential campaigning. Reporters tracking Reagan's movements closely noted that virtually everyone at a meeting of Kentucky's Republican delegates asked for a picture with him. Lou Cannon, covering the odyssey for the *San Jose Mercury News*, reported that not a single delegate at such events switched sides to Reagan. The faithful were shopping, but not buying.

Nixon certainly noticed what Reagan was doing. He recalled later that Reagan flew Southern delegates to California for conversation and courtship and, when he arrived in Miami Beach, made the rounds of key hotels, "charming the delegates with his personality and speaking ability." Perhaps the strangest part of the brief campaign was that Reagan waited until the last possible moment to publicly admit that he was running at all. On Sunday, August 4, on the eve of the convention, Reagan made official what he had been up to for nearly two years. "Once I'm placed in nomination," he announced on *Face the Nation*, "I am a candidate, if the delegates choose to consider me along with those who have been campaigning, this they are free to do."

This was a strange last-minute maneuver, so unexpected that Nancy Reagan learned about it from the radio. Meanwhile, behind the scenes, Reagan aides cornered delegates and urged them to remain uncommitted until after a first ballot. If Nixon could be halted on the first count, they argued, Reagan could emerge as the party's preferred choice later on. Even at the eleventh hour, with the feet of most of the Republican establishment locked in concrete, Reagan doubled down. "The marriage of convenience between Rockefeller and Reagan was now operating at full force," Nixon observed. "Rockefeller worked on the northern and Midwestern states while Reagan tried to breach my southern flank."

The *announced* campaign of Reagan was short-lived—a matter of just a few days. For all his team's efforts to keep questions about Nixon's viability alive, Reagan's chances slipped away fast once the voting began.

Nixon quickly rolled up the 667 delegates needed for the nomination on the first ballot. There was no need for Reagan's complex, second-ballot strategy because there was no second ballot. Sometime after 2 A.M. on August 8, as defeat neared, Reagan rushed to the podium and pleaded to be recognized. And when he finally got the floor, he asked the convention to "declare itself unanimously and unitedly behind the candidate Richard Nixon as the next President of the United States."

And that was how Reagan's first race for the presidency ended: the same man who had worked to deprive Nixon of the nomination rushed to deliver the prize once it was out of his reach.

The final delegate tally: Nixon 697, Rockefeller 277, Reagan 182.

Only one question remained: who would be Nixon's running mate? Buchanan, Sears, and Richard Whalen, a young campaign speechwriter, urged Nixon to put Reagan on the ticket as a way to peel away white Southern Democrats who were leaning toward Alabama governor George Wallace. By midsummer, Wallace was attracting nearly a quarter of the vote in some polls and Nixon's men were determined to find a way to cut that bloc down to size. By Sears's analysis, Wallace would get several dozen Electoral College votes in the South, but with Reagan as his number two, Nixon could shrink that number to perhaps half that. In a state-by-state analysis, Sears argued that Reagan was "the only officeholder in the country who can out-talk and out-campaign George Wallace." Pat Buchanan made a similar argument in a separate paper that suggested that Nixon could take the high road if Reagan were free to court the Wallace vote. "We are going to have to be bold to win this one," Buchanan argued, "and I can currently think of nothing bolder than to put the hero of Bedtime For Bonzo on the GOP ticket."

Richard Allen, Nixon's foreign policy research chief, had begun the summer thinking Nixon needed a moderate sidekick, such as Illinois's Chuck Percy, to appeal to liberal voters. But as the Wallace boomlet grew, he changed sides and argued internally for putting Reagan on the ticket because the California governor could appeal to white Southerners without sounding divisive. "With [Reagan], there is no crude appeal—his 'old time' religion is founded on the very elements which are missing today: law, order, patriotism, thrift—and in language which the common man can understand."

At the heart of all these memos was the still unproven idea that the nation was moving to the right. Not everyone in Nixon's camp believed it; not everyone had seen in the 1966 election results the beginning of a giant, forty-year tide; but conservatives in Nixon's inner circle argued that putting a liberal or moderate on the ticket would be a huge misreading of voters' growing antiliberal, antitolerant, antiestablishment mood—and would only bolster Wallace's hand.

In a memo to Nixon, Allen went so far as to say that the liberal establishment was horrified by Nixon and would be doubly horrified by Reagan—which made it all the more imperative to put Reagan on the ticket. "The Establishment *forbids* a Nixon presidency. Thus all who consume and swear by the Establishment views are votes lost forever, votes we cannot capture."

But that idea was still a little too radical for Dwight Eisenhower's vice president.

And so in the end, it came down to the human factor. Richard Whalen went so far as to personally make the case for Reagan to Nixon, who dismissed his young aide with a wave and the comment, "[Reagan's] just an actor." But veterans of that campaign say that language was Nixon's personal code for a deeper worry. Sears and others believed that Nixon feared that the telegenic Reagan might simply outshine him on the stump, just as Henry Cabot Lodge had done in 1960 when they were on the same ticket. "He didn't want to go through that again," Sears recalled. "All things being equal, Nixon probably should have picked Reagan. But Nixon would not consider it." Whalen recalled that the entire subject was a sensitive one for Nixon. "The more attractive we made Reagan appear, the less he appealed to Nixon, who would suffer from the inevitable side-by-side comparison." Buchanan, who had traveled with Nixon through much of the race, added, "Nixon clearly did not think Reagan was in his league."

In the end, Nixon surprised much of the Republican Party by picking Maryland governor Spiro Agnew, someone who would never upstage the real star of the ticket.

The battle of Dick and Ron was quickly forgotten in the ensuing fights over the general election campaign. Not many people outside conservative circles took Reagan seriously or imagined that he would run twice more before becoming president. But the Kabuki race between them altered their relationship. Years later, Nixon pointedly recalled in his memoirs that Reagan's "unifying gesture" during the roll call vote was "in keeping with his *posture* of being a strong party man" (italics added). Reagan's two-year dance of the veils left some scars.

And not just on Nixon. Reagan, for his part, left most of the 1968 story out of his memoirs; and where he did write of the campaign, he cast it almost entirely as a crusade conceived, directed, and produced by others, sometimes, if not always, against his will. Even after his name was placed in nomination, Reagan insisted, he was angry at the implications. And when Nixon won on the first ballot, he wrote, no one was happier than he was. As he put it decades later in his memoirs, "When Nixon was nominated, I was the most relieved person in the world. I knew I wasn't ready to be president."

With twenty years' hindsight, maybe not. But at the time, it seemed like a shot worth taking. In a September 1968 letter to two of his oldest friends, Lorraine and Elwood Wagner, with whom he'd maintained a long correspondence, Reagan admitted that he had boldly rolled the dice in Miami Beach. "The convention was exciting and you are right about the first ballot. If he hadn't made it on that one, the ball game was over because of the number of delegates who were pledged for only one round and intended changing votes on the second. Anyway, we'll work our heads off to elect him."

JOHNSON AND NIXON:

Two Scorpions in a Bottle

———————— 🗝 ————————

The club is bound together by an unspoken pledge to protect the presidency; but its members are often driven by an even more fierce desire to protect a legacy.

For most presidents, those missions coincide. But with the arrival at center stage of two of the century's larger and more devious characters, the club came under pressure in ways that threatened to tear it, and the country, apart. Over five years, across three continents, through two presidential campaigns, Richard Nixon and Lyndon Johnson played one of the great political chess matches of all time; great because the stakes were so high, the moves so complex—and because both sides cheated.

At issue was the Vietnam War—the war that Henry Kissinger warned was one of those tragic, cursed messes that destroy any president who touches it. More than anything, Johnson wanted to leave office as the Peacemaker, so that the sacrifices—of lives and treasure and his own presidential dreams—had not been wasted. Nixon privately promised to help end the war with honor and share the credit. Johnson believed him, embraced him, conspired with him as the 1968 campaign unfolded, right up until he discovered that Nixon had betrayed him, by secretly disrupting the Vietnam peace process to assure his own victory.

That left Johnson with a choice: protect his dream, or protect the office. He chose the latter. In a year of blood and fire, that had seen heroes slain and consensus shredded, how could he add the trauma of accusing a newly elected president of something close to treason? And so Johnson would remain silent. For the time being.

Nixon of course saw it all very differently: he had saved the country from a bad peace deal cut by a desperate president looking for redemption. If that meant denying Johnson his redemption—and perhaps missing a chance to shorten the war—it was a price Nixon was willing to pay. He was going to be a great president. The country needed him. He had earned this, after so many years of patient planning and serial humiliations. He would show them all.

What unfolded in late 1968 was the club's first dirty war. And the choices each man made would set the country on a path that would end with a president's resignation, and change American politics forever.

11

"This Is Treason"

—LYNDON JOHNSON

Unlike the Eisenhower-Truman feud, the Johnson-Nixon matchup was not personal. "I never shared the intense dislike of Richard Nixon felt by many of my fellow Democrats," Johnson wrote in his memoirs. In fact they had much in common; their humble roots, their devout mothers and loutish fathers, their resentment of the silver-spooned, their promiscuous relationship with the truth. But where Nixon was awkward, pinched, a man with his arms forever folded across his chest, Johnson was expansive, invasive, desperately needing to be loved where Nixon never expected to be.

It was the cagey, courtly Bryce Harlow, who had coached so many presidents in the ring, who explained the twisted dynamic between the two men. "I'd compare the President and Dick Nixon to a couple of fighting roosters, circling each other, with knives attached to the spurs," he said. "Nothing will happen, mind you, unless one makes the first move."

Nixon owed Johnson, among others, a debt for his restoration as a Republican contender. He may have spent the years since his 1960 defeat building his organization and collecting IOUs, but he was still a loser; the Republican Party was so thoroughly headless that in November 1965, *Newsweek* put a handsome junior congressman named John Lindsay on its cover, christening him "the most exciting and important politician" of his age. Bookies put the odds of a Nixon comeback at a thousand to one.

It would take the 1966 midterm elections to rehabilitate Nixon—thanks largely to Johnson, who alone as president had the power to elevate an adversary as his equal. That spring, the two men made a gentleman's agreement regarding their coming proxy war. At the Gridiron Dinner in March, Johnson invited Nixon to come by the White House for coffee the next morning. "He had stayed up late after the dinner," Nixon recalled. "He had developed a terrible sore throat, laryngitis, and was in bed." Eight years as Ike's vice president, and this was the first time Nixon had ever been upstairs in the private quarters, where Johnson sat in his pajamas in the great king-sized bed. They talked about Vietnam and China—and the coming campaign, in which each would be key surrogates for his party's candidates. "I know you will understand and not take any criticism I make on issues as being directed personally at you," Nixon said.

"I know, Dick," Johnson replied. "We politicians are just like lawyers who get together for a drink after fighting each other like hell in the courtroom." Then he got up and went into his dressing room, and returned with a premonitory gift: a pair of presidential cuff links.

Nixon had the midterms mapped out like a field general; he focused on helping Republican challengers in those districts where Democrats had just swept in as part of the 1964 landslide and were vulnerable now. That way he'd get credit for helping victors who would have won anyway. And all the while, he meticulously laid a trap for Johnson.

By this time the Vietnam War was such a confusing issue to most Americans that Nixon could take as many positions as he liked and find support somewhere for them all. Roughly equal numbers wanted to expand the war as negotiate a peace. Nixon had privately told aides he did not think the war could be won militarily. But he was all over the map on the value of negotiations. At one point he said negotiations would only prolong the war—yet in the summer he endorsed the idea of an all-Asia peace conference. Maybe voters didn't notice mixed messages because their own feelings were so conflicted. Loving one's country while hating the war it was fighting? Supporting the commander in chief but doubting his honesty? And most people weren't paying Nixon much attention: "It took someone with the eye of a hawk and the obsession of a neurotic to mark all the twists and turns," observes historian Rick Perlstein. That would be Lyndon Johnson, who every time he turned around found Nixon taking the opposite position as he: If you escalate, it will lead to World War III. Fail to escalate, and you'll end up with World War III. It was the perfect way to get under the skin of an insecure president in an impossible situation, fighting a war no one wanted that he could not afford to abandon.

In October, when Johnson flew to Manila for a regional summit, Nixon's worst fears ripened. All his hard work to retire his loser image by helping orchestrate a great Republican rebound would be wasted if Johnson somehow managed a breakthrough on Vietnam right before the 1966 election. "Pull the peace rabbit out of a hat" was the way Nixon and his aides talked about it; but the most he could do was gently raise doubts about Johnson's timing and motives. "Is this a quest for peace or a quest for votes?" he asked in a newspaper column. As voices of protest rose, Nixon gigged Johnson for that as well: "He is the first president in history who has failed to unite his own party in a time of war."

With election day approaching, and Eisenhower cheering him on from the bleachers ("Keep hitting!" Ike urged him), Nixon saw his opening. His inventive young aide William Safire studied the communiqué that emerged from the conference like a sacred text: Nixon's team drafted a statement denouncing the Manila proposal for a mutual drawdown of forces in Vietnam. This would leave South Vietnam at the mercy of the Vietcong, Nixon warned: the United States "should never rely on communist promises—but should always insist on guaranteed deeds." The statement was clear, cogent, and unremarkable, but for the fact that Safire called in a favor. He reached out to his friend Harrison Salisbury at the *New York Times*; you've been neglecting Nixon, he argued. Nixon had always supported the administration's goals in Vietnam, so his challenging the tactics counted as big news. He managed to persuade the *New York Times* to print the entire thing, as though it were a presidential address.

That was a crucial first step in elevating Nixon as Johnson's peer, the Republican statesman taking on the president. And it got deep under LBJ's skin. At a press conference on November 4, 1966, just days before the midterm voting, the president was snide and cutting; he brushed Nixon off as "a chronic campaigner" whose "problem is to find fault with his country and with his Government every two years." The former vice president, he added, "doesn't serve his country well" by leveling such criticism "in the hope that he can pick up a precinct or two." He even invoked Eisenhower to back him up: Nixon, Johnson said, "never did really recognize and realize what was going on when he had an official position in the Government. You remember what President Eisenhower said: that if you would give him a week or so, he'd figure out what Nixon was doing."

Through it all, Lady Bird Johnson sat against the wall, shaking her head, trying to catch her husband's eye, get him to stop. Not since Truman had flayed the music critic who dared dismiss his daughter's singing had a president leveled an attack so personal.

"I don't know what got into him," Johnson's aide Jack Valenti later told Safire. "I never saw him like that in public before. It was so obvious that Nixon had gotten his goat and that he was just playing into Nixon's hands."

Nixon, campaigning in New England, heard from his pugnacious aide Pat Buchanan how beautifully the Safire lure had worked. "He hit us," said an amazed Buchanan. "Jesus, did he hit us." All Nixon had to do now was act the part of statesman, and the title would be his once more. The president, he remarked, had been guilty of a "shocking display of temper," adding, with a more-in-sorrow-than-anger tone: "Now President Johnson and I can disagree . . . but let's disagree as gentlemen." It was a classic Nixon move: goad an opponent into attacking, then ride a wave of sympathy as you defend your honor. He'd been running this play since 1946, but seldom to such effect. "In the space of a single autumn day," Newsweek reported, "the 1,000 day reign of Lyndon came to an end."

"I suddenly found myself the center of national attention," Nixon marveled. Eisenhower called from Gettysburg: "Johnson has gone too far on this, and there will be a very strong backlash in your favor." The Republican Congressional Campaign Committee handed over its half hour of television time so Nixon could twist the knife again. "I was subjected last week to one of the most savage personal attacks ever leveled by the President of the United States against one of his political opponents," he declared, and ended by looking sagely into the camera and addressing Johnson directly: he recalled their fourteen years of service together. "I respected you then, I respect you now . . . and my respect has not changed because of the personal attack you made on me. You see, I think I understand how a man can be very, very tired and how his temper then can be very short."

Nixon emerged now as his party's senior Republican spokesman, and the Republicans went on to pick up forty-seven House seats. "The political equivalent of the batting championship for the 1966 campaign," announced the *New York Times*, "went to . . . Richard Nixon." This would have implications for 1968: "The Republican Party pros know today Richard Nixon is the only man in their party to date who has lured Lyndon Johnson in open combat and whipped him hands down. Lyndon Johnson knows who won the first round," declared the *St. Louis Globe-Democrat*.

Maybe. But Nixon too was dealing with a professional. So you had to wonder who really sprang the trap. Johnson knew the rules: never, ever lose your temper in public—except on purpose. Johnson's aide Bill Moyers recalled how calm the president had been before the press conference began, how he had planned to hit Nixon as a chronic campaigner. "Johnson thought that Nixon was the most vulnerable man in American politics," Moyers recalled. "He said so that morning."

Johnson knew exactly whom he wanted to run against in 1968. So why not help him along the way?

The Search for Peace

Of course it turned out that Johnson wouldn't be running at all. On March 31, 1968, having faced the humiliations of the Tet Offensive and the New Hampshire primary, he announced that he would not be a candidate after all. This ensured that from this point on, Johnson had only one mission: the campaign for his own redemption, a historic figure rescuing his reputation from the damn, thankless, no-win war that was destroying it.

The North Vietnamese were a shrewd and patient enemy; Johnson's resolve to get a deal to end the war with honor was probably doomed from the start. But even had it not been, there was, in any case, no way Nixon was going to let that happen.

In the spring of 1968, when Johnson announced his withdrawal from the race and a partial bombing halt as a prelude to peace talks, his approval rating jumped thirteen points. This war will not be won militarily, Clark Clifford, now the defense secretary, told Johnson in May, and so the only hope for resolution lay in the secret negotiations under way in Paris. The North Vietnamese leaders in Hanoi had long demanded that genuine peace talks could not begin as long as the United States was bombing the North. Nor were they willing to negotiate with the South Vietnamese government in Saigon—only with the United States. Johnson meanwhile had refused to consider a bombing halt so long as enemy troops and supplies from North Vietnam were pouring south to help the communist Vietcong. General Creighton Abrams, the U.S. commander in Vietnam, warned that a bombing halt would permit a fivefold increase in communist strength within a matter of days.

Saigon meanwhile demanded no halt until all North Vietnamese troops had withdrawn. Clifford traveled to Saigon in mid-July, and reported to Johnson that he was now "absolutely certain" that the weak, corrupt government there did not want the war to end—not while President Nguyen Van Thieu's regime was protected by 500,000 U.S. troops and the "golden flow of money." It was an impossible puzzle—and that was even before you counted the pieces held by the Chinese, the Soviets, and Richard Nixon.

Campaigning for his party's nomination, Nixon struck a righteous, statesmanlike stance: "Let's not destroy the chances for peace with a mouthful of words from some irresponsible candidate for President of the United States," he said in May in Evansville, Illinois. "Put yourself in the position of the enemy. He is negotiating with Lyndon Johnson and Secretary Rusk and then he reads in the paper that, not a senator, not a congressman, not an editor, but a potential *President of the United States* will give him a better deal than President Johnson is offering him. What's he going to do? It will torpedo those deliberations. . . . The enemy will wait for the next man."

The scenario was presented as a warning: but it was actually more like a plan. And as the next months unfolded, Nixon would meticulously lay the pieces in place. His first task was to make sure that Johnson did not lift a finger to get his faithful vice president, Hubert Humphrey, elected. That turned out to be simpler than you might think.

To have any chance of winning, Humphrey needed to forge an identity beyond Johnson Apologist, which would not be easy with a president who had relished through the years telling reporters about how he had Hubert's "pecker in my pocket." But any hint, any feint or whiff of breaking with Johnson over Vietnam or anything else would send Johnson into a rage. He called Humphrey "weak" and "disloyal" to his aides; he was so suspicious he had the FBI tap Humphrey's phones.

A vice president can't attack his own administration, but Humphrey couldn't win if he didn't; it was a dynamic that Nixon, as a veteran second fiddle, was uniquely well positioned to understand and exploit. Already reporters had concluded that L.B.J. was more concerned with his own place in history than with the question of succession. Clark Clifford saw the fallout: "His anger at Humphrey led him toward his old adversary, Richard Nixon."

So whoever was more likely to exalt Johnson's place in history would get his blessing. "I want to sit down with Mr. Nixon to see what kind of world he really wants," Johnson told Clifford, Secretary of State Dean Rusk, and National Security Advisor Walt Rostow at the end of July. "When he gets the nomination he may prove to be more responsible than the Democrats."

It's just another reminder of how much our politics have changed, that what unfolded over the next few weeks was not seen as anything out of the ordinary. Nixon and Johnson met twice, on either side of the Republican convention in Miami: once at the White House for an intelligence briefing, then even more intimately down at Johnson's Texas ranch. On July 26 at the White House, Johnson laid out his conditions for a bombing halt in Vietnam: the North had to agree to let the South Vietnamese government take part in the peace talks, rather than dealing only with the United States; they had to respect the Demilitarized Zone; and they had to cease their attacks on the cities. Nixon promised not to do anything that would undercut the U.S. position.

It was a promise he'd repeat two weeks later, when, fresh off his nominating convention, he shared steak and corn and Lady Bird's cookies down at the ranch; Johnson personally drove Nixon back to his helicopter, showing him on the way the modest house where he was born, and the site where his parents were buried. By the time they had finished, the two men had come to an understanding: Nixon promised to refrain from attacking Johnson, so long as Johnson promised to maintain a hard line on Vietnam and not soften his negotiating position in Paris as Humphrey and many Democrats would have liked. To Clifford, this meant to "freeze poor Hubert out in the cold."

"I was as appalled as the President was pleased," Clifford recalled.

In their phone calls, Nixon made it clear to Johnson that they saw eye to eye.

"I don't give a goddamn what the politics is," Nixon told Johnson later in August. "But we've got to stand very firm. And I won't say a damn word that's going to embarrass you. You can be sure of that."

"Oh, I know that. I know that," Johnson said. But then Nixon added, "just talking very candidly—can you keep your Vice President and others to keep them firm in this thing? Because, you know, to hell with the goddamn election, we must all stand firm on this."

"Very frankly, I don't know," Johnson said. "That's the honest answer. I just plain don't know."

Nixon was not a man to take chances. He knew how much he stood to lose if Johnson succeeded in the Paris peace talks. "If there's war, people will vote for me to end it," he told his aides. "If there's peace, they'll vote their pocketbooks—Democratic prosperity."

And so he took out some insurance. He needed to know what Johnson was offering Hanoi, how he was selling it to Saigon, and whether, after all this time, all this trouble, the way out of this benighted war might open up just in time for election day.

Anna Chennault was the cochair of Republican Women for Nixon. The Chinese-born widow of General Claire Chennault, who commanded the Flying Tigers in China in World War II, she was petite, striking, and at forty-three nicknamed the "Little Flower" or, alternatively, the "Dragon Lady." She and Nixon had met in 1954, when he made a vice presidential trip to Taiwan. She was close to President Thieu's brother, Nguyen Van Kieu. On July 12, Chennault and South Vietnamese ambassador Bui Diem, a popular, affable, and extremely well-connected diplomat, met with Nixon and his campaign manager, John Mitchell, in Nixon's New York apartment. According to Diem's account, the purpose was to open a secret back channel between the Nixon campaign and Saigon.

"Anna is my good friend," Nixon told Diem. "She knows all about Asia. I know you also consider her a friend, so please rely on her from now on as the only contact between myself and your government." If you have a message, send it though her, and he would do the same, Nixon said. "We know Anna is a good American and a dedicated Republican. We can all rely on her loyalty." He promised to make Vietnam a top priority if he won, "and to see that Vietnam gets better treatment from me than under the Democrats."

Thus had Nixon put in place a way for him to send his own messages, apply his own pressure, make his own promises to Saigon, while staying on top of Johnson's moves. He had laid the groundwork for what historian Robert Dallek calls "a fall campaign that would produce as much skullduggery and hidden actions as any in American history."

Humphrey's Hell, Nixon's Parade

In the back of his mind—and much of the front, for that matter—Johnson hoped that the Democrats might come to their senses and draft him back into service when they met to nominate their candidate in Chicago. He had picked the Windy City because he had faith in Mayor Richard Daley, who kept order like a warlord and had proposed that police shoot arsonists on sight. "Nixon can be beaten," Johnson would say. "He's like a Spanish horse who runs faster than anyone for the first nine lengths and then turns around and runs backwards. You'll see, he'll do something wrong in the end. He always does."

The president had even planned a huge sixtieth birthday party for himself in Chicago. Protesters held an "un-birthday party" hosted by the National Mobilization Committee to End the War in Vietnam, decorated with photos of butchered Vietnamese civilians. By the night of Humphrey's nomination in a convention hall ringed by barbed wire, Johnson's hopes for a political resurrection were crushed—by demonstrators hurling bricks, bottles, and nail-studded golf balls at the police lines, by cops beating and clubbing the peaceful and the protester alike.

There would at least be no softening of the party's position on Vietnam. Johnson, whose two sons-in-law were serving there, made sure of that. Many Democrats wanted the platform to endorse an *unconditional* bombing halt. "No way," Johnson told an aide in a call from his ranch. He was still the commander in chief: "I'm not about to stop this bombing unless they arrest me and take my power away from me," he said. "Because I've got some of my own right there and I'm not gonna shoot 'em in the heart. Not for a bunch of goddamn draft dodgers."

Humphrey was trapped on Vietnam, his campaign out of money. The commentariat, meanwhile, saw the emergence of a New Nixon, "a maturer and mellower man who is no longer clawing his way to the top," as Lippmann put it, loose enough to appear on the must-see TV of its day, *Rowan & Martin's Laugh-In.*

The opposite was closer to the truth. Nixon understood better than most politicians that year the new suspicions and fierce anxieties that all that fun and freedom unleashed in his Silent Majority: the people who had been rejected by their own kids with their psychedelic certainties, by Hollywood with its libertine extravagance, by the commentariat that celebrated this as "progress," cheered the revolution, disdained the heartland, and promoted social justice while sending their own kids to private schools.

His great specialty was reaching the newly wounded or resentful, uniting groups that had never united before. The union hardhats who reviled the hippie peaceniks—the "beardos and weirdos" as Nixon called them—joined politically with the Republican regulars and the Southern rejectionists and the country club moguls and the suburban strivers. This was not like an FDR coalition of labor and urban machines and minorities and the South: Nixon would cut across blocs, speak to cultural needs that didn't line up with political interests.

It was all working perfectly—so long as Nixon could keep Johnson on the sidelines. So he decided it was time to open yet another back channel. One way to persuade Johnson that he didn't need to sell the store for a peace deal would be to assure him he would get credit whenever it came—even if it came after the election. In mid-September, Nixon enlisted one of the club's honorary members to help. Evangelist Billy Graham was that rare world figure who could claim a genuine, personal relationship with both Johnson and Nixon, as he would with other presidents, past and future. He and Nixon had been close for nearly twenty years; he'd been in the room at the Republican convention in Miami as Nixon weighed his options for a running mate, before ultimately settling on Spiro Agnew. But he also delivered the invocation at the Democrats' convention in Chicago and had spent many nights and weekends at the Johnson White House. He wanted to be the bridge builder for a divided country; so in early September, when Nixon asked to meet him at the Hilton in Pittsburgh because he had a confidential message for Johnson, Graham was glad to oblige.

Graham took careful notes as Nixon talked about Johnson. "I will never embarrass him after the election," Nixon dictated. "I respect him as a man and as the president. He is the hardest working and most dedicated President in 140 years." Nixon wanted a close working relationship, drawing on Johnson's advice, sending him on special assignments, possibly overseas. And when the war was finally settled, he would make sure that Johnson received the full measure of credit he deserved.

Nixon would "do everything to make you . . . a place in history because you deserve it." He was dangling the club's sweetest benefits: you will stay in the game, I will raise you up, secure your place in history, for we will be partners in peace.

Graham flew to Washington on September 15. "It was one of the few times I had ever asked him for an appointment," Graham recalled, "and I told him it was of a private nature." Sitting in the Oval Office, he went over his notes point by point. Johnson asked him to read some of them twice. He even took the paper from Graham and studied it, struggling with Graham's angular, backward handwriting. He still intended to support Humphrey, Johnson said; but "if Mr. Nixon becomes the President-elect, I will do all in my power to cooperate with him."

Graham's message, of course, echoed what Nixon had been promising Johnson all along; but Nixon understood how much extra weight it would have coming from someone Johnson loved as much as he loved Billy Graham. Two days later, Nixon called Graham for a report. Johnson, Graham said, was "deeply appreciative of his generous gesture." It was a measure of Johnson's ego and needs that he did not realize how Nixon's courtship of him was a cunning piece of political marksmanship. Of course, if LBJ missed this, maybe it was because the message was delivered by Graham, whose enduring belief that Nixon was sincere surely helped a willing Johnson to believe likewise.

Through the month of September, even when Johnson received potentially devastating ammunition to use against Nixon, he held his fire. Johnson aide Charles Roche passed on a rumor that some Greek shipping magnates were donating $5 million to Nixon for having put Spiro Agnew on the ticket. "My source thinks the information is probably true," Roche advised. "If so, any disclosures—even the mere fact that a group of shipping representatives had met clandestinely—would be of inestimable value to Humphrey." Humphrey's campaign manager, Larry O'Brien, told Johnson about contributions to Nixon from Greece's military dictators and asked for the CIA to investigate—but Johnson refused even to leak it to reporters. When Humphrey's advisor—and Johnson's friend—James Rowe asked Johnson to make some speeches in key states, Johnson declined: "You know that Nixon is following my policies more closely than Humphrey," he told Rowe.

By the end of September, Humphrey finally tried to make a getaway. He labored over a speech he would deliver in Salt Lake City for national broadcast, working through seven drafts, typing it six times before he felt he had it right. For this was an especially delicate operation he was about to perform: somehow he needed to convince disgruntled liberals that he was separating himself from Johnson, willing to take greater risks for peace, without alienating moderates—or Johnson himself. Gone from the podium was the Vice Presidential Seal; Humphrey spoke as the Democratic Party nominee for president. "As President, I would stop the bombing of the North as an acceptable risk for peace," he declared, "because I believe it could lead to success in the negotiations and thereby shorten the war." But while the halt was unconditional, it was not irreversible: "If the Government of North Vietnam were to show bad faith, I would reserve the right to resume the bombing."

The actual proposal, advisors like Clark Clifford, George Ball, and Ambassador Averell Harriman realized, was what they had been proposing to Johnson for weeks; it was a policy departure measurable only in angstrom units, and they pointed this out to Johnson in hopes of preventing an eruption. Humphrey himself called the White House to give Johnson a heads-up. "I think I've done it carefully here," he said, "without jeopardizing what you're trying to do."

Johnson's response was cool, noncommittal. He already knew all about the speech—not because he'd read it, but because Nixon had called him and spun him blind. What better opportunity to suggest to a suspicious president that his vice president had betrayed him, personally and politically?

Nixon asked Johnson if Humphrey's speech represented a change in the official White House position—which he knew very well it did not. "It has not been discussed with me," Johnson said. "I say this in strict confidence."

"I understand."

"I don't want you to quote me or repeat me, so I'll talk freely," Johnson went on.

"I won't. I won't," Nixon assured him. "I'm not even letting anybody know I called you." Since Johnson had not had a chance to study the speech, it was easy for Nixon to portray it as both naive and treacherous. They bonded in frustration over Humphrey's foolishness in dealing with the enemy. Johnson even put Walt Rostow on the line, with the latest assessment from General Abrams. The bombing runs, Abrams reported, "have reduced the enemy's detected flow of troops from the mid-July high of 1,000 per day to less than 150 since that time. . . . If the bombing in North Vietnam ceases, a return to the level of a thousand per day would have to be expected."

Nixon needled Johnson. "I'm just seeing the AP dispatch here," he said, and noted how the wires portrayed the speech as "a dramatic moving away from the Johnson administration war policy," even though Humphrey did say his actions would depend on communist restraint in the Demilitarized Zone. "You know," Nixon said, "the press always tends to play the biggest part of the story."

But he, Nixon assured Johnson, would remain a loyal supporter. "It's my intention not to move in that direction," he said. "I think that my position has to be, in good conscience, that unless and until there is some evidence of a reciprocal step, that we could not stop the bombing." Johnson even gave him the language to use with reporters: there is only one president, one secretary of state. "They're going to be responsible until a new President is elected. Therefore, that you're not going to try to look over their shoulders without all the information and tell them what is best."

Nixon did not mention that his own double agent at the Paris peace talks had told him that Johnson too was looking for a way to announce a breakthrough sometime in October.

The Salt Lake speech marked a turning point. Liberal House Democrats finally announced their support for Humphrey, the money began flowing, and the polls started to swing in his direction. IF YOU MEAN IT, WE'RE FOR YOU read the signs now.

But relations with Johnson went downhill: the president refused to campaign for Humphrey in Texas. When the vice president proposed a meeting to make amends, he ran late and Johnson refused to see him. "That bastard Johnson. . . . I saw him sitting in his office," Humphrey told an aide. "Jim Jones [a member of the White House staff] was standing across the doorway, and I said to him: 'You tell the President he can cram it up his ass.'"

And then, things started to get really interesting.

October Surprise

On October 9, word came of progress in Paris: Hanoi was prepared to accept representatives from Saigon at the talks. Soviet embassy officials in Paris confirmed the move; Harriman, serving as the chief U.S. negotiator, suggested that Moscow wanted to prevent a victory by the Republicans and their old Cold War nemesis Nixon, and so was ready to push the peace process forward in ways likely to help the Democrats. Meanwhile intelligence reports revealed that between forty thousand and sixty thousand North Vietnamese troops had withdrawn from South Vietnam, many of them slipping into Cambodia and Laos from the northern provinces. "They just seem to have disappeared into the woodwork," said a U.S. officer.

Everyone was finally ready to talk; the question was, were the South Vietnamese? Thieu had much to lose from a peace deal that would lead to an American withdrawal. It was now three weeks before the U.S. election: on October 13, Ambassador Ellsworth Bunker met with Thieu in Saigon in a high-pressure session. For now, Thieu went along; as long as the United States would resume bombing if the DMZ or cities were attacked, he was on board. "After all," Thieu said, "the problem is not to stop the bombing but to stop the war, and we must try this path to see if they are serious."

"I thought this a statesman's view," Bunker said in his report. Back in Washington, Clifford, Rusk, and the Joint Chiefs all agreed that this was, at long last, a chance to turn the corner.

Just before noon on October 16, Johnson placed a conference call to the three candidates. Humphrey, who was still in the doghouse from Salt Lake City, got no advance warning; he took the call in the men's room of the Christian Brothers High School gymnasium in St. Louis. Nixon was in Kansas City, Wallace in L.A. He was calling, Johnson said, "so that I might review for you a matter of the highest national importance." He swore them to secrecy, assured them he had not gone soft on the communists, and warned them not to speak out of school about what he was about to tell them: Hanoi had agreed to U.S. conditions for a bombing halt and immediate talks, which would include both Saigon and the Vietcong. "I would bear in mind constantly that the enemy is looking at everything that's said in this country," he said. "I know you don't want to play politics with your country."

Humphrey had no comment. Nixon repeated his previous promise: "I've made it very clear that I will make no statement that would undercut the negotiations. So we'll just stay right on there and hope that this thing works out." They agreed to tell reporters who got wind of the call that it was a routine update on how there was no agreement yet, though all sides were still negotiating. Nixon warned his men about provoking Johnson by attacking him. "LBJ can be just as vindictive as hell," Nixon's well-sourced advisor Bryce Harlow explained to Safire, "and who knows what he might pull off on an international scale."

Over the next two weeks the plot kept twisting. First Hanoi dug in: negotiators insisted that any bombing halt be called "unconditional," and the talks be referred to as a "four power conference" to elevate the Vietcong and diminish Saigon. At the same time Thieu got tougher with Bunker, insisting that the Vietcong come to Paris only as part of a North Vietnamese delegation. Within the Nixon camp, the concern grew that Johnson was going soft, desperate for a breakthrough that would throw the election to Humphrey. "Johnson had promised to keep politics totally out of foreign policy in the campaign," explained Harlow. It was vital that they know what was going on behind the scenes, so they could plan accordingly.

Fortunately, Nixon was an able spymaster; he knew all about what Johnson and his negotiators were saying and doing. For one thing, Henry Kissinger, who had become a trusted Johnson advisor the year before, was working both sides of the game. Never mind that he referred to Nixon as "a disaster," "unfit to be President," "the most dangerous of all men running." He contacted Nixon aide Richard Allen, noting that he had close friends on the U.S. negotiating team in Paris and offering to keep Nixon informed of the progress of the talks; he was so cautious about exposing his role that he would call Allen from pay phones and once suggested they speak in German.

"It is not stretching the truth," Harriman's aide Richard Holbrooke later told Kissinger biographer Walter Isaacson, "to say that the Nixon campaign had a secret source within the U.S. negotiating team."

Harlow, who had "a double agent" working in the White House, wrote Nixon a memo about how quickly things were moving: "Expectation is that he is becoming almost pathologically eager for an excuse to order a bombing halt and will accept almost any arrangement.... Careful plans are being made to help HHH [Humphrey] exploit whatever happens.... White Housers still think they can pull the election out for HHH with this ploy."

This lit a fire in the Nixon camp. They were convinced Johnson was orchestrating the ultimate October surprise to swing the election in the final days. Harlow picked at an old Nixon scab, the dramatic October events of 1962, which had bolstered support for the Democrats when Nixon was running for governor of California. "They're going to do it to you just like they did in 1962 in the Cuban Missile Crisis. Identical. It's just a question of timing."

Two could play that game. Nixon's strategy of keeping Johnson neutral had worked nicely through the summer and into September; but now the time came to go on offense. If he thought Johnson was prepared to do anything to get a peace deal, Nixon was willing to do just about anything to stop him. Among others who were well informed on the progress of negotiations was Ambassador Bui Diem, who was briefed both by Saigon and the State Department. Anna Chennault meanwhile maintained her back channel with Nixon campaign chair John Mitchell, the former semipro hockey player and PT boat commander who had made his fortune in municipal bonds. They were now talking nearly every day: "Call me from a pay phone," Mitchell told her. "Don't talk in your office."

A warning came into the Johnson White House from the Soviets: our protégés—meaning Hanoi—are under control; are you sure yours are? With each passing day the race was tightening: even in London the bookmakers were giving the Democrat better odds, from 12 to 1 against in September to 7 to 4 now. Eugene McCarthy finally came out for Humphrey, and other dissident liberals returned to the fold.

In Washington and Paris, Hanoi, Saigon, Moscow, the signals and countersignals were flying fast. As negotiations entered their final stage, White House officials refused to give interviews, even take calls. "Fewer men are fully clued into these contacts than were involved in the Cuba missile crisis," one explained to a reporter. Diplomats in Paris were reported to be renting nondescript cars so that they could meet discreetly with North Vietnamese negotiators at various hideaways. When the White House got a crucial message from Moscow, Johnson told Clifford, Rusk, and General Wheeler to meet in the State Department basement and drive to the White House in a plain Chevrolet sedan; unfortunately CBS News reporter Marvin Kalb happened to spot them, pulled a U-turn, and followed them. His report just confirmed Republican suspicions that Johnson was preparing an October surprise.

Nixon concluded that his only course was to raise suspicions that Johnson was manipulating events to give Humphrey an edge. Having been on the record supporting the president's efforts, he could not level so cynical a charge—though other Republicans certainly could.

He had one of his allies level the accusation—which he then righteously disputed. "In the last 36 hours I have been advised of a flurry of meetings in the White House and elsewhere on Vietnam," Nixon said in a statement released on October 25. "I am also told that this spurt of activity is a cynical last minute attempt by President Johnson to salvage the candidacy of Mr. Humphrey. This I do not believe." He noted Johnson's fairness in dealing with all three presidential candidates, and praised him for resisting pressure from within his party to "contrive what he has aptly described as a 'fake peace.'"

It was a beautiful thing—a candidate praising an opponent for not doing something in a way that fueled the rumors that he was, and then making a hero of himself for not piling on. Nixon also knew that the charge that Johnson was playing politics with the war was false; Johnson had not lowered the bar or changed the conditions he had laid out privately for Nixon in July; it was Hanoi, encouraged by Moscow, that drove the timing, not Johnson. But Nixon was increasingly desperate, because the polls continued to tighten.

Indeed two days later, on October 27, word came from Paris that Hanoi had met all Johnson's conditions. If Johnson ceased bombing on October 29 then all parties could convene for talks in Paris on November 2—three days before the election.

"What do we do?" Johnson asked his top advisors that night.

"We go ahead with it," Secretary Rusk said flatly.

"Why?"

"I smell Vodka and Caviar in it," Rusk replied. "The Soviets have moved in."

"If ten steps separated us," Clifford affirmed, "they have taken eight and we have taken two." Rusk put it at nine and one; the North Vietnamese had come around.

Soviet premier Alexei Kosygin gave his assurance that Hanoi was "serious in its intentions" and that U.S. "doubts" were "without foundation." Ambassador Bunker was dispatched to get Thieu's blessing: "A burnt child dreads fire," Johnson observed, so Thieu had to be handled carefully.

But for all the talk of Johnson's desperation for a peace deal, it was he who kept holding out. Even with a breakthrough at hand, he worried that he'd be putting American soldiers at risk, giving the enemy a military advantage. Clifford even suspected that Johnson was spooked by the criticism that he was just agreeing to a deal to help Humphrey.

"I could not help asking myself, again," Clifford recalled. *"In his heart of hearts, does Lyndon Johnson really want Humphrey to win?"*

Ever respectful of his generals, Johnson wanted to hear one last assessment of the costs and benefits from his field commander. "Get him over here as soon as you can," the president ordered. General Abrams boarded a C-141 Starlifter for an unannounced flight to Washington, arriving at 2:38 A.M. on the morning of October 29, dressed in civilian clothes, to make his way discreetly to the White House.

At that hour, Johnson and his top advisors were waiting in the Cabinet Room. Abrams sat down at the president's left, and Johnson reviewed the events that had brought them to this point, and the conditions that had been met. The North Vietnamese accepting South Vietnamese participation was a huge deal: "Many experts felt Hanoi would never do this," Johnson said.

Then he asked Abrams for his assessment: it was he, after all, who had warned of the risks involved with a bombing halt. But the situation in the field had improved vastly in recent months, Abrams said, the enemy was significantly weakened, and a bombing halt might now be militarily tolerable. He did not think the North would violate the DMZ; he was a little more worried about the cities, especially Saigon.

"Can we return to full-scale bombing easily if they attack?" Johnson asked.

"Yes, very easily."

Johnson asked about supply lines and troop movements and morale. Then came the vital question. "Has it reached the point where we could reduce the bombing without causing casualties?" Abrams looked squarely at the president.

"Yes, we can."

And if you were in my shoes, Johnson wanted to know . . .

"If you were president, would you do it?"

"I have no reservations about doing it," Abrams replied. "I know it is stepping into a cesspool of comment. I do think it is the right thing to do. It is the proper thing to do."

"Will the men accept it?" the president asked.

"Yes, sir."

That was it. *Abrams has carried the ball across the goal line*, Clifford thought.

No one had slept; at dawn Johnson went upstairs to the mansion. It's "tough to be a candidate and peace seeker at the same time," he told his aides. That thought reminded him that he'd need to brief the actual candidates on what had happened.

"Where will Nixon be at 5:00 pm?" he wanted to know, and Wallace and Humphrey. "Have a phone they can cram right up their butts."

At 6:04 A.M. the call came from Rusk. He had talked to Ambassador Bunker in Saigon; Thieu was off the reservation. He said three days was too little time to get a delegation to Paris, and he needed to confer with his National Assembly, and he expressed other concerns that appeared to have come out of nowhere.

Suddenly Johnson and his men thought they understood. There was no logic to Thieu's sudden change of heart—other than what Rusk called "the under-the-table stuff." A secret CIA report had revealed that Thieu "sees a definite connection between the moves now underway and President Johnson's wish to see Vice President Humphrey elected. Thieu referred many times to the U.S. elections and suggested to his visitors that the current talks are designed to aid Humphrey's candidacy." Johnson also got word through connections on Wall Street that Nixon was working to derail the talks, with the expectation that a new offensive would break out, casualties would mount, the stock market would fall, and thus it would be easier for Nixon to cut his own peace deal once he took office, as Eisenhower had to end the Korean War. "Like Ike in 1953," read a memo from Rostow's brother Eugene, the undersecretary of state for political affairs, "he [Nixon] would be able to settle on terms which the President could not accept, blaming the deterioration of the situation between now and January or February on his predecessor." Nixon, in other words, wasn't just denying Johnson his bid to be Peacemaker; he would blame him for forcing the United States to settle for a worse deal.

Johnson had ordered the FBI to monitor contacts between Americans and the South Vietnamese embassy, put Chennault under surveillance, and tap her phones. "Follow her wherever she goes," National Security aide Bromley Smith ordered FBI deputy director Cartha "Deke" De-Loach. This would provide the hard proof: Nixon's lieutenants, if not Nixon himself, were actively trying to sabotage the peace talks. Johnson was personally watching the traffic; the National Security Agency intercepted a coded message from Diem to Saigon on October 28: "I am regularly in touch with the Nixon entourage," he said. If Saigon held out, he predicted, they would get a better deal out of Nixon than Humphrey. "The longer the situation continues, the more [we are] favored," he advised.

With the election only days away, the implications were staggering. If the Nixon sabotage was known it would "rock the world," Johnson told his aides after their all-night strategy session. "Can you imagine what people would say if this were to be known; that we have all these conditions met and then Nixon's conniving with them kept us from getting it?"

Johnson was livid at Nixon; but he also blamed Humphrey's Salt Lake City speech for spooking the South Vietnamese. "They [Nixon's allies] made Bui Diem think he could get a better deal from Nixon than us." NSC advisor Rostow wrote Johnson a confidential memo: "Mr. President, I have been considering the explosive possibilities of the information that we now have on how certain Republicans may have inflamed the South Vietnamese to behave as they have been behaving. There is no hard evidence that Mr. Nixon himself is involved."

However, "the materials are so explosive that they could gravely damage the country whether Mr. Nixon is elected or not. If they get out in their present form, they could be the subject of one of the most acrimonious debates we have ever witnessed."

That night the principals met at the White House again. Johnson worried that proceeding without Thieu would look too political. "I think we have to give Thieu some more time." The next day he pre-taped a speech announcing the bombing halt, because he was losing his voice. The broadcast was set for 8 P.M. on the 31st—Halloween, five days before the election. And Bunker was told to make it clear to Thieu that the United States was moving ahead, with or without him.

At 6 P.M., two hours before the broadcast, Johnson called the three candidates one more time. He told them what he was about to announce, and he issued a barely veiled warning. Some "old China lobbyists" are going around saying Saigon "might get a better deal" later, under a different president. That's made things harder, Johnson said, but he added, "I know that none of you candidates are aware of it or responsible for it."

Johnson insisted that he was not concerned with the election.

"I'm praying for you," George Wallace told him.

"We'll back you up," Nixon agreed.

"We'll back you up, Mr. President," Humphrey affirmed.

Nixon had every reason to inflate the hopes for peace—the better for Thieu to dash them at the very right moment and make Johnson look dishonest and manipulative. Kissinger, continuing his secret updates, had called to say that Harriman and his team had broken out the champagne. "It took some balls to give us those tips," national security aide Richard Allen told Sy Hersh years later, because it was "a pretty dangerous thing for him to be screwing around with national security."

Johnson went on the air that night; the speech promised to be the high point of his career. The North Vietnamese had backed down on their refusal to negotiate a peace settlement with Saigon. And so, "I have now ordered that all air, naval and artillery bombardment of North Viet Nam cease," he said, effective twelve hours after he spoke. "What we now expect—what we have a right to expect—are prompt, productive, serious and intensive negotiations."

When the president had finished, Mitchell tracked down Chennault, who was finishing dinner at legendary hostess Perle Mesta's apartment at the Sheraton Park Hotel in Washington. She was called to the phone, and Mitchell told her to call back on a safer line. He picked up on the first ring. "I'm speaking on behalf of Mr. Nixon," he said. "It's very important that our Vietnamese friends understand our Republican position." Chennault assured him that there was no way Thieu would agree to the peace talks. "Thieu has told me over and over again that going to Paris would be walking into a smoke screen that has nothing to do with reality."

The day after LBJ's speech, Thieu was scheduled to address the Vietnamese National Assembly. He had assured Bunker at a diplomatic reception that everything would be okay. But when he rose before the legislature, with Bunker seated right in the front row, he announced that he would not be sending anyone to the Paris talks.

That act of defiance made him a hero at home: his divided government united behind him, the local press cheered, and fifty members of the National Assembly marched in a parade to the presidential palace, cheering him and waving red and yellow national flags. THE PEOPLE ARE UNITED TO KILL THE COMMUNISTS AND SAFEGUARD THE COUNTRY, read the banners in Saigon, rejecting the idea of talks that treated the Vietcong as equals.

It was a catastrophe for Johnson and thus for Humphrey. The polls in the final weekend had shown a dead heat; now it looked as though Johnson had rushed for a deal that was not yet sealed. "S. Vietnam Spurns November 6 Talks" ran the *Washington Post* headline. Nixon aides began suggesting that Johnson had misled him—and the public—about the prospects for peace. But even as they did so, the FBI reported on November 2 that Chennault had called Bui Diem at the embassy and told him that she had just had a call from her boss, that he had a message he "wanted her to give personally to the ambassador. She said the message was that the ambassador is to 'hold on, we are going to win. . . .' She repeated that this is the only message. 'He said please tell your boss to hold on.'"

Johnson was beside himself: he was now being portrayed as a sneak, a manipulator who put his own agenda ahead of the country's, even as he concluded that his opponents were doing exactly that. But what could he do? In a secret cable from Saigon, Bunker advised that they shouldn't even try to do anything until after the election: "Thieu is convinced that Nixon will win and will follow a hawkish policy, and therefore he can afford to wait." Rostow proposed that Johnson call Nixon directly, tell him the deal really *was* locked up in mid-October, that they had negotiated the joint communiqué in a hard bargaining session on October 28, and that it only came undone at the last second. Johnson, Rostow added, should "urge Nixon [to] be extremely careful in what he says in the next few days so as not to inflame the situation."

That still left the question of what to say publicly. They had obtained the evidence against the Nixon campaign through "extremely sensitive intelligence gathering operations of the FBI, the CIA and the National Security Agency," Clifford noted, including surveillance of Chennault, a private citizen (who, as it happened, lived in the Watergate), and Diem, a foreign diplomat. Protecting the NSA's surveillance and code-breaking capabilities was essential. Johnson's men were divided about whether to use it. "I do not believe that any president can make any use of interceptions or telephone taps in any way that would involve politics," Rusk warned. "The moment we cross over that divide, we are in a different kind of society."

Early in the evening of November 2, Rusk advised that they at least brief some key Republicans about Chennault's interference. So that night, just after nine, Johnson called Senate minority leader Everett Dirksen, his old friend, and put the fear of God in him.

"We're skirting on dangerous ground," Johnson said, "and I thought I ought to give you the facts and you ought to pass them on if you choose. If you don't, why then I will a little later." He had not jumped the gun, he insisted; Thieu was on board, until Nixon's henchmen got hold of him.

"Then we got some of our friends involved, some of it your old China crowd, and here's the latest information we got." He quoted the FBI report of Chennault telling South Vietnam's ambassador to hold on.

Tell them to stand down, LBJ said. "I don't want this to get in the campaign. And they oughtn't to be doing this. This is treason."

"I know," Dirksen conceded.

And then came the threat: "I think it would shock America if a principal candidate was playing with a source like this on a matter this important," Johnson said. "I don't want to do that. But if they're going to put this kind of stuff out, they ought to know that we know what they're doing. I know who they're talking to and I know what they're saying."

"Yeah," Dirksen said.

"Well, now, what do you think we ought to do about it?"

"Well, I better get in touch with him, I think, and tell him about it."

The conversation concluded with Johnson repeating the stakes: "I know this—that they're contacting a foreign power in the middle of a war."

"That's a mistake," Dirksen agreed.

"And it's a damn bad mistake . . . and you're the only man I have confidence in to tell them. . . . If they don't want it on the front pages, they better quit it."

Dirksen's next call, frantic now, was to Nixon's aide Harlow, who was traveling with Nixon in California and staying at the Century Plaza Hotel. Johnson was "mad as all get out," Dirksen warned, threatening to unmask the plot if the Nixon camp did not "cease and desist."

Harlow hung up and ran up to Nixon's suite on the next floor, where his faithful gatekeeper H. R. Haldeman was basically standing guard outside Nixon's room.

"I've got to talk to the boss."

"He's in bed and he's asleep," Haldeman said. "You can't talk to him."

"Oh, yes I can, and I'm a gonna. I've got to talk to the boss. You'll have to get him up."

The two men fought it out, but Harlow prevailed and they woke Nixon to break the news.

"You've got to talk to LBJ," Harlow told him. "Someone has told him that you're dumping all over the South Vietnamese to keep them from doing something about peace and he's just about to believe it. If you don't let him know quickly that it's not so, then he's going to dump." He reported that Dirksen was beside himself. "He says that Lyndon is simply enraged and we ought to do something."

And so Nixon had to embark on one of the more delicate diplomatic missions of his career.

The next morning, Sunday, forty-eight hours before the election, he went on *Meet the Press* and delivered a full-throated defense of Johnson's efforts. He even offered, if elected, to go to Saigon himself if that would help.

That afternoon at 1:25, another intermediary, Florida senator George Smathers, called Johnson to soften him up. Nixon is freaking out, Smathers said, worried Johnson is about to charge him with derailing the talks. Nixon swore he had nothing to do with it, Smathers said, and was fully behind the president. "He would offer to go to any place that you might want him to go" to bring about a successful resolution of the impasse at Paris.

"The problem is not his traveling somewhere," Johnson countered. "The problem is the people on both sides of this fence getting the impression that they can get a little more for the house if they'll wait a week to sell it."

Smathers tried to argue that Nixon knew nothing of what was being said on his behalf. Then he better keep his people in line, Johnson retorted. "I'll pass this word back to him," Smathers said, "that, goddamnit, you had it set, and that someone—his people—are screwing it up."

Then it was Nixon's turn to call LBJ. Johnson was angry, accusing; Nixon poured it on thick. He'd gotten a report from Dirksen, he said, and in case Johnson had missed it, he went over his message on *Meet the Press*. "My God, I would *never* do anything to encourage Saigon not to come to the table, because basically, that was what you got out of your bombing pause. That, good God, we want them over at Paris. We've got to get them to Paris, or you can't have a peace."

It all seemed to be enough. He hung up—and "Nixon and his friends collapsed with laughter," reported the Sunday *Times* of London in an account of the episode months later. "It was partly in sheer relief that their victory had not been taken from them at the eleventh hour."

Forty-eight hours later, Nixon won the presidency by the narrowest of margins: seven tenths of one percent. Humphrey had been told of the treachery in the final days—and also agreed not to reveal it. Nineteen sixty-eight had brought too much shock, too much pain to add charges of treason into the finale of a tight presidential campaign. "Humphrey had lost to a man of shrewd cunning and inherent dishonesty," Clifford later argued, "who had outmaneuvered him in the insider game of dealing with Lyndon Johnson."

Of course wiretapping one's allies and spying on American citizens not accused of any crime was not exactly playing by the rules either, which limited what Johnson and his aides could do with the knowledge they acquired. In his account of the campaign, Safire wrote that Attorney General Ramsey Clark had never approved the surveillance, though DeLoach suggests otherwise. "The pattern of tapping by several agencies of government, confirmed to Nixon by [J. Edgar] Hoover," Safire observed, "set up a 'tolerance' of this type of activity that had disastrous ramifications later."

And it was a club secret kept for many years, until the tapes revealed all.

In 1997, Chennault confirmed publicly to Nixon biographer Anthony Summers that she had worked on his behalf to stall the peace talks. "Power overpowers all reason," she said. "It was all very, very confidential."

In 1968, Johnson did not want Nixon as his enemy. Plus he honored his club duty to defend the office of the presidency, if not the man who had just won the right to occupy it, and a confrontation at that moment would have weakened the office no matter who prevailed. It was a decision not unlike the one Nixon had made himself eight years before, when he decided not to challenge the results of the 1960 race.

It is also worth noting that, this opportunity missed, the war would continue and widen, the death toll mount, the damage deepen for years, until it finally ended on terms very much like the ones tentatively agreed to in October of 1968.

There are too many ironies to count, but among them is that the outcome left Nixon in Thieu's debt—a fact very much against the interests of a president, and a country, trying to end an unwinnable war. Nixon considered Thieu's stonewall to have been crucial, Safire concluded. "We were in real danger on Saturday," Nixon told him a few weeks after the election, referring to the moment when peace seemed at hand with seventy-two hours to go. "If they had waited one more day, they would have had the election in the bag." When he said this, he was sitting in the easy chair on Air Force One, which Johnson had lent the president-elect as a club courtesy. He pushed a button that raised a coffee table into a desk, and propped his feet up.

"It sure beats losing," he said with a smile.

The Next Transition

Given the finale, the transition from Johnson to Nixon could have been as frosty as Truman and Eisenhower in 1952. But that would not turn out to be the case.

Nixon understood how much he needed Johnson's goodwill. Democrats still controlled both houses of Congress; he would need bipartisan support to get anything done. And Johnson had no desire to have Nixon as an enemy.

He and Johnson met just a week after the election, on November 11. The Johnsons waited outside the South Portico to greet the Nixons, who pulled up in a black limousine; the greeting was so warm you'd have mistaken them for old friends. Pat and Dick had lunch with Lyndon and Lady Bird. They got a tour of the private quarters; Nixon was cautious, polite; Johnson warm, expansive.

They spent all afternoon together—and then faced reporters for one of the more extraordinary handoffs ever.

Nixon pointed out what a delicate moment it was, between the peace talks, arms control, the Middle East; the United States could not afford three months of paralysis in its foreign policy. "If progress is to be made in any of these fields, it can be made only if the parties on the other side realize that the current administration is setting forth policies that will be carried forward by the next Administration," he declared. Therefore, Nixon gave his assurances that Johnson and Rusk "could speak not just for this Administration but for the nation, and that meant for the next Administration as well."

Was Nixon essentially offering to extend Johnson's presidency longer—or start his own sooner? Nixon clarified a few days later that he presumed there would be "prior consultation and prior agreement" between himself and the White House before any major step was taken in foreign affairs. Rather than offering support, Nixon now looked like he was staging a coup, or at least demanding a co-presidency for the inter-regnum. This was not Johnson's idea of how a transition worked, so the next day he told reporters that "of course, the decisions that will be made between now and January 20th will be made by this President and by this Secretary of State and by this Secretary of Defense." Experiment over.

A month later both families met again in the mansion, while the outgoing cabinet hosted the incoming administration at the State De-partment, and the personal staff had a reception for Nixon's staff in the White House mess.

Up in the Oval Office, Nixon sat on the sofa, Johnson in his king-sized rocker. The retiring president talked about secrecy, of all things. Don't revive the NSC, he warned, it will leak like a sieve.

"Let me tell you, Dick, I would have been a damn fool to have dis-cussed major decisions with the full Cabinet present, because I know that if I said something in the morning, you could sure as hell bet it would appear in the afternoon papers.

"I will warn you now, the leaks can kill you."

12

"I Want to Go; God Take Me"

—DWIGHT EISENHOWER

In April of 1968, Eisenhower had suffered his fourth heart attack while playing golf in Palm Desert, California. "You know Lady Bird and I are thinking of you every minute and praying as deeply as we know how," Johnson said in a telegram, and offered a plane to fly Ike back to Walter Reed Army Medical Center, where the long finale played out.

Ward 8 at Walter Reed is a medical refuge like no other, something of a club infirmary. It was "a pageant, a drama unfolding every day, a corner drugstore where Senators, Generals and Presidents meet in hospital robes to trade stories and exchange gossip about the world outside," David Eisenhower observed. Established in 1946 to treat VIPs, Ward 8 was where Churchill came to visit George Marshall and John Foster Dulles, who died there in 1959. Ike put a picture of Churchill over a mantel there, in a sitting room decorated in Mamie's favorite colors. Johnson arranged to have a movie screen and projector installed, with a full-time projectionist on call, so Ike could borrow movies from the White House film library. "If you feel lonesome and need a visit from a friend, just send word," Johnson wrote at the end of June. "I might even ask you to move over and make room for me too."

And indeed he came regularly, usually arriving quietly and alone, without his entourage. He sent a steady stream of gifts and flowers, proclaimed Eisenhower Week for October to mark the general's seventy-eighth birthday. Having announced at the end of March that he would not be seeking another term, his presidency was prematurely inviting a hostile verdict from history. He would never get to be like his hero Roosevelt, David Eisenhower wrote, so "Johnson seemed drawn to the man who perhaps, though not the greatest president, had been the most loved."

Indeed, at the start of 1968, Ike was back to being the most admired man in the world in Gallup's poll. But his condition continued to weaken after three more heart attacks, followed by congestive heart failure. Walter Reed got offers from people to donate their hearts if Ike needed a transplant.

Which meant Ike was too ill to attend a most remarkable event: a club marriage. The club is a fraternity, a trade union, a secret society; but it is also something of a family, always figuratively and sometimes literally, as in December of 1968 when Nixon's daughter Julie married Ike's grandson David. If Eisenhower and Nixon had never quite managed to consummate their political union, their offspring would manage the next best thing.

Julie and David had met only a few times as children. "But each," observed the *Washington Post*, "had a mother who was forever saying 'I want my child to have a normal life'—while normal mothers were talking about their children growing up to be president."

If the club creates a natural bond among its members, something of that sympathy extends to their families as well. The first ladies share the unique burden of being perhaps the only person left on the planet who can keep the Leader of the Free World grounded, tell him to pull up his socks and quit feeling sorry for himself. They know, and their children know, what it means to live in the bell jar; to have family vacations turned into photo ops; to wonder at the sudden surfeit of friends and absence of intimacy. "People in public life, presidents, first ladies, have to make a lot of difficult choices," Lyndon Johnson's daughter Luci explained. There's a reason that even first families of very different political persuasions rarely criticize one another. "It's not necessarily because we're so classy and nice," she said. "It's because we all empathize with each other, with the vulnerability and exposure and the demands on family life. Who needs that kind of life?"

At the same time, habits run in families. When Grandfather Ike left the White House in 1961, his grandson had left "I will return" notes under the White House rugs. In the fall of 1966, David Eisenhower went off to college at Amherst; Julie Nixon went to Smith. Both were invited to address the Hadley, Massachusetts, Republican Women's Club. They conferred on the phone and decided to decline, but it was not long before David and his roommate paid a visit to Smith and took Julie and a friend out for ice cream. "I was broke," David recalled. "My roommate forgot his wallet. The girls paid."

In November 1966 they watched the midterm election returns together; in December he escorted her to her debutante ball, and it lit up the headlines. As things got serious, President Eisenhower tried to rein in his smitten grandson; finish your education, he urged, get yourself firmly established before you consider settling down. He and Mamie had set aside money for David's education.

Richard Nixon, for his part, could not have been more pleased. "Freshman year they hitchhiked between the campuses," Nixon told a reporter in Portland, Oregon, in 1967. "I'm told General Eisenhower blew his stack and urged David to get a car." By Thanksgiving in 1967, with Mamie's blessing, David gave Julie his great-grandmother's ring. "All the news reports made us sound like fugitive lovers," David said with a laugh when the news became public two weeks later.

The romance was a great blessing for Nixon, personally and politically. He and Pat genuinely liked David. Nixon was struggling to erase the old images of hatchet man, loser, stiff; now he got to be the proud father, uniting his tribe with the most popular brand name in American politics. It was a huge dose of Republican love. At a moment when college students were occupying buildings and levitating the Pentagon, the couple were like a Madison Avenue ad for respect and decency. "In a year of wee-hour skull sessions, G.O.P. strategists could hardly have cooked up such a promotional coup," *Time* wrote. "The idea would have seemed too stagy or cloyingly obvious: the candidate's perky, pretty 20-year-old daughter Julie becoming engaged to the 20-year-old grandson of Dwight Eisenhower on the very eve of the presidential primary race."

"In the realm of national politics," the *New York Times* marveled, "nothing like it has been seen since the marriage of Alice Roosevelt, daughter of President Theodore Roosevelt, and Nicholas Longworth, then Speaker of the House."

The kids had given one another joke initials reflecting their endless press coverage: Julie was NCPD—No Cream Puff Deb; Tricia was FP—Fairy Princess; David was TCC—Teen Carbon Copy, for his famous grandfather. Julie and her older sister, Tricia, "have blossomed into political charmers, paragons of wholesome comeliness in a nonconformist era," *Time* treacled.

David was actually a more loyal Nixon partisan than Ike had ever been: "You are guilty either of grave oversight or willful neglect in regard to Richard Nixon," read David's stern letter to the *New York Times* in July of 1968 as he settled into his new job as chairman of the Youth for Nixon organization. He became a star campaign attraction through the summer. "I always campaign better with an Eisenhower," Nixon would joke as he introduced David to appreciative crowds. "Inheriting both the name and his grandfather's magnificent grin," *Time* observed, "the tousled, sometimes diffident college junior lends a certain symmetry to the Nixon drive in the minds of many Republicans. His very presence recalls calmer times when Ike was in the White House."

What to give the bride whose family potentially has everything? At Julie's first bridal shower, Nixon's secretary Rosemary Woods gave her a steam iron. Others offered scented candles, nightgowns, bookends, scouring pads, and a copy of *The Joy of Cooking*. But this was no normal couple setting up house. As the December wedding approached, the gifts came in from all over the world—especially after Nixon's squeaker of a victory in November. Charles de Gaulle sent a Sèvres tea service for twelve; Israeli defense minister Moshe Dayan sent an ancient Canaanite necklace and fertility idol from 200 BC. As for the wedding dress, made by Priscilla of Boston, that was guarded like a state secret.

Julie and David could have had a White House wedding. But she wanted something more private; she said that she and David were historic enough without having their wedding in the East Room. Luci Johnson did give the incoming generation a tour after the election. The White House, she said, can either be "the loneliest" or "the warmest" place to live.

"It can be as much as you put into it."

Julie chose Marble Collegiate Church in Manhattan, where her father used to worship when he was a naval officer in World War II, stationed at the Brooklyn Navy Yard. Officiating would be Dr. Norman

Vincent Peale—another rich political irony, since it was Peale's meeting of evangelical leaders in September of 1960 that denounced the Catholic John F. Kennedy's fitness for office with such fervor that it may have helped cost Nixon the race.

One more plot twist, this one a preview, not an echo: David's best man was Fred Grandy, his Exeter roommate. In years to come, Grandy would play Watergate dirty trickster Donald Segretti in the forgettable 1979 TV adaptation of John Dean's *Blind Ambition*, and most famously, the bumbling Gopher on *The Love Boat*. In 1986, he was elected to Congress from Iowa. The reception would be at the Plaza Hotel; they requested "Edelweiss" for their first dance. "There will be no musical selections from 'Camelot,'" the *New York Times* archly observed. But there would be "The Impossible Dream."

As the big day drew near, it was clear that Eisenhower would not be well enough to attend. So Nixon took the family festivities to him. At the end of November he visited Walter Reed, had Thanksgiving with the Eisenhower family, turkey and pumpkin pie at the communal table in Ward 8. Nixon was in the process of assembling his cabinet; he asked all his cabinet choices to pay Eisenhower a visit. Soon after, Eisenhower wrote to Nixon, telling him, first, how sorry he was to miss the wedding—his grandson, he said, "is one of the luckiest young fellows in the world, to get such a girl"—and second, he had some thoughts about staffing. He attached a proposal, which he asked Nixon to destroy after he read it. It suggested that Nixon consider appointing Ike's old friend and attorney general, Herb Brownell, as chief justice of the Supreme Court.

The whole event, wedding ceremony and reception alike, was closed to the press; but NBC tried (unsuccessfully, it turned out), to televise the ceremony for an audience of two: Ike and Mamie, watching over closed circuit TV from Walter Reed. The church was decorated for Christmas, filled with red and white poinsettias and a twelve-foot wreath. The guests entered to Christmas carols and Handel's *Water Music*. It was a surprisingly nonpolitical affair; incoming cabinet members attended, and old Nixon family friends, and lots of David's and Julie's college friends. When former New York governor Thomas Dewey entered the church, an usher asked on which side he belonged, bride or groom: that was a puzzle. "Both!" he said, and the usher led him to the Nixon side.

Julie surprised her father as he stood at the front of the church to give her away, by turning to kiss him. His daughter, he said later, was not nearly as nervous as he was.

One concession to biography and the electoral map: half the champagne at the reception was from California, the other half from New York. The six-tier wedding cake stood five feet and weighed five hundred pounds. When the couple set off for their honeymoon, Julie threw her bouquet into Tricia's hands: she would turn out to have the White House wedding, on a June day in 1971. Her sense of history guiding tradition, Julie had worn the same blue garter that Mamie wore in 1916—but she gave David a different one to throw to his groomsmen.

It was a happy day for both families; it would be followed some months later by a sad one. Eisenhower continued to weaken, and developed pneumonia in March of 1969. "I want to go; God take me," he said at last, and died on March 28.

He was laid out in his Army uniform, in the $80 government-issue casket he had requested. The funeral arrangements had been made years before like a battle plan, covering every detail from the pace of the funeral march to the points at which soldiers would present arms or bands would play. The body lay in state at the Capitol, on the same black-draped bier used for Lincoln's funeral in 1865. The funeral required Johnson's first trip back to Washington since leaving office. He called on Mamie, but declined Nixon's invitation to come to the White House, trying to keep a very low profile. It was one year to the day that he had announced he would not run for another term. It was also David's twenty-first birthday.

After a service at the National Cathedral, Ike's body was borne by horses and hearse to Union Station, where a freshly painted C&O train carried the body back to Abilene, a journey that took nearly two full days. Thirty-one guns sounded as the baggage car was closed and the black crepe curtains drawn. People lined the tracks even in the chill nights. In Washington, Indiana, with a population of eleven thousand, ten thousand people gathered from as much as fifty miles away to greet the train as it stopped to change crews. Johnson had not planned to follow the body to Abilene; but the Eisenhowers invited him warmly, so after flying back to Texas, he asked the Air Force to provide him a JetStar, and he landed in Kansas just before Nixon arrived on Air Force One.

Johnson lost more than a friend and counselor; Eisenhower was the living symbol of what felt in 1969 like an easier age, when greatness was an American birthright, when the torrents of change had not yet crashed into every corner of the culture, when there was a majesty about the presidency that allowed Eisenhower to leave office as beloved, respected, and above all, trusted, as he had been when he assumed it.

"A giant of our age is gone," Johnson said. "His death leaves an empty place in my heart."

Nixon too lost a mentor whose firm, faithful guidance he sorely needed. His speechwriters debated the tone of the eulogy. It should be "gracious, eloquent, deferential . . . not obsequious."

"This is an opportunity to associate with some of the things E was known for," one speechwriter advised. "The search for peace . . . the calming of the nation; good heart, good nature, good sense . . . the rock-ribbed integrity, the moral authority."

Those were all qualities essential to Eisenhower. They would prove, like so much else about him, nontransferable. Nixon did, however, find uses for memory. After Eisenhower left office, his successors found that the cork floor of the Oval Office was scarred from Eisenhower's golf cleats; Kennedy decided not to replace the floor; Johnson didn't either. Nixon had the pocked boards pulled up and replaced, then cut up the pieces into two-inch squares, mounted them on plaques, and sent them to an appreciative coterie.

NIXON AND JOHNSON:

Brotherhood and Blackmail

———————— π—•0 ————————

Richard Nixon treated the presidency as sacred, even as he set about defiling it. He decorated the Oval Office in imperial style, instructed the White House staff not to address him directly, referred to himself in the third person; he was no longer "I," no longer an individual; he was Richard Nixon, President of the United States. He was not above the law—he was the law, as he famously explained: if a president does something, "that means it's not illegal." Especially in time of war, the president's powers, in his view, were virtually unlimited.

So Nixon would pose a particular challenge to the club, which basically meant to Lyndon Johnson. You must help me protect the presidency, he told Johnson, from all those who are trying to break it, who think they know better, the liberals, the elites, the antiwar zealots who would burn buildings, leak secrets, aid and comfort the enemy on the grounds that any act was justified if it helped end an immoral war. When the *New York Times* published the Pentagon Papers, Nixon pressed Johnson to join him in bipartisan denunciation. When his covert war against leakers led to Watergate, he wanted Johnson to help shut the Senate inquiry down. You know how this goes, Nixon reminded Johnson; a president does what is necessary.

But Johnson refused to be bullied or blackmailed; over the years he had done a great deal to help Richard Nixon, but would do no more. There were limits to how far the club would go to protect either the office or its members. But in the end that didn't matter. Harry Truman died at Christmastime 1972, just after Nixon won his landslide reelection. Johnson died a month later. And with that, for the moment, Nixon was all alone.

13

"I Want the Break-In"

—RICHARD NIXON

Richard Nixon was forever starting new clubs, not least because he was often rejected by old ones. In college he founded the Orthogonians, a mock-Latin term he invented to mean the upstanding straight shooters, the scholarship kids, who would band together against the entitled Franklins, Whittier College's elite fraternity, which had turned him down. When he got to Congress he formed the Chowder and Marching Society, fifteen junior lawmakers who united as a bloc in hopes of having some clout in a chamber controlled by the Old Bulls. It included, among others, Gerald Ford and, later, George H. W. Bush. "Chowder and Marching welded exuberant friendships," wrote *Time*'s Hugh Sidey decades later, "and accidentally founded a power matrix that helped produce three Presidents and shape an American half-century."

As for the Presidents Club, even before joining Nixon had obsessively studied it for decades—not just the institution but the members themselves. He reread every inaugural address before sitting down with his legal pads to write his own (he especially liked the baroque oratory of James K. Polk). He knew everyone's secrets; he knew that Eisenhower did not like to be touched. "He would shake hands and all the rest," Nixon later told journalist Bob Greene. "But he didn't want people to come up and throw their arms around him and say 'Hi, Ike.' Kennedy was the same way. Despite the fact that he had the reputation of being, you know, very glamorous and the rest, he had a certain privacy about him, a certain sense of dignity."

His heroes were the ones who went for the gutsy move. Nixon hung a portrait of Eisenhower in the Cabinet Room because it was expected, and maybe some of the magic would rub off. But Ike wasn't really his model. Ike had firmness; Woodrow Wilson, whose portrait he also hung, had idealism. Nixon was determined to have both.

So it was the Roosevelts—Teddy and Franklin—who were Nixon's models, combining vision and strength, ideals and the toughness to realize them. He went so far as to change the name of the conference room across from the Oval Office from the Fish Room (FDR used to keep an aquarium in it) to the Roosevelt Room; there was a bust of Teddy over the mantel. And like Franklin, Safire observed, "he took pleasure in using devious methods to reach worthy goals."

Secrets and Lies

Three conversations—two just after the 1968 election, another just after the inauguration two months later—reveal how of all those who came before, it was Lyndon Johnson whose ghost haunted Nixon's presidency and whose motives and movements, real or imagined, helped doom it.

The first encounter, right after the election on November 11, 1968, came when Nixon visited Johnson at the White House. "One of the first things [Johnson] did was to take me upstairs to show me the bedroom safe, where he kept God knows what, and the recording contraptions that Kennedy had installed under the beds," Nixon told his young aide Monica Crowley years later. "Johnson got down on the floor, lifted the bedspread and waved his hand under the bed." He was giving Nixon his first tour of the White House taping system.

The second meeting, also that November, took place on the thirty-ninth floor of the elegant Pierre Hotel in New York City, where Nixon set up his transition headquarters. FBI director J. Edgar Hoover came to call on the president-elect. Johnson had praised Hoover as a vital presidential asset: "If it hadn't been for Edgar Hoover, I couldn't have carried out my responsibilities as Commander in Chief. Period," Johnson told Nixon. "He is a pillar of strength in a city of weak men."

And that day, Hoover was a man on a mission.

"Hoover, florid, rumpled, came into the suite and got quickly down to business," recalled H. R. Haldeman. The business, Haldeman figured, was "covering his ass. And no one was more adept at sheltering that broad expanse than he."

Hoover told Nixon that Johnson had ordered the FBI to wiretap Nixon—bug his plane, for national security reasons—as well as spy on Mme. Chennault. He was embellishing; the FBI had never actually gone ahead and bugged the plane, but Nixon didn't know that, which means he had reason to fear that Johnson—and Hoover—might have hard evidence linking him with the sabotage of the Paris peace talks. Nixon's obsession with any files related to the bombing halt and peace talks in the fall of 1968 stemmed from that natural fear.

"When you get to the White House," Hoover warned, "don't make any calls through the switchboard. Johnson has it rigged, and little men you don't know will be listening." Plus a president could tape Oval Office conversations at the touch of a button.

After Hoover left, Haldeman recalled, Nixon poured himself another cup of coffee. He wasn't angry; he didn't blame Johnson for spying on him. "He's been under such pressure because of the damn war, he'd do anything," Nixon said. And he paused. "I'm not going to end up like LBJ, Bob, holed up in the White House, afraid to show my face on the street. I'm going to stop that war. Fast."

He also made one of his first presidential decisions: "We'll get that goddamn bugging crap out of the White House in a hurry."

The third conversation came about two months later, just days after Nixon took office. Haldeman found him relaxing in the Oval Office, his feet up on the desk, gesturing broadly as he explained Haldeman's first assignment. You could say that he was already acting on another piece of Eisenhower advice, that every president needs "an S.O.B."

I want you to investigate the final weeks of the campaign, and Johnson's bombing halt decision, Nixon told Haldeman, which had almost sunk Nixon's campaign. "There was plenty of phony stuff going on by LBJ, Bob," Nixon said. "I want you to make up a full report with all the documents showing just what he did. He let politics enter into a war decision, and I want the whole story on it."

"But that's all behind us," Haldeman protested. What Haldeman didn't fully realize—but what Nixon did know—was that the file also potentially contained the evidence that Nixon had played dirty during the campaign.

Nixon fiddled with his desktop pen holder. He knew what he needed. Start with the Pentagon, he ordered, they'll have all the military moves Johnson made.

Haldeman launched his investigation, "and soon felt the first shiver of a future governmental war," he wrote in his memoirs. He learned that Leslie Gelb, a former Pentagon official, had moved over to the Brookings Institution, taking key files with him including one allegedly on the bombing halt. When Haldeman asked the Pentagon for a copy, he was told the only copy was at Brookings—which functioned as a kind of Democratic government in exile.

Nixon was not pleased at this news. "I want that Goddamn Gelb material and I don't care how you get it."

That was the kind of nutty assignment Haldeman would let slide. But not Charles Colson, Nixon's "personal hit man," as Haldeman would call him, or in Colson's own words, "a flag-waving, kick-'em-in-the-nuts, anti-press, anti-liberal Nixon fanatic." Soon he and other men around Nixon would follow his orders and protect his interests, at immeasurable cost.

Thus was laid the foundation for so much of what followed: Nixon covering his tracks, while trying to get hard evidence that Johnson had done what presidents before him had done: cut corners, bent laws, helped friends, lashed enemies.

Minding Lyndon

From the moment he took office, biographer Richard Reeves observes, Nixon made resolutions: be "compassionate, bold, new, courageous," he wrote to himself less than three weeks into the job. "Most powerful office. Each day a chance to do something memorable for someone. Need to be good to do good."

It was important, he reminded himself, that he demonstrate his "zest for the job (not lonely but awesome)." But the presidency *is* a lonely job, especially when you put a lonely man in it. "I believe you should keep your troubles to yourself," Nixon would say. He could not have been more different in this way than Johnson, the man who could not stand to be alone, or Kennedy with his large family and adoring disciples, or Ike with his many comrades. His aide John Ehrlichman referred to Nixon as the Mad Monk. He'd slip away to his private office in the Old Executive Office Building to brood for hours. "No one," Republican chairman Len Hall once remarked, "would look forward to spending a week with Nixon fishing."

So Nixon was not wired to seek out club members for companionship, as Johnson had; and in any event Eisenhower had died within a few months of Nixon's taking office, and Truman was safely retired in Missouri. Nixon did travel to Independence to present for his presidential library a piano that had been in the White House when he was there. The encounter was warm, clubby; you would not have known they had hurled insults at each other for decades, as they shook hands and smiled. Nixon sat at the piano and pounded out "The Missouri Waltz." Truman actually hated the tune, but by then he was too deaf to mind.

But it was Johnson that Nixon cared about, Johnson whom he courted and flattered and watched like a hawk to make sure he did not cause trouble. It was not that Johnson retained a drop of political clout in his Texas exile. It's just that he knew too much about Nixon's past.

Handled correctly, Nixon believed, LBJ could be a valuable ally and asset in the future. Mishandled—well, anything could happen.

Nixon worried about Johnson so much he created an office inside the White House dedicated to his care and feeding. He issued Executive Order 11456, which established the new post of special assistant to the president for liaison with former presidents. It would be his job to keep the club informed on "the major aspects of such principal international and domestic problems as the President directs" and convey their views back to the president. Truman heard from his old buddy Harry Vaughan that Eisenhower's former military aide Robert Schultz earned $25,000 for that "boondoggle." "If [Schultz] does not check with you weekly," Vaughan joked, "he must bother LBJ a lot to earn his pay."

It was actually the other way around. Johnson called the White House frequently, looking for information and favors, pestering a young military aide named Brent Scowcroft for military transport at all hours. Scowcroft at first found Johnson impossible, needy, demanding, but then grew over time to look forward to his calls. Johnson called so often looking for a place to bunk down in Washington that Nixon directed Scowcroft and other aides to liberate some money from the General Services Administration to purchase a clubhouse; they found and refurbished a run-down Lafayette townhouse to be used by the former presidents.

As it turned out, Gerald Ford would be the first to actually stay there, in 1977; it was eventually run by the same staff as the adjacent Blair House, its walls lined with pictures of the former presidents. George Herbert Walker Bush would stay there when his son was in residence across the street; his wife, Barbara, was known to call the place "a dump."

But its creation was all about the managing of Johnson. Every Friday Nixon dispatched a jet carrying classified national security briefing papers to Johnson down on his ranch. Cabinet members called him regularly with updates, and Henry Kissinger came in person to discuss the progress of the peace talks. Once Lady Bird drove Kissinger back to the airstrip and asked how he thought Johnson seemed. "I mumbled something about 'serenity in retirement,' " Kissinger told Safire, "and she almost drove off the road. I supposed flattery has to be related to reality, however vaguely."

"It feels good," said Johnson, "not to have that sergeant with the little black bag a few feet behind me." But rest and relaxation did not come naturally to a man so obsessed with how he would be remembered. He was still young, just sixty years old—two years younger than Ike when he first took office. So Johnson poured his energy into building his library, a temple for study and celebration of his epic political life. He'd go over to the house where he was born, which had been turned into something of a shrine, and check the license plates in the parking lot to see how many different states were represented. He kept track of the number of postcards sold; he wanted his home to host more visitors than any other birthplace. The library staff learned to inflate the visitor count. Later, after the library was built a stone's throw from the massive University of Texas stadium in Austin, he arranged for the announcer of the Longhorn football games to remind the tens of thousands of fans as they filed out at halftime that there were plenty of bathrooms just around the corner at the LBJ library.

Nixon looked for ways to woo Johnson, bring him into the tent. In August 1969, to mark Johnson's sixty-first birthday, he flew the Johnson family to his Western White House at San Clemente for a party. It was start to finish a Nixon production, "from the original idea down to the details of a mariachi band at the helipad," Haldeman wrote in his diary.

Nixon led the group as the guests sang to him; Johnson stood smiling, holding his felt hat and looking a little dazed in the brilliant California sun. The photographers snapped pictures: Nixon turned to one and remarked, "he doesn't look that old, does he?"

Then the two presidents climbed into golf carts and rode off to Nixon's office to talk privately. Johnson complained about everything from finding the right staff to managing reporters. "He's really psychopathic," Haldeman recorded. "Raved on and on about how humiliating it all was." Johnson went back over the campaign, his decision not to run, when he had actually made it (long before McCarthy humiliated him in New Hampshire or Bobby Kennedy jumped in): "Is obviously completely absorbed in writing history the way he wants it to be," Haldeman concluded.

Then the group reassembled for lunch and a three-tiered lemon-filled birthday cake decorated with yellow roses and Texas bluebonnets. The Nixons gave Johnson a nineteen-inch-high Japanese bonsai tree, and thoughtfully included a book, *Practical Bonsai for Beginners*.

Soon California governor Ronald Reagan joined in, and Billy Graham, as Nixon and the Johnsons flew north to Redwood National Park together. On the way, Johnson urged Nixon not to listen to his critics, and found a way to remind Nixon of the reasons to keep him happy. Johnson was in the process of assembling his presidential library, and needed help getting his papers processed for the archives. "LBJ makes valid point that our interests are very much involved," Haldeman wrote, "in that there will be many of his papers we will not want made public."

The remarks at the dedication of "Lady Bird Grove" in Redwood were warm as could be. Nixon remarked on Johnson's birthday, and wished that "he may live as long as the trees," of which the average was five hundred years old.

In return, Johnson offered Nixon his first formal, public welcome into the fraternity. "One never knows what it is to be a President until you are a President," he said as he thanked the Nixons for taking the time to pay them this honor. "Presidents are lonely people, and the only ones they are really sure of all the time are their womenfolk. President Nixon and I have something else in common. We can always depend on our womenfolk. Just as Mrs. Johnson has been by my side every step of the way, so has Mrs. Nixon.

"Of one thing I am absolutely sure," he went on. "Of the 37 Presidents that have come, and 36 have gone on, I feel sure from what I have read and studied about their lives that their greatest problem was never doing what was right; their greatest problem was knowing what was right.

"No man occupied the place that you occupy who didn't want to do the best he could, and some have succeeded and some have had less success. But of this you can be sure: If all of your days are as successful as today in bringing happiness to your predecessor, you will have a most successful Presidency.

"Thank you from the bottom of our hearts."

Johnson found ways to show his gratitude a few months later: in February 1970, one of his aides let Haldeman know that reporters had been calling looking for Johnson to discuss Anna Chennault and the 1968 finale; Johnson had refused, and instructed his aides to do likewise. Haldeman, needless to say, was surprised and pleased, and thanked Johnson again for his support for the president. The night after Nixon announced the invasion of Cambodia in May of 1970, Johnson made his first speech since leaving office, at a Democratic Party fund-raiser in Chicago, and placed the blame for the violence on Hanoi. "This nation can only have one President at a time," he said, and urged that all Americans support "our president." The nation's campuses erupted; National Guardsmen killed four students at Kent State. The two presidents conferred at the White House: "You know in these times of difficulty," Johnson wrote to Nixon afterward, "I stand ready to help whenever possible."

Johnson would soon have some advice for Nixon regarding his legacy. Don Kendall, chairman of PepsiCo, was planning Nixon's presidential library, and consulted with Johnson about the whole challenge of memory management. Nixon had been foolish, Johnson told Kendall, to rip out the taping system; he would need it when the time came to write his memoirs. Nixon himself worried that there was too much room for misunderstanding or misrepresentation in his conversations with foreign leaders—or for that matter, with advisors like Kissinger, whose recollections of Oval Office conversations might conveniently shift over time. So after ripping up Johnson's recording system, he had a new one secretly installed in February of 1971; five microphones were planted in his Oval Office desk, two on either side of the fireplace; two in the Cabinet Room, then four more in his Old Executive Office Building hideaway. How could so private a man risk what became the ultimate public exposure? "Because he was convinced left-leaning historians would try to deny him his place in history," Safire argued, "because he wanted to write memoirs better than Churchill's; and because he was sure he would have the same total control of his tapes that Kennedy and Johnson had of theirs."

But unlike their manual system, his was automatic, voice-activated.

"For want of a toggle switch," one White House staffer said, "the presidency was lost."

The Pentagon Papers

One can't understand the fate of the Nixon presidency without understanding that he was a man forever at war. His critics charged that he would do anything to protect his power and his right to abuse it; he would forever insist he was protecting the presidency, which is one reason he had faith that Lyndon Johnson, for all their differences and complex history, was more ally than enemy. It was a young David Broder, writing in the *Washington Post* less than a year after Nixon took office, who foresaw the battle lines. "It is becoming more obvious with every passing day that the men and the movement that broke Lyndon B. Johnson's authority in 1968 are out to break Richard M. Nixon in 1969," he wrote. Nixon's opponents cast an unpopular and expensive war as an immoral and indecent one, which must be ended by whatever means necessary—even if that meant destroying a president's capacity to lead, to negotiate, to maneuver in the global arena. Broder all but dared them to "put their convictions to the test by moving to impeach him. Is that not, really, the proper course? . . . Rather than leaving the nation with a broken President at its head for three years, would not their cause and the country be better served by resort to the constitutional method for removing a President?" That was October 1969.

"They" had driven Johnson from office and they were out to break Nixon. Or that's the way it looked to the president's men when the first shots were fired in the battle that would end with his presidency in ashes.

The front page of the *New York Times* on June 13, 1971, featured a charming picture of Nixon with his daughter Tricia, smiling proudly on her wedding day. It was the first outdoor White House wedding in 171 years; he had gotten regular updates from the Air Force, guiding him on whether the weather would hold. Nixon used to say that only people running for sheriff danced in public; and yet there he was, dancing with Pat for the cameras, and Tricia, and Julie, and even Lynda Bird Johnson.

The article next to the photo told a different story. "Vietnam Archive: Pentagon Study Traces 3 Decades of Growing U.S. Involvement." There were three thousand pages of narrative, four thousand pages of secret supporting documents, 2.5 million words in all, a secret history of the Vietnam War commissioned by Robert McNamara, directed by Leslie Gelb, and passed to the *Times* by former Marine captain and Pentagon aide Daniel Ellsberg. It was the largest leak of classified documents in American history; and if it did nothing else, it would reveal to the American public how baldly their presidents had lied to them about a war many wished had never been fought.

Nixon's first reaction was calm; the history ended in January of 1969, five days before he took office—so it was Kennedy's secrets that were being revealed, and especially Johnson's. When Kissinger's assistant Alexander Haig first called him just after noon to discuss the leak, Nixon said he hadn't even read the *Times* story. Haig called it a devastating security breach. "It's brutal on President Johnson," he said. "They're gonna end up in a massive gut-fight in the Democratic party over this thing."

In other words, this was really just a Democratic family feud. When Nixon and Kissinger, now national security advisor, talked that afternoon, Kissinger was reassuring: "I think they outsmarted themselves," Kissinger said of the *Times*, "because . . . they had sort of tried to make it 'Nixon's War,' and what this massively proves is that, if it's anybody's war, it's Kennedy's and Johnson's."

But it didn't take much to spin the president around. Just because it was not Nixon's secrets being revealed did not mean he wouldn't be damaged by them. If one president can stand accused of barefaced lying to the American public, it damages the credibility of all of them. And if a president can't protect the country's secrets, he looks weak and vulnerable. Nixon's entire foreign policy strategy depended on secrecy: secret bombing of Cambodia, sensitive disarmament talks with the Russians, clandestine efforts to lay the groundwork for his historic opening to China. Kissinger's first secret trip to China was just three weeks away. Breakthroughs on those fronts would give him the leverage he needed in his secret negotiations with the North Vietnamese. If the revelations fueled public demands to end the war, Hanoi might feel less need to compromise.

Everything was connected; the White House could not afford to look as though it was not in control of events. "This is treasonable action on the part of the bastards that put it out," Nixon told Kissinger.

"Exactly, Mr. President," Kissinger agreed. "I'm absolutely certain that this violates all sorts of security laws."

This was indeed a Nixon soft spot, dating all the way back to the Hiss case—the way the bureaucrats, the liberals, the in-house traitors would put national security at risk to pursue their own agendas.

"People have gotta be put to the torch for this sort of thing," Nixon said.

John Mitchell, now attorney general, sought and won an injunction to halt the papers' publication while the government assessed whether they posed a national security risk. But Nixon needed to swing public opinion against the leaks, make it clear how damaging this kind of rogue operation was to national security.

He needed, in other words, some help from Lyndon Johnson. This fight was not just about Nixon's presidency. It was a fight about the presidency itself.

On Monday, June 14, Walt Rostow, Johnson's national security advisor, had called Kissinger on Johnson's behalf. "He said that it is Johnson's strong view that this is an attack on the whole integrity of government," Kissinger reported to Nixon and Mitchell. "That if whole file cabinets can be stolen and then made available to the press, you can't have orderly government anymore." If Nixon acts to defend the integrity of America's national security, "any action we take he will back publicly."

Mitchell offered his own tidbit from Rostow: that the prime suspect for the leak was "a gentleman by the name of Ellsberg."

That had to be a bad moment for Kissinger. He had assembled his own Best and Brightest at the National Security Council, including bright Democrats who had worked for Johnson as well—like Ellsberg, who consulted for both administrations and helped Kissinger on a review of Vietnam policy.

In fact it was Ellsberg, of all people, who tried to warn Kissinger about what happens when a new president and his team suddenly come into office and have access to the top secret intelligence reports. "First, you'll be exhilarated by some of this new information, and by having it all—so much! incredible!—suddenly available to you," he told Kissinger after the election. "But second, almost as fast, you will feel like a fool for having studied, written, talked about these subjects, criticized and analyzed decisions made by presidents for years without having known of the existence of all this information, which presidents and others had and you didn't, and which must have influenced their decisions in ways you couldn't even guess." You'll be amazed that the insiders tolerated the bleatings of the outsiders without divulging what they knew, he explained, and you'll feel like a fool. But soon, "after you've started reading all this daily intelligence input . . . which is much more closely held than mere top secret data, you will forget there ever was a time when you didn't have it, and you'll be aware only of the fact that you have it now and most others don't . . . and that all those *other* people are fools." The warning captured perfectly how presidents become isolated, their circle of trust constrained by knowledge that is theirs alone.

Over the next few days, Nixon's obsession grew. He instructed everyone to refer to "The Kennedy-Johnson papers," to reinforce that this was the Democrats' problem—but at the same time to emphasize the illegal interference with the government's ability to conduct foreign policy. Other papers should denounce the *Times* for giving aid and comfort to the enemy. No newspaper was above the law. Above all, get Johnson to weigh in.

At twilight on June 17, 1971, Nixon met in the Oval Office with Haldeman, Kissinger, and Ehrlichman. It was one year to the day before the Watergate break-in.

You could say that's when it all began.

Kissinger had to put some distance between himself and Ellsberg. "He's a genius," Kissinger said. "He's the brightest student I've ever had"—an interesting observation given that he had never taught him, but had indeed hired him, and invited him to speak at his Harvard seminars. "He may have been a Marine once. But at any rate, he then flipped. Late '67, he suddenly turned into a peacenik." Kissinger suggested that deviant sex and drugs were to blame. And now Ellsberg was the ultimate enemy, a fanatic with an agenda and the evidence that could paralyze policymaking if things went badly. He had gone to work at the RAND Corporation, Kissinger explained, which had a set of the Pentagon Papers.

"I think he stole one set of the RAND documents, filmed them or Xeroxed them, and put them back in."

And the *New York Times* of course would be all too eager to take them. So how to maximize the damage to the Democrats? Nixon wondered whether they could leak material on Kennedy's role in the coup that toppled Diem.

"You can blackmail Johnson on this stuff and it might be worth doing," Haldeman said.

"How?" Nixon wondered.

"The Bombing Halt stuff is all in the same file," Haldeman explained. "Or in some of the same hands."

Which reminded Nixon: why hadn't Haldeman and Kissinger come up with that file? "Damn it, I asked for that, because I need it."

"Bob and I have been trying to put the damn thing together for three years," Kissinger said.

"... But there is a file on it," Haldeman said. Now Nixon was interested. Tom Charles Huston, Nixon's enterprising young internal spymaster, swore that there was a top secret file on the bombing halt at Brookings. It was Huston who had written an infamous 1970 memo advocating burglary as a means of law enforcement, which Nixon approved but J. Edgar Hoover got cold feet about and shut down. Huston had proposed breaking into Brookings to rifle the safe.

"But couldn't we go over?" Kissinger asked. "Brookings has no right to have classified documents."

"I want it implemented on a thievery basis," Nixon said, which suggested that he didn't want anyone but him taking a second look at those files. "Goddamn it get in and get those files. Blow the safe and get it."

Haldeman came back to the Johnson gambit. "My point is, Johnson knows that those files are around. He doesn't know for sure that we don't have them."

Kissinger still didn't follow. "But what good will it do you, the bombing halt file?"

"To blackmail him," Nixon said. "Because he used the bombing halt for political purposes."

"The bombing halt file," Haldeman said, "would really kill Johnson." That assumed that it would reveal that Johnson had timed the halt for political advantage—which the record suggests he didn't—and that he had illegally bugged Nixon's plane, which he hadn't.

Kissinger knew at least some of this. He had been there, playing both sides, keeping Nixon informed even as he was being briefed by the U.S. negotiators in Paris as they worked their way toward a peace deal. He didn't see it as an election gambit—in fact, he'd never heard any discussion about timing the halt for maximum political advantage. "To the best of my knowledge," he said, "there was never any conversation in which they said we'll hold it until the end of October."

Nixon knew this too; but the point of the bombing halt file was not that it would allow Nixon to pressure Johnson; he feared that it could be used against him if his efforts to derail the peace talks were revealed.

This was getting complicated. Nixon still wanted to find a way for Johnson to join him in denouncing the leaks, make the whole issue bipartisan. "Anyway, why won't Johnson have a press conference in your view?"

"Because he's smart enough not to," Haldeman said. "If he has a press conference . . . the thing that that will accomplish is clearly put this as a battle of Lyndon Johnson's credibility versus the world."

Haldeman was right; Johnson was dragging his feet. Each day's installment of classified documents was a body blow. Johnson was accused of campaigning in 1964 on a promise not to widen the war when he was actually drawing up plans to expand it; of sending American boys to die not to stop communism or liberate the South Vietnamese, but, according to a memo from the assistant secretary of defense, "to avoid a humiliating U.S. defeat"; of pursuing a lethal bombing campaign long after he'd been informed it was militarily useless. He may have liked to protect the presidency by denouncing leaks—but he had his own legacy at stake as well. He needed to figure out how to defend it.

Half an hour later Nixon called his aide Charles Colson to find out what luck they had had getting Johnson to make a statement. "This is terribly important," Nixon said. "Johnson's got to step up to this, and he's got to step up to it on the basis that there is a hell of a lot going to come out on a lot of other things, too." Colson reported that various Johnson associates were urging him to give a press conference, lest his silence be misinterpreted. But now Rostow was advising Johnson *not* to say anything, because the legal case against the *New York Times* was pending.

"Oh, no, no, no, that's just an excuse," Nixon said. "Rostow just doesn't want to get him involved and put all the blame on us, that's all." Of course they both understood that with Johnson tucked away on his ranch and Nixon in the Oval Office suing the *Times* in court, the furor would continue to focus on the White House. If Johnson spoke out, at least it would shift the focus back to him.

This inspired Nixon to add a little threat. "Right now he is a villain," Nixon said. Even leading Democrats—Humphrey, Senator Ed Muskie—were killing Johnson in the press. "If he doesn't defend himself, he'll go down in history and by God, I'll quit defending him." Tell their mutual friend Bryce Harlow to call Johnson tonight, Nixon ordered.

"Put it this way to Johnson," Nixon said. "Either he defends himself or I have no choice but to . . . to let the chips fall where they may. Just use those terms. . . . I don't want to blame him for the war. . . . I don't think he lied. . . . But if he will not defend himself, I will have no choice but also to refuse to defend him, and I don't want to do that.

"Now you tell Bryce to get off his ass and do this now."

When Harlow called, Johnson was in a rage. He'd been reading the Texas newspapers, which were hitting him hard, and throwing them around his office. He was "just as upset as hell," Harlow warned Colson. Anything he said publicly, Johnson said, would just be turned against him by a *New York Times* eager to "re-execute" him.

Nixon's next call was to Kissinger, urging that he reach out directly to Rostow. "Johnson ought to have a press conference," Nixon said. If Rostow balks, make the same threat. "That unless he has a press conference,

I'm not prepared to defend him. Now just as cold as that. They've just got to know. I'm not going to defend him, why should I?"

Kissinger remained skeptical that Johnson would go along. "It would certainly get a tremendous brawl started between Johnson and the press."

"That's right, and it'd get off of us," Nixon replied. "You see what I mean?"

"Well, it would get it off us on the immediate problem," Kissinger agreed, "but it would also drag the whole issue down to the level of 'was Johnson guilty or not?'"

"That's a hell of a lot better than having whether I was guilty or not, Henry, that's my point."

So now Nixon had tasked both Colson and Kissinger with bringing Johnson into line. The two lieutenants conferred; Kissinger told Colson they weren't going to get anywhere calling Johnson directly. He would reach out to Rostow himself, and in the meantime, Harlow and Colson should stop pestering Johnson.

Colson suspected this was all about Kissinger currying favor with Nixon by being the one to bring Johnson into the tent. He told Kissinger that "the president wants *me* to do it." Nixon had gone to bed by this time, so Colson proposed a cease-fire.

"I'll make a deal with you," he told Kissinger. "If you promise me that you won't try to call the President tonight, I promise you I won't do anything more tonight to reach Lyndon Johnson."

Kissinger agreed. Colson didn't trust him. A few minutes later, Colson asked the White House operator whether anyone had called Nixon that evening.

"Dr. Kissinger called three or four minutes ago," she replied, "and is talking now."

In the end it didn't matter who twisted his arm: Johnson was not going to help. The next day Haldeman wrote in his diary: "Learned later this evening that Johnson had completely collapsed, was in a state of being totally unstrung, feels that the country is lost . . . and that they're out to destroy him. So that ended any participation by him."

Two weeks later, on June 30, the Supreme Court ruled 6–3 in favor of the *New York Times*'s right to publish. Nixon summoned Haldeman, Kissinger, and Mitchell to plan the next move. He still wanted Johnson's bombing halt file.

"I want Brookings, I want them just to break in, break in and take it out," Nixon said. "Do you understand?"

"Yeah," Haldeman replied, "but you have to have somebody to do it."

It was as though at that moment Nixon remembered—and then forgot—that nothing said in that office went unrecorded.

"Don't discuss it here," Nixon said. "You talk to Hunt."

That was E. Howard Hunt, man for all seasons when there was a black-bag job to be done. He had helped the CIA topple governments in the 1950s, worked on the Bay of Pigs invasion in 1961, spied on the Goldwater campaign in 1964 for Johnson. Haldeman said that CIA director Richard Helms described him as "ruthless, quiet, careful. . . . He's kind of a tiger. . . . He spent twenty years in the CIA overthrowing governments."

"I want the break-in," Nixon repeated. "Hell, they do that. You're to break into the place, rifle the files, and bring them in. . . . Just go in and take it."

Nixon needed a special kind of team for the assignments he had in mind. It wasn't as though the enemy played fair, or observed some kind of due process. "I really need a son of a bitch like [enforcer Tom Charles] Huston who will work his butt off and do it dishonorably," Nixon said in a meeting on the morning of July 1. He would direct him personally: "I know how to play this game and we're going to start playing it."

Because it wasn't as though this was going to be a fair fight.

"Do you think, for Christ sakes, that the *New York Times* is worried about all the legal niceties? Those sons of bitches are killing them. . . . We're up against an enemy, a conspiracy. They're using any means. We—are—going—to—use—any—means," he said, drawing out every word. "Is that clear? Did they get the Brookings Institute raided last night?"

"No, sir, they didn't," Haldeman admitted.

"Get it done. I want it done!" Nixon said, banging on his desk. "I want the Brookings Institute safe cleaned out."

All in all, he suggested, turnabout was fair play; it's not like Nixon invented the political dark arts. He argued to Haldeman that "the Democrats had been doing this kind of thing to us for years and they never got caught." Roosevelt secretly taped people. Johnson spied on Goldwater. "Remember that any intellectual is tempted to put himself above the law," he said. "That's the rule that I've known all my life. Any intellectual,

particularly—watch what schools they're from. If they're from any Eastern schools or Berkeley, those are particularly the potential bad ones."

In the days that followed, aides later told Senate investigators, Colson talked seriously of a plan to firebomb Brookings, then send White
House operatives in with the firemen to rifle the safes and escape in all
the confusion. That plan never was executed. But others were; it was because of the Pentagon leaks that Nixon created his Special Investigations
Unit, a secret police force nicknamed the Plumbers, to perform the kind
of operations that the FBI would not. They would orchestrate the break-
in of the office of Ellsberg's psychiatrist in September of 1971. They
would eventually be joined by the "ratfucking" antics of Donald Segretti
and his team looking to harass Nixon's potential 1972 opponents; and of
course the Watergate break-in itself, which had to be covered up lest the
long trail of "horrors," as Mitchell called them, be exposed.

It all began with Nixon and Johnson, a poisoned peace process, and
the protection of secrets—the country's, certainly, but especially the
president's.

Another Election—and Another Alliance

If Johnson was not prepared to help Nixon in the moment, events would
ensure he'd help in the future. As the Pentagon Papers further inflamed
public opposition to the war, the Senate passed an amendment calling for
mandatory withdrawal of all U.S. troops from Vietnam and an end to all
military operations. Haldeman reported to Nixon that Johnson was beside himself at the takeover of his party by the peacemongers, including
his defense secretary Clark Clifford, now an outspoken war opponent.
Clifford, Johnson said, was "a silly motherfucker."

He felt roughly the same about the rest of his party. "I'm going to do
everything I possibly can to beat the dirty rotten sons of bitches in 1972,"
Johnson vowed.

So would Richard Nixon. His reelection prospects were by no means
assured; he had not won a majority in 1968 and Republicans had lost
twelve House seats in the 1970 midterm elections. But a key to achieving
that reelection goal was finding a way to properly deploy Johnson.

For one thing, Nixon saw in Johnson a useful weapon in his mission to divide the Democratic Party in advance of 1972. All the fault lines were there—over the war, foreign policy, law and order, civil rights. Hubert Humphrey may have hesitated to break with Johnson when he was a sitting president in 1968; but his heirs felt no such compunction as the 1972 race approached. The more Democrats threw Johnson overboard, the more easily Nixon was able to reel him in. It was especially useful to Nixon when other Democrats abused Johnson, and the two men could bond in their shared antipathy.

"I am thoroughly disgusted by the outrageous attacks that have been made upon you by the likes of [Kennedy friend] Kenny O'Donnell, [NBC anchor] Chet Huntley, et al.," Nixon wrote to Johnson in the summer of 1970. "Of course, as political men, we know that we are fair game when we are holding office but attacks upon a man after he has left office and particularly when he is a former President of the United States are completely beyond the pale as far as I am concerned." He used the club to confer immunity, in the interests of dividing the enemy.

"You can rest assured that history will treat you much more kindly than some of your contemporaries."

As the 1972 campaign approached, Johnson professed no interest in getting involved: "All I could accomplish would be to make a fool of myself," he told CBS News producer Bud Benjamin. "I don't hold public office. I don't have a party position. I don't have a platform. I don't have any troops. The only thing more impotent than a former president is a cut dog at a screwing match."

But Nixon heard how disenchanted Johnson was at the prospect of South Dakota senator George McGovern as Democratic standard-bearer. This was a man who had denounced the war with eloquence and passion at every opportunity. Johnson pronounced McGovern "the most inept politician . . . in all of history. . . . I didn't know they made presidential candidates that dumb." The Democrats convened in Miami on July 10, 1972, to nominate McGovern and whomever he could convince to run with him after Ed Muskie, Ted Kennedy, consumer activist Ralph Nader, and virtually every party titan turned him down. It was a depressing spectacle for Johnson, watching from his bleacher seat back in Texas. Party elders did not invite him to attend; in fact the pantheon of pictures of the great Democratic icons—Roosevelt, Kennedy—did not include Johnson at all.

Nixon called Johnson down at the ranch after it was over. He said he kept hearing from discouraged Democrats who wanted to support Nixon. How would Johnson feel about that?

Johnson was hearing it too; he told him about "thousands" of calls and letters coming into the ranch since the convention, of people expressing "total disenchantment with the McGovernites." The revolt extended to Johnson's own family; his daughters and sons-in-law were threatening to come out against McGovern, Johnson told Nixon.

Johnson read him a letter he was preparing to send out to friends: given his long service to his party, he'd be supporting Democrats at all levels. But "I have always taken the position that what an individual does in a presidential campaign is a matter of conscience, and I am not going to interfere with that decision." It was essentially a blanket exemption for Democrats who wanted to defect.

"Now what do you think of that?" Johnson asked Nixon.

"I can only say that I'm very grateful, Mr. President."

Nixon reported the call to his other favorite Texan, John Connally, who had resigned as Nixon's treasury secretary and launched "Democrats for Nixon." He told him how Johnson had actually agreed with most of Nixon's policies and none of McGovern's. The real problem, Nixon concluded, was what LBJ would do when McGovern went to pay a formal call to get his blessing. A statement of support and picture "could be harmful to us." Connally agreed that Nixon should enlist their mutual friend Billy Graham once again, to reach out to Johnson and persuade him to keep his endorsement of McGovern as cool as possible.

Graham undertook the mission eagerly; he flew down to the ranch that weekend and reported back to Haldeman about his visit, passing along Johnson's advice to Nixon: "[Johnson] advises the P to ignore McGovern. He says he should go all out and identify with people, to ball games, factories and so on. He thinks the McGovern people will defeat themselves. He feels very strongly anti-McGovern. Says the P should not do much campaigning, stay above it, as Johnson did with Goldwater."

Graham reported that when he raised the Watergate break-in, which had been reported earlier that summer, Johnson just laughed and said, "Hell, that's not going to hurt him a bit."

The following week, Johnson hosted McGovern and his running mate, Sargent Shriver, at the ranch. He made it clear he was merely acting as a loyal Democrat, and insisted there be no press, no pictures. Johnson called Graham as they were leaving, who passed along the report to Haldeman.

Johnson had told McGovern he thought he was "crazy as hell" about his approach to Vietnam. He refused to campaign for him. "He cited all the good things the P's done for him," Haldeman recorded in his diary on August 22, "says that McGovern is associating with amateurs, that he ought to shake up half his staff and he ought to stand up and say what a wonderful place America is.

"He made it clear to Graham that he would be happy to see Nixon if he wants to come and visit him."

Watergate

Nine months later, on May 14, 1973, after Nixon had swept to a landslide victory, Walt Rostow wrote an extraordinary classified "Memorandum for the Record," summarizing what Johnson knew about Anna Chennault and the Nixon campaign's activities before the 1968 election—the decision to put her under surveillance but then remain silent about what they learned. He ended with a remarkable observation: "I am inclined to believe," Rostow wrote, "the Republican operation in 1968 relates in two ways to the Watergate affair of 1972."

First, he noted, the 1968 race was desperately close at the end, and the Nixon team had reason to believe that their shady interference with the peace talks stalled Humphrey's surge and gave Nixon his victory.

Second, "they got away with it." Though there were rumors, the matter was never fully investigated. So for those involved, as the 1972 election approached, "there was nothing in their previous experience with an operation of doubtful propriety (or, even, legality) to warn them off; and there were memories of how close an election could get and the possible utility of pressing to the limit—or beyond."

In other words, the Nixon team's success at secretly manipulating the 1968 election emboldened them to do it again four years later.

The break-in at the Democratic National Headquarters in the Watergate complex on June 17, 1972, had been such a stupid crime, such an unnecessary overreach, that it took official Washington an especially long time to realize it was directed from the very heart of the Nixon White House. Nixon was piling up triumphs on the national stage; he had made his historic breakthrough with China; he was just back from Moscow, making peace. The Democrats were self-destructing right on schedule.

But the investigation into the break-in, pursued initially by the *Washington Post*'s intrepid Bob Woodward and Carl Bernstein and eventually by the FBI and a Senate committee, did pose a threat. On September 15, 1972, the Watergate grand jury handed down indictments of the five burglars, plus co-conspirators E. Howard Hunt and G. Gordon Liddy. The evidence of a wider conspiracy, the existence of a campaign slush fund, the many markers pointing toward the White House all appeared to have been dropped. White House counsel John Dean was called to the Oval Office; Nixon and Haldeman were there, grinning and celebrating the sense that the damage had been contained. It was to this meeting that Watergate prosecutors would point to show Nixon's complicity in the cover-up. And once again, the secrets that Nixon and Johnson shared played a crucial role in what happened next.

"Is the line pretty well set now on, when asked about the Watergate, as to what everybody says and does, to stonewall?" Nixon asked Haldeman that morning, and was reassured.

That afternoon, Dean marveled at the resources that had been devoted to investigating the break-in—"It's truly a larger investigation than was conducted . . . [into] the JFK assassination."

Once again they debated putting out the story of how Johnson had bugged the Republicans in 1968—confirming, as Barry Goldwater had declared, that "everybody bugs everybody else." But whatever they knew about Johnson's 1968 wiretapping, Nixon was still respectful—and wary—enough of Johnson not to want to expose him.

"The difficulty with using it, of course, is that it reflects on Johnson," Nixon said. "He ordered it. If it weren't for that, I'd use it. Is there any way we can use it without reflecting on Johnson?" Maybe they could say the Democratic National Committee did it? No, Nixon recalled, "the FBI did the bugging, though."

Dean wondered if maybe they could blame it on Humphrey. "Oh, hell, no," Nixon said.

"He was bugging Humphrey too!" Haldeman said. And the men all laughed.

But there would be a time for vengeance, using the FBI, the Justice Department, the IRS. "I want the most comprehensive notes on all those that tried to do us in," Nixon said. "They are asking for it and they are going to get it. . . . We have not used the power in the first four years, as you know . . . but things are going to change now."

A month later, on October 10, the *Washington Post*'s front-page headline declared that "FBI Finds Nixon Aides Sabotaged Democrats." Woodward and Bernstein detailed the efforts of Donald Segretti and his merry band of dirty tricksters all through the primaries, who would, at their frat boy best, forge letters, disrupt rallies, hire a plane to fly over the Democratic convention pulling a sign saying PEACE POT PROMISCUITY— VOTE MCGOVERN, and at their worst, did much worse. The *Post* called it "a massive campaign of spying and sabotage" that represented "a basic strategy of the Nixon re-election effort."

So once again Nixon returned to the double standard of liberals and Democrats jumping up and down over dirty tricks and wiretaps when they'd never been squeamish about using them in their own campaigns. "Edgar Hoover told Mitchell that our plane was bugged for the last two weeks of the campaign," Nixon said in an Oval Office meeting on October 17 with Haldeman and John Connally. "Johnson had it bugged. He ordered it bugged. And so was Humphrey's I think. . . . But the reason he says he had it bugged is because he had his Vietnam plans in there and he had to have information as to what we were going to say about Vietnam. . . . Johnson knew every conversation. And you know where it was bugged? In my compartment. So every conversation I had for two weeks Johnson had it."

This was not actually true, at least according to the oral history Hoover's deputy DeLoach did for the Johnson library two decades later. Johnson did demand a report on any calls from the Nixon camp to the State Department or the South Vietnamese embassy. "But the President did not ask me to put a microphone on the plane," DeLoach said. He expanded the denial in his memoirs: "The bugging of a campaign plane would have to be categorized as 'Mission: Impossible.' No one could have approached such an aircraft without being apprehended and questioned by the Secret Service. You might as well try to put a bomb on board." Even that, however, doesn't mean that Hoover hadn't led Nixon to think he *had* been bugged.

Just over a week later, Haldeman told Nixon they'd figured out that leaks about Watergate to Woodward and Bernstein were coming from a high-ranking FBI agent named Mark Felt (whose identity as the key source known as Deep Throat Woodward would not confirm for another three decades). But you can't move on him, Haldeman warned, or he'll spill. "He knows everything that's to be known in the FBI. He has access to absolutely everything."

As Nixon's men celebrated their Watergate reprieve, Kissinger was in Paris preparing to exchange peace proposals with North Vietnam's Le Duc Tho. After a spring offensive that had failed to deal a decisive blow, and with Nixon's reelection looking all but certain, Hanoi had decided it was prepared to make a deal. For Kissinger, it would mean global glory, future leverage, invaluable gratitude from a president. But for Nixon, the prospect of a historic triumph before the election left him, at best, ambivalent. He wanted to be able to blame the Democrats for the war dragging on, as though the communists were hanging on in hopes of getting a better deal from the liberals: back in February, he said that the antiwar Democrats "might give the enemy an incentive to prolong the war until after the election," when actually *he* was the one prolonging the war.

History doesn't repeat itself, Mark Twain said, but it rhymes. Having feared that Johnson would steal the 1968 election for Humphrey with an October surprise, Nixon now feared what would happen if he—or more precisely, Kissinger—pulled one off. "That son of a bitch," he told Colson, accusing Kissinger of "wanting me to be in his debt for winning this election."

Kissinger's exhaustive, duplicitous, but ultimately successful negotiations with North Vietnam allowed him to pronounce that "Peace is at hand" a week before election day. Somehow even Kissinger did not always understand the convoluted calculations of the president who had never quite trusted him in the first place: Nixon was afraid that a peace deal before the election, far from sealing his victory, might actually hurt him. "Our great fear," Colson told Sy Hersh, was that a settlement "would let people say 'Well, thank goodness the war is over. Now we can go on and worry about peace and we will elect a Democrat because Democrats always do more in peacetime. . . .

"The other thing was that we didn't want to appear to be exploiting,"

Colson added, "as Johnson had done in '68 with the bombing pause, which was so blatantly and transparently political. After the 15th of October, it was definitely contrary to our interest to get an agreement." Haig and Haldeman shared that view. It was a rather beautiful bit of cosmic justice that just as Kissinger had played both sides in 1968, Haig was now keeping Nixon informed of Kissinger's actions, a loyalty for which he would be much rewarded.

So Nixon refused to pressure his old ally South Vietnamese President Thieu to accept the terms Kissinger had negotiated. He avoided a "premature" settlement to the war; he protected his reelection margin; and he inflicted enough damage on Kissinger to keep him from entering the second term as a co-president. He all but admitted this particular act of perfidy twenty years later, in a conversation with reporters before the 1992 New Hampshire primary. George H. W. Bush was already looking vulnerable in his reelection bid; but that would not have been the case, Nixon suggested, if he had just had the sense to drag out the first Gulf War a bit longer. "We had a lot of success with that in 1972."

On November 3, just four days before the election, Nixon and Johnson reached what appeared to be a temporary truce. Haldeman told Nixon that he had been in touch with George Christian, Johnson's former press secretary who had joined Connally's Democrats for Nixon. Johnson had had his staff studying all the files from 1968; he was sure Nixon would deny any wrongdoing when it came to the peace talks. Johnson reviewed with Christian the dramatic finale of the 1968 race, his confronting Nixon with charges that he or his campaign team were sabotaging the talks. "Johnson," Haldeman reassured Nixon, "said that he decided at the time to interpret this as something foolish that someone did without Nixon's knowledge." But would the FBI go along with this version? "If we try to move on this story," Haldeman said, "it could be a trap. In other words, the FBI could be prepared to leak on this."

"That's right," Nixon said.

"Johnson understood that immediately," Haldeman replied.

"Good," Nixon said.

On January 2, 1973, Nixon called Johnson, ostensibly to bring him up to date on the war, whose end seemed so tantalizingly close; but actually because he had some club business to manage. Harry Truman had died on the day after Christmas, at the age of eighty-eight; at the time he was the third most admired man in America, after Richard Nixon and Billy Graham.

Nixon proclaimed a thirty-day period of national mourning, calling Truman "one of the most courageous Presidents in our history" and "a man with guts." Truman had personally approved elaborate military plans for a five-day state funeral ("A damn fine show. I just hate that I'm not going to be around to see it," he had said). But in the end Bess (the "Boss") prevailed, and the ceremony was scaled back: no riderless horse, no muffled drums and caisson, just a caravan of cars from the funeral home to the Truman library in Independence. Nixon and his wife came and laid a wreath of red, white, and blue carnations. The modest service suited the man, Nixon told Bess: "He didn't put on airs." Johnson and Lady Bird flew up from Texas and paid tribute as well. He was "a 20th century giant," Johnson declared.

There would be another memorial service in Washington, and that was the point of Nixon's call. He had heard that Johnson was not going to attend, Nixon said, and just wanted to make sure that was the plan.

"If you *were* coming I didn't want it to appear that I was not going," Nixon said. On the other hand, since they'd already gone to the private service, "I rather thought as if we were exploiting it if we just went again. How do you feel? I don't want anyone to think that we were affronting President Truman."

Johnson affirmed that he was not coming to Washington. For one thing, he was conscious that his own health was failing; his heart pains were getting worse by the day. Men in his family tended to die young. "I don't want to linger the way Eisenhower did," he would tell friends. "When I go, I want to go fast." He had become a chain-smoker. Every afternoon the pains would come, jolting and jabbing the breath out of him.

Nixon had just the antidote Johnson needed. He renewed an offer for Johnson to make use of Bebe Rebozo's place down in Key Biscayne. "Cause ole Bebe is a great guy to have around. He cheers people up, you know. He never brings up any unpleasant subjects."

By this time Nixon was increasingly preoccupied by the prospect of the Senate's Watergate investigation, with public hearings set to begin in the spring.

It was so unfair; Nixon continued to be obsessed with how much *less* wiretapping and bugging he had done than his predecessors. "We were limited as hell," Nixon told John Dean. "I mean Hoover, good God, we could have used him forever. . . . Johnson had just apparently used him all the time for this sort of thing . . . used the FBI as his own private patrol." Get that story out, Attorney General Richard Kleindienst told Nixon, and "really turn it into something . . . it might be the thing, the thing that'll save us."

Once again, the "Johnson did it, they all did it" defense was irresistible. So many people had crossed so many lines over the years that Nixon and his men hoped they had a kind of mutual assured destruction deterrent. On January 8, 1973, the day the criminal trial of the Watergate burglars began, Dean reported on the state of the Senate investigation. He was setting up a strategy group with Colson, to figure out "the Hill guys' vulnerabilities and see if we can't turn off the Hill effort before it gets started." If the administration could just produce some hard evidence that Nixon's campaign plane had been bugged in 1968, Haldeman argued, they could "force the Congress to investigate hanky-panky in both '68 and '72," rather than just the 1972 campaign. Haldeman had heard that the *Washington Star* maybe had the story; but did they have any proof? Because the only evidence Nixon had was J. Edgar Hoover telling him . . . and Hoover was dead.

But who cared? They weren't trying to make a case in court. The point was to put the fear of God into the Democrats that if they push about Watergate, the whole ugly history of their own dirty tricks will be fair game. "All you have to do is have it out," Nixon said, "and the press will write the Goddamn story, and the *Star* will run it now."

Or else, Nixon said, maybe they could pressure Hoover's deputy DeLoach into admitting to bugging the plane.

Or, Haldeman suggested, "we could start pushing on the other buggings that Johnson did, because he did a hell of a lot of his own staff and everyone else."

The real problem they faced, Ehrlichman observed, was public ignorance. "It isn't commonly understood around the country that this is done or has been done in prior years."

"Well," Nixon concluded, "let me say we have to use the material on the Johnson thing, and if Mitchell doesn't have the hard evidence, we just put it out. We'll float it out there . . . for now."

But as they talked, the strategy, the sense of opportunity started to shift. Maybe this wasn't about changing public opinion. Maybe it was safer to play in the shadows, some quiet threats, a gentleman's agreement. As in any club, the more dubious the motive, the more underhanded the means: threaten Johnson and key Democrats with exposure, and they might have less appetite for an aggressive investigation. "LBJ could turn off the whole congressional investigation," Haldeman said. Or Hubert Humphrey: he'd been right next to Johnson in 1968; imagine how ugly the revelations would be for him if the full story of the campaign were known. They could deploy another powerful Minnesotan, Archer Daniels Midland CEO Dwayne Andreas: "Andreas has got to talk to Hubert and say now this is the situation," Nixon proposed, "what the hell do you want to do, kill Johnson?" Humphrey would deny any knowledge of wiretapping, of course, but "nobody will believe him," Nixon concluded. "Andreas to Hubert I think is the way it's got to be played. So you'll follow through rigorously on that."

On January 11, the day Johnson's old friend North Carolina senator Sam Ervin officially agreed to head the Senate's investigation, Nixon sat with a legal pad making notes called "Goals for 2d term." He had three categories: "Substance," which included "Russia—SALT; China—Exchanges," plus a Middle East settlement and better trade with Latin America. Under "Political" he wanted to strengthen the party and recruit better candidates for 1974.

And under "Personal": "Restore respect for office; New idealism—respect for flag, country; Compassion—understanding."

That day, Nixon ordered Haldeman to find out whether "the guy who did the bugging on us in '68 is still at the FBI, and then [FBI acting director L. Patrick] Gray should nail him with a lie detector and get it settled, which would give us the evidence we need," Haldeman recorded in his diary. Now he was fully on board with the blackmail strategy. The *Washington Star* was back on the story. "That'll stir Johnson up," Haldeman noted, "and that gives us a way to get back to Johnson on the basis that, you know, we've got to get this turned off, because it's going to bounce back to the other story and we can't hold them—and scare him."

"I know," Nixon agreed.

"He may decide to get word out to his troops," Haldeman said, meaning Johnson's allies in Congress, "and, if he did, that could be very helpful." They discussed reaching out to Connally and Christian, to warn

Johnson that once the whole issue of who was bugging whom becomes public, no one will emerge unscathed. Christian should "go tell Johnson that we're trying to keep an eye on it," Nixon said. "We'll do our best, but he [Johnson] better get hold of [Johnson aide Joseph] Califano and Humphrey and anybody else he knows and tell them to pipe down on this thing. . . . We will use it without question, Bob, if it comes to nut time."

That would refer to nut cutting, a favorite Nixon term for the ruthless endgame.

But to their dismay, Johnson was in no mood to be muscled. A newspaper reporter had indeed called Johnson, starting to ask questions about Johnson's own wiretapping activities. Johnson in turn had called DeLoach at home.

"If they try to give me any trouble," Johnson warned, "I'll pull out that cable from my files and turn the tables on them." DeLoach in turn warned Haldeman not to mess with Johnson "LBJ got very hot," Haldeman recorded in a handwritten note, "and . . . said to him that if the Nixon people are going to play with this," he'd play too: Johnson did not bug Nixon, he insisted; he just tapped Chennault, and if Nixon accused him of eavesdropping, he would release the intercepted cables from the South Vietnamese embassy in Washington to Saigon, showing how Nixon's campaign had interfered with the peace settlement. And just in case, there was that part about the secret contributions to the Nixon campaign from the Greek military dictatorship, which Johnson had kept to himself, a club insurance policy.

With Johnson threatening to expose Nixon for undercutting Johnson's peace talks in 1968, Nixon and his men backed off.

Inauguration day was barely a week away.

Johnson had asked a speechwriter to start working on a statement to mark the occasion when the war finally ended. He never lived to give it. Nixon was inaugurated for his second term on January 20; later that day, he announced his plans for dismantling the Great Society. It was a moment Johnson had long foreseen. Doris Kearns Goodwin recalled his telling her how he thought of his Great Society like a beautiful woman. "I figured she'd be so big and beautiful that the American people couldn't help but fall in love with her, and once they did, they'd want to keep her around forever, making her a permanent part of American life. . . .

"But now Nixon has come along and everything I've worked for is ruined. . . . I can just see him waking up in the morning, making that victory sign of his and deciding which program to kill. It's a terrible thing for me to sit by and watch someone else starve my Great Society to death. . . . Now her bones are beginning to stick out and her wrinkles are beginning to show. Soon she'll be so ugly that the American people will refuse to look at her; they'll stick her in a closet to hide her away and there she'll die. And when she dies, I, too, will die."

He turned out to be right. On January 22, Johnson was alone in his room taking a nap, when he suffered a fatal heart attack.

The next night, in a national address on all three networks, Nixon announced the end of the Vietnam War.

He handwrote a letter to Lady Bird that evening:

I only wish Lyndon could have lived to hear my announcement of the Viet Nam Peace Settlement tonight.

I know what abuse he took—particularly from members of his own party—in standing firm for peace with honor.

Now that we have such a settlement, we shall do everything we can to make it last so that he and the other brave men who sacrificed their lives for this cause will not have died in vain.

The next day's cabinet meeting started late; Nixon was in a reflective mood. When you reach the age of sixty, he told them, your days are numbered. And he started listing the ages of all the presidents when they died—many of them younger than sixty. "We need to make every day count," he said.

Years later, Nixon reflected on his sometime ally, sometime nemesis.

"I think President Johnson died of a broken heart, I really do. Here's Johnson, this big, strong, intelligent tough guy, practically getting so emotional that he'd almost cry, because his critics didn't appreciate him. He, til the very last, thought that he might be able to win them. And the point is, rather than have them love him, he should have tried to do what he could have done very well—have them respect him. And in the end, he lost. He neither gained the love nor retained the respect."

In his final remarks to the White House staff, on the day he resigned his office, Nixon applied a version of the lesson to himself.

"Always remember, others may hate you, but those who hate you don't win unless you hate them, and then you destroy yourself."

NIXON AND FORD:

Mercy at All Costs

———————— ⚷ ————————

Richard Nixon and Gerald Ford's relationship lasted forty-five years, from their earliest days in the U.S. House of Representatives together until Nixon's death in 1994. They began as colleagues; they became friends, and then allies; they served as president and vice president; at one point, they even carpooled together. Twice, in 1960 and 1968, Nixon appeared to dangle the vice presidency at Ford. But he only offered it to him once, in 1973, when he essentially had no choice—and then only on the strict understanding that Nixon favored someone else as his party's 1976 presidential nominee. That had to hurt.

Nixon, of course, was in no position to play kingmaker: in 1974, he would resign the top job.

An unelected president, Ford would soon—perhaps too soon—pardon his old friend so that his own presidency could begin. That decision, selfless and patriotic, helped consign him to a two-year term; in 1976, when he sought the voters' acceptance, the ghost of Nixon and the pardon were still too strong.

Years later, he tried to engineer a censure—to avoid an impeachment—for another president facing an implacable Congress. He would try to get it right that time.

———————— ⚷ ————————

14

"I Had to Get the Monkey off My Back"

—GERALD FORD

Only eight men in American history have served two full terms as vice president. The job, one of them noted, wasn't worth a bucket of warm piss. That was true the first two times Richard Nixon toyed with giving Gerald Ford the job.

But when round three unfolded, in October 1973, Nixon faced every kind of trouble. He had a small army of lawyers fighting the demands of a special prosecutor who was busy untangling all kinds of grimy political stunts by Nixon's henchmen. Each week seemed to bring news of yet another once-loyal West Wing aide who was peeling off and turning into a government witness. His vice president meanwhile was in even more danger. Spiro Agnew had taken $100,000 in bribes as a public official in Maryland and federal prosecutors were closing in on him fast. The White House was in no mood to mount two criminal defenses at the same time. Besides, there was an easy way out for Agnew: prosecutors hinted that the vice president could plead to a lesser charge if he simply resigned.

And so he did. It was a safe bet that Nixon would be next. Which meant, in the fall of 1973, the vice presidency was worth more than ever.

But at that point, it was no longer really Nixon's to bestow.

Friends and Allies

In the first week of 1949, a few moments after Speaker Sam Rayburn administered the oath of office to the freshman class of lawmakers, a rail-thin, dark-haired man approached Gerald Ford in the well of the House of Representatives. The thin man stuck out his hand and offered his congratulations. "I'm Dick Nixon, from California," the stranger said. "I heard about your big win in Michigan and I want to say hello and welcome you to the House."

Dick Nixon may not have been Jerry Ford's first friend in Washington, but he came close, and it is easy to see why. They were born just six months apart in 1913, a year that produced the zipper, the Federal Reserve, and Rosa Parks. They shared small-town roots, had struggled to attend nearby colleges, served in the Navy, and both gone on to law school. Nixon was elected to the House right after the war in 1946; Ford followed two years later.

And if Nixon had heard about Ford, Ford had certainly heard of Nixon, after his triumph over Alger Hiss. Ford liked to hang out on the House floor on most days in his first term, meeting other members and talking shop; he made it a point to be present when Nixon rose to speak. Ford was struck by Nixon's attention to detail, how carefully he prepared for debates, how deeply he understood the complex cast of characters who mattered on foreign policy both at home and overseas. Nixon had to be impressed by Ford's ready smile, his easy way with his colleagues, his straightforward Midwestern manner, and his obvious lack of pretense. (Ford had trouble getting into his Capitol Hill office on the first day because he came dressed to clean the place—in overalls.) "Both of us were strongly dedicated to certain domestic policies at home and US leadership abroad. In fact in political philosophy, we were about as close as two people could get," Ford said, adding, "We understood what it meant to rise on merit, not privilege."

Being the same age bonded them; so did their charter memberships in the Chowder and Marching Society. They carpooled from northern Virginia to Capitol Hill together and saw each other socially, and Pat Nixon and Betty Ford became friends as well. Nixon had big plans: by 1950, he'd graduated to the Senate and the next year, when the Republican swells in Grand Rapids pressed him to produce a big name for their annual Lincoln Day Dinner, Ford turned to Nixon for help. Sure enough, Nixon filled the hall in Ford's hometown for the event. He spent time later that night reassuring a smaller group of locals about his controversial investigation of Hiss; some of the questions were hostile, but Nixon, Ford recalled, kept his cool throughout. Later, Ford took Nixon to his parents' house to spend the night, where they stayed up late sharing a drink and talking about the coming 1952 campaign. Nixon occupied Ford's mother's four-poster bed. "Later," Ford recalled, "she hung a sign on the bed: 'The Vice President slept here.'"

Over time Ford realized that however similar their views on policy might be, their personalities were not. The sunny Ford was struck by Nixon's moodiness. He recalled one party where Nixon was playing the spirited showman inside the room but turned gloomier when he left. "On my way out I saw him on the curb waiting for a car, mumbling to himself. He seemed sad and detached." The mood swings, Ford assumed, exacted a price. "One minute he was the outgoing extrovert, the next reflective, even sullen. My impression was that his moodiness drained a lot out of him."

But Ford shared that observation with the public only late in his life. At the time, Ford was a solid Nixon man. During the 1952 campaign, he came to Nixon's defense when the nominee was discovered to have maintained a congressional slush fund for personal expenses. Ford himself had done the same and when a variety of Republicans urged Nixon to take himself off the ticket, Ford urged Nixon to stay put. "I am in your corner 100 percent," Ford wired. "Fight it to the finish, just as you did the smears by the communists when you were proving your charges against Alger Hiss. All Michigan representatives feel as I do."

A pattern emerged: Ford again led the countercharge for Nixon in 1956, when a group of Republican backbenchers, led by Harold Stassen, tried to have the vice president tossed from the ticket. This time around, Ford *organized* the defense, rallying members of the Chowder and Marching Society at the convention in San Francisco to pressure their state delegations to stick with Nixon. Ford's maneuvering took place far from any cameras and was engineered to avoid, rather than generate, publicity. But when it was over, Nixon knew whom to thank: he sent Ford four different notes of gratitude for his help over a sixteen-day period. "It is difficult to express adequately in a letter how deeply I appreciated your fine gesture of confidence," Nixon wrote. A few days later, he wrote again, despite a plea by Ford that no thanks were in order. "I know you said 'don't answer,'" Nixon wrote, "but I wanted to tell you how very much I appreciate what you did."

By 1960, it was hard to tell where friendship stopped and a strategic alliance began—to the point that Nixon arranged to have Ford's name floated as a possible vice president at the 1960 convention in Chicago. Nixon did this the old-fashioned way: he asked veteran *Newsweek* writer Raymond Moley to extol Ford's uncommon grasp of Congress in his column. Moley complied: "Watch this Ford," he wrote. "A conservative [who combines] the wisdom of age with the drive of youth."

With Ford's permission (and perhaps a little encouragement as well), Michigan Republicans picked up on the idea. About one hundred flag-waving supporters greeted his arrival at Midway Airport in Chicago that summer; the Congress Hotel on Michigan Avenue sported Ford banners and many guests pinned on blue and gold Ford buttons. Some of this hoopla was the kind of ritual courtesy a nominee paid in that era to big state delegations and their titular leaders; governors often arrived at party conventions as favorite son candidates for the top job itself, in part just to keep the delegations unified until the proper deals could be struck with the nominee. Ford later insisted that he hadn't put much stock in the 1960 vice president boomlet and instead preferred a Republican senator from Kentucky by the name of Thruston Morton for the job. Maybe so, but there is evidence that Ford did not regard his own "candidacy" as another routine Nixon head fake: he sought a lawyer's advice about whether he could, under Michigan law, run for both the vice presidency and Congress at the same time. And there is a telling aside in his wife's memoirs that some part of Ford hoped Nixon might be serious in 1960. As Betty Ford recalled the rumors in 1973 (which would, of course, come true) that Nixon was about to tap Ford to be his vice president, she wrote that she saw no reason to take them seriously then given what had happened before. "We'd done our sitting-up-until-four-in-the-morning number in 1960," she wrote, "and [Nixon] had come up with Henry Cabot Lodge, and since then we've been impervious to rumor."

As for Ford, he learned a different lesson about Nixon and the vice presidency in 1960. A day before Nixon was to announce his choice, Ford was invited by a Nixon aide to attend an urgent meeting to discuss the options. When Ford replied that he favored Kentucky's Morton, the aide said that Nixon had already decided on Lodge. So what was the point of the meeting, Ford wondered. "If Nixon had made up his mind," Ford asked later, "why would he go through the sham of asking for our advice? That wasn't the way to play the game. . . . Making up his mind and then pretending that his options were still open—that was a Nixon trait that I'd have occasion to witness again."

But if Ford was bothered, he went to Nixon's imaginary bull session at the Blackstone Hotel anyway. Which was lucky, if only because Ford too had a role to play in the psychodrama: to volunteer to stay put. Nixon at one point in that session turned to Ford and said, "I don't know of anyone whose views on domestic and foreign policy are more consonant with mine than Jerry here, but if I'm elected, I'll need him in the House." So there Ford stayed. Adding insult to injury perhaps, Nixon asked Ford to make a speech seconding Lodge's nomination. And, ever the good soldier, Ford agreed.

Nixon led Ford through a similar charade in 1968, when he was again the nominee and seeking "advice" from party elders about a running mate. At another Kabuki session, this time in his Miami Beach hotel suite, Nixon again gathered top Republicans to discuss the options. Once more he turned to Ford and said, "I know that in the past, Jerry, you have thought about being Vice President. Would you take it this year?"

It is hard to imagine that such an offer, made in such a semipublic fashion, was serious. And Ford, playing along with the charade, said that while he appreciated the "compliment," he favored New York City mayor John Lindsay instead (a choice about as far from Nixon's mind as Ford himself). But there were some candidates Ford, whatever his feelings about his own chances, could not abide. And when Nixon gently floated the name of Maryland governor Spiro Agnew later in the session, Ford let out what one man present described as a raucous whinny. Though Ford may have expressed what others in the room were thinking, his reaction was not enough to deter Nixon. When Ford, sitting poolside the next day with Betty at the Fontainebleau Hotel, heard from an aide that Nixon had indeed tapped Agnew, he was again dumbfounded. "I couldn't believe it," he said. Agnew, Ford related, "seemed like a nice enough person but he lacked national experience or recognition. And now, after just two years as governor, he was going to run for Vice President. I shook my head in disbelief."

It had to sting Ford that his old friend had picked a second-rate player as his understudy. But Nixon got exactly what he wanted with Agnew: someone who would gladly stick a knife in Nixon's enemies, a role for which the genial Ford was completely unsuited.

Third Time's the Charm

When Nixon finally tapped Ford to be his vice president—not in 1960 or in 1968 but in 1973 after Agnew resigned as part of a plea bargain agreement—it wasn't really Nixon who chose him at all.

Ford and his aides maintained in their various memoirs that being vice president was the last thing on his mind. By 1973, the story goes, Ford wanted out of politics. He had served twenty-five years in the House, made many friends, and secured a good federal pension. But he had largely missed his kids while they grew up. His gregarious wife was lonely and sought comfort in alcohol and pills. And after watching Nixon win a forty-nine-state landslide in 1972 only to have the House remain safely under Democratic control, Ford also knew, once and for all, that he'd never be speaker. By the summer of 1973, Ford was asking majority leader Tip O'Neill to consider a congressional pay raise to help boost his pension before he retired. That way, Ford figured, he could go back to Grand Rapids and practice law, as he put it to O'Neill, "three days a week and play golf the other four." O'Neill demurred, "Let me think about it."

As it became clear that Agnew could not survive in office, Ford knew he was once again a contender for the number two job. Ford and a few other lawmakers had been given the task (by Nixon) of rounding up nominations from members of Congress about who should replace Agnew; and the winner of that informal poll was none other than Ford himself. He was well known to Nixon, perfectly aligned with the president on most issues, popular on Capitol Hill, nonthreatening to Democrats, and free of any taint of scandal. Even Pat Nixon was betting on Ford.

Nixon, however, was not on board. He had long preferred John Connally, chiefly because he believed the LBJ protégé, who had joined the Nixon administration and later the Republican Party itself, could split the Democratic Party in two in the not too distant 1976 elections. Con-nally, for his part, certainly thought he was going to get it; by October 10, the day Agnew resigned, Connally was already installed at Washington's Mayflower Hotel, quietly assembling a vice presidential staff.

But Nixon had failed to anticipate the reaction of House Speaker Carl Albert, the diminutive Oklahoma Democrat who had come to Congress with Nixon in 1946 and who would later say that Dick Nixon had been the first Republican he'd ever met. Along with Senate majority leader Mike Mansfield, Albert told Nixon that only Ford would have an easy time winning confirmation in the midst of the widening Watergate crisis. Albert left no doubt that the other contenders—Ronald Reagan, Nelson Rockefeller, and especially Connally—would face a meat grinder of questions. A Congress controlled by Democrats would never allow a party turncoat like Connally to become the vice president. Nor did they want someone who might prove to be a strong contender for the presi-dency in 1976. And so, as Nixon would recall, "This left Jerry Ford."

A White House official told Richard Reeves, "Nixon hated the idea but he had to go along."

Perhaps because he had so little choice, Nixon pretended that he did, and repaired to Camp David for two days to ponder the matter. Then he flew by helicopter back to the White House on the morning of October 12 and informed his staff that he had made up his mind. They in turn laid on an East Room announcement for the evening, a Friday night. On instructions from Nixon, chief of staff Al Haig gave Connally the bad news, before calling Ford with a hint of the good news to come.

It is difficult to re-create the uncertainty about Nixon's choice that pervaded Washington in a pre-Internet, pre–cell phone, pre–cable tele-vision era. Throughout the afternoon, news organizations, including the *Washington Post*, had madly chased a rumor that Nixon would tap a relative unknown, Virginia governor Linwood Holton. Nixon phoned Ford just as the Ford family sat down to a dinner of grilled steaks at their northern Virginia home. "I've got good news," Nixon said, "but I want Betty to hear it, too." The Fords dressed and hurried to the White House, where by 9 P.M. a mix of stifling klieg lights, wild speculation—and, strangest of all, live chamber music—created a scene out of Gil-bert and Sullivan. Everyone in politics had been invited; the room was crammed with row upon row of gilt chairs to accommodate the overflow crowd. Television networks went live to the nervous and congested room, their anchormen in the dark about the outcome. As Nixon entered to "Hail to the Chief," virtually no one in the room knew the identity of the next vice president of the United States.

Yet everyone knew that whoever it turned out to be might well become the next commander in chief.

Nixon unveiled his choice slowly, first talking about his agenda and the need for the country to "build a new prosperity . . . without war and without inflation." Even when he turned to the business at hand, he moved by inches: he spent a few minutes explaining his rationale and the unnamed nominee's qualifications. Many in the crowd were madly updating their own mental short lists as Nixon ran through his reasons, trying to get there first by process of elimination. When Nixon came to the part in the remarks where he praised the nominee's twenty-five years in the House, the suspense broke and the silence began to break into whistles, cheers, and scattered applause—"Beautiful, beautiful," one lawmaker shouted from the rear of the room. By now, Jerry terHorst, who was then covering Ford for the *Detroit News*, noted in his own account, "those around Ford began pummeling him, clapping him on the back, punching his shoulders"—and he stood to accept the handshakes and congratulations of the two House leaders who were sitting near him, Albert and O'Neill; at the same time, people were nudging—shoving by some accounts—Ford out from the audience and toward the president and the podium. Those in the audience almost seemed to want to take the decision out of Nixon's hands, validating it as their own.

But Nixon was still speaking, praising the still unnamed Ford, and he broke from his text to urge the audience not to rush to judgment. "There are several here," he said, "who have served 25 years in the House of Representatives"—as if he preferred to deprive Ford of the moment. And then, a few sentences later, Nixon revealed his choice and the room exploded in sustained, unalloyed cheering. "I proudly present to you the man whose name I will submit to the Congress of the United States for confirmation as Vice President of the United States, Congressman Gerald R. Ford of Michigan."

A live microphone picked up the back-and-forth between the president and his new number two. "They like you," Nixon said to Ford, who replied, "I have a few friends out there."

It was a revealing piece of political theater that offered more than a hint of what was to come. Henry Kissinger, who had spent much of that day wrestling with the outbreak of the Yom Kippur War, spoke to Nixon after the East Room event. His analysis, recorded in his memoirs, was sharp-eyed: "He was in good form, still exuberant over achieving surprise in naming Ford, who (he reasoned) would be a short-term asset with the Congress." The choice, Nixon imagined, would slow the drive toward impeachment, since Congress would not want to run the risk of placing a supposedly inexperienced man in charge of foreign affairs. This just showed how little Nixon understood his adversaries. "He failed to recognize that [the applause] was a tribute above all to Ford," Kissinger observed. "Nor did he yet understand that his fate could no longer be changed by tactical maneuvers. Indeed, Nixon's travails had reached the point where even if Ford was as inconsequential as Nixon thought—which he emphatically was not—his designation as Vice President would accelerate Nixon's collapse rather than delay it. It was more tempting for Democrats to remove Nixon if his successor seemed to be someone they thought they could beat in the Presidential election of 1976."

Nixon resigned eight months later.

"I Haven't Cried Since Eisenhower Died"

Gerald Ford held fifty-five press conferences in his eight months as vice president, more than Nixon, as president, had held in six *years*.

So when Ford finally got to hold one as president, in mid-August 1974, he tried to do it in a way that proved that he had expunged Nixon's ghost from the White House.

Ford conducted the session in the East Room, standing in plain view of the wide-open central corridor rather than before a wall of heavy velvet drapes. Wearing no makeup, he entered from a side door that was pointedly left ajar, as if to signal a new openness. He stood comfortably, almost casually, in front of a sliver of a lectern so minimal that it hid nothing of Ford's frame and barely left room for the Presidential Seal. The whole event screamed modesty and transparency. And in case anyone missed the point, Ford opened with some lighter news from the residence: in order to hold this first press conference, he said, the commander in chief had been forced to bump his wife's first meeting with reporters into the following week. "Until then," he deadpanned, "I will be making my own breakfast, my own lunch and my own dinner."

After years of Nixon's ponderous, defensive, and sometimes leaden performances, the reporters ate it up. Over the next twenty-nine minutes, he dispensed with twenty-seven questions.

Unfortunately, ten were about Nixon and Watergate.

The most precious commodity of the United States of America is neither the gold bullion in Fort Knox nor the launch codes in its ballistic missiles. It is the time of the commander in chief: there is only so much of it, and how it is spent shapes pretty much everything else. Which is why Ford was fuming when that first press conference ended and he walked back to the West Wing with aides. "God damn it," he said as he returned to the Oval Office, "every press conference from now on, regardless of the ground rules, will degenerate into a Q and A on 'Am I going to pardon Mr. Nixon?'"

He had the same feeling the next day, when he reviewed the transcript of the East Room session: though Nixon was gone, Ford could see that questions about the former president could consume his own presidency indefinitely. On the one hand, the plainspoken, Midwestern Fords, their handsome, teenaged kids, and Betty Ford's extraordinary candor had refreshed a musty and corrupted White House. Ford hosted women and blacks and labor leaders for the first time in years; after wincing over Nixon's stilted Sunday church services in the East Room, Betty Ford banned them; Billy Graham and Lawrence Welk were out; the new first couple made news when they stayed up until 1 A.M. dancing after a state dinner to Jim Croce's "Bad, Bad Leroy Brown."

But while Nixon was gone, his shadow lingered. His fate in the courts, the continuing congressional investigations, the disposition of his secret papers—not to mention the presence of dozens of Nixon aides still on Ford's White House staff—all conspired to divert the new president for months. "I had to get the monkey off my back," he wrote later.

Two days after the press conference, Ford secretly ordered Phil Buchen, his White House counsel, to look into a pardon. Buchen and aides worked through the Labor Day weekend to find a legal basis for the decision, and particularly as to whether Ford could grant a pardon in advance of indictment or conviction. When Ford informed his political aides of what he was contemplating (and swore them to secrecy), they nearly mutinied. But as they implored him to reconsider or at least wait a few months, it became clear to all that Ford did not want to wait; and that he might have already made up his mind. "Is this the right time?" asked John Marsh, the man Ford called "the conscience of his administration." Replied Ford, "Will there *ever* be a right time?"

And while it seemed almost unthinkable then, it is easy to see now that Ford had a problem unlike any faced by an American president in history; he was the accidental president, the man who had neither wanted the job nor been elected to it. Worse, perhaps, even though he had inherited the title, the job was not yet his. That was something, because of the peculiar way he had ascended to the top, that he still had to earn. Ford needed not only to take control of the presidency in a hurry; he needed to shove his radioactive predecessor offstage for good if he had a shot at being a success himself. He needed to make Dick Nixon go away.

Ford believed that a criminal indictment and trial would take months if not years to reach a conclusion, and either way would force Ford to play an awkward sideline role throughout. He feared that the endless spectacle of a former president on trial would undercut his ability to conduct foreign policy. And Ford worried about Nixon, whose family and friends peppered the White House with reports that the former president was acting strangely, was deeply depressed, and, some feared, might be self-destructive. All these factors pointed to one solution: a full and complete pardon, even in advance of indictment and trial. "The quicker I made the decision," he believed, "the quicker that issue would get off the agenda."

While a pardon carried immense political cost, some of Ford's closest advisors worried that it might lead to something more serious than that: an investigation into possible collusion between Ford and his dishonored predecessor. Only a handful of Ford's aides knew how close Ford had come to agreeing to a deal just a month before taking over as president in exchange for granting Nixon a pardon.

The drama had unfolded eight days before Nixon resigned, on August 1, 1974, when Nixon chief of staff Al Haig requested an urgent meeting with Ford at the White House. The two men had already met earlier that morning with one of Ford's aides present, but in the later session—between the two men alone, at Haig's insistence—Haig urged Ford to be ready to take over "in a short period of time." The reason: the discovery of a new tape recording from June of 1972 that left no doubt about Nixon's role in a criminal cover-up of the Watergate break-in.

Haig warned that Nixon wasn't moving in a straight line toward stepping down; exactly how Nixon might leave the job was still unpredictable. And then he reviewed with Ford a number of options: Nixon could resign; he could fight an impeachment trial in the Senate; he could step aside briefly under the terms of the 25th Amendment—or simply resign later on if the game went bad, as it was likely to do. Also, said Haig, Nixon could pardon himself.

Until this point, everything about the August 1 conversation was unusual but fairly straightforward.

But it was also possible, Haig then explained, that Nixon could resign in return for a pardon.

This was a stunning dangle, a suggestion from the president's chief of staff that Nixon might leave the presidency in exchange for a pardon to be announced or perhaps arranged later. The presidency was being bartered—and bartered for exoneration. Nixon was offering to cut a deal with Ford, his loyal old friend, the one who had almost always come to his defense in the past.

If Ford was shocked—and there is no evidence that he was—he did not show it; in fact, Ford said nothing at all. Recalling this story years later, Ford noted that he doubted that Nixon could be pushed out—he was too stubborn, too scarred, and too much of a survivor to respond well to threats. "That's where Nixon's peculiar personality came into play," he noted. "He was not one to quit. If someone went to him and said, 'You must resign tomorrow,' that would inevitably tilt his decision to stay and fight it through."

But Haig wasn't proposing to push Nixon out; on the contrary, one of the options Haig had tabled was to buy him out, to trade the presidency for a Get Out of Jail Free Card. (In his memoirs, Haig called the suggestion that he was offering an exchange "witless." He said the list of options had come from White House counsel Fred Buzhardt and the last option had been "typed on a separate sheet of paper; I don't know why.")

In any event, Ford told Haig he'd have to think it over, talk to his wife, and thanked the general for coming by. Over the next twenty-four hours, Ford reviewed the Haig conversation with his aides and advisors. To a man, they all believed that Haig had been offering a deal and, given

Ford's equivocal response, he was now duty-bound to call Haig back and, with witnesses listening in, crush the idea in its infancy. Ford did so late the next day, repeating over the telephone words he had written out by hand to prevent any misunderstanding. "I want you to understand that I have no intention of recommending what the President should do about resigning or not resigning and that nothing we have talked about yesterday afternoon should be given any consideration in whatever decision the President may wish to make."

On at least one point, Haig was dead-on: Nixon zigzagged his way to resignation in the days that followed, leaning toward it one minute and then away from it the next. Around 5 P.M. on August 7, Nixon met a delegation of top Republicans from Congress—Arizona's Barry Goldwater and John Rhodes and Pennsylvania's Hugh Scott—who arrived to let Nixon know that his support on Capitol Hill was evaporating. "Mr. President," said Goldwater, "this isn't pleasant, but you want to know the situation and it isn't good." Goldwater said that Nixon might be able to beat some of the provisions of an impeachment resolution on the Senate floor but even the crusty Arizonan was thinking of voting for the article that charged abuse of presidential power. "I don't have many alternatives, do I?" Nixon said. At this moment, as he stared up at the ceiling, he searched for the brethren who might understand.

"Never mind, there will be no tears from me," Nixon said. "I haven't cried since Eisenhower died. My family has been fine and I'm going to be all right. I just want to thank you for coming up to tell me."

As the three men prepared to leave, Nixon was truly all alone. "Now that old Harry Truman is gone," he told his visitors, "I won't have anybody to pal around with."

"If I Can, I Must"

Given the stakes of Ford's encounter with Haig, it became imperative that Ford close the deal on a pardon for Nixon with something more than just the former president's okay; some of Ford's aides pressed their boss to extract from Nixon a genuine confession of guilt. In his legal research, Buchen had discovered a sixty-year-old court case that held that a presidential pardon carried a clear implication of guilt whether it was acknowledged by the person or not. But that was not good enough for Ford's aides. Buchen told Ford that he wanted to elicit from Nixon some explicit statement of regret or contrition as part of the pardon arrangement anyway (as well as winning access to Nixon's presidential papers).

While Ford agreed such a statement from Nixon would be acceptable, he didn't really think it was necessary. Ford didn't want negotiations to hold up the pardon; he wanted to move fast. Ford and Buchen, who had been law partners in Grand Rapids, decided to dispatch Washington criminal lawyer Benton Becker, who knew Nixon's personal lawyer, Jack Miller, well, to California. His mission: work out the exchange of presidential papers, win from Nixon an agreement to accept the pardon—and see about a statement of contrition. "Be very firm out there," Ford said to Becker as he left the Oval Office, "and tell me what you see."

What Ford had no way of knowing was that Haig, who had stayed behind in Washington to serve as Ford's interim chief of staff, was keeping some of Nixon's aides at San Clemente apprised of the new president's thinking. Which meant that as Becker was flying out to the West Coast on an Air Force plane (with Nixon's personal lawyer on board), Nixon and his aides had every advantage in the bargain: they already knew from Haig that they didn't have to give the White House much, if anything, in exchange for what looked like a certain reprieve. And so, when Becker arrived, the Nixon team pretended as an opening gambit that it was in no mood to settle. As Nixon's former press secretary Ron Ziegler told Becker, "Let's get one thing straight immediately. President Nixon is not issuing any statement whatsoever regarding Watergate, whether Jerry Ford pardons him or not." (Haig later denied playing any role in the pardon or speaking to Nixon about it.)

Nixon was playing hardball right to the end. Becker and Ziegler haggled over the wording of a Nixon statement the next day but made little progress. If Ziegler was helped by Haig's intelligence, Becker was severely constrained by time; Ford wanted to move on the pardon within twenty-four hours. The best Becker could wring from Nixon's aides carried only a whisper of contrition: "No words can describe the depths of my regret and pain at the anguish my mistakes over Watergate have caused the nation and the presidency." Becker then called on Nixon personally, as Ford had asked him to do. That encounter bordered on the bizarre; Nixon presented Becker with a set of presidential cuff links and insisted on talking about the opening of the pro football season. Becker then flew home. The subject of saying sorry did not come up.

"I had to get rid of him!" Ford later told an aide. "I couldn't get the work done. Everybody was trying to crucify the guy and I finally said to people, 'Enough is enough. Pardon him.' And Phil Buchen said, 'On what basis?' And I said, 'I don't care. Get him out of here. I can't do this job until people stop. Enough.'"

On Sunday, September 8, Ford attended church across the street from the White House and then returned to the Oval Office to speak to the nation. Though Ford was never considered a great speaker or even a very good one, his remarks that day rank among the more eloquent statements about the loneliness of the presidency. "I have sought and searched my own conscience with special diligence to determine the right thing for me to do with respect to my predecessor in this place, Richard Nixon and his loyal wife and family. . . .

"Theirs is an American tragedy in which we all have played a part. It could go on and on and on, or someone must write the end to it. I have concluded that only I can do that, and if I can, I must."

Ford explained that while he believed that no man was above the law, the nation needed to put Nixon and Watergate behind them. "I dare not depend upon my personal sympathy as a longtime friend of the former president, nor my professional judgment as a lawyer, and I do not. As President, my primary concern must always be the greatest good of all the people of the United States whose servant I am. As a man, my first consideration is to be true to my own convictions and my own conscience. . . . My conscience tells me it is my duty, not merely to proclaim domestic tranquility but to use every means that I have to insure it. I do believe that the buck stops here, that I cannot rely upon public opinion polls to tell me what is right."

It was a dramatic, all-in, bet-the-farm decision. He was, as he had said in his private conversations earlier that week, counting on the goodwill of the American people.

And then, still on camera, he signed the pardon proclamation.

Ten minutes after Ford spoke, a conference call organized for news organizations was convened by Nixon's aides in San Clemente. Nixon's final statement was then read by an aide. It wasn't what Buchen had hoped for, but it would have to do. "I know many fair minded people believe that my motivations and actions in the Watergate affair were intentionally self serving and illegal," Nixon said. "I now understand how my own mistakes and misjudgments have contributed to that belief and seem to support it. This burden is the heaviest one of all to bear. That the way I tried to deal with Watergate was the wrong way is a burden I shall bear for every day of the life that is left to me."

It was inevitable that a blanket reprieve by one club member for another would generate suspicion, but the reaction was blistering; on Capitol Hill, liberals demanded a full rendering of any secret deal Nixon may have made to arrange for a pardon before he departed. Democrats who knew nothing of Haig's furtive conversations knew enough about Nixon and his methods to fully believe that the whole resignation-and-pardon sequence had been cooked up by Nixon months before—and that Ford had been in on it.

Now the same committees that had been investigating Nixon a few months before began firing long lists of questions at Ford's lawyers: What did he know and when did he know it? What arrangements were made between Ford and Nixon before the resignation? Attempts by Ford's team to deflect those questions only made matters worse and as September turned into October, Ford was beginning to look like just another stonewalling Republican president. The man who wanted nothing more than to be Speaker of the House knew how to put a quick end to the unfolding mess. "You know," Ford told aides, "I'll bet you the best thing for me to do is just go up to Capitol Hill, testify and spell it all out."

And so it came to pass that a sitting president would testify to Congress about his relationship with a former president.

On October 17, Ford appeared before the House Judiciary Committee in the same hearing room he had testified in a year earlier when he was nominated to be vice president. Noting that his presence had "no firm precedent in the whole history of Presidential relations with the Congress," Ford added, "Yet, I am not here to make history, but to report on it."

Ford walked the lawmakers through the August 2 conversations with Haig once more—and his decision a month later to set Nixon free from prosecutors forever. "The purpose [of the pardon] was to change our national focus. I wanted to do all I could to shift our attentions from the pursuit of a fallen President to the pursuit of the urgent needs of a rising nation . . . we would needlessly be diverted from meeting those challenges if we as a people were to remain sharply divided over whether to indict, bring to trial and punish a former President, who already is condemned to suffer long and deeply in the shame and disgrace brought upon the office he held. Surely, we are not a revengeful people."

Ford dismissed the notion—advanced most aggressively by New York congresswoman Elizabeth Holtzman—that he had bartered his way into the Oval Office. "There was no deal, period, under no circumstances," Ford said. But the hearing turned on a different fear: that by pardoning Nixon, Ford had missed a chance to extract some measure of contrition from the former president—a chance that would never again present itself. To that claim, Ford made a counterargument. Courts have held, he insisted, that a pardon carries with it an implicit confession of wrongdoing. Ford was suggesting that merely by accepting his pardon, Nixon had confessed. "The acceptance of a pardon, according to the legal authorities—and we have checked them out very carefully—does indicate that by the acceptance, the person who has accepted it does, in effect, admit guilt."

It was a lawyer's argument, one that papered over Ford's failure to get something more explicitly apologetic out of Nixon in September. He remained sensitive until the end about not forcing Nixon to pay a bigger price in exchange for it, for not exacting from his old friend some admission of guilt. "It could have been better," Ford told Bob Woodward in one of their post-presidential conversations years later. But as Woodward pressed him further, Ford pulled out his wallet and removed from one of its inner pockets what Woodward described as "a folded, dog-eared piece of paper." It turned out that the Yale Law School graduate had been carrying around a portion of *Burdick v. United States*, a 1915 Supreme Court case about a newspaper editor who was pardoned by Woodrow Wilson for refusing to testify in a grand jury proceeding. Ford's personal lawyer had discovered the case and the former president had carried a piece of the decision all those years with him like a prayer card. Woodward read from the paper: "The Justices found that a pardon 'carries an imputation of guilt, acceptance, a confession of it.'"

That last part, Ford told Woodward, "was always very reassuring to me."

Intensive Care

And yet for all the trouble that Nixon caused him, for all the risks he posed to a young presidency, Ford would not abandon his old friend.

Less than two weeks after his appearance before Congress—and just four days before the congressional elections of 1974—Ford went on a ten-thousand-mile, seven-state late-October swing to campaign for Republican candidates, mostly in the West and Midwest. Ford departed just after Nixon had come out of surgery at a Long Beach, California, hospital to remove blood clots from his leg. The procedure had been touch and go; recovery was iffy. Nixon went into shock and, according to some accounts, had come close to dying.

As Ford was scheduled to headline a $500-a-plate fund-raising dinner at Los Angeles's Century Plaza Hotel on October 31, it was inevitable that his aides would be asked about whether the president was planning to visit his ailing predecessor, who was about thirty miles to the south. Ron Nessen, the new White House press secretary, urged Ford to skip the courtesy call lest he raise "new suspicions about the Ford-Nixon relationship." Coming so close to the election—and just two weeks after Ford made his unprecedented appearance on Capitol Hill—any visit with Nixon was bound to raise questions again if not resentments. But Ford dismissed Nessen's fears out of hand. "If compassion and mercy are not compatible with politics," Ford said, "then something is the matter with politics."

Ford handled the arrangements himself. After arriving in Los Angeles, he called Pat Nixon and asked whether a visit would help her husband recover. "Oh, there's nothing he'd like more," she replied. And even though there had always been a mysterious hole in the schedule for the morning of November 1, the visit was only then officially laid on, with Ford flying by helicopter down to Long Beach from his hotel in Beverly Hills. While reporters waited outside, Ford, Nessen, and a handful of other aides went in, taking the elevator to the seventh floor. There Ford greeted Pat, Julie, and Tricia Nixon with hugs and spent a few moments consoling them.

Nixon had the entire intensive care wing to himself, and Ford's del-

egation had only been there a few moments when it became clear that
there was a problem: Nixon's room was somehow locked from the inside.
The now pardoned president was bedridden behind a jammed door and
therefore, somewhat improbably, imprisoned. "Nixon was in the room all
alone," Nessen recalled, "too sick to get out of bed to unlock the door."
After about ten minutes, a maintenance man appeared and proceeded to
cut the lock with a hacksaw.

Only then was Ford able to enter the room, walk to the bedside, and
greet his predecessor. Nixon was flat on his back. "There were tubes in
his nose and mouth and wires led from his arms, chest and legs to machines with orange lights that blinked on and off," Ford remembered.
"His face was ashen and I thought I had never seen anyone closer to
death." Conversation turned out to be difficult if not impossible: the two
men talked briefly about the campaign but Nixon kept nodding off. Ford
at one point asked how the previous night had gone. Nixon's raspy reply:
"None of the nights are good." Ford realized that it was best to hurry the
engagement and let Nixon rest. As he departed, Nixon thanked him for
coming. "Mr. President, this has meant a lot to me. I'm deeply grateful."

Nessen told reporters afterward that the two presidents had chatted
for eight minutes although the real elapsed time was closer to four. (This
exaggeration led Nessen to quip in his memoirs: "Ironically, my first lie
was to cover up for Nixon.") Chatting with reporters a few minutes later,
Ford insisted that the two men had shared concerns about a variety of
foreign policy matters. "Obviously, he is a very, very sick man, but I think
he is coming along very, very well," Ford explained. "The President was
very alert." In fact, Ford left the hospital thinking Nixon might not survive and calculated that, given the odds, it was better to have visited than
not. "If he had died and I had passed up the chance to visit him," Ford
wrote later, "I wouldn't have been able to forgive myself."

Nixon and Ford, bound by time and chance, both lived long after
their presidencies ended. Nixon left office in 1974 and lived for another
twenty years; Ford left the White House in early 1977 and survived for
nearly thirty.

Ford granted many interviews over those three decades, patiently and
repeatedly explaining that he had pardoned Nixon to put the Watergate
nightmare behind the nation and restart his own unlikely presidency.

Over time, most of the people who had criticized the decision or its timing in 1974 came to believe that Ford had done the right thing—and selflessly so.

And in the end, the club recognized Ford for his decision—and perhaps for recognizing that the power of the presidency had to be preserved at all costs. In 2001, Ford was honored by another president's family—he received the John F. Kennedy Profile in Courage Award. The decision had been controversial in liberal circles: the Kennedy clan, more than twenty-five years after Watergate, was not yet in the habit of forgiving Republicans who had forgiven Richard Nixon. "Unlike many of us at the time," Senator Ted Kennedy remarked, before presenting the award to the eighty-eight-year-old former president, "President Ford recognized that the nation had to move forward, and could not do so if there was a continuing effort to prosecute former President Nixon. So President Ford made a courageous decision, one that historians now say cost him his office."

It was almost as if the Kennedys had issued Ford a pardon for pardoning Nixon.

FORD AND REAGAN:

The Family Feud

———— ⚷ ————

It would be wrong to call the relationship between Gerald Ford and Ronald Reagan a rivalry; it was more like a blood feud, a fight that broke out in the mid-1970s between the Republican Party's moderate and conservative clans, between its realist and idealist foreign policy camps, and between its old base in the East and Midwest and its fast growing new home in the West. But the fight was also a very personal one: neither man had a terribly high opinion of the other's intelligence; each believed the other to be in over his head. Reagan viewed Ford as too contented and conciliatory to lead the nation or manage its interests. Ford saw Reagan as a phony and an upstart, in no way ready for the job of commander in chief. Reagan believed Ford and his band of leftover Nixonites, led by Henry Kissinger, had turned détente into a "one-way street" that helped the Soviet Union survive. Ford regarded Reagan as a come-lately opportunist who had been staked in politics by rich oilmen after his Hollywood career cratered. Ford, Reagan believed, was a reliable party understudy but not its true star.

They would never be close, but the lure of the club would very nearly bind them together. In 1976, both men wanted so desperately to be president that they fought nonstop from New Hampshire all the way to the penultimate night of the convention. So raw was their rivalry that neither man could imagine joining forces with the other on the Republican ticket, whatever the delegates might have wanted. But four years later, they came close to hatching a curious and ill-considered power-sharing scheme designed to ensure that each man would finally get what he had long sought: Reagan would become president and Ford would finally be elected to national office.

15

"It Burned the Hell out of Me"

—GERALD FORD

E arly in January 1976, Gerald Ford explained how he expected his very first campaign for president of the United States to unfold.

After a quick sweep of the early primaries against Ronald Reagan, Ford predicted he would face his old friend Hubert Humphrey in the general election. "Hubert is a gentleman," Ford said, "and neither he nor I is going to get into any sordid political accusations. . . . That kind of contest might be very wholesome for the country."

Ford's words were sweetly naive, a reminder that even after sixteen months as president, he was still a novice. Not only had he never been elected to the presidency or the vice presidency—he had never even *run* for the office. And now he had to mount a campaign to woo tens of millions of voters who had never seen his name on a ballot. Nothing in Ford's twenty-eight years in politics prepared him for the scale of what he was about to try and very little in his prediction would come true. Many years later, he acknowledged his miscalculation: "I had always run pretty much a one man campaign for Congress," he said in 1990. "Pretty straight forward, limited money, almost certain victory. Where you just did hard work, saw everybody, campaigned as hard on a one to one basis as you could. And all of a sudden I had a different ballpark. And I must admit I didn't comprehend the vast difference."

• • •

In 1976, Ford imagined that American politics had somehow reverted to a calmer time when good men made good arguments and voters were able to make a wise choice between the two. It was a quaint notion—and a misleading one. Apart from the change in scale in running a presidential race, Ford faced a much more complex landscape than he imagined. It was easy to assume, and many did, that Democrats had gained the upper hand in the aftermath of Watergate and Nixon and the Vietnam War, now that eighteen-year-olds had been given the right to vote, now that the draft had ended, now that a sexual and gender revolution was rumbling across the United States. The culture's rapid social liberalization, went the thinking, would surely transform the nation's politics. And in a few places, that was true. But in the main, a forty-year Democratic era was already over—not in spite of, but because of, all the changes that had knocked the country back on its heels. A broad religious reawakening was under way with evangelical Christians at its forefront. An oil embargo and the gas lines it fostered, a recession and the rising deficits it created, and the cracks in the once-reliable industrial base were shifting the nation steadily to the right. A long period of productive bipartisanship was ending; Watergate and the war would turn American politics into something closer to a blood sport. The gentlemanly era that Ford imagined was already gone.

The Cat Who Came Back

When the 1976 campaign began, it wasn't only Ronald Reagan who was driving Gerald Ford nuts. It was Richard Nixon.

The president who had resigned just eighteen months earlier and whom Ford had pardoned at considerable political risk, decided that February 1976 would make an ideal time to come out of hiding and take a high-profile trip to, of all places, the People's Republic of China.

Nixon had promised Ford months earlier through intermediaries to postpone any international travel until after the 1976 election, but sometime in late 1975 Nixon changed his mind. The reasons remain murky: Nixon may have believed that Ford, under pressure from Reagan, was slowing normalization between the two countries, something Nixon as the architect of the Chinese opening could not abide. A trip to China by Ford and Kissinger a few months earlier had produced little in the way of bilateral progress and one Chinese diplomat described Nixon's visit as "a slap in the belly of Kissinger with a big wet fish." Whatever China's game, political minds in Washington thought they spied a more diabolical plot in Nixon's sudden urge to travel: to undercut Ford at the start of the primary season and somehow boost the odds that Nixon's eternal protégé, John Connally, could ride to the rescue of a divided party at the 1976 convention. More likely, Nixon was just being his usual difficult, self-centered self. In any case, even Ford had to admit that the timing was damaging. Just as he was facing a challenge from Reagan for being soft on communism, what could be worse than videotape of the disgraced president enjoying a festive homecoming in Beijing?

Ford aides discussed denying the landing rights to the Boeing 707 the Chinese sent to collect Nixon; they even discussed holding the plane hostage as a show of toughness. In the end, Ford was left to say the only thing he really could say about a man he had pardoned: "President Nixon is going there as a private citizen." Out of sight, however, Ford was seething: "If he keeps this up, we are going to crack him." National Security Advisor Brent Scowcroft put it more plainly: "Nixon is a shit."

And so after months in seclusion, Nixon and his wife turned up in Beijing three days before the New Hampshire primary.

His trip had all the trappings of a presidential visit: Nixon was attended by fifteen Secret Service agents and twenty traveling reporters; he took in the latest performance of Chinese acrobats and met for forty minutes with Chairman Mao. *Time's* editors published two pages of color photographs of the visit at a time when such vivid art direction was still a novelty. When it was over, little had been accomplished by either side and the reaction at home was savage. "There is nothing, absolutely nothing, he will not do in order to salvage for himself whatever scrap of significance he can find in the shambles of his life," wrote David Broder. Senator Barry Goldwater went further, charging Nixon with breaking the Logan Act, the 1799 law that bars private citizens from conducting unauthorized foreign policy. "If he wants to do this country a favor," he added, "he might stay over there."

There wasn't much for Ford to do but bear it stoically. Even after he returned home, Nixon showed little deference to the White House.

Nixon declined a Ford request to have deputy CIA director Vernon Walters debrief him in San Clemente and insisted instead on sending a sixty-page report to the White House about his trip. Ford read it, circulated it to Scowcroft, CIA director George Bush, and a few others who found that it contained "little of value," and then returned it without comment. With Nixon's reappearance overseas, Ford only narrowly averted a disaster in the New Hampshire primary; a switch of about seven hundred votes out of 100,000 cast would have given Reagan a first-state-in-the-nation victory over the incumbent president. It was a harbinger of the year to come.

The Fight for the Party

Ford had never been part of Reagan's plans; he was an inconvenience at best and a usurper at worst. "We had figured that Nixon would serve out two terms and then Reagan would run for President," said Reagan advisor Lyn Nofziger. "Then Nixon of course screwed up and so Ford became president. That became a problem because a lot of our people who ordinarily would have been enthused about Reagan running for president didn't want anyone to run in the primary against a sitting Republican President."

It's something of a club irony that Ford forgave Nixon all sorts of appalling personal injuries and insults during the course of their forty years in politics together chiefly because they were old friends. But because Ford and Reagan were largely strangers, the little slights and injuries common in politics alienated both men deeply. When Reagan flew to Washington in August 1974 for a meeting with some conservative activists, Ford was dismayed that Reagan had not asked to come by for a visit. Ford felt slighted when Reagan failed to meet him—or Vice President Nelson Rockefeller—at various California airports during visits to the Golden State. And Ford, the longtime party man, could not abide the fact that Reagan sometimes charged his hosts to appear at Republican fund-raisers.

Meanwhile, Reagan and his advisors saw in nearly every action taken by the Ford White House a hidden assault on the Reagan operation in Sacramento. They believed Ford's choice of Rockefeller to be vice president was designed to diminish Reagan's status in the party. And they claimed that Ford had double-crossed voters (and Reagan in particular) by breaking a promise that he would not run in 1976. Never mind that the *Newsweek* story on which this notion was based was widely discredited almost as soon as it was published.

Advisors in both camps marveled that Ford was somehow unable to buy Reagan off in 1976, as others had done before. Nixon had mollified Reagan by sending him on confected foreign trips—"it's time to stroke Ronnie," he'd tell Scowcroft, then his military aide. Nixon sent Reagan overseas four times, complete with an Air Force jet and Secret Service protection. Reagan met eighteen heads of state this way while he was still governor. Best of all, Washington paid for everything (and Reagan liked to tell the story of how he had once made a swing through European capitals with only a few dollars in his pocket).

A little of that went a long way with Reagan, but Ford never seemed to master such small strokes. By the time Ford got around to offering Reagan a spot in the cabinet, he made a hash of it. Instead of setting Reagan up somewhere in the foreign policy area that was so dear to his heart, Ford dangled the drearier job of commerce secretary. And then, rather than pick up the phone to chew the fat, seek his advice, and then ask for Reagan's help, Ford had his chief of staff Don Rumsfeld, who had his own ambitions for higher office, offer the job instead. Not surprisingly, Reagan turned it down. Reagan felt "particularly insulted" by that episode, Lou Cannon reported.

What stopped Ford from sprinkling the normal presidential holy water in Reagan's path? Jealousy, for starters. By 1974, Reagan was, at least in conservative circles, the more famous—and certainly the more favored—of the two. He was a lot of things Ford wasn't: graceful and even bold in speech, strong in conviction; and he knew how to make an entrance. Ford's pollster Robert Teeter described him in internal memos as a "conservative idol. When you think about who it is that goes to vote in a Republican primary in New Hampshire and Florida," Teeter wrote, "[Reagan] is almost perfectly attuned to them."

And where envy stopped, denial took over. Many of Ford's aides admitted later that they did not fully grasp the scale of the Reagan challenge until it was too late. They had been too busy getting their bearings in the White House to notice that many Republicans felt Ford was the

wrong man for the job. Only about 21 percent of voters by 1976 identified themselves as Republicans and a growing percentage of that group
was several turns more conservative than Ford. And yet Ford could not
believe that Reagan would upset the already perilous unity of the Republican Party and mount a challenge to a sitting president. "It burned
the hell out of me," Ford said later, "that I got the diversion from Reagan
that caused me to spend an abnormal part of my time trying to round up
individual delegates and to raise money."

Had the 1976 primaries been quick and dirty and produced a clear
winner early on, none of this might have mattered. But the opposite occurred: the Ford-Reagan grudge match went on for months, well after
the primaries, far into the summer, all the way to the convention in
Kansas City.

The primary turned on foreign policy, which was fine by both men.
Reagan wasn't really running against Ford as much he was running
against the Nixon-Ford-Kissinger foreign policy of détente—the idea
that the United States and its communist rivals could not only coex-
ist peacefully but perhaps achieve some common goals. To Nixon and
Ford, détente was an extension of containment, the bipartisan policy that
sought for decades to keep Moscow in a box. But to Reagan, détente
was akin to surrender, a grant of moral legitimacy to the communist regimes for which the United States had gained little in return. By attacking détente, Reagan was broadening a split in the Republican ranks
between its realist and idealist wings: was the Soviet Union something to
be managed—or destroyed?

Though Ford won most of the early primaries, Reagan clawed
back with wins in North Carolina, Texas, and Nebraska. Reagan was
gaining ground with claims that Ford was on the verge of recognizing
Communist-controlled Vietnam (though he wasn't) and calling on Ford
to discard plans to negotiate a new treaty that would turn the operation
and control of the Panama Canal over to the Panamanians and their "tin-
horn dictator." In a thirty-minute paid advertisement that helped him
win North Carolina, Reagan famously said of the canal: "We built it, we
paid for it, it's ours and we're going to keep it!"

The North Carolina defeat hit Ford so hard that some aides began to
talk among themselves about firing Kissinger—or at least letting some

reporters into National Security Council meetings so they could see Ford ordering him around. At the same time, there were those in Reagan's corner, most notably his wife, who wanted the governor to get out of the contest because, despite Reagan's attacks, Ford was gradually pulling away in the delegate count. Ford was helped in the final primary in California by a Stu Spencer ad that read, "When you vote Tuesday, remember: Governor Reagan couldn't start a war. President Reagan could." But even that was not enough to move California into Ford's column.

Vice President Reagan?

When the primaries ended, neither man had a lock on the nomination. Reagan was about ninety delegates short of the 1,130 needed; Ford was sixty-three short. So Reagan campaign manager John Sears uncorked several clever schemes to keep the race alive.

First, Sears convinced Reagan to name liberal Pennsylvania senator Richard Schweiker to be his running mate in the hope that some Keystone State delegates pledged to Ford would switch sides out of loyalty to the local favorite. It didn't work, but the ploy bought Sears a few weeks of continued speculation that Reagan might still be able to seize the nomination.

To keep the clock running, Sears next decided to stage a floor fight over an obscure party bylaw known as Rule 16-C, which would require a nominee to name his vice presidential pick before the voting for the top spot began. This was clever politics: having named Schweiker as his number two, Reagan would push Ford to name his own running mate. As James Baker, at the time the Ford delegate counter, explained it, "Sears wanted to force Ford's hand. He reasoned that he could pick off some Ford delegates or undecideds who were alienated by whomever President Ford selected as his running mate."

This fight, arcane though it may have been, sparked a battle that involved millions of dollars, armies of lobbyists, high-pressure arm-twisting, untold presidential favors, and plenty of nail biting. Ford's team opened a special skybox in the Kemper Arena where wavering delegates were plied with liquor—and then offered a combination of presidential favors (and boiler room threats of retribution) that usually won the day. That fight did not end until the third night of the convention. Ford prevailed by a razor-thin twenty-nine votes on the obscure rule.

Ford's team was so busy swatting away Sears's ingenious challenges that it arrived at the convention without a vice presidential nominee. Bowing to pressure from the right, Ford had informed Rockefeller in the fall of 1975 that he would not be on the ticket (a decision Ford would later describe as the most cowardly of his life). But he had yet to decide who *would* be on the ticket. John Connally? Howard Baker? William Simon? Elliot Richardson? Every imaginable name—including Reagan's—appeared on Ford's list.

But if Reagan wanted to be vice president, he did virtually nothing to help his chances and a great deal to douse them once he arrived in Kansas City. During a lunch for key supporters at the Muehlebach Hotel, Reagan heard that some Californians were starting a draft-Reagan-for-vice-president movement. Reagan whipped out a felt-tip pen and scribbled: "To my friends in the California delegation: I have learned of your concern about whether I would or would not accept the nomination for Vice President on the Ford ticket if he should be nominated for President. I thought I had made this clear—evidently I hadn't. Here is my reply as plainly as I can say it: There is no circumstance whatsoever under which I would accept the nomination for vice president. That is absolutely final."

Reagan gave the note to his brother, Moon, and told him to deliver it. Moon replied: How are they going to know it's from you? And so Reagan took the note back and scrawled his signature at the bottom of the page. Several dozen copies were made and distributed to Reagan floor leaders and delegation chiefs to quell the doubters.

Reagan wasn't closing the door; he was slamming it.

That night, by prearrangement, Ford called on Reagan in his hotel suite. The visit had been worked out days before by their aides: to preserve party unity, both camps agreed that the winner would visit the suite of the loser and then appear at a joint press conference afterward. Reagan's aides had insisted on one ground rule for the meeting: Ford could not under any circumstances offer Reagan the vice presidency. Reagan's staff said they wanted to spare Ford the embarrassment of having Reagan turn it down. But what they didn't say was that they didn't want to create any circumstances where Ford's folks might later claim that

Reagan was not interested in party unity. And so no offer was made—or expected. "Governor, it was a great fight," Ford said. "You've done a tremendous job. I just wish I had some of your talents and your tremendous organization."

After posing for photographs, Ford dismissed the press and then asked Reagan to huddle privately. "Ron," Ford then asked, "who do you recommend that I select for vice president?" This was, in Ford's retelling at least, one last dangle, a final chance for Reagan to volunteer; Ford insisted later that he phrased the question in such an open-ended way "to somehow get confirmation myself that he didn't want to be on the ticket." If so, Reagan declined the bait. The two men instead discussed a number of candidates—William Ruckelshaus, Richardson, Baker, Connally; Reagan spoke most favorably that day of Bob Dole. (Even this was according to the script: Dole had asked Nofziger earlier in the day if Reagan might put in a good word for him in the event Reagan truly didn't want the job.) And then, after asking Reagan to campaign in the fall—"I hope," Ford pleaded, "you are going to be able to help us"—Ford left. Reagan, who had been subdued throughout the entire session, said he wanted to rest and make some money, but would campaign in the fall.

The dream ticket, if that's what it might have been, was not to be.

A variety of Reagan aides and allies insisted in the years to come that Ford had missed a huge opportunity in the Muehlebach suite to bring Reagan aboard, unify the party, forge a partnership that could have defeated Jimmy Carter in November. Instead of playing by the prearranged rules, they argued, Ford should have appealed directly to Reagan's patriotism and asked him to put aside his pride for the good of the country. Reagan, they insisted, would never have turned down a commander in chief. Ford and Reagan confidant James Baker pressed Reagan on this historical what-might-have-been after he became president and came away convinced Reagan would have agreed—even if it doomed his chances to become president later. Explained Baker, "I had two or three conversations one on one [with President Reagan] in which I said, 'If President Ford had offered the vice presidency and you had taken it, you might never have been president.' Reagan replied, 'I understand that. But if he offered it to me, I would have felt duty bound to take it.'"

But all that would have required Ford to have *wanted* Reagan by his side enough to press him to come aboard. And there is very little evidence that he did. "I had mixed emotions," Ford said. "I thought he would strengthen the ticket. On the other hand, we had had such a bitter fight and we had such strong disagreements, we would have had a lot of trouble reconciling those differences publicly."

That was an understatement. "Basically, Reagan didn't want it, I know that," said Spencer, who worked for both men. "Ford didn't want it. I know that."

In any case, even if Ford had invited Reagan to be his vice president, there is no reason to think the race would have turned out differently. Reagan would have made a poor number two; the staffs would have quarreled endlessly; and while Reagan might have helped Ford in some Southern states, where Carter was strong, he would have undercut his chances in the more moderate Midwest, where Ford needed to win.

But the outcome was, in any event, a disappointment to Reagan, the second time in eight years the nomination had eluded his grasp at the convention. Before leaving Kansas City, Reagan said farewell and thanks to his aides, the California delegation, and close friends. *Time's* Dean Fischer filed a telling dispatch to his editors in New York that afternoon: at one point, confronted with a friend who began to weep, Reagan had to leave the room to control himself. During a speech he delivered to the California delegation, it was Nancy's turn to sob. Reagan himself had difficulty speaking; a nearby aide explained: "He's not a good actor."

The Impromptu Floor Speech That Wasn't

But there was one last weird drama to play out. The final scene in Kansas City was to be a reminder that Reagan left few big moments to chance— and how much he saw himself on a mission that was broader than mere politics. It was Thursday night; the balloons were poised; the band was ready; the delegates were fired up. As Ford concluded his acceptance speech, he turned to Stan Anderson, a convention manager, and said, "That went well. Now go get Reagan." And so Anderson scurried downstairs, ran headlong underneath the arena floor, through a passageway clogged with trash receptacles, and took an elevator up to a skybox on the first-tier balcony. He found Reagan, Nancy, and political aide Lyn Nofziger watching the activities on the floor below. "Governor Reagan," Anderson said, "the president would like you to join him on the podium."

"No fucking way," Nofziger replied.

"Oh Ronnie," added Nancy, "I don't think you should."

Anderson could see that the Reagans were still feeling bruised. But by now Ford was actually motioning Reagan to join him on the podium—and many on the floor were beckoning him with calls of their own. "Reagan, Reagan," the crowd chanted. Television crews panned their cameras from the skybox to the podium, waiting for one man or the other to relent. Meanwhile, Anderson pressed: "With all due respect, Governor, the President of the United States has asked you to join him for the good of the party." Anderson said it did not take Reagan long to rise to that challenge, whatever Nancy and Nofziger advised. "I'm doing it," Reagan said. And, grabbing his wife's hand, Reagan followed Anderson back toward the front of the hall.

The threesome took the elevator downstairs, back through the basement with Nancy, who implored her husband at one point, "Ronnie, why are we doing this?" But Reagan was determined, taking a comb out of his pocket to make sure his hair was in place.

What unfolded next was a performance that could have been translated: *I came close. And I'll be back.* The Reagans joined the Fords, vice presidential nominee Bob Dole, and their families onstage and the president turned the microphone over to his vanquished rival, who proceeded to give what nearly everyone at the time believed were brief, impromptu remarks. They certainly *seemed* improvised. But Reagan had in fact been warned by his aides (who had been warned by Ford aides) that the president might ask him to speak. Though he prepared no remarks for such a moment, Reagan took those warnings seriously enough to at least discuss with policy advisor Martin Anderson what he might say should Ford call him to the podium. He did not arrive without the outline of a speech in his head.

And those remarks are surely one of the more curious speeches of any modern political convention.

Reagan did not mention, much less endorse, Ford beyond a brief thank-you at the top of the speech. He took credit for forcing the adoption of a robust foreign policy platform, which he described as "a banner of bold, unmistakable colors, with no pastel shades." But at the core of the roughly one-thousand-word riff was a story of how he had been recently asked to write a letter to Americans in the year 2076. As Reagan pondered what to say to those people in the future, he noted, he realized that far too much hung in the balance in 1976 to be certain that they would even be around to read it.

"Will they look back with appreciation and say, 'Thank God for those people in 1976 who headed off that loss of freedom, who kept us now 100 years later free, who kept our world from nuclear destruction?' . . . This is our challenge; and this is why here in this hall tonight, better than we have ever done before, we have got to quit talking to each other and about each other and go out and communicate to the world that we may be fewer in numbers than we have ever been, but we carry the message they are waiting for. We must go forth from here united, determined that what a great general said a few years ago is true: There is no substitute for victory, Mr. President."

It was powerful, self-glorifying—and a little strange. It was as much a challenge to Ford and his team as it was to the rival party—and maybe more so.

Reagan departed Kansas City more resentful of Ford than before he had arrived—and no less determined to become president the next time around. "He thought Gerald Ford had stolen the nomination from him," Nofziger said later. "Gerald Ford had not. But I think Reagan just couldn't conceive that Ford could have got that from him honestly. So he determined that he would run."

In the months that followed, Reagan traveled to twenty states on Ford's behalf. Ford later complained that Reagan had not pulled his weight for the ticket—a not entirely fair assessment. But it is true that Reagan declined Ford campaign requests that he campaign in Texas and Mississippi, where Ford was weak and Jimmy Carter was stronger. Lou Cannon recounted in his biography that Reagan appeared with Ford on one California swing during the fall but then found a reason not to join the president on a second—a decision that Ford surely did not forget. "The best way to say it is that Reagan didn't bust his tail to help," Spencer said later. "Ford knows that. That's not the reason he lost. But the point is, when you come out of the Nixon school of politics, you take your poison. You do your dishes and you go out and bust your tail for the next guy. That's the way I was raised. Reagan never had that philosophy."

What philosophy did move Reagan? Spencer believed that Reagan always heard a different music than other politicians—and that rhythm was anticommunism. Having come from an impoverished, dysfunctional background, and then having made it big as a radio announcer and Hollywood actor in the midst of the Depression, Reagan's love for America was always shot through a prism of good and evil. His experience as leader of the Screen Actors Guild had taught him that communism could damage all that was dear to him. And when Spencer would ask Reagan why, at the very core of things, he wanted to *be* president, the answer was always the same: ending communism. "It was the only thing he really thought about in depth, intellectualized, thought about what you can do, what you can't do, how you can do it," Spencer said. "With everything else . . . he went through the motions." Some years would pass before the rest of the country caught up to Spencer's insight.

Before the year was over, Ford came to believe that Reagan—and not Jimmy Carter—had cost him the 1976 election. By distracting him with a primary challenge, depleting him of time, resources, and party delegates, dragging the fight all the way to the third night of the convention—and then slow-walking through the fall, Reagan had, in Ford's view, prevented him from winning his first national election. "They didn't give a damn whether I won or not," Ford said, "because they were already planning to run in 1980." And Ford carried this grudge with him for years. As he told Cannon a few months before he died, "It was not in [Reagan's] nature to help someone else. He believed in winning on his own."

Dream Ticket, Reversed

Through the late 1970s, the club limped along on life support. Though Ford and Carter worked closely during the transition between their presidencies, Carter wanted little to do with his predecessor once he was sworn in and wanted even less to do with Nixon. Carter invited Nixon to a state dinner in January 1979 honoring Deng Xiaoping, and included the former president in a small reception he and Rosalynn hosted for Deng in the White House residence. Carter recognized, as an aide said later, that Nixon had begun the process of normalization with Beijing and "so he should be invited." But Carter refused to let Nixon stay in the special Lafayette Square guesthouse that Nixon himself had created for Johnson.

Nixon would never stop trying to rehabilitate his image in the years that followed and he often used the club as a lever to get it done. Ford's challenge after his defeat in 1976 was more basic: to get legitimately elected in the first place. In June 1978, Ford's old friend Jack Marsh wrote a long memo laying out the rationale, the timelines, and the various steps Ford would have to take to win the 1980 nomination. It was an utterly serious look at the challenges and Marsh's memo did not understate the difficulty. Reagan started the race as the clear favorite but other hopefuls, including George Bush, John Connally, and Howard Baker all had their own claim on the party. Robert Teeter, Ford's longtime pollster, worried that Ford might not have the stomach for the fight. Ford had his doubts as well. "It nauseated me that I would have to go out and raise four or five million dollars to put on a campaign, to beat Reagan, even though I thought I could."

But as the primaries approached, Ford kept putting the idea on the table. In October 1979, Ford turned up in Washington to confuse everyone about his plans. At a breakfast with reporters, many of whom he had known for years, Ford sounded like a coy teenager. "If I came here as a candidate, I'd have to be answering tough questions," he teased. "Now I don't come here having to make some point, having to seduce you. I'm seeing good friends, old acquaintances. Isn't that a nice way to spend the morning?" Pressed a second time, then a third, and then over and over about his plans, Ford said he wasn't running, but made it clear he would welcome a draft. "I will speak out on SALT [strategic arms talks], other issues. That doesn't indicate I'm sitting in a smoke filled room with charts and experts, scheming. If something happens, it happens. I'm a fatalist. . . . I never say 'never' in politics."

And then, sensing perhaps that those comments hadn't fully clarified things, he proceeded to muddle them further. "I'm not a candidate, I'm not. Somehow you all don't believe it. On the other hand, if a scenario developed, I'd have to take another look at it."

If Ford had a strategy, it amounted to praying the party would turn to him in desperation. As Reagan began to roll through the primaries in early 1980, some of the more moderate members of the Republican

Party began to privately express doubts about Reagan's ability to beat Carter, which fueled speculation about a Ford return. In truth, some of those moderates weren't worried that Reagan couldn't win; they were worried that he could. On February 1, Ford told Adam Clymer of the *New York Times* that Reagan could not win and volunteered to get in if he was "asked." As if there were a Standing Committee on Invitations.

This comment provoked another round of emergency planning inside the Ford camp. It was now very late to be jump-starting a campaign: the Iowa caucuses (which Reagan had lost to George Bush) were already past; New Hampshire was only three weeks away. On February 12, longtime Ford aides Doug Bailey and John Deardourff prepared a long memo to Ford outlining the pros and cons of a last-minute bid. The memo was mostly con: key deadlines for some of the primaries had passed; there was little time left for fund-raising; at age fifty-five, Bush seemed to have a good shot of winning moderate Republicans who did not care for Reagan. That day, three years after leaving the Oval Office, Ford finally (but privately) put the idea of a second run to bed for good. A few weeks would pass before he told reporters on a sunny afternoon in mid-March that he would not be a candidate. "America needs a new president," Ford said. "I will support the nominee of my party with all the energy I have." As Ford turned to go back into his house, he said to Betty, "If I were a drinking man I'd have myself a drink." He later called it the hardest decision of his life.

Twelve days later, pollster Richard Wirthlin sent Reagan a memo urging the candidate to direct his campaign manager, Bill Casey, to "develop ties" to Ford. It was time to schmooze and court the former president. Wirthlin predicted that nothing would really shake Ford loose until Reagan himself took control of the courtship. But he had to be won over before the convention in July.

> *Of all Republicans, Gerald R. Ford potentially can hurt us or help us more than any other. He is respected a great deal by the electorate at large, and even more so in the Republican ranks. Because he considered his own presidential candidacy . . . his whole-hearted and active conversion to our cause will carry a significant political impact. The clincher will come only when Gerald Ford and Ronald Reagan sit*

*down amicably one on one, and resolve for the near, and hopefully long
term, the major difficulties that arose out of the 1976 election.*

And so on June 5, 1980, two days after he had won the California
primary with 80 percent of the vote, Reagan paid a ninety-minute call on
the former president in Rancho Mirage. They quickly worked through
the old grudges: Reagan asked Ford for his help in the fall against Carter
and made the case to Ford that he had not, as Ford had long assumed,
slacked off after the 1976 convention. Lou Cannon reported that the two
men, both inclined toward forgiveness and common purpose, seemed to
patch things up. "Ford found himself strangely drawn to this old foe who
shared with him a midwestern upbringing and a natural friendliness,"
Cannon wrote. "Ford also thought that Carter had been a terrible president and wanted to help defeat him."

At some point during the Rancho Mirage peace talks, Reagan made
Ford an unexpected and secret offer. He proposed that Ford join him on
the ticket. Ford declined.

But the courtship was just getting under way. Several factors put Ford
into play. First, Reagan didn't love his other choices. A Wirthlin poll in
early summer showed that only three men could help Reagan against
Carter: Bush, who had finished second in the primaries, Ford, and Howard Baker. Though Baker had withdrawn months before, Bush had
stayed in the primary race until late May, upsetting some Reagan insiders who had waited since 1968 for the boss to win the nomination. Reagan, furthermore, had some doubts about Bush's judgment. "He thought
George Bush was a wimp," Lyn Nofziger said later, "and he was still mad
at Howard Baker for opposing him on the Panama Canal." Finally, Ford
was a former president; his experience and credentials could go a long
way toward mollifying voters who worried about Reagan's inexperience
in Washington. While Carter was floundering at home and overseas,
deep doubts about Reagan's suitability as commander in chief remained;
Ford's presence at his side would be reassuring. Still, for much of June
and early July, various emissaries to and from the Ford camp reported to
the Reagan high command that the former president did not want to be
considered.

Then, on the first night of the Detroit convention in August, Ford delivered a blistering attack on Carter. "You've all heard Carter's alibis," Ford said, sounding like the prosecutor in chief. "Inflation cannot be controlled. The world has changed. We can no longer protect our diplomats in foreign capitals, nor our workingmen on Detroit's assembly lines. We must lower our expectations. We must be realistic. We must prudently retreat. Baloney!" And then came a tantalizing passage: "Elder statesmen are supposed to sit quietly and smile wisely from the sidelines," Ford said. "I've never been much for sitting. I've never spent much time on the sidelines. This country means too much to me to comfortably park on the bench. So when this convention fields the team for Governor Reagan, count me in."

The line played to thunderous applause and got Reagan, watching from his hotel suite, thinking that Ford might be warming to the idea of joining forces after all. When a delegation of six party leaders stopped by Reagan's suite on the sixty-ninth floor of the Detroit Renaissance Center Hotel the next morning to discuss various vice president options, Reagan asked: "What about Ford?"

Reagan's guests were hesitant. "Of course," said Delaware governor Pete du Pont, "Jerry Ford would be the very best choice." But few if any of Reagan's visitors believed that Ford could be induced to take the job—and most doubted whether it would be wise to try. Former presidents don't stoop to being vice president and even if Ford might be convinced to do so, melding the two staffs would get messy very quickly. But in the hothouse atmosphere of a national convention, logic sometimes evaporates. House minority leader Bob Michel urged Reagan to make a personal appeal to Ford: "It ought to be on a one to one basis and not handled by staff, so there's no mistake. You bare your breast to him and tell him how it is. He appreciates forthrightness."

Ford, who somewhat improbably was staying just one flight above Reagan at the Renaissance Center, stepped downstairs later that afternoon to huddle once more. In the sixty-five-minute session, Reagan again—and more directly—asked Ford to join him on the ticket. He had been watching Ford closely over the last several weeks, he said, and this was not a spur-of-the-moment impulse. But then Reagan went further, proposing as a sweetener that Ford might want to add a second job to his portfolio, such as secretary of defense. In their accounts of this session, Ford's aides said that he replied, essentially, by saying, "I don't think it will work" and "I don't want to encourage you."

These vaguely discouraging comments were all that Reagan needed to keep the talks going.

The ironic replay of 1976 was unmistakable: Reagan had shut the door in 1976 before Ford could offer him the vice president's job; in 1980, Reagan was unquestionably offering it and Ford couldn't bring himself to say no. Being vice president after being president was unimaginable— unless you had not been elected president in the first place.

The Reagan lobbying team then swung into action. Paul Laxalt, who regarded a Reagan-Ford ticket as "a political marriage made in heaven," called Henry Kissinger, Ford's secretary of state and now foreign policy advisor, and recruited him to the matchmaking mission. Kissinger met early Tuesday evening with Reagan aides Bill Casey, Ed Meese, and Mike Deaver and agreed to push Ford on the idea. Around midnight, Ford gathered members of his family, along with aides Alan Greenspan, John Marsh, and Kissinger, to discuss the idea in his suite. Even later, Ford and Kissinger talked alone for forty-five minutes. During that session, Kissinger pressed Ford to take the offer seriously. One of those in the Ford suite later reported that Kissinger alternated that night between cajoling Ford into yes one minute and then warning him the next of the perils of saying no. "The country needs you," Kissinger told Ford at one point. "But, Henry," Ford replied, "it won't work." The two men did not finish until nearly 2 A.M.

On Wednesday morning, Ford was a riot of ambivalence and ambition, unable to move forward, unable to let go. Robert Teeter circulated a private poll that morning showing that Ford would move a Reagan ticket by eleven points nationwide, more than any other vice presidential candidate. On the *Today* show, Ford was no better than Delphic when asked if pride was an obstacle to him taking the number two spot. "Jerry left a crack in the door," Bob Michel said, watching from a Republican breakfast in party chairman Bill Brock's Plaza suite. At a breakfast with *Time* editors at the Detroit Athletic Club a few minutes later, Ford said he'd had a good meeting with Reagan the day before and that he continued to think the idea was unworkable. But he hedged on the question of whether he or his aides had sent a definitive answer to the Reagan camp. At 10:30 A.M., Ford told aides Robert Barrett, Marsh, Kissinger, and Greenspan that he wanted to break off talks. But then Casey, Reagan's campaign manager, called at 11:15 and asked to meet with Ford's advisors. Ford agreed, as long as everyone understood that he was still against it. And still Ford just couldn't say no. At a lunch with *Newsweek*'s editors, he imagined a possible relationship between himself and Reagan not unlike that used in some European capitals "where you have a head of state and a head of government." An eleven-hour marathon of intense negotiations began around noon. Greenspan, Kissinger, and Marsh huddled with counterparts from the Reagan camp: Casey, Ed Meese, Wirthlin, Deaver. By mid-afternoon, Reagan's group presented a ten-point, double-spaced, page-and-a-half talking paper that gave Ford an outsized role as chief of staff and authority over the National Security Council, the budget office, and the Council of Economic Advisors, while Reagan would maintain final decisions on everything. It was not a formal proposal, more like a basis for future discussion. But it was in any form an extraordinary offer: Reagan, in effect, proposed to give Ford day-to-day control over most if not all of the important White House offices and agencies and control over all the documents that would reach the president. Ford and his aides understood just how dramatic a devolution of power Reagan's aides were proposing. They weren't even sure it was constitutional. Ford's team also realized that their counterparts had little or no idea how the White House really worked, that you couldn't have one man run the senior staff who was not in every way loyal to—and fireable by—the president. But that was what the Reagan team was proposing. By now—it was Wednesday afternoon, July 16—Ford was tired and feeling pressured. The roll call vote on Reagan's nomination was just hours away. A parade of governors and lawmakers trooped through Ford's suite throughout the day, urging him to join the ticket. "Maybe there's a way," he said around 5 P.M., "but I don't think there is."

By dinnertime, the plot was not merely thickening, it was congealing. The notion that an incoming president would share anything like this kind of clout with a former president was awkward at best and dangerous at worst. Reagan would say later that troubled times called for abnormal approaches and yet this was too clever by half. Foreign policy hard-liners were horrified by any partnership with Ford that meant a return of Kissinger. Traditionalists just thought the whole thing was a risky experiment with the presidency itself. "It can't happen," Arizona congressman John Rhodes said of any co-presidency. "If it does, a lot of people have taken leave of their senses." Rhodes believed in the end the plan would never get off the ground and, if it somehow did, would tear the White House apart. "Would it be good for the country to bifurcate the presidency?" he asked. Later, he told a reporter from *Time*, "I couldn't believe what I was hearing."

When Reagan and Ford met again early that evening, for fifteen minutes in Reagan's suite, Ford had become insistent that Reagan name Kissinger as secretary of state. Ford felt like he was making a huge concession to leave private life and asked for Reagan to make a concession in return. "Ron, I'm making a sacrifice here. And now I'm asking you to make a sacrifice." It was an astonishing request, given the way Reagan had made Kissinger an issue in the 1976 primary. And this time, it would be Reagan's turn to politely but firmly decline. "Jerry, I know all of Kissinger's strong points and there's no question that he should play a role. I would use him a lot but not as Secretary of State. I've been all over the country the last several years and Kissinger carries a lot of baggage. I couldn't accept that. My own people, in fact, wouldn't accept it."

Over the next three hours, the talks fell apart. But not before Ford did an awkward interview with Walter Cronkite of CBS News in which he floated the notion of some kind of power sharing. Repeating versions of this idea as he made the rounds to the network TV booths Wednesday night, Ford did not fully realize that the idea of a joint ticket came as news to most of the delegates and reporters attending the convention. His remarks sent a wave of celebration—pandemonium might be a better word—through the ranks of delegates on the floor and unleashed every reporter at the convention into a citywide hunt for confirmation. The wave had a name: the dream ticket.

But up in Reagan's suite, Ford's media tour had fallen flat. Negotiations were still under way, aides marveled, and here was Ford giving the public an update. Reagan, watching Ford on TV, could hardly believe it. Years later, in his autobiography, Reagan claimed this was his breaking point. "Wait a minute," Reagan thought to himself, "this is really two presidents he is talking about." Reagan and his aides felt pressured all of a sudden, even though they were the ones who had put the power-sharing idea on the table. Meanwhile, in the rooms upstairs where the details were being worked out, Ford's aides were weary of the murkiness of the Reagan proposals; Reagan's aides were growing tired of the scope of the Ford demands. There was a nagging feeling among some of the more hard-line Reagan aides that Ford was not as interested in returning to power as some of his more ambitious wingmen. Moreover, it didn't much help that Kissinger, a bone of contention in the talks, was a key part of Ford's negotiating team, practically reprising his storied shuttle diplomacy in the Middle East as he moved between the Reagan and Ford suites in pursuit of a deal.

Reagan called Ford at 9:15 saying they needed to close on the deal that night. By 10 P.M., the pieces had yet to fall into place. Ford's team asked for an extension until Thursday; Meese, after checking with Reagan, declined the request. The media frenzy to get the scoop on the dream ticket was by now reaching a peak and sometime after ten CBS announced, as flat-out fact, that Ford would be Reagan's running mate; moreover, the network added, the two men would be coming to the hall later in the evening. Other networks ordered their floor reporters to confirm the story; but in fact the whole idea was dead. At 10:30, Ford told his wife he was pulling the plug. He changed into a business suit and walked downstairs thirty minutes later to tell Reagan himself. "This isn't gonna work," Ford said. Lou Cannon reported that Ford, over the course of a brief but emotional meeting, thanked Reagan, hugged him, vowed to campaign in the fall. The two men parted on amicable terms and Reagan proceeded to place a call to a long-suffering Bush, asking him to be the vice president. "He was a gentleman," Reagan said of Ford later. "I feel we are friends now."

In its review of the convention a few days later, *Time* ruled that the whole gambit was "ill-considered," "unseemly," and "a stunning spectacle" that raised questions "about the nominee's judgment and how far he was willing to go to win election in November." In fact, the Detroit episode was a prologue to the presidency: Reagan would exhibit a tendency to reach for the ideal and then settle for something short of it, an instinct that would become a key component of his success in the White House. At the same time, he displayed a tendency to let others perform duties vested in the presidency if it suited his needs—and that would very nearly tip his presidency over in its second term.

Both camps would try in later years to dispel any notion that a co-presidency was ever on the table or, if it was, to play down the idea that either man ever took it seriously. And each side did its share of blaming the entire episode on the other. The Ford folks, Lyn Nofziger charged later, "would be nice and let Reagan go to funerals and he—Ford—would pick the Secretary of State and Secretary of Defense. Anybody who wanted to see the president would have to go through him."

Ford, for his part, made it sound like he merely wanted to be the First Gatekeeper. "I firmly believe, and this is, in effect, what I told my people they had to put on paper, that as Vice President I would be chief of staff. I didn't want to make the decisions. But I had to know what was going on and would pass on recommendations. But, the president would have to be the decision maker. . . . I think I would have been a very good chief of staff. That's what . . . I was aiming at."

Just as he did with his 1968 run, Reagan wrote almost fancifully of the whole episode as if it had been someone else's idea. And a small army of Reagan historians, interpreters, and expungers rushed in to say that there was far less to the whole episode than it appeared at the time. "There was never any love lost between these two guys," Stu Spencer would later say. "If 50 people had come and said he had to do it, [Reagan] wouldn't have done it. He wouldn't have put Ford on the ticket." Spencer believed Ford's advisors were just playing games. "They were talking about power sharing. You get this acre and I get these two acres and you get this acre. It was ludicrous."

And yet it very nearly happened.

NIXON, FORD, AND CARTER:

Three Men and a Funeral

———————— ⚷ ————————

Jerry Ford and Jimmy Carter disliked each other for five years until they realized they both disliked Ronald Reagan even more.

And then they became friends.

They discovered that more united than divided them while flying back from the funeral of Anwar Sadat in Cairo in 1981. Stuck on a 707 for sixteen hours, Ford and Carter put aside what were largely petty disagreements and decided, in the space of a few hours, to become partners and friends. This reconciliation required no intermediaries, as it had with Nixon and Kennedy, or weeks of behind-the-scenes negotiations, as it had with Hoover and Truman. They did it themselves, in the cramped forward cabin of the plane that had functioned as Air Force One during each man's presidency. Though one was an exacting and difficult engineer and the other an easygoing former jock, they had just enough in common to see the advantages of getting over it: each had been an unexpected president; each had been tossed out of office by voters; each had at least twenty years to live—and each blamed Reagan for his defeat.

It helped that both men were confident in their faith—Ford an Episcopalian and Carter a Baptist—and each bent toward forgiveness. It surely helped too that both men had just gotten a big dose of Nixon, who was back onstage and acting like he was still the commander in chief. The club can be a competitive place. Both Carter and Ford sensed that they might need each other just to keep up with Nixon's never-ending quest for redemption. In time, Ford and Carter would create a place all their own, a powerful, productive club inside the club, which would go a few rounds with Reagan, and later with Bush and Clinton as they all tried to square their places in history.

16

"Why Don't We Make It Just Dick, Jimmy and Jerry?"

—GERALD FORD

Even by Air Force One standards, it was a mission for the ages. Air Force corpsmen cleaned, fueled, watered, and then checked over the Boeing 707, the one that had brought JFK's body home from Dallas and carried Richard Nixon on his first trip to China. Special provisions were brought aboard for this trip: lead steward Terry Yamada ordered up some Don Diego cigars, a guilty pleasure of Nixon's. He stuck a quart of butter brickle ice cream in the freezer for Ford. Grits for Carter were stowed somewhere in the cramped, starboard aft galley along with an electric frying pan, extra eggs, beef tenderloins, and crab claws. White House advance man Joe Canzeri somehow got his hands on some vintage blue and white Air Force One matchbooks bearing the names of Nixon, Ford, and Carter and left them strewn around the cabin for old times' sake.

And somewhere, just in case, airmen stashed a trio of bulletproof vests.

Three former presidents were about to fly fifteen thousand miles from Washington to Cairo to attend the funeral of Egyptian president Anwar Sadat and it was going to take all the ingenuity White House aides could muster to make this strange trip a success. Gerald Ford cared little for Jimmy Carter. Carter had even less use for Richard Nixon. And Nixon was, unbeknownst to the other two, about to peel off for a secret mission of his own. And all three had a complex relationship with Ronald Reagan, the man who summoned them all to duty and was about to send them halfway around the world. What unfolded in October 1981 would herald the rebirth of the Presidents Club. And it happened at 35,000 feet, more or less in full view of nearly twenty-five other people. After years of lying dormant, the club was about to wake up.

Only hours after Islamic extremists had assassinated Sadat and eleven others during a military parade in Cairo, White House officials decided that security concerns made it impossible for Reagan to attend. Reagan had survived an assassination attempt six months earlier—and it had come much closer to claiming his life than the public, as yet, knew. Nor was the Secret Service keen to permit Vice President George Bush to go in Reagan's place. "Our friends in Egypt understand that," Bush said the next day. But who should attend?

Secretary of State Alexander Haig proposed an unexpected alternative: a delegation of three former presidents, led by Haig himself, to pay respects to a man who had done so much to advance the cause of peace. Nixon volunteered for duty; Carter had balked at first, briefly peeved that Reagan was unwilling to make the journey himself. When Carter relented, after a number of phone calls from former aides urging him to make the journey, Carter's lone condition was that his wife, Rosalynn, be allowed to accompany him. White House aides eventually won the participation of Ford, whose family was wary of the trip, and Air Force jets were scrambled to collect all three parties. They arrived at Andrews Air Force Base on the same afternoon, each within one minute of the others.

This mission had uncommon possibilities—the power to redeem, the potential to explode. Each man had left Washington disgraced, disappointed, or rejected in some way. Carter had not been back to the White House at all; Nixon only once before at Carter's invitation. Now they were returning together, taking up their old places on a world stage for a few brief hours. The mere fact that there were three of them was confusing even to them: which man, they wondered, should be first to board the Marine helicopter for the ride downtown? It was Nixon, Carter recalled, who suggested the most recent president should lead the way because he was technically the senior member of the delegation. Even after this vital matter of protocol had been cleared up, there was considerable tension on board the brief chopper flight and so the ever amiable Ford suggested a way to adjust the mood as they flew from Andrews to the White House. "Look," he said, "for the trip, why don't we make it just Dick, Jimmy and Jerry?" The other two men quickly agreed.

Old White House hands sensed that this was an unusual, even an unprecedented, moment. Several hundred White House staffers met the trio on the South Lawn and applauded as they stepped, one by one, off the helicopter, again in order of service. The applause mounted with each successive president. The men walked three abreast (four, counting Rosalynn) across the South Lawn, where they were greeted by the Reagans. Watching the arrival with her husband from a window upstairs, Barbara Bush marveled at the sight of four presidents standing together: "It all rather amused me. I don't really think they liked each other very much," she recalled. "Rosalynn came also, and I don't believe that she and Nancy liked each other very much."

Everyone was ushered inside the White House and up to the Blue Room, where coffee and canapés were served. The Bushes joined the group as well. It was, Reagan noted in his diary, the first time four presidents had been together at the White House—ever. (Though, with Bush there, it could be argued that there were five.) Reagan thanked his guests for standing in his place and the group exchanged brief memories of Sadat. "Ordinarily, I would wish you happy landing," Reagan told them, "but you're all Navy men, so I wish you bon voyage."

Then, almost as quickly, they were all outside again. A quick South Lawn ceremony, redolent with unity, unfolded as dusk fell. Then the three former presidents headed to the chopper. Carter annoyed Reagan aides when he stepped away from their carefully organized tableau to speak briefly to reporters. "I'm glad to be going," he said, "but it's a sad occasion." Then protocol took over again: Carter reboarded first, followed by Ford and then Nixon. The Marine chopper lifted into the night. Total elapsed time at the old stomping grounds: about thirty-six minutes. The club might be reforming, but that did not mean its members were ready to spend time communing with each other. Peering out the window of the helicopter, a vantage point he had experienced seven years earlier on the August afternoon when he had resigned, Nixon said to his brethren, "I kind of like that house down there, don't you?"

The First Leg

Special Air Mission 26000 would have been a memorable flight even without the extra cargo of former presidents. Led by Haig, the U.S. delegation included Defense Secretary Caspar Weinberger, former secretary of state Henry Kissinger, singer Stevie Wonder, U.N. representative Jeane Kirkpatrick, and a sampling of lawmakers that included Senator Strom Thurmond of South Carolina, Chuck Percy of Illinois, and majority leader Jim Wright of Texas. Rounding out the delegation were Army Chief of Staff Edward C. Meyer, former Carter aide Jody Powell, and Middle East envoy Sol Linowitz, as well as a fourteen-year-old boy from Liberty, South Carolina, named Sam Brown who had been pen pals with Sadat. Fold in Nixon, Ford, and Carter and the mood, those on board noticed, was electric.

"This is," said Haig dryly, "quite a planeload."

The historical baggage alone would have been enough to ground any normal aircraft. It is easy to forget that Nixon submitted his resignation to Kissinger in 1974 in a deal that was largely engineered by Haig—or that Ford pardoned Nixon a month or so later in a decision that was regarded by many as a payback. Or that Carter would come along out of nowhere two years later to toss Ford out of office; and that Reagan, whose picture lined the fuselage's interior now, had just as abruptly unseated Carter in 1980.

There was nowhere to hide on this flight: the aging 707 was a thin, noisy, single-aisle plane with only a few not very private rooms. Haig took the tiny presidential cabin up front, leaving Nixon and Ford to share a cramped four-person compartment with Kissinger and Weinberger. Nearby, Carter and his wife shared another two-person row. Rosalynn Carter got things going, walking through the plane and greeting everyone, particularly Nixon, whom she found polite and unexpectedly talkative. Nixon urged Haig, in front of his peers, to allow Mrs. Carter to have the president's stateroom, which came with a bed. Haig declined, citing protocol. (It was not the first time Nixon had come to Rosalynn's defense: after Carter had left office just months before, he sent an aide to see Nixon for advice about setting up a post-presidential operation. Nixon offered the Carter emissary one particularly pointed piece of advice: "Make sure Mrs. Carter has her own office," he said.)

By contrast, Ford and Carter seemed determined to not get along. Their wounds were deeper, their anger fresher. "Oil and water," Carter himself explained early in the flight, smiling slightly for reporters. "They had no use for each other," said a Ford aide later. At one point, when an Air Force steward asked all three men for a photograph, Carter seemed uncertain. "How long will it take," he asked, before agreeing to smile for the cameras. Later, Ford murmured to a fellow member of the delegation, "You know, that just goes to show you can't make chicken salad out of chicken shit."

Carter later said he found Nixon fascinating, perhaps because Nixon worked so hard to lighten the mood, walking stiffly through the plane in his blue serge suit, greeting people, moving away from Ford and Carter when others on board approached the group for photographs. "They don't want pictures with me," Nixon demurred, making sport of his own misfortunes. "Nixon was being very gregarious," said Barrie Dunsmore, diplomatic correspondent for ABC News and one of three reporters on the first leg of the flight. "He was walking up and down the aisle and really trying to be gracious." But the old awkwardness was there too: Nixon at one point wandered back to the small section in the rear where the reporters were sequestered, looked around, uttered an enigmatic few words—"This is all," he observed—and then headed back up front.

From the very start of the trip, security was an obsession. Sadat's assassination had been sudden, brazen—and caught on videotape. At this time, very few people, even in government, understood the seismic forces at work in the Muslim world. "There was a real fear, everyone was uneasy," recalled Haynes Johnson of the *Washington Post*, also on the trip. "You didn't know what was going to happen." And even if there was a bulletproof vest for every president, there were not enough for all the other VIPs along for the ride. There were some morbid jokes about the plane flying close to the Gulf of Sidra, which Libyan leader Colonel Muamar Gaddafi had threatened to defend with his life—or that of his air force pilots.

Things seemed to ease a bit once the plane was airborne. The sweaters came out: Carter wore a beige cardigan; Ford put on a red one, while Nixon, martini in hand, wore blue. It may have been the nostalgic fact that they were now all aboard a plane that had once been, in a way, their own. Or it may have been the symbolism and sheer power of the 707 itself: to walk through Air Force One, even in its older, narrower, louder, cramped incarnation, was a heady experience; to do so when it was fully loaded, thick with Air Force personnel, on a high-stakes mission overseas under full power could be intoxicating. "Every time you got on that airplane, you were flying into history," Haynes Johnson recalled. "Everybody feels that. You know you are on history itself."

The former presidents quickly found something to talk about: Anwar Sadat, what he meant to each man, each man's presidency, and the world. All three commanders in chief had tried to prevent this day: Nixon sold Sadat Sikorsky helicopters; under Ford, the CIA had given Egyptian security agents special encryption devices so they could communicate about Sadat's movements in secret. Carter even sent a radar plane to patrol the skies over Cairo in the event Gaddafi sent fighters in Sadat's direction. Carter recalled that Begin, Sadat, and Carter jointly phoned Ford in 1978 to inform him that they had completed the Camp David Accords. Carter told the small group of traveling reporters that he could not believe his ears when he learned that Sadat was dead. "The only time I had that bad a day," he said, "was when my own Daddy died."

Sadat, Kissinger would observe, "handled four American presidents with consummate psychological skill. He treated Nixon as a great statesman, Ford as a living manifestation of good will, Carter as a missionary almost too decent for the world and Reagan as the benevolent leader of a popular revolution, subtly appealing to each man's conception of himself and gaining the confidence of each." They then discussed the broader situation in the Middle East—and agreed that Reagan was right to push the Senate to approve early-warning aircraft, known as AWACS, for Saudi Arabia; it was Carter, after all, who had proposed that sale in the final year of his term and had pressed Reagan during the transition in 1980 to see it through.

But just when things seemed to be settling down, Nixon steered the ship into turbulence. A few hours into the flight, Haig came out of his cabin to speak to Kissinger about some cables he had received just before boarding in Washington. The cables, Haig explained, were from officials at the State Department seeking guidance now that Nixon was apparently expected in a few days at a private dinner in Jidda, Saudi Arabia. Haig was taken aback by this news—landing as it did amid the uphill fight for AWACS in Congress and the very real regional confusion in the wake of Sadat's assassination. Haig asked Kissinger to find out what Nixon was up to. About the same time, White House signal operators called to say that Reagan aide Mike Deaver was on the line, also asking about Nixon's mystery dinner in Jidda: was Nixon running his own secret mission inside the public one?

Kissinger pressed Nixon for an explanation. "Ever the conspirator," Hugh Sidey reported, "Nixon threw his hands in the air. He was not sure, he claimed. He had invitations to visit several nations in the Middle East. Whether the Saudis would let him come had not yet been resolved." Nixon was once more up to his old tricks, keeping his host, the U.S. government, in the dark about his next move. By the time the plane bounced into Spain's Torrejón Airbase near Madrid to refuel, even Kissinger's head was spinning. Asked by Haynes Johnson how everyone was getting along up front, Kissinger set the stage as the reporter and the diplomat strolled around the Spanish tarmac. "They are all being themselves. Ford is being Ford. Carter is being Carter and Nixon? Nixon is all over the place!"

When the party arrived in Cairo that night, the trio boarded armor-plated limos flown in from Washington and sped to their hotel downtown. Robert Barrett, a Ford aide who was assisting with advance work on the journey, approached all three men before each event, his arms outstretched, and recalled later how awkward it was to keep saying "Mr. President" as he guided them from place to place. They paid courtesy calls on Sadat's handpicked successor, Hosni Mubarak, and then spent thirty minutes with Sadat's widow, Jehan, at her home in Giza. They visited the Egyptian parliament and met with the parliamentary speaker. They even made a visit to a group of U.S. government officials living in Cairo, each man speaking extemporaneously. In his remarks, Nixon self-consciously noted that the sad occasion had attracted people from around the world, both famous "and infamous."

The next day, wearing the bulletproof vests that made each man seem stiff, the three presidents attended the sprawling funeral held on the outskirts of the city. It proved to be a spooky and unsettling occasion. Mindful of the way several million Egyptians had disrupted Gamal Abdel Nasser's funeral in 1970, Egyptian authorities held services for the decidedly less popular Sadat well away from the city's teeming population. The former presidents gathered in a large pavilion and then began a half-mile walk with leaders from dozens of other nations to Sadat's final resting place—a tomb directly opposite the very reviewing stand where he had been assassinated just four days before. "It was like being in Aida," recalled Johnson. "There was something almost operatic about it."

And something frightening. The mourners marched eight hundred yards through a gauntlet of well-armed Egyptian troops, who lined the parade route on both right and left. Everyone was thinking the same dark thought: a repeat of the massacre of just a few days before, when Islamic radicals dressed as Egyptian army troops came rolling out of a truck to murder Sadat and many of his party. "We were walking in a long line, very spread out," Dunsmore recalled. "I was close to Kissinger, who was walking with Menachem Begin. I think the presidents were just ahead of us. At a certain point in the procession, a group of Egyptian guards, their rifles not pointed directly at us but certainly in a ready position, blocked our way. All of a sudden, everyone went stiff and turned white with fear because there were at least a dozen of these soldiers in front of us. Given what had happened here just a few days before, we were all terrified. It was one of the scariest moments of my life."

Finally, someone barked an order in Arabic and the soldiers parted. The experience left nearly everyone in the party convinced that Reagan and Bush had been right not to attend. Ford in particular found it unnerving. "The whole thing was surreal," said Johnson. "The assassination hung in the air. We reached the grandstand and we could see the blood that was still there." A makeshift tomb awaited nearby. So did a plaque that read: *President Mohommed Anwar Sadat, hero of war and peace. He lived for peace and he was martyred for his principles.* Apparently, Sadat himself had written the epitaph three years earlier. Then a twenty-one-gun salute began, but most of the VIPs dashed for their limos before it was over. The whole thing felt like an anticlimax. But the trip was only half over.

Where Did Nixon Go?

Earlier that morning, an ABC producer woke up the network's Steve Bell, who was in Cairo covering the funeral for *Good Morning America*. Dunsmore was breaking off from the trip, the producer explained. Might Bell be willing to fly back to Washington with the former presidents later that day? Count me in, said Bell. The flight back could be historic. And thanks in no small measure to Bell, it was.

When the U.S. delegation arrived at the Cairo airport later that morning for the flight home, Egyptian ground personnel had wheeled one—and only one—boarding stairs up to the blue, white, and gold-trimmed 707. That may not sound remarkable, but to the three reporters, it was nothing short of miraculous: it meant that they would get the chance to board the plane through the same door as the presidents, dignitaries, and other VIPs for the ride back home, rather than the rear door. And that meant that they would get thirty seconds, perhaps more if they were lucky, to strike up a conversation as they moved through the front of the plane.

That was all Bell needed. He climbed the stairs, entered the plane near the cockpit, and then turned right to head back to the press section. He ran almost immediately into Carter and, after introducing himself (he had covered the Carter White House), Bell said, "Mr. President, would you consider doing a joint interview with the other presidents?" Carter replied, "I don't think so," to which Bell responded, "Forgive me, Mr. President, but sharing the experience of being president I'd think you would be closer to each other than anyone but your wives." Carter said with his trademark smile, "I'll think about it."

Bell was no sooner back in the rear of the plane with Johnson and UPI's Jim Anderson than the three made a formal request for a joint interview with the former presidents through advance man Robert Barrett. The interview would have to be on the record—and would be pooled to all news organizations upon landing. Barrett took the request back to the front of the plane.

But on the way forward, Barrett met a Secret Service agent who reported that Nixon would not be coming along for the ride. The news startled Barrett, who had not heard about Nixon's clandestine mission to Jidda. Barrett quickly secured the consent of Ford and Carter for an interview and returned to the press section. "I have some good news and bad news," he said. "The good news is that the presidents would be delighted to talk on the way back. The bad news is that there are only two of them."

Said a stunned Haynes Johnson, "That goddamned Nixon! Where did he go?"

"Beats the hell out of me," replied Barrett, "but I will try to find out."

Meanwhile, in the front of the plane, something even more important was unfolding. For Carter and Ford, time was collapsing. Their four-year feud was dissolving during the long, relaxed flight home.

How did that happen? For starters, they had the magical plane to themselves again. The absurd Haig had stayed behind in the region and the furtive Nixon had diverted to Saudi Arabia. "The absence of Nixon made a huge difference," Johnson recalled years later. "Not having that pallid, viral figure meant it was much more relaxed." And there was another factor too: "We had survived," he said. "The bulletproof vests came off, we moved around more freely, everyone was talking about how strange the funeral was." Alcohol was served on Air Force One if you knew which steward to ask and there were surely a few requests for cocktails after the events in Cairo.

Besides, death has a way of rearranging perspective and Carter and Ford realized how silly their grievances and disagreements had been. Barrett recalled that Ford, Carter, Kissinger, and Rosalynn spent part of the first leg back conducting what he called a Ph.D. course in Middle East politics. The conversation grew very animated, even heated at times, particularly as the men discussed the lingering hostilities in the United Nations toward Israel. When the three reporters came forward after a refueling stop for their interview, they found Ford and Carter sitting opposite each other at a table, each in shirtsleeves. Carter wore a tie; Ford's collar was open. There was no camera crew; only a still photographer. Johnson and Anderson took notes while Bell kneeled on the floor of the plane and moved his tape recorder back and forth between the two presidents so that his tiny device picked up all the words over the roar of the engines.

What the reporters got was an unusually frank—and bipartisan—dissection of dysfunction in the Middle East. "It is almost impossible for an Arab to step forward [in favor of peace] because of a threat of assassination or violence within their own fragile government," Carter said. "They don't have the stability of Sadat. Jordan has a weak nation. [Jordan's King Hussein] is a weak leader. . . . And of course the Saudi Arabians also have a fragile country with a tiny population, no great military strength and enormous wealth. So they don't have the courage of a Sadat." Ford was no less candid when he more or less accused moderate Arab leaders of hypocrisy, of being "as anxious as Sadat was for peace. For various internal reasons, they can't publicly come out and say what they tell me or tell President Carter or tell others."

Each man provided the other a lot of cover; and the club began to speak with one voice. Carter and Ford said the United States must recognize the Palestine Liberation Organization in order to advance the cause of Middle East peace. Ford said the United States needed to take that step and then predicted it would happen; Carter sketched the outlines of a possible deal: the United States should recognize the PLO at the same time the PLO recognized Israel's right to exist. "At some point it has to happen," said Ford. "I don't want to pick a date, but in a realistic way, that dialogue has to take place." Carter was more emphatic: "There is no way for Israel ever to have an assured permanent peace without resolving the Palestinian issue so I think Jerry is certainly right in saying these discussions have to be done." Taken together, their comments were a significant departure from official U.S. policy and everyone who was listening knew it. Johnson reported that the "frankness of the former presidents' comments troubled some of the diplomats aboard the plane."

But the two men were just warming up. Though somewhat formal at the outset, their conversation had quickly turned more casual and everyone noticed that the presidents were virtually finishing each other's sentences by the end, using their first names, going out of their way to praise each other on various issues. The session was a complete turnaround from the brittle formality of a few days before. "You could see the two of them were really engaged," recalled Johnson. And when they were asked about the roles former presidents could play, the two men all but declared the club was back in business. "I believe this example of President Carter, President Nixon and myself participating in a mission," said Ford, "is an excellent example of how former presidents can be brought back into service."

The session had gone on for more than thirty minutes, both men leaning toward each other. Someone asked, "Final thoughts?" Carter replied, "No, that is good." And then the two men shook hands.

Anderson, Johnson, and Bell returned to the rear of the plane and pinched themselves. Something astonishing had just taken place, they agreed, something none of them had really expected. Johnson and Anderson began to type out their notes. A transcript was produced and before the plane landed, Jody Powell was back in his old role as press wrangler, charged with running the Xerox. Within days, the presidents' remarks shook official Washington. Columnist Mary McGrory called the session a rare burst of "out of office outspokenness." Reagan had to distance himself from what his predecessors said. And in a reminder of the days when Washington reporters routinely self-censored, Joseph Alsop, the aging voice of Washington's wisest elders, chastised the pool scribes for reporting the interview in the first place.

But up front, the parley continued. The two men talked about how Carter's arms control work on SALT II had built on Ford's work at Vladivostok. They talked about the difficulty of safeguarding cruise missiles. They commiserated about how difficult it was to organize their presidential papers in a timely way. After five years of distrust, they mutually disarmed. "We found," Ford said later, "that we had a lot of things in common."

Before long, they weren't just talking about partnerships, they were forging them. Carter agreed to attend a conference at the Ford library; Ford volunteered to cochair several projects being launched by the Carter Center. Both men were somewhat surprised by their change in feelings. "We had hours in the plane, in a private compartment, just the two of us, to talk over previous relationships and what our children were doing and the interests Betty and Rosalynn had," Carter said. "One of the things that we felt bound us together particularly was an onerous and mandatory task of raising money to build our presidential libraries."

Even among the few people who were privy to the fact that the two men had buried the hatchet at 35,000 feet, none could have imagined how harmonious the relationship would become over time. During the next three decades, Ford and Carter would team up on dozens of projects. They wrote a *Reader's Digest* article in 1983 that was critical of Israel. They joined forces to push the North American Free Trade Agreement in 1993 and jointly opposed a plan to legalize drugs in California in 1996. Their wives even teamed up from time to time.

Perhaps most remarkably, they each agreed, whichever died first, to give the eulogy at the funeral of the other, a job that fell to Carter in December 2006—more than twenty-five years after the historic flight to Cairo.

REAGAN AND NIXON:

The Exile Returns

Jerry Ford may have pardoned Richard Nixon, but it was Ronald Reagan who put him back in the game. Which was a little ironic because Nixon never thought much of Reagan, at least not when he first contemplated him as commander in chief. "Decent" but "shallow" were the words he used to describe Reagan in a 1971 Oval Office conversation with Henry Kissinger, a chat during which Nixon kept returning to the frightening prospect of Reagan becoming president. Nixon had been leery of Reagan since their strange primary contest in 1968; by 1973, with the race to replace Nixon already visible on a distant horizon, Nixon again found the prospect of Reagan taking his place unthinkable. "Good God," Nixon waxed. "Can you imagine—can you really imagine—him sitting here?"

But Reagan's election in 1980 gave Nixon a chance to make a new start, to enjoy at least probationary privileges in the club whose other members—Carter and Ford—had little or no use for him. Enough time had passed since his resignation in 1974 for Nixon to start stepping out in public and working his levers behind the scenes. Nixon would earn Reagan's confidence, offering advice as a private, back-channel problem solver, one president to another. This was a role that conveniently matched both Nixon's preference for secrecy and, given his still tarnished public reputation, made it easier for Reagan to swallow. While that role took shape, Nixon worked to rehabilitate himself in public, writing books, giving speeches, holding forth on foreign policy questions as a private citizen. In his public remarks, Nixon was always careful to support Reagan even if he didn't agree with him. Reagan repaid Nixon in the way Ford and Carter had not, by asking for his advice early and often—and then taking it.

17

"I Am Yours to Command"

—RICHARD NIXON

The help started even before Reagan reached the Oval Office. In September 1980, Nixon wrote Reagan a three-page, single-spaced letter offering detailed suggestions about how to handle Carter in the final weeks of the campaign. Nixon urged Reagan to dodge any debate with Carter unless third party candidate John Anderson was included. Nixon pressed Reagan, a seasoned performer, to feign political stage fright, in order to lower expectations about his competence as a debater. He advised Reagan to hire Pat Buchanan to "come up with some good lines" but strongly urged him to take a few days off before the big event. "How you look is if anything more important than what you say," Nixon said. "Let Carter come over uptight, nitpicking and mean. You should be a contrast, strong but not shrill; in command, poised, the big man versus the little man."

Nixon even urged Reagan to hold his final campaign rallies indoors, the better to preserve his voice.

Once Reagan had crushed Carter and tossed all hopes for a new Democratic revival aside, Nixon turned from being a campaign consultant to an unofficial White House guide. What would a former California governor know of all the traps and traditions of the nation's capital? Nixon would be Reagan's Baedeker, reclaiming some of his old powers by helping Reagan deploy his new ones. On November 17, Nixon quietly handed Reagan another, longer letter, this one a blueprint for constructing his presidency, along with specific recommendations for most of the top cabinet positions (as well as far less important posts such as head of the General Services Administration). It included shrewd prescriptions for making the White House work better: Nixon urged Reagan to focus on diversity in his appointments to subcabinet posts. ("It is time once and for all to erase the image of the Republican party as white, Anglo Saxon and Protestant.") He proposed that Reagan make certain that none of his National Security Council aides were closet liberals; and he suggested that Reagan kick senior White House aides out of the cabinet meetings, and instead invite in promising deputies to groom a second-term farm team.

But at the heart of Nixon's single-spaced, eleven-page letter was a thinly disguised plea that Reagan tap Nixon's longtime spear-carrier and spy Alexander Haig as secretary of state. This campaign was a twofer: Nixon had written the letter on the very day that press reports were hinting that former Nixon labor and treasury chief George Shultz was the odds-on favorite for State. Nixon was never a Shultz fan; their enmity dated to a flat-out refusal by Shultz in 1972 to unleash the IRS on a number of Nixon enemies. But Nixon was pushing Haig for another reason: having the former four-star general on the seventh floor of the State Department would give him a direct line to both foreign intelligence and U.S. decision making. Nixon naturally did not mention this to Reagan; instead he sold the president-elect an unusually large helping of hokum about how Haig would "reassure the Europeans, give pause to the Russians, and in addition, because of over five years as Henry [Kissinger]'s deputy in the White House and two years at NATO, he has acquired a great deal of experience in dealing with the Chinese, the Japanese, the various factions in the Mideast, the Africans and the Latin Americans. Those who oppose him because they think he is 'soft' are either ignorant or stupid. Others who raise the specter that he was somehow involved in Watergate simply don't know the facts."

And then Nixon added a final grace note, though it would prove a promise far easier to make than to keep. "As far as my own personal situation is concerned, I do not, as you know, seek any official position. However, I would welcome the opportunity to provide advice in areas where I have special experience to you," he wrote. "President Eisenhower said to me when I visited him at Walter Reed Hospital after the election of 1968, 'I am yours to command.'

"I now say the same to you. I trust that that can be our relationship in the years ahead."

In a handwritten note five days later, Reagan thanked Nixon for the "sound" suggestions in both letters. "I followed your advice regarding those last campaign days although I couldn't manage to get all the [rallies] indoors. But I did stick with the proven campaign speech and the polls kept going up a point or two each day. I can't thank you enough for the guidelines you have [given] me on personnel and the cabinet meeting suggestions—this will be done."

Reagan named Haig as secretary of state a few weeks later.

Nixon would bombard Reagan over the next six years with letters and telegrams, offering foreign policy tips, intelligence gleaned on overseas trips, and occasional political predictions. He sent many short notes of encouragement, usually after big speeches, and a stream of welcome-home notes after overseas trips. He offered suggestions, historical artifacts, personal recollections (usually self-serving), and countless pieces of advice about everything from minor political stagecraft to grand geostrategy. The substance of all these messages, good as some of the advice was, mattered less than the mere fact of it. Nixon had lots of advice for Reagan; he offered it freely, and even if Reagan didn't always take it (though much of the evidence suggests that he did), Nixon for the first time *felt* like he was being heard.

He was no longer persona non grata. On the eve of the 1982 midterms, Nixon wrote Reagan to buck him up, urging him to overhaul his political team before Christmas. "Shaking up a team at midterm is not a sign of weakness," he counseled. "Done the right way, it increases your status at home and abroad as a strong leader who will not tolerate ineffectiveness let alone disloyalty or dishonesty. I speak from experience. Some charged me with being too tough on subordinates . . . in retrospect, had I been tough, I might have avoided some of the problems that plagued me at the last." When Reagan struggled to find his footing in the early days of the 1986 Iran-contra scandal, Nixon was there with a list of steps to take quickly. "After Christmas you might consider making several changes in order to strengthen your team for the last two years."

Three days later, Nixon wrote again, this time playing nurse. "Your continued good health is the free world's greatest asset. Do whatever the doctor advises you and don't delay treatment even a day because of concern about the PR effect."

How the Club Became a Weapon

But if there was one topic that dominated the two men's correspondence, it was how to manage the U.S.-Soviet relationship, and Nixon's tone in these letters is that of a nervous coach who still longed to be on the field himself. One gets the sense that Nixon may have praised Reagan on all sorts of matters that he didn't much care about in order to win the president's ear on U.S.-Soviet affairs. At the very least, Nixon paid Reagan the courtesy of candor when it came to the USSR; the tone of these letters is different, more emphatic, almost unvarnished when compared to his other notes. You can almost hear Nixon straining not to lecture. And yet, at the end of one such note in February 1983, Nixon is careful to acknowledge who is in the chair. "As usual, these thoughts are not for the record or for history but for your private consideration. Whatever you finally decide I will of course support."

Mikhail Gorbachev's emergence as Communist party general secretary tested this promise. Gorbachev began to rattle and then reform an ossified Soviet system. His changes at first were minor, mostly in how the Communist Party chose its leaders. But as he moved to make broader economic reforms in the USSR, he turned his attention to the most sacred of Soviet cows: shrinking Moscow's military spending and the strategic nuclear forces at its core. American Sovietologists disagreed for months about how seriously to take Gorbachev's vision or whether he would be allowed by Kremlin hard-liners to advance it or even remain in power. If the West were to take Gorbachev at his word, it could have vast implications for America's place in the world, prospects for freedom around the globe, and its own defense industrial base. Nixon, the aging Red hunter, was a skeptic from the start. While Reagan would come to believe that the new Soviet leader was a real if imperfect departure from the past, Nixon was still too much of an unalloyed Cold Warrior to see it. Nixon worked behind the scenes and often in public to undermine

Gorbachev's reformist image, warning that no matter how appealing and friendly Gorbachev may seem, he was nonetheless a classic Soviet apparatchik. "Anyone who reaches the top in the Soviet Hierarchy," Nixon wrote in a *New York Times* op-ed in September 1985, "is bound to be a dedicated Communist and a strong, ruthless leader who supports the policy of extending Soviet domination into the non-communist world." Nixon published the column two months before Reagan and Gorbachev would meet for the first time in Geneva. Nixon expanded on his worries in an eleven-page article in *Foreign Affairs* that fall. Summits for summits' sake, he argued, are silly. "This is a long struggle with no end in sight," Nixon wrote. "Gorbachev, at 54, is a man who does not need to be in a hurry. He may live long enough to deal with as many as five American presidents."

Nixon was practically telling Reagan that the club needed him to be firm.

And there is a lot of evidence that Reagan was listening. In late 1985, just before he was set to fly to Geneva to meet Gorbachev, Reagan recorded in his diary, "Dick had a hell of a good idea on the arms negotiations. . . . His suggestion is that we state what we have agreed on, that we will continue negotiating on the other points and as a token of our resolve to achieve results, we each take 100 missiles out of the silos and store them for a set time. If we can't come to reduction agreement, we put them back in the silos."

Reagan's first meeting with Gorbachev in Geneva that fall had produced little beyond the requisite communiqué and good pictures, but provided a basis for a second meeting a year later. By the spring of 1986, Nixon had decided to take the measure of Gorbachev himself and scheduled a six-day, "private, fact finding" trip to Moscow. Some of Reagan's aides—who by now were engaged in an almost daily skirmishing with one another about how seriously to take Gorbachev—were skeptical of Nixon's mission and voiced their objections. But Reagan opted to let Nixon go, in part because he assumed that Nixon would also be granted time with Gorbachev. Nixon and Reagan spoke by phone for fifteen minutes before takeoff; the more eyes and ears on his counterpart, Reagan felt, the better.

Nixon arrived in Moscow on July 12, 1986. Once again, he was in his element, quietly working as a one-man back channel between the White

House and the Kremlin. Just as he had predicted to Reagan, Nixon got to spend more than two hours with Andrei Gromyko, president of the Supreme Soviet Presidium, two hours with longtime Soviet envoy to Washington Anatoly Dobrynin, and an hour and forty-five minutes with Gorbachev himself. A week later, Nixon sent Reagan a remarkably detailed, twenty-six-page memo about his trip with advice ranging from the gastronomic to the strategic. Should a trip to Moscow ever be planned, he wrote, "Get ready to eat plenty of tomatoes, cucumbers, caviar and sturgeon. They still serve them for breakfast, lunch and dinner. Incidentally, Gorbachev may not be able to change Soviet foreign policy but he has made one significant change on the domestic front. This was the first time in six trips to Moscow I was never served even a drop of vodka!"

The memo made clear that Nixon played multiple roles during his trip—and relished his own performance. He gathered intelligence, noting who in Gorbachev's circle was up and who was down; he took it upon himself to explain Reagan to the Soviets and then, in great detail, reported back to Reagan on how the men in the Kremlin viewed the U.S. president. Nixon played the advocate too, urging the Soviets to cut an arms deal with Reagan rather than wait for a more moderate successor, who, he shrewdly explained, would have a much harder time shepherding any treaty through the U.S. Senate. He toggled back and forth between hard-nosed Cold Warrior and avuncular American. "I had known President Reagan for 30 years," he recalled telling the Russians. Reagan, he said, "was a man of very strong convictions but that he was a reasonable man and if he could be convinced that an agreement was in our interests, he would make one. But I also emphasized that he did not need an agreement for his own political purposes because he would leave office with very high popularity even if he made no agreement with the Soviets."

But then Nixon added, "However, I expressed my personal belief that [Reagan's] major foreign policy goal in his second term was to reduce tensions between the Soviet Union and the US, negotiate the first nuclear arms *reductions* agreement in history and leave his successor a new, less confrontational relationship which could survive long after he left office."

Nixon was not running a rogue operation, but the former president was operating with enormous latitude in both capitals. And it is easy to imagine how much Nixon loved being back in the mix, simultaneously applying both grease and pressure at all the universal joints. At one point, Dobrynin asked Nixon for ideas to move the stalled arms talks along and Nixon complied, making a few proposals, including the idea of putting one-hundred-odd missiles into "escrow" as a confidence-building measure until a final deal could be done. Nixon did not tell the Russians he had already discussed the idea with Reagan; instead, he reminded them on several occasions that he was speaking only as a private citizen and had "no way of knowing what the reaction of US negotiators" might be. The Russians then asked Nixon to put those ideas on paper so that they could be translated and given to Gorbachev. Nixon agreed.

The former president came away from his 105-minute session with Gorbachev more impressed than he had been going in; still he found him to be "charismatic," but also a "crude and vulgar man," "more skillful, more subtle" than Leonid Brezhnev but less "rash" and "irresponsible" than Nikita Khrushchev. "He is the most affable of all the Soviet leaders I have met," Nixon wrote Reagan, "but at the same time without question the most formidable because his goals are the same as theirs and he will be more effective in attempting to achieve them."

Nixon was wrong about this, of course—Gorbachev would emerge as a clear break from his predecessors. But he was right about one thing: the value of the club as an instrument of American power. And it was that power that Nixon made sure Gorbachev understood. He reminded him that an arms deal before 1988 would "ensure that Reagan would strongly support his successor's efforts to carry out the Reagan initiatives." And he warned: "Failure to reach agreement while President Reagan is in office might run the risk of developing a situation where President Reagan might become a powerful critic of his successor's Soviet American initiatives." In other words, a current former president was warning the Soviets about the potential opposition of a future former president. Don't mess with the club, Nixon advised.

Coming from Nixon, this was not an idle threat. And in his memo to Reagan, Nixon added, "I don't believe anything I said during the conversation had a greater impact on him than this statement."

Nixon's relations with Reagan and the White House cooled after Reagan flew to Reykjavík in October 1986 and, in a spasm of wishful thinking, proposed to Gorbachev that the United States and the USSR abolish *all* their nuclear weapons. Nixon, who had long worried about Reagan's judgment, found the idea alarming, maybe even reckless. And though that idea fizzled in Iceland, Reagan was determined to move forward on arms control, even by small steps, in his final two years in office. His chief target was a proposal by his secretary of state, George Shultz, to reduce intermediate-range nuclear forces (INF) in Europe.

For some Republicans, Reagan's second-term push for arms reduction may have seemed like a head-snap: Reagan made his name as an anti-communist crusader and had broken with Nixon and his détente wing of the GOP because it had been too accommodating to Moscow. But it was nearly as strange that Nixon, who had made his own march from fevered anticommunist to dispassionate arms controller over twenty-five years, did not approve of the bilateral route that Reagan was now traveling. And Nixon was complaining about Reagan's approach to anyone who would listen.

On April 28, 1987, Nixon was summoned to the White House for reprogramming. He arrived by helicopter; National Security Advisor Frank Carlucci and chief of staff Howard Baker greeted the former president on the South Lawn and the three men slipped inside and proceeded upstairs to the residence. Careful White House advance work meant that Nixon's arrival through the White House back door went unseen by the several dozen reporters who worked there.

Nixon arrived after spending the previous seventy-two hours driving the White House crazy. First, on Sunday, April 26, Nixon had published a syndicated op-ed column with Kissinger that suggested that Reagan was being seduced by Gorbachev into a shared but perilous vision of a nuclear-free world. In the *New York Times* the next morning, former Nixon speechwriter William Safire added his tart voice to the realists' chorus: "Who'd a thunk it: a dozen years after the death of détente, after a decade of Reaganaut criticism about a 'fatally flawed' pair of SALT treaties, comes now Richard Nixon and Henry Kissinger—together again—to warn that the Reagan administration may be going soft on the Russians.... Who's right: the out of office former detenteniks turned neo-hardliners or the in office former hardliners turned neo-detenteniks?" (Safire's call: Nixon was right.)

And just that morning, in case anyone had missed either of those columns, *Time* had published an interview with Nixon in which the former president again tried to knock some sense into Reagan's head. "Nuclear weapons aren't going to be abolished," he warned, "and they're not going to be uninvented."

Never mind that Reagan had laid aside his dream of a nuclear-free world and was merely trying to shrink the number of atomic weapons in Europe. Nixon was determined to play the antagonist—and it would not be the last time. Perhaps as a result, Baker and Carlucci had modest goals for the meeting: they hoped to convince Nixon to back their proposed reductions for medium-range missiles in Europe. And if Nixon wouldn't agree to that, could he just pipe down?

Nixon rode the private elevator to the second floor with Baker and Carlucci and then joined Reagan in his private study, which had served as both LBJ's and Nixon's bedroom. It was his second visit to the White House since his resignation thirteen years earlier and his first in the private quarters. Nixon was astonished by how much the place had changed and found the furnishings extravagant compared to those he had known.

The two men had used the residence and its perks differently. Nixon preferred the nearby Lincoln Sitting Room as a smoker: he'd go in, build a fire in the fireplace, and then crank up the air conditioner. Reagan installed a weight room in the White House living quarters and worked out every day. Nixon had the trails at Camp David paved over so that his golf carts could scoot along faster; Reagan had them torn up and taken out so he could use them as horseback-riding trails.

But this was a room that had seen some strange club gatherings before: Nixon told Reagan how he had once sat in that same room in 1966 while Lady Bird had crawled into bed with LBJ. Reagan, trying to ease the tension, offered cocktails, but Nixon declined. Baker, an avid photographer, took pictures. Nixon urged Carlucci to take notes, adding weirdly: "I assume that the place isn't taped!" Later, even Nixon admitted the mood was awkward; Nancy Reagan was nowhere to be found and Nixon noted the absence of Shultz as well. "I don't know whether Nancy was in the Residence at the time, but if she was, he did not suggest that she come in and say hello. My guess is that she is probably as teed off as Shultz is."

Nixon did what he always did in such sessions: he delivered a long opening statement, confessing from the start that he knew Reagan's aides believed he and Kissinger were trying to "sabotage" the INF deal. Not so, said Nixon; he was just trying to make what looked like an inevitable INF arms pact stronger. Deep down, Nixon felt Reagan was playing a strong hand badly and did not possess the same patient, supple, and sometimes devilish feel for high-stakes negotiation he and Kissinger had in their heyday. He was not ready to trust Reagan on something as important as arms control.

Baker then asked Nixon if he might see a way to get behind the INF deal.

Nixon declined. The best he could do for Reagan, he said, was not to oppose any deal he struck with the Russians. But support it? No way.

"If the agreement was too unbalanced I would simply remain silent," Nixon told himself later, "since opposing it, when there was no chance of getting it rejected [by the Senate], would be totally irresponsible."

Nixon found it interesting that Reagan himself had not asked Nixon for his support. "Reagan did not enter into this dialogue with Baker and I am not sure he was aware that Baker was going to make this proposal. I am quite sure that Shultz had put him up to it. In any event, I did not agree to it."

Baker returned to the point before the meeting was over and once again Nixon declined to help out.

Nixon was no longer Reagan's to command.

The session had lasted an hour—a fair amount of time for any president and, apparently, something close to an eternity for Reagan. Nixon came away worried about the president's focus. He seemed tired, Nixon wrote afterward, "particularly so as the hour drew to a close. He was simply having difficulty concentrating, even though I made the presentation as simple and direct as possible." Nixon was alarmed that Reagan continued to speak of eliminating all nuclear weapons, as though that was going to happen in his lifetime.

The two men, each in his own way, had come full circle. Forty years after Nixon had helped turn a fledgling union president into a well-known voice on anticommunism, he was now worried that the great, fire-breathing Reagan had gone soft on the reds. But Nixon was completing a revolution of his own. Once again, a former president, having been criticized from the right for being too quick to conduct détente with an enemy, found himself complaining about a successor being too quick to conduct détente with the enemy.

And the veteran, once again, found his onetime protégé wanting. "I must regretfully observe," Nixon concluded in a four-thousand-word memo to himself on the White House visit, "that Reagan looks far older, more tired, and less vigorous in person than in public. There is no way he can ever be allowed to participate in a private meeting with Gorbachev."

The meeting effectively ended the partnership between the two men on U.S.-Soviet relations; they had grown too far apart in outlook to team up behind the scenes again. Their work together in Reagan's final year would be limited to politics—and the lessons each had learned the hard way.

Ike and Dick and Ron and George

From: The Reagan Diaries

Thursday, July 28, 1988

> *. . . Lunch with George B. We talked possible V.P. cand's. Both of us are without a firm choice. . . . Then the Bush campaign spot ads and finally upstairs to await visit by Richard Nixon. As always, he had some campaign suggestions that make great good sense.*

By now, Reagan was a lame duck, modestly popular at home, wrapping up a handful of items on his to-do-before-I-go list. The men around him were busy trying to figure out how to continue the Reagan revolution in spirit since they couldn't extend the Reagan presidency itself. And because of his Eisenhower days, no one had a more acute understanding of what was involved in extracting a vice president from the shadow of a popular president—while retaining the incumbent's sheen of power—than Richard Nixon.

Sometime during the early summer of 1988, Reagan White House chief of staff Ken Duberstein called Nixon at home in New Jersey with a question: What should a sitting president do—or not do—in his final months to help his vice president win the top job? Might Nixon be available sometime to discuss the problem?

It had been a busy winter for Nixon, finishing another book, talking privately with select reporters at his home in New Jersey, and above all keeping a close eye on the 1988 campaign. Nixon watched that contest with a mixture of pride and wonder as two of his protégés, Bush and Bob Dole, arm-wrestled for the Republican nomination. Though Nixon had groomed, promoted, and advised both men at different points over several decades, he had long favored Dole. Bush was a turn too smooth and well-born for Nixon's taste and he feared that Bush might not be tough enough to stand up to a Democratic challenge—much less a Russian one. By contrast, Dole was the kind of small-town scrappy infighter that Nixon imagined himself to be; indeed, Dole's great weakness was that he sometimes came off as too tough and unforgiving—as a little too much like Nixon himself. Though he struck a pose of neutrality in the months leading up to 1988, "Nixon was for Dole," explained a Bush aide who managed the relationship, "Quietly." In a private memo to just a few friends that winter, Nixon described Bush as "weak" while praising Dole as "strong and courageous." After Bush lost the early caucuses in Iowa to Dole, Nixon diagnosed the vice president with a case of "insufficient drive." But when Bush battled back in mid-February to win in New Hampshire, Nixon reported that Bush had "really come into his own." If Nixon admired the winner in Bush, he admired the survivor even more. "It is necessary to struggle, to be embattled, to be knocked down and to have to get up," he told *Time* that spring. "Renewal. Americans are crazy about renewal."

Nixon was betting on that. He appeared on *Meet the Press* on April 10, his first appearance on TV in eight years, and led viewers on a tour of world affairs and his controversial presidency. He admitted to fouling up Watergate and regretted only that he hadn't bombed Vietnam earlier. During the commercial breaks, he joked about his habit of perspiring on camera. ("I'm famous for that," he said.) He dismissed all the criticism of Reagan for trading arms for hostages in the Iran-contra affair and then reviewed some of the 1988 campaign's most memorable performances. "The best politics is poetry, not prose," Nixon said. "Jesse Jackson is a poet. Mario Cuomo is a poet and [Michael] Dukakis is a word processor." As for the national mood, Nixon said he sensed "a restlessness amid prosperity." A few days later, Nixon told a gathering of newspaper editors that Bush would beat Dukakis in November. "The election is close with Bush winning by a nose and it will be decided in California." He urged Bush to pick Dole as his running mate but noted, "Bush can pick anyone—nobody is going to hurt him."

In mid-April, Nixon dined privately with the vice president and his wife, Barbara, as well as campaign advisor Lee Atwater and his wife, all at the Naval Observatory. After the meal, Bush and Nixon met alone for an hour to talk. Nixon told Bush that his path to the presidency was clear but not by any means assured. According to the definitive account of the session by Jules Witcover and Jack Germond, Nixon urged Bush to take a hard line on crime and the Soviet Union to keep any Democratic rival off balance (Bush would do both); to develop a persona independent of Reagan's while campaigning, but to wait until after the convention in August to do so (Bush followed this advice down to the letter, even when advisors were close to pulling out their hair). In addition, Nixon warned, Bush needed to be mindful about the reaction of the Republican right wing to his eventual choice of running mate—a lesson Nixon had learned the hard way in 1960, when he chose moderate Massachusetts senator Henry Cabot Lodge and his party's conservative flank howled.

And finally, Nixon urged Bush to do everything he could to lure Reagan back onto the campaign trail. Nixon had long believed that he had made a mistake by not pressing Eisenhower to help him in 1960.

Bush took this all on board, well aware that much had changed since 1960 and that while Reagan had never been as widely popular as Ike, he remained plenty popular with Republicans.

A few months later, in July, Nixon was in Washington and called Duberstein at the White House. If you come to my hotel, Nixon proposed—he preferred One Washington Circle in Foggy Bottom to the Lafayette Square clubhouse—we can discuss the 1988 campaign. Duberstein immediately took a car over from the West Wing.

Nixon launched into a history lesson. He spoke about how difficult the separation problem had been for him in 1960, how little Eisenhower had done to help him. Nixon urged Duberstein to think carefully about how to deploy Reagan, but to find a way to get him out there on Bush's behalf. Barely an hour had passed when Duberstein, sensing his oppor-

tunity, told the former president that while he was being extremely helpful, it would be even better if he could come back with him to the White
House to brief Reagan in person.

Nixon replied, "I would enjoy that if you think it would be helpful."
But then Nixon added: "I have a tendency to lecture." No president likes
lectures, particularly from former presidents with whom they have had
textured relations—much less disagreements going back a generation or
more. And so Nixon offered some strategic stage management. When we
sit down with Reagan, he told Duberstein, "You could ask me questions."

Later that evening, Nixon was ushered in a back door of the West
Wing and then up the small elevator to the residence. Nixon and Duberstein were joined in the West Sitting Hall by Reagan and Nancy.

Reagan sat in an armchair, flanked by Nixon nearby on a red and
white chintz sofa, hands folded in his lap. Nancy Reagan sat on Nixon's
left, on the same couch but at a safe distance. This was never going to be
a fun visit; the events of the year before had put a strain on the friendship. Virtually throughout the unusual tutorial, there was little to no eye
contact between Nixon and Reagan. Nixon, Duberstein guessed, knew
that Nancy had her misgivings about any contact between her husband
and the thirty-seventh president. And then there was that item in *U.S.
News & World Report* a few months earlier, which quoted Nixon telling
friends privately that Reagan could survive the Iran-contra mess simply
by acting "stupid."

Still, the conversation about how to help Bush lasted an hour and
before it ended, Nixon offered an unusually specific prophecy: Bush, he
told Reagan, is going to call you in the last week of October and say that
he needs you to campaign in California. *Southern* California in particular,
Nixon predicted.

Even Reagan rolled his eyes at this last touch, Duberstein recalled.
Such was Nixon's obsession with politics and power: he didn't need
merely to guide a president about how to handle the future; he needed to
be able to predict it for him as well.

The Last Campaign

Over the next few months, Nixon would check in with Duberstein every week or so, getting the latest gossip, offering a running commentary on events at home and abroad, passing along political tips and hunches from his fraying network of listening posts around the country. Nixon urged Reagan to attack the Democrats in order to keep Dukakis off balance, particularly on national security. In mid-August, after the Republican convention in New Orleans, Nixon dashed off a handwritten note to Reagan praising his speech. "You have given George a great sendoff; it will be close but if he can make ideology the issue, it could mean 4 more years for the Reagan revolution."

In late October, just slightly more than a week before the election, Bush campaign manager James Baker phoned Duberstein. "We need the President in California on the final weekend, Ken. That will sew up the race so that we won't have to worry about the other states."

Duberstein was speechless: Nixon's prophecy had come true. And right on schedule too. Bush was running only slightly ahead of Dukakis in Illinois, Missouri, and, most critically, California. If the Republican team could simply hold California and its fifty-five electoral votes, Bush would not need to win the other close states to capture the presidency. Thus unfolded Baker's plan for an eleventh-hour club fly-in—just as Nixon had predicted.

The Bush campaign, Baker told Duberstein, hoped to send both Reagan and Gerald Ford to California during the final weekend of the campaign. The two-pronged club attack would energize voters and help nail down the Republican win.

The next day, Duberstein called Nixon. "Are you sitting down?" he asked, explaining how he had heard from Baker and, just as Nixon had foreseen, the Bush forces had called on the White House for help in California. Then Duberstein added: "Thanks for the heads up."

Which is how it happened that, on the last weekend of the 1988 campaign, Ford went to Contra Costa County near San Francisco while Reagan flew south; first to Long Beach, where he addressed a rally of four thousand in a parking lot next to the *Queen Mary*, on which Reagan had traveled to England some forty years before. White House advance teams spared no expense: fireworks, water-spitting fireboats, a flyby of eleven World War II vintage T-6 airplanes in tight formation, and a dramatic launch of hundreds of red, white, and blue balloons.

Then it was on to San Diego's Civic Center where Reagan gave his final campaign speech. He played it for all it was worth: "Now please forgive me if from time to time over the next few minutes there seems to be a lump in my throat and a catch in my voice. This is a special moment for me in a special place and yes with special people. I closed both of my campaigns for the Presidency right here in San Diego . . . and when I finish in San Diego, I feel I'm with family and I know I'm with friends."

Reagan talked about his hardworking underemployed father, a shoe salesman who tried to keep his family fed through the Depression but who preferred to sleep in his car to staying in a hotel that would not allow Jews; and he fondly recalled his mother, Nelle, who despite her own modest means never turned down a panhandler at the back door and whom Reagan brought out to California when he was in Hollywood, where he bought them "a home, the first they had ever owned." It was a marvelous piece of storytelling, mythic and emotive—punctuated by calls for "four more years," as well as "Bush, Bush, Bush." He was campaigning one last time, he told the crowd, for his mom and dad.

"So, now we come to the end of this last campaign, and I just hope that Nelle and Jack are looking down on us right now and nodding their heads and saying their kid did them proud. And I hope someday your children and grandchildren will tell of a time that a certain President came to town at the end of a long journey and asked their parents and grandparents to join him in setting America on a course to the new millennium and that a century of peace, prosperity, opportunity and hope had followed.

"So, if I could ask you just one last time: Tomorrow, when the mountains greet the dawn, would you go out there and win one for the Gipper?"

Nixon had been right. The race in California had become too close to call in the last days of the contest. Exit polls would later reveal that those who made up their minds in the final days broke five to four for Dukakis. But in Southern California, experts on both sides said later, it was the election eve visit of Reagan that turned the tide for the Republicans. The next day, when the totals were completed, Bush had won California 51 to 48 percent. Bush held the land of Reagan and Nixon by 300,000 votes. And in some small way, he had Reagan, Ford, and Nixon to thank for it.

BUSH AND NIXON:

No Good Deed Goes Unpunished

───────── ⚷ ─────────

The story of Nixon and George Herbert Walker Bush is a tale of loyalty and its limits. Eleven years apart in age, they were miles apart in origins. Nixon grew up poor, smart, and striving on the West Coast; Bush was the son of a Connecticut senator, whose own parents had hailed from powerful Midwestern industrial clans. Nixon spent his summers working as a house painter, a chicken plucker, and a carnival barker; Bush worked at a summer camp. Nixon was the first of two California Republicans who would ride a powerful conservative tide into the White House; Bush's political roots and instincts were decidedly more eastern seaboard and moderate; he wrestled with distrust on his right flank throughout his career.

But when the two men finally crossed paths in the 1960s, Bush found a mentor who would change his life. The older man helped lift Bush from political obscurity and propelled him to the front ranks of the Republican lineup. Nixon had his doubts about Bush—about his politics, his judgment, and that all-important Nixon metric, his toughness. Bush admired Nixon's brains and large parts of his agenda, but worried about his character, his expediency, and the men he kept around him. He would remain loyal to Nixon as president virtually until his resignation; and as a person long after.

When Bush became president a decade and a half later, Nixon had a curious way of paying that loyalty back.

───────── ⚷ ─────────

18

"I'm Convinced . . . He Feels I'm Soft"

—GEORGE H. W. BUSH

L ong before he became president, George Bush had learned when to listen to Richard Nixon and when to ignore him.

The two men got to know each other in 1964, when Nixon flew to Houston to help Bush raise money for his campaign for a Texas Senate seat. It was an unlikely bid: there weren't many Republicans in Texas in the early 1960s. One year after the Kennedy assassination in Dallas, Lyndon Johnson and the Democrats had little to fear from Barry Goldwater and the Republicans. "We got whipped and whipped soundly," Bush reported to Nixon a week after losing in the Johnson landslide. Bush didn't dwell on the loss: in 1966, he won a seat in Congress from Houston's Westside.

And so it was something of a miracle that, just two years later, the forty-four-year-old freshman congressman was on Nixon's short list as a possible running mate in 1968. How did that happen? An unlikely but potent coalition of leading Republican lights had mentioned the young comer to Nixon: Eisenhower, who knew Bush's father, Prescott, urged Nixon to consider him during a 1967 chat at his Gettysburg farm. So had Billy Graham, whom Nixon trusted implicitly and who had been holding irregular Bible study for Bush's parents for nearly a decade. Chase Manhattan Bank CEO George Champion was a Bush man; and so was former New York governor Thomas Dewey, who had been the Republican nominee in 1948 against Truman. It was as if the oldest of the Republican moderates had caucused in secret and voted to put a Bush on the ticket.

Bush never had much of a chance in Nixon's Miami Beach gambling parlor—he was too green to be Nixon's vice president. But it got him thinking that he might have what it took to go all the way. He later thanked Dewey for lending a hand to "this Silky Sullivan longshot," a reference to an early-1960s thoroughbred who specialized in dramatic, come-from-behind victories. "Though we finished out of the money," Bush wrote Dewey, "it was a great big plus for me."

It was just the first of many times Nixon would call. In 1970, Nixon pressed Bush to quit his safe House seat and run again for the Senate in Texas. This push, coming from the president himself, was heady stuff and it appealed to Bush as he watched others in his generation climb the House leadership ladder, move to the Senate, or even get White House jobs. Bush took everyone's temperature on the matter and even made a pilgrimage to the Texas Hill Country to get a second opinion from another president. The club verdict was unanimous: though a Democrat, Lyndon Johnson urged Bush to run by invoking a salty aphorism: the difference between the House and the Senate, LBJ advised his fellow Texan, was the difference between "chicken shit and chicken salad." Recalling that moment more than four decades later, Bush noted, "You never had to guess what Lyndon was thinking. He was many things but 'mysterious' was not one of them." Bush's father, who had stepped down after a decade in the Senate for health reasons, argued against making the race, fearful his son was giving up a safe seat to make a stab at a longer shot. But in the end, the offer of White House help was too good to pass up and so Bush agreed to do what Nixon asked.

But not the Nixon way—and that quickly became the problem. Instead of facing the liberal Ralph Yarborough in the general election, Bush instead found himself facing moderate Lloyd Bentsen, a Democrat who was nothing like Yarborough: he was rich, popular in the Rio Grande Valley, and conservative enough to appeal to Texas Republicans. He had also been out of politics for twenty years. Nixon's henchmen dug up everything nasty they could find on Bentsen and shipped it down to

Houston for Bush to use against him in ads and speeches, along with more than $100,000 from Nixon's secret campaign slush fund funneled through seventeen different accounts. But after reading through all of the anti-Bentsen material, Bush set it aside. This isn't how the game is won, Bush thought. The White House even offered to send down political ax men Bob Dole and Spiro Agnew to go after Bentsen if Bush wouldn't. No thanks, Bush said, I'll do this my way. "George and Lloyd were gentlemen running a gentleman's race," said Richard Whalen, a former Nixon speechwriter who worked for Bush that year. "But the men in the White House were not gentlemen."

Bush lost his 1970 Senate bid, capturing fewer votes statewide than he had in 1964. He summed up the landscape on election night: "Like Custer, who said there were just too many Indians, I guess there were too many Democrats." And though everyone else in his family was distraught, Bush smiled through the worst of it and at five the next morning got out his list of several hundred people he needed to thank and reached for the phone. He got off sixteen hours later. For his trouble, Nixon rewarded Bush with a pair of administration jobs: first as U.N. ambassador and then as chairman of the Republican Party.

Nixon was gimlet-eyed about Bush: he liked him because he was young and seemed to represent a new breed of Southern Republicans the party had never seen before. In part because Eisenhower had plucked him to be his running mate at age thirty-nine, Nixon was well known in Republican circles for nurturing young talent long before he got the top job himself. But Nixon already had a Texas favorite in John Connally and there was the added problem that Nixon and his aides found Bush too much of a Boy Scout for their no-prisoners style of politics. In April 1971, while Bush was U.N. envoy, Nixon and Kissinger had agreed that Bush was "too soft and not sophisticated enough" to handle what was then the beginning of the Nixon opening to China. Nixon later mentioned to Bob Haldeman that Bush was "a worrywart" when it came to Watergate.

Bush's doubts about Nixon were nearly as great as Nixon's about Bush. While neither of the posts Nixon had handed to Bush were backwaters, each was in its own way at a thankless remove from Nixon's highly centralized West Wing. Bush's letters to Nixon, written as he either weighed or accepted these appointments, are still painful to read; you can hear the protégé swallow his doubts and say, *Taking this job goes against my instincts but I will do it for you anyway.* If Bush was too nice for Nixon and his heavies, they were too dodgy for him. As chairman of the Republican Party in 1973–74, Bush watched Nixon virtually destroy the party in order to save his own skin. Between 1973 and 1974, Bush logged 97,000 miles raising money as Republican Party boss; for this, Bush was told by the White House to do things that were, he told his wife, Barbara, "just wrong." He often simply refused to follow orders.

Bush, who never loved politics as much as policy and resisted the game when it turned dirty, found Watergate wrenching, dreadful, embarrassing. In public, he stuck by Nixon virtually until the very end, defending the boss's record, criticizing his tormentors, clinging to the narrowing evidence that Watergate was just a Democratic fantasy. But privately, he was in agony—not only because of what Nixon was doing to the party and the presidency, but because he knew, deep down, that Nixon had doubts about him. In July 1974, three weeks before the resignation, Bush wrote his four sons a long, revealing letter about Nixon's record and his character. It's as good a psychological profile of Nixon as any that exists. Nixon was a great leader, he told his boys, and a first-rate intellect but also a third-rate person. "He is enormously complicated. He is capable of great kindness. . . . I am not that close to him as a warm personal friend, for he holds people off some. But I've been around him enough to see some humor and to feel some kindness." Then Bush went on: "He has enormous hang-ups. He is unable to get close to people. It's almost like he's afraid to be reamed in some way—people who respect him and want to be friends get only so close—and then it is clear—no more!"

Bush told his sons that Nixon had little respect for Congress or his party machinery and felt outright contempt for the Ivy League, partly because it tilted left but also because of what Bush described as Nixon's habit of equating the Ivy League with "privilege and softness in a tea sipping, martini drinking tennis playing sense." Bush took this cultural bias of Nixon's personally: "It stings but doesn't bleed because I know if I said, 'Mr. President, do you mean me . . .' he'd say no. But I must confess that I'm convinced that deep in his heart he feels I'm soft, not tough enough, not willing to do the 'gut job' that his political instincts have taught him must be done. . . . He surrounded himself on his personal staff with people unwilling to question the unlovely instincts we all have—and that he has in spades."

The letter is even more remarkable because one of its recipients is a future president himself. In one aside to his twenty-eight-year-old eldest son about Nixon's Ivy League resentments, Bush wrote, "Thank God, George, you got the best from Yale but you retained a fundamental conviction that a lot of good happens for America south and west of Woolsey Hall." And then, in perhaps the best advice one future president gave to another, not to mention from a father to his sons, Bush added: "I shall stop with this gratuitous advice. Listen to your conscience. Don't be afraid not to join the mob—if you feel it's wrong. Don't confuse being 'soft' with seeing the other guy's point of view."

The day after Bush wrote that letter, the Supreme Court ruled 8–0 that Nixon had to turn over the June 23, 1972, tapes in which he had ordered the FBI cover-up of the Watergate break-in. Once those "smoking gun" transcripts were released and Bush read them, he reluctantly changed course. On August 7, Bush sent Nixon a letter urging him to step down for the good of the country, praising his "massive achievements," and expecting Nixon "in his lonely embattled position" to see Bush's request as "an act of disloyalty." Indeed, Nixon noted in his memoirs how Bush had backed away from him in the final days. But if Bush had given up on the president, he didn't abandon *the man*: he trooped down to the White House early on August 9 and found Nixon's family, his staff, and the president himself were all in tears or "close to breaking down" that final morning. "One couldn't help but look at the family and the whole thing and think of his accomplishments and then think of the shame," he wrote in his diary, "and wonder what kind of a man is this really? No morality—kicking his friends in those tapes—all of them. Gratuitous abuse. Caring for no one and yet doing so much."

Bush checked in on Nixon a month later, partly to seek his advice about whether to go to China as Gerald Ford's first envoy, and partly just to see how he was. The call did not go well. Bush noted in his diary that Nixon was "reserved, very reserved . . . he was less than warm personally." Nixon ignored Bush's offer to fly out to San Clemente and pay him a visit. And when Bush tried to give Nixon credit for the new position he was about to undertake, Nixon ignored him. "He never warmed up at that," he wrote. "The conversation was very brief."

Would You Like a Secure Phone With That?

Fifteen years later, Bush was still reaching out. Only now, he was president and Nixon had spent nearly fifteen years fighting to redeem his place in history.

Bush had a wide range of talent in the club at his disposal and the temperament to use it. Nixon, Ford, Carter, and Reagan were all still alive and Bush had worked directly for three of the four. In February and March 1989, Bush sent National Security Advisor Brent Scowcroft to personally visit every former president. Scowcroft asked what, now that Bush was president, they might want in the way of regular briefings and other logistical favors. This was self-protective on Bush's part: he knew that his predecessors could be excellent allies on all sorts of issues; and regular briefings in advance of big decisions could keep them sounding supportive when reporters called.

In return, Bush offered the usual club benefits: special government airlift when necessary and extra security as it might be required. These were standard privileges, just like those Bush's predecessors had doled out for years. But Bush offered new club perks as well. Scowcroft proposed to install in each of their offices a secure telephone so that Bush could reach them night or day. In an era before cell phones, Bush was regarded even by his aides as a little manic about the phone; he liked to have one at his side constantly, and used it at all hours, even at the dinner table in some cases. The scrambled telephone lines, encoded in order to prevent electronic surveillance, would also permit Bush to call and consult his predecessors at moments of crisis without fear of being overheard.

Over the next four years, Bush filed a series of semiregular dispatches to his predecessors to keep them up to date. These memos, a kind of club newsletter, were usually stamped SECRET or Confidential, and often explained various problems of foreign policy. Bush would write these himself—the prose bears his distinctive style—and they lack the stilted formality that so many previous presidents used when corresponding with their predecessors. For example, Bush's seven-page, single-spaced explanation of the coming Gulf War on December 11, 1992, is lucid, candid, and distinctly nonpartisan.

Scowcroft made the rounds to New Jersey, Plains, Beaver Creek, and Pacific Palisades, taking every ex-president's temperature and letting them know they could call at any time. This was territory the retired Air Force general knew well, having worked for two of the four and having had responsibility as a young colonel in Nixon's White House for fielding what seemed like endless requests for airplanes from Lyndon Johnson. Yet most of the former presidents declined Bush's special phone line because, as one official familiar with the conversations explained, they valued their independence and did not want to be part of even a semiofficial network. Only Ford accepted Bush's offer, but even he came to regard the larger-than-normal desktop handset as something of a bother. The Scowcroft missions remained a secret but the private message to the club was clear: Bush was counting on their help and advice; and if he couldn't get that, perhaps he could at least win their silence.

That was unlikely in Nixon's case. "He used to call all the time," recalled Scowcroft. "It was his way of unburdening himself. Sometimes it would be to find out what was going on. Sometimes he wanted to assuage his ego. But it was always helpful. He knew it would get to Bush and he didn't always want to bother him." Nixon knew Bush's strengths and weaknesses and wasn't shy about listing them. Bush, he told reporters, was steady, not flashy—but not a big risk taker, either. "He is highly intelligent. He is hands-on. He's not a bomb thrower but because he isn't a bomb thrower he doesn't have any interceptions. . . . He's the Joe Montana. The short, sure pass. He has a very high percentage."

Nixon was tougher on Bush than he was on Reagan, in part because, at least as president, Reagan paid more attention to what Nixon advised. And this really was the heart of what turned out to be a difficult Nixon-Bush relationship: unlike Reagan, Bush wasn't looking for foreign policy advice. Thanks to Nixon and Ford, he had already served at the U.N., in China, and at the CIA. He had a broad network of contacts overseas and didn't really need Nixon whispering in his ear about statecraft and strategy. Nixon at times felt pushed away, even by Scowcroft, his old military advisor. "Brent was always correct in his dealings with Nixon," recalled Dimitri Simes, a Soviet émigré who was serving as Nixon's foreign policy advisor in Washington. "But Nixon did not feel that Brent was really listening."

On China, specifically, Bush had developed his own outlook, which happened to align with Nixon's. The day after Chinese tanks broke up a peaceful demonstration in Tiananmen Square by more than 100,000 students in June 1989, Nixon counseled Bush in an 8 A.M. phone call not to overreact. Here, the architect of the Chinese opening in 1972 was urging his successor not to turn back the clock. "Don't disrupt the relationship," Nixon told Bush, who recorded his words in his diary. "What's happened has been handled badly and is deplorable, but take a look at the long haul." Bush, who took the entire U.S.-Chinese relationship "personally," as he put it, was already thinking in those terms. He would secretly send Scowcroft to Beijing later that month in an unmarked C-141 cargo jet for private conversations with Chinese leaders to make certain bilateral relations were not sidetracked. When word of those talks leaked weeks later, Bush and Scowcroft were pilloried by Democrats for coddling Beijing.

A few months later, in November 1989, Bush and Nixon met upstairs in the White House. Bush was preparing to meet Gorbachev in Malta for their first face-to-face talks; Nixon had just returned from a trip to the People's Republic of China. Nixon had been helpful to Bush during that journey, telling a gathering of Chinese leaders in private that the breach over the Tiananmen shootings with the American public was "large and unbridgeable." Now, at a working dinner in the residence that Scowcroft and Barbara Bush attended, Nixon urged Bush to send Treasury Secretary Nicholas Brady or another envoy to Beijing to try to nudge the relationship forward again. Bush had a shrewder idea: he would indeed send an envoy—it would again turn out to be Scowcroft—to Beijing but only *after* the meetings in Malta with Gorbachev. As he listened to Nixon, Bush knew that he would be making something of an ally of Gorbachev at Malta; and a visit to Beijing by Scowcroft in the aftermath of that summit would be more persuasive if Washington was coming off a successful meeting with the Soviet leader. But Bush liked what he was hearing from Nixon and agreed that the two nations needed to continue their progress. As he noted in his diary: "[Nixon] lectured the Chinese pretty clearly when he was there and gave them a realistic view of how things were in this country. He thinks the best thing to do is send Brady over there. I'm not sure. I still think we ought to put it in the context of my meetings with Gorbachev and make clear to China that we're not overlooking their views or their positions."

But if Nixon and Bush mostly saw eye to eye on China, the USSR was another matter. Managing the U.S.-Soviet relationship, at least for Nixon, was the whole shooting match, the most important part of being president. When it came to relations with Moscow, Nixon felt duty-bound to express his opinions, even if it meant breaking with the president. Normal club rules did not apply.

So in April 1991, Nixon issued his own personal declaration of independence from Bush. It began over something small: the month before, Nixon had gone to Europe to check on Mikhail Gorbachev's progress toward economic and political reform, making stops in Lithuania, Georgia, and Ukraine, and then spending two days in talks with a variety of political figures in Moscow, including Gorbachev and Boris Yeltsin, the chairman of the Russian parliament. Nixon came away certain that Gorbachev was, by most measures, moving backward on reform. He was drawn, however, to Yeltsin, a former mayor of Moscow and member of the Supreme Soviet. "I'd say this," Nixon concluded at the end of the trip, when he sat down to render his findings with three carefully chosen American reporters in Moscow. "Gorbachev is Wall Street and Yeltsin is Main Street; Gorbachev is Georgetown drawing rooms and Yeltsin is Newark factory gate."

What Nixon really thought was more dire: he told his friends that Gorbachev's time was short and that the United States must start looking beyond the charismatic Soviet leader. "It's really all over for the Soviet Union," Nixon remarked, returning to his Moscow hotel room after an hour-long meeting with the Soviet leader. "Gorbachev still doesn't get it. He still talks like the clock can be stopped, like he can find a formula to outsmart history. But the poor bastard belongs to the past. The Soviet Union is beyond salvation. It's time for Bush to understand that."

But when Nixon returned to the United States a few days later, he discovered that few in the White House shared his doubts about Gorbachev's longevity—or really cared what he thought. It's easy to see why. Just five weeks before, Bush and his foreign policy team had completed a dramatic, nine-month diplomatic and military campaign to oust Saddam Hussein's Iraqi army from Kuwait. Bush was enjoying a 90 percent approval rating at home in part because he organized dozens of countries against the Iraqi tyrant and then launched, won, and halted the ground war after five days. It was a tour de force by an American president and had unfolded with Moscow's acquiescence if not always its outright help. Bush, Scowcroft, and Secretary of State James Baker were on top of what they regarded as a new world order; they didn't really need a lot of kibitzing from an old Cold Warrior who was still trying to redeem himself for Watergate.

Besides, Bush and Baker had already spent a year sizing up Gorbachev to make sure that he had legs. At the Malta meetings they had offered the Soviet leader unprecedented inducements to move toward economic and political reform. And while there were those on Bush's team who had their own doubts about Gorbachev's staying power, Bush was not about to abandon him. To Bush, Nixon was the worrywart now.

But Nixon did not like being ignored. And so he laid out his plans to get the attention he felt he deserved in a letter to Dimitri Simes, his informal advisor on foreign affairs, who was increasingly serving as Nixon's point man in Washington. "In view of the Administration's obvious lack of interest in what we learned, the only way we can get across a point of view different from the conventional Washington beltway wisdom is through going public. I would prefer that you not follow up on trying to get people in the White House to talk to me with reference to that trip. I think they have their plate full and that apart from that, they are quite reluctant to hear any view point which is inconsistent with the line that both Bush and Baker have taken that Gorbachev is our best and only hope if we want constructive discussions and agreements with the Soviet Union.

"Under the circumstances, I would prefer to have a more arms-length relationship. This will give me more freedom to be constructively critical of Administration policy, when I think it is appropriate to do so. I would prefer not to run the risk of being co-opted by cozy little suppers in the White House family dining room since I prefer substantive conversation to substantive meals! Since that does not appear to be in the cards at the moment, I have decided to follow an entirely different course of action to get my views across and to affect the course of the foreign policy debates in other forums."

This was a dramatic departure, even for Nixon. If he had promised to be Reagan's "to command," Nixon was now organizing a rebellion. Over the next year, Nixon waged a deliberate campaign to reshape U.S. policy toward Moscow, enlisting much of the foreign policy establishment and his dwindling disciples in the press to his cause—all in opposition to the policy of a sitting president from his own party. Nixon would do this just as Bush was facing a primary challenge from, of all people, a combative conservative whose feel for the jugular was legendary and whose primary sponsor had been none other than Nixon himself. That would be Pat Buchanan.

Nixon made the first move, offering an essay in *Time* that would disclose his view that Gorbachev was a goner. Nixon jotted a few notes on paper for Simes, who would draft the essay, to follow: "You may not agree with me but with the exception of an occasional piece by [Charles] Krauthammer, I have found most of TIME's essays erudite, elegant, fashionable and virtually irrelevant as far as affecting the course of events. I want our essay to be totally different. Instead of elegant poetry, I want to use muscular prose. While TIME's essays are usually for those who pride themselves on being intellectuals, I want ours to be one that can be understood and will appeal to the silent majority."

The final version of the two-page essay, which appeared in *Time* in the third week of April, read like Gorbachev's death warrant. "Gorbachev seems unable to realize that there is no halfway house between a command system and a free market. He is unable to cut the umbilical cord to the Marxist Leninist philosophy that has nurtured him all his life." Nixon then carefully prescribed a new approach for Bush. "I'm not saying that the US should start interfering in Soviet internal affairs and side with Yeltsin against Gorbachev. The US must continue to deal with whoever is in charge of the other nuclear superpower's foreign policy. Today that happens to be Gorbachev and for the time being there is no alternative to him. But at the same time we can and should strengthen our contacts at all levels with the reformers in Russia and other republics. Gorbachev will not like that. But we must remember that he needs us far more than we need him."

Just as Nixon had pushed Reagan to toughen his terms with Moscow, Nixon was now pressing Bush to take the longer view, to look beyond the Soviet Union to a time when it might no longer exist. Nixon's message had not really changed; he was just as focused on the destruction of the

Soviet Union in 1991 as he had been on squeezing it in 1987, when he believed Reagan was offering far too generous terms on an arms control deal and refused to back the president in public. Now, Nixon was refusing to cooperate in private. And in public, he was preparing to go rogue.

Whatever the wisdom of those tactics, events soon proved Nixon's instincts right. In June, Yeltsin became the first democratically elected leader of Russia, which was the largest state in Gorbachev's USSR. Then, in August, right-wing military officers tried to overthrow Gorbachev himself while he was on vacation in the Crimea. Bush's reaction was uncertain for the first twenty-four hours; he called the coup "extra-constitutional" and noted that "coups can fail." But he also half dangled an olive branch to the plotters. Gorbachev certainly looked finished: in the Crimea, KGB officers surrounded his villa; they cut his phone lines, including his direct links to the Ministry of Defense. Plotters parked farm tractors across the runways at a nearby airfield in case Gorbachev tried to fly back to Moscow to assume command. It looked like a classic putsch.

In Moscow, however, a different story was taking shape: the next morning Yeltsin and a small band of perhaps two hundred Russians armed with rifles, grenades, and shovels gathered at the Russian parliament. Around noon that day, Yeltsin climbed atop an armored truck and denounced the coup, called for a general strike, and demanded the reinstatement of Gorbachev's post of president of the USSR (if not the man himself). With only a few hundred supporters facing the prospect of a military attack on his office, Yeltsin cabled Washington and pleaded for Bush to back him up. Bush changed course and began to call for the coup plotters to back off. Over the next twenty-four hours, the crowd outside the Russian White House mushroomed to more than 150,000. The Russian air force simply declined to lend a hand to the army generals. Russian tank crews, a handful of which were arrayed around the parliament, refused to fire on protesters. Within seventy-two hours the coup began to fizzle. A day later, it was dead. Gorbachev returned to Moscow four days after being taken prisoner, but Yeltsin had become the man to see in Moscow. Bush now realized that the Gorbachev era was finished. So, in many ways, was the old Soviet Union—just as Nixon had predicted.

The Secret Memo

By autumn 1991, with a brief recession getting under way in the United States, Nixon was privately astounded by Bush's lack of vigorous leadership. His daily comments to his research assistant Monica Crowley reveal a man who was itching to be back in the game, fearful that Bush was "in over his head" and unable to seize the economic initiative. But more than these specific concerns, Nixon was angry generally that while a political campaign was looming and the world was unwinding in historic fashion, no one was paying him any attention.

And then, someone did: in late 1991, former Nixon speechwriter Pat Buchanan decided to challenge Bush for the nomination. His campaign would be isolationist, protectionist, and heavy on conservative social issues—positions that Nixon had long opposed. In fact, Nixon was alarmed when he first learned of Buchanan's campaign. On December 5, Buchanan called Nixon and informed him of his plans. The two men talked and while Buchanan could not recall if Nixon discouraged him or not, Nixon afterward told Crowley that perhaps Buchanan would help galvanize Bush into action. Nixon said a few weeks later that Buchanan might take as much as 40 percent of the New Hampshire vote from Bush—another prediction that would prove to be on target.

With the 1992 campaign getting under way, Nixon was ramping up his profile in every direction, whatever the cost to Bush. In December, he wrote an op-ed in the *Wall Street Journal* calling on the White House to act more aggressively in the former Yugoslavia, which was on the verge of ethnic civil war. He prepared a second column criticizing a thawing trend between Washington and Hanoi. It was almost as if Nixon wanted a confrontation with Bush: when Billy Graham engineered a pacifying phone call from Bush to Nixon one evening in late January, Nixon complained afterward that Bush hadn't thought of making the call himself. "Bush put me on with Graham and Barbara, who thanked me for 'all I was doing for George.' That's a laugh. This was the first time in a long time that he's really called for me and it took Graham to put him up to it." Crowley recalled how Nixon saw the deals: "If he cultivated Nixon, Bush would get valuable advice and a prominent ally. If he ignored him, he would face a troublesome adversary."

Adversary it would be. For weeks, Nixon and Simes had been planning a high-profile conference on the future of U.S. foreign policy. The confab would mark the opening of the Nixon Center, a Washington-based think tank on foreign and domestic affairs that was designed to put another tent pole in Nixon's revival show. Nixon and Simes wanted the conference to be bipartisan and wide-ranging; they spent months planning the speakers and choosing the topics for discussion. They were shooting for scale: the conference would turn on nothing less than the future of American diplomacy in a one-superpower world. And it would be a flashy club event too: Nixon would speak at lunch on the first day; Bush would be invited to speak at a black-tie dinner that night. As for dates, Nixon and Simes chose March 11–12, 1992, the two days after the big Super Tuesday primary contests that were designed to pick, if not confirm, both the Republican and Democratic nominees. With the primaries largely over, Nixon was hoping to set the agenda for the fall campaign.

Nixon knew that inviting Bush to kick off something called "The Nixon Center" in the middle of a presidential campaign was politically awkward. This slowed Nixon down, but it did not stop him. He agonized how best to invite Bush: he wanted to give the president a chance to come (and enhance Nixon's own stature) but also the option of saying no (in case the politics were simply too toxic). And so a host of lesser players were tapped to invite the president first by writing pleading letters to White House aides. When those efforts yielded no response, Julie Nixon Eisenhower wrote Bush herself.

But what Nixon did next, even before he had heard back from Bush, made his conference scheme look positively charitable.

In late February 1992, Nixon condensed his greatest worries about the overall direction of U.S.-Russia policy into a withering 1,800-word memo. He chose a provocative title—"How to Lose the Cold War"—and rather than send it only to the president, Nixon decided he would share it instead with several dozen columnists and foreign policy thinkers around the country. Nixon would not tell his correspondents to keep the memo to themselves; instead, he hoped that they would talk it up, write about it, or leak it to others who would.

Nixon did not tell anyone—not even Simes, who was busy trying to get the president to attend the Nixon Center dinner—about his memo.

But Nixon knew exactly what he was doing, and he proceeded as meticulously as a bomb maker. He mailed his memos out from his home in New Jersey in plain brown envelopes. Each copy included a handwritten note ("Dear Bill") followed by a simple, one-sentence typed explanation: "I have enclosed some thoughts on a vital issue that deserves priority attention during the '92 campaign."

The gist of the memo was that Bush needed to propose millions more in foreign aid to Russia to prevent the former Soviet Union from falling back into tyranny or, worse, into chaos. It was implicitly critical of Bush for being too cautious. His language was as pointed as it was apocalyptic: "In light of the stakes involved, the West must do everything it can to help President Yeltsin succeed. . . . The stakes are high and we are playing as if it were a penny-ante game."

Nixon was turning a club rule—when giving advice, try to do it privately in order to minimize friction—on its head: he was sending out his private advice in order to pick a fight in public and elevate his stature at the president's expense. Even the delivery system was designed for effect: as Marvin Kalb later reported, "The memos left New Jersey in two batches, one dated February 25, 1992 and the other dated March 3, 1992, a week later." Before the days of blogs and email, the secret memos caused a chain reaction in Washington. William Safire said the fifty-odd people who got it were part of the most prestigious cabal to come out of Washington since Nixon's "enemies" list of 1972. One who made both lists—reporter Daniel Schorr—brought the memo to the attention of the *New York Times* by submitting a column about it to the op-ed page. Former Nixon speechwriter turned *New York Times* columnist William Safire called the secret memo a "swift kick in the teeth"; Crowley called it "revenge," for being ignored, which was hard to square with the fact that it was Nixon who had ordered Simes to break off further relations with the White House a few months earlier.

Whatever it was, it hit the front pages right on schedule—the day before the Nixon Center conference opened in Washington at which Bush was set to be the keynote speaker. This, of course, was excellent political theater, just as Nixon had planned, and it offered everyone in the audience a story line of their choice: one Republican president going into battle against one of his protégés; two foreign policy masters fighting it out through means fair and foul; not to mention the spectacle of a man nicknamed *Tricky Dick* mounting a comeback at the expense of a man whose childhood nickname was *Have-Half* because he readily shared his candy bars with friends. The *New York Times*'s Thomas Friedman's analysis story the next day twisted the knife: "Nixon's Save Russia Memo: Bush Feels the Sting."

Not everyone found Nixon's cleverly timed proposal for massive Russian aid wise. The United States was slowly coming out of a recession in the first quarter of 1992 and there was little interest in either party in spending more on foreign aid. The United States was already dropping more than $1 billion on Russia in 1992 in commercial and security credits, and not many people believed the Russians could responsibly absorb more. Former Pentagon official Leslie Gelb, writing in the *New York Times*, pointed out the flaws in Nixon's logic. "Russia is not ours to win or lose," Gelb wrote. "If democracy fails there, the blame will belong almost exclusively to the Russians."

That view was widely held inside the White House. Bush got a copy of the Nixon memo from Scowcroft and sent its author a private reply from Air Force One. "I certainly agree with the major principle of this paper, namely, that we have an enormous stake with the democratic Russia," he wrote. And then Bush went on to firmly dispute much of what Nixon had claimed about the extent and the feasibility of further Western aid to the disintegrating Soviet Union. Bush called Nixon to talk about the memo as well.

He explained to reporters the next day that he and Nixon weren't that far apart. "I didn't read it as criticism," he said, "because I talked with the man. And I learned to go to the source. . . . You know he's got very good ideas on this subject and we're in very close touch on it." The next morning, Bush sounded far more circumspect. "There isn't a lot of money around," he said at one of his regular press briefings. "We are spending too much as it already is. So to do the things I would really like to do—I don't have a blank check for all of that."

Bush was being polite, as usual. Scowcroft said later that Bush was "amazed" by the brazen, self-promotional nature of Nixon's campaign. "We had bent over backwards to scrape together the money we were providing," Scowcroft recalled, "and here Nixon was pushing—pushing hard—for more."

The Speech

Just as Bush was gently dismissing Nixon's memo in public, Nixon's long-awaited conference, "America's Role in the Emerging World," was getting under way at what was then Washington's swankiest hotel. The Four Seasons ballroom was packed with foreign policy heavyweights: former secretaries of state, aging spooks, U.N. ambassadors, as well as a huge helping of people who had worked for Nixon over the previous fifty years. It was as much a reunion as it was a policy conference. "Our speaker," former Pentagon boss James Schlesinger said by way of introducing Nixon, "is a man who has weathered a storm that would have been fatal to most other men."

And then Nixon rose to speak. For the next thirty-five minutes, Nixon held forth, talking without notes, his hands clasped in front of him, warning that both parties were flirting with a "new isolationism." Unless the United States came to Russia's aid, he added, a new kind of despotism in the former Soviet Union would reemerge, forcing the United States to spend more on defense than it had before the Cold War ended. He called on the United States to make $20 billion available to Russia immediately. When he finished, he received a standing ovation. Veteran Nixon hands were convinced the old man had memorized his remarks.

Nixon had certainly succeeded in restarting the debate. That very afternoon, Bush officials defended their allegedly measly Russian aid requests in hearings on Capitol Hill; Edward Hewitt, an NSC official, told attendees at the conference that the West had already shipped some $40 billion to Russia in the previous two years and that no one could account for its whereabouts. Sending more, therefore, made little sense. After his luncheon speech had ended, Nixon was asked by reporters why he was "attacking" Bush. Nixon disputed the suggestion. He was, he said, merely trying to "focus attention on what I consider to be the major foreign policy issue of our time."

That evening, it was Bush's turn. After a dinner of filet of sole with salmon mousseline had been cleared, Nixon introduced the forty-first president as "without question . . . the best qualified to lead the United

States and the free world in the years ahead." But Bush's speech was a dud. Some of it was a predictable broadside against the kind of isolationism that Pat Buchanan had been advocating. Some of it was a review of Bush's foreign policy accomplishments. But most of it was a lukewarm tribute to Nixon and all he had done for Bush over the years. There was little or nothing in the way of new ideas or more investment in Russia. Instead, Bush simply said he valued Nixon's advice. "I get it. I appreciate it," Bush said. ". . . we invested so much to win the cold war. We must invest what is necessary to win the peace. If we fail, we will create new and profound problems for our security."

Who Lost Nixon?

After all that, it would have been reasonable for Nixon to declare victory and head back to New Jersey. Instead, four days later, on March 16, he wrote Bush another memo and sent this one directly to the president. In it, he urged Bush to focus not on Buchanan but on Bill Clinton, who was poised to capture the Democratic nomination and whom Nixon had been watching for some time. And, like a dog with a bone, Nixon called again for a new round of aid for Russia.

A day later, Bush won both the Michigan and Illinois primaries, effectively ending Buchanan's quixotic but damaging campaign. Though he never won a single contest, Buchanan attracted between a quarter and a third of the vote every place he was on the ballot. His campaign was finished, but it had left the strong impression on political observers that the incumbent president might be beatable. Buchanan called Nixon for advice. "I'm ten for ten," he joked, referring to his unbroken string of defeats by Bush.

"Buchanan, you are the only extremist I know with a sense of humor," Nixon replied. "Come on up and see me."

Nixon quietly alerted a few friends in the press to Buchanan's visit— and then phoned White House chief of staff Sam Skinner with a heads-up too.

That was enough to provoke a call the next day from Bush, who was understandably concerned about whether Nixon would press Buchanan to get out of the race or would quietly encourage him to stay in a while longer. Nixon promised Bush, according to conversations he had the same day with Crowley, that he would apply some "pressure" on his old speechwriter to get out quickly.

On March 21, Buchanan and his wife flew to New Jersey to huddle with Nixon for seventy-five minutes. It was a very friendly session, Buchanan recalled. But Nixon never came out and told him to get out of the race—at least not directly. Instead, about halfway through the conversation, Nixon invited Crowley to step in and asked whether *she* thought Buchanan should exit the race.

"Tell him what you told me," Nixon urged Crowley, who proceeded to tell Buchanan that she—then twenty-three years old—thought it would be a good idea if he brought the curtain down on his campaign.

"I got the impression," Buchanan said dryly, "that she was conveying a message from the old man."

The two men did a brief appearance with reporters afterward in which Buchanan made no commitment to quit the race and Nixon praised Buchanan after a fashion. "There's only one thing worse in politics than being wrong and that's being dull. And Pat Buchanan is far from dull."

Buchanan departed and Nixon was immediately on the phone to Skinner at the White House. "I told Buchanan to get out of the race," Nixon said as Crowley listened nearby. But he really hadn't.

Two weeks later, Nixon had some satisfaction in seeing Bush reverse course on Russia, announcing a $24 billion aid package on April 1 for the former Soviet republic. Bush argued that he had been putting the pieces together for months, but no one really believed that. What they did believe was that aid to Russia—how much, how soon, in what form—had become a proxy issue in the presidential campaign, which was already about which candidate could embrace an uncertain future and which could not. Nixon had seen to that.

In fact, on that same morning and in the same hour that Bush had made his new offer of assistance, Clinton announced his own multibillion-dollar Russian aid package.

"Now, prodded by Democrats in Congress, rebuked by Richard Nixon and realizing that I have been raising this issue in the campaign since December," Clinton said, "the president is finally, even now as we meet here, putting forward a plan of assistance. . . . I'd really like it if I could have as much influence on his domestic policy."

Bush had beaten Bill Clinton by exactly twenty-one minutes. He would not beat him again.

BUSH AND CARTER:

The Missionary Goes Rogue

——————— ⚿ ———————

James Earl Carter was always a problem for the presidents club. Where most other members stepped back from public life after the White House, Carter spent the next thirty-some years getting even more deeply involved in world affairs, remaking himself as a global action figure, and eventually winning the Nobel Peace Prize. As Carter would be the first to tell you, no other president was so dedicated to saving the world after leaving the White House.

But his campaign of good works overseas and political redemption at home did not make him an easy man to work with. Stubborn, fiercely independent, and on occasion unusually sensitive, Carter had the habit of saying the wrong thing at the wrong time. He could be relied upon to engage in awkward self-promotion when cool modesty was in order. Even when he volunteered to run secret missions for his successors, he sometimes strayed beyond his brief or could not resist taking to the airwaves to brag about his achievements. Though Carter would set something of a club record by teaming up with Gerald Ford more than two dozen times between 1980 and 2000 to address a range of national problems, at times even Ford believed that Carter had gone too far and put some distance between himself and his partner.

All presidents compare themselves to those who came before and after, but Carter had a way of doing it rather gracelessly. "I feel that my role as a former President is probably superior to that of other presidents," he declared in 2010. His fellow club members kept their reaction to those kinds of remarks to themselves.

And yet, Carter gave the club a great gift: something for all the others to complain about. When nothing else seemed to unite its members, the club often bonded over what an annoying cuss Carter could be. Every club needs a black sheep and after Nixon died, Carter stepped seamlessly into this role. More than Nixon, who had obvious demons, Carter was the driven, self-righteous, impatient perfectionist who united the other club members around what seemed like an eternal question: was Jimmy Carter worth the trouble?

19

"I Am a Better Ex-President Than I Was a President"

—JIMMY CARTER

O utside of Sumter County, Georgia, Jimmy Carter was never much of a joiner. He came to Washington as a self-described outsider and he and his close-knit team of top advisors never saw the need to court the high priests of his new hometown. He asked voters outside the capital to turn down their thermostats, put on sweaters, and, just when they could have used a drink, forgo the tax-supported three-martini lunch. Carter wore his righteousness on his sleeve; he was a born-again Christian who taught adult Sunday school. His abstemiousness was the opposite of clubbable; he even replaced the open bars at White House events with pitchers of sweet tea and lemonade. He dismissed the White House drivers and promised that 10 percent of all state dinner guests would be "ordinary" citizens. He auctioned off the presidential yacht *Sequoia* that nearly every president since Hoover had used to wine and dine political allies and opponents. He insisted on acting as his own chief of staff for the first three years but then cited his twelve-year-old daughter as an authority on priorities in a presidential debate.

He seems doomed now to have been a one-term president. Carter was unlucky in his timing, taking over as the nation was losing its industrial competitiveness to Asia. His technocratic approach to governing made him impatient with the backslapping and logrolling that for years made Washington function. His treasury secretary at first thought Carter's spooky silences in meetings were time-outs for consideration but came to believe they were long apneas of incomprehension at the questions placed before him. He achieved an astonishing breakthrough at Camp David with Israeli prime minister Menachem Begin and Egyptian leader Anwar Sadat. But at other times he seemed uneasy with power and uncertain about how to use it. On the eve of the 1980 hostage rescue mission, he asked his generals if the student guards outside the U.S. embassy in Tehran could be immobilized by tranquilizer guns, rather than bullets. (No, came the reply.) Just three years after executing a breathtaking, come-from-nowhere campaign that had dazzled Democratic Party veterans for its deft reading of the public mood, Carter was beset by a revolt inside his own party when the time came to run again. Even his final concession speech was a minor botch: he acknowledged his loss to Reagan so early on election day in 1980 that many Democrats blamed Carter for reducing turnout on the West Coast, where polls were still open.

Carter had returned to Plains in 1981 beaten, bitter, depressed, and at age fifty-six, at a loss for what to do next. The youngest ex-president since Calvin Coolidge, he was not ready to retire and give speeches. "When I got out of the White House," he recalled, "I had a life expectancy of 25 years and so I needed to figure out how to use it." And so he wrote his memoirs, rediscovered woodworking, built his library, and then, in his late fifties, invented something entirely new: a full-time career as an international problem solver. Though other former presidents had dabbled in troubleshooting, Carter made it a full-time job, traveling to scores of foreign countries negotiating peace deals, opening agrarian and health centers, planning and monitoring elections. The Carter Center, which would grow into a $150 million organization, became the instrument of this ambitious campaign. He imagined the center as a kind of private sector Camp David, he said: "I want to provide a place where conflicts around the world can be solved." It grew into something of a shadow government at times as it pushed for peaceful engagement in Latin American, African, and Middle Eastern affairs. Carter established himself as the world's leading expert on election integrity, raised millions of dollars, hired dozens of experts, and launched scores of projects to foster better sanitation, healthier diets, and economic rights overseas. He lent his name and his face (as well as his hands) to Habitat for Humanity, a shelter-building enterprise that had its world headquarters just a few miles from his boyhood home. He campaigned against river blindness and guinea worm disease in Africa; he helped free political prisoners in Cuba and dissidents in the Soviet Union; he looked for solutions to border disputes between Thailand and Vietnam and was a constant champion of Palestinian rights. More than all this, he renewed his contacts with leaders all around the world, particularly in the Middle East. In time, Carter's influence in some parts of the world rivaled and even exceeded his clout when he was commander in chief. "I can't deny that I am a better ex-president than I was a president," Carter admitted in 2005.

So even though he left the White House in 1981, Carter's presidency never really ended. It was as if he spent a generation out of office completing a mission he never fulfilled as president. And if you happened to be president of the United States in the years that Carter was busy redefining what it meant to be an ex-president, you might just find yourself in his way.

The Baker Opening

Carter spent most of Reagan's first term minding his own business. He and Reagan would never become close and their relationship ran the gamut from merely correct to icy. At one point Carter grew so tired of Reagan insisting in public that Carter had weakened America's defenses that he phoned Reagan to insist that he stop. In late 1985, Reagan sent a "Dear Jimmy" note about the state of Middle East peace talks that was a brush-off dressed up as a thank-you note. "Forgive the informality," Reagan wrote, "but since we are both members of a somewhat exclusive club, I thought maybe we could forgo protocol." The letter went on to thank Carter for his interest in the region and politely set aside the former president's offer to serve as a diplomatic go-between.

During Reagan's second term, Carter began to step out around the globe, reestablishing contacts with foreign leaders, both friendly and hostile. It pleased no one on Reagan's team that Carter was back on the road, making stops in places where U.S. diplomats didn't often go. He made a point as he traveled of sitting down with tyrants to whom the United States was often actively opposed or sometimes covertly working to weaken, such as Hafez al-Assad in Syria in 1983 and Daniel Ortega in Nicaragua in 1986. These conversations were chiefly businesslike but Carter often treated them like personal ministries, bringing up religion and spirituality in an effort to scratch out some common ground with despots. Conservatives complained that merely by offering an audience with a former U.S. president, Carter was conveying legitimacy on men who were, by most measures, little more than thugs. But Carter did not see the trade-off in those terms. Instead he believed that his meetings were opportunities to reset the table and perhaps extract concessions—or future concessions—in return. Peter Bourne, who worked for Carter and later wrote a book about his presidency, observed that Carter "knew that leaders would exploit their meetings to try to enhance their own stature and that he would be subjected to criticism by traditionalists in the United States who believed you should never talk to your enemies." Through the entire Reagan era, Carter was marginalized by an adminis-tration that had kicked him out of office.

So it had to come as something of a surprise in December 1988, as the Reagan White House was turning into the Bush White House, that James Baker, Bush's choice to be secretary of state, stopped by Plains for a post-election visit. Carter quickly sensed that his status as outcast in Washington was changing. Bush and Baker had some specific goals in mind: in particular, they hoped to moderate U.S. policy in Latin Amer-ica, which had become politically polarized in the Reagan era. After years of bitter partisan bickering about the U.S. role in the region, Baker believed both parties in Congress could unite behind a reasonable U.S. push for democratic elections in Latin America, stepping away from po-litically unpopular support for right-wing juntas and counterproductive covert campaigns against leftist regimes. Unlike Reagan, who brushed Carter off, Bush and Baker were looking to him as an ally.

Carter was soon recalled to active duty. His mission: Panama City. During Reagan's last year in office, a federal grand jury had indicted Panamanian strongman Manuel Noriega on charges of drug trafficking. Reagan—and later Bush—gradually beefed up U.S. forces in the Canal Zone while tightening economic sanctions in hope of squeezing Noriega out of power. Those moves didn't budge the pockmarked general from his perch; within a few months of taking office, Bush quietly authorized covert support for Noriega's opponents—and waited for an opening.

It came in May 1989, when Carter and Ford volunteered to lead a group of international officials to monitor and observe the Panamanian elections. The bipartisan nature of the delegation gave the Bush team some useful cover for action in case the elections proved to be fraudulent. Bush, Baker, and Scowcroft, who was now Bush's NSC advisor, assumed—correctly, it would turn out—that Noriega couldn't win the election and would simply try to steal it. Carter flew down to Panama City on May 5 and met with Noriega soon after. Though the voting unfolded largely without incident on May 7, once the polls had closed, bands of armed goons fanned out to polling stations, stealing the tabulation sheets, and replacing the official results with fake counts of their own. Not long after, Noriega's murderous "dignity battalions" began to sweep the streets of dissenters, clubbing opposition candidates in Panama City and killing some of their supporters. Carter roamed the darkened countryside that night (the electricity had been shut off), checking in at polling stations while an independent count revealed that the opposition party led by Guillermo Endara had won. As it became clear that Noriega was stealing the vote, Carter phoned Noriega's headquarters, but was told the general was too busy to speak to him.

By now, Carter was angry that the election had been stolen, angry that Noriega was dodging him, and even angrier that he was using violence to cement the results on the street. Stopping at one tabulation center where vote tampering was obviously under way, Carter remonstrated in his rudimentary Spanish: "Are you honest or are you thieves?" And then he began to swing the spotlight on the fraud. Carter tried to call a press conference, but ran into Panamanian Defense Force regulars, complete with fixed bayonets, who proceeded to cordon off the former president and his aides in a conference center in downtown Panama City. Carter simply held his forty-five-minute press conference right there. "I hope there will be a worldwide outcry," he declared, "against a dictator who stole this election from his own people." As the session came to an end, one of Noriega's intelligence officers quietly warned a Carter aide that he needed to get his team and its famous leader out of town soon. As Carter's delegation departed a few hours later, Noriega's armored units moved into Panama City.

This was a gutsy performance by any measure. For most Americans, and much of the world, the verdict was clear and Carter had delivered it: Noriega was a tyrant and his elections were a charade. For the first time since he stepped down as president, Carter earned worldwide praise for making a hard and fast call at a tense and dangerous moment. (Nor had it gone unnoticed that Ford had skipped the messy election monitoring to attend a charity golf tournament.) The Bush White House was quite pleased with Carter's work; it helped to have a prominent former Democratic president on its side calling Noriega a tyrant. Within a few months, Bush would invade Panama and push Noriega from power.

The next stop was Nicaragua. In early 1989, Sandinista leader Daniel Ortega, as well as leaders of Nicaragua's opposition parties, invited Carter and the Carter Center to monitor their pending national elections. The Marxist Sandinistas had seized power in an armed revolt in the late 1970s and then resisted U.S.-backed revolts against their regime in the Reagan era. Now, in the late fall of 1989, Ortega was betting he was popular enough to try democracy. This was a huge gamble. And so, once again, Carter gathered a team of fifty observers, toured the country three times before the voting began, and worked behind the scenes to win the confidence of Ortega both in the event the Sandinistas won—and if they lost. Armed with a $500,000 grant from Congress, the Carter Center observers held seminars in how to hold an election and even staged a small-scale mock election as practice. Carter (as well as many independent pollsters) expected the Sandinistas to win, in part because the party controlled the nation's media outlets. Carter went so far as to predict it.

After almost ten years of trying unsuccessfully to overthrow the Sandinistas by force, Washington was ready for a different approach. Congress passed, and Bush signed, a measure to spend $9 million on get-out-the-vote campaigns. Bush also cut a deal with Democrats in Congress to continue aid for food and housing, as long as genuinely free elections were held. While it wasn't a unanimous sentiment, a thin majority in Washington was prepared to recognize the Sandinistas if they somehow managed to win.

In the weeks leading up to the February 1990 vote, Carter kept Bush, Baker, and Scowcroft apprised of developments on the ground. Carter also spent time preparing members of Congress for a Sandinista victory. Coming on the heels of Noriega's electoral theft, he argued, it was incumbent on Congress to honor the results if the Sandinistas managed to win one fair and square. And then he flew back to Managua to watch the vote come in.

But the voting did not unfold as expected. Carter's observers, divided into more than a dozen patrols and dispersed throughout Nicaragua, reported only minor voting problems on election day. But midway through the evening, a preliminary vote count by U.N. officials showed that Violeta Chamorro and her opposition National Opposition Union (UNO) party were on the verge of tossing Ortega and the Sandinistas from power. The margin appeared to be large—perhaps as much as fifteen points. If it held, it could add up to an upset that neither Ortega nor Carter had expected. The next question was obvious: would Ortega and the Sandinistas abide by the vote?

Carter left nothing to chance. With fellow observer Elliot Richardson, a former U.S. attorney general, he hastily arranged a meeting with Ortega to make sure the Sandinista leader understood the implications of the early count. Carter was uniquely qualified to speak plainly to Ortega on this score: his administration had recognized the Sandinistas when they first came to power in 1979 (at some political cost at home) and he'd later called on Ortega in his years out of office. He was as close to a real friend as the Sandinistas had in the United States. Arriving at party headquarters after midnight, Carter and Richardson found the ruling party bosses in despair, if not utter shock. Pressed by Carter to accept the inevitable, Ortega resisted. Then Carter spoke plainly: "I've won an election, Daniel. I've lost an election. I can tell you from my own experience that losing is not the end of the world." (This prompted Rosalynn Carter, who was also in attendance, to remark, "I thought it was the end of the world!") But Carter added: "Your greatest accomplishment as president will be if you lead a peaceful transition of power."

It takes at least two sides to play that game and so the Carters next called on UNO's Chamorro and made it clear to the incoming president that an orderly transition would not be helped by any sort of gloating victory remarks. Then, around 4 a.m., Carter called Baker back in Washington with a request that the secretary issue a no-Ortega-bashing order to government officials later that day. Carter, the aging fly fisherman, was trying to bring in a ten-pound fish on a five-pound test line. He knew who to call and what to say, and had the stature to say it.

Carter in Managua was one of the club's finest moments. While countless issues of security and personnel remained to be worked out over the weeks that followed, many of which Carter helped arrange, Ortega took Carter's advice. Chamorro was sworn in on April 15. When it was over, both Baker and Bush paid tribute to Carter for his role in the peaceful transfer of power, both at the time and later in their memoirs. For the first time since leaving office, Carter was earning a reputation as a wise man worthy of the name. By early 1990, an ABC/*Wall Street Journal* poll revealed that Carter's popularity among Americans nearly equaled that of Ronald Reagan.

"Carter is really quite easy to deal with," Baker said later. "He just wants to be useful. He never complains. But if you don't clearly spell out his assignment and then ride herd over him, then he can get in your way."

And that's exactly what happened next.

When Carter Went Rogue

The most delicate task of the Bush presidency was the high-stakes bid to expel Saddam Hussein from Kuwait. The United States was the world's clearly dominant military power; but the stability of the region and the security of the world's oil supplies required more than a unilateral response, and Bush set about assembling his unprecedented coalition and lining up support for an invasion if Saddam refused to retreat.

But Carter saw things differently. In late 1990, Carter secretly and repeatedly lobbied the United Nations Security Council and other foreign leaders to vote against a resolution, proposed by President Bush, authorizing the use of force to remove Saddam from Kuwait. Carter's little-known campaign to delay and perhaps even derail the 1991 Gulf War would remain a secret for several years and is one of the strangest chapters in club history, in part because Carter had worked so hard in 1989 and 1990 to develop the kind of working relationship with the Bush White House that he could never have had with Reagan. Bush put Carter back in business, gave him some jobs to do and some missions to execute. And then Carter turned around and threw it over the side.

Carter's behavior on Iraq was not merely coloring outside the lines. His performance, several former Bush advisors said later, bordered on treason.

The episode was all the more remarkable because it wasn't George Bush who declared, for all time, that an attack on one of the oil-rich states of the Persian Gulf would be treated as an attack on the United States. That president was Carter, who in his 1980 State of the Union address to Congress said, "An attempt by any outside force to gain control of the Persian Gulf region will be regarded as an assault on the vital interests of the United States of America, and such an assault will be repelled by any means necessary, including military force." It even had a name: the Carter Doctrine.

After Saddam overran Kuwait in August 1990, George Bush decided to make the Carter Doctrine stick. He appeared before reporters a few days after the invasion and said, "This will not stand," a remark that surprised even some of Bush's own top aides. Soon after, Bush asked Pentagon officers for an estimate of the number of troops it would take to eject the Iraqis; when the generals came back with a half million— what they thought would be a prohibitively high number—Bush coolly said, "Fine. Move 'em." The generals gulped. Meanwhile, Bush, Baker, and Scowcroft began to lay down a series of deadlines and timetables for Saddam to meet—or be forced out of Kuwait.

Not everyone in Washington realized just how serious Bush was. But Carter did and he recoiled. He believed that the invasion of Kuwait by Iraq could somehow have opened the door to a new round of Middle East peace talks between Israel and Egypt—unless the U.S. overreacted. But more importantly, Carter in general was opposed to the use of force to solve problems. That was what the Carter Center was all about and that was how he defined his post-presidency. Carter took his crusade for negotiations to the op-ed pages, fearful that a U.S. invasion would be bloody and upend decades of work in the region by the United States (and by Carter himself). These op-eds were curious documents: they dodged the central question of whether Saddam should be ejected from Kuwait by force—Carter seemed to think not, but he wouldn't exactly say—and called instead for talks to avert war, if not before the shooting started, then afterward to settle the peace.

But it is also clear that Carter completely misunderstood Bush's war *aims*; he assumed Bush would not be content to merely throw Saddam out of Kuwait but would instead chase him all the way to Baghdad. "There is little doubt that an attack on Iraq without further provocation from Saddam will erode US support in the Middle East," he argued in *Time* in mid-October. Maybe so, but Bush wasn't planning to invade Iraq; the remarkable coalition of thirty-two nations had been assembled solely to eject Saddam from Kuwait, and it was that very limited goal that enabled him to build such a broad alliance. In any case, the best that can be said about Carter's efforts in this period is that he meant well. He even held a conference in Atlanta on the Gulf crisis and how to avoid war through negotiations. Through October, Carter was dancing on the edge of opposition, but had not crossed over.

Then he did. In mid-November, in a personal letter to the leaders of the countries on the U.N. Security Council, Carter called for good-faith negotiations with Saddam Hussein. And then he secretly sent that letter to twelve *other* heads of state, hoping they would put pressure on the other four permanent members of the Security Council to put peace talks before military action. It was the second letter that was in some ways the most egregious because Carter was urging the allied nations to drop out of the U.S.-led coalition and give "unequivocal support" to an Arab League effort to resolve the conflict through talks.

"Recent statements from Washington and other national capitals make it increasingly clear that patience and persistence are being abandoned and that great pressures are being exerted for approval of a military solution to the present Gulf Crisis," he wrote. "History has shown that momentum of this kind is extremely difficult to reverse. Since armed intervention by forces of the United States and other nations is predicated on prior approval of the United Nations Security Council, your own decision can be a deciding factor in making this momentous judgment."

The meaning of the letter could not be clearer: a former president was lobbying foreign heads of state to work against a sitting U.S. president as war loomed.

Rather than alerting Bush in advance of his plans, Carter sent Bush a copy of the letter the day after he mailed it around the world and then couched it in a fashion that it might have seemed, as his biographer Douglas Brinkley noted later, that the letter was "written directly

Bush was a loyal Nixon protégé during the 1960s and 1970s, breaking with him only in the final days of Watergate. Once Bush became president in 1989, Nixon often seemed determined to undermine him. (*George Bush Presidential Library and Museum*)

Clinton received foreign policy advice from Nixon, usually in late-night telephone calls, that he described as hardheaded and matchless. Nixon told an aide that no other president had ever confided in him so completely. (*Courtesy William J. Clinton Library*)

RIGHT: During his visit to the White House residence in 1993, Nixon discussed with the Clintons both the challenges of raising daughters in the White House and passing health care reform. (*Courtesy William J. Clinton Library*)

LEFT: Clinton hosted three of the five living former presidents for a sleepover at the White House in October of 1993. Bush went to bed early and Ford preferred a hotel; Carter and Clinton stayed up late talking and mending fences. (*Courtesy William J. Clinton Library*)

BELOW: Ford (and to a lesser degree, Carter) secretly tried to help Clinton avoid impeachment and a trial in the Senate in 1997 and 1998. In 1999, Clinton awarded Ford the Presidential Medal of Freedom. (*Reuters/Win McNamee*)

George Herbert Walker Bush, pictured at Yale in 1947, with his son George W. Bush, age nine months. The father was sworn in at age sixty-four; the son, having closely followed in many of his father's footsteps, was sworn in at age fifty-four. (*George Bush Presidential Library and Museum*)

The younger Bush did not often talk about his father when he ran for president in 2000; when they met in the Oval Office on Inauguration Day in 2001, neither man could speak. (*Eric Draper, Courtesy of the George W. Bush Presidential Library*)

Four presidents gathered to celebrate the opening of the Clinton Library in November of 2004. Clinton and the elder Bush fell behind the main party during the tour; it was the beginning of a real friendship. (*Eric Draper, Courtesy of the George W. Bush Presidential Library*)

Bush and Clinton teamed up to help coordinate U.S. aid to Asian countries ravaged by the December 2005 tsunami, and later to assist Gulf coast states hit hard by hurricanes Katrina and Ike. (© *Gerald Herbert/Pool/Reuters/Corbis*)

The friendship between Bush and Clinton, shown here in 2005, was a rare display of bipartisanship in an era when the United States was deeply divided about politics. Bush even said that he might have been the father Clinton never had. (*Associated Press*)

Born just forty-four days apart, Bush and Clinton struck up a friendship long before they joined forces on Haiti in 2010. Bush appreciated the way Clinton had treated his father; Clinton respected Bush's skills as a politician. (*Associated Press*)

Bush invited Carter, Clinton, and his father to have lunch with incoming president Obama in January of 2009. The four men warned the Club newcomer that living in the White House was hard on parents and children. (*Associated Press*)

RIGHT: As a candidate, Obama criticized many of Bush's national security policies; as president, he adopted a number of them. The two men reunited at the ten-year anniversary of the 9/11 attacks in New York City. (*Associated Press*)

BELOW: Obama welcomed Bush and Clinton back to the White House before the two men took charge of coordinating U.S. aid to Haiti. By the winter of 2012, they had raised more than $50 million for Haitian relief. (© *Brooks Kraft/Corbis*)

and only" for Bush when in fact Carter had already distributed his views widely.

Even in his worst post-presidential mischief, Nixon had never gone this far. Nixon may have differed with Reagan about arms control strategy, and opposed Bush's gentle handling of Gorbachev, but he made his arguments in public and always kept a line to the Oval Office open. And Nixon's arguments were largely academic differences about the shape and size of foreign aid levels and what sort of concessions Washington might make in arms control talks. Carter, by comparison, had gone operational: he had mounted a lobbying campaign in the run-up to a war in which the United States had organized and was leading a global coalition.

Given the distribution list, it is unlikely that Carter intended his gambit to remain a secret for very long. After Canadian prime minister Brian Mulroney called Pentagon chief Dick Cheney and read him Carter's letter word for word, the White House came unhinged. Bush was privately furious. Scowcroft told Carter through back channels to cease and desist. Decades later, top Bush officials still complained that Carter's actions were tantamount to treason, a probable violation of the 1799 Logan Act, which made it a crime for any private citizen to try to conduct U.S. foreign policy without proper authority from the U.S. government. "He heard from us," Scowcroft recalled, still a bit amazed. "I recognized his right to speak out," Bush said later. "What I violently disagreed with was his writing to heads of foreign governments, urging them to stand against what we were trying to do in the UN." If Carter ever apologized for his action, there is little evidence of it. On the contrary, when we asked him years later if he would do the same all over again, Carter quickly replied, "Yes, I would because I sent exactly the same letter to President Bush as I did to the other members of the Security Council, and I just expressed my opinion that the war was not necessary. Because I knew from my own sources that the Iraqis were willing to withdraw from occupied territory and then pay reparations and so forth, but that's ancient history."

But Carter did not stop with the letter to the Security Council. In January, just days before the deadline set by Bush for Saddam to withdraw from Kuwait or face air strikes, Carter wrote Egypt's Hosni Mubarak, Saudi Arabia's King Fahd, and Syria's Hafez al-Assad (all of whom were

members of Bush's anti-Saddam coalition) urging each to "call publicly
for a delay in the use of force while Arab leaders seek a peaceful solution
to the crisis." This last-minute move was never designed to become public; it was a one-man end run around U.S. foreign policy. In fact, in an especially divisive suggestion, he informed his counterparts that U.S. voters
might in some way support his personal search for peace. "You may have
to forego approval from the White House, but you will find the French,
Soviets and others fully supportive. Also, most Americans will welcome
such a move." And unlike the letter of a few months before, there is no
evidence that Carter ever told the White House about it.

Why had Carter done it? What made him take matters in his own
hands in such a dramatic and furtive fashion? Those who have known
him longest say it is a combination of factors even beyond his deep aver-
sion to violence; a personal faith that the Middle East was a province
only he understood clearly; and the fact that he didn't really care what
anyone else thought. Perhaps the most remarkable thing about the entire
episode was not that it happened but that it remained a club secret for
years. Despite the fact that his letters had been sent around the world
and to the White House itself, word of Carter's insurrection was not
made public until three years later, when the *New York Times* disclosed
the story. His last-minute plea to Arab leaders on behalf of peace would
remain largely unknown until Brinkley unearthed it. Though the Bush
White House believed that Carter had committed an unpardonable sin,
it was not in the administration's interest to disclose Carter's strange maneuvering in the midst of a national mobilization. Besides, leaking word
of Carter's behavior would itself have been a violation of the club's genteel rule against intra-member warfare. Instead, Bush aides took more
punitive but discreet action: they simply cut Carter out of future foreign
policy partnerships. There would be no more teaming up on overseas hot
spots or elections; Carter's requests for aircraft and other assistance now
went unanswered by Baker's State Department. Unable to trust Carter,
the Bush team discarded him as an ally.

He would have to wait until someone else became commander in
chief.

SIX PRESIDENTS:

The Golden Age of the Club

——————— ⚷ ———————

Bill Clinton was lucky in many ways; but when it came to former presidents, he won the lottery.

When he was elected president, he had five former commanders in chief at his disposal: Nixon, Ford, Carter, Reagan, and Bush, the most of any president in the twentieth century. Not all of them had been helpful to one another, in or out of office. But some combination of his charm, their needs, and the new global challenges of the post–Cold War age allowed Clinton to deploy nearly all to his advantage—especially, as it turned out, the Republicans.

Clinton studied their personalities and presidencies closely; he wanted to know more about each of them. When he invited the entire club to breakfast during the fall of his first year, he had an aide find out the last time that had happened (answer: never). And in turn, the veterans wanted to meet the new boy, were curious about his instincts, eager for his attention, and in need of help for the missions and projects that kept their retirements interesting. He'd turn out to have the least rapport with the one with whom he had the most in common. Clinton shared with Carter, his fellow Southern Baptist political prodigy, a colorful mother, a strong-willed wife, and deep roots in the loamy soil of pragmatic liberalism. Clinton began his political life as a Carter man; but by the time he had become a once and future Arkansas governor, he felt Carter had betrayed him, and so had little compunction about ignoring him completely as he made his own bid for the White House. As he had before with Bush, Carter would prove to Clinton just how useful, and how enraging, a former president could be.

The Republicans, on the other hand, were more valuable assets. Reagan would fade quickly from view during Clinton's first term, but not before he taught the young president a lesson. Clinton turned to Ford for help in escaping Washington— and later to elude a trial by the Senate. He marveled at, and later modeled himself after, George Herbert Walker Bush. Most improbably of all, Clinton found in Nixon a welcome tutor and a helpful confessor.

And when Nixon died, Clinton likened the loss to that of his mother.

20

"The Guy Knows How the Game Is Played"

— RICHARD NIXON

Fate and modern medicine conspired to make January 20, 1993, a milestone in the annals of the club. For the first time since Lincoln's inauguration in 1861, five former presidents were alive to see the swearing in of a sixth.

The five—Nixon, Ford, Carter, Reagan, and Bush—represented twenty-four years in the Oval Office. This historic expansion in club membership was chiefly the result of presidents getting elected younger, being thrown out of office faster, and then living much longer than their nineteenth- and twentieth-century counterparts. But as a quintet, they were particularly distinctive. Except for Reagan, all had left the White House under unhappy circumstances: Nixon resigned; Ford was defeated after two years; Carter and Bush were rejected after one term. Nixon spent twenty years in retirement, Ford more than twenty-five, and Carter is likely to become the longest-living former president in history (he is set to surpass Herbert Hoover, who spent thirty-one years in retirement before dying in 1964). Nixon, the thirty-seventh president, was elected to Congress in 1946, the same year that Clinton, the forty-second president, was born.

As Clinton took the oath, he had the club on his side. All his predecessors had pledged to be helpful; several secretly wanted to be recruited;

and one had solemnly vowed to do no harm—provided Clinton played by the rules.

The Golden Age of the club had begun.

Two months earlier, on November 18, Bill Clinton paid a courtesy call on George Bush at the White House during a quick, thirty-six-hour visit to Washington.

Bush had taken the defeat very hard. His aides told him, right up until election day itself, that the race was close and that he'd probably squeak by. He told himself that voters would never dismiss all his experience as president and opt for someone so much younger and of such different bearing and character. Neither hunch turned out to be right.

On the evening of his defeat, Bush stayed up well past midnight, writing in his diary that it "hurt, hurt, hurt and I guess it's the pride, too. . . . On a competitive basis I don't like to see the pollsters right at the end; I don't like to see the pundits right; and I don't like to see all of those who have written me off right. I was absolutely convinced we would prove them wrong but I was wrong and they were right and that hurts a lot. . . . Now to bed, prepared to face tomorrow: Be strong, be kind, be generous of spirit, be understanding and let people know how grateful you are. Don't get even. Comfort the ones I've hurt and let down. Say your prayers and ask for God's understanding and strength. Finish with a smile and some gusto and do what's right and finish strong."

Clinton came by to visit two weeks later. The presidents huddled in the Oval Office for close to two hours, sitting in wing chairs by the fireplace and talking mostly about foreign affairs. "Yugoslavia, Kosovo, Serbia and Bosnia," Bush recalled. "I told him I thought that was mostly likely to be the prime trouble spot." Bush also told Clinton he felt the same sense of excitement and wonder at the end of the four years as he had on the first day. But he was already preparing for life after the White House. He had made plans to build a new house in Houston and was dabbling more with personal computers. He chose a self-mocking email username and shared it only with his closest friends: "former leader of the free world." As Clinton prepared to leave, Bush offered a benediction. "Bill, I want to tell you something. When I leave here, you're going to have no trouble from me. The campaign is over, it was tough and I'm out of here. I will do nothing to complicate your work and I just want you to know that."

Bush kept his promise. One day, Clinton would return the favor.

• • •

The very next morning, on November 19, 1992, a peculiar valentine appeared on the op-ed page of the *New York Times*.

"President Elect Bill Clinton deserves high marks for aggressively addressing a number of important issues during the transition period," it began, a pretty watery compliment given the fact that the transition was barely two weeks old. "But as was the case during the campaign, the most important issue since the end of World War Two has received minimal attention."

The rest of Richard Nixon's essay went on at some length about how Boris Yeltsin's government was in "mortal danger" and needed an infusion of Western aid. But the sorry state of U.S.-Russian relations wasn't the reason Nixon wrote the op-ed; the sorry state of Nixon-Clinton relations was.

Nixon wanted the new president's ear. And despite its mostly positive tone, Nixon's *Times* essay was actually the second stage of one of his trademark good cop/bad cop routines. The thirty-seventh president had already sent Clinton a handwritten letter on the morning after the election, in which he congratulated Clinton on his win, calling it "one of the best" in memory and giving a special "never-give-up" shout-out to Clinton for overcoming doubts about his Arkansas background and character as he won the White House. Nixon promised to be a help and not a hindrance to the forty-second president, and stroked him to the point that Nixon apologized to his research assistant Monica Crowley for laying the frosting on a little thick. "The guy's got a big ego," Nixon said, "and you gotta flatter the hell out of him if you are going to get anywhere."

But the secret, morning-after letter had produced no reply. Frustrated and angry, Nixon decided to escalate things a step or two. He wrote the *Times* op-ed in mid-November as a kind of friendly shot across Clinton's bow, one that was designed to say, "if you don't get back to me in private, we can have this conversation in public if you prefer."

Nixon wanted a back channel to a new president. And he would get it, one way or another.

Eight days after the *Times* op-ed, Clinton's motorcade pulled up to the Century City skyscraper in Los Angeles where Ronald Reagan had his post-presidential office. Clinton was spending a few days in town with friends and had sent word to Reagan, now eighty-one years old, that he wanted to stop by and chat.

A meeting was quickly arranged. The two men were thirty-five years and a world apart in outlook, a gap nearly as great as the forty-three years that had separated Herbert Hoover and John F. Kennedy when they met four decades before. Reagan had met Clinton before, in the White House, when Clinton attended a reception for the governors with his wife, Hillary. But the seventy minutes the two men spent in L.A. were historic. They talked about the need for a line item veto and how to hold down spending. And then Reagan offered Clinton two vital pieces of advice. First, he said, get out of Washington every weekend you can and make thorough use of Camp David. The fresh air, the chance to freely roam the complex's roughly 150 acres, even the brief time away from Washington, Reagan told Clinton, were all good for body and soul.

That piece of advice was predictable. The other was not. Clinton, Reagan insisted, needed to learn how to salute. The older man had noticed during the campaign that Clinton didn't have any idea how to execute a proper military greeting. As commander in chief, Reagan suggested, Clinton would need a good, crisp up-and-down slash of the hand to get the job done right.

This was not strictly true. Until Reagan came along and made it part of the role, U.S. presidents rarely, if ever, saluted men in uniform. Uniformed personnel are required to salute the president but not the other way around. As president, Reagan had been concerned enough about his preference for returning salutes that he consulted ahead of time with the Marine commandant to make sure there was no formal reason that he could not repay the gesture to the men who stood like stone griffins at the feet of the Marine One and Air Force One stairways. The general told Reagan he could do pretty much whatever he liked when it came to saluting people, regardless of what tradition dictated or what his predecessors had done. And so Reagan, astute in all ways a president performed his role, started doing it.

It helped that Reagan knew how to salute, both as a former Army cavalry officer and a former actor who played one in the movies. The trick was pacing, he told Clinton. Soldiers liked to bring the hand up slowly, as if dripping with honey, and then shake it off briskly, as if it were covered with something less pleasant. Clinton, having never served in uniform (and having spent a small portion of his campaign explaining his youthful draft evasion), was more than ready to hear Reagan's message.

And so the eighty-one-year-old Reagan proceeded to give the forty-six-year-old Clinton a private tutorial. The two men stood there in Reagan's L.A. office, thirty-four floors above Beverly Hills, perfecting their salutes.

When the lesson was over, Reagan rewarded Clinton with a jar of red, white, and blue jelly beans, explaining that they had prevented him from becoming a nicotine addict. Clinton thanked him, shook hands, and headed downstairs to his car. Clinton later spent time practicing his salutes with aides who had served in the military—and some who had not. The jelly beans remained in Clinton's office for the next eight years.

The Club Gets a Crush

A month later, by January 1993, Nixon had tried everything short of voodoo to get Clinton's attention. He'd done the private letter. He'd unleashed his flirty op-ed piece. He pressed his former aide Roger Stone to make contact with Clinton types who could push the president to call the old man in New Jersey. When all that yielded nothing, Nixon asked Dick Morris, a Clinton advisor, to make some calls and get it done. Still nothing. Stone, an old Nixon hand, kept at it, pressing longtime Democratic sachem Tony Coelho to put in a good word, implying that Nixon was about to come unglued. Finally, Stone made contact with White House speechwriter Paul Begala. Nixon, Stone said, was drafting another op-ed piece that, depending on whether Clinton picked up the phone, could be friendly or hostile. Begala managed to get a memo about Nixon's desperation in front of the president. Word came back: Clinton would call.

Nixon, now eighty, was in a hurry. He was scheduled to make his ninth trip to Russia in early February and desperately wanted Clinton's blessing before he departed; such things gave him added maneuvering room overseas, of course, but also guaranteed a second hearing when the trip was over. Foreign policy advisor Dimitri Simes put in a call to Strobe Talbott, Clinton's new point man on the former Soviet Union, and asked: might they meet before the trip? Certainly, Talbott replied.

Talbott and Nixon went back a few years. As *Time*'s Washington bureau chief in the mid-1980s and later as the magazine's editor at large, Talbott had interviewed Nixon several times in the Reagan and Bush eras—interviews that usually turned on U.S.-Soviet relations or foreign policy. He was also part of an irregular group of reporters—most of whom were too young to have covered Watergate—who received occasional invitations to dine off the record with the Sage of Saddle River. Talbott understood that Nixon's private hospitality and his public obsession with U.S.-Russian relations were part of an elaborate rehabilitation scheme, designed to blur lingering memories of Watergate while serving as a reminder of his own, widely praised foreign policy accomplishments when he was president.

So when he and NSC aide Toby Gati finally turned up at Nixon's hotel on March 4, 1993, Talbott knew exactly what was about to unfold. It was "an encounter that was awkward bordering on weird," Talbott recalled in his memoirs. "Nixon opened with five minutes of stilted bonhomie laced with phony compliments and strained jokes, followed by a 30 minute lecture that was carefully prepared, artfully crafted, substantively dense and delivered as though Toby and I were an auditorium, full of people whose hostility Nixon took for granted but whose views he was sure he could influence by the sheer force of his experience, intelligence and—his favorite word—hard headedness."

Nixon was certainly unplugged. At times, his language was coarse; he called the leaders of the G7 nations "assholes" for shortchanging Russian aid; he repeatedly referred to Yeltsin as "Yelstin." Talbott told Nixon that the new administration supported his upcoming trip and wanted to hear more when he returned. Nixon made it clear he was keen to help Yeltsin, despite the Russian's well-known tendency to drink too much and speak too expansively. Finally, Nixon urged Talbott not to make the same mistake that Bush and his team had made when it came to the club. Translation: take me seriously. After an hour, Talbott and Gati thanked Nixon for his advice and departed. That night, Talbott reported the gist of the conversation to Clinton, who had dropped by Talbott's Calvert Street home for dinner. Clinton needed no convincing when it came to boosting aid to Yeltsin. "He's preaching to the converted," Clinton said. "In fact, he's preaching to the preacher."

Nixon left for Russia on February 7. He spent two weeks in the region and even from Moscow continued to sound the don't-ignore-Boris alarm. Foreign and domestic policy, he told the *New York Times*'s Moscow correspondent, were indivisible. "Separate them and they die," he warned a faraway White House. Without further aid to Russia, "you can kiss the peace dividend goodbye."

Nixon returned home on February 23 and waited by the phone. When several days passed without a word from the White House, he unsheathed his pen and began writing another *New York Times* op-ed piece. But before he could send it in, Clinton called. A White House operator telephoned on March 3 asking Nixon to stand by for the president. Five minutes passed. Then another eight. Then the operator came back on to apologize: Clinton could not be found. "I'll wait," Nixon replied. "He's a helluva lot busier than I am." Just after ten, the White House called again and this time Clinton came on the line.

The conversation swept Nixon off his feet. The two men talked for forty minutes that night and the policy was just the appetizer. They discussed Russia and the Chinese economy, as well as defense spending at home. Nixon delivered a report on his trip and his assessment of Yeltsin (upshot: wounded but salvageable) and Clinton told Nixon he admired Yeltsin's nerve. They talked of the approaching U.S.-Russia summit in Vancouver, scheduled in April. "Will he last?" Clinton wanted to know of Yeltsin. Yes, Nixon assured him.

Nixon was impressed by the substance of the conversation, but he was astonished by what came next. A president he had never met, the leader of the opposite party, a man nearly half his age, seemed to take him completely into his confidence. It was like alchemy, Nixon thought, an almost instant partnership that comes when two men have sat at the big desk. And yet Jerry Ford had never talked to him this way, nor Reagan, nor Bush. And Nixon had the sense that Clinton *needed* to talk. There are some questions that no one else can answer, and Clinton began asking them: How did *you* do this job? What is the best way to organize your day? Clinton gave Nixon the hour-by-hour breakdown of his daily work schedule—how he rose early, jogged, ate breakfast with his daughter, and then worked through the day until retiring around eleven—in order to ask Nixon if his routine was typical for a president. This exchange delighted Nixon; he had harbored a similar curiosity some forty years earlier as he watched Eisenhower in the job. "You want to know," he recalled, after his exchange with Clinton, "if you are doing it right." As he recounted the conversation the following morning, Nixon was still impressed. "He was very respectful with no sickening bullshit," Nixon said. Best of all, Clinton invited him to the White House on March 8.

And for that meeting, Nixon prepared like a grad student before his oral exams. He made notes, aligning his arguments and his evidence just as he had for the session with Talbott and Gati. He knew, he told Crowley, how he wanted to "structure" the conversation with Clinton.

And the White House knew how it wanted to structure the conversation as well. White House aides didn't go out of their way to boast about the meeting, but they didn't try to hide it either. Clinton aides brought Nixon in and out by a side door, divulging both the meeting and the earlier phone call in the course of regular press briefings. Nixon was under no illusion about Clinton's game. He guessed that a young Democratic president with virtually no foreign policy experience calculated that he could only be helped if he was occasionally seen consulting a president with a black belt in diplomacy. But Nixon didn't care. He was thrilled to be back in the loop. And just in case the larger world somehow missed the development, he leaked word of the late-night call to his old friend Bill Safire, who wrote a *New York Times* column that appeared on the very morning of their March 8 meeting.

As he stepped off the private elevator and out into the second-floor residence that afternoon, Nixon was met by Hillary and Chelsea Clinton. Nixon found Hillary a little unnerving—she had worked on the House Judiciary staff charged with preparing the impeachment case against him nineteen years earlier—and so that day he was all charm. He reminded the first lady that he was raised as a Quaker and that his own daughters, Julie and Tricia, had also attended Sidwell Friends, where Chelsea was in school. Trying to bond over the one thing he knew Hillary cared most about, he said, "You know I tried to fix the health care system more than twenty years ago. It has to be done sometime."

"I know," Hillary replied, stroking him right back. "And we'd be better off today if your proposal had succeeded."

When the two presidents finally sat down, alone, over Diet Cokes,

Nixon did most of the talking. He told Clinton that how he managed Russia would matter far more to history than how he managed the economy (an unlikely but provocative thesis). He urged the president to press Congress for more aid to Russia and to recruit top American business leaders to lobby lawmakers for that aid as well. Nixon urged Clinton to be tactical as well as strategic; there were many ways to help Yeltsin succeed, he said. U.S. pipeline builders, for example, could boost the performance of key Russian natural gas pipelines if more American aid was authorized. That would help Yeltsin too.

Then Nixon suggested that Clinton consider the past before moving forward. LBJ and Carter lost control of their presidencies, he said, because of foreign policy failures. If Clinton failed to meet this challenge, his presidency might end prematurely as well. This was a lopsided comparison; it was never clear that the challenge of helping Russia modernize in the 1990s was as existential a threat to Clinton as Vietnam or Iran had been to LBJ or Carter. But it was on the Washington-Moscow axis that Nixon had made his mark as president and it served his larger purpose to make his stand there in his twilight years.

Clinton paid Nixon the compliment of not trying to flatter him. What Clinton liked most about Nixon's advice was that it was well prepared, tough-minded, and as far as he could tell did not carry some hidden agenda beyond Nixon's personal need for redemption, which Clinton could weigh well enough for himself. Nixon, Clinton realized, had a rare ability to see past the minor worries and considerations that often dominated foreign policy debates and take the long view.

Clinton told enough people that he found Nixon's advice helpful that word of his appreciation made its way quickly back to New Jersey. Democratic Party wise man Bob Strauss told Nixon that Clinton said that it had been the best conversation he had had with any former president. In public, Clinton praised Nixon—at least on Russia policy. "We are pretty much on the same wavelength, and we have been pretty much on the same wavelength on this issue for more than a year now." And Nixon paid him right back. "I think Clinton is making a gutsy call, really the mark of a leader," he told *Time* a few weeks later, speaking about Russian aid.

But apart from the theatrics, Clinton genuinely appreciated Nixon's help. Soon after, he sent Nixon an autographed snapshot of their meeting and in an attached note asked for one in return. Nixon complied, sending a photograph to Washington turning his inscription into an odd joke, thanking Clinton for his help with "aid to China." "It was," one Clinton aide recalled, "something of a mutual admiration society." A few weeks later, the White House released a single picture of the Clinton-Nixon conversation.

It was—what else could you call it?—a Nixon-to-China moment: though Nixon's own Republican contemporaries had treated him like something of a pariah, the much younger Democratic president was embracing him like a long-lost uncle. Clinton called his new friend on March 24 and again Nixon marveled at Clinton's confiding nature. This time, the two men had a more detailed conversation about how to handle Yeltsin in Vancouver. Clinton was now cramming for his early-April summit and wanted to know if Nixon thought he should consult Henry Kissinger in advance as well. Nixon instead urged him to talk to Brent Scowcroft, but he gave Clinton a tip: when seeking advice from people who are more experienced than you, Nixon urged, tell them what you plan to do first—and then ask for their reaction. Don't ask for advice and then ignore it. That way, Nixon coached, you save on bruised feelings. The détente continued as Nixon prepared to leave for China in early April and Clinton's national security advisor, Tony Lake, phoned Nixon with a few messages to deliver to the Chinese leadership. At a refueling stop in Alaska, Nixon tuned in to the news from Vancouver to see how his new protégé was doing.

In late April, after Nixon returned, Clinton called once more, this time to discuss the worsening situation in the Balkans. Before signing off, Clinton told Nixon he wanted to talk about China soon. That tease, Nixon guessed, was designed to keep Nixon thinking he was indispensable—at least, for a while longer. "The guy knows how the game is played," Nixon remarked.

The Club Strikes Back

Monica Crowley's extensive accounts about her years at Nixon's side during this period make it clear that Nixon's appreciation for Clinton was never unalloyed. Whatever satisfaction Nixon felt for finally winning

Clinton's ear on Russia or China or Bosnia, he was routinely dismayed by many of Clinton's personnel choices, domestic priorities, and what Nixon saw as the president's decision to virtually share power with his wife. He admired Clinton's brains, his guts, his confidence, and surely his energy. But he disliked, at least as Crowley related his remarks, his sloppiness and his reliance on multilateral solutions; and he distrusted his youth. Nixon also found Clinton graceless: he noticed during his White House meeting that Clinton had not inquired after his wife, Pat, who was suffering from lung cancer.

Human nature makes it easy to root both for, and against, someone who comes along to do the job you once held. But at times, an element of competition seemed to have Nixon by the throat. After returning from China in late April, for example, Nixon remarked several times that he never enjoyed the kind of favorable press coverage that Clinton did—a comment Clinton would have found amusing given that his own press clips were withering during his first year in office. Nixon also complained that late-night comics continued to make fun of him decades after he left the White House—but seemed to give Clinton a pass. Presidents, even when they get some things right, never cease to be punch lines, and it was telling that Nixon regarded his comic potential as a metric for comparing himself to his successors.

On June 22, Pat Nixon passed away at the age of eighty-one. Clinton phoned his condolences in an awkward call later that day. Both Clinton and his wife skipped the funeral in California. Instead, he issued a statement and sent his old friend Vernon Jordan, who carried a personal letter of sympathy from one president to another. Crowley recorded that Nixon "exploded" at Clinton's absence after the funeral service.

But if Clinton was distracted, it was in part because he had a more pressing club problem: someone had tried to kill one of its members.

A few weeks earlier on April 14, former president George Bush and his wife, Barbara, along with former secretary of state James Baker, former secretary of the treasury Nicholas Brady, and former White House chief of staff John Sununu, visited Kuwait to take part in a celebration of the allied invasion two years before that had driven Iraqi forces under Saddam Hussein out of the country. A few weeks afterward, Kuwaiti authorities informed their U.S. counterparts that they had uncovered a plot to kill Bush and captured a Toyota Land Cruiser carrying 180 pounds of explosives in its door frames, along with detonators and timers. They had arrested fourteen men and charged them with conspiracy to assassinate Bush by detonating a car bomb. U.S. officials sent CIA and FBI investigators to find out who was behind the plot, though they could well have guessed the source. One of the plotters cooperated with investigators and on June 24, two days after Pat's death, FBI officials informed Clinton that they had traced the evidence back to Saddam's intelligence ministry.

The next question was what to do about it. The politics were not complicated: an attack on any American overseas was unacceptable and merited a response; a premeditated attack on a former president was outrageous and required one. But what response, exactly? Attempting to kill a sitting president might justify a full-bore declaration of war; but what is the commensurate response for trying to kill a former president? The United States was still in a half war with Iraq: the U.S. Air Force and Navy maintained a no fly zone over most of the country and had to routinely destroy Iraq's antiaircraft radars to keep the skies clear.

But the attempt on Bush's life was a far bolder assault against American sovereignty than anything Iraq had done since the end of the Gulf War. A more dramatic response was required and other forces may have fueled Clinton's need to respond. Sheer inexperience, bad luck, and almost nonstop internal second-guessing lent Clinton's first six months in office a chaotic, amateurish quality. Clinton had an excellent cabinet but a weak White House staff, which struggled to keep up with events, expectations, and an unforgiving press corps. He suffered a heart-stopping twenty-point drop in the polls in June, overhauled his staff, and brought in David Gergen, a former aide to Nixon, Ford, and Reagan, to steady his listing West Wing. *Time*'s cover on June 7 summed up the problem: *The Incredible Shrinking President.*

Clinton met with his advisors on June 24, to review the evidence from Kuwait as well as his options. There was general agreement among Clinton's aides for a coordinated cruise missile attack on the government ministry that had hatched the plot. Clinton and his team discussed the best time for an attack and how to explain it to the public. Secretary of State Warren Christopher identified the only yardstick that mattered: "You'll be judged on whether you hit the target." Clinton signed the orders; the attack would come in forty-eight hours.

As the president prepared to address the nation two days later, he made a few calls to alert key foreign leaders and then phoned Bush himself. An unusual exchange followed: here was Clinton, an embattled young president who defeated the Prospero of the Gulf War just the year before, calling to explain why he couldn't let an attempt on Bush's life go unanswered. The impending U.S. attack would be Clinton's first use of military force as president; he wasn't merely informing his predecessor of his decision; he was seeking his advice.

And perhaps, in a way, his consent. As Clinton's advisor George Stephanopoulos recalled it, Clinton said, "We completed our investigation. Both the CIA and the FBI did an excellent job. It was directed against you. I've ordered a cruise missile attack." Stephanopoulos recalled that Bush seemed to be concerned most about the possibility of collateral damage in Baghdad, and Clinton assured him that the United States was taking every precaution. "I think he thinks we are doing the right thing," Clinton said when the conversation ended. "Thought it was a tough call."

Clinton dispatched Christopher to Maine to brief Bush in person. That was in part to seal the deal with Bush. In his memoirs, Stephanopoulos tried to capture the implicit transaction between Bush and Clinton at this unprecedented moment. "Clinton wanted and needed Bush's approval as much as Bush needed—although he may not have wanted—Clinton's protection. Bush may have been the only man in the country, with the possible exception of Colin Powell, who could have single-handedly stopped the attack. All it would take is a well-placed leak to the press or a sotto voce call from Brent Scowcroft to Tony Lake. The message would suggest, perhaps, that Bush would publicly criticize Clinton for a hollow, opportunist gesture—a hasty retaliation, based on shaky evidence—that was more about propping up Clinton's political fortunes than punishing Saddam Hussein. But that wasn't Bush's style. Whatever made him diffident at the prospect of having a military strike ordered in his defense, he kept to himself. Presidents, especially gentlemen presidents, didn't do that to each other."

On June 26, the U.S. Navy launched twenty-three Tomahawk cruise missiles, nine from a destroyer in the Red Sea and fourteen from a cruiser in the Persian Gulf, at the Iraqi intelligence services headquarters in Baghdad. The raid was only a partial success: the missiles destroyed a section of the building but three of the missiles missed their target and landed in a residential neighborhood, killing eight and wounding twelve. The news broke early on a perfect midsummer Saturday evening in Washington; reporters turned up at the briefing room near dusk to hear the president announce the first military strike of his presidency: "From the first days of our Revolution," Clinton said, "American security has depended on this phrase: Don't tread on me."

Nine years later, another president, George W. Bush, launched a war that led to the overthrow, capture, and eventually the execution of Saddam Hussein—the man he once referred to as "the one who tried to kill my dad."

A Vacation . . . and a Sleepover

A few weeks later, Gerald Ford invited Clinton, his wife, and his daughter to Vail for a few days of R & R. Ford barely knew Clinton. But he knew that Clinton's daughter, Chelsea, a budding ballerina, wanted to take part in the Bolshoi Academy, which was in residence in Vail that summer. So he invited Chelsea and her parents to join him for a weekend.

Ford arranged for the first family to stay a few doors down from his own mountainside house. The two presidents played golf by day and then had dinner each night with their families. However brief, the few days in Colorado were the first real vacation Clinton had taken during his first seven months in office. Ford was enchanted by Chelsea and charmed by Hillary, the Republican-turned-Democrat who regaled Ford with stories about her formative days as a Goldwater Girl in Illinois. Hillary presented Ford with a framed copy of a photograph of her standing between Ford and former congressman Melvin Laird when she was a college intern on Capitol Hill. (The original photo was one of Hillary's father's proudest possessions; it had still been hanging in his bedroom when he died just a few months before.) When she gave Ford a copy, Hillary apologized for having "strayed from the fold."

Ford was touched by the gift and sent it to his own presidential library. After attending a performance of the Bolshoi on the first night, Ford and Hillary danced together at a tented, post-ballet reception while a band played "New York, New York."

• • •

Ford was struck—dazzled might be a better word—during the two-day break by Clinton's political skills, and he would liken him in conversations with friends to an evangelist, a Chautauqua charmer, and the ultimate salesman. He found Clinton much more affable than he expected and much more persuasive as well. He could see that Clinton was more sure-footed on domestic affairs than foreign policy though he wasn't sure what, if anything, Clinton really believed in. The new president, Ford said later, "moves in, seduces everybody and then starts to compromise his position based on the pressures that he gets politically and otherwise. . . . This guy can sell three day old ice."

But if Ford admired some of Clinton's political talents, he was alarmed by what he saw of his golf game. The forty-second president's habit of repeated mulligans and outrageous gimme putts unnerved and even upset the thirty-eighth president. Locals as well as reporters hovered nearby as Clinton, dressed in a blue golf shirt, beige slacks, and a panama hat, hooked drives, missed putts, was swallowed by sand traps, and sometimes voiced his frustration ("Owww, you idiot!") as part of a foursome of Ford, Jack Nicklaus, and Enron chairman Ken Lay. At the end of the first day of golf together, the First Duffer proclaimed, "That was great; let's do it again tomorrow." Ford wasn't sure that was such a great idea.

Asked about the conspicuously bipartisan nature of his golf quartet, Clinton remarked from his cart, "It's the way I'm going to try and run the rest of my administration. I don't ever want the kind of polarization we had the last six months." His host was more circumspect: "We've got a few things," Ford said, "where we have similar views."

One of those things was free trade. In late summer, Clinton invited all five former presidents to join him at the White House for a pep rally to support the North American Free Trade Agreement, launched by Bush but now languishing in the Congress.

But with Clinton things are never simple, and so the invitation had two parts. Clinton wanted the former presidents to join him on the South Lawn on the first day for the signing of a Middle East peace treaty between Yassir Arafat and Yitzhak Rabin, sleep over that night in the White House, and then join him for a NAFTA booster event the next day.

Nixon, who was still sore at Clinton's missing Pat's funeral, declined. Reagan was limiting his appearances with the onset of Alzheimer's. Ford and Carter agreed to participate. But what about Bush? It had been less than a year since Clinton had won the election and White House officials worried it might be too soon to ask for a favor. It was easier for Kennedy to tap Eisenhower, who had retired with honors after two terms, than for Clinton to invite a man he had defeated back into the fray after eight months. And so chief of staff Mack McLarty checked with former secretary of state James Baker first, just to be sure an invitation wouldn't upset the former president. Baker guessed that Bush would rise to the challenge and when McLarty finally called, Bush quickly agreed. Somewhat to Clinton's surprise, Bush agreed to stay overnight in the White House. So did Carter. Ford begged off, staying at a downtown hotel.

The next morning, when the presidents met for breakfast, Clinton told his guests they were making history over bacon and eggs: it was the only time four presidents had dined together at the White House. The conversation dragged until someone brought up Ross Perot, who had emerged that summer as the leading opponent to the NAFTA treaty. And then the four presidents went around the table, one after the other, criticizing the Texas industrialist. The club contest for who disliked Perot the most was spirited: Ford said he regarded Perot as a fraud, who sought and won government contracts and then turned around and pretended to be a spokesman for free enterprise. Carter, who had dismissed Perot as a demagogue, recalled how Perot had stoked the fever to rescue the Iranian hostages in the late 1970s without understanding the risks. Clinton insisted later that he had remained relatively quiet during the breakfast but, of the four, no one seemed to take more pleasure in deriding Perot than Bush, who had known him for years in Texas and then faced him as a candidate in 1992. Asked later if he among the quartet was the most outspoken about Perot, Clinton would only say, "There were other candidates for the prize."

At the East Room event a few hours later, it was Ford who made the most convincing case for ratifying the treaty. Recalling his own votes for reciprocal free trade in the late 1940s, Ford said it had required bipartisan teamwork to undo the "stupidity of what had been done in 1930 and '31 by the . . . Smoot Hawley Tariff Act" and it would take such partnership again. Otherwise, he warned, "We, the United States, could not sell abroad."

Nixon watched the NAFTA event on television and dismissed the bonhomie as a presidential dog and pony show. "I see where Bush [spent] the night at the White House. What is wrong with him? I can't understand why they all want to go back to the goddamned place." But when Israel's Rabin called to thank Nixon for his contributions to Middle East peace, the exiled president began to have second thoughts about having skipped the slumber party. He had missed his chance to go back. He would only get one more.

The Club Buries Its Own

By fall, Clinton was relying on Nixon again. He called in October to talk about Somalia, where his administration had stumbled and lost nineteen U.S. servicemen as part of a U.N. peacekeeping force. Nixon urged Clinton to use the U.N. as a tool, but not become a prisoner to its strange ways and means. And then Clinton called again later in the month to discuss Haiti, where the corrupt military regime of General Raoul Cédras was turning an impoverished country into a lawless and bloody one as well. Whatever anger Nixon had harbored at Clinton for missing Pat's funeral had passed; Nixon once more was serving as a part-time Clinton advisor.

In December of 1993, the two men watched as parliamentary elections in Russia produced a popular comeback for the nationalists and communists—exactly the sort of regression Nixon had been warning about for the previous two years. The uneasy clarity of 1993 had shattered as Russians went to the polls, and within a few weeks some of Yeltsin's top aides quit and Russian officials began to sound a lot like their Soviet predecessors. Clinton called Nixon in January before the president flew to Moscow to meet with Yeltsin.

In February, Nixon decided he too needed to see what was going on in Russia and laid on a trip to Moscow. Nixon's final trip to Russia revealed how closely he was coordinating with Clinton by early 1994. Working through Dimitri Simes in Washington, Nixon checked to make sure every visit on his six-day itinerary was approved by Clinton aides. NSC aide Nicholas Burns made a special trip to New Jersey to brief Nixon a few days before the departure. U.S. officials called Nixon's trip a private fact-finding mission. Clinton phoned to talk through the itinerary.

Before leaving, Nixon wrote an op-ed for the *New York Times* that he would have been better off sticking in a drawer. The column asked whether Yeltsin was "losing his grip." And then he urged, much as he had to Bush in 1992, that the United States should look beyond Yeltsin and build bridges to other players on the Russian political scene. As strategic advice to the president, Nixon's observation was spot-on. As a public, prearrival calling card, it was unwise.

But this was a minor misstep compared to the trip itself. Soon after arriving in Moscow, Nixon was photographed virtually embracing a Yeltsin rival. The sight of that on Russian TV led Yeltsin to abruptly cancel his own appointment with the former president and yank both Nixon's security detail and motorcade. It was a rash overreaction—but the damage was done: Nixon had been blackballed at the highest levels.

Clinton came to Nixon's defense back in the United States, urging Yeltsin to sit down with Nixon in part because he feared the snub would weaken Republican support for Russian aid in Congress. Bob Dole, the Senate majority leader, made a similar plea. And before Nixon left Russia, Yeltsin backed off a little, permitting his aides to meet with Nixon but leaving town himself to attend his mother-in-law's funeral.

When Nixon got back, he sent Clinton a seven-page letter on his findings. Clinton pored over the memo, wowed by its intelligence, showing it only to his wife and Vice President Al Gore. Never made public, Clinton paraphrased it briefly in his memoirs: "Nixon said I had earned the respect of the leaders he visited and could not let Whitewater or any other domestic issue 'divert attention from our major foreign policy priority—the survival of political and economic freedom in Russia.'" But the letter went further than that: Nixon urged Clinton to maintain his relationship with Yeltsin but make contact with other democrats in Russia. He warned Clinton away from some ultranationalists and toward those interested in liberty and reform. He pressed Clinton to replace his ambassador in Kiev and concentrate future U.S. economic aid on Ukraine, where it would matter most. And he predicted that the former Soviet Union would come under even greater pressure internally from ethnic and subnational groups in the future. Clinton told Taylor Branch a few weeks later that it was the smartest document on foreign policy he'd received as president. "The letter was a tour de force," Clinton recalled. "Nixon at his best."

And it turned out that Nixon would continue to be a small source of some inspiration long after Clinton left the presidency. In an interview in late 2011, Clinton could still recall in some detail the contents of Nixon's last letter. "The thing that struck me about Nixon was that he really cared about [Russia] and that his mind was working great and his ability to write coherent thoughts in a compelling way was still there. . . . It was so lucid, so well written, and some of it seems dated today."

And how did he know that?

"I reread it every year," he said.

It would also turn out to be Nixon's farewell address. Just before 6 P.M. on April 18, 1994, Nixon suffered a stroke while working at home. The galleys of his last book, *Beyond Peace*, had arrived only that morning. He was preparing to speak to a group of Republican fund-raisers in a few days. *Time* was preparing to excerpt the book in its next issue. Instead, Nixon was transferred to New York–Cornell Medical Center in Manhattan where he slipped into a coma the next day. Billy Graham, who was in New York at the time, called the White House when he heard the news, got Clinton on the phone, and asked the president which hospital Nixon was in so that the preacher could visit. Clinton didn't know but said he'd find out. A few minutes later, Clinton called Graham back with the details. Within minutes, Graham was at Nixon's bedside, praying with his daughters. At the White House, Clinton worried about Nixon's condition. "I hope it hasn't affected his mind," he told Gergen.

Graham, who had known Clinton for nearly a decade and prayed with the then Arkansas governor at the deathbed of a mutual friend in 1989, kept Clinton informed about Nixon's deterioration over the next twenty-four hours. During one call, after it became clear Nixon would not recover, Clinton asked Graham if the family would permit him to attend the funeral in Yorba Linda. Graham assumed so but said he would check with Julie and Tricia. A few minutes later, Graham called back and gave Clinton the okay. Nixon's daughters later called Clinton and asked him more formally to attend. By this point, Clinton was ruminating with advisors about the meaning of Nixon's life, both his achievements and shortcomings. He believed that Nixon had been a brilliant, troubled, emotionally complicated man. "He was one of those husbands," he told Branch, "who couldn't live with or without his wife."

When Nixon passed away just after 8 P.M. on April 22, several hours passed before the news was made public. And who made the announcement? The former president's new best friend, in a somber Rose Garden statement later that night that Johnny Apple of the *New York Times* described as "unstinted." Clinton praised Nixon as a statesman who redefined resiliency. "It's impossible to be in this job," he added, "without feeling a special bond with the people who have gone before." In a proclamation, Clinton declared the following Wednesday a national day of mourning. He closed the federal government, canceled postal delivery, and ordered that the U.S. flag be lowered to half-staff, both at home and at U.S. bases overseas, for a month. "I encourage the American people to assemble on that day in their respective places of worship to pay homage to the memory of President Nixon and seek God's continued blessing on our land." Nixon would have liked that most of all.

Clinton offered the Nixon family a state funeral, but Nixon had made it clear before he died that he wanted only to lie in repose at his library in Yorba Linda in Orange County. Clinton put a backup military transport once used as Air Force One at the Nixon family's disposal. Meanwhile, White House aides argued about how to properly eulogize a former president whose name was still something of an epithet in Democratic circles. Clinton wanted, among other things, to reframe Nixon as the last liberal Republican before Reagan had ushered in a more conservative era. Moderates, led by Gergen, wanted to throw a light blanket of redemption over Nixon's life now that it was over. George Stephanopoulos worried that a wholesale absolution would inflame Clinton's base and cause him no end of trouble. And so Clinton changed the one key line in the eulogy—"The day of judging Richard Nixon based on one part of his life alone has finally come to an end"—at Stephanopoulos's suggestion to: "*May* the day of judging President Nixon on anything less than his entire life and career come to a close."

The club was smaller now, but newspapers and magazines splashed the dramatic image of Clinton, the four remaining members, and their wives all sitting in the front row at the funeral in Yorba Linda. Nearly as memorable were Clinton's remarks. After praising Nixon for making strong advances in cancer research and environmental protection, he said: "For the past year, even in the final weeks of his life, he gave me his wise counsel, especially with regard to Russia. One thing in particular left a profound impression on me. Though this man was in his ninth decade, he had an incredibly sharp and vigorous and rigorous mind. As a public man, he always seemed to believe the greatest sin was remaining passive in the face of challenges. And he never stopped living by that creed."

Less than a week later, musing on the death of his mother in January, Clinton told CNN's Larry King that he missed Nixon in similar fashion. "Just today I had a problem and I said to the person working with me, 'I wish I could pick up the phone and call Richard Nixon and ask him what he thinks we ought to do about this.'"

"I'm Sending Carter. You Think It
Will Be OK, Don't You?"

—BILL CLINTON

When Bill Clinton became the nation's youngest governor in 1978, President Jimmy Carter sent a note that was as much challenge as congratulation: "You and I will succeed in meeting the goals for our country by working closely together to serve those whom we represent."

Well before the start of one man's presidency in 1976 and well after the end of the other's in 2000, the Carter-Clinton relationship would always be fraught. Despite the fact—or maybe because—they shared Southern roots, a Baptist's faith, and bragging rights as the only Democrats to win the White House between 1964 and 2008, the two men quarreled as much as they got along. Each man would test the other's ability to forgive.

The relationship began well enough. Carter had spotted Clinton as a rising political star, helped him in his first run for Congress in 1974, and then offered him a job in the 1976 presidential campaign. (Clinton declined that offer in order to run for Arkansas attorney general.) By the time Clinton was governor, Carter invited Clinton to the White House on occasion and named his wife, Hillary, as the first female chair of the Legal Services Commission. All this made the Clintons certified Carter people: though he had many liberal friends, Clinton was never tempted by Teddy Kennedy's bid to unseat Carter for the Democratic nomination in 1980. Carl Wagner, who was close to Clinton but worked as one of Kennedy's top political aides in that contest, recalled that Clinton wasn't even worth trying to peel away from Carter's camp. "He was loyal to Carter," Wagner explained, "no matter what."

That loyalty was soon tested. In May 1980, Carter sent eighteen thousand Cuban refugees, most of whom had come ashore illegally along the Gulf Coast, to be interned at Fort Chaffee in northwest Arkansas. When several hundred Cubans broke out of the facility and began to roam the streets shouting "Libertad! Libertad!" Clinton had to send in state police and the National Guard to maintain order. He called Carter to complain, but was told to take his problems to a midlevel White House official instead.

Clinton briefly won a White House promise not to send any more Cubans to Fort Chaffee but that vow was soon broken. On August 1, three months before the election, Carter ordered that all the Cubans that he had already sent to refugee centers in the politically more important states of Florida, Wisconsin, and Pennsylvania be shipped to the less important state of Arkansas. Fort Chaffee's population quickly tripled. This was a political disaster and a personal double-cross for Clinton. "You're fucking me," Clinton screamed at his midlevel Carter White House contact. "How could you do this to me? I busted my ass for Carter. You guys are gonna' get me beat. I've done everything I could for you guys. This is ridiculous. Carter's too chicken-shit about it to tell me directly!" Carter eventually phoned; the call did not go well.

Clinton kept his anger to himself, but his ties to Carter quickly frayed. Frank White, Clinton's Republican opponent in 1980, ran a television ad that featured footage of the Cuban refugees running amok with the line, "Bill Clinton cares more about Jimmy Carter than he does about Arkansas." Within a few months, both Clinton and Carter had been unseated. Clinton later blamed Carter in part for his defeat.

Twelve years later, there had been little thaw. Carter had been no more than lukewarm about Clinton's candidacy in 1991 and 1992 and it was simply not in Clinton's interest in 1993 to be in any way associated with someone who was perceived as a failed, one-term Democratic president. In Little Rock, where Clinton was putting together his transition team, Carter's advice was not sought and his presence not welcome. The Georgian's calls to the Arkansas Governor's Mansion—Carter wanted to discuss a variety of foreign policy challenges with the incoming president—went unanswered. Clinton went so far as to ask Warren Christopher, who had been the deputy secretary of state under Carter and was poised to take the top job for Clinton, to break his long-standing ties with Carter as a condition for employment. When Carter called Christopher to congratulate him, the secretary of state designate let days pass before returning the call. Maybe worse, he delegated the job of handling Carter to a deputy; who in turn attempted to delegate it to his deputy. These slights did not go unnoticed in Plains.

Carter soon found a way to express his grievance. While promoting a new book in early January 1993, Carter told the *New York Times* that he was "very disappointed" the Clintons had elected to send their daughter, Chelsea, to the Sidwell Friends private school rather than to the Washington, D.C., public schools, as the Carters had done with their young daughter, Amy. Carter also shared his low opinion of Clinton's skills with a hammer and nail, which he had observed when Bill and Hillary swung through Georgia over the previous summer and spent a day with Carter building houses for Habitat for Humanity. "He was obviously not an experienced carpenter," Carter recalled.

This was accurate; Clinton had been hopeless in shop class. But such remarks were unhelpful to a former president trying to establish diplomatic relations with a new commander in chief. A week later, at the Clinton inaugural festivities in Washington, Carter and his wife were kept conspicuously at arm's length from the new president and his inner circle—a snub that Rosalynn Carter certainly detected. Carter understood that Clinton needed to blaze his own trail as the first Democrat in the White House in a dozen years. But it galled him that Clinton's foreign policy team was shot through with veterans from his own presidency and yet he could not get his phone calls returned. When he finally sat down with Christopher in March and argued that he was uniquely positioned to perform some missions that U.S. diplomats could not, he got a polite, but firm, brush-off from his old friend. "When George Bush senior came into office, I had the best relationship I have ever had since I left the White House," Carter recalled. "When President Clinton came into office, that relationship dissipated."

Savior or Stuntman?

The first real chance for partnership came in April 1994, when North Korean leader Kim Il Sung began to remove plutonium-packed fuel rods from one of his country's aging Soviet-style nuclear reactors without permitting international inspectors to monitor the procedure. North Korea's decision to refuel its reactors, often a precursor to diverting plutonium from peaceful to military purposes, sparked a crisis in Washington about how to respond. Clinton's foreign policy advisors suspected that Kim probably had enough plutonium for a handful of ten-kiloton bombs and feared that if he continued defueling the reactor, he could double or triple his atomic stockpile very quickly. The question with North Korea was familiar: was this a hostile act—or just a play for more wheat? When the threat of further economic sanctions did nothing to halt Kim's direction, Clinton asked his generals to review plans for a possible invasion involving as many as 400,000 U.S. troops—and to do it quickly.

Clinton was in a difficult spot: Kim warned that he would treat every move from economic sanctions to further deployment of U.S. troops as a provocation for war with South Korea—and no one in Washington believed a shooting war would end well for either side. Some U.S. military officials were genuinely worried that Kim might launch a preemptive strike on the south. Over the course of several weeks in late April and May, the United States quietly deployed extra combat troops, attack helicopters, Patriot missile batteries, spare parts, and ammunition to South Korea. It was no exercise.

Clinton had already spent a lot of time in early 1994 trying to find the best scout to send to Pyongyang to figure out what Kim really wanted. He urged Billy Graham to travel there in January and gave Graham a letter to deliver to Kim. When that mission went slightly awry, Clinton floated the idea internally of sending Senators Sam Nunn and Richard Lugar, an idea Kim at first welcomed and later spurned. Clinton wanted a dialogue with Kim, but had no way to start one.

Which is how Clinton, after keeping Carter at bay for months, finally turned to him for help. Carter had kept at his courtship of the new president: he spent the night at the White House in September 1993, when Clinton invited all the former presidents to witness the signing of the Oslo Accords between Israeli Yitzhak Rabin and the Palestinian Liberation Organization's Yassir Arafat and then stay on for an event the next morning, all in support of the North American Free Trade Agreement. Clinton and Carter stayed up late talking the first night; Carter explained that he felt ignored by Christopher and the State Department; Clinton pretended to know nothing of this arm's-length treatment and promised to turn to him for help more often. So when Carter called Clinton on June 1, 1994, and expressed his concern that the war of words with Pyongyang was getting out of control, Clinton saw an opening. He dispatched his top Korean negotiator, Robert L. Gallucci, to Georgia to brief the former president on possible next steps.

Gallucci came away from his three-hour meeting in Plains on June 5 convinced Carter would probably go to North Korea whether the administration okayed such a visit or not. Carter came away convinced the Clinton administration had no idea how to bring the situation under control. *Someone* had to keep war from breaking out. And who better than the thirty-ninth president?

The North Koreans trusted Carter: as president, he had reduced by 10 percent the number of U.S. forces on the peninsula, and had hoped to make even larger troop withdrawals. Since then, Kim had invited Carter to Pyongyang three times, in 1991, 1992, and 1993. Each time, the White House, whether under Bush or Clinton, had declined Carter's request to go.

Five days after the Gallucci visit, Carter informed Vice President Al Gore that he wanted to go to North Korea and see what he could do.

After some back-and-forth negotiations between Carter and Gore about how exactly to word this "request" from a former president to a sitting one, Gore called Clinton, who was on his way to Europe to attend the fiftieth anniversary celebration of the Normandy invasion, and made the case for Carter to go. Warren Christopher opposed the trip, aware of just how unpredictable Carter could be to work with. But Gore liked the idea and so did Clinton, who was looking for a way to help Kim step back from the brink. It couldn't hurt, Clinton figured, and it might help. He needed to do something; as he landed in Europe, *Time*'s editors chose a cover depicting a menacing-looking Kim with a fiery nuclear explosion in the background. "Is Kim Il Sung bluffing or will he go to war?" A few days later, Gore called Carter to approve the visit.

On June 10, Carter flew to Washington for pre-trip briefings. The sessions went badly. For starters, the Clinton White House was so sensitive about turning to Carter for foreign policy help that National Security Advisor Tony Lake, Gallucci, and NSC aide Dan Poneman opted to meet the former president and his wife at National Airport; that was as close to Pennsylvania Avenue as they wanted him to get. Lake told Carter that he would be traveling as a private citizen and would have no authority to negotiate on behalf of the United States. His mission, Lake added, was not to cut a deal, or make promises, but simply to divine Kim's intentions—were they peaceful or not?—and remind the North Korean leader that the United States had the right to take reasonable defensive steps until the crisis passed. Carter, Poneman observed, "seemed to chafe at these limits. [He] clearly viewed his own role far more expansively than as a messenger between Washington and Pyongyang."

The State Department briefings a few hours later went just as poorly. One assistant greeted the Carters as "Mr. President and Mrs. Mondale." Aides offered the two Georgians Pepsi to drink once the background-ers began— something of an insult to anyone who had spent any time in Coca-Cola-proud Atlanta. And as the detailed session began on nuclear weapons, nonproliferation, and internal North Korean politics, the former nuclear engineer made it clear he was nobody's errand boy. "How many times have you visited North Korea?" he inquired of each expert. And each time Carter asked, the answer was "none."

The contradictions about Carter's role were hard to ignore, but both sides did so: he was traveling as a private citizen but he was charged with carrying out a vital, presidentially sanctioned mission. At the same time, though he was serving as Clinton's official, unofficial envoy, he openly opposed the administration's push for U.N. sanctions against Pyongyang and had a well-deserved reputation for ignoring orders. When Carter left for Korea two days later, some of Clinton's own aides believed that they had launched an unguided missile.

A Breakthrough, and Then Breakdown

Carter stopped in South Korea on the way to Pyongyang. Both Douglas Brinkley and Don Oberdorfer, in their fine, separate accounts of Carter's visit to Seoul, reported that he found the city on war footing. The U.S. embassy was working up plans to evacuate more than eighty thousand Americans from the Korean Peninsula. Locals were stripping the food markets of rice, candles, and noodles, stockpiling water, building makeshift bomb shelters. The Korean stock market had plunged 25 percent in forty-eight hours and the U.S. ambassador was making arrangements to airlift his own family out of the country. South Korea's president, Kim Young Sam, met with Carter and gave the American his own letter to deliver: a secret offer to Kim Il Sung to start bilateral talks between the North and South.

So by the time he left the South Korean capital and headed north, Carter was on multiple missions: one for President Clinton and another for South Korean president Kim. And Carter had his own goal: he believed that economic sanctions could be avoided if Pyongyang agreed to let U.N. inspectors monitor the fuel rods they had removed from the Yongbyon reactor and promised not to refuel it. He was not going to just take Kim's temperature. He was determined to cut a deal to defuse the crisis.

The Carter delegation—made up of several aides and a State Department official, and a CNN news crew—crossed the Demilitarized Zone on June 15 and climbed into armored military trucks for the trip along an utterly deserted four-lane highway to Pyongyang. Carter's official reception was predictably weird: the North Korean foreign minister treated the Carters to a dinner headlined by an all-girl rock 'n' roll group, dressed in crinolines, who sang "My Darling Clementine" and "Oh! Susanna." Carter's earnest dinner toast included a push for clarity on nuclear inspectors; the foreign minister gave a hostile toast in return—so hostile that Carter went to bed that night fearing his mission might be a lost cause.

With that prospect in mind, Carter dispatched an aide to the DMZ before dawn with a secret note for Clinton urging him to quickly launch direct and official communications with Pyongyang should his mission fail. Carter feared the worst; the situation was so grave that nothing short of direct intervention by Clinton himself would defuse the crisis. But U.S. diplomats, certain that Carter was overreacting, intercepted Carter's courier at the DMZ and prevented his letter from reaching Washington. And as it turned out, relations had not quite reached the breaking point. Later that morning, Kim greeted his American visitor with a big smile and a bear hug and the two men got quickly down to business. Carter told Kim he had to give the U.N. the authority to monitor all fuel rods immediately. Kim said he would happily exchange his aging graphite block reactors (which made lots of plutonium) for light water reactors supplied by the United States; and if those could be provided, he would abide by the nonproliferation treaty and its terms.

As to the all-important matter of whether the international inspectors could return, Kim claimed ignorance that they had been barred in the first place but quickly announced that they could go back. In a very short time, the two men were on the verge of a deal. Carter huddled with Kim's aides after lunch to work out the details; in these sessions, Carter had to push back against almost constant attempts by Kim's aides to retract Kim's verbal promises.

Despite his instructions, Carter now had the makings of a breakthrough in hand. He phoned the White House just as Clinton and his national security advisors, meeting in the Roosevelt Room, had agreed to propose stricter sanctions in the U.N. Security Council and were finalizing plans to send an additional Army division to South Korea. Gallucci took the call in another room and heard Carter report from Pyongyang that Kim had agreed to let International Atomic Energy Agency monitors back in and freeze its nuclear program. Carter informed Gallucci that he would be making the announcement on CNN in a few moments.

Gallucci returned to the Cabinet Room with the news of Carter's apparent fait accompli and his plans to announce it. The room was aghast. Lake asked Gallucci, "You did tell him not to go on CNN, didn't you?" No, came the reply. "Did you try?" asked Christopher. Gallucci admitted that he had not. It was hard to tell what upset Clinton and his aides more: that Carter had cut a deal they couldn't read on paper or that he was about to announce it to the world. "Not since the presidency of Lyndon Johnson had so many barnyard expletives echoed off the Cabinet room wall," Brinkley wrote in his account. So the group scattered to watch the thirty-ninth president announce on CNN a "new breakthrough" with the Hermit Kingdom. "The reason I came over here," he explained, "was to prevent an irreconcilable mistake." Carter even praised Kim for taking "important" and "positive" steps, though all the North Korean leader had done was return to the terms of a previous promise by his government. And then Carter suggested that all that remained was for Clinton to okay a new round of direct bilateral talks.

This was simply bizarre: a former American president, having been sent on a fact-finding mission, was now pitching a deal he cut in private on international television. Rather than serving discreetly as Clinton's envoy, Carter was negotiating in public for a deal of his own and explaining to the world what Clinton had to do next. White House officials, gathered around a television in the West Wing, did not try to contain their contempt. "The problem is that North Korea now has a former president as its spokesperson," one official remarked. One cabinet member saw it more starkly; he called Carter "a treasonous prick."

But the immediate question was how, exactly, to respond. The White House had little faith that Kim would keep his word to Carter and no desire to barter away the threat of sanctions in case its instincts were correct. Clinton aides decided on a two-part approach. First, they hammered out a brief statement that offered no more than tentative support for Carter's apparent breakthrough. Clinton delivered it himself in the White House briefing room and answered a question or two.

Behind the scenes, meanwhile, Carter was getting spanked. Lake called him in Pyongyang and told the former president in what one official later described as "unvarnished language" that the administration would not agree to Carter's terms unless the North Koreans specifically agreed not to replace removed fuel rods with new ones. Clinton, moreover, was not satisfied with a verbal agreement from Kim; Lake told Carter he wanted the deal in writing. Carter listened to Lake's demands as he sat on the edge of his bed before sunrise in Pyongyang. They would be an affront to Kim, he told Lake.

The normally mild-mannered Lake fought back, raising his voice with his old boss and demanding that the former president follow the instructions of the current commander in chief. "A difficult exchange," Lake recalled.

Carter didn't forget that he had never been authorized to hold negotiations in the first place; he had simply ignored his instructions. But now that he had walked into the Korean bazaar, started making deals, and announced them on TV, he knew he would have to abide by his master's demands. He agreed to send Kim a letter explaining the new conditions. "That man used to work for me as a young pup," Carter complained after hanging up with Lake. Taking no chances, Lake sent a copy of his new conditions to Pyongyang's mission to the U.N. in New York City, just in case Carter didn't follow orders again.

Kim agreed to the new U.S. conditions later that day, after he and Carter had taken a leisurely three-hour cruise down the Taedong River. Carter's Atlanta-based CNN crew was on hand to capture the voyage. Both Carter and Kim brought along their wives, which made things easier; pressed by Carter and Kim's wife, Kim agreed to take steps to help find the remains of some three thousand U.S. servicemen still missing from the Korean War. But then Carter, in an inexplicable move, turned to the CNN crew and announced that, thanks to his actions the day before, the United States had backed away from its push for U.N. sanctions against North Korea.

This was plainly untrue—the United States still held out the threat of sanctions in order to force Kim to keep his word on the nuclear deal. In Washington, the response to Carter's latest gambit was immediate: White House press secretary Dee Dee Myers dismissed Carter's assertion as inaccurate. South Korean ambassador James Laney was instructed to meet Carter the next morning at the DMZ with a clear message: knock it off about sanctions. Laney had another message to deliver: don't even think about returning to Washington from Seoul. Nobody there wants to see you now. In fact, nobody at the White House can see you for a week or two.

But that message didn't take either. Before leaving Seoul, Carter called Gore and informed the vice president he wanted to come to Washington to debrief the president or his aides in person. Gore declined that offer; Carter pressed again to come to Washington and, after a few more phone conversations—including one where the vice president had Carter in one ear and Lake in the other—Carter was permitted to visit Washington on his return. Carter's end of the discussion with Gore had been so heated that aides later reported that it could be heard all through the American ambassador's residence.

And yet for all the collateral damage, the trip was a success: Carter won acceptance from Kim to hold bilateral talks with South Korea, as Kim Young Sam had proposed. He cleared the way for a joint Korean War remains commission. Most of all, he had helped defuse the fuel rod crisis. Carter expected, at the very least, some thanks for that. But Carter had a way of making gratitude difficult. Before leaving Seoul, Carter issued another slap at the White House, saying sanctions would be "a personal insult to their so called Great Leader."

When Carter arrived in Washington on Sunday, June 19, Clinton's aides hoped to smooth over any lingering resentments. But it quickly became apparent that Carter was not interested in making peace at home. The former president entered Lake's office, sat down on the sofa, and proceeded to read his written report—word for word—as if he was lecturing a roomful of schoolboys. Hope for reconciliation faded further when Carter announced that he would circulate his final report on the trip only to Clinton, Gore, Christopher, and what he called "my mailing list of supporters."

It was all evidence, if any more proof were needed, that Carter could be a complicated partner. When it was over, Clinton was circumspect, telling his aides that he had relied on the club to get the deal done. Even when they go rogue, he said, former presidents could still be a useful instrument of presidential power. For all the problems they cause at home, the club had special influence with some foreign leaders. "Look, I knew I was going to take some heat for letting Carter go there," Clinton said. "But I also knew we needed to give the North . . . some way to climb down without losing face. I figured if they could say to themselves that a former president had come to their country, it would allow them to do that."

It was a lesson Clinton would remember.

Mission to Haiti

Just three months later, Clinton deputized Carter again. The assignment, this time, was even riskier. Carter's secret mission in June had simply been to make contact with a reclusive leader in a troublesome kingdom.

His much more public journey to Haiti in September was to remove a gangster from power as war loomed.

By mid-1994, Haiti's military boss, General Raoul Cédras, had been waging a campaign of terror against the supporters of former president Jean-Bertrand Aristide since he and a handful of other military officers kicked Aristide out as president in 1992. An estimated three thousand Haitians had died under Cédras's rule, many of them hacked to death by his goons and left in pieces to die on the streets. In cities where Aristide had once been strongest, women and girls were routinely raped or assaulted while Cédras's security forces filled Haitian prisons under a new arbitrary arrest policy. Dozens of people just vanished.

It is easy to forget now just how close the United States came to invading Haiti in 1994. Clinton spent much of 1993 and 1994 trying different nonmilitary approaches to dislodge Cédras's generals from their perch: an oil embargo, economic sanctions, special envoys, tighter sanctions; nothing moved them. If anything, the Haitian military and its allies in the ruling class were only getting richer on the shortages resulting from the sanctions. Clinton finally pushed through a unanimous United Nations Security Council resolution in late July 1994 authorizing the use of force to restore democracy—a first for the U.N.—on the hunch that the mere threat of a U.S. invasion would force the junta to give way. But it was possible that global sanctions would not budge Cédras from power, and by midsummer invasion planning was already under way at the Pentagon. Against an army that was estimated to be no larger than seven thousand men, the thinking went, U.S. forces would face only token opposition.

But the idea of sending troops to Haiti was a deeply unpopular one. Public confidence in Clinton's handling of foreign policy during his first term was never very high and the prospect of invading the hemisphere's poorest country made little sense to most Americans. Arkansas senator Dale Bumpers warned Clinton that an invasion might provoke the Senate to pass a resolution of disapproval. Reputable alternatives to Cédras weren't easy to come by; former chairman of the Joint Chiefs of Staff Colin Powell had warned Clinton that exiled Haitian leader Jean-Bertrand Aristide was unreliable and hardly worth the American lives it would cost to reinstall him. "Nobody is for this," Clinton complained.

"Nobody." Still, he was fatalistic. "I'll get through this," he told Taylor Branch. "Don't worry about it. I can always find something else to do to make a living."

His defensiveness wasn't much different when he talked about Haiti in public. On September 15, Clinton gave an Oval Office address explaining his rationale for an invasion. "I have bent over backwards. I have used sanctions and everything else. I have also not had the United States be the Lone Ranger. We had the UN come in here."

As he finished the speech, he gave no indication that he was working secretly to give peace one last chance. For several months, Carter had been urging Clinton to let him go to Haiti and try to make a deal with Cédras to step aside. Clinton thought it was worth a shot: Carter had known both Cédras and Aristide for years and had visited Haiti seven times in the previous decade. It was Cédras, after all, who had helped to install Aristide in February 1991 before kicking him out eight months later. If Cédras could be convinced to step down beforehand, Carter argued, the Marines would be able to go in peacefully. Carter volunteered to fly to Haiti and negotiate Cédras's departure ahead of the invasion.

Carter's return made Clinton's aides pull at their hair. Gore and Christopher flatly, and loudly, opposed the idea, recalling what had happened that summer in Korea. Perhaps mindful of that episode, Carter came up with a solution to his own problem: he called Sam Nunn of Georgia and Powell, neither of whom favored an invasion, and asked if they would be interested in taking on the mission as well. Both men said yes, they would go, if the president agreed. Clinton, Carter recalled, "wouldn't let me go until I got Sam Nunn and Colin Powell to go with me."

Clinton then called each man, laid out the parameters of the mission, and officially invited them to take it on together. The goal: tell Cédras the Marines were on the way and see if he would step down in exchange for a peaceful takeover.

The exact terms of Cédras's departure were left up to the trio—in part because everyone knew they would need some flexibility to pull it off. The anxiety was over how much flexibility that would turn out to be. Powell recalled that Clinton was worried that Carter might cut a deal that went well beyond what Clinton had authorized in advance. After Carter's gambits in Korea, George Stephanopoulos, Clinton's senior advisor, recalled, "We couldn't afford more freelancing." Clinton himself spent part of a day talking himself into his decision. "I'm sending Carter," he told Stephanopoulos. "You think it will be OK, don't you?"

In the end, Clinton again decided to trust his instincts, in part because the alternative—in this case, an invasion—was worse. As he explained it to Powell, "Jimmy Carter is sometimes a wild card. But I took a chance on him in North Korea and that didn't turn out too badly."

Clinton gave Carter, Powell, and Nunn one secret weapon before they departed: "I told them to feel free to tell the Haitians they disagree with my policy because they [the Haitians] would be more likely to believe I was going to invade." With a small group of aides, Carter, Powell, and Nunn arrived in Port-au-Prince just after noon on Saturday, September 17, and went immediately to see Cédras at Haitian military headquarters. The Americans sensed they were literally walking into a trap: the run-down building was ringed by several thousand of Cédras's irregulars, who were chanting slogans and brandishing machetes. Upstairs, in a corner room, Carter coolly explained to the general and his lieutenants that a massive U.S. invasion was imminent and urged the Haitians to lay down their weapons and step down from power. Nunn reported that the Congress was completely behind the president, while Powell, the former general, played the heavy, explaining how the U.S. military would come at Cédras with two carriers, two and a half infantry divisions, the usual array of helicopter gunships, artillery, tens of thousands of troops, and support from two dozen other nations. The show of force from Powell prompted Cédras to joke, "We used to be the weakest nation in the hemisphere. After this we'll be the strongest."

That cut the tension but it did nothing to clear the way for a deal. Cédras told his guests he wasn't budging. So the U.S. team took a break, met with local business leaders for dinner, and then reconvened with Cédras later that night. That meeting, which began at 11 P.M., went well past one and still produced little movement. But Carter won from Cédras an invitation to meet his family the next morning at his home. By now, four U.S. naval vessels were staging offshore, along with at least sixteen thousand soldiers and Marines. U.S. troops were set to move at midnight Monday, which meant the trio had less than twenty-four hours to do a deal. But the three men had perhaps eighteen hours remaining if they wanted to get out of the country before the shooting started.

Clinton began Sunday at the Pentagon, where he reviewed the invasion plans and talked by phone to the operational commanders in the region. In Haiti, meanwhile, Carter, Nunn, and Powell headed for Cédras's home at dawn to meet his wife and family. Yannick Prosper Cédras sounded just as entrenched as her husband, telling the Americans "we would rather die with American bullets in our chests than as traitors with Haitian bullets in our backs." It was a stirring piece of bravado but Powell deftly set it aside. "My wife would understand perfectly your loyalty as a general's wife," he said, "but I tell you there is no honor in throwing away lives when the outcome is already determined."

That altered the dynamics and, by noon Sunday, Cédras proposed to step down as soon as a new government was in place. When Carter relayed that offer to Washington by fax, Clinton rejected it as too vague and insisted on Cédras's departure by October 15. Cédras balked at the timetable and Clinton in return urged Carter and his team to leave the island quickly. The last-ditch mission was now operating several hours past its deadline. The invasion was just twelve hours away, and some forward elements were expected in half that time. Nerves in Washington were starting to fray; the only thing worse than having to invade an impoverished neighboring country was having three sainted American political figures martyred in the crossfire. Military officials put a Delta Force team on standby to rescue the trio in the event it ran into trouble. General Hugh Shelton, who commanded the U.S. operation offshore, was frantically telephoning the White House that afternoon urging Clinton to extract Carter and his team immediately.

Around 4 P.M., Cédras's top deputy warned Cédras that the invasion was imminent and urged him to leave the building. (Haiti's generals, whatever the condition of their army, apparently had some spotters near Fort Bragg's Pope Field in North Carolina—a bit of foreign intelligence that impressed Powell, the former paratrooper. "Not bad for a poor country," he noted.) Clinton phoned again to tell the three Americans to leave immediately, but Carter begged for still more time. Clinton was skeptical but willing to extend the deadline until the last possible minute, perhaps an hour away.

What Carter did next is not in any Carter Center Peaceful Mediation Handbook.

He wheeled on Cédras and all but shouted, "You must accept this agreement right now or your children will be killed! Your country will be burned!" It was an astonishing change of tactics and Powell recalled being stunned as he watched it unfold. And yet it seemed to work: Cédras was close to capitulating but needed some face-saving political cover for stepping aside. So Carter rolled the dice, proposing to take Cédras to see Emile Jonassaint, the eighty-one-year-old figurehead president named by the generals a few months earlier. Though the United States did not regard Jonassaint as legitimate leader of anything, the Haitian generals did and Carter imagined that if Jonassaint could be convinced to order Cédras to step down, Cédras might just agree to do it. The delegation hurriedly left the military HQ in two cars: Nunn and Carter in one vehicle and Cédras and Powell in the other, along with several hand grenades, which rolled around on the floor of the backseat as they sped through the streets of Port-au-Prince.

By the time they arrived at Jonassaint's office, Carter had written a one-page proposal that permitted American forces to enter the country peacefully if the ruling junta stepped down by October 15. Jonassaint asked the generals if they could hold out against the Americans. Cédras said no. Two lower-level ministers objected to the surrender and threatened to resign. "We have too many ministers already," Jonassaint replied. "I choose peace." As the agreement was being translated into French, Carter called Clinton on an unsecured telephone to make sure that Jonassaint was, considering the urgency of the situation, now an acceptable official with whom to cut the final deal.

Clinton agreed, and soon after Jonassaint signed. When Powell reminded the Haitians that the agreement meant that U.S. troops could not be fired upon, Cédras agreed. "I will obey the orders of my president." Carter then phoned the White House with the news. U.S. paratroopers were only thirty minutes away when Clinton ordered them back home.

The War Over the Peace

As the U.S. team headed to the airport late that night for the flight back to Washington, it was hard to see how Carter had underperformed. Facing long odds and a ticking clock, he had moved quickly and, at key moments, creatively, to get a deal while sticking for the most part to the White House guidance. He had wavered at times during the negotiations, but came out in the end where he and Clinton could call it a win. And, so far, he had stayed out of public view.

Then, inevitably, he overplayed his hand. The American delegation landed in Washington at 3:30 A.M. and dispersed to get a few hours of sleep. The three men were supposed to regroup with Clinton for breakfast and then hold a four-man press conference to put a nice, tidy bow on the deal. But Carter went AWOL, turning up on CNN at 7 A.M., putting his own spin on the previous seventy-two hours and taking the opportunity to criticize the White House for insisting that Cédras leave Haiti for a third country, while praising Cédras for being willing to step down.

And all this occurred before he had briefed the president on whose behalf he was working.

When Carter got to the White House, he found Clinton in a breathless fury, outraged that Carter had once again taken to the airwaves before talking to the boss. But rather than simply apologize for his misjudgment, Carter gave as good as he got, shouting at Clinton for launching an invasion while the negotiating team was still in Haiti. This must have annoyed Clinton even more, as Carter knew it was the threat of the invasion that had given the negotiators their leverage. The conversation, such as it was, degenerated into a shouting match.

It fell to Sam Nunn to restore order and the quartet somehow made it to the East Room for pictures and questions. Once again, Carter had saved Clinton a lot of trouble, one president coming to the rescue of another. But he had fouled the finish, much as he had in Korea.

In many ways, the prickly yet productive Clinton-Carter relationship was about second chances, a twenty-five-year test of how many times the younger man could forgive the older and whether the older could get over the fact that his protégé turned out to be a better politician. Clinton never gave up. In August 1999, as his time in the White House began to wind down, Clinton flew to Atlanta to award both Carter and his wife, Rosalynn, the Presidential Medal of Freedom. The Medal of Freedom is the nation's highest civilian award but it is also one that is normally distributed in East Room ceremonies.

Once in Atlanta, the president ran through a long litany of the Carters' charitable works around the globe. "There have been other presidents who have contributed to the public good once they left office," Clinton remarked, reaching back to Taft and Jefferson to make clear he had studied the entire record. "To call Jimmy Carter the greatest former president in history . . . does not do justice to either him or to his work." He made an equally gracious speech about Rosalynn.

Carter, moved by the honor, thanked Clinton right back but with an asterisk. "You still have some months to go before you join our small fraternity of former presidents," Carter said. "Now, just imagine, Mr. President, you'll be able to play golf without any television, telephoto lenses, focused on your stroke. Isn't that great? But I think I have to warn you that there are some downsides to being out of office as well. I understand that golfing partners don't give as many mulligans to ex-presidents as they do to presidents."

By 2000, it was practically a club bylaw: even when you were doing Carter a favor, you never knew what you might get in return. But it probably won't feel good.

22

"Bill, I Think You Have to Admit That You Lied"

—GERALD FORD

The shocking but not entirely surprising news in early 1998 that Bill Clinton may have had sex with a twenty-one-year-old intern sent a scandalized Presidents Club into silence.

Reagan by that time was not making public appearances or statements. Bush had no reason to comment: his eldest son was facing reelection in Texas and mulling a run at the White House. The club's two closest members, Ford and Carter, agreed during a private conversation that spring not to say anything in public about Clinton's deepening political problems. A House impeachment probe was certain; a Senate trial was likely. They agreed that their influence, such as it was, might be more valuable if they banked and deployed it later.

But by August, Clinton had admitted to a grand jury—and then on national television—that he had had an inappropriate relationship with Monica Lewinsky. In late September, an incoming Emory University student asked Carter to comment on the deepening mess in Washington. In more than fifteen years, Carter explained, he had never dodged a single question in his annual orientation session with Emory freshmen. And though this might have been an ideal time to make an exception, Carter apparently did not see it that way. He predicted, boldly but accurately, that Clinton would be impeached, but would not be convicted in the Senate. The club's silence had been broken.

A Moment of Majesty

Within days, Ford had written an op-ed column for the *New York Times* in close coordination with his longtime friend, historian Richard Norton Smith. Ford felt that Clinton was still not leveling with the public about his own behavior nor showing sufficient shame about what he had done. "Ford believed Clinton needed to show more contrition," said Smith. "He thought Clinton needed to impress upon the nation that he understood what he had put the country through."

But Ford had other worries. A House veteran who had risen from obscurity over a quarter century to become his party's leader in the lower chamber, Ford feared that zealous House Republicans were in danger of damaging themselves were they to follow their instincts and pursue impeachment over a sordid sexual affair. The public, Ford guessed, might punish them for overreaching. Smith suspected that Ford had a third agenda as well. Born in a more genteel era, he said, Ford believed that it was one thing for the public to be obsessed with Clinton's sex life but it was another for the government to be. Ford had a deep faith in the power of contrition and its salutary effect on the body politic. In pardoning Richard Nixon twenty-five years earlier, Smith noted, Ford had tried to win from Nixon an admission of guilt for his crimes in exchange. But while Nixon had made some minor comments along those lines, he had never really come right out and apologized. Ford pardoned Nixon anyway, but spent some part of his remaining years rationalizing the trade-off. Here, perhaps, was a chance for Ford to prove his case.

And yet what Ford was suggesting in his *Times* op-ed was highly irregular. He urged members of the House Judiciary Committee to proceed with their inquiry, but suggested the full House resolve the crisis with a parliamentary device that had no name. Clinton, Ford argued, should voluntarily go to the well of the House during a joint session of Congress and receive "not an ovation from the people's representatives, but a harshly worded rebuke as rendered by members of both parties. I emphasize: this would be a rebuke, not a rebuttal by the President . . . the President would accept full responsibility for his actions, as well as for his subsequent efforts to delay or impede the investigation of them. . . .

Let it be dignified, honest and, above all, cleansing. The result, I believe, would be the first moment of majesty in an otherwise squalid year."

And that was the most important mission: members of the club tend to put protecting the presidency above protecting individual presidents, and the Oval Office, sullied by the whole episode, needed a ritual bath. However appalled they were at Clinton's private conduct, the former presidents understood the profound but intangible costs of putting him on trial before the United States Senate. A certain amount of the president's power comes from the "majesty" that adheres to the office; they did not want to see it diminished by the squalor of one individual's conduct.

But Ford's proposal seemed almost Edwardian in its quaintness. The notion that the House Republican leadership, a mostly male group led by Newt Gingrich that had developed a seething dislike of Clinton, would somehow limit its yearlong probe was unimaginable. Even the Democrats who had agreed in 1986 not to pursue impeachment against Ronald Reagan after Iran-contra nonetheless opted to continue their investigations for months. "At 85, I have no personal or political agenda, nor do I have any interest in 'rescuing' Bill Clinton. But I do care, passionately, about rescuing the country I love from further turmoil or uncertainty."

When the op-ed was published, conservatives howled. Republicans dismissed Ford's notion out of hand, and Ford's aides heard that majority whip Tom DeLay was annoyed at Ford for meddling in what was shaping up to be a constitutional showdown. If Republicans hated Ford's idea, however, Clinton was intrigued enough to approve a very private follow-up. Sometime in October, longtime Democratic Party insider Robert Strauss called Ford with a question. Acting on White House instructions, Strauss asked Ford if he would consider testifying in the upcoming House Judiciary Committee impeachment hearings on Clinton's behalf. In fact, Strauss told Ford that the White House was hoping that Ford would serve as the *sole* witness on Clinton's behalf at the House hearings.

Even from an old friend like Strauss, this was an astonishing thing to ask: would a former president from a different party take up arms for a sitting president in a free-fire zone against much younger, more conservative, more vengeful Republicans? "I told Bob there was just no way," Ford recalled. "I mean, can you imagine me, a longtime House Republican, testifying for Bill Clinton before a Republican House?" But Ford didn't rule out helping entirely. Privately, Ford told Strauss, he could play a more useful role as the crisis unfolded. If the Republicans pushed the matter to a trial in the Senate, Ford said, he would make calls to wavering Republicans. But as a *character* witness? That was asking too much.

On November 3, midterm elections confirmed one of Ford's hunches. While leaving the Republicans' ten-seat Senate margin unchanged, voters handed the Democrats an unexpected pickup of five House seats. That sparked an internal revolt against Speaker Newt Gingrich, who had predicted a six- to thirty-seat gain. Three days later, Gingrich announced he was stepping down as Speaker.

On December 11, the House Judiciary Committee voted along party lines for impeachment. By now, the vast majority of Americans favored some sort of censure over the impeachment and trial, but the House panel had opted to press ahead at all costs. That afternoon, Clinton appeared in the Rose Garden and tried to open the door to a possible censure again. "Should they determine that my errors of word and deed require their rebuke and censure I am ready to accept that." A week later, the full House approved two of four proposed articles of impeachment on a mostly party-line vote. Clinton became the second president in history to be impeached.

Calling the Club

And that was when the White House really started leaning on the former presidents. After a nudge from Al Gore, who managed the sometimes rocky channel between the West Wing and Plains, Carter called Ford and suggested a second op-ed, again in the *New York Times*. Let's make another stab at the censure idea, Carter proposed, and Ford went along. By this time the two men had been conducting successful joint operations at home and abroad for close to twenty years. They traded drafts for a few days—there were six versions in all—before agreeing on a mutually satisfactory version. The commentary appeared December 21, just two days after the House impeachment vote. In it, Ford and Carter argued for a "unique" punishment, one even more unconventional than Ford's original proposal. "We personally favor a bipartisan resolution of censure by the Senate. Under such a plan, President Clinton would have to accept rebuke while acknowledging his wrongdoing and the very real harm he has caused. The Congressional resolution should contain language stipulating that the President's acceptance of these findings—including a public acknowledgment that he did not tell the truth under oath— cannot be used in any future criminal trial to which he may be subject."

The authors had one eye on history and another on the country; once again, they feared, the presidency itself was at risk. "Fortunately, Senate procedures, through their flexibility and freedom, provide the means to end this national ordeal in ways that can uphold the rule of law without permanently damaging the presidency." The op-ed was titled "A Time to Heal Our Nation," echoing the title of Ford's memoir about his own turn in the White House two decades earlier.

Ford and Carter made it sound simple, but their proposal was laced with problems: How, exactly, might the immunity that the two presidents imagined be granted? How might special prosecutor Ken Starr be forced to abide by it? What guarantee existed that the terms of the deal would ever satisfy the president's lawyers, who by now had a reason to distrust just about everyone at the table, including their own client? And how would the most conservative Republicans, who could practically taste Clinton's hide in their teeth, ever be convinced to let him go now? The club's last-ditch effort was as short on time as it was on specifics. The momentum toward a trial was gaining speed, whatever common sense Ford and Carter were hoping to impart.

But the White House continued to explore alternative scenarios. After the second op-ed, White House counsel Charles Ruff called Ford directly. Ruff, who was in charge of the president's defense team, asked Ford what else he might be able to do to lend Clinton a hand. Ford replied that he could only be of service if Clinton copped to the perjury plea, one of four impeachment counts. Ruff told Ford that Clinton would never agree to that. And so Ford informed Ruff that he could not do any more to help. There was some history at work here: unable to wrest a clear admission of guilt out of Nixon in 1974, Ford was reluctant to embrace a similar deal in 1998.

Five days after Christmas, on December 30, Clinton picked up the phone and called Ford. The most unusual club negotiation since Ford pardoned Nixon then commenced, only this time it involved no intermediaries. Clinton told Ford that he had not committed perjury, but Ford would have none of it. And though the tone of the conversation was even and businesslike, Ford was resolute: "Bill, I think you have to admit that you lied," Ford said. "If you do that, I think that will help, and I will help you. If you'll admit perjury, I'll do more." But Clinton stuck to his story. He had not lied when he testified in January 1998 in a sexual harassment suit, he insisted, and wasn't about to change his story now to avoid a Senate trial. "I won't do that," Ford recalled Clinton saying, "I can't do that."

Ford reminded Clinton that Congress could grant immunity in exchange for a confession. But Clinton said he doubted that a bloodthirsty Republican Congress would provide such a shield for him. To which Ford replied, "Bill, I spent 25 years up there and came to the conclusion that they can pretty much do whatever they want to do." Immunity, Ford reminded Clinton, was still possible. But Clinton would not budge. The two presidents had arrived at an impasse. One had done all he could to help the other.

Or almost all. Ford remarked that the coming Senate trial would be long and unpleasant for the nation. To which Clinton replied: can you call Senate majority leader Trent Lott and impress upon him the downside of an extended trial? Ford agreed. When he did call Lott, he warned him that Clinton was in no mood to make a deal, and then made the case for a short trial.

It was common in those days to observe of Clinton, "That which doesn't kill him only makes him stronger." And by now, it occurred to Ford that Clinton might not really be looking for a way out, that he no longer feared a fight with the Republicans, and that, in some ways, he actually relished one. Coming on the heels of an election that had cost the Republicans seats in the Congress, how much worse could it get for Clinton? Why not just fight it out? While Ford was willing to reenter a conversation about rebuke or censure, it was clear to him that Clinton had decided the politics were working *for* him.

One More Bouquet

Clinton did not mention his secret negotiations with Ford in his memoir, *My Life*. And Ford only talked about them with *New York Daily News* reporter Tom DeFrank on an embargoed-until-I-die basis for DeFrank's

2007 book, *Write It When I'm Gone*. In August 1999, months after the Senate acquitted him of all charges, Clinton presented Ford with the Presidential Medal of Freedom.

The following year, Clinton watched Ford steal the show at the two hundredth birthday party for the White House, when the East Room swelled with club members. Ford wowed the crowd with embarrassing stories, particularly one about dancing with Queen Elizabeth while the Marine Band played "The Lady Is a Tramp." "I only wish I could be in such good shape when I'm 87," Clinton said of Ford afterward. "Of course, I don't think I'll ever see 87."

Ford lived to be ninety-three, the longest post-presidential tenure since Herbert Hoover. Ford chose other presidents—Carter and George W. Bush—to speak at his funeral. But Clinton found his own way to pay tribute. A few months after Ford's death, in June 2007, Clinton flew to Grand Rapids to speak at the annual black-tie dinner of the local Economics Club. Before his speech that night, he turned up at the Ford Museum downtown, bearing a bouquet of flowers and asking if he might visit the former president's tomb alone. Marty Allen, chairman of the Gerald R. Ford Foundation, escorted Clinton to the gravesite, which is set along the Grand River in a semicircular garden of gently sloping stone. Engraved in the sheltering wall above the tomb are the words "Lives Devoted to God, Country and Love." Clinton went in the gated area by himself, with no aides or photographers around, and laid his bouquet at the foot of Ford's grave, lingering longer than his hosts had expected. He then emerged, Allen recalled, obviously moved. The simplicity of the grave, Clinton remarked as he departed, "was reflective of President Ford."

And then the two men took a stroll around Grand Rapids at dusk. The bustling commercial activity downtown surprised Clinton, as did the numerous construction sites and tower cranes. Ford's hometown reminded Clinton, he told Allen, of Little Rock.

BUSH AND CLINTON:

The Rascal and the Rebel

———————— ⚷ ————————

Born forty-four days apart in the summer of 1946, the closest birth dates of any two American presidents, Bill Clinton and George W. Bush would become the political polar icons of the baby boom generation. One seemed a model conformist, who followed the pedigreed path of his Greatest Generation father almost step for step: Andover, Yale, the military, and then to West Texas for the oil business. The other was, at least in appearances, an American mutt, born into a family of mystery in Arkansas, who marched into the turmoil of the 1960s, dodged the draft, and missed a lot of law school to work on improbable Democratic political campaigns. But that contrast is what appears in a wide-angle lens. Close up, Clinton was the establishment's idea of a dream date: he was marching band and Boys State, Georgetown and a Rhodes Scholar, the earnest undergrad who interned for senators and talked at age twenty-two of deferring his military commitment in order to maintain his "political viability." And while Clinton was elected a governor at the record age of thirty-two, Bush was going nowhere until he was forty, caught in the whirlpool of entitlement and rebellion: the grandson of a senator and son of a vice president who was wrestling with booze, struggling at business, trying to find his place in the world. Bush was far more of a renegade in his family than Clinton had ever been in his: as a teenager, Bush snuck out of the family compound in Kennebunkport to smoke and drink; Clinton snuck out of his house in Hot Springs to send his allowance to Billy Graham.

One man never met his father; the other couldn't escape his father's shadow. Each would serve eight years as president; each would divide, polarize, and at times infuriate a nation; both would endure implacable criticism for their actions. One would be impeached for lying about sex; the other accused of lying to justify a war. Both would be blamed, each in his own way, for failing to stop the attacks on September 11, 2001. And each would limp out of Washington battered, exhausted, unapologetic; the club would become their infirmary. In their post-presidencies, a sense of purpose was welcome; a sense of peace even more so.

23

"He's Never Forgiven Me for Beating His Father"

—BILL CLINTON

In November 1997, the club had a reunion. Nine presidents or their kin shared the stage to mark the opening of the George Herbert Walker Bush Library in College Station, Texas. Bush thanked everyone for coming—David Eisenhower, Caroline Kennedy, Lady Bird Johnson, Julie Nixon, Nancy Reagan, plus presidents Ford, Carter, and Bill Clinton, all of whom made it to the Texas A&M campus to be a part of what a grateful Bush called a gathering of "this rather unique club of former presidents."

Of course, a future president was there too, and when the governor of Texas stepped to the microphone to welcome the crowd, he praised his father as a man who "left office with his integrity intact." That was widely seen as a dig at the man who had forced his father from power. From that day on, the relationship between Clinton and Bush the younger had nowhere to go but up.

Clinton got his next good look at Bush eighteen months later and he didn't much like the view. The encounter came at a governors' conference in Washington in February 1999, ten days after the Senate had voted to acquit Clinton of all charges stemming from his affair with Monica Lewinsky. That was merely the official conclusion to the outlandish episode; the aftershocks would unsettle the political terrain for months, even years, to come. At that moment, Bush was ascendant: he had won a second term as Texas governor and would soon announce his own bid for the White House; he was traveling the nation raising money, testing themes, quietly promising a restoration of Republican rule after the nation's embarrassing experiment with a Democrat. The Bushes were coming back and the son made it sound like a combination of rescue and revenge.

So that February, when Bush turned up at the White House, the Boomer Head Game was on: Clinton found room in his remarks to praise both Bush's father and brother Jeb, the newly elected governor of Florida, but omitted any mention of George W. Maybe as a result, Clinton got along with Jeb but found George downright surly that night, recalling later that the son seemed a lot like his mother, Barbara: smooth and gracious on the outside but sharp and unforgiving beneath the veneer. He assumed the hostility was personal, not ideological. "Of course, he's never forgiven me for beating his father," Clinton said afterward, "but that's about as deep as his political conviction gets." Years later, Clinton recalled the unusual experience of hosting both George W. and Jeb Bush at the White House when they were governors, noting that the Bush boys reacted differently to being a guest of the enemy. "Jeb was a better actor than W. was. Jeb would come to the governor's conferences and pay attention and ask questions in a very respectful way." By contrast, he added, "W. didn't like being in the White House when I was there. Now, I don't believe that Jeb Bush was a bit happier about me defeating his father." The elder son, he said, just didn't believe in pretending to be gracious.

When Clinton's aides noted that George W. seemed particularly uncomfortable that night in the White House, Clinton came to his defense: "Look, the guy's just being honest. What's he supposed to do, like me? I defeated his father, he loves his father. It doesn't bother me, this is a contact sport."

The Shadow

There's no way to measure what portion of Bush's presidential ambition arose from the desire to punish Clinton and the Democrats for ejecting his father from office. As Bush noted in his memoirs, if he had always longed to be president, he would have done a lot of things differently when he was younger. But politics was always part of the picture. He dabbled in campaigns as early as 1964; he had run for Congress in 1978 and lost; ten years later, he was in Dallas buying into a baseball franchise and plotting a race for Texas governor. Some part of Bush's interest in the top job was simply about wanting to beat the odds: after his father was elected, Bush allowed an old friend to produce a report for him measuring how the children of all previous forty presidents had fared in life. This telling exercise produced a discouraging forty-four-page result: many, it turned out, couldn't hold jobs, died young, struggled with addictions and depression. While one had gone on to be president himself, none had been elected governor. Bush had groaned when he learned that. His memoirs make only the most cursory mention of why he wanted the top job—cutting taxes, reforming education and entitlements—but the truth is he had a natural feel for the game. "I love campaigns," he said in 2000. "My heritage is a part of who I am."

Watching his father lose to Clinton in 1992 was also part of that heritage, an experience that capped what he called the "worst year of my life." But if Bush was running in part to avenge his father's defeat, Clinton's sexual escapades certainly helped to make Bush's candidacy credible. Bush never mentioned Clinton's womanizing on the campaign trail, but when he promised at every stop to "restore honor and dignity to the White House," everyone knew what he meant. Close friends reported that Bush was privately appalled by Clinton's behavior, not only what he had done but where he had done it. For Bush, the sex was a metaphor for Clinton's general lack of discipline. Watching one of Clinton's epic State of the Union speeches, which were usually lengthy to-do lists for the coming year, Bush remarked impatiently, "A good leader sets priorities— he doesn't just list."

All that may explain why, by the time the Republican race got fully under way in early 2000, *Clintonian* was such a nasty, room-clearing label that even Republicans hurled it at one another to gain an advantage. When dirty tricks in the days before the South Carolina primary led John McCain to charge that Bush "twists the truth like Clinton," Bush's advisors portrayed the remark as outrageous, unthinkably unfair, "the worst insult one Republican could hurl at another," Bush advisor Karl

Rove said. And so Bush made a point of firing back in these words: "When John McCain compares me to Bill Clinton and said I was untrustworthy, that's over the line. Disagree with me, fine. But do not challenge my integrity."

Clinton assumed, if only because of his name and his money, that Bush would win the nomination easily. And as he watched Bush push McCain out of the race, he gained a grudging respect for the Texan as a political combatant. But as the prospect of a Bush matchup against Gore emerged, he grew concerned. He believed that Bush was running a shrewd, virtually substance-free campaign, and that his "compassionate conservative" slogan was fresh enough to sound appealing but vague enough to avoid criticism. "I studied him closely," Clinton told us in 2011. "The first time he did that compassionate conservative thing, I picked up the phone and called Gore's guy and I said, 'Bush is the only one that can beat you. Because you don't get what this compassionate conservative thing is really about. Forget what is in the headlines, this is saying to the swing voters, we'll give you the same economy Clinton did with a smaller government, bigger tax cut, how can you be against it?' I said, 'It's a genius slogan. It's a genius slogan.'"

Clinton was conflicted; on the one hand, he didn't think much of a personality-based campaign that argued, in effect, that voters should choose the candidate they'd rather have a beer with. On the other hand, he could see that it was working. Whatever he thought of Bush's policy positions, even Clinton found Bush personally appealing. Attending the funeral mass in New York of John Cardinal O'Connor in May, Clinton reached across four other worshippers to pass the peace to Bush, telling a friend afterward, "I don't always respect the guy, but you just gotta' like him."

While many Americans assumed that Bush II would be a reprise of the kinder, gentler era of Bush I, Clinton could see that the younger Bush was a much tougher customer than his father and Bush's choice of Dick Cheney as a running mate in midsummer confirmed that for him. Clinton feared that Bush would roll back his accomplishments—not the centrist ones like NAFTA and welfare reform, but certainly the tax increases of 1993 that set the nation on a path toward a balanced budget as well as some of his anticrime initiatives. He wanted Gore to enlist him as a fellow soldier in the campaign, but the vice president kept Clinton at arm's length. Clinton tried to help anyway: he slipped into full-blown parody of Bush at a private midsummer Democratic fund-raiser, complete with a Texas twang, that suggested just how worried he really was. "Well, how bad could I be? I'm a governor. My Daddy was president. I owned a baseball team. They *like* me down in Texas."

That was an honest rendering of how Clinton felt but a sloppy thing for a president to have said. Bush deftly swatted away the parody, warning the White House that Clinton would be wise to stay on the sidelines. Asked in October about Clinton's infidelity, Bush replied, "I'm not running against President Clinton. That's a chapter . . . most of us would rather forget. I don't think there's a lot of politics to be gained by talking about him. As a matter of fact, I think most Americans would rather move on, and that's what I'm going to do." But, Bush added, "if he decides he can't help himself and gets out there and starts campaigning against me, the shadow returns."

The shadow, of course, was the Lewinsky affair, the very thing that Gore believed was costing him votes and made it impossible for Gore to ask Clinton for help the way Bush had relied on Reagan. Clinton doubted this logic, telling a few friends, "There isn't one person in America who thinks Al would have had an affair with Monica Lewinsky."

When the votes were counted, no clear winner emerged. Gore won the popular vote by more than 500,000, but Bush was ahead by a few hundred votes in Florida, which meant he would win the Electoral College and the presidency if the tallies held. The recount in Florida—and the legal fight about whether to have one—lasted five weeks, until the Supreme Court voted 5–4 to uphold Bush's victory in mid-December.

Four days later, Bush flew to Washington, spent fifteen minutes with Gore at the Naval Observatory, and then met Clinton at the White House. By then, with the election over, his wife, Hillary, safely elected to the Senate, and his own future wide open, Clinton could afford to be the gracious host. This was an especially unusual handoff; Bush wasn't so much moving in, as moving back. So aware was Clinton of how many nights and weekends Bush had already spent in the White House while his father was president that he joked that his guest already knew where the light switches were. Now the terms of their fraternal relations were shifting; they clicked virtually from hello this time, talking first in the Oval Office and then moving to the residence for a ninety-minute lunch.

They talked about the transition, some last-minute judicial appointments, free trade (where they agreed), and the economy (where they didn't). Clinton asked Bush to protect his beloved AmeriCorps national service program, just as Bush's father had asked Clinton to preserve the Points of Light Initiative eight years before. The conversation quickly turned personal: Bush asked Clinton if he minded the mention of "the shadow" during the campaign; he had done it, Bush explained, to keep Gore off balance. Must have worked, Clinton replied, as Gore rarely wanted me at his side.

Before leaving, Bush made a surprising request. Recalling Clinton's comically dull 1988 Democratic convention speech in Atlanta at which Clinton had droned on so long he was eventually heckled and booed, Bush said: "With all due respect, you used not to be so great a speaker. You're good now." How, Bush was asking, did Clinton become so deft at shaping the national conversation?

The incoming president was trolling for tips on how to give a good speech.

The question was especially striking, coming from a man who had just been elected and never seemed to lack for confidence. But rallying your base or even running a national campaign is not the same as leading a country—all of it—through whatever passage might lie ahead. Could the club help with that?

Clinton had to relish this moment, just as Reagan had relished teaching Clinton how to salute eight years earlier. And so the sitting president proceeded to hold a mini-clinic of his own for the new kid: timing, Clinton replied, it's all in the timing, the pacing, and the careful parsing of the words on the page, letting it unfold like a good sermon or lecture. But Clinton liked what he saw; he said to friends, "Bush really connects. It's a mistake to underestimate him."

By the time inauguration day approached, it was clear that Clinton did not really want to leave, despite—or maybe because of—all the blows he had survived. He was only fifty-four years old, younger than any two-term president other than Teddy Roosevelt. It was not just the reflexive reluctance to relinquish vast power; this departure scraped at him so deeply he took it upon himself to study the 22nd Amendment closely, concluding that there was no other way to read it than as a lifetime ban on more than two terms. It might be possible to slip back in if he was somehow elected vice president and then ascended to the top job in the event of the commander in chief's death, he explained. But he realized that the idea would seem outrageous to most people. "I love this job," he said in the final weeks in office. "I think I'm getting better at it. I'd run again in a heartbeat if I could."

But the strange and slippery manner of Clinton's exit only helped remind people why they were ready for him to leave. The outgoing president issued more than 175 pardons in his final days, including one absolving Marc Rich of fifty-one charges of tax evasion, fraud, and racketeering. Clinton ignored virtually all of his top aides' advice when he signed the Rich pardon and, to make matters worse, it turned out that some of the people who had been pushing hardest for Rich behind the scenes had also sent "going away" presents to Clinton and his wife that totaled nearly $200,000. As the weeks passed, the Rich affair took on a life of its own. Rich's ex-wife, Denise, turned out to be a $450,000 donor to Clinton's presidential library fund, which was just being launched. At best, the arrangement reeked of poor judgment; at worst it looked like a slimy quid pro quo. Jimmy Carter labeled the arrangement "disgraceful." Outgoing commerce secretary Bill Daley described it as "terrible, devastating and rather appalling."

The pardons, and the congressional hearings they engendered, guaranteed that Clinton's ghost would linger in Washington well after Clinton himself had left. In early February, *Time* put a tiny picture of Clinton wearing a sweatshirt and tennis shoes on its cover with the line "The Incredible Shrinking ex-President" and noted how strange it was "to watch a shiny new ex-president disappear under a freak mudslide." The next week, Clinton wrote an op-ed in the *New York Times* trying to explain "what he did and why." Former aides explained that Clinton would happily call everyone in the country and explain it to them in person if it would help.

All this noise sweetened Bush's honeymoon. Clinton "is making the honesty and integrity case for us," an aide said. "We don't have to do anything." In fact, they were doing plenty. The Bush White House pulled out every stop to make it clear that a new team was in town, that it was nothing like the last, and no matter what the outcome of the election, there would be no doubting who was president now. They claimed departing Clinton aides had vandalized the White House, prying the letter W off computer keyboards and pilfering government property. Meanwhile Bush aides moved to freeze all new regulations before the inaugural parade was over, rolled back as many of Clinton's executive orders as they could find, and announced over and over that the old king was gone and living in Chappaqua, New York, where the Clintons had bought a new home. The comparisons kept coming: Where Clinton could second-guess all night, Bush didn't "do nuance." Where Clinton was tardy, Bush was punctual to the point of arriving at events a few minutes early. Where Clinton was often the best-informed person in White House meetings, Bush was only too happy to be tutored by aides. If Bubba had wandered into the Oval Office around nine and worked past midnight, Dubya was a straight eight-hours man, in by 7:15 A.M., gone by dinner, and asleep by ten, if not earlier. "I don't like to sit around in meetings for hours and hours and hours," Bush told *Time* in March. "People will tell you, I get to the point."

If Bush was determined to show who was now in charge, Clinton was equally prepared to respect the club's rules of succession. In early 2001, for example, Clinton appealed to National Security Advisor Condoleezza Rice for permission to give a speech in Hong Kong at the very moment that the White House was trying to negotiate the release of twenty-four detained servicemen after their U.S. Navy EP-3 aircraft had been forced down over China in April.

Clinton wanted to go and give the speech—in part because he needed the money. But he didn't want to get in the way of delicate administration efforts to retrieve the crew, if not the airplane itself. Complicating the journey, Clinton knew, was the presence at the Hong Kong event of Jiang Zemin, the Chinese president and an old Clinton friend. Clinton could not go and ignore Jiang. But he didn't want to take the meeting and run afoul of Bush's efforts to bring the crisis to a close—much less be seen interfering. And so he put in a call to Rice, whom he knew well because she had been the Stanford University provost when his daughter, Chelsea, had been an undergraduate there.

"I said, 'Condi, I need to give a speech, they're gonna pay me a ridiculous amount of money and you guys nearly bankrupted me. I'm an American first and here's the problem, Jiang Zemin is going to be there and the airplane's still on the island and I cannot go there without seeing him. He's my friend and I will not insult him or be rude or do anything. So you have to tell me what to do. If you don't want me to go, I won't go. If you want me to go, I'll deliver the message and I will make sure he knows it's President Bush's message, not mine. There's only one president at a time, whether I agree with it or not.'

"And Condi called me back and said 'we'd like for you to go.' And so I said 'Okay, what am I supposed to say?' . . . I wanted them to have the confidence that I would never try to undermine their policy. He had to know that I would never stab him in the back."

It would not be long before that promise would be tested.

Who Lost bin Laden?

The attacks on September 11, 2001, brought everyone together—including the members of the club. This is the one sure summons, when the nation is startled out of its habits and hopes by cataclysm, in this case a shocking ambush that was all the more terrifying for its simple efficiency; nineteen men, four planes, one morning that forever changed the meaning of the date. It was the bloodiest day on American soil since the Civil War, and by the time the day was over it was clear that this untested president whose eight months had been no better than average was now facing an act of war by an enemy unlike any in the nation's history.

It wasn't just the country under attack; it was the presidency itself. Bush was traveling in Florida when a "credible threat" forced the evacuation of the White House, and eventually State and Justice and all the federal office buildings. The west side of the Pentagon was already in flames. Secret Service officers had automatic weapons drawn as they patrolled Lafayette Park, across from the White House. A security detail rushed Vice President Dick Cheney to a bunker by the seat of his pants; he told Bush aboard Air Force One that security agencies believed both the White House and Bush's plane were targets. In Bush's airborne office, aides heard Bush on the phone. "That's what we're paid for, boys," he said. "We're gonna' take care of this. We're going to find out who did this. They're not going to like me as President."

Ford, Carter, the senior Bush, and Clinton all flew to Washington for a grim and moving memorial service at the National Cathedral three days later. The president invoked FDR's phrase about "the warm courage of national unity" to heal and then bind Americans. After the speech, the world watched as Bush's father, now seventy-seven, reached over and squeezed his son's hand in the front pew.

But once America's dramatic invasion of Afghanistan gave way to a less satisfying occupation, whatever unity had existed within the club cracked under the pressure of political scapegoating. By midsummer 2002, a much broader argument broke out about which president—Bush or Clinton—was most responsible for permitting Osama bin Laden's al Qaeda network to get big enough to attack the United States in the first place. This line of inquiry, which would eventually become a focus of a huge bipartisan commission, had the potential to leave permanent marks on both presidents. The best way to avoid being blamed, both camps realized, was to point a finger at the other. Former Clinton national security officials began telling reporters in mid-2002 that they had clearly and repeatedly warned Bush, Cheney, NSC advisor Condoleezza Rice, and other Bush aides about the dangers of al Qaeda during the transition. Richard Clarke, Clinton's top terrorist advisor, presented the Bush team with a plan to aggressively target al Qaeda's leaders after Bush was sworn in, and though Clarke remained on Bush's NSC staff for a time, his plan was ignored. Clinton partisans alleged that the Bush team was much more interested in halting nuclear proliferation in North Korea and Iran and revising a missile defense treaty with Russia than it was in finding a rich Saudi troublemaker in Afghanistan. This was a serious charge—not only because it would amount to negligence if true, but also because it threatened to become a useful weapon for the Democrats as the 2004 election approached.

In response, the Republicans gave as good as they were getting. Vice President Cheney led the White House effort to kill the bipartisan 9/11 Commission to investigate the roots of the attacks and warned Democrats in private that Clinton and his party would be damaged if the inquiry went forward. Other Bush allies charged that Clinton had missed multiple chances to kill bin Laden in the 1990s either because he lacked the will or because he was distracted by the Lewinsky scandal. If anyone was asleep at the switch, they argued, it was Bubba not Dubya. This line of argument had some merit as well: though Clinton launched air strikes on bin Laden's training camps in August 1998, right in the middle of some of the most unpleasant days of the sex scandal, several other military operations against al Qaeda were planned and readied on his watch but never activated. On the rare occasions when Clinton's intelligence officers could claim that they were certain of bin Laden's whereabouts, his legal advisors were reluctant to authorize attacks that were thinly veiled assassination efforts. "Almost all of the 'authorities' President Clinton provided to us with regard to bin Laden were predicated on the planning of a capture operation," CIA director George Tenet noted. "Bin Laden could resist and might be killed in the ensuing battle. But the context was almost always to attempt to capture him first."

When the bipartisan 9/11 panel released its findings in July 2004, it was praised for being detailed, well written, and evenhanded. But it laid barely a glove on either president. The final 567-page report was a strange, no-fault document that seemed to presume that the two commanders in chief, at least, did nothing wrong: Clinton was cleared of any charges that he had missed a chance to kill bin Laden in advance of the 2001 attacks; the report noted that he had instead tried a variety of tactics and strategies designed to degrade al Qaeda. At the same time, Bush was spared any direct criticism for failing to act when he came into office and reported that some of his aides had their own doubts about the wisdom of targeting individuals. And where there was evidence of either president underperforming in the war on terrorism, the report detailed those in such neutral terms that the reader could be forgiven for not knowing how many opportunities had been missed. The club would have surely supported this narrative technique had it been put to a vote.

And in the matter of what Clinton had told Bush about bin Laden in their pre-inaugural conversation in December 2000? The two presidents had different recollections about that. Clinton specifically recalled warning Bush about bin Laden before the swearing in. "I think you will find that by far your biggest threat is bin Laden and the al Qaeda," Clinton claims to have told Bush. "One of the great regrets of my presidency is that I didn't get him for you, because I tried to." But Bush remembered it differently. He told the 9/11 Commission that while the two men discussed terrorism in general that day, he had no recollection of any specific mention of al Qaeda by Clinton.

In the most critical conversation between an outgoing and an incoming president since Eisenhower briefed Kennedy, Clinton and Bush could not agree on who said what.

By the time their differing memories became public in the panel's final report in July 2004, Bush and Clinton were well down the road toward a friendship. The first sign of warming came in late spring of 2004, when Bush and Clinton saw each other three times in the space of fifteen days. The men, along with Bush's father, sat three abreast at the dedication ceremonies for a new World War II monument on the National Mall on Memorial Day; Clinton's lengthy memoirs had just been released and Bush ribbed his predecessor that he would read the first half and his father would read the second.

The next week, Ronald Reagan died at the age of ninety-three; and so the presidents sat side by side at Reagan's funeral at the National Cathedral. Three days after that, Bush welcomed the Clintons back to the White House for the unveiling of their official portraits. Bush praised Clinton at some length, but singled out his "far ranging knowledge of public policy, a great compassion for people in need, and the forward looking spirit Americans like in a president." Laura Bush praised her predecessor as well. Clinton said he was humbled by Bush's "kind and generous words. . . . Made me feel like I was a pickle stepping into history."

Four days later, in a lengthy conversation over Diet Cokes at home in Chappaqua, Clinton had nearly as much sympathy for Bush as he had criticism. He worried that Bush had squandered a rare moment in American history to build national unity after years of partisan division. And he wondered whether Bush's all-in focus on terrorism had consumed his presidency and led to headlong decisions like the invasion of Iraq. "I think we needed a little missionary zeal after 9/11," he said. "But the exercise of power in the grip of any obsession is always a risk. There's a difference between having convictions and obsessions. And, by the way, I had to fight this. I was almost obsessed with bin Laden and the record will reflect that. And you know, I have repeatedly defended President Bush against the left in Iraq, even though I don't agree. I think he should have waited until the UN inspections were over."

But Clinton had grudging admiration for the way Bush had managed the politics of 9/11 and how effectively he had neutralized the Democrats both in the way he got credit for creating the Department of Homeland Security in 2002 and over the war in Iraq that followed. "I always thought Bush was a good politician," Clinton said. "I never thought he was dumb. There's a difference between not knowing certain things and being dumb. But I never bought that. Not ever, not for a minute. I never believed it."

As his wife's campaign for the 2008 Democratic nomination got under way in 2007, Clinton explained to Bush that he may have to take a swing at him every now and then. "I said, 'You know Hillary is in politics and because she is, sometimes it's necessary for me to disagree with you. But I will always do it respectfully.'"

As Bush's days in office began to wind down, he reached out to Clinton more, usually on weekends. The two men would talk on the phone, aides reported, discussing the ups and downs of the fall campaign, speaking in what one advisor said was a kind of shorthand code about voting blocs and state polls and political messaging. Bush's aides made trips to Little Rock and tapped their counterparts for tips about how to plan, site, and build a presidential library.

Bush and Clinton would, in time, find something to agree—and team up—on when they both retired. Clinton called him before the election to welcome him to emeritus status and promise Bush that there was plenty of life after politics. They talked again in November, the day before President-elect Barack Obama was to visit Bush in the White House. "I remember how gracious you were to me," Bush told Clinton. "I hope I can be as gracious [to his successor] as you were to me." As George and Laura flew home to Texas after the inauguration, his friends and departing aides screened a surprise, twenty-minute video tribute—which featured, among others, Bill Clinton, previewing life after the White House.

BUSH AND BUSH:

Father and Son

——————— ⊤—•○ ———————

By the time the younger man joined the club, the older man had known him for fifty-four years—all his life. They had already worked through a series of nicknames: Big George and Little George. Poppy and Junior. Now they could just use numbers, which they had stitched on their baseball caps: 41 and 43.

But mostly, obviously, ultimately, they were father and son. Of all the benefits the club could offer any president, none compared to the prospect of having someone a phone call away who knew the job better than any of your advisors but also knew your strong suits and blind spots, not to mention the birthdays of your children. Imagine having someone on speed dial who had also carried the punishing burdens of being commander in chief, but who had no agenda except your success. That would be quite a resource.

The ingredients were all there; starting in 2001, the club was poised for its finest hour ever.

And yet, both men tell a story of a relationship that was circumscribed. It started out that way for reasons of politics; it finished that way for reasons of policy. The two men functioned, as they explain it, not as nearly consecutive presidents but almost entirely as family; George W. Bush was not a president looking for advice but a son looking for understanding.

This was a bond that should have been tighter than any club. But families are more complicated than politics.

——————— ⊤—•○ ———————

24

"I Love You More Than Tongue Can Tell"

—GEORGE H. W. BUSH

George W. Bush carried a much bigger burden into the Oval Office than his father had.

His father *was* the burden. How would he measure up?

It was commonplace in liberal circles to explain nearly everything about the second Bush presidency in the context of a mad, Oedipal mission that went like this: Bush so longed for his father's approval that he spent the early part of his life trying to be just like him. And when that didn't work out so well, he spent the next part of his life trying to defy him, overlearning the lessons of his presidency, overreaching overseas to come up with a cogent foreign policy of his own—only to lead the nation into a disastrous, unnecessary war and ultimately an economic disaster. And all this supposedly happened because once upon a time there was a distant and distracted father, perpetually disappointed in a son who consistently underperformed the family's expectations.

It would be easier to dismiss that idea as too tidy if the son did not occasionally seem to acknowledge it. "I know there is a lot of psychobabble out there, that you know he and I compete and was trying to overshadow the father and all this," George W. Bush said in 2010. "Look, I think people would be surprised to learn that this relationship is based on love. It's not as complex as some would like it to be. I admired him. And he never disappointed me. He was always a great father. He was always a man who gave unconditional love. And so when it came time to run for president, I was motivated in large part—look I wanted to run. I had an agenda. You know I had a team of people I was coming with. The truth of the matter is that the final motivating factor was my admiration for George Bush and I wondered whether or not I had what it took to get in the arena like he did."

But the notion that the relationship between father and son defined the younger man's presidency has it backward. It was the younger man's presidency that defined the father-son relationship.

Two Men, Two Visions

Inside the Bush clan, George W. had always been larger than life. He was the firstborn, the biggest personality of the five children, the one with the "slightly outrageous streak," said his aunt Nancy Ellis. He smoked cigarettes as a teenager, whacked golf balls at cars along the coast road in Kennebunkport, and was arrested for drunk driving at the age of thirty. Because he was seven years older than the next surviving child, he was the leader of a large brood of brothers and cousins, the Spanky of his gang, the one they all looked up to. He was, a cousin recalled, "a very broad personality but he always kept just within the lines of truly offensive. The parents would roll their eyes and say, 'Oh my God, you didn't,' but there was some appreciative eye rolling in that."

But like most young men, he could stray over the line too. His critics would make much of the fact that he once squared off with his father after banging up the family car; years later, the encounter sounds more banal than formative. "There is an infamous story about me driving home late one night, running over the neighbors' trash can and then smarting off to Dad. When some people picture that scene, they envision two presidents locked in some epic psychological showdown. In reality, I was a boozy kid and he was an understandably irritated father."

What was different was that being the oldest and sharing (most of) his father's famous name meant that George W. faced challenges his siblings never did. He simply took his parents—and their expectations—more seriously than the children who followed him. "The others almost felt, 'That's W's job,'" said a cousin. "'We don't have to measure up. We're just living our lives here.'" That was partly because George carried scars the others did not: he alone among his siblings had lived at age seven through the death of his younger sister Robin from leukemia in 1953. That childhood trauma made the eldest son live much more in the moment, search for the fun in everything—and bound him even more closely to his blunt-spoken mom. He took his role as protective oldest brother seriously, which sometimes meant playing the role of family clown. "Half the time," recalled brother Marvin, "he acts younger than all of us combined." If George took after his mother, he revered his father, which meant that when he was hauled in for discipline, even a mild verdict of "disappointed" from the father could be crushing to the son. He once skipped out a week early on a summer job; when his father called him to his Houston office for a dressing-down, the young man found the experience devastating. His siblings watched the oldest boy collapse at such moments. George "could be made to feel that he had committed the worst crime in the world," Marvin once said.

He followed his father's path through early life: to Andover and then Yale, into the military as a pilot, and then to graduate school at Harvard. But the old investments no longer paid the same dividends: coming from West Texas instead of Greenwich, he found Andover and Yale to be a culture shock; he wore defiantly cowboy boots and a bomber jacket around Cambridge, which was far less hospitable to legatees in the 1960s and 1970s than New Haven had been to his father's generation in the 1940s and 1950s. After business school, he scratched out a living in the oilfields of the Permian Basin, where his father had prospered and eventually made millions. He made a lunge at a congressional seat at the age of thirty-two, won the primary, and then lost to a seasoned Democrat who painted him as an Eastern-educated carpetbagger who was simply trading on his father's name. He married a librarian from Midland named Laura Welch, had twins in 1981, and waited for daylight.

But the oil business turned sour, his drilling ventures languished, and his drinking problem continued until his wife put her foot down. Once he got sober, he still needed a way out from under his father's shadow and he found one by stepping into it again. In 1986, he moved his family into a townhouse in Washington, where he began work on his father's 1988 presidential campaign. Bush didn't much like D.C., but around the campaign's 14th Street headquarters, where everyone called him Junior, he needed no introduction. He established himself as the family enforcer and took responsibility for bringing in the fast-growing and elusive evangelical vote, memorizing names of religious leaders across the Midwest, sometimes giving seven speeches a day, and realizing for the first time that he might actually be good at the family business. Inside the New Orleans Superdome in August, the son took the microphone to deliver the votes of the Texas delegation that put his father over the top.

They turned out to be a better team than either man expected. Where his father was methodical, thoughtful, sometimes slow to act, the son was instinctive, impulsive, and famously impatient. If the old man gave all newcomers an even chance, the son regarded strangers as guilty until proven innocent. The incoming president was quick to forgive; his son could hold a grudge forever. "I tend to be a quick judge of people," he said in 1989. "I don't know how accurate I am, but all that matters is what I think." The father delighted in creating an imaginary panel called the Ranking Committee to judge his aides on how well they golfed or played tennis or even slept through important meetings, all in order to keep things light and breezy. By contrast, the son created a truly genuine and completely secret board when his father was elected in 1988 called the Silent Committee, which he convened to make sure that the most ardent Bush loyalists found government jobs. By the time the campaign was over Bush felt that he had expunged any doubts about his utility and won his father's appreciation. "In the campaign, he and I attained a new level of friendship," he said afterward, somewhat awkwardly. "I know there were times—I could just tell—when he respected my opinion."

Somehow that success freed Bush to go his own way. After his father was sworn in, the son moved his family back to Texas and recruited a team of investors to buy the Texas Rangers baseball team. Bush was laying the foundation for his first genuine business success as well as another run at political office. And, for once, he was not rushing things. The *Dallas Morning News* caught him one morning in early 1989 in his office, too busy with backroom negotiations to talk to his father, who was calling from Tokyo. "Dad, I'm fixin' to give a speech," he said, just slightly annoyed. "Everything is fine. Call me when you get back from Japan." He raised millions, did the big deal, took over as general manager—and became a fixture in the Metroplex by prowling the old Arlington Stadium at every home game, sometimes with a bat in hand. "I want the folks to see me sitting in the same kind of seat they sit in, eating the same popcorn, peeing in the same urinal," he said. More than anything else, said brother Marvin, baseball was "a real opportunity for him to be George W. Bush and not George Bush, Jr."

The son stayed away from his father's White House, except for the occasional family visit, and stuck to the baseball diamond instead. He kept tabs by phone, and he had a few old friends working at key choke points in the White House who kept him up to speed on office politics. When his father asked him in mid-1991 to speak to John Sununu about stepping aside as chief of staff, the suggestion from the son did not budge the president's top aide. Around the Bush White House, the son was still widely known as "Junior."

He bragged in late 1991 that there was no way that the Democrats could defeat his father in 1992 but otherwise had little to do with the reelection campaign. When Bill Clinton prevailed in that contest, both father and son were devastated, though the son was less surprised. Still, it made his 1994 victory over Texas governor Ann Richards all the sweeter and set the stage for his own run for the White House.

Four years later, he was openly running for president, raising record amounts of money, and acting as if his father didn't exist. The first two years of the first Bush's presidency had delivered solid bipartisan achievements at home: a new clean air measure, a historic civil rights act for disabled Americans, and a landmark deficit reduction deal. But each was anathema to the party's right wing. Which meant the younger Bush would need to take a harder line on economic and social issues while signaling to uncertain independent voters that he wasn't a hopeless ideologue. Hence the mantle of the "compassionate conservative." He campaigned for lower taxes, greater participation in government programs by churches and other faith-based groups, and tougher educational standards in the public schools. If his father had run as a kinder and gentler successor to Ronald Reagan, the son would instead run as Reagan.

At the heart of the son's strategy was a belief that the first Bush's presidency had failed because the father didn't properly manage intra-party politics and, as a result, had failed to win a second term. Bush and his top strategist, Karl Rove, were determined not to make the same mistakes. The first Bush's record, over time, would come to be recognized for its many successes: the older man dramatically revised the nation's finances and put them on a path toward a balanced budget; he deftly managed the fall of the Soviet Union, the main enemy of the United States for nearly forty years; he reduced the footprint of U.S. forces overseas and, using overwhelming military force, he ousted Manuel Noriega from power in Panama in a matter of weeks and pushed Saddam Hussein's army out of Kuwait and back to Iraq in a matter of days.

His recession lasted two quarters only.

But it was an article of faith in conservative circles that the presidency of Bush 41 was a failure at best and a betrayal of conservatism at worst—mainly for raising taxes and losing to Clinton. And so while many of the same people who helped the older man in office all pitched in to get the son elected, there was some unspoken awkwardness from the start; the record of the older Bush was never brought to bear to help the younger.

But if the father was rarely visible, direct criticism of him would not be tolerated. After Nebraska senator Chuck Hagel turned up in Austin to take Bush's measure in person, he announced to waiting reporters that the younger man was tougher, more conservative, and more disciplined than his father. And though that was exactly the message Rove was hoping to send to the party's ever-suspicious rank and file, Hagel's remarks upset the son because they impugned the father. Bush might criticize his father's way of doing business, but no one else could.

These protective feelings traveled in both directions. By 2000, with the younger man on the verge of capturing the nomination only eight years after his father had done so, the older man's feelings of pride surpassed his ability to actually say them out loud. When the time came for the father to shoot the Republican Party's official biographical video about his son, he broke down on camera and the session had to be halted. On January 21, 2001, the younger Bush was sworn in as the forty-third president wearing the same cuff links his father had worn twelve years earlier. When they finally met alone in the Oval Office later that day, now as club members, neither man could speak. "The moment," the new president recalled, "was more moving than either of us could have expressed."

The Son Becomes the Comforter

For most of the campaign, an unspoken rule had been observed: the father would be seen and not heard. It followed that any reports of the two men trading tips and pointers were routinely denied. After Bush had secured the nomination—and suddenly needed independent and moderate voters to give him a chance—a few exceptions to that rule were made. "I'm a warrior for my Dad," he said before the Philadelphia convention during one particularly wide-ranging interview with Walter Isaacson of *Time*. "My Dad gives me advice when I ask for it," like when he inquired about how to pick a vice president. "If someone says no," W. asked his father, "do they mean it?" They talked specifically about the merits of Dick Cheney; the older man knew Cheney's strengths and weaknesses and believed he would make a good match. (In fact, the younger man's second choice for the vice president's job, Senator John Danforth, had been high on his father's short list in 1988 as well.)

But after the 9/11 attacks, when Bush was under pressure to be seen as the confident commander in chief, the father stepped back and you could be forgiven for thinking the older man was in another line of work entirely. "Now and then George will ask me about something," he said, "but I am out of the line. I'm not up on things any longer. And I don't want to get crossways with his people." The father knew the battle against Islamic terrorists would be harder and more complicated than those he had waged as president. He urged his son to reach out to Muslims in the United States after 9/11, mindful, he said, of how many American leaders mishandled the Japanese internment issue during World War II. He also told his son that the unity of 9/11 would not last forever. But beyond that, he said, his role was limited to something more basic: "What I can do these days is kind of put my arm around him from hundreds of miles away."

"As for making the tough decisions—I knew George could handle it," Bush recalled to us. "So I didn't worry too much about that. But on 9/11, I couldn't quit thinking about George and what he was facing. The whole world changed the minute that the second plane hit the second tower. None of George's recent predecessors faced a moment like that. None of us."

When the president decided in early 2002 that he was going to invade Iraq and topple Saddam Hussein, he was undertaking the grandest deviation from his father yet. The elder man had faced the same question in 1991 and pointedly decided trying to overthow Saddam was military folly as well as a diplomatic nightmare. He and Brent Scowcroft had said as much in their joint memoir. Even the son thought his father had done the right thing at the time. But this George Bush believed that times had changed: that 9/11 made the world a more dangerous place, that al Qaeda could either join forces with Saddam to threaten the region or conspire with him to develop nuclear weapons.

Bush's march toward war split Bushworld in half in 2002. Many of the father's advisors were skeptical of war, fearing it would cost billions, distract the United States from its focus on terror, and lead to a military quagmire. The son's A-team—Cheney, Don Rumsfeld, Paul Wolfowitz—were all gung ho, overconfident, uninterested in dissent. James Baker wrote an op-ed in the *New York Times* in August urging prudence (but stopping short of opposing an invasion). Scowcroft wrote a commentary in the *Wall Street Journal* that flatly opposed military action. The two articles were widely seen by both those who backed Bush and those who opposed him as a coded message from father to son: *I wouldn't do this if I were you.*

What made Scowcroft's piece remarkable wasn't that he opposed the invasion; it was that he, alone in the realm of Bush retainers, came out and said what so many of them were privately thinking. Much of the realist Republican cosmos opposed the idea of invading another country on a hunch but was either too conflicted or too scared to take on the popular president a year after 9/11. But Scowcroft, having worked for Nixon, knew too well the dangers of just saluting the commander in chief. "We need to think about this issue very carefully," Scowcroft wrote. "There is scant evidence to tie Saddam to terrorist organizations, and even less to the Sept. 11 attacks."

When the piece appeared, Bush 43 was furious. Though Scowcroft had never sworn an oath to the son, Bush felt he had violated the family's code of loyalty. "I was angry that Brent had chosen to publish his advice in the newspaper instead of sharing it with me," he recalled. "I knew critics would later exploit Brent's article if the diplomatic track failed." As for the popular notion that the op-ed was a smoke signal from father to son, Bush said, "that was ridiculous. Of all people, Dad understood the stakes. If he thought I was handling Iraq wrong, he damn sure would have told me himself."

When the son complained to his father, the older man put Scowcroft in a different category from all other retainers—and granted him the immunity that came with it. "Son," he said, "Brent is a friend."

That ended that. But what *did* the father think? One top official who supported the war explained that in the period leading up to the invasion, the father avoided all interviews and speeches, certain that anything he said about any aspect of the war or its implications would explode into its own sideshow. Whether he supported or opposed the war apart from his son, the official said, is moot, because the father could never separate the one from the other. Instead, the father believed that his son had plenty of advisors who were far more clued in than he was; but he had only one father to offer unconditional support when everyone else had doubts. And so even if the father had his reservations, he decided what role he would play. "With 41, it was, I'm supporting this guy 100 percent," this official said. "No distance."

Where he did speak out, he did so according to club rules. "I want the US president to have as much worldwide support as possible," Bush 41 said in a September 2002 interview with *Time*. "But I want to do it the way the President wants it done. If he decides we must act alone, I'm with him all the way."

Those who spoke to the father said he worried less about the policy than the burden on the son. The two did discuss the looming war at Camp David on Christmas 2002 and the gist of that conversation, at least as the son related it in his memoirs, amounted to a blessing. "For the most part, I didn't seek Dad's advice on major issues," Bush wrote. "He and I both understood that I had access to more and better information than he did." But what is also clear is that the father was very troubled. It's not that the decision was unpopular at the time: polls were running 63 percent in support of an invasion in February 2003; it's that he couldn't ignore the critics. The static level was very difficult for the father to bear. Laura Bush told her father-in-law to stop watching the television; the president told his father not to worry. But he worried anyway. "It's my job to worry," he told *Time*'s Hugh Sidey in early March. Few better understood how paralyzing the pressure of the decision could be. Before sending troops to Panama in 1989, the elder Bush had lain in bed the night before, literally unable to move his neck or arms. "The tension had taken hold, the responsibility for those lives, even though I had been in combat myself," he said. "The decision on the war cannot finally be made by a committee or a general. It must be made by one person—the President."

It was that burden—more than the merits of the enterprise itself— that the two men discussed when the decision was actually made. Bush signed off on the war on March 19, 2003, with the words "for the peace of the world and the benefit and freedom of the Iraqi people, I hereby give the order to execute Operation Iraqi Freedom. May God bless America." He left the Situation Room, walked up one flight of stairs, through the Oval Office, and out on the South Lawn for a walk and prayer. His father had done much the same thing in 1991 when he launched the Gulf War. When Bush returned, he sat down in the Treaty Room and wrote his father a letter, he said later, because "There was one man who understood what I was feeling."

> *Dear Dad,*
>
> *In spite of the fact that I had decided a few months ago to use force, if need be, to liberate Iraq and rid the country of WMD, the decision was an emotional one. . . . I know I have to take the right action and do pray few will lose life. Iraq will be free, the world will be safer. The emotion of the moment has passed and now I wait word on the covert action that is taking place. I know what you went through.*

Bush faxed the letter to his father in Texas; a few hours later, his father replied, invoking the most sacred name in the family to bolster the commander in chief.

> *Your handwritten note, just received, touched my heart. You are doing the right thing. Your decision, just made, is the toughest decision you have had to make up until now. But you made it with strength and with compassion. It is right to worry about the loss of innocent life be it Iraqi or American. But you have done that which you had*

to do. Maybe it helps a little bit as you face the toughest bunch of problems any president since Lincoln has faced. You carry the burden with strength and grace. . . . Remember Robin's words: I love you more than tongue can tell.

    Well, I do.

Devotedly, Dad

The Father-Son Thing

The familial comfort the two men shared became more valuable when the substance became more uncomfortable.

The senior Bush, who had been known to spend entire mornings at his computer scanning the Internet for news, gossip, criticism, and even wild conspiracy theories if they amused him, sometimes took it on himself to wage a quiet one-man campaign against his son's critics. He would often start the day by firing off an angry letter to some columnist or pundit who had disapproved of something his son had done or said, sometimes letting the offender have it for several paragraphs before deleting his message entirely or just saving it to DRAFT. But he sometimes hit SEND. Exactly eleven years after the head of the Episcopal Church criticized him for invading Kuwait (Bush had held his tongue at the time), he fired back in private letters when the new head of the church opposed his son's intervention in Iraq.

The president, sensing his father's agitation, fell into a predictable pattern. "I would call him and mother would answer the phone and [she would] say, 'Your father . . . I can't believe he's listening to all this stuff. George, you need to talk to your Dad.' And I became the comforter. I'd say, 'Hey Dad, I'm doing great. I know it's tough out there, but don't worry about me.' And so our roles got reversed." The elder Bush explained later that "watching your son take a pounding from his critics was much, much harder" than being president. "Barbara quit reading the papers and watching the news, but I couldn't do that."

Bush often called his parents first thing in the morning, when they were still in bed in Houston or Maine, drinking coffee and sharing the newspapers as they had done for years. The phone would ring, and they would put their son on speakerphone. Ever sensitive to charges of puppeteering, Mrs. Bush let it be known that certain restrictions were observed. "The rules are: no repeating what he tells you and no giving unsolicited advice and no passing on things that people ask you to give the President . . . gifts or advice or ideas or wanting jobs," his mother recalled. "We just have made that deal because we were there. We know what it's like."

Father and son joined forces on one project: keeping Mom from un-leashing her famously wicked tongue. While the former president knew how to mince his words in public, the former first lady was not as reliable. So husband and son conspired against her; specifically, they worked on her individually to make sure she didn't sound off when a microphone was nearby. "It took a joint effort to keep her quiet," one key advisor ex-plained. Sometimes, she was a useful early-warning system. After Bush called in 2002 for a two-state solution to the Israeli-Palestinian conflict that did not include PLO leader Yassir Arafat, his mother phoned one day with a question: "How's the first Jewish president doing?" Bush later said he "laughed off Mother's wisecrack," but guessed that if she was unimpressed by his speech, so was his father.

When Bush defeated John Kerry in 2004, he snapped the family's one-term curse. Bush finally reached his father on the telephone the next day. "I could tell he was happy I would not have to go through what he did." But by then, the father was well over his own defeats. "I am not trying to build a legacy," he explained in late November 2004. "I will leave that to the historians. If I get a good shake, then fine. If I don't, I'll be in heaven." And he came back to those who imagined he was some-how pulling strings, secretly guiding policy—or as his son's liberal critics imagined, being shut out of the conversation altogether. Those critics, he said, "do not, maybe cannot, understand what it is like for a father who wants to stand by his son, close up, cheering him on, arguing his case, being there for him if he gets down. We can talk on issues, but it's not real in depth. It's not his saying to me, 'What do I do now?' It's the pride of a father in a son and it transcends or avoids the issues. You know, the idea that George wanted to redeem me after my loss, all this crazy stuff like that, it has nothing to do with that."

Just as likely, something subtler was also going on. The elder Bush's foreign policy had been a constant crusade against instability; he, Baker, and Scowcroft worked at every level, but particularly in the Middle East, to slow the pace of change and build in hedges, usually well out of public view, against an unknown future. They got little credit for keeping bad things from happening. But they kept the ship in the channel.

But after 9/11, the younger Bush's team looked at the old order as managed by the father's generation and said, "That won't work; we need something new." They then set out to change it, first in Afghanistan, and then Iraq, and ultimately with a highly public "freedom agenda" across the globe that was as bold as it was unsustainable. It is likely that the father watched this unfold desperately hoping the son was right, and that times had changed, that the era of quiet diplomacy had ended and something new was needed, all the while fearing that the new strategy might be wrong. Meanwhile, the son was thinking that no one from his father's generation could really grasp the risks and perils that now beset the United States, that their outlook was great for its time but obsolete in this newer age; and that U.S. strategy, whatever the risks and uncertainties, had to move quickly to embrace the change.

Between father and son, it was virtually impossible to reconcile the two worldviews, which meant there was no point in talking about it and so they fell back on family—a safer place anyway, where everyone knows what to say. "What people can't possibly imagine," George W. Bush explained, "is what it's like to have two presidents who have a relationship as father and son—they envision us sitting around the table endlessly analyzing the different issues and strategies and tactics. It's much simpler than that and more profound."

In all families, some things are just better left unsaid; in the Bush family, the subjects that were off-limits sometimes included their two presidencies.

As the roadside attacks on American troops in Iraq increased in 2005 and 2006, the father struggled to keep his balance. In November 2006, a woman rose to question him after a speech in Abu Dhabi. "We do not respect your son," she said. "We do not respect what he's doing all over the world." While other members of the crowd expressed their agreement with whoops and whistles, the father fought back. "This son is not going to back away," he replied, his voice catching. "He's not going to change his view because some poll says this or some poll says that. You can't be president of the United States and conduct yourself if you're going to cut and run. This is going to work out in Iraq. I understand the anxiety. It's not easy."

He went on: "I have strong opinions on a lot of these things. But the reason I can't voice them is, if I did what you ask me to do, tell you what advice I give my son, that would then be flashed all over the world. If it happened to deviate one iota, one little inch, from what the president's doing or thinks he ought to be doing, it would be terrible. It would bring great anxiety not only to him but to his supporters."

Having made this candid admission, he then asked for mercy. "He is working hard for peace." It takes a lot of nerve, he said, "to get up and tell a father about his son in those terms when I just told you the thing that matters in my heart is my family."

A Model for the Afterlife

As Bush's second term wound down, the old taboo against joint appearances lifted. They began to talk about each other in public more; they occasionally even referred to each other by number, a signal that they no longer had to pretend that the other didn't exist. "It's quite an honor to be introduced by your dad," Bush said as he opened a new embassy in China in mid-2008. "This has got to be a historic moment, father and son, two presidents, opening up an embassy. I suspect it's the first, although I must confess I haven't done a lot of research in the itinerary of the Adams boys." It was a rare reference to the other father-son dynasty. "My dad was a fabulous president. And I tell people one reason why was not only did he know what he was doing. He was a fabulous father."

Finally, it is a measure of how much changed in eight years that, though Bush was not inclined to credit his father for helping him win the White House, he was quick with praise for teaching him how to leave it. He studied the post-presidencies of Reagan and Truman; during a trip to New York in his final year in office, he told aides he did not want to spend his time hanging around the United Nations the way Bill Clinton did. Instead, he looked once more to his father. He went back to Texas and began to tell some of the same daily stories of housework and chores that his father had retailed after he left office in 1993. "I watched him carefully and how he moved on with his life. He didn't linger. He didn't have a sense of needing to hang on to the presidency. I learned from him that when it's over, it's over. . . . Once you're off the stage, you're off the stage."

25

"Tell 41 and 42 That 43 Is Hungry"

—GEORGE W. BUSH

George Herbert Walker Bush was wrapping up some meetings in Manhattan late in 2006 when he learned that the private jet that was to take him home needed some unscheduled maintenance.

Restless even at age eighty-two and suddenly footloose in the city for a couple of hours, Bush turned his small motorcade around and headed toward Harlem to see his new best friend. "I'm gonna visit Bill," he told an aide. "Can you let him know we are coming?" As Bush sped north toward 125th Street, his Secret Service detail scrambled to alert their counterparts shadowing Bill Clinton that his predecessor was on the way over for a spontaneous howdy-do.

Clinton wasn't in the office that day; in fact, he wasn't even in New York. But that did not prevent the forty-first president from favoring the forty-second with a visit. Bush's motorcade pulled up in front of Clinton's offices in a federal building on Harlem's main thoroughfare, where Bush and his entourage got out and headed to the fourteenth floor. Undeterred by Clinton's absence, Bush made the rounds in Clinton's suite anyway, posing for pictures, signing autographs, chatting up staffers. And when he came to Clinton's office, he walked in, sat down, put his feet up on the massive desk, and said, "Let's call Bill!"

Soon a connection was made: "Hey Bill, nice office up here in Harlem! Great view! Nice people! Where are you, anyway?"

Through the ages, the Presidents Club has seen its share of rivalries, alliances, even some true friendships. But no relationship is quite like the bond between George H. W. Bush and the man who defeated him in 1992. The connection surprised both men, and astonished many of their longtime aides. Bush would go so far as to suggest more than once that he might be the father that Clinton had always lacked—a notion that the younger man did not dispute. And if the closeness of the relationship surprised people, so did its origin: it was Bush's actual son who made it happen.

Rescue Mission

Fifty-eight minutes after midnight on December 26, 2004, a tremor erupted thirty miles below the surface in waters off the coast of Sumatra. Though earthquakes in that region are a normal occurrence, tremors of this size were not; at 9.0 on the Richter scale, the Boxing Day quake was at the time among the two or three largest ever recorded. Two massive tectonic plates gave way, shifting in some places twenty meters or more. That sudden wrinkle in the earth's crust roared upward through the sea, creating a series of massive tsunamis, some more than twenty meters high, which began barreling toward the coasts of more than a dozen countries. When these waves came ashore hours later, parts of towns and cities—and their residents—along the coasts of Indonesia, Sri Lanka, and Thailand were swept away.

The tsunami left more than 165,000 dead, tens of thousands missing, and millions homeless. The sheer number of corpses choked morgues and medical facilities and raised fears of famine and disease. Dramatic videos, shot by awestruck tourists, turned up on the Internet. Millions of dollars in aid pledges poured in from all over the world, including more than $350 million from the U.S. government. Back in Washington, George W. Bush and his advisors searched for an appropriate way to coordinate and direct the outpouring of aid from private sources, which would quickly grow to dwarf anything governments could bring to bear.

It was the president who came up with the idea of asking his two predecessors to work together. Both were proven fund-raisers in very different realms and both had world-class Rolodexes.

Bush and Clinton were described many times as the Oscar and Felix of American politics, one proper and prudent, the other all appetite and instinct. Clinton's presidency tested the question of whether you could run the country like a series of all-night bull sessions while one of Bush's favorite questions—what if we do nothing?—defined the best and worst of his presidency. Their hard-fought 1992 campaign had left scars. Clinton, then forty-six, made repeated reference to Bush's age, and called the incumbent president "old." Bush had called Clinton a "bozo," and at one point suggested that his dog knew more about foreign policy than Clinton did. Bush assumed he was going to win right up to the end and when he lost, took the defeat hard.

But Bush the younger had good reason to think, ten years on, that the scars had healed. It helped that both men were now former presidents. At the opening of the Clinton library in Little Rock in November 2004, the elder Bush delivered gracious remarks about Clinton that delighted the huge crowd gathered in a driving rainstorm. "It has to be said that Bill Clinton was one of the most gifted American political figures in modern times. Believe me, I learned that the hard way. He made it look too easy and oh, how I hated him for that." Inside the museum, the two paired off: while touring the modern, glass-wrapped facility that overlooks the Arkansas River, Bush and Clinton got lost in conversation and fell far behind the main party of dignitaries. Bush 41 peered at one point outside a window and asked Clinton what he was going to do with all the empty property that lay fallow to the east of the library. When Clinton seemed uncertain, Bush urged him to think about making it his gravesite; and to decide soon, so that he could oversee arrangements for the media and crowds. It's the kind of thing a president has to think about—or be reminded to think about by another president: that your death, your funeral, and your burial ground are very public matters.

Bush 43 noticed that his father was lagging behind with Clinton. At one point, eager to eat lunch and then leave, Bush sent a search party out to find them. "Tell 41 and 42," Bush said to Clinton Foundation boss Skip Rutherford, "that 43 is hungry."

Chief of staff Andy Card was certain the two men would team up well; Clinton, he knew, was keen to get back into action. During George W. Bush's first term, Card would occasionally call New York senator Hillary Clinton at her home in Northwest Washington. More often than not, the former president would pick up the receiver. Card often found himself in extended conversations with 42, doing mini-briefings for the former president, exchanging information, even passing along the latest gossip. "He would talk to me and ask me what was going on and we would sort of trade information," Card recalled. On one occasion, the Card-Clinton conversation went on so long that Clinton finished talking and Card would have to call back and say it was Hillary he had called for in the first place.

After the tsunami hit, Card called both men separately and had them signed up in minutes. Within days, 41 and 42 were in the West Wing with 43, getting their orders for what was supposed to be a fairly narrow assignment: tour the region, ask local governments for advice about how to target and deliver private aid, and then come back to the United States and get busy raising money. The White House put an Air Force Boeing 757 and a small team of State Department handlers at their disposal.

The two men worked virtually nonstop on their four-day swing through the region. Each man was greeted like a pasha at every stop, but in some places the crowds leaned toward the younger man. "If you've ever had an ego problem," Bush said later, "don't travel with President Clinton to the Maldives. It was like traveling with a rock star: 'Get out of the way, will you? Clinton's coming.' It was terrible." Along the way, they rediscovered that they had been allies before they had become rivals: Clinton backed Bush early in his presidency on a variety of controversial education initiatives when other Democrats declined to help; Clinton recalled that Bush had hosted his family at Kennebunkport in the early 1980s and how, on one occasion, when three-year-old Chelsea explained that she had to go to the bathroom, Bush took the little girl by the hand and led her to the nearest loo. In midair, each man insisted the other guy take the lone bed. (Bush slept in the state room while Clinton stayed up all night playing cards with Bush aide Jean Becker.) "You get into a campaign and there's understandable hostility," Bush said later. "But I've always had a rather pleasant personal relationship with him and he said . . . he felt the same way about me. So it's not surprising to us. But it is surprising to everybody else."

Clinton told friends that Bush made the alliance work, because the older man had to swallow his pride and embrace a former opponent. "He deserves far more credit than I do," said Clinton. But it is also important to remember that post-presidencies have their own challenges; finding something appropriately challenging can be difficult. Raising money for a natural disaster was a job that approached in scale the size of things that used to keep them both up late at night. "You feel like you're doing something bigger than your own political lives," Bush said, "or bigger than your own self."

The Buddy Movie

Once back in the States, the two men became an item. The club had, in its sixty-year history, no precedent for this public display of affection. They greeted fans together at the Super Bowl in January and they played golf with Greg Norman in a rainy charity tournament in March; the next day, Clinton checked himself into a New York hospital to remove scar tissue and fluid from around his left lung, and within hours his predecessor was on the phone checking up on him. How do you feel? What do your doctors say? Are you sore? How much can you exercise? Are you using your treadmill? Dr. Bush was back on the case a few weeks later when the White House asked 42 and 41 (as well as President Carter, who declined) to join Bush 43 on the Air Force One flight to Rome for the funeral of Pope John Paul II. The senior Bush told Clinton not to worry, the pace would be manageable and, besides, there would be a doctor on board at all times. When Clinton told his own skeptical physicians he was making an overseas trip so soon after major surgery, he explained that his friend in Maine said everything would be okay.

By the time Clinton flew to Maine in June for a weekend of fishing, golfing, and boating with Bush, the Secret Service was no longer in charge of transport and transfer. Bush made it clear that he would personally pick Clinton up at the Portland, Maine, airport—in his speedboat. Bush wanted to take his high-performance racer up the coast in the morning, and bring Clinton back himself, riding the waves at 50 mph in time for lunch. It was a slightly harebrained idea, and happily, a dense Maine fog intervened to kill it. When lunchtime arrived, Bush proposed to make that journey by sea, explaining how he and Clinton would go down the coast about twenty minutes to a local seafood joint called Barnacle Billy's, with the Secret Service following in chase boats. But the seas still looked sketchy to Clinton, who, suddenly begging a weak stomach, opted to go by car instead. (At the restaurant, Clinton ordered fried clams and then ate heartily.) But Bush ultimately got his wish, taking Clinton out on the waves later that afternoon when the visibility improved for a ride that Clinton later likened to wingless flight. "He drove like a bat out of hell," Clinton recalled. "He's got these three giant engines that were so quiet . . . until he revs 'em up, right, and then it was well, we were practically levitating across the water at the speed of sound. I thought the G-forces were gonna kill me." A framed picture of the moment rests on Bush's sideboard in his private office in Houston.

The rest of the Bush family looked on with amusement. Barbara Bush began referring to the two men as "the odd couple." Jeb Bush, the Florida governor, announced that he was going to refer to Clinton as "Bro." And at the white-tie Gridiron Dinner in Washington that spring, Bush 43 joked about how Clinton, recovering from the March surgery, "woke up surrounded by his loved ones: Hillary, Chelsea . . . my Dad."

Teaming up as they did in the middle of an ugly political era, the odd couple was a hit with the public. It had been a long time since Americans had actually seen politicians of different parties work together to achieve anything—much less two presidents—and then invite the rest of the country to join in the effort. Both men knew they were modeling an alternative method in an age of partisan political cagefights. "I think people see George and me and they say, 'That is the way our country ought to work,'" Clinton said.

The arrangement also had obvious advantages for both men—and their deeply political families. A friendship with the older, steadier Bush conferred a legitimacy on Clinton that he had partly squandered in his final years in office. For Bush, the political math was just as obvious—and even closer to home: his son, the president, was a divisive figure across the nation and having the spiritual leader of the Democratic Party as a partner made it more likely that the forty-second president would deliver his criticisms of the forty-third in a kinder, gentler fashion. "He's been very good about not criticizing the president," Barbara noted in 2005. "As of today's paper, he did not criticize the president. And I appreciate that."

If the public cheered the sight of adversaries as partners, longtime Bush and Clinton seconds were not so charmed. Partisan allies both to the Bushes' right and Clintons' left found the string of public performances disturbing, almost like sleeping with the enemy. Clinton told aides that he took numerous calls from Democrats who asked, in effect, "What the hell are you doing, letting them use you?" Another of Clinton's more liberal former advisors took up the matter with Clinton directly, only to hear 42 explode on the phone: "This is much more important than politics." Bush endured the same treatment. A longtime Bush aide told *Time* in 2005 that he phoned his former boss to discuss the partnership that summer but discovered Bush would brook no criticism of it. "Don't start with me," Bush told his old ally. "Clinton's been very deferential and we've been doing good things."

And the relationship had limits. Clinton confessed at one point that he practically "needed a rabies shot" whenever the topic of the Iraq War came up at public events. Bush, the father, sometimes tired of Clinton's nonstop chattering. "They are truly good friends," said one of Bush's oldest allies. "Bush genuinely likes him—but he will be quick to say that it has to happen in small doses. Clinton just talks too much for Bush." Bush explained it this way: "We have a lot in common and I cherish it. But I'm out of the game. He's not. He's going to be active for a good while longer."

But by the middle of 2005 it was clear they just liked each other. Too many of their meetings took place too far from cameras for the relationship to have been designed for public consumption. Each man visited the other's library to raise money and then meet with major donors. They both flew to Little Rock in the spring to shoot the public service announcements that would become ubiquitous on cable TV. Afterward, they stopped for conversation in the half-sized mock Oval Office on the Clinton museum's third floor, one man sitting in one wing chair, the other relaxing in another. Peeking in from a doorway, a visitor remarked, "It looked like the wax museum in there."

Common Ground

Bearing winds of 125 mph, Hurricane Katrina smashed into the east side of New Orleans on August 29, 2005. The storm left a debris field that stretched nearly five hundred miles, from the eastern Texas Gulf Coast to the Florida Panhandle. Katrina would turn out to be the costliest natural disaster in U.S. history and the deadliest in seventy-five years.

It took a piece out of George W. Bush too. For while the storm looked like a wanton attack by Mother Nature, it soon became clear that man-made forces, some years in the making, had done far worse damage. The flood protections designed by the Army Corps of Engineers were wholly inadequate and ill-conceived, the response plans by local and state officials a mess; but it was the White House and especially the Federal Emergency Management Agency, run by Bush crony Michael Brown, that became the all-purpose target of disgust among people who watched in horror as hours, then days, passed without help reaching those trapped in the broken soup bowl that was New Orleans.

Thousands of people who waited out the storm in the Superdome were stranded there without food, hygiene products, or medical care. At the hospitals, nurses hand-pumped the ventilators of dying patients after the generators and then the batteries failed. As the temperature rose, the whole city was poached in a vile stew of chemicals, corpses, gasoline, snakes, canal rats; many could not escape their flooded homes without help. The pictures of so many African Americans standing on roofs literally dying to be rescued suggested that the U.S. government had lost the ability—and the will—to take care of its own.

How could it be, after so many commissions and commitments, bureaucracies scrambled and agencies wired, emergency supplies stockpiled and pre-positioned, that when a disaster struck, the whole newfangled system just seized up and couldn't move? By the time President Bush touched down in the tormented region days after the storm, more than just the topography had changed. Fifty-five nations had already offered aid—including Sri Lanka. So Bush once again drafted his father and his surrogate brother. And, once again, Bush and Clinton quickly signed on.

Both men had deep emotional ties to the region. Clinton had grown up in Hot Springs and Little Rock, Arkansas, two towns for which New

Orleans is a regional mecca. Bush was likewise anchored in the Gulf: it was as a Houston oilman in the early 1950s that he had made his fortune in offshore oil drilling—and then made his name as a politician. And it was in the now infamous Superdome where Bush had secured the Republican nomination in 1988 and where he made his call for a "kinder, gentler nation." For Bush and Clinton, Katrina had devastated what was literally common ground.

And so once more they hit the road, taping the public service announcements, doing the interviews, and dividing up the big lists of likely donors. They did their fact finding separately—one man took New Orleans and everything east; the other took everything to the west. They begged governors and mayors for ideas and then swapped what they had heard by email and phone. Rather than direct the funds they raised to private charities, as they had with the tsunami, Bush and Clinton set up their own joint nonprofit foundation and asked people to send their checks directly to their offices in Houston and New York. This new feature was a huge boon, for nearly everyone in the country liked one man or the other, or the remarkable fact that they were in this together.

Millions poured in: it came from bands of Girl Scouts and dozens of foreign governments; from corporate moguls and little kids running lemonade stands. Some of the envelopes contained checks made out to the two men personally; others were paid to the order of the Red Cross or Toys for Tots but mailed to Bush and Clinton with the confidence that the two former presidents would get it in the right hands. Golfer Michelle Wie donated $500,000 and got to play a round of golf with Clinton in Las Vegas on a Sunday morning in October. Another woman, who would remain anonymous, asked only to meet Bush in person so she could present the check herself. Bush made arrangements to simply cross paths with her on a tarmac in Boston, where the woman quietly handed him a check for a half million dollars. Even Bush was dumbfounded. "People just wanted to give to *them*," said Clinton aide Jay Carson.

Before they were done, they had raised $130 million. Then they had to sit down and figure out together how best to spend it. Both believed the private money would best be spent to fill in the cracks that the government response missed. But the government response was so hapless that the two men, as one aide put it, "saw cracks on about Day 3." Bush wanted to help small business and tap churches and faith-based groups to distribute it; those ideas were fine with Clinton but he wanted to do direct aid, particularly to educational institutions—an idea that Bush liked as well. "We had mini–public policy discussions," recalled Clinton, "as if we were all still in government." In the end, millions went to schools and colleges to help them reopen; but smaller amounts went to buy new fiberglass boats for fishermen who had lost their vessels in the storm. The two men named a bipartisan board of trustees to distribute additional funds that rolled in during 2006. "I never asked him and he never asked me to discard our convictions where we honestly disagreed," Clinton explained. "But if you do it in the right way, you are always working for that more perfect union." When the money stopped coming in, the two men decided to shut down the charity, divide up the remaining cash, and let each man spend their portion in the region as he saw fit. "He made one hundred percent of the decisions on [his] money and I made one hundred percent of decisions [on mine]," Clinton explained, adding wistfully, "It all worked well. . . . If we can just get that trust up again, all over the world . . ."

Brother of Another Mother

The partnership between Clinton and Bush set the stage for Clinton and Bush's son to do the same a few years later, after George W. Bush had left the White House and retired to Dallas. But it wasn't automatic: after a 7.0 magnitude earthquake rocked Haiti in January 2010, leaving tens of thousands dead and millions more homeless, Clinton called Bush 41 about swinging back into action, hitting the road again, doing the joint appearances, raising money, and then handing out cash. But the elder man, now eighty-five, begged off. Talk to my son, he said. I'm too old; it's George's turn.

"I can't do this without you," Clinton told the older man. But Bush insisted, urging Clinton to call the White House, offer his services, and propose that President Barack Obama reach out to his predecessor in Dallas and invite him to join Clinton in a club mission on Haiti's behalf. Soon after, when the father privately floated the notion of joining forces with Clinton, the son had just one request: it was a matter of club protocol. Obama had to be the one who does the asking.

Meanwhile, Clinton proposed the idea to the White House. Not long after, Obama called both Bush 43 and Clinton and asked them to pitch in. The trio met at the White House three days later. Obama looked appreciative; Clinton, something of a Haiti expert, looked serious. Bush got to the point faster than either of them: "I know a lot of people want to send blankets or water," he told a press conference, pausing for a second. "Just send your cash."

A few weeks later, the two men flew on separate airplanes to Haiti to make a tour of the ravaged capital area. Bush arrived in Port-au-Prince first, stepped out of his plane, and was ready to go. Clinton was late and when his plane finally arrived, Bush walked over to the aircraft and waited on the tarmac below, like he was the mayor of Port-au-Prince welcoming some foreign dignitary. But Clinton stayed onboard a few minutes longer, unaware that his buddy was waiting below. It was all the famously impatient Bush could do, an aide later explained, not to climb the stairs to find out what was holding things up. But during their Haiti partnership, each man found ways to defer to the other: Bush let Clinton, who was a special UN envoy to Haiti, take the lead with organizing the relief effort; Clinton's much larger staff shouldered much of the heavy lifting associated with raising and distributing funds. Clinton made sure that a former Bush aide ran the overall charitable effort, a move that was appreciated in Dallas. By mid-2011, the two men had raised more than $53 million. And they were exchanging birthday and Christmas presents: Bush sent Clinton foodstuffs from Texas; Clinton liked to send books and music.

Several government officials who knew and served both men suggested that both Bush and Clinton left office with such deep scars—impeachment for one, Iraq for the other—that it was inevitable that they would find in each other some unexpected solace in private life. No one else—not even one's spouse—can really imagine what it is like to go through what each man endured, these officials said; so who better to understand the challenge of living with all those bruises for the rest of your life? Helping cure the relationship was another factor: Bush and Clinton were, in effect, the club's first two business partners. From 2009 on, the two men occasionally appeared at joint speaking events around the world, where they would take questions for an hour or so and each receive a six-figure check in return. These marquee assemblies drew big audiences in civic arenas and convention centers from Toronto to Tokyo, where people paid several hundred dollars to see a pair of global celebrities sit in comfortable armchairs and talk about what it is like to be president.

Clinton's deep regard for Bush senior, coupled with his friendship with the son, meant that he was soon operating almost like family in Kennebunkport, inviting himself up for weekends, arranging to keep an eye on the eighty-six-year-old Barbara Bush at Betty Ford's July 2011 funeral, even helping Bush's daughter Jenna land a big scoop after she became a special correspondent for the *Today* show (the scoop would be an interview with Clinton himself). The elder Bush enjoyed watching his son and Clinton become friends and spied a common thread. "They both like to get things done," he said. "Neither is afraid to say what they think. Each considers the other a friend."

Clinton treated his new brother with a respect that not everyone in his party appreciated. In interviews he was careful never to criticize the younger Bush by name. In private, he said, he urged his friends to take the long view. "Let's take something we disagree about, the decision on Iraq and everything else," he explained. "I said, 'I tell you one thing about that man, whether you think it's right or wrong, he believed it was the right thing to do. And he did it.' And I said, 'So right now, it doesn't look too good, [but] who knows what it will look like a hundred years from now?'"

In late March 2011, Carter, Clinton, and George W. Bush turned up in tuxedos at the Kennedy Center in Washington to pay tribute to the oldest member of the club. A few months shy of his eighty-seventh birthday, the elder Bush was slowing down; he had developed a mild form of Parkinson's disease, which made his legs wobbly and upset his balance. After jumping out of an airplane for his eighty-fifth birthday in 2009, he had cut back on public appearances in 2010, declining most interviews. The Kennedy Center event was held to celebrate Bush's support for voluntarism and raise $30 million for the Points of Light Initiative, a nonprofit outfit named after the federal initiative he started while in office. But it was also something of a last waltz. Garth Brooks, Reba

McEntire, Carrie Underwood, and Mavis Staples sang; two choirs and an orchestra backed them up; eloquent volunteers from all around the nation testified about their volunteer projects, and the three American presidents (as well as Barack Obama, via video) praised Bush's lifetime commitment to national service. Carter spoke first; then Bush's son. But it was clear from the start that Clinton would perform the cadenza.

He had been fiddling with his remarks as he sat next to the guest of honor throughout the show's first half. When Clinton finally spoke, he began with a club secret. "You know, when a president is about to leave office, most of the time most people are dying for him to go on and get out of there. But there are a few little rituals that have to be observed. One of them is that the president must host the incoming president in the White House, smile as if they love each other and give the American people the idea that democracy is peaceful and honorable and there will be a good transfer of power.

"You might be interested to know that the only thing George Herbert Walker Bush asked me to do is to preserve the Points of Light. I've always been grateful that he asked and I listened. So when I was leaving, and George W. Bush was coming in, the only thing I asked him to do was to preserve AmeriCorps . . . and he did. And I thank you . . ." When it's time to depart the White House, he explained, you want to leave something ennobling behind.

"Then George W. Bush did me one of the great favors of my life," Clinton went on. "He asked me not once, but twice, to work with his father. We took 7 trips together. This man who'd I'd always liked and respected and run against . . . I literally came to love . . . and I realize all over again how much energy we waste fighting with each other over things that don't matter. . . . He can virtually do no wrong in my eyes, even though every 5 years he makes me look like a wimp by insisting on continuing to jump out of airplanes."

With that, Clinton bowed his head, stretched out his arms, and said, in front of several thousand people, looking straight at Bush senior, "I love you."

And in what amounted to an official baptism into the tribe, the family paid Clinton right back, conferring on him the highest possible honor: a family nickname. Before the Kennedy Center event concluded, Laura Bush asked all twenty-seven Bushes in attendance to gather for a family picture. The Carters and Clinton were standing quietly off to the side backstage, watching the big family take its places for a photographer when the call from Neil Bush rang out: "Bill, Bill! Brother of Another Mother! Get in here!"

And so he did, taking his place in the back row, near some grandchildren. "Yeah," Clinton mused, recalling the moment a few months later, "the family's black sheep. Every family's got one."

OBAMA AND HIS CLUB:

The Learning Curve

———————— ⚷ ————————

In the Presidents Club, there are many rooms: a Situation Room for secret briefings, an office of management consulting, a confession booth, an annex for charitable works. But by the second decade of the twenty-first century, with Barack Obama in the White House, the family room had to be enlarged. Because the club by 2009 was beginning to resemble a sprawling, modern, blended family, with George H. W. Bush as the father figure.

The three brothers, Clinton, George W. Bush, and Obama, had plenty to quarrel about: Clinton, christened by novelist Toni Morrison as "America's first black president," did not have an easy time welcoming a new messiah, let alone the man who beat his wife for the nomination. Meanwhile, relations between the younger Bush and Obama would never be much more than just correct after Obama spent most of the first two years in office blaming nearly everything on his predecessor.

But when Obama was elected, the club swooped in to pat him on the back, teach him the secret handshake—and let him in on its oldest secret. "You know, they were all incredibly gracious," Obama said, after hearing from the brethren a few days after his election. "I think all of them recognized that there's a certain loneliness to the job. You'll get advice and you'll get counsel. Ultimately, you're the person who's going to be making decisions. You can already feel that fact."

• • •

Obama's bond with the club would grow as he got his hands dirty in office, cutting deals, falling short of expectations, and simply getting through the day when you have two wars to fight and a recession is picking your pocket. Bush refused to criticize him; Clinton found ways to help him. And the club's presiding officer, George H. W. Bush, understood maybe better than any of them what a young president needed most, which had nothing to do with problems solved or messages delivered. Sometimes it was as simple as quietly stopping by the White House and telling him jokes.

26

"We Want You to Succeed"

—GEORGE W. BUSH

At a key moment in his 2008 campaign for the Democratic nomination, Barack Obama declared that Ronald Reagan was a more transformative president than Bill Clinton. Clinton's reaction—defensive and excessive—suited Obama's needs perfectly: it fed directly into one of his central arguments, that he was a new kind of Democrat, cooler, more cerebral, and far less obsessed with ancient gripes and grudges than the generation of Democrats who had come of age in the 1960s and 1970s.

This was a clever, and entirely deliberate, intra-club smackdown: Obama had invoked the ghost of one former president to provoke a second into overreacting, in ways that served Obama's ambitions nicely. But the feud between Clinton and Obama was really a fight between Clintonism and Obamaism, two supposedly different strains of the Democratic genome. Both men coveted the same prize: to be the leader who changed the way Americans thought about Democrats. Each man believed he could, through sheer force of personality and argument, lure an electorate that had been trending conservative since the mid-1960s back to the center or perhaps even further. Reagan had figured out how to talk to restless voters and carted them away; each man thought he knew the melody for whistling them back home. Obama watched how that had turned out for Clinton, watched the grand progressive vision shrink and the compromises accrue, and saw that presidency as a great opportunity lost.

There was little chance of the two men making peace until the new president had learned for himself what all the former presidents understood: that promising great change and delivering it are two entirely different things.

The Change Agents

Obama all but dismissed Clinton's claim to transformational change when he announced, "We are the ones we have been waiting for." Yes, he admired the way Clinton tried to "transcend" the divisive politics of the Reagan era and advance progressive policies at a time when voters were suspicious of big government. But Clinton never pulled it off, Obama argued in his book *The Audacity of Hope*, and he thought one of the reasons was Clinton himself. The forty-second president was a less than perfect vehicle, Obama believed, for transforming a largely conservative electorate into a permanent progressive majority. Obama noted how "frighteningly coldhearted" Clinton had been when as Arkansas governor he declined to stay the execution of a mentally disabled death row inmate during the 1992 campaign. Obama derided that decision as a "clumsy and transparent" effort to woo Reagan Democrats back into the party fold. That might yield short-term successes, Obama argued, but nothing like permanent transformation. Obama also believed that Clinton's goals had been essentially "modest," and "hardly radical." It became something of an Obama campaign mantra that at a moment when the end of the Cold War and the arrival of the Information Age allowed for a great leap forward, Clinton squandered the opportunity, settling for small steps and superficial accomplishments. In his sales catalogue for Hope and Change, Obama promised he had grander things in mind.

This was a conveniently selective reading of the Clinton presidency: true, Clinton's second term was shot through with initiatives to make sure that children's car seats were simple to install and to provide cell phones for neighborhood watch groups. But Clinton also oversaw the passage of NAFTA, the first genuine reform of welfare in thirty years, the first balanced budget in a generation, and the first crime bill in a decade. None of these measures had been easy to pass; all, it should be noted, were deeply unpopular on the left. So if Obama had a gripe, it was that Clinton had failed to do enough big *liberal* things, which was a little like accusing him of failing to do the impossible.

By 2007, however, memories of Clinton's achievements were fading, which helped to explain the third Obama criticism of the Clintons and Clintonism: they were, to Obama's mind, just increasingly passé, no longer suited to solving the nation's problems in a new century. Obama believed that for too long American politics had been following a script written at the height of the Vietnam War by a generation that was fixed in its ideological ways. Younger leaders were needed, who could "bring us together as Americans," he argued, playing to his obvious advantage. "In the back and forth between Clinton and [Newt] Gingrich and in the elections of 2000 and 2004," he wrote, "I sometimes felt as if I were watching the psychodrama of the Baby Boom generation—a tale rooted in old grudges and revenge plots hatched on a handful of college campuses long ago—and played out on the national stage."

Obama implied on the stump that he, unlike the Clintons, could run and govern as a post-partisan leader. And though the Clintons and their supporters quietly rolled their eyes at this gauzy notion, it was an appealing vision at the end of the Bush era. As Obama said in Des Moines in late 2007, "I don't want to spend the next year or the next four years refighting the same fights we had in the 1990s."

Clinton's performance on his wife's behalf played into Obama's hands. Both from behind the scenes and in his public appearances, Clinton leveled the kind of criticisms at Obama that Obama could claim had poisoned American politics. It was Clinton who said on *Charlie Rose* in December 2007 that a vote for Obama was a "roll of the dice." It was Clinton who alleged on the eve of the New Hampshire primary that Obama had fudged his opposition to the Iraq War. "Give . . . me . . . a . . . break," he croaked before a crowd at Dartmouth. "This whole thing is the biggest fairy tale I've ever seen." Obama's operatives absorbed these shots and then returned them to sender. "We put the Clinton attacks front and center as a rationale to vote for change," campaign manager David Plouffe noted.

The Obama campaign even invited the attacks. In a January 14 interview with the *Reno Gazette-Journal,* Obama let fly a rocket straight at the Clinton brand: "I think Ronald Reagan changed the trajectory of America in a way that, you know, Richard Nixon did not and in a way that Bill Clinton did not," Obama said. "He put us on a fundamentally different path because the country was ready for it . . . he tapped into what people were already feeling, which was that we want clarity, we want optimism and a return to a sense of entrepreneurship that had been missing."

And then Obama added the coup de grâce. It was "fair to say," Obama added, "that Republicans were the party of ideas for a pretty long chunk of time over the last ten to 15 years, in the sense that they were challenging the conventional wisdom."

Obama knew exactly what he was doing. To Bill Clinton, being called idea-free was like being told your mama was ugly and your pickup was for sissies. "It aggravated something about which the Clintons felt a great deal of pride," said a longtime Clinton aide. Clinton was so aggrieved he hyped Obama's remarks into something even worse, telling an audience in New York that Obama had said that "President Reagan was the engine of innovation and did more, had a more lasting impact on America than I did."

This exaggeration gave Obama the opening to swoop in and say Clinton was overheating again. At a January debate in Myrtle Beach, South Carolina, he made Clinton the issue in his race against Clinton's wife. "President Clinton asserts that I said that the Republicans had had better economic policies since 1980. That is not the case."

Then it was Obama's turn to make it personal. He told Hillary during the debate: "What I said is that Ronald Reagan was a transformative political figure because he was able to get Democrats to vote against their economic interests to form a majority to push through their agenda, an agenda that I objected to. Because while I was working on those streets watching those folks see their jobs shift overseas, you were a corporate lawyer sitting on the board at Walmart."

Hillary replied that she had never mentioned Ronald Reagan by name.

"Your husband did," Obama replied.

"Well, I'm here," Hillary said. "He's not."

"Okay, well, I can't tell whom I'm running against sometimes."

The riposte did its work: Obama tied Hillary even more tightly to her husband, who was to Obama's way of thinking, ancient history.

The 2008 primary went on for months, longer than any presidential heat in either party since 1976. By the time Clinton finally suspended her campaign in early June, her husband had withdrawn from the scene and both camps were putting out cautious feelers to the other side. When the former president reemerged to endorse Obama in Denver, he wore his club robes. "I want all of you who supported [Hillary] to vote for Barack Obama in November," he said, "and here's why: I have the privilege of speaking here, thanks to you, from a perspective that no other American Democrat, except President Carter, can offer." That would be, of course, the perspective than can only come from knowing what it takes to do the job. As for the unpleasant primary season, he quipped, "That campaign generated so much heat, it increased global warming."

When Obama asked Hillary to be his secretary of state, she was worried about her campaign debt, uncertain about leaving the Senate, fearful that she might not get along with the president-elect. Her husband was a factor too: he moved around the world virtually at light speed, uncontrolled and uncontrollable. The list of donors to his foundation and library were many, secret, and almost certainly full of foreign personalities and factions that would raise issues for his wife if she became America's top diplomat. It's not going to work, she said. But Obama was undaunted. I need you, he replied.

Bill Clinton, for his part, sounded game. "I'll do whatever they want."

That turned out to be a lot. On December 12, top aides to Obama and Clinton signed a "memorandum of understanding" that was unlike any arrangement between a president and one of his predecessors. Under its terms, Clinton released a previously secret list of more than 200,000 contributors to his foundation. He also agreed to publish his donor list every year that his wife served as secretary of state, separate his foundation from his charitable work at the Clinton Global Initiative, forgo annual meetings of the CGI outside the United States, and stop taking contributions from overseas or soliciting them worldwide. Clinton also consented to running future speeches by administration officials for their okay.

Clinton aides noted in private that the terms of the memorandum of agreement ran well beyond what was required by law; his allies griped that it went too far. But then no other former president had ever lived to see his wife in someone else's cabinet, either. It would have been inappropriate for the foreign governments with which Hillary Clinton was negotiating to have been able to make donations, secret or otherwise, to an entity that directly or indirectly supported her husband. But there was also a sense that the Obama team pushed for more in the way of concessions than it needed for its own protection. Some of the terms seemed designed in part to remind everyone who had won and who had lost.

Exit Gracefully, Stage Right

At Obama's suggestion, Bush the younger held a White House lunch for the club in January 2009. The lunch itself was a historic event, the first time since Sadat's death in 1981 that all living presidents had gathered at the White House (only this time there would be five, not four). The five men met in the small private dining room adjacent to the Oval Office. Lunch was a little on the thin side, not much more than a sandwich, Carter recalled. The conversation turned less on policy and politics than simply on the difficulty of making a home in Washington. "We spent an hour talking about how we dealt with the White House staff and what living accommodations were and what to do about putting our kids in school in Washington . . . and how much of an intrusion it was on our private affairs to have security," Carter said. "We were trying to educate President-elect Obama in a nice way without preaching to him, by letting him hear us just exchange ideas, back and forth, about what experiences we had." The five also discussed the Congress and foreign policy briefly.

"We want you to succeed," the younger Bush told Obama. "Whether we're Democrat or Republican, we all care deeply about this country. . . . All of us who have served in this office understand that the office transcends the individual." During the car ride to the swearing-in a few days later, Bush urged Obama to move early in his tenure to lay down a clear and unalterable policy about presidential pardons, which had bedeviled both Bush and Clinton in their final days in office. "I gave him a suggestion," Bush recalled. "Announce a pardon policy early on and stick to it."

It was hard to tell the difference between Obama and Clinton as the new president assembled his White House team. On the one hand, it sure looked a lot like a Clinton Revival: Obama turned to John Podesta, a former Clinton chief of staff, to run the transition. He tapped Rahm Emanuel, a Clinton troubleshooter, as his chief of staff. There was Larry Summers, Clinton treasury secretary, back as top White House economic advisor. And Carol Browner, Clinton's Environmental Protection Agency director, as his environmental czar. And of course, his secretary of state was named Clinton. Virtually everywhere you looked, many of the people who had served in the White House a dozen years before were now back, some in the same job they had held before.

With so many Clinton veterans on hand, the White House seemed to bend over backward to remind people there was actually a new president. Inside the West Wing, this sensitivity was palpable: the quickest way to kill an idea in the Obama White House was to call it Clintonian. Former Clinton officials who worked in the Obama White House— and there were many—had to breathe deeply at such moments. And yet the fact that the word "Clintonian" could be a slur inside a Democratic White House was a reminder of the fundamental differences between the two men's personalities. Clinton loved politics and his instinctive feel—hunger, really—for the never-ending contest for voters' hearts got him up in the morning and recalled no one so much as Lyndon Johnson. Obama seemed to have less of this drive once he got into the White House; the instincts that had served him so well in his campaign seemed at times to turn less on action than intellect. It was too much to say the forty-fourth president was all head and the forty-second was all heart, but it wasn't far off, either.

Even the agenda seemed like a reproof: at the top of Obama's to-do list—as important in some ways as repairing the economy—was health care reform. To the Obama way of thinking, the Clintons had blown their big chance for a health fix by refusing to compromise with moderates. Instead of writing their own legislation, as the Clintons had in 1993, Obama would leave the details to Congress. "We've tried the stone tablet route of depositing a bill on the steps of the Capitol," said senior Obama advisor David Axelrod. "It wasn't well received."

While Obama was defining himself against Clinton, Bush was busy redefining himself as an ex-president. The Bushes bought a comfortable home on a North Dallas cul-de-sac near Southern Methodist University. Friends reported that he was friendlier and more relaxed than he had been in years, all the burdens gone, all the worries now in someone else's inbox. "The relief is visible to anyone who knows him," an old friend told the *Washington Post*. "This is where he's comfortable." He began working on his memoirs, planning his library, and raising money: in the first one hundred days of Obama's presidency, Bush managed to bring in $100 million.

Bush otherwise kept his head down. About Obama, he said virtually nothing. "He deserves my silence," Bush said in March. "I'm not going to spend my time criticizing him. There's plenty of critics in the arena. I think it's time for the ex-president to tap dance off the stage and let the current president have a go at solving the world's problems." It was a smart move, given the weak economy; smarter still when compared to that of his old sidekick. Like Bush, Dick Cheney had moved out of Washington, but the former vice president resettled only a few miles away in McLean, Virginia, where he laid siege to the new administration, criticizing any number of foreign policy decisions by the new president. While these assaults were cheered by many conservatives, many Bush loyalists disapproved. Once again, being in the club, and not just merely near it, made a difference. "I love my country a lot more than I love politics," Bush said. "I think it is essential that Obama be helped in the office."

Friends insisted Bush was untroubled by the tell-all books or the damning assessments about his eight years in office, "confident to the point of serene," one said, that history would offer him a better place than the journalism of the moment. After reading several books on George Washington, he remarked to an aide that if the first president was still being scrutinized, what did he have to worry about? "Bush is totally zen-like about his eventual resurrection," a former advisor explained. "He is incredibly disciplined about not criticizing Obama, despite what he thinks of him. He has never raised the comparison himself. And even when he is asked directly about something Obama has done, the most he will say is, 'Well, I might have done it differently.' But in most cases, like financial reform, he is big enough to add, 'Something had to be done.'"

If Obama had little contact with Bush the son, the father was a different story; he instead seemed to go out of his way to woo the older man. "I have enormous sympathy for the foreign policy of George H. W.

Bush," he told *New York Times* columnist David Brooks in May 2008. Bush for his part had admired the way then Senator Obama had turned up on the Gulf Coast in the aftermath of Hurricane Katrina, anxious to help but not interested in publicity. "He came without fanfare," Bush recalled. "I could quickly see that he was someone who genuinely cared about others." Early in 2009, the White House established some friendly back channels to Kennebunkport; Obama aides invited Bush to Washington to mark the twentieth anniversary of the Americans with Disabilities Act, which he had signed in 1989; they let Bush know the president would like to arrange a courtesy visit sometime, preferably in Texas. Which is how it happened that in October of 2009, Obama arranged to attend the twentieth anniversary of the Points of Light Initiative at the Bush School of Government and Public Service on the campus of Texas A&M. This was Bush 41's sentimental home; for all the time the Bushes had spent in Houston and Kennebunkport, it was to College Station that they would come in the end: Bush and his wife had made plans to be buried in a secluded creekside woods on campus. The Bushes' first daughter, Robin, had already been reinterred there on a gently sloping hill framed by oak trees.

Texas A&M is a famously traditional campus with proud military customs and when it was announced that Obama was stopping by, not everyone was pleased. Fearing an imperfect reception for the president, Bush wrote the entire Aggie community an open letter pleading for a warm welcome. "Howdy," the letter began, "I am honored that the president, our president, is taking the time and making the effort to come to College Station," noting that it would put A&M in the global spotlight. "I cannot wait for President Obama to experience the open, decent and welcoming Aggie spirit for himself." Bush wanted the Obama visit to take place outdoors, but the Secret Service refused to go along.

Obama used the visit to offer Bush a full-throated salute. "George Bush isn't just a president who promoted the ethic of service long before it was fashionable," Obama said. "He's a citizen whose life has embodied that ethic. . . . He could easily have chosen a life of comfort and privilege, and instead, time and again, when offered a chance to serve, he seized it."

When it was over, Bush feared he would slow the president down and so urged Obama to leave without him. But Obama delayed his motorcade's departure until Bush could join him in the presidential limousine for the brief ride to the airport. The visit to Texas, the images of two men from two parties together, were all good politics for Obama; inside the Bush family, where the club is more than just an idea, the little tributes the younger man paid to the older counted for a lot. And Bush would repay the favor. A few months later, when Bush slipped into Washington for the annual Alfalfa Club dinner, he spent the night at the clubhouse on Lafayette Square. When Obama heard he was there, he invited him over for coffee. The snow was blowing sideways when Bush's limousine pulled up to the West Wing entrance. Within minutes, Obama and Bush were together in the Oval Office, telling stories. It was Bush, mostly, who did the telling. One picture of the meeting, which Obama sent Bush a few days later, shows the two men in shirtsleeves and Obama laughing as Bush, a renowned storyteller, gets to the punch line.

Bubba to the Rescue

While Obama and Bush parleyed, relations between Obama and Clinton gradually thawed. Once a president takes office, he learns that the office is its own arena, and that the tactics, tools, and talents that had helped him rise so far so fast were useful only to a point. And so what had seemed to separate Clinton and Obama so dramatically at first—personally, politically, philosophically—became harder to detect as time went by.

Obama may have disparaged Clinton's politics and the cynical tactics they sometimes entailed. But when he decided that the time had come to resort to them, he did not hesitate to ask the master for help. As long as it was all done in secret. When the White House needed to make a Pennsylvania Senate primary challenger disappear in June 2009, Clinton got the assignment. White House chief of staff Rahm Emanuel asked Clinton to find out if Democratic representative Joe Sestak, a former Clinton aide, might accept an executive branch appointment of some kind in exchange for not challenging incumbent (Republican-turned-Democrat) senator Arlen Specter. Sestak declined the White House offer—and the offer remained a secret for months until Sestak disclosed it to rally listless Pennsylvania Democrats in his uphill primary battle against Specter.

Obama even turned to Clinton for help in public, although the request came with strings attached. In May 2009, a North Korean tribunal convicted two American journalists, Laura Ling and Euna Lee, of illegal entry and other crimes after they were found shooting TV footage on the border with China. During June and July, Al Gore, Hillary Clinton, and Jimmy Carter all volunteered to travel to Pyongyang to negotiate the women's release. But the North Koreans wanted a special tribute, a man who represented a kind of golden age of diplomatic relations, when the Hermit Kingdom claimed the attention, if not exactly the respect, of the rest of the world. They wanted Bill Clinton.

The former president was game, in part because he had hoped to visit the country during his final year in office as president and because, while talking it over with his wife and daughter, Chelsea had said, "Dad, you have to go. What if it was me over there?" But as he explained later, "I can't do it if the president doesn't want me to." Some State Department officials worried about what Clinton's return would mean for his wife, who was scheduled to be in Africa during the rescue mission. What would Hillary's role be? What would prevent Clinton from going too far with Kim Jong Il, as Jimmy Carter had nearly done on a similar mission (but with Kim Il Sung, his father) for Clinton in 1994? What if Clinton somehow failed to win the journalists' release? At the White House, meanwhile, National Security Council aides weren't crazy about a former president negotiating with a rogue nation on a sitting president's behalf. And there was, on top of all that, some White House discomfort with turning to Clinton for help on any front, especially after they had worked so hard to build a fence around him just a few months earlier.

But when those aides briefed Obama, he didn't see much of a downside. As one official involved in the conversation put it, "Obama was like, 'Are you kidding me? If he is willing to go, let's send him.'"

And so off Clinton went to Pyongyang, in a private plane, as a private citizen, much as Carter had done for Clinton years before. Little about the visit was pleasant, except the outcome; the women were freed, and as they all flew home together, Clinton called the White House to share the good news. The *New York Times* practically hyperventilated: "The riveting tableau of a former president, jetting into a diplomatic crisis while his wife was embarking on a tour of Africa in her role as the nation's chief diplomat, underscored the unique and enduring role of the Clintons, even in the Obama era."

But that role had its limits and in the view of the Obama administration needed careful management. On the way home, the White House notified Ling's sister Lisa that when Clinton's plane landed in Southern California, the two women would descend the steps alone while Clinton remained, unseen, in the cabin.

Ling, an ABC news contributor, could not believe what she was hearing: was the Obama White House really so concerned about Clinton's role in this diplomatic success story that it was trying to erase him from the arrival and reunion picture? Apparently so. She pressed the White House official to reconsider. "I'm sorry, Lisa," came the reply. "We feel very strongly about this decision." Ling argued her case in a subsequent call and again was waved off. Later that evening, she fired off a stiff email to some friendlier State Department officials. "As someone who works in the media, I would be remiss if I didn't say one more time that keeping President Clinton on the plane may very well invite a whole shit-storm of speculation and chatter that you may not want. I'm fairly certain that he'd be fine with not saying anything, but to have him stay on the plane is just plain awkward." Ling was right, of course, and in the end, the White House relented and Clinton was permitted to come down the steps with the rest of the party. But it was a reminder that the White House was not really comfortable having Clinton back in the picture.

A few weeks later, Clinton met privately for forty minutes with Obama in the Situation Room delivering his firsthand assessment of Kim, who had not been seen in public for some time and who U.S. analysts had believed was ailing. Instead, Clinton found him to be very much in charge while his son, Kim Jong-un, was nowhere in evidence. Afterward, Obama invited Clinton to the Oval Office to continue talking. Mindful of how Carter had overstepped his role sixteen years earlier, Clinton was careful to observe club protocols in public: when asked about his mission on CNN, he explained that he had found Kim "alert, in better health than most people thought and clearly in command of the situation. . . . But beyond that, I think I shouldn't say anything because I don't have any policymaking authority anymore."

By this time Clinton had a chance to assess how Obama was holding up as well. "I can tell that it has worn on him," he told Larry King a few weeks later, "but I think he's also growing into the job. As I did, as nearly everybody does. Nobody shows up just ready to be president." Obama was working hard, and is very smart, Clinton noted. But "you really can't tell until, you know, like a couple of years pass, as to how it all works. . . . He's trying to do the right thing and he can keep a lot of balls in the air at the same time, which is exceedingly important in a complicated time."

The reset of American politics that Obama had imagined in 2008 was premature; the economy had restarted, then stalled; the explosion in federal spending gave voice to the Tea Party tribunes, who saw the massive auto, insurance, and bank bailouts not as a capitalist lifeline but as a socialist death sentence. By midsummer 2010, Obama's ratings were wilting; it was clear that the Democrats would lose the House, and they might lose the Senate as well.

Obama's aides believed the midterm elections were a matter of divide and conquer: they would remind voters that Bush and the Republicans had run the economy into the ditch then ask for more time to finish the cleanup. Clinton privately questioned this line of argument. In conversations with senior Obama officials, Clinton argued that it made more sense for Obama to brag—and loudly—about the things he had accomplished—health care reform, a massive stimulus, and new financial regulations—than simply attack the Republicans and then plead for more time. "The Democrats need to say, 'This is what we did, this is what happened, this is what we are going to do,'" Clinton explained in mid-September. "I think their only chance here is to shake their own voters out of their apathy and respond to the legitimate voter anger by saying, 'What do we need to do and who's more likely to do it?'" But the White House resisted this strategy, partly because it looked backward, and partly because it required defending the wildly unpopular stimulus bill; it preferred to emphasize Republican faults over Democratic strengths.

Democrats facing reelection found it useful, however, to have Clinton at their side. A Gallup survey in mid-October revealed that all voters, but particularly independent voters, would be more likely to vote for candidates if Clinton campaigned on their behalf than if Obama did. Clinton jumped back into the game like a man starved for a meal. He campaigned for sixty-five candidates at more than a hundred events, appeared on *Meet the Press, The Daily Show*, even Fox News. He drew crowds of two thousand in Denver, five thousand in San Jose, and six thousand on the campus of UCLA. While Obama could draw many more, Clinton had more room to take the Tea Party on directly: "Some of these positions people haven't held for 110 years," he said in Denver. "Don't be fooled, don't be played and don't stay home," he told a crowd in Washington State. Clinton went to West Virginia, where Obama had a 29 percent approval rating, and warned Mountaineer voters: "I am old enough to know that if you make a decision when you are mad—and I am not just talking about politics here—there is an 80 percent chance you will make a mistake." Remarked Pennsylvania governor Ed Rendell, a longtime supporter, "He's all upside and no downside. He's welcome anywhere in the country."

Though Clinton was careful in all his conversations never to say anything critical about Obama, he often sounded like the lifeguard who was trying to save a drowning man. "Most of the things they're saying about him they said about me," said Clinton, "so I'm much more sympathetic to him than most people. And when you get in there, if you're an earnest policy wonk like he is and I was, it's hard to believe there are people who really don't want you to do your job."

But all of Clinton's public testimony could not avert the inevitable. Voters turned Election 2010 into a revolt, tossing dozens of incumbent House Democrats overboard. Republicans gained sixty-three seats (and majority control) in the House, and narrowly missed gaining control of the Senate; they captured more state legislative seats than at any time since 1928. At his postmortem press conference Obama called it "a shellacking." Now the two presidents, whatever their personal differences, had more in common than ever. Both had been elected against great odds, both had seemed to promise a politically moderate agenda; both had veered further to the left than many of their supporters had expected; both had been rebuked by the voters in the midterms.

Obama needed some club magic; so on December 10 he summoned the spirit of one predecessor and the presence of another. He invited several former aides to Ronald Reagan to come in for a chat, pressing them for details about how the Great Communicator had coped with uncertainty and doubt when he was in office. Did he worry about his direction? Did he have trouble hiding his doubts from the public? How did he get through those passages? When the Reagan séance ended,

Clinton arrived and the inquiry moved from temperament to tactics. Obama wanted to know what Clinton thought of the $858 billion tax cut package that was making its way through Congress.

As they sat in the Oval Office, Clinton told him it was the best deal he could get and volunteered to help Obama sell it to liberal House Democrats. But Obama declined and instead asked him to go before the cameras in the White House Briefing Room and endorse it there. This was a reversal: only months after his aides had worked to restrict Clinton's movements and visibility, Obama now needed him back onstage to defend the kind of compromise with Republicans that he had seemed to criticize Clinton for forging just a few years before. Obama may not have cared for Clinton and Clintonism in 2007 and 2008, but after two years it was hard to see what exactly set them apart from Obama and Obamaism. Maybe it was a measure of Obama's growing confidence that he felt no need anymore to keep Clinton in a box; maybe it reflected the inevitable learning curve, as a president comes to understand the complexity of the job, the luxury of the theory versus the limits of the practice.

In any event, Obama needed the Good Housekeeping Seal of Approval from Clinton on, of all things, a massive tax cut deal and, by the way, could he possibly do it in the Briefing Room?

"I'm a little out of practice," Clinton said.

"You'll be fine," Obama replied. "It's like riding a bicycle."

Obama was certainly right about that. The two men strolled into the Briefing Room around 4:20 P.M. "I just had a terrific meeting with the former President, President Bill Clinton. . . . And I thought, given the fact that he presided over as good an economy as we've seen in our lifetimes, that it might be useful for him to share some of his thoughts. I'm going to let him speak very briefly," he added before saying he might have to leave soon for a Christmas party.

And then the former president, as if ten years had never passed, held forth for the next half hour. He explained that Obama's tax bill was "the best bipartisan agreement we can reach to help the largest number of Americans." Asked what advice he had given the president, Obama interrupted to say, "I've been keeping the First Lady waiting for about a half an hour, so I'm going to take off."

Clinton didn't seem to mind going solo. "I don't want to make her mad," he said with a smile. "Please go."

Clinton carried on alone for another twenty minutes. It felt like time travel, as though a decade were rewound and replayed. Asked if he preferred consulting to governing, Clinton replied, to some laughter, "Oh, I had quite a good time governing. I am happy to be here, I suppose, when the bullets that are fired are unlikely to hit me, unless they're just ricocheting." Clinton's performance led *The Daily Show*'s Jon Stewart to remark, "Barack Obama, I'm not saying you don't have Jedi potential, but maybe you want to wait until term two before you get Obi Wan back in the briefing room."

It would not be the last time Obama invoked the club to fortify himself. In the summer of 2011, when Obama was fighting his toughest battle yet to pass a budget deal, raise the debt limit, and avert a global economic meltdown, he invoked them all, living and dead, as he campaigned for a superdeal that would force both parties to compromise in taxes and spending. The only solution to America's problems, he argued before a crowd in Maryland on the hottest of summer days, was shared sacrifice. "It's a position that's been taken by every Democratic and Republican President who've signed major deficit deals in the past, from Ronald Reagan to Bill Clinton."

And then he reached further, higher. Compromise can be framed as selling out your convictions, he admitted. But "I think it's fair to say that Abraham Lincoln had convictions. But he was constantly making concessions and compromises." It's a president's prerogative to decorate the Oval Office with his vision and trophies; on the wall of Obama's office hangs the Emancipation Proclamation. If you read that document, he told the crowd, you'll discover that it doesn't emancipate everybody. There were all sorts of gimmicks and giveaways, provinces carved out that would be allowed to stay in the union but keep their slaves.

"Now think about that," he said. " 'The Great Emancipator' was making a compromise in the Emancipation Proclamation because he thought it was necessary . . . in preserving the Union and winning the war.

"So you know what? If Abraham Lincoln could make some compromises as part of governance, then surely we can make some compromises when it comes to handling our budget."

It was a speech that Bill Clinton—or anyone else in the club—could have given.

CONCLUSION

Margaret Truman told a story of a small dinner that her father hosted for Winston Churchill just before leaving the White House. Defense Secretary Robert Lovett was there, and Secretary of State Dean Acheson, Ambassador Averell Harriman, General Omar Bradley—wise men all.

Churchill was not one to miss an opportunity or let a conversation lag, so he threw out a challenge to a president soon to relinquish his office: "Mr. President," he said to Truman, "I hope you have your answer ready for that hour when you and I stand before Saint Peter and he says 'I understand you two are responsible for putting off those atomic bombs. What have you got to say for yourselves?'"

Well, that could have been an awkward moment. But Lovett came to the rescue.

"Are you sure, Mr. Prime Minister, that you are going to be in the same place as the president for that interrogation?"

Churchill sipped his champagne, and pronounced himself confident that the great creator of the universe would not condemn a man without a hearing—a trial by jury of his peers.

With that the game was on. Imagine they were gathered at the gates of heaven: "Oyez, Oyez," cried Acheson. "In the matter of the immigration of Winston Spencer Churchill, Mr. Bailiff, will you empanel a jury?"

That would be a jury of Churchill's peers, the other great men of history, who, like Churchill and Roosevelt and Truman, had faced the mortal threats, wrestled impossible choices, and left to history the judgment of their crimes, follies, and misfortunes.

Each guest assumed his role as a member of the jury, conjuring up any great leader they liked. General Bradley decided he would be Alexander the Great, Margaret Truman recalled; others cast themselves as Julius Caesar, Aristotle, though Churchill blocked Voltaire (an atheist) or Oliver Cromwell, on the grounds that he did not believe in the rule of law. When Acheson stood in as George Washington, Churchill decided he would be better off if he waived the jury; he was prepared to trust in the presiding judge—Harry Truman—who proceeded to acquit him of all charges. Truman certainly understood as well as anyone: forced to choose between the unacceptable and the intolerable, leaders nonetheless have no choice but to lead.

During that visit, Churchill made a confession to Truman: he too, he admitted, had been pretty discouraged when Truman suddenly succeeded Roosevelt. "I misjudged you badly," said the prime minister. "Since that time, you, more than any other man, have saved Western Civilization."

If the Presidents Club had a seal, around the ring would be three words: *cooperation, competition,* and *consolation.* On the one hand, the presidents have powerful motives—personal and patriotic—to help one another succeed and comfort one another when they fail. But at the same time they all compete for history's blessing. Praise or blame in the moment means little: it is how their decisions play out over time that matters, and so the redemption they're looking for is of a more lasting kind. They are one another's peers; who else can really judge them? Truman "had strong opinions about the presidents who succeeded him," Margaret recalled, but he would not voice them; he believed that "more time must pass before anyone, even an ex-president, can evaluate the performance of a man in the White House."

So they take the longer view; that perspective is, among other things, more forgiving. Just about every president becomes a presidential historian. They read the diaries, devour the biographies, decide whose portrait should hang where, so that the eyes that follow them through their day are sympathetic. Hoover even wrote an entire book about Woodrow Wilson. Late at night, Nixon would walk around the White House, look at the paintings. "You cannot walk in those old rooms," he said, "without feeling or hearing the footsteps of those who have gone before you." They had all left office tattooed onto history. How would he compare, he wondered? "Presidents noted for—FDR—Charm. Truman—Gutsy.

Ike—smile, prestige. Kennedy—charm. LBJ—vitality," he wrote in notes to himself. But then . . . "RN—?"

A whole wall of Bill Clinton's study was filled with books on the presidents: Truman, Kennedy, FDR, Lincoln. "At times," his aide George Stephanopoulos recalled, "it seemed as if his predecessors were the only people who could understand him."

Maybe it's not surprising that they all find themselves drawn to Lincoln, the one who started lowest, rose highest, faced the great test, and triumphed. Abraham Lincoln was the archetype of presidential greatness. Eisenhower identified so strongly that he bought a farm in Gettysburg, painted a portrait of Lincoln, and gave prints of it to the White House staff for Christmas. As Kennedy flew home from his grueling summit with Khrushchev in June of 1961, his secretary found a slip of paper that fell to the floor, in his handwriting: it was a quote from Lincoln. "I know there is a God—and I see a storm coming. If He has a place for me, I believe I am ready." It was as though Lincoln had given him a pep talk, across a century. Among Nixon's most prized possessions was the framed picture of Lincoln his grandmother gave him on his thirteenth birthday. On the strangest, most revealing night of his presidency—May 9, 1970, in the wake of the Kent State shooting—Nixon and his valet, Manolo Sanchez, left the White House at 4:15 A.M. and, to the horror of the Secret Service, drove to the Lincoln Memorial and talked to some student protesters camped out there. He copied the monument's inscription in his diary: "In this temple, as in the hearts of the people for whom he saved the Union, the memory of Abraham Lincoln is enshrined forever."

Clinton read David Herbert Donald's epic Lincoln biography: "I don't know if he could get elected today with his mental health history," Clinton said of Lincoln. "But what I learned was that when Lincoln became president and the country was coming apart at the seams and he was trying so hard to hold it together, he almost became so absorbed in the work and the mission and the suffering of others that it lifted the burden off of him." George W. Bush admired his vision so much, he read seventeen different biographies of him while in office. "I've got his painting right there," he said one day in the Oval Office. "I have sat here and thought about what it would be like to be the President when brother was fighting brother and cousin killing cousin. He clearly saw what needed to happen about keeping this country united." Barack Obama, the first

African American president, looked to the Great Emancipator to console himself about his own instincts; even the acts for which Lincoln was most exalted were themselves compromises.

Historians measure and rank presidents. But when they take the longer view, presidents do not just compare themselves to one another; they weigh their leadership against what might have been. A president knows, each day, that if he makes the wrong call on fiscal policy a million more people could lose their jobs, or the wrong judgment about an enemy means thousands lose their lives. Presidents rise or fall according to how they handle a crisis—an invasion, a depression, a massive oil spill—but there's no glory in prevention, in foreseeing and forestalling and keeping the bad from getting worse. We know what happened when each president presided; they are often just as proud of what didn't happen. They wind their way toward solutions, commuting back and forth to the alternative reality where they glimpse the damage if things don't go as planned. When the weight of office is finally off their shoulders, this is often what they remember most. Eisenhower the general was honored for winning the great war. But Eisenhower the president was proudest of not fighting one. "The United States never lost a soldier or a foot of ground in my Administration," he argued in retirement. "We kept the peace. People asked how it happened. By God, it didn't just happen, I'll tell you that." Johnson, retired to his ranch in Texas, refused to talk about the mistakes he might have made. "I will not let you take me backward in time in Vietnam," he growled to his biographer, Doris Kearns Goodwin. "Fifty thousand American boys are dead. Nothing we can say will change that fact. Your idea that I could have chosen otherwise rests upon complete ignorance. For if I had chosen otherwise, I would have been responsible for starting World War III."

Every president lives with his own version of this. Ford's aides sat mute as he explained his plan to pardon Nixon and spare the country prolonged agony. "The President's logic was unassailable," one advisor recalled, "yet I felt as if I was watching someone commit hara-kiri." George W. Bush owned the legacy of Abu Ghraib and waterboarding and the costs of making "hard calls" but left office able to say, We were not successfully attacked a second time on my watch. Every time his aides told him he had to admit his mistakes, he brushed them off. It is far too soon to tell. "I truly believe that the decisions I made will make the world a better place," he said. "Unfortunately, if you're doing big things, most of the time you're never going to be around to see them. . . . And I fully understand that. If you aim for big change, you shouldn't expect to be rewarded by short-term history."

This is another reason for the club's protocols, of support and silence and solidarity. All presidents are fellow travelers in the parallel universe where past, present, and future blur, where the terrain of regret looks very different and where there is hardly ever such a thing as a perfect outcome. They are the jurors who will not pronounce a verdict, because they know they have not heard all the evidence—and they are predisposed to be merciful.

ACKNOWLEDGMENTS

It is not often, as E. B. White suggested, that someone comes along who is both a true friend and a good editor. Priscilla Painton was excited about *The Presidents Club* from the very first, when even we could barely glimpse its dimensions. She put up with our peculiar way of writing books without betraying any doubts about our speed or direction. She is precise, passionate, provocative, and loyal. Priscilla would be a once-in-a-lifetime editor for most writers, and yet we have been lucky enough to work with her, more or less on a daily basis, for more than twenty years. If this book bears any signs of success, they are as much hers as ours.

We were lucky to have in John Huey and Rick Stengel two bosses who know history is told best through big personalities and long narratives. Rick and John supported this project from its inception and never complained when we occasionally seemed more interested in 1968 than 2012.

At *Time*, we were assisted and encouraged by too many colleagues to name; but we would be remiss not to thank D.W. Pine and Lon Tweeten, for technical and artistic advice on the jacket; Paul Moakley, Kira Pollack, and Diana Walker for missions and matters photographic; and Angela Thornton and Susan Weill for research. We are grateful as well for the patience and insights of Melissa August, Massimo Calabresi, David von Drehle, Michael Grunwald, Radhika Jones, Ratu Kamlani, Kim Kelleher, Michael Scherer, Mark Thompson, and Ali Zelenko. And we were at all times aware of the legions of *Time* correspondents from years past whose private memos and detailed dispatches to a different generation of editors remind us that there is nothing better than great reporting and storytelling knit carefully together.

We are indebted to those who marched through this wilderness years before and left blazes for us to follow: Michael Beschloss, Douglas Brinkley, David Coleman, Robert Dallek, Doris Kearns Goodwin, Marvin Kalb, James Mann, Jon Meacham, Rick Perlstine, Richard Reeves, and Richard Norton Smith. Bob Woodward was generous with his time and his own archive of club materials. Mike Meece, Doug Band, and Jean Becker lent a hand when we needed it most.

At the presidential libraries and foundations, John Heubusch, Mark Updegrove, Roman Papadiuk, Skip Rutherford, and Tim Naftali were unstinting in their time and help. Maryrose Grossman at the Kennedy Library assisted us with pictures. Barbara Cline at the LBJ library helped excavate the Nixon-Johnson relationship. Mary Lukens dove into the stacks in Ann Arbor to help find answers. Martin and Annelise Anderson at the Hoover Institution provided help at all hours and, at times, food and drink. Kristen Julian gave us a crash course in citation.

We were saved from many errors by research assistants Maya Curry, Bayly Buck, Rick Eberstadt, and Sophia Yan. Chief researcher Mavis Baah hunted down countless requests for information and then kept track of every article, book, picture, and footnote. Her unseen hand is somewhere on every page.

At Simon & Schuster, Michael Szczerban was our unflappable and wise handler. Senior production editor Jonathan Evans and two peerless copy editors, Fred Chase and Ben Holmes, scoured and polished the manuscript with great skill and care.

At every turn, we stepped firmly thanks to the sure and confident guidance of Bob Barnett at Williams & Connolly. We are lucky to have him as our agent, advisor, and friend.

For the four years we have lived with this book, our families endured and indulged our distractions and our disappearances. Janet Gibbs and Robert Duffy laid the foundations, modeled on curiosity and the pursuit of far-fetched aspirations. Through countless nights and weekends, the space and encouragement to press on came from those who know us best and inspire us most: Demetra and Waits, Niko, Charlotte, Luke, Galen, and Jake. With love and gratitude, we dedicate this book to them.

NOTES

Introduction

2 *"There's just a general sympathy"*: Author interview with Bill Clinton, November 16, 2011.

2 *"Educate president-elect Obama in a nice way"*: Author interview with Jimmy Carter, December 2, 2011.

2 *"And you respect that"*: Author interview by email with George H. W. Bush, October 7, 2011.

4 *"You are the only one"*: Marie B. Hecht, *Beyond the Presidency: The Residues of Power* (New York: Macmillan, 1976), 51.

5 *"I will be the Secretary"*: Harry S. Truman, *Mr. Citizen* (New York: Geis Associates; distributed by Random House, 1960), 18.

5 *"the presidential machinery should keep on running"*: Richard Norton Smith, *An Uncommon Man: The Triumph of Herbert Hoover* (New York: Simon & Schuster, 1984), 150.

6 *"I need you more than ever now"*: Lyndon B. Johnson to Dwight D. Eisenhower, November 23, 1963, Presidential Papers: Special Files: White House Famous Names, Papers of Lyndon B. Johnson, LBJ Library.

6 *"And your bedroom is up there"*: Lyndon B. Johnson, Harry S. Truman, Bess Truman, WH6411-04-6166 (phone call), November 1964, transcript and MP3 and FLAC audio, Miller Center of Public Affairs, University of Virginia, http://whitehouse tapes.net/transcript/johnson/wh6411-04-6166.

6 *A year later*: Michael Beschloss, ed., *Reaching for Glory: Lyndon Johnson's Secret White House Tapes, 1964–1965* (New York: Simon & Schuster, 2001), 384.

6 *He and his wife, Pat*: Richard M. Nixon, *RN: The Memoirs of Richard Nixon* (New York: Grosset & Dunlap, 1978), 535.

8 *"There is no experience"*: Arthur M. Schlesinger, *A Thousand Days: John F. Kennedy in the White House* (New York: Fawcett Premier, 1971), 674.

8 *"They behaved as though history had begun"*: Clark Clifford, *Counsel to the President: A Memoir* (New York: Random House, 1991), 334.

8 *"The nakedness of the battlefield"*: "The Loneliness of Office," Republicans, *Time*, November 14, 1960.

9 *"They'll come sliding in"*: David McCullough, *Truman* (New York: Simon & Schuster, 1992), 440.

9 *Poison of the Presidency*: Schlesinger, *A Thousand Days*, 667.

9 *"I am sure that the problems"*: Steve Neal, *Harry and Ike: The Partnership That Remade the Postwar World* (New York: Scribner, 2001), 303.

9 *"No one," Kennedy told historian*: Robert Dallek, *An Unfinished Life: John F. Kennedy, 1917–1963* (New York: Oxford University Press, 2011), 557–58.

10 *"We surely do," Eisenhower agreed*: David Eisenhower, *Going Home to Glory: A Memoir of Life with Dwight D. Eisenhower, 1961–1969* (New York: Simon & Schuster, 2010), 122.

10 *" 'I wish I could pick up the phone' "*: Bowling Green Daily News, April 29, 1994.

11 *"I've got a much better appreciation"*: *Time*, Dec. 19, 2004; interview with George W. Bush.

11 *"There is no conversation so sweet"*: Margaret Truman, "After the Presidency," *Life*, December 1, 1972.

12 *White House officials*: Douglas Brinkley, *The Unfinished Presidency: Jimmy Carter's Journey Beyond the White House* (New York: Viking, 1998), 405.

12 *"No one who has been in the Presidency"*: Robert Dallek, *Nixon and Kissinger: Partners in Power* (New York: HarperCollins, 2007), 613.

13 *"Some indications of national unity"*: Richard M. Nixon, *Six Crises* (Garden City, NY: Doubleday, 1962), 404.

13 *When Kennedy and then Johnson*: David S. Broder, "Eisenhower Backs Stand on Vietnam," *New York Times*, August 20, 1965.

14 *" 'That is the way our country ought to work' "*: Michael Duffy, "Interview," *Time*, December 19, 2005.

Truman and Hoover: The Return of the Exile

15 *"I'm not big enough"*: Robert J. Donovan, *Conflict and Crisis: The Presidency of Harry S. Truman 1945–1948* (New York: Norton, 1977), 15.

16 *"We talked," Truman said*: Merle Miller, *Plain Speaking: An Oral Biography of Harry S. Truman* (New York: Berkley Publishing Corporation; distributed by Putnam, 1974), 221.

16 *"Yours has been a friendship"*: Herbert Hoover to Harry S. Truman, December 19, 1962; available in Timothy Walch and Dwight M. Miller, eds., *Herbert Hoover and Harry S. Truman: A Documentary History* (Worland, WY: High Plains Publishing Co., 1992), 237.

Chapter 1: "I'm Not Big Enough for This Job"

17 *He'd been in office less than two months*: Lansing Warren, "Europe in Dire Need of U.S. Food," *New York Times*, May 13, 1945.

17 *One in three Belgian children*: Herbert Hoover, *An American Epic, vol. IV, The Guns Cease Killing and the Saving of Life from Famine Begins 1939–1963* (Chicago: Henry Regnery Company, 1964), 103.

17 *one in four children in Belgrade*: Ibid., 170.

17 *"I knew just the man I wanted to help me"*: Harry S. Truman, *Mr. Citizen* (New York: Geis Associates; distributed by Random House, 1960), 119.

18 *And such a sentimental whitewash*: Whether Truman or Merle Miller was doing the fabricating will never be known for sure. The quotes in the above paragraph are from Miller's *Plain Speaking*, a problematic book; the tapes on which it was allegedly based do not include the Hoover story.

18 *While pleased at being back inside*: Edgar Rickard, diary entry of May 30, 1945; this and other diary citations are available in Walch and Miller, *Herbert Hoover and Harry S. Truman*.

18 *"Nothing more would come of it"*: Herbert Hoover, personal memo reflecting on his meeting with Truman and relating the issues they discussed, May 28, 1945; available in Walch and Miller, *Herbert Hoover and Harry S. Truman*.

19 *When he ran for reelection*. Miller, *Plain Speaking*, 153.

19 *By 1945 as Truman moved into the White House*: Richard Norton Smith, *An Uncommon Man: The Triumph of Herbert Hoover* (New York: Simon & Schuster, 1984), 292.

19 *"His father was a blacksmith in West Branch"*: Harry S. Truman, *Where the Buck Stops: The Personal and Private Writings of Harry S. Truman*, ed. Margaret Truman (New York: Warner Books, 1989), 87–88.

19 *until that point, it was not uncommon*: Harry S. Truman, *Mr. Citizen*, 117.

19 *"There certainly couldn't be a better one"*: David Burner, *Herbert Hoover: A Public Life* (New York: Atheneum, 1984), 151.

19 *A poll of the Harvard faculty*: William E. Leuchtenburg, *Herbert Hoover* (New York: Times Books, 2009), 47.

20 *"The poorhouse is vanishing from among us"*: "Hoover's Speech," National Affairs, *Time*, August 20, 1928.

20 *Four years later Franklin Roosevelt would carry*: "President-Reject," Election Results, *Time*, November 14, 1932.

20 *the lame-duck Congress considered impeachment*: "I Impeach. . . . ," National Affairs, *Time*, December 26, 1932.

20 *"We'll hang Herbert Hoover to a sour apple tree"*: "72nd's Last," The Congress, *Time*, December 12, 1932.

20 *"I think he and his administration were blamed"*: Harry S. Truman, *Where the Buck Stops*, 87.

20 *"I'll not kiss any babies"*: Leuchtenburg, *Herbert Hoover*, 72.

20 *"the needs of the American people"*: Harry S. Truman, *Where the Buck Stops*, 88.

21 *"But the bank closings were an absolute necessity"*: Harry S. Truman, *Where the Buck Stops*, 363.

21 *When stock markets rose*: Smith, *An Uncommon Man*, 185.

21 *His own party pretended he didn't exist*: Leuchtenburg, *Herbert Hoover*, 154.

21 *"He deserved better treatment"*: Harry S. Truman, *Mr. Citizen*, 118.

21 *After Pearl Harbor*: Herbert Hoover to Harry S. Truman, December 19, 1962; available in Walch and Miller, *Herbert Hoover and Harry S. Truman*.

21 *"Roosevelt couldn't stand him"*: David E. Lilienthal, *The Journals of David E. Lilienthal, vol. II, The Atomic Energy Years, 1945–1950* (New York: Harper & Row, 1964), 564; cited in Walch and Miller, *Herbert Hoover and Harry S. Truman*.

22 *"I'm not raising him from the dead"*: Smith, *An Uncommon Man*, 309.

22 Newsweek *cast doubt on the sincerity*: Ibid., 279.

22 *At the Democratic convention in 1944*: "The Man Who Wasn't There," Democrats, *Time*, July 31, 1944.

22 *"We ought to be eternally grateful"*: Leuchtenburg, *Herbert Hoover*, 149.

23 *At this point*: Harry S. Truman, *Mr. Citizen*, 119.

23 *"I've got a limousine on the way"*: Miller, *Plain Speaking*, 219–20.

23 *He helped lead a nationwide drive*: "Big Clothing Drive Opens Here Today," *New York Times*, April 2, 1945.

23 *He blasted the inefficiency*: "Hoover Assails UNRRA on Food," *New York Times*, April 8, 1945.

23 *"It is now 11:59"*: "Feed Victims Now, Hoover Appeals," *New York Times*, May 9, 1945.

24 *"You have the right to call for any service"*: Herbert Hoover to Harry S. Truman, April 12, 1945, President's Personal File, Harry S. Truman Papers, Harry S. Truman Library.

24 *"Thanks for the offer"*: Harry S. Truman to Herbert Hoover, April 19, 1945, Post-Presidential Individual Correspondence File, Herbert Hoover Papers, Herbert Hoover Library.

24 *His hopes unleashed*: Edgar Rickard, diary entry of April 14, 1945, Edgar Rickard Collection, Herbert Hoover Library.

24 *Republican congresswoman Clare Boothe Luce*: "U.S. Europe's Hope, Mrs. Luce Reports," *New York Times*, May 3, 1945.

24 *It's time to call Hoover*: Henry L. Stimson, diary entry of May 2, 1945, Henry L. Stimson Papers, Yale University Library; cited in Walch and Miller, *Herbert Hoover and Harry S. Truman*.

24 *"I had to explain that I would not go to Washington"*: Herbert Hoover, notes of meeting between Hoover and Bernard Baruch, May 6, 1945, Post-Presidential Individual Correspondence File, Herbert Hoover Papers, Herbert Hoover Library.

24 *Friends kept telling him*: Rickard, diary entry of May 8, 1945.

24 *"Because of the pettiness"*: Hoover, notes of meeting between Hoover and Bernard Baruch.

25 *But he was softening*: Rickard, diary entry of May 14, 1945.

25 *"making a mountain out of a molehill"*: Memo of phone conversation between Herbert Hoover and Henry Stimson, May 17, 1945, Post-Presidential Individual Correspondence File, Herbert Hoover Papers, Herbert Hoover Library.

25 *The only way he would get a real hearing*: Ibid.

25 *Harry S. Truman*: Harry S. Truman to Herbert Hoover, May 24, 1945, Post-Presidential Individual Correspondence File, Herbert Hoover Papers, Herbert Hoover Library.

25 *The Roosevelt loyalists*: Harry S. Truman, *Mr. Citizen*, 183.

26 *As aide Eben Ayers remembered it*: Eben A. Ayers, *Truman in the White House: The Diary of Eben A. Ayers*, ed. Robert H. Ferrell (Columbia, MO: University of Missouri Press, 1991), 27.

26 *Hoover wrote back immediately*: Rickard, diary entry of May 27, 1945.

26 *"Mr. Hoover's advice has been available"*: "Mr. Truman Calls Mr. Hoover," *New York Times*, May 28, 1945.

26 *"Bare subsistence meant hunger"*: Herbert Hoover, personal memo, May 28, 1945, Post-Presidential Individual Correspondence File, Herbert Hoover Papers, Herbert Hoover Library.

26 *The meeting lasted nearly an hour*: "Truman Speeds Up Tempo Of White House Activity," *New York Times*, May 13, 1945.

27 *"This is the same answer"*: Harry S. Truman, *Mr. Citizen*, 121.

27 *"The President of the United States"*: Lansing Warren, "Truman Hears Hoover on Food," *New York Times*, May 29, 1945.

27 *"In one master stroke"*: "Era of Good Feeling?" *Time*, June 4, 1945.

27 *In his own notes*: Herbert Hoover, personal memo, May 28, 1945, Post-Presidential Individual Correspondence File, Herbert Hoover Papers, Herbert Hoover Library.

27 *Hoover went back to the Waldorf*: Herbert Hoover to Harry S. Truman, May 30, 1945, President's Secretary's Files, Harry S. Truman Papers, Harry S. Truman Library.

27 *Hoover publicly praised the president*: "Hoover Hails Truman on His Food Policies," *New York Times*, June 7, 1945.

28 *Truman had once observed*: David McCullough, *Truman* (New York: Simon & Schuster, 1992), 467.

28 *"I have no one to raise a fuss"*: Harry S. Truman, *Off the Record: The Private Papers of Harry S. Truman*, ed. Robert H. Ferrell (New York: Harper & Row, 1980), 40.

28 *"It gave me a lift"*: Harry S. Truman to Herbert Hoover, June 1, 1945, Post-Presidential Individual Correspondence File, Herbert Hoover Papers, Herbert Hoover Library.

28 *No war president*: McCullough, *Truman*, 406.

28 *"an absolute ruin"*: Dwight D. Eisenhower, *The Eisenhower Diaries*, ed. Robert H. Ferrell (New York: Doubleday, 1967), 52.

29 *"He does not have the abilities of his predecessor"*: Herbert Hoover to John C. O'Laughlin, December 27, 1945, Post-Presidential Individual Correspondence File, Herbert Hoover Papers, Herbert Hoover Library.

29 *Hoover could sympathize*: Leuchtenburg, *Herbert Hoover*, 93.

29 *"If I can get the use"*: Harry S. Truman, *Strictly Personal and Confidential: The Letters Harry Truman Never Mailed*, ed. Monte M. Poen (Boston: Little, Brown and Company, 1982), 172–73.

29 *There were food riots in Hamburg*: "The March of Famine," *New York Times*, March 25, 1946.

29 *Drought and locusts wrecked crops*: "The Bad News," The Nation, *Time*, February 18, 1946.

29 *Attlee, Truman said*: Harry S. Truman, *Memoirs: 1945: Year of Decisions* (Garden City, NY: Doubleday, 1955), 468.

30 *Agriculture Secretary Clinton Anderson*: "Anatomy of Failure," The Administration, *Time*, April 29, 1946.

30 *But Hoover didn't believe*: "Hoover Urges U.S. to Heed Food Plea," *New York Times*, February 9, 1946.

30 *"More people face starvation"*: "The Bad News," *Time*, February 18, 1946.

30 *Hoover immediately pitched in*: "Hoover Urges U.S. to Heed Food Plea," *New York Times*.

30 *Hoover was on a fishing trip*: Hoover, *An American Epic*, 4, 113.

31 *Lest Hoover worry about a trap*: Clinton Anderson, notes of phone conversation between Anderson and Herbert Hoover, February 25, 1946, Herbert Hoover Papers, Hoover Institution at Stanford University.

31 *He then walked Anderson*: Herbert Hoover, telegram to Clinton Anderson, February 26, 1946, Herbert Hoover Papers, Hoover Institution at Stanford University.

31 *"I count on your support"*: Harry S. Truman, press release, February 27, 1946, White House Press Release Files, Harry S. Truman Papers, Harry S. Truman Library.

31 *Truman didn't care*: Leuchtenburg, *Herbert Hoover*, 157.

31 *He called this "the most important meeting"*: Felix Belair Jr., "New 'Famine' Board Asks U.S. Cut Wheat Use By 25%," *New York Times*, March 2, 1946.

32 *"You know more about feeding nations"*: Smith, *An Uncommon Man*, 352.

32 *Recalling the request later*: Hoover, *An American Epic*, 4, 123.

32 *And everyone smiled*: Belair Jr., "New 'Famine' Board Asks U.S. Cut Wheat Use By 25%."

33 *"Mr. Hoover taking up where he left off"*: "An Old Trail for Mr. Hoover," *New York Times*, March 6, 1946.

33 *If your neighbor were starving*: Address by Herbert Hoover on world famine, March 16, 1946, Post-Presidential Articles, Addresses, and Public Statements File, Herbert Hoover Papers, Herbert Hoover Library. Quoted in Walch and Miller, *Herbert Hoover and Harry S. Truman*.

33 *After a week of consultations*: Walch and Miller, *Herbert Hoover and Harry S. Truman*, 72.

33 *Touring Warsaw*: Hoover, *An American Epic*, 4, 143.

33 *He visited slums and soup kitchens*: "Hoover Finds Poland Hardest Hit, 5 Million Children Badly Underfed," *New York Times*, April 1, 1946.

33 *When the team went to Rome*: Hoover, *An American Epic*, 4, 136.

34 *"Because of his experience"*: John W. Snyder, interview by Jerry N. Hess, March 12, 1968, transcript, Oral History Interviews, Harry S. Truman Library.

34 *"An urgent need has developed"*: Harry S. Truman to Herbert Hoover, April 18, 1946, Post-Presidential Individual Correspondence File, Herbert Hoover Papers, Herbert Hoover Library.

34 *"Millions will surely die"*: Harry S. Truman, *Memoirs*, vol. 1, 473–74.

35 *It was "a part of the moral and spiritual reconstruction"*: Hoover, *An American Epic*, 4, 173–77.

35 *A few days later he warned Truman*: Herbert Hoover to Harry S. Truman, April 21, 1946, White House Central Files: Confidential File, Harry S. Truman Papers, Harry S. Truman Library.

35 *"I fully recognize the personal sacrifice"*: Harry S. Truman, telegram to Herbert Hoover, May 7, 1946, Post-Presidential Individual Correspondence File, Herbert Hoover Papers, Herbert Hoover Library.

35 *"there was only one method"*: Notes of meeting between Herbert Hoover and Harry S. Truman, May 16, 1946, Post-Presidential Individual Correspondence File, Herbert Hoover Papers, Herbert Hoover Library.

35 *Hoover even drafted a telegram*: Herbert Hoover, notes of meeting between Hoover and Harry S. Truman, May 16, 1946, Post-Presidential Individual Correspondence File, Herbert Hoover Papers, Herbert Hoover Library.

36 *"All of the values of right living"*: Herbert Hoover, *Addresses Upon the American Road: 1945–1948* (New York: D. Van Nostrand Company, 1949), 221–22.

36 *relations with Argentina were so bitter*: Herbert Hoover, diary entries, June 6–10, 1946, Post-Presidential Subject File, Herbert Hoover Papers, Herbert Hoover Library.

36 *"Colossus of the North"*: Hoover, *An American Epic*, 212.

37 *"I sent a cordial telegram to President Perón"*: Ibid., 214.

37 *"With justified pride"*: "Goal Attained," Food, *Time*, July 8, 1946.

37 *"I am going away for a rest"*: Walch and Miller, *Herbert Hoover and Harry S. Truman*, 90.

37 *"I know that I can count upon your cooperation"*: Harry S. Truman to Herbert Hoover, November 29, 1946, Post-Presidential Individual Correspondence File, Herbert Hoover Papers, Herbert Hoover Library.

Chapter 2: "Our Exclusive Trade Union"

38 *He was called stupid*: McCullough, *Truman*, 520.

38 *In the 1946 midterm elections*: Ibid., 522.

39 *"President Hopes Investigator's Findings"*: James Reston, "Truman's Choice of Hoover Called Political Maneuver," *New York Times*, January 24, 1947.

39 *German economic unification*: Felix Belair Jr., "Hoover Weighs Bid to Study Germany," *New York Times*, January 22, 1947.

40 *"I was not in a particularly conciliatory mood"*: Hoover, *An American Epic*, 4, 226.

40 *"If the views expressed by Mr. Hoover"*: Felix Belair Jr., "Congress Gives Clear Indication That It Is Not Forgetting About 1948," *New York Times*, January 26, 1947.

40 *When Hoover reached the White House*: Hoover, *An American Epic*, 4, 226.

40 *He agreed to undertake*: Felix Belair Jr., "Hoover Accepts Mission to Europe to Ease U.S. Taxpayers' Burden," *New York Times*, January 23, 1947.

40 *Food was once again terribly scarce*: Hoover, *An American Epic*, 4, 228.

40 *He testified before the House*: Walch and Miller, *Herbert Hoover and Harry S. Truman*, 103.

41 *"You have made a very decided contribution"*: Harry S. Truman to Herbert Hoover, March 11, 1947, Post-Presidential Individual Correspondence File, Herbert Hoover Papers, Herbert Hoover Library.

41 *No longer could the United States sit back*: Ayers, *Truman in the White House*, 171.

41 *The stunned lawmakers seemed*: C.P. Trussell, "Congress Is Solemn," *New York Times*, March 13, 1947.

41 *"Blair House may be wired"*: Rickard, diary entry, May 22, 1947.

42 *In April he signed a congressional resolution*: "The Restoration," Power, *Time*, May 12, 1947.

42 *When Hoover finished*: Smith, *An Uncommon Man*, 371.

43 *Early in 1949*: "The Laundry Is Free," National Affairs, *Time*, January 24, 1949.

43 *There had been at least a half dozen attempts*: John D. Morris, "A Modern Government Is Hoover Group's Aim," *New York Times*, October 5, 1947.

43 *"The overlap, waste and conflict of policies"*: Herbert Hoover to Representative George H. Bender, October 3, 1945, White House Central Files: Official File, Harry S. Truman Papers, Harry S. Truman Library.

43 *"It is heartening to know"*: Harry S. Truman to Herbert Hoover, October 11, 1945, Post-Presidential Individual Correspondence File, Herbert Hoover Papers, Herbert Hoover Library.

44 *A single salmon in the Columbia River*: "One Way to Save Money," Boards & Bureaus, *Time*, December 13, 1948; and Smith, *An Uncommon Man*, 373–74.

44 *Those most intent on rolling back*: Herbert Hoover, *The Memoirs of Herbert Hoover, Volume 1: Years of Adventure, 1874–1920*, v–vi, quoted in Marie B. Hecht, *Beyond the Presidency: The Residues of Power* (New York: Macmillan, 1976), 301.

44 *"Mr. Hoover was not about to take part"*: Peri E. Arnold, "The First Hoover Com-

mission and the Managerial Presidency," *Journal of Politics* 38, no. 1 (February 1976): 56.

44 *Truman told the commission*: Hecht, *Beyond the Presidency*, 169.

45 *"Now Sam, that's all"*: Smith, *An Uncommon Man*, 342.

45 *The commission had a mandate*: John D. Morris, "A Modern Government Is Hoover Group's Aim," *New York Times*, October 5, 1947.

45 *Hoover predicted*: "Red Tape Costs U.S. $250,000,000 In Buying Supplies, Hoover Reports," *New York Times*, November 24, 1948.

45 *"They weren't very well written"*: James H. Rowe, interview by Jerry N. Hess, September 30, 1969, transcript, Oral History Interviews, Harry S. Truman Library.

45 *"Who is there who ought to know"*: Ronald C. Moe, "A New Hoover Commission: A Timely Idea or Misdirected Nostalgia?" *Public Administration Review* 42, no. 3 (May–June, 1982): 272.

46 *"From my several conversations"*: James E. Webb, memo to Harry S. Truman, October 1947, James E. Webb Papers, Harry S. Truman Library.

46 *At a staff meeting*: Ayers, *Truman in the White House*, 250.

46 *"If you follow the counsel"*: "The Big Show," Republicans, *Time*, June 28, 1948.

46 *Truman wrote to him*: Harry S. Truman to Herbert Hoover, June 23, 1948, Post-Presidential Individual Correspondence File, Herbert Hoover Papers, Herbert Hoover Library.

46 *"If you can't win an election"*: Miller, *Plain Speaking*, 261.

47 *"Well, I suppose he does"*: Rowe, interview.

47 *"Hoover didn't have any more to do with the Depression"*: Donovan, *Conflict and Crisis*, 427.

47 *"Mr. Hoover and his staff"*: James Reston, "Hoover Ponders How Much to Ask in Reorganization," *New York Times*, January 1, 1949.

48 *Acheson urged*: Peri E. Arnold, "The First Hoover Commission and the Managerial Presidency," 59.

48 *His best hope*: Cabell Phillips, "Hoover Board Plans Affected By Election," *New York Times*, November 14, 1948.

48 *"FDR kicked him around"*: Charles S. Murphy, David H. Stowe, James E. Webb, and Richard E. Neustadt, joint interview by Hugh Heclo and Anna Nelson, February 20, 1980, transcript, Oral History Interview with the Truman White House, Harry S. Truman Library.

48 *"If that can be managed"*: James E. Webb, memo to Harry S. Truman, November 5, 1948, James E. Webb Papers, Harry S. Truman Library.

49 *"It is not our function"*: William E. Pemberton, "Truman and the Hoover Commission," *Whistle Stop* (newsletter of the Harry S. Truman Library Institute) 19, no. 3, 1991.

49 *"The task, as you and I have seen"*: Harry S. Truman to Herbert Hoover, November 12, 1948, Post-Presidential Individual Correspondence File, Herbert Hoover Papers, Herbert Hoover Library.

49 *"I believe we can really accomplish"*: Harry S. Truman to Herbert Hoover, November 26, 1948, Post-Presidential Individual Correspondence File, Herbert Hoover Papers, Herbert Hoover Library.

49 *"They went along until November"*: Rickard, diary entry of December 4, 1948.

49 *Hoover came to suspect*: Herbert Hoover, Commissions on the Organization of the Executive Branch, Post-Presidential Hoover Commission I Files, Herbert Hoover Papers, Herbert Hoover Library.

49 *You now had two presidents*: Herbert Hoover, notes of meeting between Hoover and Harry S. Truman, January 7, 1949, Post-Presidential Individual Correspondence File, Herbert Hoover Papers, Herbert Hoover Library.

50 *Congress would still have the right*: Clayton Knowles, "Reorganization Bill Voted In House As Hoover Report Asks Cut In Executive Units," *New York Times*, February 8, 1949.

50 *Finally, columnist Arthur Krock wrote*: Arthur Krock, "In the Nation: The Senate and the Reorganization Plans," *New York Times*, February 10, 1949.

50 *"Yet it was approved"*: "An Impressive Vote," *New York Times*, February 9, 1949.

51 *"Senator, don't try to create"*: "Hoover Approves Reorganizing Acts," *New York Times*, July 1, 1949.

51 *In fact on his last night in office*: Matthew Connelly, interview by Jerry N. Hess, August 21, 1968, transcripts, Oral History Interviews, Harry S. Truman Library.

51 *"And least of all, our former Presidents"*: Truman, *Mr. Citizen*, 121–22.

52 *"Mr. Truman's treatment affected him"*: Frank Pace Jr., interview by Jerry N. Hess, January 17, 1972, transcript, Oral History interviews, Harry S. Truman Library.

52 *"I think we need an agreement"*: Herbert Hoover to Harry S. Truman, March 27, 1960, Post-Presidential Papers, Harry S. Truman Papers, Harry S. Truman Library.

52 *Hoover, rearranging his travel plans*: Herbert Hoover to Harry S. Truman, May 10, 1957, Post-Presidential Papers, Harry S. Truman Papers, Harry S. Truman Library.

52 *"I am all swelled up about it"*: Harry S. Truman to Herbert Hoover, May 20, 1957, Post-Presidential Individual Correspondence File, Herbert Hoover Papers, Herbert Hoover Library.

52 *"I feel that I am one of his closest friends"*: Truman speech at the dedication of the Hoover Library, August 10, quoted in Walch and Miller, *Herbert Hoover and Harry S. Truman*, 235.

53 "I am deeply grateful": Herbert Hoover to Harry S. Truman, December 19, 1962, Post-Presidential Papers, Harry S. Truman Papers, Harry S. Truman Library.

Chapter 3: "The News Hounds Are Trying to Drive a Wedge Between Us"

57 *Like millions of his countrymen*: Dwight D. Eisenhower, *Crusade in Europe* (Garden City, NY: Doubleday, 1948), 409.

58 *A "rush and storm of joy"*: William S. White, "Capital Hails Eisenhower," *New York Times*, June 19, 1945.

58 *"Stand up, so they can see you"*: Harry C. Butcher, *My Three Years with Eisenhower: The Personal Diary of Captain Harry C. Butcher, USNR, Naval Aide to General Eisenhower, 1942 to 1945* (New York: Simon & Schuster, 1946), 869.

58 *"I am nevertheless proud and honored"*: *New York Times*, June 19, 1945.

58 *"The U.S. liked what it saw"*: "Home to Abilene," Heroes, *Time*, July 2, 1945.

58 *"That is my hardest decision"*: Truman diary, "6/17/45," Harry S. Truman Library, http://nuclearfiles.org/menu/library/correspondence/truman-harry/corr_diary_ truman.htm.

59 *"I was informed that event"*: Harry S. Truman, notes regarding June 18, 1945 meeting, President's Secretary's Files, Harry S. Truman Papers, Harry S. Truman Library.

59 *Missouri National Guard*: This Day in Truman History: June 14, 1905, Harry S. Truman Library.

59 *I'd rather have the medal*: Steve Neal, *Harry and Ike: The Partnership That Remade the Postwar World* (New York: Scribner, 2001), 18.

59 *"What he saw and heard, he liked"*: Butcher, *My Three Years with Eisenhower*, 871.

59 *"I'd turn it over to him now"*: David McCullough, *Truman* (New York: Simon & Schuster, 1992), 398, and Harry S. Truman, *Dear Bess: The Letters from Harry to Bess Truman, 1910–1959*, ed. Robert H. Ferrell (New York: Norton, 1983), 516.

59 *"The same goes for politics"*: "Home to Abilene," *Time*.

60 *Truman and Eisenhower's brother*: Stephen E. Ambrose, *Eisenhower: Soldier and President* (New York: Simon & Schuster, 1990), 223.

60 *While Truman's popularity was high in 1945*: McCullough, *Truman*, 572.

60 *He was surrounded by "moochers"*: William E. Leuchtenburg, *In the Shadow of FDR: From Harry Truman to George W. Bush* (Ithaca, NY: Cornell University Press, 2001), 21.

60 *Far from feeling like the seat*: Ibid., 18.

61 *"Mr. President, I don't know"*: Dwight D. Eisenhower, *Crusade in Europe*, 444.

61 *Eisenhower called Truman*: Ibid.

61 *"Presented to President Harry S Truman"*: Neal, *Harry and Ike*, 46.

61 *"And that's all there was to it"*: Merle Miller, *Plain Speaking: An Oral Biography of Harry S. Truman* (New York: Berkley Publishing Corporation; distributed by Putnam, 1974), 338, and Harry S. Truman, *Talking with Harry: Candid Conversations with President Harry S. Truman*, ed. Ralph E. Weber (Wilmington, DE: SR Books, 2001), 131–32.

61 *But Bradley confirmed Ike's account*: According to International News Service Correspondent Robert Nixon, who was covering the trip, Truman revealed to him that "I told Ike that if he wanted to be President, I'd help him be." Robert G. Nixon, interview by Jerry N. Hess, October 16, 1970, transcript, Oral History Interviews, Harry S. Truman Library.

61 *"I told him I'd much rather retire"*: Dwight D. Eisenhower, *At Ease: Stories I Tell to Friends* (Garden City, NY: Doubleday, 1967), 316.

62 *Retooling a war machine*: Neal, *Harry and Ike*, 63.

62 *Eisenhower appreciated Truman's commitment*: Ibid., 67.

62 *"Maybe you and I could think up"*: Harry S. Truman to Dwight D. Eisenhower, October 30, 1946, Pre-Presidential Papers: Principal File: Box 112, "Truman, Harry S.," Dwight D. Eisenhower Papers, Dwight D. Eisenhower Library.

62 *"What a job he can do there"*: Libby Quaid, "National Archives Unveils Newly Found 1947 Truman Diary," Associated Press, July 11, 2003.

63 *The conversation ended*: Harry S. Truman, diary entry of July 25, 1947, Harry S. Truman 1947 Diary, Harry S. Truman Library.

63 *"Ike, no matter what you do"*: David Eisenhower, *Going Home to Glory: A Memoir of Life with Dwight D. Eisenhower, 1961–1969* (New York: Simon & Schuster, 2010), 19.

63 *"All journalists know"*: Dwight D. Eisenhower, *At Ease*, 333.

63 *A majority of people*: "Is He Is or Is He Ain't?" Political Notes, *Time*, September 1, 1947.

63 *Beginning that fall*: "Everything to Gain," National Affairs, *Time*, October 6, 1947; and "Snowball," National Affairs, *Time*, January 26, 1948.

63 *"Draft Eisenhower" groups*: "Second Wind," Political Notes, *Time*, January 19, 1948.

63 *"The tossing about of my name"*: Dwight D. Eisenhower, *The Eisenhower Diaries*, ed. Robert H. Ferrell (New York: Norton, 1981), 147.

63 *But, one reporter remarked*: "Snowball," *Time*.

64 *Among his reasons*: "Back to Normal," Republicans, *Time*, February 2, 1948.

64 *" 'My decision to remove myself' "*: Dwight D. Eisenhower, *At Ease*, 335.

64 *In a warm letter to Truman*: Dwight D. Eisenhower to Harry S. Truman, January 22, 1948, Pre-Presidential Papers: Principal File: Box 112, "Truman, Harry S.," Dwight D. Eisenhower Papers, Dwight D. Eisenhower Library.

64 *"Our dear President Truman"*: "Wake & Awakening," Democrats, *Time*, July 12, 1948.

64 *"You have the choice of retiring voluntarily"*: Robert J. Donovan, *Conflict and Crisis: The Presidency of Harry S. Truman 1945–1948* (New York: Norton, 1977), 389.

64 *He is "an incompetent"*: McCullough, *Truman*, 844.

64 *"No President in memory"*: Ibid., 633.

65 *"They weren't interested in a liberal candidate"*: Clark M. Clifford, interview by Jerry N. Hess, May 10, 1971, transcript, Oral History Interviews, Harry S. Truman Library.

65 *"I will not at this time identify"*: *Time*, July 12, 1948.

65 *"When the President in the White House"*: Harry S. Truman, *Talking with Harry*, 132.

65 *Eisenhower reaffirmed his loyalty*: Dwight D. Eisenhower to Harry S. Truman,

November 18, 1948, Pre-Presidential Papers: Principal File: Box 112, "Truman, Harry S.," Dwight D. Eisenhower Papers, Dwight D. Eisenhower Library.

66 *After a long session with Truman*: Dwight D. Eisenhower, *The Eisenhower Diaries*, 157.

66 *"My father made it clear"*: McCullough, *Truman*, 775.

66 *A mere twelve Western divisions*: Robert H. Ferrell, *Harry S. Truman and the Cold War Revisionists* (Columbia, MO: University of Missouri Press, 2006), 49.

67 *Eisenhower stood right by Truman's side*: William G. Weart, "Eisenhower Calls Korea Step a Duty," *New York Times*, July 5, 1950.

67 *"I'm not so sure we met full comprehension"*: Dwight D. Eisenhower, *The Eisenhower Diaries*, 176.

67 *"If his wisdom could only equal"*: Ibid., 181.

67 *Truman meanwhile shared*: "Bradley's Case," National Affairs, *Time*, May 28, 1951.

68 *"I rather look on this effort"*: Ambrose, *Eisenhower: Soldier and President*, 250.

68 *" 'If that's what we need, that's what we need' "*: Henry Byroade, interview by Niel M. Johnson, September 19, 1988, transcript, Oral History Interviews, Harry S. Truman Library.

69 *"I am forced to believe"*: Dwight D. Eisenhower, *The Eisenhower Diaries*, 189.

69 *"He would have to do it"*: "Again, Ike," NATO, *Time*, January 15, 1951.

69 *He landed in Oslo*: Dwight D. Eisenhower, *At Ease*, 366.

70 *"We should all stand behind him"*: Harry S. Truman, "Annual Message to the Congress on the State of the Union" (speech, chamber of the U.S. House of Representatives, January 8, 1951), transcript, Harry S. Truman Library.

70 *"Few speeches"*: Dwight D. Eisenhower, *At Ease*, 368.

70 *"We can't give this fellow pneumonia"*: "The Man with the Answers," The Nation, *Time*, February 12, 1951.

70 *"American policy and purpose"*: William Bragg Ewald, *Eisenhower the President: Crucial Days, 1951–1960* (Englewood Cliffs, NJ: Prentice-Hall, 1981), 37.

71 *"Congress and the people"*: "The Man with the Answers," *Time*.

71 *So with an eye toward killing*: Dwight D. Eisenhower, *At Ease*, 371.

71 *After Taft left*: Ibid.

71 *"I finally concluded"*: Dwight D. Eisenhower, *Mandate for Change, 1953–1956: The White House Years, A Personal Account* (Garden City, NY: Doubleday, 1963), 14.

72 *The headline practically wrote itself*: "The Oracle," Political Notes, *Time*, August 20, 1951.

72 *"I don't think that would do him any good"*: Press Conference, August 9, 1951, transcript, Public Papers of the Presidents: Harry S. Truman, 1945–1953, Harry S. Truman Library.

72 *That summer of 1951*: "That Old Feeling," Republicans, *Time*, June 25, 1951.

72 *He cabled George Marshall*: Dwight D. Eisenhower, *The Papers of Dwight David Eisenhower*, ed. Alfred D. Chandler Jr. et al., vol. 12 (Baltimore: Johns Hopkins Press, 1989), 426.

73 *"I'm accustomed to it"*: Harry S. Truman to Dwight D. Eisenhower, July 20, 1951, Pre-Presidential Papers: Principal File: Box 112, "Truman, Harry S.," Dwight D. Eisenhower Papers, Dwight D. Eisenhower Library.

73 *"You are doing a grand job"*: Harry S. Truman to Dwight D. Eisenhower, September 24, 1951, Pre-Presidential Papers: Principal File: Box 112, "Truman, Harry S.," Dwight D. Eisenhower Papers, Dwight D. Eisenhower Library.

73 Collier's *magazine*: Theodore Achilles, interview by Richard D. McKinzie, December 18, 1972, transcript, Oral History Interviews, Harry S. Truman Library.

73 *"What reason have you"*: Arthur Krock, "Truman's Bid to Eisenhower Climax of Party Proposals," *New York Times*, November 9, 1951.

73 *"He believed in Democrats so much"*: Neal, *Harry and Ike*, 227.

74 *Both Eisenhower and Truman*: Press Conference, November 15, 1951, transcript, Public Papers of the Presidents: Harry S. Truman, 1945–1953, Harry S. Truman Library.

74 *"There is a lure in power"*: Harry S. Truman, *Off the Record: The Private Papers of Harry S. Truman*, ed. Robert H. Ferrell (Columbia, MO: University of Missouri Press, 1997), 177.

74 *In mid-December he wrote*: Ibid., 220.

74 *"As I told you in 1948"*: Ibid.

74 *"I do not feel that I have any duty"*: Dwight D. Eisenhower, *Mandate for Change*, 19.

75 *"I won't stand in his way"*: Press Conference, January 10, 1952, transcript, Public Papers of the Presidents: Harry S. Truman, 1945–1953, Harry S. Truman Library.

75 *"As far as I am concerned"*: Dwight D. Eisenhower, *The Papers of Dwight David Eisenhower*, ed. Alfred D. Chandler Jr. et al., vol. 13 (Baltimore: Johns Hopkins Press, 1989), 908.

75 *"I deeply appreciate your determination"*: Ibid., 907.

75 *"You can rest assured"*: Harry S. Truman to Dwight D. Eisenhower, January 31, 1952.

75 *"I clearly miscalculated"*: Eisenhower letter to Truman, April 2, 1952, quoted in Neal, *Harry and Ike*, 239.

76 *"He's as fine a man as ever walked"*: Press Conference, May 1, 1952, transcript, Public Papers of the Presidents: Harry S. Truman, 1945–1953, Harry S. Truman Library.

76 *"But I still like him"*: Press Conference, June 19, 1952, transcript, Public Papers of the Presidents: Harry S. Truman, 1945–1953, Harry S. Truman Library.

Chapter 4: "The Man Is a Congenital Liar"

77 *Already the incoming fire seemed fierce*: Ambrose, *Eisenhower: Soldier and President*, 268.

77 *"If that's all it is, Ike"*: Neal, *Harry and Ike*, 240.

77 *"You're going to need it"*: Margaret Truman, *Harry S. Truman* (New York: William Morrow, 1973), 536.

78   *"I shall conclude that I made a mistake"*: Herbert S. Parmet, *Eisenhower and the American Crusades* (New York: Macmillan, 1972), 112.

78   *"The whole atmosphere is so different"*: Eisenhower, *The Papers of Dwight David Eisenhower*, vol. 13, 1277.

79   *Party officials speculated*: James Reston, "Stevenson and Truman Meet Today on Campaign Strategy," *New York Times*, August 12, 1952.

79   *Some Taft loyalists*: Arthur Krock, "Top G.O.P. Rift Closed but Not the Democrats'," *New York Times*, September 14, 1952.

79   *"Ike is running like a dry creek"*: "Eisenhower Urged to Start 'Swinging,' " *New York Times*, August 26, 1952.

79   *"I am amazed to find out"*: Dwight D. Eisenhower, *The Papers of Dwight David Eisenhower*, vol. 13, 1323–24.

79   *In public*: W.H. Lawrence, "Eisenhower Scores Briefing Session," *New York Times*, August 13, 1952.

80   *"I've made arrangements"*: Harry S. Truman to Dwight D. Eisenhower, August 13, 1952, Presidential Papers: Box 33, "Ann Whitman File: Truman, Harry S.," Dwight D. Eisenhower Papers, Dwight D. Eisenhower Library.

80   *"Consequently I think it would be unwise"*: Dwight D. Eisenhower to Harry S. Truman, August 14, 1952, Presidential Papers: Box 33, "Ann Whitman File: Truman, Harry S.," Dwight D. Eisenhower Papers, Dwight D. Eisenhower Library.

80   *The telegram was a little piece*: Neal, *Harry and Ike*, 259.

80   *Bradley said he would have*: W.H. Lawrence, "Eisenhower Spurns Truman Invitation to Policy Briefing," *New York Times*, August 15, 1952.

80   *"Most of this information"*: Press Conference, August 14, 1952, transcript, Public Papers of the Presidents: Harry S. Truman, 1945–1953, Harry S. Truman Library.

81   *"Sincerely, HST"*: Truman, *Off the Record*, 266.

81   *Truman's letter*: Dwight D. Eisenhower, *The Papers of Dwight David Eisenhower*, vol. 13, 1331.

82   *Churchill referred to Marshall*: Robert G. Nixon, interview, October 16, 1970.

82   *"I never saw one"*: W.H. Lawrence, "Eisenhower to Back M'Carthy If Named, But Assails Tactics," *New York Times*, August 23, 1952.

82   *If Republican primary voters*: W.H. Lawrence, "Eisenhower Assails 'Bareface Looters,' " *New York Times*, September 10, 1952.

83   *"I felt dirty"*: Parmet, *Eisenhower and the American Crusades*, 128.

83   *"That was the end of the line"*: Robert G. Nixon, interview by Jerry N. Hess, November 20, 1970, transcript, Oral History Interviews, Harry S. Truman Library.

83   *Ike blamed a staff "blunder"*: Eisenhower, *Mandate for Change*, 317.

83   *Afterward McCarthy told reporters*: W.H. Lawrence, "Eisenhower Wants Koreans to Bear Brunt of Fighting," *New York Times*, October 3, 1952.

83   *"I never heard the General"*: Ewald, *Eisenhower the President*, 60.

84   *At one point Eisenhower returned*: Parmet, *Eisenhower and the American Crusades*, 131.

84 *Eisenhower later told people*: Fletcher Knebel, "The Inside Story of the Ike-Truman Feud," The National Scene, *Look Magazine*, September 6, 1955.

84 *"By thus arousing new public clamor"*: Eisenhower, *The White House Years*, 318.

84 *"The differences apply to method"*: W.H. Lawrence, "Eisenhower Scores President on Reds," *New York Times*, October 4, 1952.

85 *"I have been privileged for 35 years"*: Neal, *Harry and Ike*, 267.

85 *Then the photographers finally*: "Why Not Better?", *Time,* October 13, 1952.

85 *"Do I need to tell you"*: McCullough, *Truman*, 911.

85 *"It was a mistake"*: Ewald, *Eisenhower the President*, 58.

85 *Marshall himself*: Neal, *Harry and Ike*, 269.

85 *Truman had been restrained*: Press Conference, September 11, 1952, transcript, Public Papers of the Presidents: Harry S. Truman, 1945–1953, Harry S. Truman Library.

85 *But Truman later charged*: Harry S. Truman, *Where the Buck Stops: The Personal and Private Writings of Harry S. Truman*, ed. Margaret Truman (New York: Warner Books, 1989), 69.

86 *One of the last things*: Miller, *Plain Speaking*, 339–40.

86 *"I would feel far more comfortable"*: Dwight D. Eisenhower to George Marshall, June 4, 1945, Pre-Presidential Papers: Principal File: Box 32, "Marshall, George," Dwight D. Eisenhower Papers, Dwight D. Eisenhower Library.

86 *He apologized to Marshall*: Ambrose, *Eisenhower: Soldier and President*, 209–10.

87 *Eisenhower's very public failure*: "Halfway; Campaign Gets Rough," *New York Times*, October 5, 1952.

87 *Any man who would bow*: Anthony Leviero, "Truman Declares General Betrays Moral Principles," *New York Times*, October 8, 1952.

87 *"I skinned old Ike"*: Edward T. Folliard, interview by Jerry N. Hess, August 20, 1970, transcript, Oral History Interviews, Harry S. Truman Library.

87 *But now Ike*: "The Other McCarthy," The Campaign, *Time*, October 13, 1952.

87 *Truman called Eisenhower a liar*: Harry S. Truman, Rear Platform and Other Informal Remarks in New York, October 10, 1952, Public Papers of the Presidents: Harry S. Truman, 1945–1953, Harry S. Truman Library.

87 *"I thought he stood for"*: McCullough, *Truman*, 911.

88 *Truman ran higher and hotter*: Harry Truman, Rear Platform and Other Informal Remarks in New York.

88 *Eisenhower wasn't exactly wearing*: "Ike in the West," National Affairs, *Time*, October 20, 1952.

88 *"Three times during the tour of Minneapolis"*: Richard H. Rovere, *The Eisenhower Years: Affairs of State* (New York: Farrar, Straus and Cudahy, 1956), 36.

88 *"Many Believe He Is Harming"*: "Many Believe He Is Harming Stevenson's Chances," *New York Times*, October 6, 1952.

88 *"He had no idea of the difference"*: David Eisenhower, *Going Home to Glory: A Mem-*

oir of Life with Dwight D. Eisenhower, 1961–1969 (New York: Simon & Schuster, 2010), 156.

89 *Obediently, he went to the phone*: Ambrose, *Eisenhower: Soldier and President*, 287.

89 *"Underneath, the venom worked"*: Ewald, *Eisenhower the President*, 240.

89 *"Congratulations on your overwhelming victory"*: "Orderly Transfer," *Time*, November 17, 1952.

90 *"Ike and his advisors"*: Harry S. Truman, *Off the Record*, 273.

90 *"I could have clotted things up"*: "Inertia," The Nation, *Time*, January 19, 1953.

90 *"It has never been done"*: Harry S. Truman, *Off the Record*, 273.

90 *When Eisenhower came to the White House*: Arthur Krock, "White House Meeting Recalls '32 Precedent," *New York Times*, November 16, 1952.

90 *It was Eisenhower's first time*: Peter Braestrup, "Eisenhower Plans to Greet Kennedy," *New York Times*, December 4, 1960.

90 *"He accepted that"*: Dwight D. Eisenhower, *The Eisenhower Diaries*, 274.

91 *"It was a friendly gesture"*: Neal, *Harry and Ike*, 282.

91 *"If that is so"*: Harry S. Truman, *Memoirs, Volume 2: Years of Trial and Hope* (Garden City, NY: Doubleday, 1956), 521.

91 *Ike reported no such reaction*: Eisenhower, *Mandate for Change*, 85, quoted in Stephen E. Ambrose, *Eisenhower the President*, vol. II (New York: Simon & Schuster, 1984), 15.

91 *"Sunk back in a chair"*: Neal, *Harry and Ike*, 283, and Dean Acheson, *Present at the Creation: My Years in the State Department* (New York: Norton, 1969), 706.

91 *Before Ike left*: "Setting the Course," The President-Elect, *Time*, December 1, 1952.

91 *"This fellow," he told reporters*: Rovere, *The Eisenhower Years*, 72.

91 *"Why you'd have thought"*: McCullough, *Truman*, 917.

92 *"Mr. Truman has been every inch the President"*: Ibid., 920.

92 *Ike had warned an aide*: Neal, *Harry and Ike*, 286.

92 *"everybody goes over to a tailor"*: Robert Nixon Oral History, Harry S. Truman Library.

92 *"get into any hat controversy"*: Neal, *Harry and Ike*, 285.

92 *Eisenhower was aiming for*: "Great Day," National Affairs, *Time*, February 2, 1953.

93 *"Well, I wouldn't do it"*: Truman, *Where the Buck Stops*, 62.

93 *"We were disappointed"*: Harry S. Truman, *Mr. Citizen* (New York: Geis Associates; distributed by Random House, 1960), 19.

93 *"He showed his superiority"*: McCullough, *Truman*, 921.

93 *"It's interesting that a single thing"*: Harry S. Truman, *Where the Buck Stops*, 62.

93 *"President assumes full responsibility"*: Harry S. Truman, *Mr. Citizen*, 16.

93 *He thanked Truman*: Dwight D. Eisenhower to Harry S. Truman, January 23, 1953, Presidential Papers: Box 33, "Ann Whitman File: Truman, Harry S.," Dwight D. Eisenhower Papers, Dwight D. Eisenhower Library.

93 *"I would never have mentioned"*: Harry S. Truman to Dwight D. Eisenhower, Janu-

ary 28, 1953, Presidential Papers: Box 33, "Ann Whitman File: Truman, Harry S.,"
Dwight D. Eisenhower Papers, Dwight D. Eisenhower Library.

94 *"One trying to be nice"*: Robert Nixon Oral History, October 16, 1970, Harry S.
Truman Library.

94 *"I'll never forget it"*: "Plain Mr. Truman," Democrats, *Time*, February 2, 1953.

94 *"Hoover has handled himself perfectly"*: Ibid.

94 *"Harry that comes to town"*: "The Missouri Traveler," Political Notes, *Time*, June 29,
1953.

94 *"If we point out the Republicans' errors"*: "Now Is the Time," National Affairs, *Time*,
September 14, 1953.

95 *Truman's portrait was removed*: Neal, *Harry and Ike*, 289; and Knebel, "The Inside
Story of the Ike-Truman Feud."

95 *"I'm Julius Caesar"*: Neal, *Harry and Ike*, 291.

95 *"Oh, that was wrong"*: Edward T. Folliard Oral History, August 20, 1970, Harry S.
Truman Library.

95 *"The man is a congenital liar"*: Ewald, *Eisenhower the President*, 32.

95 *"The effort of Herbert Brownell"*: Clayton Fritchey, interview by Jerry N. Hess,
July 1, 1969, transcript, Oral History Interviews, Harry S. Truman Library.

96 *"cheap political trickery"*: "I Have Been Accused" National Affairs, *Time,* November 23, 1953.

96 *He never appeared*: James Giglio, "Harry S. Truman and the Multifarious Ex-
Presidency," *Presidential Studies Quarterly* 12, no. 2 (1982).

96 *"Best of luck"*: Harry S. Truman, *Off the Record*, 341.

96 *"I can't tell you why"*: Harry S. Truman, *Where the Buck Stops*, 54.

97 *"But the really terrible thing"*: Ibid., 108.

97 *"you could almost see the icicles"*: J. Leonard Reinsch Oral History, March 13, 1967,
Harry S. Truman Library.

97 *"Only if he had sent the GSA employee"*: Neal, *Harry and Ike*, 301.

97 *"I don't believe in attacking"*: "Truman Defends Eisenhower's Trip," *New York Times*,
February 26, 1958.

98 *On another occasion Acheson questioned*: Giglio, "Harry S. Truman and the Multifarious Ex-Presidency."

98 *"How are you"*: Alvin Shuster, "President Meets Truman at Rites," *New York Times*,
October 21, 1959.

98 *When the service was over*: Neal, *Harry and Ike*, 308.

98 *how to place a phone call*: Ambrose, *Eisenhower the President*, vol. II, 617.

99 *"The other fellow"*: "Eisenhower Policy Scored by Truman," *New York Times*, November 3, 1961.

99 *"Ike applied for membership"*: Neal, *Harry and Ike*, 317.

99 *"I want to have some time"*: Rufus B. Burrus, interview by Niel M. Johnson,
November 8, 1985, transcript, Oral History Interviews, Harry S. Truman Library.

99 *"Then if anything is missing"*: Donald Janson, "Eisenhower Visits with Truman," *New York Times*, November 11, 1961.

99 *Truman also pointed out*: Burrus, interview.

99 *" 'Former Presidents' Club' "*: Janson, "Eisenhower Visits with Truman."

100 *"I'm glad we had the chance"*: Burrus, interview.

Kennedy and His Club: The Hazing

101 *"And so . . . he always went out of his way"*: Robert F. Kennedy, *Robert Kennedy In His Own Words: The Unpublished Recollections of the Kennedy Years*, eds. Edwin O. Guthman and Jeffrey Shulman (New York: Bantam, 1988), 55.

Chapter 5: "He Had No Idea of the Complexity of the Job"

103 *"the pay is pretty good"*: "A Way with the People," *Time*, January 5, 1962.

104 *"So Jack met Ike"*: Robert Dallek, *An Unfinished Life: John F. Kennedy, 1917–1963* (Boston: Little, Brown and Company, 2003), 116–17.

104 *"American way of life"*: Arthur M. Schlesinger, *A Thousand Days: John F. Kennedy in the White House* (New York: Fawcett Premier, 1971), 726.

104 *"It's the way"*: Richard Reeves, *President Kennedy: Profile of Power* (New York: Simon & Schuster, 1993), 65.

104 *Finally, there was something*: Dallek, *An Unfinished Life*, 302.

105 *"All his golfing pals"*: Schlesinger, *A Thousand Days*, 18.

105 *Kennedy was the golden boy*: Christopher Matthews, *Kennedy & Nixon: The Rivalry that Shaped Postwar America* (New York: Simon & Schuster, 1996), 24.

105 *They even shared*: Ibid., 52.

105 *He told Jackie*: Ibid., 18.

106 *"From that time on"*: Rick Perlstein, *Nixonland: The Rise of a President and the Fracturing of America* (New York: Scribner, 2008), 25.

106 *press conference early in 1960*: Ambrose, *Eisenhower: Soldier and President*, 503.

107 *"I've spent my life in this"*: Ibid., 500.

107 *"failure of nerve"*: Herbert S. Parmet, *JFK: The Presidency of John F. Kennedy* (New York: Dial Press, 1983), 9.

107 *"I am not dissatisfied"*: Dwight D. Eisenhower, "The President's News Conference, February 3, 1960," The American Presidency Project, http://www.presidency.ucsb.edu/ws/?pid=11884

107 *He managed to deliver*: Dwight D. Eisenhower, "Address at the Republican National Convention" (speech, Chicago, July 26, 1960), transcript, The American Presidency Project, http://www.presidency.ucsb.edu/ws/index.php?pid=11890&st=1960&st1=#axzz1eME0rmh8.

108 *He demolished the experience argument*: Theodore C. Sorensen, *Kennedy* (New York: Harper & Row, 1965), 152.

108 *"Now, he might get the nomination"*: Dallek, *An Unfinished Life*, 261.

108 *As he told interviewer*: Ibid., 274.

109 *"I'll do anything to beat him"*: Ibid., 278.

109 *"Listen, dammit"*: "Biggest Gun," The Campaign, *Time*, October 10, 1960.

109 *"Little Boy Blue"*: Dallek, *An Unfinished Life,* 302.

109 *"U.S. moving forward again"*: "Candidate in Orbit," Democrats, *Time*, November 7, 1960.

109 *But he charged in*: "On the Firing Line," The Presidency, *Time*, November 7, 1960.

109 *"Where did this young genius"*: Felix Belair Jr., "Eisenhower Gibes at 'Young Genius' in Campaign Tour," *New York Times*, November 5, 1960.

110 *"If the election were held tomorrow"*: Matthews, *Kennedy & Nixon*, 175.

110 *"We Back Jack"*: Peter Kihss, "Crowds Are Huge," *New York Times*, November 3, 1960.

110 *Ike's popularity averaged*: "They Still Like Ike," The Presidency, *Time*, November 28, 1960.

110 *"I wouldn't criticize anything"*: Sorensen, *Kennedy*, 114.

110 *Never mind that the first*: John W. Finney, "A G.O.P. Peace Bid," *New York Times*, November 7, 1960.

110 *He was so angry*: William Bragg Ewald, *Eisenhower the President: Crucial Days, 1951–1960* (Englewood Cliffs, NJ: Prentice-Hall, 1981), 312–13.

111 *"Nixon's late surge"*: Dallek, *An Unfinished Life*, 295.

111 *"Dick Nixon in 1960"*: "Ike on the Frontier," Nation, *Time*, October 19, 1962.

111 *"My father had said to Ike"*: William Safire, *Before the Fall: An Inside View of the Pre-Watergate White House* (Garden City, NY: Doubleday, 1975), 623.

111 *The votes had barely been counted*: Richard M. Nixon, *RN: The Memoirs of Richard Nixon* (New York: Grosset & Dunlap, 1978), 224.

112 *The initial overture*: Richard Norton Smith, *An Uncommon Man: The Triumph of Herbert Hoover* (New York: Simon & Schuster, 1984), 271.

112 *"He was completely depressed"*: Matthews, *Kennedy & Nixon*, 183.

112 *"I knew he would not be calling"*: Richard M. Nixon, *Six Crises* (Garden City, NY: Doubleday, 1962), 404.

113 *"This is a generous gesture"*: Smith, *An Uncommon Man*, 424.

113 *Back at the table*: Matthews, *Kennedy & Nixon*, 184.

113 *"As I hung up and walked slowly"*: Nixon, *Six Crises*, 405.

114 *"Republicans don't have to do"*: Schlesinger, *A Thousand Days*, 125.

114 *"Maybe I'll ask him"*: Dallek, *An Unfinished Life*, 201.

114 *Kennedy sat in the backseat*: Matthews, *Kennedy & Nixon*, 185.

114 *Pat and the girls*: W.H. Lawrence, "Talk Is 'Cordial,'" *New York Times*, November 15, 1960.

114 *the purpose of the meeting*: W.H. Lawrence, "Kennedy to Meet with Nixon Today in Move for Unity," *New York Times*, November 14, 1960.

114 *"I shall never join in any criticism of you"*: Nixon, *Six Crises*, 410.

115 *He got a standing ovation*: Matthews, *Kennedy & Nixon*, 188–89.

115 *"put an end to the bitter charges"*: Sorensen, *Kennedy*, 232.

115 *"It was political"*: "Reunion at Key Biscayne," *New York Times*, November 15, 1960.

115 *" 'What in the world do I do now' "*: Schlesinger, *A Thousand Days*, 121.

115 *The Constitution provides no machinery*: "The Morning After," The Presidency, *Time*, November 14, 1960.

116 *"Governing has got to be a pleasure"*: Richard E. Neustadt, *Preparing to Be President: The Memos of Richard E. Neustadt*, ed. Charles O. Jones (Washington, DC: AEI Press, 2000), 3.

116 *"I regarded this"*: Clark Clifford, *Counsel to the President: A Memoir* (New York: Random House, 1991), 334.

116 *"I never heard him talk"*: McGeorge Bundy, interview by Richard E. Neustadt, March 1964, transcript, Oral History Program, John F. Kennedy Library.

116 *"In the Kennedy Administration"*: Sorensen, *Kennedy*, 282.

116 *"He paid little attention"*: Ibid., 281.

116 *The new president*: Stephen Hess, *Organizing the Presidency* (Washington, DC: Brookings Institution, 1976), 78.

117 *"Kennedy would never have"*: Frederick G. Dutton, interview by Charles T. Morrissey, May 3, 1965, transcript, Oral History Program, John F. Kennedy Library.

117 *In its place*: Sorensen, *Kennedy*, 262.

117 *There would be no such figure*: "The Nation," *New York Times*, November 27, 1960.

117 *"In the first months"*: Sorensen, *Kennedy*, 281.

117 *"I'm just telling you"*: Bryce Harlow, interview by Michael L. Gillette, May 6, 1979, transcript, Oral History Collection, LBJ Library.

118 *For all the formal machinery*: Ernest R. May, "The Replacements," *National Interest*, January–February, 2009, http://nationalinterest.org/bookreview/the-replacements-2955.

118 *"Did you want me"*: Bob Schieffer, "Advice and Dissent: What LBJ Could Have Learned from Ike," *Washington Monthly*, July–August 1990, 50.

118 *"His thoughts far outraced his speech"*: Nixon, *Six Crises*, 161.

118 *Thanking Eisenhower for his invitation*: "Answers & Questions," The President-Elect, *Time*, November 21, 1960.

118 *Then with a bow*: Reeves, *President Kennedy*, 21.

119 *"I feel," he told friends*: Felix Belair Jr., "Kennedy to Visit President Today," *New York Times*, December 6, 1960.

119 *But on that Monday*: Felix Belair Jr., "Meeting Cordial," *New York Times*, December 7, 1960.

119 *And Ike ushered him*: "Changing of the Guard," The President-Elect, *Time*, December 19, 1960.

119 *They seemed, the* New York Times *suggested*: Belair Jr., "Meeting Cordial."

119 *Ike stressed that the NSC*: Michael Gordon Jackson, "Beyond Brinkmanship: Eisen-

hower, Nuclear War Fighting, and Korea, 1953–1968," *Presidential Studies Quarterly* 35, no. 1, (March 2005): 62.

119   *It proposed drastically*: James R. Locher, *Victory on the Potomac: The Goldwater-Nichols Act Unifies the Pentagon* (College Station, TX: Texas A&M University Press, 2002), 29.

119   *Eisenhower knew something*: Dwight D. Eisenhower, memo of December 6, 1960, Presidential Papers: Ann Whitman File: Presidential Transition Series, Dwight D. Eisenhower Papers, Dwight D. Eisenhower Library.

120   *"If they are easy"*: Reeves, *President Kennedy*, 23.

120   *"Certainly his attitude"*: Dwight D. Eisenhower, memo of December 6, 1960.

120   *"Of course," Eisenhower replied*: Dwight D. Eisenhower, *The Eisenhower Diaries*, ed. Robert H. Ferrell (New York: Norton, 1981), 382.

120   *In case Kennedy wasn't getting*: memo by Wilton Persons, December 6, 1960, Presidential Papers: Ann Whitman File: Presidential Transition Series, Dwight D. Eisenhower Papers, Dwight D. Eisenhower Library.

120   *"What impressed the President most"*: Clifford, *Counsel to the President*, 342.

121   *Ike called him*: Dallek, *An Unfinished Life*, 303.

121   *"He had no idea"*: Dwight D. Eisenhower, Post-Presidential Papers, 1961–69; Gettysburg, Palm Desert, Indio File Box 2 JFK 1960–61 (1)(2) JFK 1962–67 (1) (2) (1)-14 pp. Malcolm Moos interview, 1966

121   *"Eisenhower was a 'non-President'"*: Clifford, *Counsel to the President*, 342.

121   *"I can handle it"*: Reeves, *President Kennedy*, 666.

121   *"And if he is a five star general"*: David Eisenhower, *Going Home to Glory: A Memoir of Life with Dwight D. Eisenhower, 1961–1969* (New York: Simon & Schuster, 2010), 16.

122   *Kennedy wanted to get together*: John F. Kennedy, memo, January 19, 1961, Eisenhower, Dwight D., 1961: January–December file, Special Correspondence, Papers of John F. Kennedy, John F. Kennedy Library.

122   *He introduced the nondescript man*: Michael Korda, *Ike: An American Hero* (New York: HarperCollins, 2007), 720; Reeves, *President Kennedy*, 30.

122   *"I've shown my friend here"*: "The 35th: John Fitzgerald Kennedy," The Presidency, *Time*, January 27, 1961.

122   *Had he not been briefed*: Paul P. Kennedy, "U.S. Helps Train an Anti-Castro Force at Secret Guatemalan Air-Ground Base," *New York Times*, January 10, 1961.

122   *"In the long run"*: memo by Wilton Persons, January 19, 1961, Dwight D. Eisenhower Post-Presidential Papers: Augusta–Walter Reed Series, Dwight D. Eisenhower Papers, Dwight D. Eisenhower Library; Reeves, *President Kennedy*, 31.

123   *"In retrospect, I believe"*: Clifford, *Counsel to the President*, 344.

123   *Having himself resisted*: Ewald, *Eisenhower the President*, 316.

123   *When it was over*: Dwight D. Eisenhower, memo to Wilton Persons, January 19, 1961.

123   *"It is not a partisan question"*: "The 35th: John Fitzgerald Kennedy," *Time*.

123 *"It is invulnerable"*: Reeves, *President Kennedy*, 33.

124 *"He was fascinated"*: Kennedy, *In His Own Words*, 55.

124 *"If that smoke indicates a bomb"*: Richard J. Cardinal Cushing, interview by Edward M. Kennedy, 1966, transcript, Oral History Program, John F. Kennedy Library.

124 *At that point*: Parmet, *JFK*, 4.

125 *"And there was the oldest of them all"*: "Eisenhower: Soldier of Peace," Nation, *Time*, April 4, 1969.

125 *They realized, Ike wrote later*: Stephen E. Ambrose, *Eisenhower the President*, vol. II (Norwalk, CT: Easton Press, 1987), 616.

125 *"I'm going to be heard from"*: "Last Days," National Affairs, *Time*, January 27, 1961.

125 *When they arrived at the farm*: David Eisenhower, *Going Home to Glory*, 3.

125 *"I would be back here"*: Nixon, *RN*, 227–28.

125 *"I am sure that your generous assistance"*: John F. Kennedy to Dwight D. Eisenhower, January 21, 1961, Eisenhower, Dwight D., 1961: January–December file, Special Correspondence, Papers of John F. Kennedy, John F. Kennedy Library.

125 *As the story goes*: David Eisenhower, *Going Home to Glory*, 17.

Chapter 6: "The Worse I Do, the More Popular I Get"

126 *"I believe the President did not realize"*: Richard M. Bissell Jr., Jonathan E. Lewis, and Frances T. Pudlo, *Reflections of a Cold Warrior: From Yalta to the Bay of Pigs* (New Haven, CT: Yale University Press, 1996), 183.

126 *Again the CIA went along*: Lucien S. Vandenbroucke, "The 'Confessions' of Allen Dulles: New Evidence on the Bay of Pigs," *Diplomatic History* 8, no. 4 (October 1984): 369.

126 *"The Cuban armed forces are stronger"*: McGeorge Bundy, "Memorandum from the President's Special Assistant for National Security Affairs (Bundy) to President Kennedy," April 18, 1961, *Foreign Relations of the United States, 1961–1963*, vol. X, *Cuba, 1961–1962*, ed. Louis J. Smith, http://www.mtholyoke.edu/acad/intrel/baypig8.htm.

127 *"It was a marvelous demonstration"*: Deborah Hart Strober and Gerald S. Strober, *The Kennedy Presidency: An Oral History of the Era* (Washington, DC: Brassey's, 2003), 349.

127 *"He was very in awe of Eisenhower"*: Ibid., 333.

128 *"No man entering upon this office"*: "Man Meets Presidency," The Nation, *Time*, February 10, 1961.

128 *"But he had discovered"*: Ibid.

128 *"I will reserve to myself"*: Strober and Strober, *The Kennedy Presidency*, 324.

128 *"Everyone must be prepared"*: Reeves, *President Kennedy*, 70.

128 *" 'That's just the problem' "*: Strober and Strober, *The Kennedy Presidency*, 323.

129 *But they didn't mention that*: Jack B. Pfeiffer, *Official History of the Bay of Pigs Opera-*

tion, vol. III, *Evolution of CIA's Anti-Castro Policies, 1959–January 1961*, Central Intelligence Agency, December 1979, http://www.gwu.edu/~nsarchiv/NSAEBB/NSAEBB355/bop-vol3.pdf.

129 *George Ball recalled*: Strober and Strober, *The Kennedy Presidency*, 333.

129 *"The Joint Chiefs"*: Schlesinger, *A Thousand Days*, 250.

130 *"He respected the Supreme Allied Commander"*: Strober and Strober, *The Kennedy Presidency*, 333.

130 *"He was really trapped"*: Schlesinger, *A Thousand Days*, 337.

130 *"It was on their recommendations"*: Kennedy, *In His Own Words*, 246.

130 *Not to mention*: Sorensen, *Kennedy*, 295.

131 *"And I say to you now"*: Dallek, *An Unfinished Life*, 362; and Reeves, *President Kennedy*, 73.

131 *Bissell sensed that Kennedy*: Bissell Jr., Lewis, and Pudlow, *Reflections of a Cold Warrior*, 335.

131 *By this point*: Reeves, *President Kennedy*, 72.

131 *Something about large meetings*: Dutton, interview.

132 *"But you always assume"*: Schlesinger, *A Thousand Days*, 258.

132 *"There were twelve of us"*: Strober and Strober, *The Kennedy Presidency*, 158.

132 *"More than once"*: Reeves, *President Kennedy*, 84.

133 *"Hell, Mr. President"*: Ibid., 93.

133 *"He seemed to me"*: Sorensen, *Kennedy*, 308.

133 *"And he cared so much"*: Rick Klein, "Jacqueline Kennedy's Audio Tapes Describe 'Our Happiest Years,'" September 12, 2011, ABCnews.com, http://abcnews.go.com/Politics/Jacqueline_Kennedy/jacqueline-kennedy-audio-tapes-describe-happiest-years-jfk/story?id=14478313.

133 *"How can you people do this"*: Jack Hawkins, "Classified Disaster," *National Review*, December 31, 1996.

133 *"Here for the first time"*: Chester Bowles, Notes on Cabinet Meeting, April 20, 1961, *Foreign Relations of the United States, 1961–1963*, vol. X, *Cuba, 1961–1962*, ed. Louis J. Smith, http://www.state.gov/www/aboutstate/history/frusX/index.html.

134 *"He didn't say"*: Dutton, interview.

134 *"I am the responsible officer"*: News Conference 10, April 21, 1961, transcript, Press Conferences of President Kennedy, John F. Kennedy Library.

134 *"How could I have been so stupid"*: Sorensen, *Kennedy*, 309.

134 *"Well, they had me figured"*: Dallek, *An Unfinished Life*, 365.

134 *"You failed in Cuba"*: "Grand Illusion," Foreign Relations, *Time*, April 28, 1961.

134 *"They had tremendously high expectations"*: Dean G. Acheson, interview by Lucius D. Battle, April 27, 1964, transcript, Oral History Program, John F. Kennedy Library.

134 *The administration, he argued*: Walter Lippmann, "Walter Lippmann, 1961," interview by Howard K. Smith, *CBS* Reports, June 15, 1961, transcript, http://archives-trim.un.org/webdrawer/rec/423553/view/Items-in-Public%20relations%20files

%20-%20interviews%20-%20TV%20broadcast%20-%20CBS%20Reports%20
%28Walter%20Lippman%29.PDF.

135 *"It wouldn't be long"*: Nixon, *RN*, 234.

135 *"I felt empathy for a man"*: Ibid., 236.

135 *"I'd end the thing forthright"*: Smith, *An Uncommon Man*, 23.

135 *"In fact, you'd better go"*: Ewald, *Eisenhower the President*, 316.

136 *"I don't run no bad invasions"*: Michael R. Beschloss, "A Tale of Two Presidents," *Wilson Quarterly* (Winter 2000).

136 *"He seemed himself at that moment"*: Dwight D. Eisenhower, Post-Presidential Papers, 1961–69; Gettysburg, Palm Desert, Indio File Box 2 JFK 1960–61 (1)(2) JFK 1962–67 (1) (2)(1)-14 pp. Malcolm Moos interview, 1966.

137 *"Kennedy's most irritating campaign promise"*: Eisenhower, *Going Home to Glory*, 32.

137 *"You must get courageous men"*: Schieffer, "Advice and Dissent."

138 *But the American people*: Dwight D. Eisenhower, notes on meeting with John F. Kennedy, April 22, 1961, Post-Presidential Papers: Augusta–Walter Reed Series, Dwight D. Eisenhower Papers, Dwight D. Eisenhower Library.

139 *"I want you to see"*: W.H. Lawrence, "Eisenhower Urges Nation to Back Kennedy on Cuba," *New York Times*, April 23, 1961.

139 *When New York's Republican congressman*: Parmet, *JFK*, 155.

139 *"Don't go back and rake over the ashes"*: *New York Times*, May 2, 1961.

139 *He invited some old friends*: David Eisenhower, *Going Home to Glory*, 38.

140 *" 'Profile in Timidity and Indecision' "*: Dwight D. Eisenhower, *The Eisenhower Diaries*, 389.

140 *His report, one of the most secret*: Jon Wiener, "SECRECY: The American Experience," *The Nation* 267, no. 21 (December 21, 1998).

141 *The operation was doomed*: For the full account, see Peter Kornbluh, ed., *The Bay of Pigs Declassified: The Secret CIA Report on the Invasion of Cuba* (New York: The New Press, 1998).

141 *"Calling three meetings"*: Reeves, *President Kennedy*, 113–14.

141 *"how you like to begin the day"*: Reeves, *President Kennedy*, 113.

141 *The Bay of Pigs*: Clifford, *Counsel to the President*, 350.

141 *After the Bay of Pigs*: Ibid., 350–51.

142 *"I send them with my best wishes"*: Eisenhower, *Going Home to Glory*, 65.

142 *Gray agreed*: Ambrose, *Eisenhower the President*, vol. II, 640.

142 *"Did we inherit these problems"*: Sorensen, *Kennedy*, 293–94.

143 *"The worse I do"*: Schlesinger, *A Thousand Days*, 292.

143 *Kennedy's great fear*: Pierre Salinger, *With Kennedy* (Garden City, NY: Doubleday, 1966), 255.

143 *"He treated me like a little boy"*: Reeves, *President Kennedy*, 166.

143 *"He savaged me"*: Ibid., 172.

143 *In the "Single Integrated Operation Plan"*: Fred Kaplan, "JFK's First-Strike Plan," *Atlantic*, October 2001.

144   *"'And we call ourselves the human race' "*: Reeves, *President Kennedy*, 230.

144   *Kennedy struck people*: "John F. Kennedy, a Way with the People," Man of the Year, *Time*, January 5, 1962.

144   *How do we drain*: Schlesinger, *A Thousand Days*, 298.

144   *The United States had too little*: Ibid., 316.

144   *"It's not a very nice solution"*: Dallek, *An Unfinished Life*, 426.

144   *He doubled the arsenal*: Reeves, *President Kennedy*, 245.

144   *"Well, I thought you should have"*: Schlesinger, *A Thousand Days*, 496.

145   *"Therefore the missiles have one purpose"*: Dallek, *An Unfinished Life*, 536.

145   *Conservative senators*: Reeves, *President Kennedy*, 347.

145   *"The reason we're in trouble"*: "The Durable Doctrine," The Presidency, *Time*, September 21, 1962.

145   *Kennedy meanwhile said*: Dallek, *An Unfinished Life*, 541.

145   *"He said that"*: Kennedy, *In His Own Words*, 346.

146   *"The Nation's engine was idling"*: John F. Kennedy, "Remarks in Harrisburg at a Democratic State Finance Committee Dinner, September 20, 1962," The American Presidency Project, http://www.presidency.ucsb.edu/ws/?pid=8886.

146   *"One more attack"*: David Eisenhower, *Going Home to Glory*, 94.

146   *"No threatening foreign bases"*: Tom Wicker, "Eisenhower Calls President Weak on Foreign Policy," *New York Times*, October 16, 1962.

146   *"But partisan discussions of foreign policy"*: "Two Presidents," *New York Times*, October 17, 1962.

146   *"I want you over here"*: Reeves, *President Kennedy*, 368.

147   *Bobby Kennedy rode to the White House*: Ibid., 381.

147   *The White House mess stayed open*: Salinger, *With Kennedy*, 261.

147   *"He thought they were the only ones"*: Dallek, *An Unfinished Life*, 557–58.

147   *"He initially suspected Kennedy"*: David Eisenhower, *Going Home to Glory*, 94.

147   *McCone told Kennedy*: Kennedy, *In His Own Words*, 346.

148   *"Eisenhower Bars Any Crisis"*: *New York Times*, October 22, 1962.

149   *"Well, we'll hang on tight"*: Dwight D. Eisenhower, Dictabelt recording of phone call with John F. Kennedy, October 22, 1962, transcript, Post-Presidential Papers: Augusta–Walter Reed Series, Dwight D. Eisenhower Papers, Dwight D. Eisenhower Library.

149   *"YOUR ACTION DESPERATE"*: "The West's Response," World, *Time*, November 2, 1962.

149   *There was a run*: "The Showdown," Nation, *Time*, November 2, 1962.

149   *McCone offered*: Sheldon M. Stern, "What JFK Really Said," *Atlantic*, May 2000.

150   *"I felt we were on the edge"*: Reeves, *President Kennedy*, 378.

150   *"So far as Cuba and Soviet Russia"*: "Eisenhower Backs Kennedy in Crisis," *New York Times*, October 24, 1962.

150   *"Here, Kennedy's talent for crisis management"*: Beschloss, "A Tale of Two Presidents."

151   *"In effect the members walked"*: Schlesinger, *A Thousand Days*, 801.

151   *Part of the problem*: "The Talker," World, *Time*, November 23, 1962.

151   *Tiffany president Walter Hoving*: Reeves, *President Kennedy*, 416.

152   *"The advisors may move on"*: "John F. Kennedy, a Way with the People," *Time*.

152   *He had come, Schlesinger the younger concluded*: Schlesinger, *A Thousand Days*, 674.

153   *"Now he's mad to save"*: Ibid., 675.

153   *"The old man"*: David Eisenhower, *Going Home to Glory*, 74.

153   *"Apparently we have avoided this one"*: Marie B. Hecht, *Beyond the Presidency: The Residues of Power* (New York: Macmillan, 1976), 313.

153   *"It is my hope"*: Ibid., 180.

Chapter 7: "How About Coming in for a Drink?"

154   *"I am ready to serve our government"*: Smith, *An Uncommon Man*, 426; and Lyndon B. Johnson, *The Vantage Point: Perspectives of the Presidency, 1963–1969* (New York: Holt, Rinehart and Winston, 1971), 31.

155   *"Oswald had been planning to kill me"*: Nixon, *RN*, 252.

155   *"Now he wasn't so sure"*: William Manchester, *The Death of a President: November 20–25, 1963* (New York: Harper & Row, 1967), 260.

155   *"He can ride with me"*: Ibid., 504.

155   *In the river of people behind*: "The Funeral," Nation, *Time*, December 6, 1963; "A Hero's Burial," *New York Times*, November 26, 1963.

156   *And they talked about the old days*: Steve Neal, *Harry and Ike: The Partnership That Remade the Postwar World* (New York: Scribner, 2001), 321; and Manchester, *The Death of a President*, 592.

156   *Eisenhower looked at Mamie*: Edward T. Folliard, interview by Jerry N. Hess, August 20, 1970, transcript, Oral History Interviews, Harry S. Truman Library.

156   *"I don't know where the magic came from"*: Admiral Robert L. Dennison, interview by Jerry N. Hess, November 2, 1971, transcript, Oral History Interviews, Harry S. Truman Library.

157   *Truman had already planned*: Neal, *Harry and Ike*, 322.

157   *Neither was at all inclined*: Margaret Truman, *Harry S. Truman* (New York: William Morrow, 1973), 576.

157   *And she thanked him*: Folliard, interview.

158   *"It was a long, lingering, silent handshake"*: Neal, *Harry and Ike*, 322.

158   *"President Truman does too"*: "June 17, 1966," People, *Time*, June 17, 1966.

158   *"They had been very closely associated"*: E. Clifton Daniel, interview by J.R. Fuchs, May 4, 1972, transcript, Oral History Interviews, Harry S. Truman Library.

Johnson and Eisenhower: Blood Brothers

160 *Pulling back from Vietnam*: George Ball, interview by Paige E. Mulhollan, July 8, 1971, transcript, Oral Histories, LBJ Library.

160 *"And, for the fact that no one"*: Lyndon B. Johnson to Dwight D. Eisenhower, March 10, 1966, Presidential Papers: Special Files: White House Famous Names, Papers of Lyndon B. Johnson, LBJ Library.

Chapter 8: "The Country Is Far More Important Than Any of Us"

161 *"No one but my family"*: Lyndon B. Johnson, *The Vantage Point: Perspectives of the Presidency, 1963–1969* (New York: Holt, Rinehart and Winston, 1971), 13.

161 *"I always felt sorry for Harry Truman"*: Robert Dallek, *Lyndon B. Johnson: Portrait of a President* (New York: Oxford University Press, 2004), 145.

162 *"as useful as a cow's fifth teat"*: "Some Day You'll Be Sitting in That Chair," Nation, *Time*, November 29, 1963.

162 *"Every time I came into"*: Doris Kearns Goodwin, *Lyndon Johnson and the American Dream* (New York: Harper & Row, 1976), 164.

162 *More than a quarter million people*: "Sympathy & Scrutiny," The Nations, *Time*, December 6, 1963.

162 *"The whole thing was almost unbearable"*: Goodwin, *Lyndon Johnson and the American Dream*, 170.

162 *The secretaries had already cleared*: Cartha D. "Deke" DeLoach, interview by Michael L. Gillette, January 11, 1991, transcript, Oral Histories, LBJ Library.

163 *"you give me a call"*: Michael Beschloss, ed., *Taking Charge: The Johnson White House Tapes 1963–1964* (New York: Simon & Schuster, 1997), 20.

163 *"Us three Texans got to stand together"*: James J. Hagerty, interview by Joe Frantz, November 16, 1971, transcript, Oral History Collection, LBJ Library.

164 *This helped explain how*: Dallek, *Lyndon B. Johnson*, 80.

164 *"Ike," Harlow said*: Bryce Harlow, interview by Michael L. Gillette, May 6, 1979, transcript, Oral History Collection, LBJ Library.

164 *Republicans dragged their feet*: John Whiteclay Chambers II, "Presidents Emeritus," *American Heritage Magazine* 30, no. 4 (June/July, 1979).

165 *"For the moment we can content ourselves"*: Lyndon B. Johnson, statement on Senate floor, February 4, 1957, Presidential Papers: Special Files: White House Famous Names, Papers of Lyndon B. Johnson, LBJ Library.

165 *"It's easily possible"*: Andrew J. Goodpaster, interview by Joe Frantz, June 21, 1971, transcript, Oral History Collection, LBJ Library.

165 *"Every impulse of the man"*: Horace W. Busby, *The Thirty-First of March: An Intimate Portrait of Lyndon Johnson's Final Days in Office* (New York: Farrar, Straus and Giroux, 2005), 158.

166 *Let a decent interval pass*: David Eisenhower, *Going Home to Glory: A Memoir of Life*

with Dwight D. Eisenhower, 1961–1969 (New York: Simon & Schuster, 2010), 205.

166 *"It is better to be"*: Dwight D. Eisenhower, November 23, 1963, Post-Presidential Papers: Appointment Book Series, Dwight D. Eisenhower Papers, Dwight D. Eisenhower Library.

166 *He asked if a secretary he'd known*: Johnson, *The Vantage Point*, 31.

166 *He asked that she burn her notes*: Dwight D. Eisenhower, memo to Lyndon B. Johnson, November 23, 1963, Presidential Papers: Special Files: White House Famous Names, Papers of Lyndon B. Johnson, LBJ Library.

166 *And he should vow to work*: Ibid.

166 *"Any hesitation or wavering"*: Robert Dallek, *Flawed Giant: Lyndon Johnson and His Times, 1961–1973* (New York: Oxford University Press, 1998), 54; and Johnson, *The Vantage Point*, 12, 18.

167 *Then Lady Bird got on the phone*: Beschloss, *Taking Charge*, 131.

167 *"Of all the things to which Kennedy was born"*: Theodore H. White, *The Making of the President, 1964* (New York: Atheneum Publishers, 1965), 35.

167 *Indeed Johnson tended to build*: Goodwin, *Lyndon Johnson and the American Dream*, 79.

168 *" 'I talked to the President' "*: Robert B. Anderson, interview by Paige E. Mulhollan, July 8, 1969, transcript, Oral History Collection, LBJ Library.

168 *"I want people around me"*: Dallek, *Lyndon B. Johnson*, 181.

168 *"Outside of that"*: Hagerty, OH interview.

168 *" 'This is what I would have done' "*: Anderson, OH interview.

169 *"If you asked him a question"*: Hagerty, OH interview.

169 *He moved Eisenhower's portrait*: Memorandum for the President from Bob Fleming, October 13, 1967, Presidential Papers: Special Files: White House Famous Names, Papers of Lyndon B. Johnson, LBJ Library.

170 *"I think that one day"*: Dwight D. Eisenhower to Lyndon B. Johnson, November 25, 1966, Presidential Papers: Special Files: White House Famous Names, Papers of Lyndon B. Johnson, LBJ Library.

170 *"And your bedroom is up there"*: Lyndon B. Johnson, Harry S. Truman, Bess Truman, WH6411-04-6166 (phone call), November 1964, transcript and MP3 and FLAC audio, Miller Center of Public Affairs, University of Virginia, http://whitehouse tapes.net/transcript/johnson/wh6411-04-6166.

170 *It was, Truman told Johnson*: Harry S. Truman to Lyndon B. Johnson, November 9, 1965, Presidential Papers: Special Files: White House Famous Names, Papers of Lyndon B. Johnson, LBJ Library.

170 *"I wonder if anyone will do the same"*: Goodwin, *Lyndon Johnson and the American Dream*, 250.

Chapter 9: "I Need Your Counsel, and I Love You"

171 *"We hardly discussed it"*: Gregory Allen Olson, *Mansfield and Vietnam: A Study in Rhetorical Adaptation* (East Lansing, MI: Michigan State University Press, 1995), 126.

171 *At least until he won*: Beschloss, *Taking Charge*, 266–67.

172 *And then he would wake up*: Goodwin, *Lyndon Johnson and the American Dream*, 253.

172 *He opened a press conference*: Dallek, *Flawed Giant*, 145.

172 *"And it's just the biggest damn mess"*: Ibid.

172 *"I don't know all the answers"*: Michael Beschloss, ed., *Reaching for Glory: Lyndon Johnson's Secret White House Tapes, 1964–1965* (New York: Simon & Schuster, 2001), 165.

173 *A special National Intelligence Estimate*: Rick Perlstein, *Nixonland: The Rise of a President and the Fracturing of America* (New York: Scribner, 2008), 102.

173 *Stalwart establishment columnists*: "One Problem, Two Solutions," Columnists, *Time*, January 1, 1965.

173 *That would yield*: Goodwin, *Lyndon Johnson and the American Dream*, 251–52.

173 *"a defeat for the American people"*: Dallek, *Flawed Giant*, 244.

173 *"That's why I am suspicious of the military"*: Goodwin, *Lyndon Johnson and the American Dream*, 252.

173 *"I'm going to come running"*: Beschloss, *Reaching for Glory*, 154.

173 *"The time has come for harder choices"*: Dallek, *Flawed Giant*, 246.

174 *Bundy, after a quick trip*: Johnson, *The Vantage Point*, 127.

174 *The problem was not political*: Clark Clifford, *Counsel to the President: A Memoir* (New York: Random House, 1991), 408.

174 *"I'm too sentimental to give the orders"*: Beschloss, *Reaching for Glory*, 175.

175 *"Don't be in a hurry"*: Ibid., 178.

175 *"I don't want to tax you"*: Ibid., 180.

176 *Goodpaster reported in his notes*: Memorandum of meeting with President Johnson, February 17, 1965, Presidential Papers: Special File: Meeting Notes (Top Secret), Papers of Lyndon B. Johnson, LBJ Library.

177 *But it ensured that the North Koreans*: Beschloss, *Reaching for Glory*, 182.

177 *(That may have been how he chose)*: Michael Gordon Jackson, "Beyond Brinkmanship: Eisenhower, Nuclear War Fighting, and Korea, 1953–1968," *Presidential Studies Quarterly* 35, no. 1 (March 2005).

177 *But the United States has now put its prestige*: Lyndon B. Johnson, Presidential Papers: Special Files: Meeting Notes, Papers of Lyndon B. Johnson, LBJ Library.

177 *"Eisenhower advocated a variety"*: Clifford, *Counsel to the President*, 407.

178 *"This country is in an undeclared and unexplained war"*: James Reston, "Washington: The Undeclared and Unexplained War," *New York Times*, February 14, 1965.

178 *And yet all the while*: Dallek, *Flawed Giant*, 281.

178 *"The Republican leaders"*: Lyndon B. Johnson to Dwight D. Eisenhower, March 5, 1965, Presidential Papers: Special Files: White House Famous Names, Papers of Lyndon B. Johnson, LBJ Library.

179 *"I wonder why people don't recognize"*: Eric F. Goldman, *The Tragedy of Lyndon Johnson* (New York: Knopf, 1969), 406.

179 *The* Dallas Morning News: Dror Yuravlivker, " 'Peace without Conquest': Lyndon Johnson's Speech of April 7, 1965," *Presidential Studies Quarterly* 36, no. 3 (September 2006), 475.

179 *Nearly two thirds of voters*: Dallek, *Lyndon B. Johnson*, 217.

179 *"We're in a hell of a mess"*: Beschloss, *Reaching for Glory*, 348.

179 *"I've exaggerated in both cases"*: McGeorge Bundy, interview by Paige E. Mulhollan, January 30, 1969, transcript, Oral History Collection, LBJ Library.

179 *"I don't see that he's overeager"*: Beschloss, *Reaching for Glory*, 348.

180 *"It could only be serious and bad"*: Ibid., 377.

180 *"a thorn stuck in his throat"*: Dallek, *Flawed Giant*, 283.

180 *"I'm beginning to feel like a martyr"*: Ibid., 258.

180 *"Louisiana swamp . . . that's pulling me down"*: Ibid., 282.

181 *"I've got to rely on you on this one"*: Beschloss, *Reaching for Glory*, 383.

182 *"We just cannot now dishonor our word"*: "The Press Conference," Nation, *Time*, August 6, 1965.

182 *He had never made a unilateral military commitment*: Max Frankel, "Eisenhower Denies Pledge to Saigon," *New York Times*, August 18, 1965.

182 *He had refused to provide fighter planes*: "Dwight David Eisenhower: A Leader in War and Peace," *New York Times*, March 29, 1969.

182 *"Military Pledge to Saigon Is Denied by Eisenhower"*: *New York Times*, August 18, 1965.

182 *"Indeed the whole effort"*: "The Eisenhower Demurrer," *New York Times*, August 19, 1965.

182 *"They want to get us in a fight"*: Transcript of telephone conversation between Lyndon B. Johnson and Dwight D. Eisenhower, August 18, 1965, 6:15 p.m., Citation #8555, Recordings and Transcripts of Conversations and Meetings, LBJ Library.

183 *"Next to the operations in Vietnam"*: McGeorge Bundy to Andrew J. Goodpaster, August 19, 1965, Presidential Papers: National Security File, Papers of Lyndon B. Johnson, LBJ Library.

183 *The Churchill letter asserted*: Eisenhower to Churchill, April 4, 1954, copy included in Bundy memo to Goodpaster, August 19, 1965, LBJ Library.

183 *"Patriot, soldier, President"*: Johnson to Eisenhower, August 19, 1965, Presidential Papers: National Security File, Papers of Lyndon B. Johnson, LBJ Library.

183 *Eisenhower assured Goodpaster*: Goodpaster memo for the record, August 20, 1965, Presidential Papers: National Security File (Country File: Vietnam), Papers of Lyndon B. Johnson, LBJ Library.

184 *And at a time of crisis*: David S. Broder, "Eisenhower Backs Stand on Vietnam," *New York Times*, August 20, 1965.

184 *He promised that the Republicans*: John W. Finney, "Johnson Asks 'Unified Support' in Meeting at State Department," *New York Times*, August 20, 1965.

184   *Ike declined to endorse the Republican*: "The One-Two Punch," Foreign Relations, *Time*, September 3, 1965.

184   *Johnson called him*: "Greyer, Graver—and Growing," The Presidency, *Time*, September 3, 1965.

184   *The talks with Johnson would be very warm*: Eisenhower, *Going Home to Glory*, 166.

185   *And he tore up the pages*: William Bragg Ewald, *Eisenhower the President: Crucial Days, 1951–1960* (Englewood Cliffs, NJ: Prentice-Hall, 1981), 28.

185   *But when the year came to an end*: Dallek, *Flawed Giant*, 340.

185   *The chairman of the Federal Reserve*: Perlstein, *Nixonland*, 181.

185   *"I frankly am lukewarm"*: Ibid., 205.

185   *Johnson wasn't just looking*: David Eisenhower, *Going Home to Glory*, 204.

185   *"And he said it was like drinking"*: Jack Valenti, interview by author, June 16, 2005.

186   *"God had set out to torture him"*: Goodwin, interview by author, September 26, 2006; Goodwin, *Lyndon Johnson and the American Dream*, 342.

186   *"He had no hobbies or interests outside of politics"*: David Eisenhower, *Going Home to Glory*, 304.

186   *"I wish I had some of that quality"*: Goodwin, *Lyndon Johnson and the American Dream*, 349.

186   *"I don't believe it's possible"*: "The War Pinch," *Time*, January 14, 1966.

186   *Johnson's popularity sank*: "No Cure in Consensus," The Presidency, *Time*, June 10, 1966.

186   *"Lee Harvey Oswald"*: Dallek, *Flawed Giant*, 452.

187   *Half the country didn't know*: Ibid., 462.

187   *And then there was the March*: Ibid., 487.

187   *The White House watched in growing frustration*: Max Frankel, "Six Different Views on How to End the War in Vietnam," *New York Times*, October 29, 1967.

187   *Advisor James Rowe warned*: Dallek, *Flawed Giant*, 468.

187   *The task of taking on the protesters*: Joseph G. Morgan, *The Vietnam Lobby: The American Friends of Vietnam, 1955–1975* (Chapel Hill, NC: University of North Carolina Press, 1997), 132.

187   *Roche was a classic Cold War liberal*: Wolfgang Saxon, "John P. Roche, 70, Scholar and Counselor to Presidents," *New York Times*, May 7, 1994.

187   *"I will argue to my dying day"*: John P. Roche, "Ten Years After Vietnam," *National Review* 37 (May 31, 1985), quoted in William F. Buckley, *Happy Days Were Here Again: Reflections of a Libertarian Journalist* (New York: Basic Books, 2008), 194.

187   *When Johnson was desperate for allies*: Morgan, *The Vietnam Lobby*.

187   *He even promised squads*: Perlstein, *Nixonland*, 207.

188   *"the majority voice of America is heard"*: "Voice from the Silent Center," *Time*, November 3, 1967.

188   *"Despite your implication"*: Peter Grose, "Public Figures Warn on Impatience in Peace Talks," *New York Times*, May 24, 1968.

188 " '*Why, I'd just go ahead and smack them*' ": Goodwin, *Lyndon Johnson and the American Dream*, 349.

189 "*That's one of the few things*": Tom Wicker, "In the Nation: Eisenhower Rides Again," *New York Times*, December 28, 1967.

189 *Peace candidate Eugene McCarthy*: Perlstein, *Nixonland*, 232.

Chapter 10: "You'll Have My Promise—I'll Speak No Evil"

194 "*Just sit tight in the buggy*' ": Richard M. Nixon to Ronald Reagan, June 9, 1966, Reagan Personal Collection, Ronald Reagan Library.

195 "*Reagan would make a particularly good witness*": Richard M. Nixon to Herman L. Perry, June 17, 1947, Herman L. & Hubert C. Perry Collection, Richard M. Nixon Library.

195 *And so the Nixon-Reagan partnership*: transcript of Committee On Un-American Activities hearing, October 20–30, 1947, National Archives.

196 *In a brief postscript*: Richard M. Nixon to Ronald Reagan, June 18, 1959, National Archives Pacific Region, Laguna Niguel.

196 "*As a matter of fact*": Ronald Reagan to Richard M. Nixon, June 27, 1959, National Archives Pacific Region, Laguna Niguel.

196 "*Those of us who have spent*": Richard M. Nixon to Ronald Reagan, July 6, 1959, National Archives Pacific Region, Laguna Niguel.

196 *Nixon was helping to launch*: Hedda Hopper, "Peter Palmer Seen on 'Li'l Abner' Set," *Los Angeles Times*, July 8, 1959.

196 *Nixon replied overnight*: Ronald Reagan to Richard M. Nixon, September 7, 1959, National Archives Pacific Region, Laguna Niguel.

197 *But Nixon begged off*: Ronald Reagan to Richard M. Nixon, December 11, 1959, National Archives Pacific Region, Laguna Niguel.

197 *Nixon sent Reagan*: Ronald Reagan to Richard M. Nixon, July 15, 1960, Richard Nixon Pre-Presidential Materials, Richard M. Nixon Library.

197 *A second scribbled note*: Ronald Reagan to Richard M. Nixon, July 23, 1960, National Archives Pacific Region, Laguna Niguel.

198 "*This is no longer the Democratic Party*": "40 Section Chairmen for Nixon Drive Named," The Watchman, *Los Angeles Times*, October 2, 1960.

198 "*He tried to persuade me*": Ronald Reagan, *An American Life* (New York: Simon & Schuster, 1990), 135.

199 "*I signed it and became a Republican*": Ibid., 132.

199 "*He was only 49*": "California: Career's End," Nation, *Time*, November 16, 1962.

199 "*CBS canceled the show*": Lou Cannon, *Governor Reagan: His Rise to Power* (New York: Public Affairs, 2003), 113.

200 "*I am sure that no one can beat Brown*": Richard M. Nixon to Ronald Reagan, November 28, 1966, Richard Nixon Pre-Presidential Materials, Richard M. Nixon Library.

200 *"I'll speak no evil"*: Ronald Reagan to Richard M. Nixon, May 7, 1965, Richard Nixon Pre-Presidential Materials, Richard M. Nixon Library.

200 *Reagan made sure of that*: Daryl E. Lembke, "Reagan May Shun Nixon, Goldwater," *Los Angeles Times*, January 26, 1966.

201 *"He said a lot of things that Barry said"*: Stuart Spencer, interview by Paul B. Freedman, Stephen F. Knott, Russell L. Riley, and James Sterling Young, November 15–16, 2001, transcript, Miller Center of Public Affairs, University of Virginia.

201 *Elite opinion makers on the East Coast*: Rick Perlstein, *Nixonland: The Rise of a President and the Fracturing of America* (New York: Scribner, 2008), 92.

202 *"The only thing I know about his politics"*: Dwight D. Eisenhower to Jim Murphy, September 8, 1965, Eisenhower Post-Presidential Papers, Dwight D. Eisenhower Library.

202 *"Our party deserves to have a voice"*: Robert J. Donovan, "Eisenhower Endorses Reagan, Talks of Candidate's Future," *Los Angeles Times*, June 16, 1966.

202 *George Murphy (also a former actor), to coach Reagan*: Perlstein, *Nixonland*, 93.

202 *"That's as far as my dreams go"*: Ibid.

203 *"Any member of the society"*: Lou Cannon, *Governor Reagan*, 153.

203 *"You might have some thoughts on this"*: Freeman Gosden to Dwight D. Eisenhower, July 7, 1966, Eisenhower Post-Presidential Papers, Dwight D. Eisenhower Library.

203 *" 'There are not minority groups' "*: Dwight D. Eisenhower to Freeman Gosden, July 11, 1966, Eisenhower Post-Presidential Papers, Dwight D. Eisenhower Library.

204 *"He is a decent American"*: Dwight D. Eisenhower to Mrs. Edwin C. Hilson, Office of President Reagan, Ronald Reagan Library.

204 *It's no secret I deplore racism"*: Richard Bergholz, "Cranston Confronts Reagan at Airport on Birch Society Issue," *Los Angeles Times*, August 2, 1966.

204 *"The old man told me to do it"*: Pat Buchanan, interview by author, January 14, 2011.

205 *Then the whole Nixon party*: William Safire, *Before the Fall: An Inside View of the Pre-Watergate White House* (Garden City, NY: Doubleday, 1975), 941.

205 *Dick*: Richard M. Nixon to Ronald Reagan, November 28, 1966, Reagan Personal collection, Richard M. Nixon Library.

206 *According to Lou Cannon's definitive account*: Lou Cannon, *Governor Reagan*, 258.

206 *Reed personally briefed Reagan*: Robert Novak, *The Prince of Darkness: 50 Years Reporting in Washington* (New York: Crown Forum, 2007), 166.

206 *"Reagan was not a candidate"*: Ibid.

206 *Stuart Spencer recalled*: Spencer, interview.

207 *"Equally dangerous would be a serious intraparty split"*: Richard M. Nixon, *RN: The Memoirs of Richard Nixon* (New York: Grosset & Dunlap, 1978), 304.

207 *But Reagan was enough of a concern*: Safire, *Before the Fall*, 43–44.

208 *Dick*: Richard M. Nixon to Ronald Reagan, February 24, 1967, Richard Nixon Pre-Presidential Materials, Richard M. Nixon Library.

208 *"That was part of his idea"*: John Sears, interview by author, October 22, 2010.

208 *In late April 1967*: "Sam Pan," Nation, *Time*, May 5, 1967.

209 *"Who the fuck got me into this"*: Lou Cannon, *Governor Reagan*, 260.

209 *It was a boffo performance*: "Welcome to the Fraternity," Nation, *Time*, May 19, 1967.

209 *Dick*: Richard M. Nixon to Ronald Reagan, May 31, 1967, Richard Nixon Pre-Presidential Materials, Richard M. Nixon Library.

209 *"We want Reagan"*: "Omaha Handshake," Republicans, *Time*, June 30, 1967.

210 *"But that isn't going to happen"*: "Waiting Game," Republicans, *Time*, July 7, 1967.

210 *"Any guy who can lose to Pat Brown"*: Ibid.

210 *"I am sorry that at a time"*: "Polls & Portents," Political Notes, *Time*, July 21, 1967.

210 *Ron*: Ronald Reagan to Richard M. Nixon, July 12, 1967, Richard Nixon Pre-Presidential Materials, Richard M. Nixon Library.

211 *Dick*: Richard M. Nixon to Ronald Reagan, July 18, 1967, Richard Nixon Pre-Presidential Materials, Richard M. Nixon Library.

211 *It was something of a clubhouse*: Stephen E. Ambrose, *Eisenhower: Soldier and President* (New York: Simon & Schuster, 1990), 248.

211 *Echoing many of their previous conversations*: Nixon, *RN*, 286.

212 *Reagan also told Nixon*: Ibid.

212 *Reagan historian James Mann*: James Mann, *The Rebellion of Ronald Reagan: A History of the End of the Cold War* (New York: Viking, 2009), 10.

212 *"Let Ronnie have the kooks"*: Rowland Evans and Robert Novak, "Nixon's New Strategy Is: 'Let Ronnie Have Kooks,'" *Pittsburgh Post-Gazette*, July 25, 1967.

212 *Dick*: Richard M. Nixon to Ronald Reagan, August 4, 1967, Richard Nixon Pre-Presidential Materials, Richard M. Nixon Library.

213 *Ron*: Ronald Reagan to Richard M. Nixon, August 16, 1967, Richard Nixon Pre-Presidential Materials, Richard M. Nixon Library.

213 *"For those of you who don't know"*: "Reagan's Road Show," Republicans, *Time*, October 13, 1967.

213 *Reagan campaigned in Oregon*: "Chubbmanship," Nation, *Time*, December 15, 1967.

214 *"It can't be his first World Series"*: "Anchors Aweigh," Republicans, *Time*, October 20, 1967.

214 *"The only one who can stop us"*: Safire, *Before the Fall*, 47.

214 *Dick*: Richard M. Nixon to Ronald Reagan, April 4, 1968, Richard Nixon Pre-Presidential Materials, Richard M. Nixon Library.

215 *Ron*: Ronald Reagan to Richard M. Nixon, April 10, 1968, Richard Nixon Pre-Presidential Materials, Richard M. Nixon Library.

215 *(CBS declined)*: "Nixon's Steppingstones, Reagan's TV Show," Republicans, *Time*, May 24, 1968.

216 *He recalled later that Reagan flew Southern delegates*: Nixon, *RN*, 309.

216 *"I am a candidate"*: Novak, *The Prince of Darkness*, 167.

216 *This was a strange last-minute maneuver*: Lou Cannon, *Governor Reagan*, 163–64.

216 *"Rockefeller worked on the northern"*: Nixon, *RN*, 309.

217 *And when he finally got the floor*: Ibid., 311.

218 *"Establishment* forbids *a Nixon presidency"*: Richard Whalen, *Catch a Falling Flag: A Republican's Challenge to His Party* (Boston: Houghton Mifflin, 1972), 178.

218 *"He didn't want to go through that"*: Author interview with John Sears, October 22, 2010.

219 *Years later, Nixon pointedly recalled*: Nixon, *RN*, 311.

219 *"I knew I wasn't ready to be president"*: Ronald Reagan, *An American Life*, 178.

219 *"Anyway, we'll work our heads off"*: Ronald Reagan to Mr. and Mrs. Elwood Wagner, September 3, 1968, Lorraine Wagner Letter Collection at the Reagan Ranch, Young America's Foundation.

Johnson and Nixon: Two Scorpions in a Bottle

221 *At issue was the Vietnam War*: David S. Broder, "A Risky New American Sport: 'The Breaking of the President,'" *Washington Post*, October 7, 1969.

Chapter 11: "This Is Treason"

223 *"I never shared the intense dislike"*: Lyndon B. Johnson, *The Vantage Point: Perspectives of the Presidency, 1963–1969* (New York: Holt, Rinehart and Winston, 1971), 547.

223 *"Nothing will happen"*: William Safire, *Before the Fall: An Inside View of the Pre-Watergate White House* (Garden City, NY: Doubleday, 1975), 84.

223 *He may have spent the years*: Rick Perlstein, *Nixonland: The Rise of a President and the Fracturing of America* (New York: Scribner, 2008), 65.

224 *Bookies put the odds*: Ibid., 17.

224 *Then he got up*: Bob Greene, *Fraternity: A Journey in Search of Five Presidents* (New York: Crown Publishers, 2004), 66; and Richard M. Nixon, *RN: The Memoirs of Richard Nixon* (New York: Grosset & Dunlap, 1978), 272–73.

224 *"It took someone with the eye of a hawk"*: Perlstein, *Nixonland*, 138.

225 *"Is this a quest for peace"*: Nixon, *RN*, 273.

225 *Nixon gigged Johnson*: Perlstein, *Nixonland*, 528.

225 *Ike urged him*: Dwight D. Eisenhower to Richard M. Nixon, October 21, 1966, Post-Presidential Papers: Special Names Series, Dwight D. Eisenhower Papers, Dwight D. Eisenhower Library.

225 *He managed to persuade the* New York Times: Safire, *Before the Fall*, 37–38.

226 *"You remember what President Eisenhower said"*: "Operation Withdrawal," The Campaign, *Time*, November 11, 1966.

226 *"Nixon had gotten his goat"*: Safire, *Before the Fall*, 46.

226 *"Jesus, did he hit us"*: Ibid., 39.

226 *"In the space of a single autumn day"*: Perlstein, *Nixonland*, 163.

226 *"I suddenly found myself"*: Nixon, *RN*, 276.

227 *"my respect has not changed"*: Ibid.

227 *"Lyndon Johnson knows who won"*: Richard H. Amberg, *St. Louis Globe-Democrat*, December 3–4, 1966, quoted in Andrew L. Johns, "A Voice from the Wilderness: Richard Nixon and the Vietnam War, 1964–1966," *Presidential Studies Quarterly* 29, no. 2 (June 1999).

227 *"Nixon was the most vulnerable"*: Safire, *Before the Fall*, 47.

228 *General Creighton Abrams*: "Assessing the Bombing," World, *Time*, September 13, 1968.

228 *Clifford traveled to Saigon*: Clark Clifford, *Counsel to the President: A Memoir* (New York: Random House, 1991), 551.

228 *"The enemy will wait for the next man"*: Jules Witcover, *The Resurrection of Richard Nixon* (New York: Putnam, 1970), 293.

229 *To have any chance of winning*: Perlstein, *Nixonland*, 267.

229 *He called Humphrey "weak"*: Robert Dallek, *Flawed Giant: Lyndon Johnson and His Times, 1961–1973* (New York: Oxford University Press, 1998), 576.

229 *"L.B.J. seems at the moment"*: "What Should Humphrey Do?" Nation, *Time*, September 27, 1968.

229 *"His anger at Humphrey"*: Clifford, *Counsel to the President*, 563.

229 *"When he gets the nomination"*: Ibid.

230 *"I was as appalled as the President"*: Ibid.

230 *"I just plain don't know"*: Robert "KC" Johnson, "Did Nixon Commit Treason in 1968? What the New LBJ Tapes Reveal," History News Network, January 26, 2009, http://hnn.us/articles/60446.html.

230 *"If there's peace"*: Safire, *Before the Fall*, 58.

230 *The Chinese-born widow*: Bui Diem with David Chanoff, *In the Jaws of History* (Boston: Houghton Mifflin, 1987), 236–37.

230 *On July 12*: Robert Dallek, *Nixon and Kissinger: Partners in Power* (New York: HarperCollins, 2007), 75.

231 *He promised to make Vietnam*: Nguyen Tien Hung and Jerrold L. Schecter, *The Palace File* (New York: Harper & Row, 1986), 23.

231 *He had laid the groundwork*: Dallek, *Flawed Giant*, 575.

231 *"He always does"*: Doris Kearns Goodwin, *Lyndon Johnson and the American Dream* (New York: Harper & Row, 1976), 351.

231 *Protesters held an "un-birthday party"*: James Reston Jr., *The Lone Star: The Life of John Connally* (New York: Harper & Row, 1989), 366.

231 *By the night of Humphrey's nomination*: "Dementia in the Second City," Nation, *Time*, September 6, 1968.

232 *"Not for a bunch of goddamn draft dodgers"*: Johnson, "Did Nixon Commit Treason in 1968?"

232 *This was not like an FDR coalition*: Safire, *Before the Fall*, 62.

233 *"It was one of the few times"*: Bob Faiss, memo to James R. Jones, September 10,

1968, Presidential Papers: Special Files: White House Famous Names: Billy Graham, Papers of Lyndon B. Johnson, LBJ Library.

233 *He even took the paper from Graham*: Billy Graham, notes of meeting with Lyndon B. Johnson concerning Nixon's secret overture to Johnson, Special Name File: Billy Graham, Papers of Lyndon B. Johnson, LBJ Library.

233 *Johnson, Graham said*: Billy Graham, handwritten notes and an undated typewritten account, Special Name File: Billy Graham, Papers of Lyndon B. Johnson, LBJ Library.

234 *"If so, any disclosures"*: Charles D. Roche, memo to Lyndon B. Johnson, September 28, 1968, Presidential Papers: White House Famous Names File: Richard M. Nixon, Papers of Lyndon B. Johnson, LBJ Library.

234 *"You know that Nixon is following"*: Dallek, *Nixon and Kissinger*, 67.

234 *"If the Government of North Vietnam"*: R.W. Apple Jr., "Humphrey Vows Halt in Bombing if Hanoi Reacts," *New York Times*, October 1, 1968.

234 *The actual proposal*: Clifford, *Counsel to the President*, 572.

234 *"I think I've done it carefully here"*: Perlstein, *Nixonland*, 345.

235 *"I think that my position has to be"*: Lyndon B. Johnson, Richard M. Nixon, Jim Jones, Walt Rostow, WH6809-04-13432-13433 (phone call), September 30, 1968, transcript and MP3 and FLAC audio, Miller Center of Public Affairs, University of Virginia, http://whitehousetapes.net/transcript/johnson/wh6809-04-13432 -13433.

236 *Liberal House Democrats*: "Some Forward Motion for H.H.H.," Nation, *Time*, October 11, 1968.

236 *" 'You tell the President' "*: Dallek, *Flawed Giant*, 580.

236 *Soviet embassy officials in Paris*: Clifford, *Counsel to the President*, 575.

236 *"They just seem to have disappeared"*: "Watching for the Peace Signals," Nation, *Time*, October 25, 1968.

237 *"I thought this a statesman's view"*: Ellsworth Bunker, report on meeting with Nguyen Van Thieu, November 10, 1968, Presidential Papers: National Security File, 1963–1969: Files of Walt W. Rostow, Papers of Lyndon B. Johnson, LBJ Library.

237 *Humphrey, who was still in the doghouse*: "Watching for the Peace Signals," *Time*.

237 *They agreed to tell reporters*: Lyndon B. Johnson, Richard M. Nixon, Hubert H. Humphrey, George Wallace, WH6810-04-13547-13548 (phone call), October 16, 1968, transcript and MP3 and FLAC audio, Miller Center of Public Affairs, University of Virginia, http://whitehousetapes.net/transcript/johnson/wh6810-04 -13547-13548.

237 *"LBJ can be just as vindictive"*: Safire, *Before the Fall*, 84.

238 *It was vital that they know*: Bryce Harlow, interview by Michael L. Gillette, May 6, 1979, transcript, Oral History Collection, LBJ Library.

238 *Never mind*: Anthony Summers, *The Arrogance of Power: The Secret World of Richard Nixon* (New York: Viking, 2000), 313.

238 *He contacted Nixon aide Richard Allen*: Walter Isaacson, *Kissinger: A Biography* (New York: Simon & Schuster, 1992), 130.

238 *"It is not stretching the truth"*: Ibid., 131.

238 *Harlow, who had "a double agent"*: Harlow, interview.

238 *"White Housers still think"*: Nixon, *RN*, 326.

238 *"It's just a question of timing"*: Harlow, interview.

239 *"Don't talk in your office"*: Summers, *The Arrogance of Power*, 300.

239 *A warning came into the Johnson White House*: Dallek, *Flawed Giant*, 584.

239 *Eugene McCarthy finally came out*: "Down to the Wire," Nation, *Time*, November 8, 1968.

239 *"Fewer men are fully clued into"*: "Keeping the Secret," Nation, *Time*, November 8, 1968.

239 *When the White House got a crucial message*: Clifford, *Counsel to the President*, 579; "Johnson's Gamble for Peace" *Time*, November 8, 1968

239 *"salvage the candidacy of Mr. Humphrey"*: Statement from Richard M. Nixon, October 25, 1968, Presidential Papers: White House Famous Name File: Nixon, Richard, Papers of Lyndon B. Johnson, LBJ Library.

240 *Rusk put it at nine and one*: Tom Johnson, "Notes on President's Meeting with Group of Foreign Policy Advisors," October 27, 1968, *Foreign Relations of the United States, 1964–1968*, vol. VII, *Vietnam, September 1968–January 1969*, ed. Kent Sieg, http://history.state.gov/historicaldocuments/frus1964-68v07/d129.

240 *Soviet premier Alexei Kosygin*: Walt W. Rostow, "Information Memorandum from the President's Special Assistant (Rostow) to President Johnson," October 28, 1968, *Foreign Relations of the United States, 1964–1968*, vol. VII, *Vietnam, September 1968–January 1969*, ed. Kent Sieg, http://history.state.gov/historicaldocuments/frus1964-68v07/d138.

240 *"A burnt child dreads fire"*: Tom Johnson, "Notes of the President's Meeting," October 28, 1968, *Foreign Relations of the United States, 1964–1968*, vol. VII, *Vietnam, September 1968–January 1969*, ed. Kent Sieg, http://history.state.gov/historical documents/frus1964-68v07/d139.

240 "In his heart of hearts": Clifford, *Counsel to the President*, 580.

240 *General Abrams boarded a C-141 Starlifter*: "A Halting Step Toward Peace," World, *Time*, November 15, 1968.

241 *"Yes, sir"*: Tom Johnson, "Notes of the President's Meeting," October 29, 1968, *Foreign Relations of the United States, 1964–1968*, vol. VII, *Vietnam, September 1968–January 1969*, ed. Kent Sieg, http://history.state.gov/historicaldocuments/frus1964-68v07/d140.

241 "Abrams has carried the ball": Clifford, *Counsel to the President*, 586.

241 *It's "tough to be a candidate"*: Johnson, "Notes of the President's Meeting," October 29, 1968.

241 *"Where will Nixon be"*: Robert Dallek, "Three New Revelations about LBJ," *Atlantic Monthly*, April 1998.

242 *"Thieu referred many times"*: Central Intelligence Agency, "President Thieu's Views Regarding the Issues Involved in Agreeing to a Bombing Halt," memo to Walt W. Rostow and Dean Rusk, October 26, 1968, Presidential Papers: Reference File: South Vietnam and U.S. Policies, Papers of Lyndon B. Johnson, LBJ Library.

242 *Nixon, in other words*: Eugene V. Rostow, memo regarding Anna Chennault to Walt W. Rostow, October 29, 1968, Presidential Papers: Reference File: South Vietnam and U.S. Policies, Papers of Lyndon B. Johnson, LBJ Library. The South Vietnam and U.S. Policies file is sometimes referred to as the "X- File"; it contains a set of photocopied documents concerning Anna Chennault's involvement in the October 1968 bombing halt. These documents were retained by Walt Rostow in a special file at President Johnson's request because of their sensitivity. Most, but not all, have been declassified.

242 *Johnson had ordered the FBI*: Walt W. Rostow, "Memorandum for the Record," May 14, 1973, Presidential Papers: Reference File: South Vietnam and U.S. Policies, Papers of Lyndon B. Johnson, LBJ Library; and Dallek, *Nixon and Kissinger*, 75. FBI officials would later deny they actually bugged Agnew's plane.

242 *If Saigon held out*: National Security Agency, "Delays Improve South Vietnam's Position," cable to White House, October 28, 1968, Presidential Papers: Reference File: South Vietnam and U.S. Policies, Papers of Lyndon B. Johnson, LBJ Library.

242 *"Follow her wherever"*: Cartha D. "Deke" DeLoach, *Hoover's FBI: The Inside Story by Hoover's Trusted Lieutenant* (Washington, DC: Regnery, 1997), 397.

242 *get a better deal out of Nixon*: "Delays Improve South Vietnam's Position," October 28, 1968, memo from the Director of the National Security Agency to the White House, Reference File: South Vietnam and U.S. Policies, LBJ Library.

242 *"Can you imagine what people would say"*: Johnson, "Notes of the President's Meeting," October 29, 1968.

243 *"They [Nixon's allies] made Bui Diem think"*: Clifford, *Counsel to the President*, 589.

243 *"If they get out in their present form"*: Walt W. Rostow, "Information Memorandum from the President's Special Assistant (Rostow) to President Johnson," October 29, 1968, *Foreign Relations of the United States, 1964–1968*, vol. VII, *Vietnam, September 1968–January 1969*, ed. Kent Sieg, http://history.state.gov/historicaldocuments/frus1964-68v07/d145#fn1.

243 *And Bunker was told to make it clear*: Clifford, *Counsel to the President*, 590.

243 *"We'll back you up"*: Transcript of telephone conversation between Lyndon B. Johnson, Hubert H. Humphrey, Richard M. Nixon, and George Wallace, October 31, 1968, 6:05 p.m., Citation #13618, Recordings and Transcripts of Conversations and Meetings, LBJ Library.

243 *Allen told Sy Hersh*: Seymour M. Hersh, *The Price of Power: Kissinger in the Nixon White House* (New York: Summit Books, 1983), 20.

244 *"What we now expect"*: "Johnson's Gamble for Peace," The Bombing Halt, *Time*, November 8, 1968.

244 *He picked up*: Summers, *The Arrogance of Power*, 301.

244 *"Thieu has told me over and over again"*: Dallek, *Nixon and Kissinger*, 74.

244 *THE PEOPLE ARE UNITED*: "A Halting Step Toward Peace."

245 *" 'He said please tell your boss' "*: Federal Bureau of Investigation, "Message from Anna Chennault to Bui Diem," November 2, 1968, Presidential Papers: Reference File: South Vietnam and U.S. Policies, Papers of Lyndon B. Johnson, LBJ Library.

245 *"Thieu is convinced"*: Ellsworth Bunker, cable to White House, November 2, 1968. Presidential Papers: National Security File, 1963–1969: Files of Walt W. Rostow, Country File: Vietnam, Papers of Lyndon B. Johnson, LBJ Library.

245 *They had obtained the evidence*: Clifford, *Counsel to the President*, 583.

245 *"The moment we cross over that divide"*: Robert T. Garrett, "LBJ Library Releases Last Set of Secret Recordings," *Dallas Morning News*, December 5, 2008.

246 *"And it's a damn bad mistake"*: Telephone conversation between Lyndon B. Johnson and Everett Dirksen, November 2, 1968, quoted in Johnson, "Did Nixon Commit Treason in 1968?"

246 *"He says that Lyndon is simply enraged"*: Harlow, interview.

247 *"I'll pass this word back to him"*: Transcript of telephone conversation between Lyndon B. Johnson and George Smathers, November 3, 1968, 1:25 p.m., Citation #13709, Recordings and Transcripts of Conversations and Meetings, LBJ Library.

247 *"It was partly in sheer relief"*: "The Woman who Scared Nixon," *Sunday Times*, March 2, 1969.

248 *"The pattern of tapping"*: Safire, *Before the Fall*, 90.

248 *"It was all very, very confidential"*: Summers, *The Arrogance of Power*, 299.

249 *"It sure beats losing"*: Safire, *Before the Fall*, 107.

250 *Experiment over*: "An Interregnum without Rancor," Nation, *Time*, November 22, 1968.

250 *"I will warn you now"*: Nixon, *RN*, 357.

Chapter 12: "I Want to Go; God Take Me"

251 *"You know Lady Bird and I"*: Lyndon B. Johnson, telegram to Dwight D. Eisenhower, April 30, 1968, Presidential Papers: Special File: White House Famous Names (Folder "Eisenhower, Dwight D., 1968"), Papers of Lyndon B. Johnson, LBJ Library.

251 *It was "a pageant"*: David Eisenhower, *Going Home to Glory: A Memoir of Life with Dwight D. Eisenhower, 1961–1969* (New York: Simon & Schuster, 2010), 250.

251 *Established in 1946*: Michael E. Ruane, "A Hospital's Storied Halls," *Washington Post*, January 15, 2006.

251 *"I might even ask you to move over"*: Lyndon B. Johnson to Dwight D. Eisenhower, June 27, 1968, Presidential Papers: Special File: White House Famous Names (Folder "Eisenhower, Dwight D., 1968"), Papers of Lyndon B. Johnson, LBJ Library.

252 *"Johnson seemed drawn to the man"*: David Eisenhower, *Going Home to Glory*, 252.

252 *Indeed, at the start of 1968*: "People," *Time*, January 19, 1968.

252 *Walter Reed got offers from people*: David Eisenhower, *Going Home to Glory*, 260.

252 " *'I want my child to have a normal life'* ": Judith Martin, "Julie and David," *Washington Post*, December 22, 1968.

252 *"Who needs that kind of life?"*: Interview with Luci Johnson, September 12, 2006.

253 *"The girls paid"*: David Eisenhower, *Going Home to Glory*, 210.

253 *He and Mamie had set aside money*: Ibid., 213.

253 *By Thanksgiving in 1967*: "Eisenhower's Grandson to Wed a Nixon Daughter," *New York Times*, December 1, 1967.

253 *"The idea would have seemed too stagy"*: "Love Ticket: David and Julie," Nation, *Time*, September 27, 1968.

253 *"In the realm of national politics"*: R.W. Apple Jr., "Julie Nixon and David Eisenhower Pick Date and Place: Sunday, Dec. 22, Here," *New York Times*, November 24, 1968.

254 *The kids had given one another*: Summers, *The Arrogance of Power*, 326.

254 *Julie and her older sister, Tricia*: "Bring the Girls," Nation, *Time*, June 7, 1968.

254 *David was actually a more loyal Nixon partisan*: "People," *Time*, July 5, 1968.

254 *"His very presence"*: "Love Ticket: David and Julie."

254 *As the December wedding approached*: Charlotte Curtis, "Just What Julie Nixon Needs—Scouring Pads and a Cookbook," *New York Times*, November 27, 1968.

254 *Charles De Gaulle sent a Sèvres tea service*: Martin, "Julie and David."

254 *But she wanted something more private*: William E. Farrell, "750 Wait to Glimpse Wedding Party," *New York Times*, December 23, 1968.

254 *"It can be as much"*: "Of Nixon Daughter," *Los Angeles Times*, December 16, 1968.

255 *"The Impossible Dream"*: Charlotte Curtis, "When It's Mr. and Mrs. Eisenhower, the First Dance Will Be 'Edelweiss,' " *New York Times*, December 14, 1968.

255 *At the end of November*: Robert B. Semple Jr., "Nixons See Eisenhowers," *New York Times*, November 29, 1968.

255 *It was that Nixon consider appointing*: Dwight D. Eisenhower to Richard M. Nixon, December 13, 1969, Presidential Papers: Special File: Post-Presidential, 1961–69 (Folder "Nixon, Richard M., 1968"), Eisenhower Library.

255 *"Both!" he said*: Safire, *Before the Fall*, 623.

256 *One concession to biography*: Charlotte Curtis, "Julie Nixon Wed to David Eisenhower," *New York Times*, December 23, 1968.

256 *Her sense of history guiding tradition*: Nixon, *RN*, 361.

256 *The funeral arrangements had been made*: "Eisenhower: Soldier of Peace," Nation, *Time*, April 4, 1969.

257 *Nixon had the pocked boards pulled up*: David Eisenhower, *Going Home to Glory*, 18.

Chapter 13: "I Want the Break-In"

261 *"Chowder and Marching"*: Hugh Sidey, "Richard Nixon: Fanfare for an Uncommon Man," Nation, *Time*, May 9, 1994.

261 *He reread every inaugural address*: "Nixon's Message: Let Us Gather the Light," Nation, *Time*, January 24, 1969.

262 *"Despite the fact that he had the reputation"*: Bob Greene, *Fraternity: A Journey in Search of Five Presidents* (New York: Crown Publishers, 2004), 30.

262 *And like Franklin*: William Safire, *Before the Fall: An Inside View of the Pre-Watergate White House* (Garden City, NY: Doubleday, 1975), 103–4.

262 *He was giving Nixon his first tour*: Monica Crowley, *Nixon Off the Record* (New York: Random House, 1996), 17.

262 *The second meeting*: "An Interregnum without Rancor," Nation, *Time*, November 22, 1968.

263 *"He is a pillar of strength"*: Richard M. Nixon, *RN: The Memoirs of Richard Nixon* (New York: Grosset & Dunlap, 1978), 358.

263 *"Fast"*: H.R. Haldeman and Joseph DiMona, *The Ends of Power* (New York: Times Books, 1978), 80–81.

263 *"We'll get that goddamn bugging crap"*: Anthony Summers, *The Arrogance of Power: The Secret World of Richard Nixon* (New York: Viking, 2000), 315.

263 *You could say that he was already acting*: Haldeman and DiMona, *The Ends of Power*, 54.

264 *"I want that Goddamn Gelb material"*: Ibid., 219–20.

264 *But not Charles Colson*: Ibid., 5.

264 *"a flag-waving, kick-'em-in-the-nuts"*: Summers, *The Arrogance of Power*, 312.

264 *"Need to be good to do good"*: Richard Reeves, *President Nixon: Alone in the White House* (New York: Simon & Schuster, 2001), 21.

265 *"I believe you should keep your troubles"*: Greene, *Fraternity*, 36.

265 *His aide*: Haldeman and DiMona, *The Ends of Power*, 26.

265 *"No one"*: Stephen E. Ambrose, *Nixon, Vol. 1: The Education of a Politician 1913–1962* (New York: Simon & Schuster, 1987), 350.

265 *Nixon sat at the piano*: "The First Two Months: Between Brake and Accelerator," Nation, *Time*, March 28, 1969.

265 *It would be his job*: Richard M. Nixon, "Executive Order 11456—Providing for a Special Assistant to the President for Liaison with Former Presidents," National Archives, http://www.archives.gov/federal-register/codification/executive-order/11456.html.

265 *"If [Schulz] does not check with you"*: James Giglio, "Harry S. Truman and the Multifarious Ex-Presidency," *Presidential Studies Quarterly* 12, no. 2 (1982).

266 *"I supposed flattery has to be related"*: Safire, *Before the Fall*, 158.

266 *"It feels good"*: "L.B.J.: Hurting Good," Nation, *Time*, January 31, 1969.

266 *The library staff*: Doris Kearns Goodwin, *Lyndon Johnson and the American Dream* (New York: Harper & Row, 1976), 363.

267 *In August 1969*: "The Politics of Reconciliation," Nation, *Time*, September 5, 1969.

267 *It was start to finish a Nixon production*: H.R. Haldeman, *The Haldeman Diaries: Inside the Nixon White House* (New York: G.P. Putnam's Sons, 1994), 82.

267 *The photographers snapped pictures*: "The Politics of Reconciliation," *Time*.

267 *"Is obviously completely absorbed"*: Haldeman, *The Haldeman Diaries*, 82.

268 *"Thank you from the bottom of our hearts"*: Richard M. Nixon, "Remarks at the Dedication of Lady Bird Johnson Grove in Redwood National Park in California," August 27, 1969; The American Presidency Project, http://www.presidency.ucsb.edu/ws/index.php?pid=2213.

268 *Haldeman, needless to say*: Robert Dallek, *Flawed Giant: Lyndon Johnson and His Times, 1961–1973* (New York: Oxford University Press, 1998), 616.

268 *"This nation can only have one"*: "The New Burdens of War," Nation, *Time*, May 11, 1970.

268 *"I stand ready to help"*: Dallek, *Flawed Giant*, 617.

269 *"Because he was convinced"*: Safire, *Before the Fall*, 664.

269 *"For want of a toggle switch"*: Haldeman and DiMona, *The Ends of Power*, 81.

269 *"Rather than leaving the nation"*: David S. Broder, "A Risky New American Sport: 'The Breaking of the President,'" *Washington Post*, October 7, 1969.

270 *It was the largest leak*: Neil Sheehan, "Vietnam Archive: Pentagon Study Traces 3 Decades of Growing U.S. Involvement," *New York Times*, June 13, 1971.

270 *"They're gonna end up in a massive gut-fight"*: Richard M. Nixon and Alexander Haig, 005-050 (phone call), June 13, 1971, transcript and MP3 audio, Miller Center of Public Affairs, University of Virginia, http://whitehousetapes.net/transcript/nixon/005-050.

271 *"People have gotta be put to the torch"*: Richard M. Nixon and Henry Kissinger, 005-059 (phone call), June 13, 1971, transcript and MP3 audio, Miller Center of Public Affairs, University of Virginia, http://whitehousetapes.net/transcript/nixon/005-059.

272 *Mitchell offered his own tidbit*: Richard M. Nixon, John Mitchell, and Henry Kissinger, 005-070 (phone call), June 14, 1971, transcript and MP3 audio, Miller Center of Public Affairs, University of Virginia, http://whitehousetapes.net/transcript/nixon/005-070.

272 *But soon, "after you've started reading all this"*: Daniel Ellsberg, *Secrets: A Memoir of Vietnam and the Pentagon Papers* (New York: Viking, 2002), 238.

274 *"Lyndon Johnson's credibility versus the world"*: Richard M. Nixon, John Ehrlichman, Henry Kissinger, and Bob Haldeman, 525-001 (phone call), June 17, 1971, transcript and MP3 and FLAC audio, Miller Center of Public Affairs, University of Virginia, http://whitehousetapes.net/transcript/nixon/525-001; and Stanley I. Kutler, ed., *Abuse of Power: The New Nixon Tapes* (New York: Free Press, 1997), 3.

275 *"Now you tell Bryce"*: Richard M. Nixon and Charles Colson, 005-113 (phone call),

June 17, 1971, transcript and MP3 audio, Miller Center of Public Affairs, University of Virginia, http://whitehousetapes.net/transcript/nixon/005-113.

275 *Anything he said publicly*: Nixon, *RN*, 510.

276 *"That's a hell of a lot better"*: Richard M. Nixon and Henry Kissinger, 005-117 (phone call), June 17, 1971, transcript and MP3 audio, Miller Center of Public Affairs, University of Virginia, http://whitehousetapes.net/transcript/nixon/005-117.

276 *"Dr. Kissinger called"*: Seymour M. Hersh, *The Price of Power: Kissinger in the Nixon White House* (New York: Summit Books, 1983), 388.

276 *"So that ended any participation"*: Haldeman, *The Haldeman Diaries*, 367.

277 *"He spent twenty years in the CIA"*: Reeves, *President Nixon*, 339.

277 *"Just go in and take it"*: Kutler, *Abuse of Power*, 6.

277 *"I want the Brookings Institute"*: Richard M. Nixon and Bob Haldeman, "I want the Brookings Institute safe cleaned out" (phone call), July 1, 1971, transcript and MP3 and FLAC audio, Miller Center of Public Affairs, University of Virginia, http://whitehousetapes.net/transcript/nixon/i-want-brookings-institute-safe-cleaned-out; and Kutler, *Abuse of Power*, 7–8.

277 *He argued to Haldeman*: Nixon, *RN*, 637.

278 *"If they're from any Eastern schools"*: Richard M. Nixon, 534-002 (meeting tape), July 1, 1971, transcript and MP3 and FLAC audio, Miller Center of Public Affairs, University of Virginia, http://whitehousetapes.net/transcript/nixon/534-002.

278 *In the days that followed*: Hersh, *The Price of Power*, 391.

278 *"I'm going to do everything"*: Robert Dallek, *Nixon and Kissinger: Partners in Power* (New York: HarperCollins, 2007), 313.

279 *"You can rest assured"*: Richard M. Nixon to Lyndon B. Johnson, August 10, 1970, Presidential Papers: Reference File: Nixon, Richard M., Papers of Lyndon B. Johnson, LBJ Library.

279 *"The only thing more impotent"*: Richard Norton Smith and Timothy Walch, eds., *Farewell to the Chief: Former Presidents in American Public Life* (Worland, WY: High Plains Publishing Company, 1990), 106.

279 *"I didn't know they made presidential candidates"*: Dallek, *Flawed Giant*, 617.

280 *The revolt extended to Johnson's own family*: Bruce Oudes, *From the President: Richard Nixon's Secret Files* (New York: Harper & Row, 1989), 520.

280 *"I can only say"*: Nixon, *RN*, 673.

280 *A statement of support*: Oudes, *From the President*, 520.

280 *Connally agreed that Nixon*: Haldeman, *The Haldeman Diaries*, 493.

280 *"Hell, that's not going to hurt him a bit"*: Ibid., 494–95; Nixon, *RN*, 674.

281 *"He made it clear to Graham"*: Haldeman, *The Haldeman Diaries*, 497.

281 *So for those involved*: Walt W. Rostow, "Memorandum for the Record," May 14, 1973, Presidential Papers: Reference File: South Vietnam and U.S. Policies, Papers of Lyndon B. Johnson, LBJ Library.

282 *Nixon asked Haldeman*: Kutler, *Abuse of Power*, 144.

283 *"We have not used the power"*: Richard M. Nixon, John Dean, and Bob Haldeman,

"Everybody Bugs Everybody Else" (meeting tape), September 15, 1972, transcript and MP3 and FLAC audio, Miller Center of Public Affairs, University of Virginia, http://whitehousetapes.net/transcript/nixon/everybody-bugs-everybody -else; and Kutler, *Abuse of Power*, 146–52.

283 *"PEACE POT PROMISCUITY"*: Rick Perlstein, *Nixonland: The Rise of a President and the Fracturing of America* (New York: Scribner, 2008), 713.

283 *The* Post *called it*: Carl Bernstein and Bob Woodward, "FBI Finds Nixon Aides Sabotaged Democrats," *Washington Post*, October 10, 1972.

283 *"So every conversation I had"*: Kutler, *Abuse of Power*, 168.

283 *"But the President did not ask me"*: Cartha D. "Deke" DeLoach, interview by Michael L. Gillette, January 11, 1991, transcript, Oral Histories, LBJ Library.

283 *He expanded the denial*: DeLoach, *Hoover's FBI*, 407.

284 *"He has access"*: Reeves, *President Nixon*, 532.

284 *He wanted to be able to blame*: Perlstein, *Nixonland*, 709.

284 *"That son of a bitch"*: Hersh, *The Price of Power*, 582.

285 *"After the 15th of October"*: Ibid., 591.

285 *"We had a lot of success"*: Perlstein, *Nixonland*, 709.

285 *"Good," Nixon said*: Kutler, *Abuse of Power*, 175–76.

286 *He was "a 20th century giant"*: "The World of Harry Truman," The Presidency, *Time*, January 8, 1973.

286 *Every afternoon the pains would come*: Leo Janos, "The Last Days of the President: LBJ in Retirement," *Atlantic*, July 1973.

286 *"He never brings up"*: Richard M. Nixon, phone call to Lyndon B. Johnson, January 2, 1973, MP3 audio, http://nixontapes.org/lbj/035-067.mp3.

287 *"Johnson had just apparently used him"*: Fred Emery, *Watergate: The Corruption of American Politics and the Fall of Richard Nixon* (New York: Times Books, 1994), 253.

287 *Get that story out*: Ibid., 252.

287 *He was setting up a strategy group*: Dallek, *Nixon and Kissinger*, 457.

287 *If the administration could just produce*: Haldeman, *The Haldeman Diaries*, 563; and Kutler, *Abuse of Power*, 198.

287 *"We'll float it out there"*: Kutler, *Abuse of Power*, 197–98.

288 *"So you'll follow through rigorously"*: Ibid., 200–201.

288 *"Restore respect for office"*: Reeves, *President Nixon*, 558–59.

288 *That day, Nixon ordered Haldeman*: Haldeman, *The Haldeman Diaries*, 565.

289 *"We will use it without question"*: Kutler, *Abuse of Power*, 203–4.

289 *"turn the tables on them"*: DeLoach, *Hoover's FBI*, 409.

289 *And just in case*: Dallek, *Flawed Giant*, 618–19.

290 *"And when she dies"*: Doris Kearns Goodwin, *Lyndon Johnson and the American Dream* (New York: Harper & Row, 1976), 286–87.

290 *Now that we have such a settlement*: Safire, *Before the Fall*, 681.

290 *"We need to make every day count"*: Haldeman, *The Haldeman Diaries*, 573.

290 *"He neither gained the love"*: Greene, *Fraternity*, 55.

Chapter 14: "I Had to Get the Monkey off My Back"

294 *The thin man*: Hugh Sidey, "Richard Nixon: Fanfare for an Uncommon Man," Nation, *Time*, May 9, 1994.

294 *"I heard about your big win"*: James M. Cannon, *Time and Chance: Gerald Ford's Appointment with History* (New York: HarperCollins, 1994), 53.

294 *Ford liked to hang out*: Gerald R. Ford, *A Time to Heal: The Autobiography of Gerald R. Ford* (New York: Harper & Row, 1979), 68.

294 *(Ford had trouble)*: Douglas Brinkley, *Gerald R. Ford* (New York: Times Books, 2007), 14.

294 *"In fact in political philosophy"*: James M. Cannon, *Time and Chance*, 57.

294 *"We understood what it meant"*: Brinkley, *Gerald R. Ford*, 16.

294 *They carpooled from northern Virginia*: William A. Arnold, *Back When It All Began: The Early Nixon Years* (New York: Vantage Press, 1975), 6.

295 *" 'The Vice President slept here' "*: Gerald R. Ford, *A Time to Heal*, 69.

295 *"He seemed sad and detached"*: Ibid.

295 *"My impression was"*: James M. Cannon, *Time and Chance*, 57.

295 *"All Michigan representatives"*: Richard M. Nixon, *RN: The Memoirs of Richard Nixon* (New York: Grosset & Dunlap, 1978), 101–2.

295 *But when it was over*: Jerald F. TerHorst, *Gerald Ford and the Future of the Presidency* (New York: Third Press, 1974), 70.

296 *"I know you said 'don't answer' "*: Richard M. Nixon to Gerald R. Ford, August 1 and 10, 1956, Gerald R. Ford Scrapbooks, vol. 6, February 1956–December 1956, Gerald R. Ford Library.

296 *Nixon did this the old-fashioned way*: James M. Cannon, *Time and Chance*, 68.

296 *"A conservative [who combines] the wisdom"*: Ibid.

296 *With Ford's permission*: TerHorst, *Gerald Ford and the Future of the Presidency*, 73.

296 *About one hundred flag-waving supporters*: Ibid.

296 *Maybe so, but there is evidence*: Ibid.

296 *"We'd done our sitting-up"*: Betty Ford and Chris Chase, *The Times of My Life* (New York: Harper & Row, 1978), 146.

297 *"Making up his mind"*: Gerald R. Ford, *A Time to Heal*, 73.

297 *And, ever the good soldier*: TerHorst, *Gerald Ford and the Future of the Presidency*, 73.

297 *"Would you take it"*: Ibid., 85.

297 *And when Nixon gently floated*: Robert T. Hartmann, *Palace Politics: An Inside Account of the Ford Years* (New York: McGraw-Hill, 1980), 6–7.

298 *"I shook my head in disbelief"*: Gerald R. Ford, *A Time to Heal*, 86.

298 *"Let me think about it"*: James M. Cannon, *Time and Chance*, 175.

298 *Even Pat Nixon was betting*: Nixon, *RN*, 927.

299 *Connally, for his part*: James Reston Jr., *The Lone Star: The Life of John Connally* (New York: Harper & Row, 1989), 457–58.

299   *Republican he'd ever met*: Carl Albert with Danney Goble, *Little Giant: The Life and Times of Speaker Carl Albert* (Norman, Oklahoma: University of Oklahoma Press, 1990), p. 159.

299   *This left Jerry Ford*: Nixon, *RN*, 926.

299   *"Nixon hated the idea"*: Richard Reeves, *A Ford, Not a Lincoln* (New York: Harcourt Brace Jovanovich, 1975), 40.

299   *On instructions from Nixon*: Alexander M. Haig Jr. and Charles McCarry, *Inner Circles: How America Changed the World: A Memoir* (New York: Warner Books, 1992), 170.

299   *"I've got good news"*: Betty Ford and Chase, *The Times of My Life*, 146.

300   *"They like you"*: TerHorst, *Gerald Ford and the Future of the Presidency*, 142.

301   *"It was more tempting for Democrats"*: Henry Kissinger, *Years of Upheaval* (Boston: Little, Brown and Company, 1982), 514.

301   *Wearing no makeup*: "Off to a Helluva Start," The Press, *Time*, August 26, 1974.

302   *"my own lunch and my own dinner"*: Gerald R. Ford: "The President's News Conference," August 28, 1974. Online by Gerhard Peters and John T. Woolley, *The American Presidency Project*. http://www.presidency.ucsb.edu/ws/?pid=4671.

302   *"every press conference from now on"*: James M. Cannon, *Time and Chance*, 372.

302   *Ford hosted women and blacks*: Gerald R. Ford, *A Time to Heal*, 139–41.

302   *"I had to get the monkey off my back"*: Ibid., 159.

303   *"Will there ever be a right time"*: James M. Cannon, *Time and Chance*, 374.

303   *And Ford worried about Nixon*: "The Pardon that Brought No Peace," *Time*, September 16, 1974.

303   *"The quicker I made the decision"*: Thomas M. DeFrank, *Write It When I'm Gone: Remarkable Off-the-Record Conversations with Gerald R. Ford* (New York: G.P. Putnam's Sons, 2007), 117.

303   *take over in a "short period of time"*: Gerald R. Ford, *A Time To Heal*, 3.

304   *resign in return for a pardon*: Ibid., 4.

304   *" 'You must resign tomorrow' "*: Ibid., 4.

304   *He said the list of options*: Haig Jr. and McCarry, *Inner Circles*, 481–86.

305   *"I want you to understand"*: Gerald R. Ford, *A Time to Heal*, 13.

305   *"this isn't pleasant"*: Nixon, *RN*, 1073.

305   *"Now that old Harry Truman is gone"*: Ibid.

306   *"Be very firm out there"*: James M. Cannon, *Time and Chance*, 378.

306   *What Ford had no way of knowing*: Ibid., 380.

306   *"President Nixon is not issuing any statement"*: Ibid.

306   *(Haig later denied)*: Haig Jr. and McCarry, *Inner Circles*, 513.

307   *Becker then flew home*: Gerald R. Ford, *A Time to Heal*, 171.

307   *" 'Enough' "*: Bob Woodward, *Shadow: Five Presidents and the Legacy of Watergate* (New York: Simon & Schuster, 1999), 30.

307   *"opinion polls to tell me what is right"*: Gerald R. Ford, Remarks on Signing a Proclamation Granting Pardon to Richard Nixon, September 8, 1974.

308 *"a burden I shall bear for every day"*: Richard M. Nixon, former president Nixon's response to the full pardon granted to him by President Ford, September 8, 1974.

308 *"I'll bet you the best thing"*: Gerald R. Ford, *A Time to Heal*, 197.

308 *"Yet, I am not here to make history"*: Gerald R. Ford, "Statement and Responses to Questions from Members of the House Judiciary Committee Concerning the Pardon of Richard Nixon," October 17, 1974, Papers of Gerald Ford, American Presidency Project, http://www.presidency.ucsb.edu/ws/index.php?pid=4471#axzz1evl7qDIZ.

309 *"Surely, we are not a revengeful people"*: Ibid.

309 *"There was no deal"*: Ibid.

309 *That last part*: Woodward, *Shadow*, 38.

310 *"If compassion and mercy are not compatible"*: Ron Nessen, *It Sure Looks Different from the Inside* (Chicago: Playboy Press, trade distribution by Simon & Schuster, 1978), 36.

310 *"Oh, there's nothing he'd like more"*: Gerald R. Ford, *A Time to Heal*, 201–2.

311 *"I'm deeply grateful"*: Gerald R. Ford, *A Time to Heal*, 202; and Nessen, *It Sure Looks Different from the Inside*, 35.

311 *("Ironically, my first lie")*: Nessen, *It Sure Looks Different from the Inside*, 36.

311 *"If he had died"*: Gerald R. Ford, *A Time to Heal*, 202.

312 *"President Ford made a courageous decision"*: Edward Kennedy, "Remarks by Senator Edward M. Kennedy," May 21, 2001, available online at John F. Kennedy Presidential Library and Museum.

Chapter 15: "It Burned the Hell out of Me"

315 *"That kind of contest"*: " 'I Don't Expect to Lose,' " The Nation, *Time*, January 26, 1976.

315 *"And I must admit"*: Gerald R. Ford, interview by James M. Cannon, April 29, 1990, transcript, James M. Cannon Research Interviews, Oral Histories, Gerald R. Ford Library.

317 *Whatever China's game*: "Nixon's Embarrassing Road Show," The Ex-President, *Time*, March 8, 1976.

317 *"Nixon is a shit"*: Ron Nessen, *It Sure Looks Different from the Inside* (Chicago: Playboy Press, trade distribution by Simon & Schuster, 1978), 198.

317 *"If he wants to do this country a favor"*: "Nixon's Embarrassing Road Show," *Time*.

318 *Ford read it*: Nessen, *It Sure Looks Different from the Inside*, 201.

318 *"run in the primary against a sitting Republican President"*: Miller Center, "Interview with Lyn Nofziger (2005)," available online at http://millercenter.org/president/reagan/oralhistory/lyn-nofziger.

318 *And Ford, the longtime party man*: Robert T. Hartmann, *Palace Politics: An Inside Account of the Ford Years* (New York: McGraw-Hill, 1980), 337.

319 *Never mind that the* Newsweek *story*: Nessen, *It Sure Looks Different from the Inside*, 193.

319 *Best of all, Washington paid*: James Mann, *The Rebellion of Ronald Reagan: A History of the End of the Cold War* (New York: Viking, 2009), 11.

319 *Not surprisingly*: Hartmann, *Palace Politics*, 336.

319 *Reagan felt "particularly insulted"*: Lou Cannon, *Governor Reagan: His Rise to Power* (New York: Public Affairs, 2003), 403.

319 *"[Reagan] is almost perfectly attuned"*: Robert Teeter, interview, Gerald R. Ford Library Oral History Projects, Gerald R. Ford Library.

320 *"It burned the hell out of me"*: James M. Cannon, *Time and Chance: Gerald Ford's Appointment with History* (New York: HarperCollins, 1994), 406.

320 *"We built it"*: Nessen, *It Sure Looks Different from the Inside*, 206.

320 *The North Carolina defeat*: Ibid., 208.

321 *"He reasoned that he could pick off"*: James A. Baker III and Steve Fiffer, *Work Hard, Study—and Keep Out of Politics! Adventures and Lessons from an Unexpected Public Life* (New York: G.P. Putnam's Sons, 2006), 50.

322 *Bowing to pressure*: Gerald R. Ford, *A Time to Heal: The Autobiography of Gerald R. Ford* (New York: Harper & Row, 1979), 328; James M. Cannon, *Time and Chance*, 406–7; Thomas M. DeFrank, *Write It When I'm Gone: Remarkable Off-the-Record Conversations with Gerald R. Ford* (New York: G.P. Putnam's Sons, 2007), 175.

322 *Several dozen copies were made*: Laurence Barrett, unpublished file, August 18, 1976, Time Life News Service.

323 *This was, in Ford's retelling*: Ford, interview.

323 *Reagan, who had been subdued*: Dean Fischer, "Unpublished Files, Take 27," Time-Life News Service, August 19, 1976.

324 *"On the other hand"*: Ford, interview.

324 *"He's not a good actor"*: Dean Fischer, "Unpublished Files, Take 27."

325 *Though he prepared no remarks*: Martin Anderson, interview by Stephen F. Knott, James Sterling Young, and Allison Asher, December 11–12, 2001, transcript, Miller Center of Public Affairs, University of Virginia.

326 *"There is no substitute for victory, Mr. President"*: Ronald Reagan, "Address at the Republican National Convention in Kansas City," August 19, 1976, The American Presidency Project, http://www.presidency.ucsb.edu/ws/?pid=85204.

326 *"So he determined"*: Lyn Nofziger, interview by Stephen F. Knott and Russell L. Riley, March 6, 2003, transcript, Miller Center of Public Affairs, University of Virginia.

326 *"Reagan never had that philosophy"*: Miller Center, "Interview with Stuart Spencer (2005)," available at http://millercenter.org/president/reagan/oralhistory/stuart-spencer.

327 *"With everything else"*: Stuart Spencer, interview by Paul B. Freedman, Stephen F.

Knott, Russell L. Riley, and James Sterling Young, November 15–16, 2001, transcript, Miller Center of Public Affairs, University of Virginia.

327 *"They didn't give a damn"*: Ford, interview.

327 *"He believed in winning"*: DeFrank, *Write It When I'm Gone*, 123.

327 *Carter recognized*: Martin Schram, "The Return of Richard Nixon," *Washington Post*, January 30, 1979.

328 *Nixon himself had created for Johnson*: David Frost with Bob Zelnick, *Frost/Nixon: Behind The Scenes of the Nixon Interviews* (New York: Harper Perennial, 2007), 165.

328 *"It nauseated me"*: Ford, interview.

328 *"I'm not a candidate, I'm not"*: Elizabeth Drew, *Portrait of An Election* (New York: Simon & Schuster, 1981), 18.

329 *Reagan couldn't win*: Adam Clymer, "Ford Declares Reagan Can't Win; Invites GOP to Ask Him to Run," *New York Times*, March 2, 1980.

329 *On February 12*: Bailey, Deardourff & Eyre, memo to Gerald R. Ford, March 12, 1980; in unopened collection at the Gerald Ford Library used by permission from Mary C. Lukens.

329 *That day*: Ford, interview.

329 *"If I were a drinking man"*: DeFrank, *Write It When I'm Gone*, 92.

329 *the hardest decision of his life*: Ibid., 91.

329 "The clincher will come": Richard Wirthlin memo to Ronald Reagan, March 28, 1980, quoted in Drew, *Portrait of an Election*, 355.

330 *Ford declined*: Lou Cannon, *Governor Reagan*, 471.

330 *"He thought George Bush was a wimp"*: Nofziger, interview.

331 *"I've never been much for sitting"*: Gerald Ford convention speech, Detroit, July 1980.

331 *The line played to thunderous applause*: Lou Cannon, *Governor Reagan*, 473.

331 *"He appreciates forthrightness"*: Ed Magnuson, "Inside the Gerry Ford Drama," *Time*, July 28, 1980.

332 *Paul Laxalt*: "The G.O.P. Gets Its Act Together," *Time*, July 28, 1980.

333 *At a lunch with* Newsweek's *editors*: Elizabeth Drew, *Richard M. Nixon* (New York: Times Books, 2007), 214.

334 *"I couldn't believe what I was hearing*: Magnuson, "Inside the Gerry Ford Drama."

334 *"Kissinger carries a lot of baggage"*: Walter Isaacson, *Kissinger: A Biography* (New York: Simon & Schuster, 1992), 719.

334 *"this is really two presidents"*: Ronald Reagan, *An American Life* (New York: Simon & Schuster, 1990), 215.

335 *The media frenzy to get the scoop*: Drew, *Richard M. Nixon*, 211.

335 *"I feel we are friends now"*: Lou Cannon, *Governor Reagan*, 475.

335 *In its review of the convention*: "The G.O.P. Gets Its Act Together," *Time*.

336 *"Anybody who wanted to see the president"*: Nofziger, interview.

336 *"That's what . . . I was aiming at"*: Gerald R. Ford, interview by James M. Cannon,

April 30, 1990, transcript, James M. Cannon Research Interviews, Oral Histories, Gerald R. Ford Library.

336 *"It was ludicrous"*: Spencer, interview.

Chapter 16: "Why Don't We Make It Just Dick, Jimmy and Jerry?"

339 *White House advanceman*: Hugh Sidey, "Flight of Three Presidents," *Time,* October 26, 1981.

340 *White House aides*: Mark K. Updegrove, "Flying Coach to Cairo," *American Heritage Magazine* 57, no. 4 (August/September 2006), 131.

340 *They arrived at Andrews Air Force Base*: Ibid.

340 *Each man had left Washington*: Haynes Johnson, " 'Oil and Water' Mix on Air Force One," *Washington Post,* October 10, 1981.

341 *"Dick, Jimmy, and Jerry"*: Updegrove, "Flying Coach to Cairo."

341 *The applause mounted*: Howell Raines, "Sadat's Successor Invited by Reagan to Visit U.S. in '82," *New York Times,* October 9, 1981.

341 *"Rosalynn came also"*: Barbara Bush, *Barbara Bush: A Memoir* (New York: Scribner's Sons, 1994), 173.

341 *It was, Reagan noted*: Ronald Reagan, *The Reagan Diaries,* ed. Douglas Brinkley (New York: HarperCollins, 2007), 43.

341 *"Ordinarily, I would wish you"*: Ibid.

341 *Total elapsed time*: Lee Lescaze, "The Tragedy Brings 4 Presidents Together," *Washington Post,* October 9, 1981.

342 *"I kind of like that house"*: Sidey, "Flight of Three Presidents."

342 *"This is," said Haig dryly, "quite a planeload"*: "Alexander Haig Takes Charge in Cairo," *Telegraph,* October 10, 1981.

343 *"You know, that just goes to show"*: Thomas M. DeFrank, *Write It When I'm Gone: Remarkable Off-the-Record Conversations with Gerald R. Ford* (New York: G.P. Putnam's Sons, 2007), 158.

343 *There were some morbid jokes*: " 'Act of Infamy,' " *Newsweek,* October 19, 1981.

343 *The sweaters came out*: Sidey, "Flight of Three Presidents."

344 *Carter even sent a radar plane*: " 'Act of Infamy,' " *Newsweek.*

344 *"The only time I had that bad a day"*: R. Gregory Nokes, "U.S. Moves Swiftly to Bolster Arabs," Associated Press, October 13, 1981.

344 *"He treated Nixon as a great statesman"*: Henry A. Kissinger, "Sadat: A Man with a Passion for Peace," *Time,* October 19, 1981.

345 *"Ever the conspirator"*: Sidey, "Flight of Three Presidents."

345 *They paid courtesy calls*: Nokes, "U.S. Moves Swiftly to Bolster Arabs."

346 *Ford in particular*: Updegrove, "Flying Coach to Cairo."

346 *Then a twenty-one-gun salute began*: " 'Act of Infamy,' " *Newsweek.*

349 *"the former presidents' comments troubled some"*: Haynes Johnson, "Ford, Carter United on Mideast," *Washington Post,* October 12, 1981.

350 *A transcript was produced*: Sidey, "Flight of Three Presidents."

350 *Columnist Mary McGrory*: Mary McGrory, "As Former Presidents Show the Flag, Bush Helps Mind the Store," *Washington Post*, October 13, 1981.

351 *Their wives even teamed up*: Ibid.

Reagan and Nixon: The Exile Returns

353 *"Decent" but "shallow"*: Richard M. Nixon, Henry Kissinger, and Bob Haldeman, 620–008 (meeting tape), November 17, 1971, transcript and MP3 and FLAC audio, Miller Center of Public Affairs, University of Virginia, http://whitehouse tapes.net/transcript/nixon/620–008.

353 *"Good God"*: White House tapes, Richard M. Nixon Library.

Chapter 17: "I Am Yours to Command"

356 *This campaign was a twofer*: Walter Isaacson, "New Team in Town," Nation, *Time*, November 24, 1980.

356 *Nixon was never a Shultz fan*: Bob Woodward, *Shadow: Five Presidents and the Legacy of Watergate* (New York: Simon & Schuster, 1999), 101.

357 *" 'I am yours to command' "*: Richard M. Nixon letter to Ronald Reagan, November 17, 1980, Presidential Papers: Richard Nixon Post-presidential Correspondence with Ronald Reagan, Richard M. Nixon Library.

357 *"I can't thank you enough"*: Ronald Reagan letter to Richard M. Nixon, November 22, 1980, Presidential Papers: Richard Nixon Post-presidential Correspondence with Ronald Reagan, Richard M. Nixon Library.

357 *"Some charged me with being too tough"*: Richard M. Nixon to Ronald Reagan, November 1, 1982, Presidential Papers: Richard Nixon Post-presidential Correspondence with Ronald Reagan, Richard M. Nixon Library.

357 *"After Christmas you might consider"*: Richard M. Nixon to Ronald Reagan, December 12, 1986, Presidential Papers: Richard Nixon Post-presidential Correspondence with Ronald Reagan, Richard M. Nixon Library.

358 *"Do whatever the doctor advises"*: Richard M. Nixon to Ronald Reagan, December 19, 1986, Presidential Papers: Richard Nixon Post-presidential Correspondence with Ronald Reagan, Richard M. Nixon Library.

358 *"these thoughts are not for the record or for history"*: Richard M. Nixon letter to Ronald Reagan, February 25, 1983, Presidential Papers: Richard Nixon Post-presidential Correspondence with Ronald Reagan, Richard M. Nixon Library.

359 *"Anyone who reaches the top"*: Richard M. Nixon, "Meeting the Russians at the Summit," *New York Times*, September 1, 1985.

359 *"He may live long enough"*: Richard M. Nixon, "Reagan and Gorbachev: Superpower Summitry," *Foreign Affairs* 64, no. 1 (Fall 1985).

359 *"If we can't come to a reduction agreement"*: Ronald Reagan, *The Reagan Diaries*, ed.
     Douglas Brinkley (New York: HarperCollins, 2007), 365.

359 *Nixon and Reagan spoke*: "Nixon Arrives in Soviet," *New York Times*, July 13, 1986.

361 *"the conversation had a greater impact on him"*: Richard M. Nixon letter to Ronald
     Reagan, July 1985, Presidential Papers: Richard Nixon Post-presidential Corre-
     spondence with Ronald Reagan, Richard M. Nixon Library.

362 *Careful White House advance work*: James Mann, *The Rebellion of Ronald Reagan:
     A History of the End of the Cold War* (New York: Viking, 2009), 4.

362 *First, on Sunday, April 26*: Richard M. Nixon and Henry A. Kissinger, "To With-
     draw the Missiles We Must Add Conditions," *Los Angeles Times*, April 26, 1987;
     Richard M. Nixon and Henry Kissinger, "An Arms Agreement—On Two Condi-
     tions," *Washington Post*, April 26, 1987.

362 *(Safire's call)*: William Safire, "The Kissnix Factor," *New York Times*, April 27, 1987.

363 *"Nuclear weapons aren't going to be abolished"*: "An Interview with Richard Nixon,"
     Time, May 4, 1987.

363 *Nixon preferred the nearby Lincoln Sitting Room*: Nancy Reagan, *My Turn: The
     Memoirs of Nancy Reagan* (New York: Random House, 1989), 258; and Ron Rea-
     gan, "My Father, the President," *Parade*, January 16, 2011.

365 *"Reagan looks far older, more tired, and less vigorous"*: Richard M. Nixon, "Memoran-
     dum RE: Meeting with President Reagan at the White House," April 18, 1987,
     Richard M. Nixon Library.

365 *As always, he had some campaign suggestions*: Ronald Reagan, *The Reagan Diaries*,
     634.

366 *In a private memo*: Marvin L. Kalb, *The Nixon Memo: Political Respectability, Russia,
     and the Press* (Chicago: University of Chicago Press, 1994), 55.

366 *But when Bush battled back*: Robert B. Semple Jr., "The Editorial Notebook: Nixon
     Re-Re-Redux," *New York Times*, April 15, 1988.

366 *"Americans are crazy about renewal"*: Roger Rosenblatt, "Richard Nixon: The Dark
     Comedian," *Time*, April 25, 1988.

366 *As for the national mood*: Richard M. Nixon, interview, transcript, *Meet the Press*,
     NBC, April 11, 1988.

367 *"Bush can pick anyone"*: Helen Thomas, "Nixon on Bush, Jackson, Dukakis—and
     Gorbachev," UPI, April 15, 1988.

367 *And finally, Nixon urged Bush*: Jack W. Germond and Jules Witcover, *Whose Broad
     Stripes and Bright Stars? The Trivial Pursuit of the Presidency* (New York: Warner
     Books, 1989), 371.

367 *Bush took this all on board*: But on one front, Bush flatly ignored Nixon. The old
     warhorse urged Bush to hold a broad and public search for a vice presidential
     nominee, in part to signal to a variety of party factions that he took them and their
     views seriously. In the end, Bush went another way, running a selection process so
     secretive and idiosyncratic that when he made his final choice and tapped Indiana
     senator Dan Quayle to be his number two, most of his own campaign aides were

caught off guard. But as Nixon had predicted on television, even that choice did not hurt him.

369 *"You have given George a great sendoff"*: Richard M. Nixon letter to Ronald Reagan, August 16, 1988, Presidential Papers: Richard Nixon Post-presidential Correspondence with Ronald Reagan, Richard M. Nixon Library.

370 *White House advance teams*: Lee May, "Impassioned Goodbye: 'Stand by Me,' Reagan Urges State's Voters," *Los Angeles Times,* November 8, 1988.

370 *"Tomorrow, when the mountains greet the dawn"*: Ronald Reagan, "Remarks at a Republican Campaign Rally in San Diego, California," November 7, 1988, Public Papers of President Ronald W. Reagan, Ronald Reagan Library.

Chapter 18: "I'm Convinced . . . He Feels I'm Soft"

375 *"We got whipped and whipped soundly"*: letter from George Bush to Richard M. Nixon, November 10, 1964, in George Bush, *All the Best, George Bush: My Life in Letters and Other Writings* (New York: Scribner, 1999), 89.

375 *An unlikely but potent coalition*: Herbert S. Parmet, *George Bush: The Life of a Lone Star Yankee* (New York: Scribner, 1997), 135.

376 *"Though we finished out of the money"*: George Bush, "Rewriting History," Talk of the Town, *New Yorker,* October 5, 1992; and Parmet, *George Bush,* 135.

376 *The club verdict was unanimous*: George Bush with Victor Gold, *Looking Forward* (New York: Doubleday, 1987), 101.

376 *"'mysterious' was not one of them"*: Author interview with George H. W. Bush, October 7, 2011.

377 *"gentlemen running a gentleman's race"*: Author interview with Richard Whalen, March 4, 2011.

377 *"I guess there are too many Democrats"*: Parmet, *George Bush,* 145.

377 *He got off sixteen hours later*: Richard Ben Cramer, *What It Takes: The Way to the White House* (New York: Random House, 1992), 596.

378 *He often simply refused*: Barbara Bush, *Barbara Bush: A Memoir* (New York: Scribner's Sons, 1994), 105.

378 *"He surrounded himself"*: George Bush, *All the Best, George Bush,* 179.

379 *"George, you got the best from Yale"*: Ibid., 182.

379 *On August 7, Bush sent Nixon*: Ibid., 193.

379 *"Caring for no one"*: Ibid., 194.

379 *"The conversation was very brief"*: Ibid., 197.

380 *Scowcroft asked what*: Brent Scowcroft, interview by author, February 9, 2009.

381 *Only Ford accepted Bush's offer*: The story of Ford's secure phone was first reported in Thomas M. DeFrank, *Write It When I'm Gone: Remarkable Off-the-Record Conversations with Gerald R. Ford* (New York: G.P. Putnam's Sons, 2007). Ford's feelings about it—and Scowcroft's offer to install them elsewhere—were detailed in subsequent reporting by the authors.

382   *"I still think we ought to put it"*: George Bush and Brent Scowcroft, *A World Trans-formed* (New York: Knopf, distributed by Random House, 1998), 157.

383   *"Gorbachev is Wall Street"*: David Remnick, "Gorbachev's the One, Nixon Says," *Washington Post,* April 4, 1991.

383   *"It's time for Bush to understand that"*: Dimitri K. Simes, *After the Collapse: Russia Seeks Its Place as a Great Power* (New York: Simon & Schuster, 1999), 15.

384   *"Since that does not appear to be in the cards"*: Richard M. Nixon to Dimitri K. Simes, April 16, 1991, courtesy of Simes.

385   *"While* TIME's *essays are usually for those"*: Richard M. Nixon to Dimitri K. Simes, April 5, 1991, courtesy of Simes.

385   *"he needs us far more"*: Richard M. Nixon, "A Superpower at the Abyss," *Time,* April 22, 1991.

386   *So, in many ways*: Lance Morrow, "The Russian Revolution," *Time,* September 2, 1991.

387   *But more than these specific concerns*: Monica Crowley, *Nixon Off the Record* (New York: Random House, 1996), 45–50.

387   *The two men talked*: Ibid., 49.

387   *"This was the first time in a long time"*: Ibid., 67.

387   *"If he ignored him"*: Ibid., 56.

388   *When those efforts yielded*: The story of the invitation is reported in Marvin L. Kalb's *The Nixon Memo: Political Respectability, Russia, and the Press* (Chicago: University of Chicago Press, 1994).

389   *"The memos left New Jersey"*: Ibid., 75.

390   *Thomas Friedman's analysis story*: Thomas Friedman, "Nixon's Save Russia Memo: Bush Feels the Sting," *New York Times,* March 11, 1992.

390   *"If democracy fails there"*: Leslie H. Gelb, "Foreign Affairs: Nixon's Tricky Crusade," *New York Times,* March 13, 1992.

390   *"I don't have a blank check"*: Norman Kempster, "Briefing Book: U.S. Candidates' Stands on Foreign Issues: All of President Bush's major challengers want a sterner line on China. Democrats say he is too tough on Israel. Free trade is a bit of a free-for-all," *Los Angeles Times,* March 17, 1992.

390   *"We had bent over backwards"*: Scowcroft, interview.

391   *He was, he said*: Kalb, *The Nixon Memo,* 108.

393   *Nixon promised Bush*: Crowley, *Nixon Off the Record,* 80.

393   *"I got the impression"*: Pat Buchanan, interview by author, January 21, 2011.

393   *"And Pat Buchanan is far from dull"*: "Nixon's Advice for Buchanan," *New York Times,* March 22, 1992.

393   *"I told Buchanan to get out"*: Crowley, *Nixon Off the Record,* 82.

Bush and Carter: The Missionary Goes Rogue

395 *"I feel that my role"*: Jimmy Carter, interview by Brian Williams, *NBC Nightly News*, September 21, 2010.

Chapter 19: "I Am a Better Ex-President Than I Was a President"

398 *"Carter's spooky silences in meetings"*: Hugh Sidey, "Accessing the Presidency," *Time*, August 18, 1980.

398 *"I had a life expectancy of 25 years"*: Monitor breakfast transcript, November 3, 2005.

398 *"I want to provide a place"*: Eleanor Clift, "A Man with a Mission," *Newsweek*, October 3, 1994.

399 *"I can't deny"*: Monitor breakfast transcript, November 3, 2005.

399 *At one point Carter grew so tired*: Douglas Brinkley, *The Unfinished Presidency: Jimmy Carter's Journey Beyond the White House* (New York: Viking, 1998), 41.

399 *The letter went on to thank Carter*: Ibid., 122.

400 *Peter Bourne, who worked for Carter*: Peter G. Bourne, *Jimmy Carter: A Comprehensive Biography from Plains to Post-Presidency* (New York: Scribner, 1997), 496.

400 *Carter quickly sensed*: Brinkley, *The Unfinished Presidency*, 269.

401 *As Carter's delegation departed*: Ibid., 285.

402 *Within a few months*: One spoil from that invasion would end its days at Camp David: a life-size photograph of Bush with five bullet holes in its head, liberated from Noriega's private pistol range.

402 *And so, once again*: The details of Carter's legwork before the election are outlined in Brinkley, *The Unfinished Presidency*, 297–99.

403 *"I can tell you from my own experience"*: Ibid., 306.

403 *"Your greatest accomplishment"*: Bourne, *Jimmy Carter*, 494.

404 *By early 1990*: Burton I. Kaufman, *The Presidency of James Earl Carter, Jr.* (Lawrence, KS: University Press of Kansas, 1993), 213.

404 *"But if you don't clearly spell out"*: Brinkley, *The Unfinished Presidency*, 270.

406 *"Since armed intervention"*: Ibid., 339.

406 *Rather than alerting Bush in advance*: Ibid.

407 *"What I violently disagreed with"*: Douglas Brinkley, "Jimmy Carter's Modest Quest for Global Peace: The Missionary Man," *Foreign Affairs* 74, no. 6 (November/December 1995).

407 *"sent exactly the same letter to President Bush"*: Author interview with Jimmy Carter, December 2, 2011.

408 *"Also, most Americans will welcome"*: Brinkley, *The Unfinished Presidency*, 341.

408 *There would be no more teaming up*: Ibid., 345.

Chapter 20: "The Guy Knows How the Game Is Played"

412 *"Finish with a smile"*: Diary of George Herbert Walker Bush, November 4, 1992, quoted in George Bush, *All The Best, George Bush: My Life in Letters and Other Writings* (New York: Lisa Drew/Scribner, 1999), 572; see also James A. Baker III and Steve Fiffer, *Work Hard, Study—and Keep Out of Politics! Adventures and Lessons from an Unexpected Public Life* (New York: G.P. Putnam's Sons, 2006), 332–33.

412 *Bush also told Clinton*: Diary of George Herbert Walker Bush, January 20, 1993, quoted in George Bush, *All The Best*, 583.

412 *"I will do nothing to complicate your work"*: Ibid., 567.

413 *"The guy's got a big ego"*: Monica Crowley, *Nixon Off the Record* (New York: Random House, 1996), 131.

413 *And he would get it*: Ibid.

415 *Word came back*: The details of Nixon's insinuation into the Clinton White House are explained in detail in Marvin L. Kalb's *The Nixon Memo: Political Respectability, Russia, and the Press* (Chicago: University of Chicago Press, 1994), 144–47.

416 *"Nixon opened with five minutes"*: Strobe Talbott, *The Russia Hand: A Memoir of Presidential Diplomacy* (New York: Random House, 2002), 46.

417 *"In fact, he's preaching to the preacher"*: Ibid., 47.

417 *"kiss the peace dividend goodbye"*: Serge Schmemann, "Moscow Journal: Who'll Speak Up For Russia Now? Nixon, No Less," *New York Times*, February 19, 1993.

418 *"He was very respectful"*: Crowley, *Nixon Off the Record*, 166.

418 *Clinton invited him to the White House*: Ibid., 171.

418 *He reminded the first lady*: Bill Clinton, *My Life* (New York: Knopf, 2004), 505.

418 *"And we'd be better off today"*: Hillary Rodham Clinton, *Living History* (New York: Simon & Schuster, 2003), 226.

419 *If Clinton failed to meet this challenge*: Kalb, *The Nixon Memo*, 153–54.

419 *Bob Strauss told Nixon*: Crowley, *Nixon Off the Record*, 169

419 *"Clinton is making a gutsy call"*: Hugh Sidey and Christopher Ogden, "Advice From Two Old Pros," *Time*, April 5, 1993.

420 *picture of the Clinton-Nixon conversation*: Kalb, *The Nixon Memo*, 150.

420 *Nixon tuned into the news from Vancouver*: Crowley, *Nixon Off The Record*, 177.

420 *"how the game is played"*: Ibid., 180.

421 *Nixon "exploded" at Clinton's absence*: Ibid., 189.

422 *One of the plotters cooperated*: Eventually, Kuwait sentenced six of the plotters to death.

422 *The Incredible Shrinking President*: Michael Duffy, "The Incredible Shrinking President," *Time*, June 7, 1993.

422 *the attack would come in forty-eight hours*: George Stephanopoulos, *All Too Human: A Political Education* (Boston: Little, Brown and Company, 1999), 160.

423 *"Thought it was a tough call"*: Ibid., 161–63.

423 *Clinton dispatched Christopher*: James Collins, "Bill Clinton: Striking Back," *Time*, July 5, 1993.

423   *"Presidents, especially gentlemen presidents"*: Stephanopoulos, *All Too Human*, 163.

424   *"Don't tread on me"*: Bill Clinton, White House statement, June 26, 1993.

424   *Nine years later*: "Bush Calls Saddam 'the guy who tried to kill my dad,'" CNN .com, September 27, 2002.

424   *Hillary apologized for having "strayed from the fold"*: Hillary Rodham Clinton, *Living History*, 35.

425   *"can sell three day old ice"*: Thomas M. DeFrank, *Write It When I'm Gone: Remarkable Off-the-Record Conversations with Gerald R. Ford* (New York: G.P. Putnam's Sons, 2007), 135.

426   *Clinton insisted later*: Taylor Branch, *The Clinton Tapes: Wrestling History with the President* (New York: Simon & Schuster, 2009), 51.

426   *"There were other candidates"*: Margaret Carlson, "I Didn't Get Hired to Fix Everything: Bill Clinton," *Time*, September 27, 1993.

427   *"We, the United States, could not sell abroad"*: Gerald R. Ford, speaking in the East Room, September 14, 1993, White House transcript available at http://www.4uth .gov.ua/usa/english/facts/speeches/clinton/93–4.txt.

427   *He would only get*: Crowley, *Nixon Off the Record*, 202.

427   *Raul Cédras was turning an impoverished country*: Ibid., 208.

427   *Clinton called Nixon in January*: Kalb, *The Nixon Memo*, 168.

428   *Other players on the Russian political scene*: Richard M. Nixon, "Moscow, March '94: Chaos and Hope," *New York Times*, March 25, 1994.

428   *to attend his mother-in-law's funeral*: Kalb, *The Nixon Memo*, 175.

428   *"Nixon said I had earned the respect of the leaders"*: Bill Clinton, *My Life*, 593.

429   *"Nixon at his best"*: Ibid.

429   *"I hope it hasn't affected his mind"*: Apple Jr., "For Clinton and Nixon, a Rarefied Bond."

429   *Nixon's daughters later called*: Billy Graham, *Just As I Am: The Autobiography of Billy Graham* (San Francisco: HarperSanFrancisco, 1997), 462–63.

430   *"He was one of those husbands"*: Branch, *The Clinton Tapes*, 135.

430   *"pay homage to the memory of President Nixon"*: Bill Clinton, "Presidential Proclamation on Richard Nixon's Death, April 24, 1994," available online at nytimes.com.

430   *Clinton offered the Nixon family*: Apple Jr., "For Clinton and Nixon, a Rarefied Bond."

430   *Clinton wanted, among other things*: Branch, *The Clinton Tapes*, 153.

430   *And so Clinton changed the one key line*: Stephanopoulos, *All Too Human*, 265.

431   *"seemed to believe the greatest sin was remaining passive"*: Bill Clinton, "Remarks at the Funeral Service for Richard Nixon, April 27, 1994," available online at The American Presidency Project.

431   *" 'I wish I could pick up the phone' "*: Ibid.

Chapter 21: "I'm Sending Carter. You Think It Will Be OK, Don't You?"

432   *"You and I will succeed"*: Douglas Brinkley, *The Unfinished Presidency: Jimmy Carter's Journey Beyond the White House* (New York: Viking, 1998), 357.

433 *"Carter's too chicken-shit"*: Ibid., 355.

433 *"Bill Clinton cares more about Jimmy Carter"*: Hillary Rodham Clinton, *Living History*, 89.

433 *Clinton later blamed Carter*: David Maraniss, *First in His Class: A Biography of Bill Clinton* (New York: Simon & Schuster, 1995), 38.

434 *The Georgian's calls*: David Halberstam, *War in a Time of Peace: Bush, Clinton, and the Generals* (New York, Scribner, 2001), 175.

434 *These slights did not go unnoticed*: Brinkley, *The Unfinished Presidency*, 366.

434 *"He was obviously not an experienced carpenter"*: Alessandra Stanley, "On Tour with Jimmy Carter; Words of Advice, Bittersweet," *New York Times*, January 14, 1993.

434 *This was accurate*: Maraniss, *First in His Class*, 330.

434 *A week later*: Brinkley, *The Unfinished Presidency*, 370.

434 *When he finally sat down with Christopher*: Ibid., 371–73.

434 *"When President Clinton came into office"*: Monitor breakfast transcript, November 3, 2005.

435 *The question with North Korea*: Don Oberdorfer, *The Two Koreas: A Contemporary History* (Reading, MA: Addison-Wesley, 1997), 306.

435 *When the threat of further economic sanctions*: Ibid., 312–13.

435 *When that mission went slightly awry*: Details of the Nunn-Lugar non-mission are recounted in Joel S. Wit, Daniel B. Poneman, and Robert L. Gallucci's *Going Critical: The First North Korean Nuclear Crisis* (Washington, DC: Brookings Institution Press, 2004), 185–86.

436 *Clinton pretended to know nothing*: Brinkley, *The Unfinished Presidency*, 383.

436 *Carter came away convinced*: Ibid., 398.

436 *The North Koreans trusted Carter*: Ibid., 392.

436 *After some back-and-forth negotiations*: Oberdorfer, *The Two Koreas*, 318.

437 *"Is Kim Il Sung bluffing"*: Cover, *Time*, June 13, 1994.

437 *"[He] clearly viewed his own role"*: Wit, Poneman, and Gallucci, *Going Critical*, 207.

437 *And each time Carter asked*: Ibid., 207–8.

438 *Locals were stripping the food markets*: Brinkley, *The Unfinished Presidency*, 399.

438 *The Korean stock market*: Oberdorfer, *The Two Koreas*, 322.

438 *Carter went to bed*: Wit, Poneman, and Gallucci, *Going Critical*, 222.

439 *But U.S. diplomats*: Ibid.

439 *Carter huddled with Kim's aides*: Ibid., 224–25.

439 *Gallucci admitted that he had not*: Brinkley, *The Unfinished Presidency*, 404.

439 *"Not since the presidency of Lyndon Johnson"*: Ibid.

440 *"The problem is that North Korea"*: Wit, Poneman, and Gallucci, *Going Critical*, 228.

440 *One cabinet member saw it*: Brinkley, *The Unfinished Presidency*, 405.

440 *"A difficult exchange"*: Wit, Poneman, and Gallucci, *Going Critical*, 232.

441 *But then Carter*: Wit, Poneman, and Gallucci, *Going Critical*, 232.

441 *In fact, nobody at the White House*: Ibid.

441   *Carter's end of the discussion*: Ibid., 234.

441   *Before leaving Seoul*: Ibid.

442   *Hope for reconciliation faded further*: Ibid., 235–36.

442   *"I figured if they could say to themselves"*: Ibid., 240.

443   *If anything, the Haitian military*: Cathy Booth, "Still Punishing the Victims," Haiti, *Time,* April 11, 1994.

443   *Arkansas senator Dale Bumpers*: Branch, *The Clinton Tapes,* 187–88.

443   *Reputable alternatives to Cédras*: Ibid.

444   *"I can always find something else"*: Ibid., 186, 192.

444   *"United States be the Lone Ranger"*: William J. Clinton, "Address to the Nation on Haiti, September 15, 1994," audio file available online at http://www.presidency.ucsb.edu/mediaplay.php?id=49093&admin=42.

444   *Perhaps mindful of that episode*: Branch, *The Clinton Tapes,* 199.

444   *"Sam Nunn and Colin Powell to go"*: Author interview with Jimmy Carter, December 2, 2011.

444   *Powell recalled that Clinton*: Colin L. Powell and Joseph E. Persico, *My American Journey* (New York: Random House, 1995), 598.

445   *"You think it will be OK"*: Stephanopoulos, *All Too Human,* 313.

445   *"I was going to invade"*: Author interview with Bill Clinton, November 16, 2011.

445   *"But I took a chance"*: Powell and Persico, *My American Journey,* 398.

445   *"We used to be the weakest"*: Ibid., 600–601.

446   *"My wife would understand"*: Ibid., 600.

446   *General Hugh Shelton*: Brinkley, *The Unfinished Presidency,* 427.

446   *("Not bad for a poor country")*: Powell and Persico, *My American Journey,* 601.

447   *The delegation hurriedly left*: Ibid.

447   *"I will obey the orders"*: Ibid., 601–2.

447   *U.S. paratroopers*: Bill Clinton, *My Life,* 618.

448   *The conversation, such as it was*: Brinkley, *The Unfinished Presidency,* 432–33.

448   *It fell to Sam Nunn*: Ibid., 433.

449   *"golfing partners don't give as many mulligans to ex-presidents"*: Bill Clinton, "Remarks on Presenting The Medal of Freedom to Former President Jimmy Carter and Rosalyn Carter," August 9, 1999.

Chapter 22: "Bill, I Think You Have to Admit That You Lied"

450   *The club's two closest members*: Stacey Jones, "Carter Breaks Silence on Clinton, Says Nation Will Heal," *Emory Report* 51, no. 6 (September 28, 1998).

452   *"But I do care, passionately"*: Gerald R. Ford, "The Path Back to Dignity," *New York Times,* October 4, 1998.

452   *"I mean, can you imagine me"*: DeFrank, *Write It When I'm Gone,* 145.

453   *"my errors of word and deed require their rebuke"*: Bill Clinton, White House speech, December 11, 1998.

454 *echo of Ford's bestselling memoir*: Gerald R. Ford and Jimmy Carter, "A Time to Heal Our Nation," *New York Times,* December 21, 1998.

454 *There was a historical echo*: DeFrank, *Write It When I'm Gone,* 146.

455 *"I won't do that"*: Ibid., 147.

455 *When he did call Lott*: Bob Woodward, *Shadow: Five Presidents and the Legacy of Watergate* (New York: Simon & Schuster, 1999), 499.

455 *While Ford was willing*: Amid all these secret negotiations, the club gathered for a funeral. One week before the Senate acquitted Clinton of all charges, Clinton, Ford, Carter, and Bush all flew on Air Force One to Amman, Jordan, for the funeral of King Hussein. The four men got along well, Clinton said later, mostly because Carter maintained a pleasant disposition on both legs of the journey. Clinton repeatedly offered his predecessors a chance at some kip in the presidential beds, but all three refused. Ford, at eighty-five, could not keep up the pace as the official party trudged through Amman's snaggletoothed backstreets and soon dropped out, but Clinton was amazed that he made the effort at all.

456 *"Of course, I don't think"*: Branch, *The Clinton Tapes,* 633.

456 *Ford's hometown reminded Clinton*: Bill Clinton, interview by Marty Allen, July 18, 2010.

Bush and Clinton: The Rascal and the Rebel

457 *Born forty-four days apart*: The next closest are Andrew Johnson (December 29, 1808) and Abraham Lincoln (February 12, 1809), born forty-five days apart.

Chapter 23: "He's Never Forgiven Me for Beating His Father"

459 *"left office with his integrity intact"*: C-SPAN Video Library, "Bush Presidential Library Dedication," November 6, 1997, http://www.c-spanvideo.org/program/LibraryD&showFullAbstract=1.

460 *"Of course, he's never forgiven me"*: Taylor Branch, *The Clinton Tapes: Wrestling History with the President* (New York: Simon & Schuster, 2009), 539.

461 *Bush had groaned when he learned that*: Michael Duffy and Nancy Gibbs, "The Quiet Dynasty," *Time,* August 7, 2000.

461 *"My heritage is a part"*: Walter Isaacson, "George Bush: My Heritage Is Part of Who I Am," Republican Convention, *Time,* August 7, 2000.

461 *the "worst year of my life"*: George W. Bush, *Decision Points* (New York: Crown Publishers, 2010).

461 *"A good leader sets priorities"*: Robert Draper, *Dead Certain: The Presidency of George W. Bush* (New York: Free Press, 2007), 295.

462 *"But do not challenge"*: Ibid., 68–70

462 " *'It's a genius slogan'* ": Author interview with Bill Clinton, November 16, 2011.

462 *"I don't always respect the guy"*: Margaret Carlson, "The Shadow Moves On," *Time*, January 29, 2001.

463 *"They* like *me"*: Branch, *The Clinton Tapes*, 620.

463 *But, Bush added*: Frank Bruni, "Bush Ridicules Gore's Proposals For Tax Cuts," *New York Times*, October 25, 2000.

464 *Must have worked*: Carlson, "The Shadow Moves On."

464 *The incoming president was trolling*: Draper, *Dead Certain*, 91–92; see also Carlson, "The Shadow Moves On."

464 *"It's a mistake to underestimate him"*: Carlson, "The Shadow Moves On."

465 *"I'd run again in a heartbeat"*: Branch, *The Clinton Tapes*, 633–34.

465 *Clinton ignored virtually all*: The Clintons either returned or paid for these gifts.

465 *Bill Daley described it as "terrible, devastating and rather appalling"*: Michael Hedges, "Even Loyal Liberals Join In The Clinton Bashing," *Houston Chronicle*, February 19, 2001.

465 *"to watch a shiny new ex-president disappear under a freak mudslide"*: Karen Tumulty, "How Can We Miss You If You Never Go Away?", *Time*, February 26, 2001.

465 *Clinton wrote an op-ed*: William Jefferson Clinton, "My Reasons for the Pardons," *New York Times*, February 18, 2001.

465 *"We don't have to do anything"*: Tumulty, "How Can We Miss You If You Never Go Away?"

466 *"People will tell you"*: James Carney, "Easy Does It," *Time*, March 19, 2001.

466 *aircraft had been forced down*: "China-U.S. Aircraft Collision Incident of April 2001: Assessments and Policy Implications," CRS Report for Congress, available online at www.fas.org, updated October 10, 2001 (pdf file).

467 *"They're not going to like me"*: Nancy Gibbs, "If You Want to Humble an Empire," *Time*, September 14, 2001.

467 *"never stab him in the back"*: Author interview with Bill Clinton, November 16, 2011.

468 *The president invoked FDR's phrase*: George W. Bush, "Remarks at the National Day of Prayer and Remembrance," September 14, 2001, transcript available online at the American Presidency Project, http://www.presidency.ucsb.edu/ws/index .php?pid=63645#axzz1g3ecaWlh.

468 *Vice President Cheney*: Philip Shenon, *The Commission: The Uncensored History of the 9/11 Investigation* (New York: Twelve, 2008), 29–30.

469 *"But the context"*: George Tenet and Bill Harlow, *At the Center of the Storm: My Years at the CIA* (New York: HarperCollins, 2007), 109; Philip Shenon, in his study of the 9/11 commission, reported that Clinton signed orders authorizing the killing of bin Laden in December 1998 and early 1999.

469 *He told the 9/11 commission*: National Commission on Terrorist Attacks upon the United States, *The 9/11 Commission Report: The Final Report of the National Commission on Terrorist Attacks upon the United States* (New York: Norton, 2004), 199.

470   *The men, along with Bush's father*: Elisabeth Bumiller, "White House Bond: Teamed by No. 43, 41 and 42 Hit It Off," *New York Times,* February 19, 2005.

470   *"I was a pickle stepping into history"*: Transcript from portrait unveiling ceremony, June 14, 2004, available online at washingtonpost.com.

471   *"I never believed it"*: Author interview with Bill Clinton (never published), June 18, 2004; see also Branch, *The Clinton Tapes,* 588.

471   " *'Hillary is in politics' "*: Author interview with Bill Clinton, November 16, 2011.

471   *"I hope I can be as gracious"*: Alexander Mooney, "Bush: Obama's Win 'Good For Our Country,' " CNN.com, November 12, 2008, http://www.cnn.com/2008/POLITICS/11/12/bush.obama/index.html?iref=allsearch.

Chapter 24: "I Love You More Than Tongue Can Tell"

476   *"the final motivating factor was my admiration for George Bush"*: NBC News special on *Decision Points,* November 8, 2010.

476   *"slightly outrageous streak"*: Larry Barrett, *Time,* March 1989.

476   *"parents would roll their eyes"*: Nancy Gibbs and Michael Duffy, *The Preacher and the Presidents: Billy Graham in the White House* (New York: Center Street, 2007), 327.

476   *"In reality, I was a boozy kid"*: George W. Bush, *Decision Points* (New York: Crown Publishers, 2010), 20–21.

477   " *'That's W's job' "*: Gibbs and Duffy, *The Preacher and the Presidents,* 328.

477   *"Half the time"*: George Bush and Doug Wead, *Man of Integrity* (Eugene, OR: Harvest House Publishers, 1988), 121.

477   *George "could be made to feel"*: Laurence I. Barrett, "Junior Is His Own Bush Now," *Time,* July 31, 1989.

478   *"I don't know how accurate I am"*: Ken Stephens, "Partners in Perseverance," *Dallas Morning News,* March 30, 1989.

478   *"I know there were times"*: Barrett, "Junior Is His Own Bush Now."

478   *"Call me when you get back"*: Kevin Sherrington, "More Than Meets the Name," *Dallas Morning News,* May 2, 1989.

479   *More than anything else*: Barrett, "Junior Is His Own Bush Now."

480   *Bush might criticize*: Karl Rove, *Courage and Consequence: My Life as a Conservative in the Fight* (New York: Threshold Editions, 2010), 120.

480   *"The moment"*: George W. Bush, *Decision Points,* 109.

481   *"I'm a warrior for my Dad"*: Walter Isaacson, "Republican Convention: George Bush: My Heritage Is Part of Who I Am," *Time,* August 7, 2000.

481   *"What I can do these days"*: Hugh Sidey, "Conversations with a Father," *Time,* September 24, 2001.

481   *"The whole world changed"*: Author interview with George H. W. Bush, October 7, 2011.

482   *Even the son thought*: Bob Woodward, *Bush at War* (New York: Simon & Schuster, 2002), 328–29.

482 *"There is scant evidence"*: Brent Scowcroft, "Don't Attack Saddam," *Wall Street Journal*, August 15, 2002.

483 *"If he thought I was handling Iraq wrong"*: George W. Bush, *Decision Points*, 238.

483 *"If he decides we must act"*: Hugh Sidey, "What Makes Dad Clench His Jaw," The Presidency, *Time*, September 16, 2002.

483 *It's not that the decision was unpopular*: "Poll: Bush Gaining Support on Invading Iraq," CNN.com, February 10, 2003, http://www.cnn.com/2003/US/02/10/sprj .irq.iraq.poll/index.html?iref=allsearch.

484 *"The tension had taken hold"*: Hugh Sidey, "Former President George H.W. Bush," *Time*, March 9, 2003.

485 *Exactly eleven years after the head of the Episcopal Church*: Hugh Sidey, "He Had No Respect For Our Military Then," *Time*, March 17, 2003.

485 *"And so our roles got reversed"*: George W. Bush interview with Mark K. Updegrove, *Texas Monthly* transcript, October 26, 2010.

485 *"watching your son take a pounding"*: Author interview with George H. W. Bush, October 7, 2011.

486 *"We know what it's like"*: Hugh Sidey, "They're Talking About . . . Our Kid," *Time*, December 19, 2004.

486 *"How's the first Jewish president doing"*: George W. Bush, *Decision Points*, 404.

486 *"I could tell he was happy"*: Ibid., 296.

486 *"You know, the idea that George"*: Hugh Sidey, "Savoring Victory, Family-Style," 2004 Election, *Time*, November 15, 2004.

487 *"It's much simpler than that"*: George W. Bush interview with Mark K. Updegrove.

488 *"the thing that matters in my heart is my family"*: Jim Krane, Associated Press, November 22, 2006.

488 *"He was a fabulous father"*: George W. Bush, "Remarks by President George W. Bush and President George H.W. Bush at Dedication of United States Embassy Beijing," Reuters, August 7, 2008.

Chapter 25: "Tell 41 and 42 That 43 Is Hungry"

492 *"how I hated him for that"*: George Bush, "Former President George H.W. Bush Comments At Clinton Library Dedication," November 18, 2004, transcript available online at washingtonpost.com.

493 *"It was terrible"*: George Bush, "Acceptance Speech" (National Constitution Center, Philadelphia, PA, October 5, 2006), transcript, http://constitutioncenter.org/ libertymedal/recipient_2006_speecha.html.

493 *"But it is surprising"*: Ibid.

494 *"He deserves far more credit"*: Michael Duffy, "When Opposites Attract," *Time*, December 19, 2005.

494 *"You feel like you're doing something bigger"*: George Bush and Barbara Bush, in-

terview by Larry King, *Larry King Live,* CNN, May 31, 2005, transcript, http://transcripts.cnn.com/TRANSCRIPTS/0505/31/lkl.01.html.

495 *" 'That is the way our country ought to work' "*: Michael Duffy, "Interview," *Time,* December 19, 2005.

496 *"And I appreciate that"*: George Bush and Barbara Bush, interview.

496 *"This is much more important"*: Ibid. President Obama used this quote in a speech at the George Bush Presidential Library on October 16, 2009.

498 *And it was in the now infamous Superdome*: George Bush made his fateful promise not to raise taxes here as well.

499 *"But if you do it in the right way"*: Bill Clinton, "Acceptance Speech" (National Constitution Center, Philadelphia, PA, October 5, 2006), transcript, http://constitutioncenter.org/libertymedal/recipient_2006_speechb.html.

499 *When the money stopped coming*: Author interview with Bill Clinton, November 16, 2011.

500 *"Just send your cash"*: "Remarks by President Obama, Former President Bill Clinton, and Former President George W. Bush on the Recovery and Rebuilding Effort in Haiti," January 16, 2010, available online at whitehouse.gov.

501 *"Each considers the other a friend"*: Author interview with George H. W. Bush, October 7, 2011.

501 *"the right thing to do"*: Author interview with Bill Clinton, November 16, 2011.

502 *And with that, Clinton bowed his head*: Point of Light Institute, *All Together Now: A Celebration of Service,* DVD Copyright © 2011 Point of Light Institute.

Obama and His Club: The Learning Curve

505 *"there's a certain loneliness to the job"*: Emily Friedman, "Presidency Can Feel Isolated, Lonely," ABC News, November 18, 2008.

Chapter 26: "We Want You to Succeed"

508 *That might yield short-term successes*: Barack Obama, *The Audacity of Hope: Thoughts on Reclaiming the American Dream* (New York: Crown Publishers, 2006), 35.

509 *"I sometimes felt as if I were watching"*: Ibid., 36–37.

509 *"refighting the same fights we had in the 1990s"*: Barack Obama, "Remarks at the Iowa Jefferson-Jackson Dinner in Des Moines," November 10, 2007, available online at The American Presidency Project.

509 *"the biggest fairy tale I've ever seen"*: Bill Clinton, *Charlie Rose,* December 2007.

509 *"We put the Clinton attacks front and center"*: David Plouffe, *The Audacity To Win,* (New York: Penguin, 2010).

510 *"He put us on a fundamentally different path"*: James Ball, "Obama: Reagan Changed Direction; Bill Clinton Didn't," YouTube video, posted January 14, 2008, http://www.youtube.com/watch?v=HFLuOBsNMZA.

510 *"President Reagan was the engine of innovation"*: Dan Balz and Haynes Johnson, *The Battle For America 2008: The Story of an Extraordinary Election* (New York: Viking Penguin, 2009), 160–61.

510 *"I can't tell whom I'm running against sometimes"*: "Democrats Clinton, Obama Clash at S.C. Debate," January 22, 2008, msnbc.com.

511 *"That campaign generated so much heat"*: Bill Clinton, "Convention Speech" (Denver, CO, August 27, 2008), transcript, http://www.nytimes.com/2008/08/27/us/politics/27text-clinton.html?pagewanted=all.

511 *It's not going to work*: John Heileman and Mark Halperin, *Game Change* (New York: HarperCollins, 2010), 435.

511 *"I'll do whatever they want"*: Azi Paybarah, "Bill Clinton Has No Problem with Vetting: 'Talk to Them,'" *New York Observer,* November 19, 2008.

512 *"educate President-elect Obama"*: Author interview with Jimmy Carter, December 2, 2011.

512 *"the office transcends the individual"*: Kenneth T. Walsh, "Bush and Ex-Presidents Counsel President-Elect Obama," January 8, 2009, USNews.com.

512 *"I gave him a suggestion"*: Bush, *Decision Points,* 105.

513 *"It wasn't well received"*: Jonathan Alter, *The Promise: President Obama, Year One* (New York: Simon & Schuster, 2010), 113.

514 *"This is where he's comfortable"*: Eli Saslow, "Back in Texas, Bush Enjoys A Simpler Life," *Washington Post,* April 11, 2009.

514 *"He deserves my silence"*: Mike Allen, "Bush Promises Not To Attack Obama," *Politico,* March 18, 2009.

514 *"I love my country a lot more"*: Ibid.

514 *After reading several books*: Saslow, "Back in Texas, Bush Enjoys a Simpler Life."

514 *"I have enormous sympathy"*: Sheryl Gay Stolberg, "The Political Revival of George Herbert Walker Bush," On the White House, *New York Times,* August 1, 2008.

515 *"I could quickly see"*: Eamon Javers, "41 and 44 Together in Texas," *Politico,* October 16, 2009.

515 *"I cannot wait for President Obama"*: "Open Letter From Bush 41 To Aggie Family," October 14, 2009, KBTX.com.

515 *"when offered a chance to serve"*: Barack Obama, "Remarks by the President At Points of Light 20th anniversary," October 16, 2009, available online at whitehouse.gov.

517 *"What if it was me"*: Laura Ling and Lisa Ling, *Somewhere Inside: One Sister's Captivity in North Korea and the Other's Fight to Bring Her Home* (New York: William Morrow, 2010), 297.

517 *"if the president doesn't want me to"*: Author interview with Bill Clinton, November 16, 2011.

517 *Little about the visit was pleasant*: Evan Ramstad and Jay Solomon, "North Korea Frees Americans," *Wall Street Journal,* August 5, 2009.

517 *"The riveting tableau of a former president"*: Mark Landler and Peter Baker, "Clinton Secures 2 Pardons; All 3 Leave North Korea," *New York Times,* August 5, 2009.

518 *"I'm fairly certain that he'd be fine"*: Ling and Ling, *Somewhere Inside,* 285–303.

518 *Instead, Clinton found him to be*: Ibid.

518 *Afterward, Obama invited Clinton*: Mark Landler and Mark Mazzetti, "In North Korea, Clinton Helped Unveil a Mystery," *New York Times,* August 19, 2009.

519 *"He's trying to do the right thing"*: Bill Clinton, interview by Larry King, *Larry King Live,* CNN, September 21, 2009, transcript, http://transcripts.cnn.com/TRAN SCRIPTS/0909/21/lkl.01.html.

519 *" 'What do we need to do' "*: Bill Clinton, interview by David Gregory, *Meet the Press,* NBC, September 19, 2010, transcript, http://www.msnbc.msn.com/id/39235412/ ns/meet_the_press-transcripts/t/meet-press-transcript-sept/.

519 *A Gallup survey in mid-October*: Frank Newport, "Bill Clinton's Impact More Positive for Democrats Than Obama's," Gallup.com, October 19, 2010, http://www .gallup.com/poll/143798/Bill-Clinton-Impact-Positive-Democrats-Obama-aspx.

520 *"Don't be fooled"*: Charles Babington, "Bill Clinton Races to Help Democratic Candidates, Treading Where Obama Won't," Associated Press, October 22, 2010.

520 *"I am old enough to know"*: Edward Luce, "Clinton's Aim Is True as Democrats' Top Gun," *Financial Times,* October 12, 2010.

520 *"He's welcome anywhere in the country"*: Jim Rutenberg and Kate Zernike, "Bill Clinton, In Demand, Stumps for Obama," *New York Times,* September 21, 2010.

520 *"And when you get in there"*: Ibid.

520 *At his postmortem press conference*: Press Conference, November 3, 2010, transcript available online at http://www.whitehouse.gov/the-press-office/2010/11/03/press -conference-president.

521 *"It's like riding a bicycle"*: Bill Clinton, *Larry King Live,* December 16, 2010.

522 *"I am happy to be here"*: Remarks by President Obama and former president Clinton, December 10, 2010, transcript, http://www.whitehouse.gov/the-press -office/2010/12/10/remarks-president-obama-and-former-president-clinton.

522 *"Obi Wan back in the briefing room"*: Jon Stewart, *The Daily Show with John Stewart,* December 14, 2010.

522 *"surely we can make some compromises"*: Barack Obama, "Remarks by the President at University of Maryland Town Hall," July 22, 2011, available online at white house.gov.

Conclusion

524 *Margaret Truman recalled*: Margaret Truman, *Harry S. Truman* (New York: William Morrow, 1973), 555.

524 *"Since that time"*: Ibid., 556.

524 *"more time must pass"*: Margaret Truman, "Harry Truman," *Life,* December 1, 1972.

524   *"You cannot walk in those old rooms"*: Bob Greene, *Fraternity: A Journey in Search of Five Presidents* (New York: Crown Publishers, 2004), 34.

525   *But then*: Richard Reeves, *President Nixon: Alone in the White House* (New York: Simon & Schuster, 2001), 24.

525   *"At times," his aide George Stephanopoulos recalled*: George Stephanopoulos, *All Too Human: A Political Education* (Boston: Little, Brown and Company, 1999), 164.

525   *"If He has a place for me"*: Richard Reeves, *President Kennedy: Profile of Power* (New York: Simon & Schuster, 1993), 174.

525   *"In this temple"*: William Safire, *Before the Fall: An Inside View of the Pre-Watergate White House* (Garden City, NY: Doubleday, 1975), 205.

525   *"He clearly saw what needed to happen"*: "Interview with George W. Bush," *Time,* December 19, 2004.

526   *"We kept the peace"*: Stephen E. Ambrose, *Eisenhower the President,* vol. II (Norwalk, CT: Easton Press, 1987), 626.

526   *"Fifty thousand American boys are dead"*: Doris Kearns Goodwin, *Lyndon Johnson and the American Dream* (New York: Harper & Row, 1976), 310.

526   *"aim for big change"*: "Interview with George W. Bush," *Time.*

BIBLIOGRAPHY

Acheson, Dean. *Present at the Creation: My Years in the State Department*. New York: W.W. Norton and Co., 1987.

Albert, Carl, with Danney Goble. *Little Giant: The Life and Times of Speaker Carl Albert*. Norman, Oklahoma: University of Oklahoma Press, 1990.

Alter, Jonathan. *The Promise: President Obama, Year One*. New York: Simon & Schuster, 2010.

Ambrose, Stephen E. *Nixon, Vol. I: The Education of a Politician 1913–1962*. New York: Simon & Schuster, 1987.

———. *Nixon: The Triumph of a Politician 1962–1972*. New York: Simon & Schuster, 1989.

———. *Eisenhower: Soldier and President*. New York: Simon & Schuster, 1990.

———. *Eisenhower*. New York: Simon & Schuster, 1991.

American Agenda, Inc. *American Agenda: Report to the Forty-First President of the United States of America*. Camp Hill, PA: Book-Of-The-Month-Club.

Arnold, Peri E. "The First Hoover Commission and the Managerial Presidency." *The Journal of Politics* Vol. 38.1 (February 1976): 49–50.

Arnold, William A. *Back When It All Began: The Early Nixon Years*. New York: Vantage Press, 1975.

Ayers, Eben A. *Truman in the White House: The Diary of Eben A. Ayers*. Ed. Robert H. Ferrell. Columbia, Missouri: University of Missouri Press, 1991.

Baker, Peter. *The Breach: Inside the Impeachment and Trial of William Jefferson Clinton*. New York: Lisa Drew/Scribner, 2000.

Balfour, Michael Leonard Graham. *The Adversaries: America, Russia, and the Open World, 1941–62*. London: Routledge and Kegan, 1981.

Balz, Dan, and Haynes Johnson. *The Battle For America 2008: The Story of an Extraordinary Election*. New York: Viking Penguin, 2009.

Barber, James David. *The Pulse of Politics: Electing Presidents in the Media Age*. New York: W.W. Norton, 1980.

Barrett, Laurence I. *Gambling with History: Reagan in the White House*. New York: Penguin Books, 1983.

Beschloss, Michael R. "A Tale of Two Presidents." *The Wilson Quarterly* (Winter 2000).

———. *Reaching for Glory: Lyndon Johnson's Secret White House Tapes, 1964–1965*. New York: Simon & Schuster, 2001.

———, ed. *Taking Charge: The Johnson White House Tapes 1963–1964*. New York: Simon & Schuster, 1997.

Bissell, Richard, with Jonathan E. Lewis and Frances T. Pudlo. *Reflections of a Cold Warrior: From Yalta to the Bay of Pigs*. New Haven: Yale University, 1996.

Branch, Taylor. *The Clinton Tapes: Wrestling History with the President*. New York: Simon & Schuster, 2009.

Brinkley, Douglas. *The Unfinished Presidency: Jimmy Carter's Journey Beyond the White House*. New York: Viking Penguin, 1998.

Brownstein, Ronald. *The Power and the Glitter: The Hollywood-Washington Connection*. New York: Pantheon Books, 1990.

Burner, David. *Herbert Hoover: A Public Life*. New York: Knopf, 1979.

Butcher, Harry C. *My Three Years With Eisenhower: The Personal Diary of Captain Harry C. Butcher, USNR Naval Aide to General Eisenhower 1942–1945*. New York: Simon & Schuster, 1946.

Busby, Horace. *The Thirty-First of March: An Intimate Portrait of Lyndon Johnson's Final Days in Office*. New York: Farrar, Straus and Giroux, 2005.

Bush, Barbara. *Barbara Bush, A Memoir*. New York: Lisa Drew/Scribner, 1994.

Bush, George, with Victor Gold. *Looking Forward*. New York: Doubleday, 1987.

———, with Doug Wead. *George Bush: Man of Integrity*. Eugene, Oregon: Harvest House Publishers, 1988.

———, and Brent Scowcroft. *A World Transformed*. New York: Vintage Books, 1998.

———. *All The Best, George Bush: My Life in Letters and Other Writings*. New York: Lisa Drew/Scribner, 1999.

Bush, George W. *A Charge To Keep*. New York: William Morrow and Company, Inc., 1999.

———. *Decision Points*. New York: Crown Publishers, 2010.

Bush, Laura. *Spoken from the Heart*. New York: Scribner, 2010.

Califano, Joseph A. *The Triumph & Tragedy of Lyndon Johnson*. College Station, Texas: Texas A & M University Press, 1991.

Cannon, James. *Time and Chance: Gerald Ford's Appointment with History*. New York: HarperCollins, 1994.

Cannon, Lou. *Reagan*. New York: G.P. Putnam's Sons, 1982.

———. *President Reagan: The Role of a Lifetime*. New York: Public Affairs, 1991.

———. *Governor Reagan: His Rise To Power*. New York: Public Affairs, 2003.

Caro, Robert A. *The Years of Lyndon Johnson: Master of the Senate*. New York: Knopf, 2002.

Carter, Jimmy. *White House Diary*. New York: Farrar, Straus and Giroux, 2010.

Cheney, Dick, with Liz Cheney. *In My Time: A Personal and Political Memoir*. New York: Threshold Editions, 2011.

Clifford, Clark, with Richard Holbrooke. *Counsel to the President.* New York: Random House, 1991.

Clinton, Bill. *My Life: The Presidential Years.* New York: Vintage Books, 2005.

———. *Back to Work: Why We Need Smart Government for a Strong Economy.* New York: Knopf, 2011.

Clinton, Hillary Rodham. *Living History.* New York: Scribner, 2003.

Commager, Henry Steele. *Documents of American History.* Upper Saddle River, New Jersey: Prentice-Hall, 1975.

Congressional Quarterly, Inc. *National Party Conventions 1831–1984.* Ed. Evamarie Socha. Washington, D.C.: Congressional Quarterly, Inc., 1987.

Cormier, Frank. *LBJ: The Way He Was.* New York: Doubleday, 1977.

Crowley, Monica. *Nixon Off the Record.* New York: Random House, 1996.

———. *Nixon in Winter.* New York: Random House, 1998.

Dallek, Robert. "Three New Revelations about LBJ." *The Atlantic Monthly* (April 1998).

———. *Flawed Giant: Lyndon Johnson and His Times.* New York: Oxford University Press, 1998.

———. *Ronald Reagan: The Politics of Symbolism.* Cambridge: Harvard University Press, 1999.

———. *An Unfinished Life: John F. Kennedy 1917–1963.* New York: Little, Brown and Company, 2003.

———. *Lyndon B. Johnson: Portrait of a President.* New York: Oxford University Press, 2004.

———. *Nixon and Kissinger.* New York: HarperCollins, 2007.

———. *John F. Kennedy.* New York: Oxford University Press, 2011.

DeFrank, Thomas M. *Write It When I'm Gone: Remarkable Off-the-Record Conversations with Gerald R. Ford.* New York: Berkley Books, 2007.

D' Este, Carlo. *Eisenhower: A Soldier's Life.* New York: Henry Holt, 2002.

Donovan, Robert J. *Conflict and Crisis: The Presidency of Harry S. Truman 1945–1948.* New York: W.W. Norton & Company, Inc., 1977.

Draper, Robert. *Dead Certain: The Presidency of George W. Bush.* New York: Free Press, 2007.

Eisenhower, David, with Julie Nixon Eisenhower. *Going Home To Glory: A Memoir of Life With Dwight D. Eisenhower, 1961–1969.* New York: Simon & Schuster, 2010.

Eisenhower, Dwight D. *Crusade in Europe.* Garden City, New York: Doubleday, 1948.

———. *Mandate for Change, 1953–1956: The White House Years, A Personal Account.* New York: Doubleday, 1963.

———. *At Ease: Stories I Tell to Friends.* New York: Doubleday, 1967.

———. *The Eisenhower Diaries.* Ed. Robert H. Ferrell. New York: W.W. Norton and Company, 1981.

Emery, Fred. *Watergate: The Corruption of American Politics and the Fall of Richard Nixon.* New York: Random House, 1994.

Evans, Hugh E. *The Hidden Campaign: FDR's Health and the 1944 Campaign*. Armonky, New York: M.E. Sharpe, 2002.

Ewald, William Bragg, Jr. *Eisenhower, The President: Crucial Days, 1951–1960*. Englewood Cliffs, New Jersey: Prentice-Hall, 1981.

Ferrell, Robert H., ed. *Dear Bess: The Letters from Harry to Bess Truman, 1910–1959*. Columbia, Missouri: University of Missouri Press, 1983.

———. *Harry S. Truman and The Cold War Revisionists*. Columbia, Missouri: University of Missouri Press, 2006.

Ford, Gerald R. *A Time to Heal*. New York: Harper & Row, 1979.

Frost, Sir David, with Bob Zelnick. *Frost/Nixon: Behind the Scenes of the Nixon Interviews*. New York: Harper Perennial, 2007.

Gates, Robert M. *From the Shadows: The Ultimate Insider's Story of Five Presidents and How They Won the Cold War*. New York: Simon & Schuster, 1996.

Gibbs, Nancy, and Michael Duffy. *The Preacher and the Presidents*. New York: Center Street, 2007.

Giglio, James. "Harry S. Truman and the Multifarious Ex-Presidency." *Presidential Studies Quarterly* Vol 12.2 (Spring 1982): 239.

Goldman, Eric F. *The Tragedy of Lyndon Johnson*. New York: Knopf, 1969.

Goodwin, Doris Kearns. *Lyndon Johnson and the American Dream*. New York: St. Martin's Griffin, 1991.

Gormley, Ken. *The Death of American Virtue: Clinton vs. Starr*. New York: Crown Publishers, 2010.

Green, Fitzhugh. *George Bush: An Intimate Portrait*. New York: Hippocrene Books, 1989.

Greene, Bob. *Fraternity: A Journey in Search of Five Presidents*. New York: Crown Publishers, 2004.

Greenstein, Fred I. *The Hidden Hand Presidency: Eisenhower As Leader*. New York: Basic Books, 1982.

Haig, Alexander M., with Charles McCarry. *Inner Circles: How America Changed the World, A Memoir*. New York: Warner Books, 1992.

Haldeman, H.R. *The Ends of Power*. New York: Dell Publishing, 1978.

———. *The Haldeman Diaries*. New York: Putnam, 1994.

Halberstam, David. *War in a Time of Peace: Bush, Clinton, and the Generals*. New York: Scribner, 2001.

Harris, John F. *The Survivor: Bill Clinton in the White House*. New York: Random House, 2005.

Hartmann, Robert T. *Palace Politics: An Inside Account of the Ford Years*. New York: McGraw-Hill, 1980.

Hawkins, Jack. "Classified Disaster: The Bay of Pigs Operation Was Doomed by Presidential Indecisiveness and Lack of Commitment." *National Review* Vol. 48.25 (December 31, 1996).

Hecht, Marie B. *Beyond the Presidency: The Residues of Power*. New York: MacMillan Publishing Co., Inc., 1976.

Heileman, John, and Mark Halperin. *Game Change*. New York: HarperCollins, 2010.

Herbert Hoover Presidential Library Association, Inc. *Farewell to the Chief: Former Presidents in American Public Life*. Ed. Richard Norton Smith and Timothy Walch. Worland, Wyoming: High Plains Publishing Company, 1990.

————. *Herbert Hoover and Harry S. Truman: A Documentary History*. Ed. Timothy Walch and Dwight M. Miller. Worland, Wyoming: High Plains Publishing Company, 1992.

Hersh, Seymour M. *The Price of Power: Kissinger in the Nixon White House*. New York: Summit Books, 1983.

Herskowitz, Mickey. *Duty, Honor, Country: The Life and Legacy of Prescott Bush*. Nashville: Rutledge Hill Press, 2003.

Hess, Stephen. *Organizing the Presidency*. Washington, D.C.: The Brookings Institution, 1988.

Hoover, Herbert. *An American Epic, vol. IV, The Guns Cease Killing and the Saving of Life from Famine Begins 1939–1963*. Chicago: Henry Regnery Company, 1964.

Hughes, Karen. *Ten Minutes from Normal*. New York: Viking Penguin, 2004.

Isaacson, Walter. *Kissinger: A Biography*. New York: Simon & Schuster, 1992.

Isikoff, Michael. *Uncovering Clinton: A Reporter's Story*. New York: Crown Publishers, 1999.

Johnson, Lyndon Baines. *The Vantage Point: Perspectives of the Presidency, 1963–1969*. New York: Holt, Rinehart and Winston, 1971.

————, and Michael R. Beschloss. *Reaching for Glory*. New York: Touchstone, 2002.

Kalb, Marvin. *The Nixon Memo*. Chicago: The University of Chicago Press, 1994.

Kaplan, Fred. "JFK's First-Strike Plan." *The Atlantic Monthly* Vol.288.3 (October 2001): 81.

Kennedy, Robert. *Robert Kennedy in His Own Words: The Unpublished Recollections of the Kennedy Years*. Ed. Edwin O. Guthman and Jeffrey Shulman. New York: Twenty First Century Books and Bantam Books, 1988.

Kissinger, Henry. *Years of Upheaval*. New York: Little, Brown and Company, 1982.

Korda, Michael. *Ike: An American Hero*. New York: HarperCollins, 2007.

Kutler, Stanley I. *Abuse of Power: The New Nixon Tapes*. New York: Free Press, 1997.

Larson, Arthur. *Eisenhower, the President Nobody Knew*. New York: Popular Library, 1968.

Leuchtenberg, William E. *In the Shadow of FDR: From Harry Truman to George W. Bush*. Ithaca: Cornell University Press, 1983.

————. *Herbert Hoover*. New York: Henry Holt and Co., 2009.

Lilienthal, David E. *The Journals of David Lilienthal, Volume II: The Atomic Energy Years 1945–1950*. New York: Harper & Row, 1964.

Ling, Laura, and Lisa Ling. *Somewhere Inside: One Sister's Captivity in North Korea and the Other's Fight to Bring Her Home*. New York: HarperCollins, 2010.

Locher, James R. III. *Victory on the Potomac: The Goldwater-Nichols Act Unifies the Pentagon*. College Station: Texas A&M University Press, 2004.

Maier, Thomas. *The Kennedys: America's Emerald Kings*. New York: Basic Books, 2003.

Manchester, William. *The Death of a President: November 20-November 25, 1963*. New York: Harper & Row, 1967.

Mann, James. *The Rebellion of Ronald Reagan*. New York: Viking Penguin, 2009.

Maraniss, David. *First In His Class: The Biography of Bill Clinton*. New York: Touchstone, 1995.

Matthews, Christopher. *Kennedy and Nixon: The Rivalry That Shaped Postwar America*. New York: Simon & Schuster, 1996.

———. *Jack Kennedy: Elusive Hero*. New York: Simon & Schuster, 2011.

May, Ernest R. "The Replacements." *The National Interest* Vol. 99 (January–February 2009): 73.

McCullough, David. *Truman*. New York: Simon & Schuster, 1992.

McPherson, Harry. *A Political Education*. Austin, Texas: University of Texas Press, 1995.

Miller, Merle. *Plain Speaking: An Oral Biography of Harry S. Truman*. New York: G.P. Putnam's Sons, 1973.

Moe, Ronald C. "A New Hoover Commission: A Timely Idea of Misdirected Nostalgia?" *Public Administration Review* Vol. 42.3 (May–June 1982).

Morris, Edmund. *Dutch: A Memoir of Ronald Reagan*. New York: Modern Library, 1999.

Neal, Steve. *Harry and Ike: The Partnership That Remade the Postwar World*. New York: Touchstone/Simon & Schuster, 2001.

Nessen, Ron. *It Sure Looks Different from the Inside*. Chicago: Playboy Press, 1978.

Neustadt, Richard E. *Preparing to Be President: The Memos of Richard E. Neustadt*. Ed. Charles O. Jones. Washington, DC: The AEI Press Publisher for the American Enterprise Institute, 2000.

Nguyen, Gregory Tien Hung, and Jerrold L. Schecter. *The Palace File*. New York: HarperCollins, 1989.

Nixon, Richard M. *Six Crises*. New York: Pyramid Publications, Inc., 1968.

———. *The Memoirs of Richard Nixon*. New York: Grosset & Dunlap, 1978.

———. *In the Arena: A Memoir of Victory, Defeat, and Renewal*. New York: Simon & Schuster, 1990.

———. *Seize the Moment: America's Challenge in a One-Superpower World*. New York: Simon & Schuster, 1992.

Novak, Robert D. *The Prince of Darkness: 50 Years Reporting in Washington*. New York: Crown Forum, 2007.

Obama, Barack. *The Audacity of Hope: Thoughts on Reclaiming the American Dream*. New York: Crown Publishers, 2006.

Oberdorfer, Don. *The Two Koreas*. New York: Basic Books, 1997.

Olson, Gregory Allen. *Mansfield and Vietnam: A Study in Rhetorical Adaptation*. East Lansing, Michigan: Michigan State University Press, 1995.

O'Neill, Tip, with William Novak. *Man of the House: The Life and Political Memoirs of Speaker Tip O'Neill*. New York: St. Martin's Press, 1987.

Osborne, John. *The Nixon Watch*. New York: Liveright, 1970.

Oudes, Bruce, ed. *From the President: Richard Nixon's Secret Files*. New York: HarperCollins, 1989.

Pach, Chester J., and Elmo Richardson. *The Presidency of Dwight D. Eisenhower*. Lawrence, Kansas: University Press of Kansas, 1991.

Parmet, Herbert S. *Eisenhower and the American Crusades*. New York: The MacMillan Company, 1972.

———. *JFK: The Presidency of John F. Kennedy*. Norwalk, CT: The Easton Press, 1983.

———. *George Bush: The Life of a Lone Star Yankee*. New York: Lisa Drew/Scribner, 1997.

Perlstein, Rick. *Barry Goldwater and the Unmaking of the American Consensus*. New York: Nation Books, 2001.

———. *Nixonland: The Rise of a President and the Fracturing of America*. New York: Scribner, 2008.

Perry, Mark. *Partners in Command: George Marshall and Dwight Eisenhower In War*. New York: The Penguin Press, 2007.

Phillips, Kevin P. *The Emerging Republican Majority*. New Rochelle, N.Y.: Arlington House, 1969.

Pietrusza, David. *1960: LBJ vs. JFK vs. Nixon: The Epic Campaign That Forged Three Presidencies*. New York: Union Square Press, 2008.

Plouffe, David. *The Audacity to Win: How Obama Won and How We Can Beat the Party of Limbaugh, Beck, and Palin*. New York: Penguin Group, 2010.

Powell, Colin L., with Joseph E. Persico. *My American Journey*. New York: Random House, 1995.

Prados, John. *The White House Tapes: Eavesdropping on the President*. New York: The New Press, 2003.

Reagan, Nancy, with William Novak. *My Turn: The Memoirs of Nancy Reagan*. New York: Random House, 1989.

Reagan, Ronald. *An American Life*. New York: Simon & Schuster, 1990.

———. *Reagan: A Life In Letters*. New York: Free Press, 2003.

———. *The Reagan Diaries: Unabridged*. Ed. Douglas Brinkley. New York: HarperCollins, 2009.

Reeves, Richard. *President Kennedy: Profile of Power*. New York: Simon & Schuster, 1993.

———. *President Nixon: Alone in the White House*. New York: Simon & Schuster, 2002.

———. *President Reagan: The Triumph of Imagination*. New York: Simon & Schuster, 2005.

Remnick, David. *The Bridge: The Life and Rise of Barack Obama*. New York: Knopf, 2010.

Reston, James, Jr. *The Lone Star: The Life of John Connally*. New York: Harper & Row, 1989.

Roberts, Charles. *LBJ's Inner Circle*. New York: Delacorte Press, 1965.

Rove, Karl. *Courage and Consequence: My Life as a Conservative in the Fight*. New York: Threshold Editions, 2010.

Rovere, Richard H. *The Eisenhower Years: Affairs of State*. New York: Farrar, Straus and Cudahy, 1956.

Rumsfeld, Donald. *Known and Unknown*. New York: Sentinel/Penguin Group, 2011.

Safire, William. *Before the Fall: An Inside View of the Pre-Watergate White House*. New York: Da Capo Press, 1975.

Sanger, David E. *The Inheritance: The World Obama Confronts and the Challenges to American Power*. New York: Crown, 2009.

Salinger, Pierre. *With Kennedy*. New York: Doubleday, 1966.

Schieffer, Bob. "Advice and Dissent: What LBJ Could Have Learned from Ike." *Washington Monthly* Vol. 22.6–7 (July–August 1990).

Schlesinger, Arthur. *A Thousand Days: John F. Kennedy in the White House*. Boston: Houghton Mifflin, 1965.

Schoenebaum, Eleanora W., ed. *Facts on File Yearbook 1980*. New York: Facts on File, Inc., 1981.

Shirley, Craig. *Reagan's Revolution: The Untold Story of the Campaign That Started It All*. Nashville: Thomas Nelson, Inc., 2005.

Shultz, George P. *Turmoil and Triumph: Diplomacy, Power, and the Victory of the American Ideal*. New York: Touchstone, 1993.

Skidmore, Max J. *After the White House: Former Presidents as Private Citizens*. New York: Palgrave MacMillan, 2004.

Simes, Dimitri K. *After the Collapse: Russia Seeks Its Place as a Great Power*. New York: Simon & Schuster, 1999.

Smith, Richard Norton. *An Uncommon Man: The Triumph of Herbert Hoover*. New York: Simon & Schuster, 1984.

———, and Timothy Walch, eds. *Farewell to the Chief: Former Presidents in American Public Life*. Worland, Wyoming: High Plains Publishing Co. Inc., 1990.

Sorensen, Theodore. *Kennedy*. New York: Harper & Row, 1965.

Starr, Kevin. *California, a History*. New York: Modern Library, 2005.

Stephanopoulos, George. *All Too Human: A Political Education*. Boston: Little, Brown and Company, 1999.

Stout, Richard T. *People*. New York: Harper & Row, 1970.

Strober, Deborah Hart, and Gerald S. Strober. *The Kennedy Presidency*. Dulles, Virginia: Potomac Books, Inc., 2003.

———. *The Kennedy Presidency: An Oral History of the Era*. Washington, DC: Brassey's, Inc., 2003.

Summers, Anthony, and Robbyn Swan. *The Arrogance of Power*. New York: Viking Press, 2000.

Suskind, Ron. *The One Percent Doctrine: Deep Inside America's Pursuit of Its Enemies Since 9/11*. New York: Simon & Schuster, 2006.

Takiff, Michael. *A Complicated Man: The Life of Bill Clinton as Told by Those Who Know Him*. New Haven: Yale University Press, 2010.

Talbott, Strobe. *The Russia Hand: A Memoir of Presidential Diplomacy*. New York: Random House, 2002.

Tenet, George, with Bill Harlow. *At the Center of the Storm: My Years at the CIA*. New York: HarperCollins, 2007.

terHorst, J.F. *Gerald Ford and the Future of the Presidency*. New York: Joseph Okpaku Publishing, 1974.

The 9/11 Commission Report: Final Report of the National Commission on Terrorist Attacks upon the United States. New York: W.W. Norton & Company.

Truman, Harry S. *Memoirs, Volume One, 1945: Year of Decisions*. Garden City, New York: Doubleday, 1955.

———. *Memoirs, Volume Two: Years of Trial and Hope*. Garden City, New York: Doubleday, 1956.

———. *Mr. Citizen*. New York: Random House, 1960.

———. *Off the Record: The Private Papers of Harry S. Truman*. Ed. Robert H. Ferrell. New York: Harper & Row, 1980.

———. *Strictly Personal and Confidential: The Letters Harry Truman Never Mailed*. Ed. Monte M. Poen. Boston: Little, Brown and Company, 1982.

———. *Where the Buck Stops: The Personal and Private Writings of Harry S. Truman*. Ed. Margaret Truman. New York: Grand Central Publishing, 1990.

Updegrove, Mark K. *Second Acts: Presidential Lives and Legacies After the White House*. Guilford, CT: The Lyons Press, 2006.

Walsh, Kenneth T. *Air Force One: A History of the Presidents and Their Planes*. New York: Hyperion, 2003.

Weber, Ralph Edward, ed. *Talking with Harry: Candid Conversations with President Harry S. Truman*. Wilmington, Delaware: Scholarly Resources, 2001.

Weisberg, Jacob. *The Bush Tragedy*. New York: Random House, 2008.

Whalen, Richard J. *Catch the Falling Flag: A Republican's Challenge to His Party*. Boston: Houghton Mifflin Company, 1972.

White, Theodore H. *The Making of the President 1960*. New York: Atheneum Publishers, 1961.

———. *The Making of the President 1964*. New York: Harper Perennial, 1965.

———. *The Making of the President 1968*. New York: Atheneum Publishers, 1969.

———. *The Making of the President 1972*. New York: Harper Perennial, 1973.

———. *Breach of Faith: The Fall of Richard Nixon*. New York: Atheneum, 1975.

Wicker, Tom. *One of Us: Richard Nixon and the American Dream*. New York: Random House, 1991.

Wills, Garry. *Nixon Agonistes*. Boston: Mariner Books, 2002.

Wit, Joel S., Daniel B. Poneman, and Robert L. Galluci. *Going Critical: The First North Korean Nuclear Crisis*. Washington, D.C.: The Brookings Institution Press, 2004.

Wolffe, Richard. *Renegade: The Making of a President*. New York: Crown Publishers, 2009.

———. *Revival: The Struggle for Survival Inside the Obama White House*. New York: Crown Publishers, 2010.

Woodward, Bob. *Shadow*. New York: Simon & Schuster, 1999.

———. *Bush At War*. New York: Simon & Schuster, 2002.

INDEX